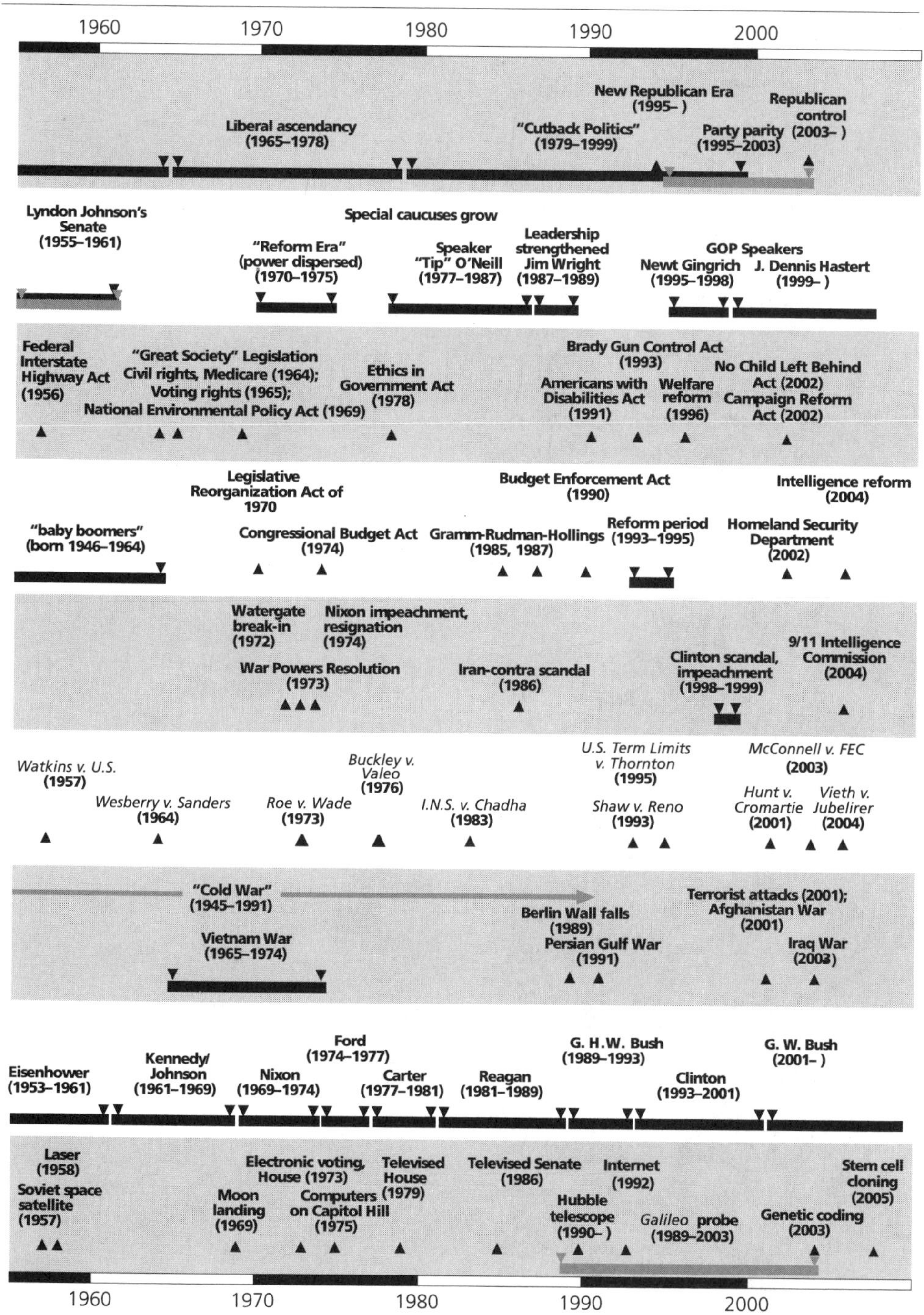
1960
1970
1980
1990
2000
Liberal ascendancy (1965–1978)
"Cutback Politics" (1979–1999)
New Republican Era (1995–)
Party parity (1995–2003)
Republican control (2003–)
Lyndon Johnson's Senate (1955–1961)
Special caucuses grow
"Reform Era" (power dispersed) (1970–1975)
Speaker "Tip" O'Neill (1977–1987)
Leadership strengthened Jim Wright (1987–1989)
GOP Speakers
Newt Gingrich (1995–1998)
J. Dennis Hastert (1999–)
Federal Interstate Highway Act (1956)
"Great Society" Legislation Civil rights, Medicare (1964); Voting rights (1965);
National Environmental Policy Act (1969)
Ethics in Government Act (1978)
Brady Gun Control Act (1993)
Americans with Disabilities Act (1991)
Welfare reform (1996)
No Child Left Behind Act (2002)
Campaign Reform Act (2002)
Legislative Reorganization Act of 1970
"baby boomers" (born 1946–1964)
Congressional Budget Act (1974)
Budget Enforcement Act (1990)
Gramm-Rudman-Hollings (1985, 1987)
Reform period (1993–1995)
Intelligence reform (2004)
Homeland Security Department (2002)
Watergate break-in (1972)
Nixon impeachment, resignation (1974)
War Powers Resolution (1973)
Iran-contra scandal (1986)
Clinton scandal, impeachment (1998–1999)
9/11 Intelligence Commission (2004)
Watkins v. U.S. (1957)
Wesberry v. Sanders (1964)
Roe v. Wade (1973)
Buckley v. Valeo (1976)
I.N.S. v. Chadha (1983)
U.S. Term Limits v. Thornton (1995)
Shaw v. Reno (1993)
McConnell v. FEC (2003)
Hunt v. Cromartie (2001)
Vieth v. Jubelirer (2004)
"Cold War" (1945–1991)
Vietnam War (1965–1974)
Berlin Wall falls (1989)
Persian Gulf War (1991)
Terrorist attacks (2001); Afghanistan War (2001)
Iraq War (2003)
Eisenhower (1953–1961)
Kennedy/ Johnson (1961–1969)
Nixon (1969–1974)
Ford (1974–1977)
Carter (1977–1981)
Reagan (1981–1989)
G. H.W. Bush (1989–1993)
Clinton (1993–2001)
G. W. Bush (2001–)
Laser (1958)
Soviet space satellite (1957)
Moon landing (1969)
Electronic voting, House (1973)
Computers on Capitol Hill (1975)
Televised House (1979)
Televised Senate (1986)
Hubble telescope (1990–)
Internet (1992)
Galileo probe (1989–2003)
Genetic coding (2003)
Stem cell cloning (2005)
1960
1970
1980
1990
2000

CLASSICAL MOMENTS IN CONGRESSIONAL POLITICS

Lyndon B. Johnson, Senate majority leader (1955–1961), vice president (1961–1963), and president (1963–1969), master of one-on-one communication and what was termed "The Treatment," interacts at close range with Supreme Court justice Abe Fortas, left; Sen. Richard B. Russell, D-Ga., top right; and Sen. Theodore Francis Green, D-R.I., bottom right.

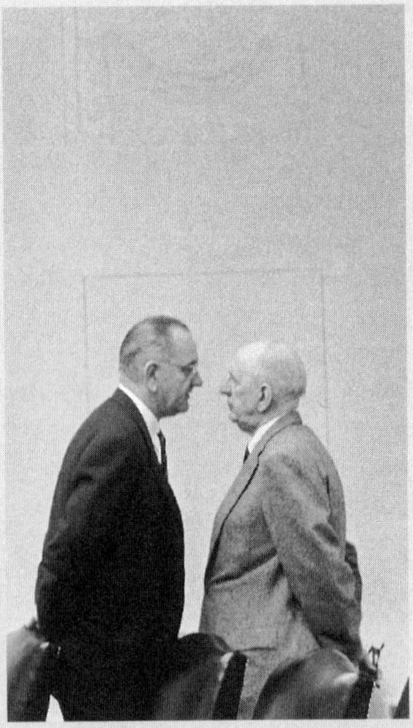

TENTH EDITION

Congress and Its Members

Roger H. Davidson
University of Maryland

Walter J. Oleszek
Congressional Research Service

CQ PRESS A Division of Congressional Quarterly Inc., Washington, D.C.

CQ Press
1255 22nd Street, NW, Suite 400
Washington, DC 20037

Phone, 202-729-1900; toll-free, 1-866-427-7737 (1-866-4CQ-PRESS)

Web: www.cqpress.com

Photo Credits: Agence France-Presse, 477 (middle); AP/Wide World Photos, 2 (middle), 38 (middle, bottom), 80 (top, middle, bottom left, bottom right), 272 (bottom), 304 (bottom), 334 (top, bottom), 362 (middle, bottom left, bottom right), 394 (top), 420 (top, bottom), 450 (top, bottom left, bottom right); Scott J. Ferrell, Congressional Quarterly, 12 (bottom), 116 (middle, bottom), 192 (middle, bottom), 236, 272 (middle right), 477; Landov/Reuters, 148 (top, bottom left, bottom right), 192 (top), 272 (top), 304 (top), 362 (top); LBJ Library, frontispiece (left, top right); Library of Congress, 12 (top); *New York Times*, frontispiece, (bottom right); Office of Congressman Roy Blunt, 116 (top); Office of Representative Jerrold Nadler, 2 (bottom); Reuters, 2 (top), 28 (top), 304 (middle), 334 (middle), 394 (bottom)

Text Design: Judy Myers
Cover Design: Tony Olivis, Circle Graphics

♾ The paper used in this publication exceeds the requirements of the American National Standard for Information Sciences—Permanence of Paper for Printed Library Materials, ANSI Z39.48-1992.

Printed and bound in the United States of America

09 08 07 06 05 1 2 3 4 5

ISBN: 1-56802-935-7
ISSN: 1539-1779

FOR *Nancy; Douglas, Victoria, Elizabeth, Thomas, James, Alexander; Chris, Teddy, Emily, and Olivia*

—*R. H. D.*

FOR *Janet, Mark, and Eric*

—*W. J. O.*

CONTENTS

PART II A CONGRESS OF AMBASSADORS

PART IV Policy Making and Change in the Two Congresses

Part V Conclusion

Reference Materials

TABLES, FIGURES, AND BOXES

Tables

Figures

Boxes

PREFACE

As authors of the tenth edition of a book that first appeared in 1981, we are perforce believers in the maxim that in politics six months is a long time and four years practically a lifetime. Events of recent years surely bear out this wisdom.

George W. Bush entered the presidency after a 2000 presidential contest that ended in the political equivalent of a tied score resolved by a judicial coin toss. But his moderately successful presidency was dramatically transformed by the terrorist attacks of September 11, 2001, which enabled him to reinvent himself as a wartime leader. This image helped him in the 2004 election, when voters narrowly reelected him over Democratic candidate John Kerry, a Massachusetts senator who had been a Vietnam War hero. Bush's firmness in the face of the terrorist attacks overcame voters' leanings toward Kerry's stances on many leading issues, including foreign policy and various economic and social questions. Bush in his second term faced increased resistance to his administration's policies from emerging fissures within the majority Republicans' coalition and from heightened Democratic opposition.

Political forces on Capitol Hill reflect a recent partisan realignment. The two parties are at fairly close parity. The Republicans began the 109th Congress (2005–2007) with 232 House seats, a sufficient but not overwhelming majority. In the Senate the GOP edge was 55–44 (one Independent caucused with the minority Democrats), a modest majority in a chamber whose traditions value independence and often require supermajorities to conduct business.

The fluctuating fortunes of recent presidents and congressional majorities remind us of the pervasive pluralism of the American political system, with its diversity of viewpoints and interests. What presidents and congressional majorities see as their mandates sooner or later bump against the founders' intricate "auxiliary precautions" for preventing majorities from winning quick or total victories. Not the least of the system's attributes is what we call the "two Congresses" dilemma: Congress is both a conduit for localized interests and a maker of national policy.

In this edition we discuss new developments and fresh research findings regarding nearly every aspect of Congress. The impact of the 2001 terrorist attacks cannot be minimized. A wartime context—thus far embracing two wars and reconstruction efforts in Afghanistan and Iraq and ongoing offensives against terrorism—placed extreme pressures on Congress. Deliberative legislative processes may seem out of place when people demand immediate, concerted actions. But hasty actions invariably are regretted, and sober reflections require legislative oversight and remediation.

The strength of partisanship and party leadership is probably the biggest Capitol Hill story. Capitol Hill is a vortex of the so-called permanent campaign, in which electioneering goals and techniques are routinely used to influence the content of lawmaking. The role of the 2004 elections in ratifying and strengthening the recent partisan realignment is analyzed, along with the implications for congressional operations and decision making. We record changes in party leadership, the committee system, floor procedures, and the Capitol Hill community. Shifting relationships with presidents, the bureaucracy, and the courts illustrate the centrality of Congress to the entire federal government apparatus.

Amid all these global and political changes, there are underlying constants in Congress's character and behavior. Most important is the dual nature of Congress as a collection of career-minded politicians and at the same time a forum for shaping and refining national policy. We employ the two Congresses theme to explain the details of congressional life as well as the scholarly findings about legislators' behavior. Colorful personalities and practical examples illustrate the enduring topics essential for understanding Capitol Hill. We strive to describe recent events and trends precisely and perceptively; more than that, we try to place these developments in the broader historical and conceptual frameworks necessary for understanding how Congress and its members function.

For those who believe in representative democracy, these are troubling times. True, Congress has—with varying levels of success—absorbed astonishing changes in its membership, partisan control, structural and procedural arrangements, and policy agendas. Yet Congress has all too often retreated from its constitutional stature as an initiator of national policy and an overseer of government operations. Its prerogatives are under siege from executive decision makers, federal judges, and elite opinion makers—who constantly belittle its capacities and evade its scrutiny. Yet lawmakers themselves must accept blame for yielding too often to the initiatives of others, for failing to ask hard questions and to insist upon straight answers, and for at times substituting partisan allegiance for independent judgment. Today's Congress often falls short of the founders' vision that it is the "first branch of government"—for reasons that this book explains.

This edition, like its predecessors, is written for general readers seeking an introduction to the modern Congress as well as for college or university students taking courses on the legislative process or national policy making. We have tried to present accurate, timely, and readable information, along with thoughtful and influential insights from scholars and practitioners alike. Although wrapped around our core theme, the book's chapters are long on analysis. For this we do not apologize. Lawmaking is an arduous business that demands special skills; those who would understand it must encounter its details and nuances. At the same time, we hope to convey the energy and excitement of the place. After all, our journalist friends are right: Capitol Hill is the best beat in town.

We have incurred more debts to friends and fellow scholars than we could ever recount. We thank especially our colleagues at the Congressional Research Service and elsewhere: Mildred Amer, Richard Beth, Colton Campbell, Joe Cantor, Thomas Carr, Kevin Coleman, George Costello, Royce Crocker, Christopher Davis, Paul E. Dwyer, C. Lawrence Evans, Louis Fisher, Kevin Gates, Richard Grimmett, William Heniff, Henry Hogue, David Huckabee, Frederick Kaiser, Robert Keith, Johnny Killian, Mike Kolakowski, Betsy Palmer, Harold Relyea, Sula P. Richardson, Morton Rosenberg, Steve Rutkus, Elizabeth Rybicki, James Saturno, Judy Schneider, Barbara Schwemle, Stephen W. Stathis, Sean M. Theriault, and Donald Wolfensberger.

We also wish to thank our reviewers, Michelle Chin, Arizona State University; Jeff Jenkins, Northwestern University; Matthew Streb, Loyola Marymount University; and Stephen Wirls, Rhodes College, for their generous assistance. Their thoughtful comments provoked us to consider new questions and revisit enduring ones, and helped us to shape the current edition.

Our friends at CQ Press deserve special appreciation. Brenda Carter, director of the college division, has inspired and prodded us over the last seven editions. Elise Frasier, our editor, capably reviewed the book's overall structure and helped us tighten this edition. Colleen McGuiness provided skilled and probing editorial assistance. Anna Socrates supervised the book into production and, with the assistance of Daphne Levitas, gave invaluable advice on photo research. Jessica Forman ably composed the pages.

Our deep appreciation for our families, for their love and support, cannot be fully expressed in words. As a measure of our affection, this book is dedicated to them.

—Roger H. Davidson
Santa Barbara, California

—Walter J. Oleszek
Fairfax, Virginia

June 2005

TENTH EDITION

Congress and Its Members

Rep. Jerrold Nadler, D-N.Y., and the "two Congresses" after the 2001 attack on the World Trade Center in the heart of his congressional district: Above, a masked Nadler and, beside him, then-Democratic leader Richard A. Gephardt of Missouri inspect the devastation at Ground Zero. Right, Nadler confers with New York City mayor Michael Bloomberg. Born and raised in his district, Nadler reflects the liberal views of his constituents. Below, Nadler addresses a pro-choice rally.

chapter 1

The Two Congresses

A U.S. representative rarely gets to see a part of his constituency attacked and destroyed. But Rep. Jerrold Nadler, D-N.Y., did on the morning of September 11, 2001. Nadler, who represents Wall Street, the Upper West Side of Manhattan, and portions of Brooklyn, was watching television in his Washington, D.C., apartment when the second jetliner hit the World Trade Center, his district's most prominent landmark.

"Holy God, this is a terrorist act," Nadler exclaimed. "I immediately decided I had to get back to my district."[1] With a steadily fading cell phone his only link to the outside world, he and his wife coped with several disrupted train rides, reaching the Hudson River eight hours later. Meanwhile, his staff members—in Washington, Brooklyn, and lower Manhattan—struggled to follow developments and to field inquiries from frantic constituents.

"What's amazing is when you come up to New York on the train, you can normally see the twin towers from [northern New Jersey]," Nadler recalled. "All we could see was a plume of smoke. I can't tell you how empty I felt. I felt violated. This is my New York I'm coming home to."[2] Since then, he has worked tirelessly to rebuild the devastated neighborhood and aid the thousands of families whose lives were forever changed.

Nadler's experiences illustrate the themes in this book. The work of Congress is conducted not only on Capitol Hill but also in states and districts hundreds or thousands of miles away. Nadler has lived all his life in or near his district, where he is known simply as "Jerry." His representational style, his language, and his brash liberalism speak in the distinct accents of his hometown.

Nadler's Capitol Hill role is an extension of his district's character—with its large concentration of liberal Jewish voters and gay and lesbian activists. As a member of the Judiciary Committee, he defended President Bill Clinton in the 1998-1999 impeachment imbroglio and upholds his party's positions on most key issues. His liberal voting record (Americans for Democratic Action) is 100 percent; his lifetime American Conservative Union score is 3 percent.[3] In 2004 he was reelected by nearly four-fifths of the district's voters.

THE DUAL NATURE OF CONGRESS

The crisis in lower Manhattan underscores the dual nature of Congress. Like all members of Congress, Nadler inhabits two very different but closely linked worlds. His activities highlight the dual character of the national legislature—Congress as a lawmaking institution and as an assembly of local representatives. The question is how these disparate elements can be reconciled.

The answer is that there are two Congresses. One is the Congress of textbooks, of "how a bill becomes a law." It is Congress acting as a collegial body, performing constitutional duties and debating legislative issues. And it is an intriguing subject. To tourists and Cable Satellite Public Affairs Network (C-SPAN) viewers no less than to veteran analysts, Capitol Hill is a fascinating arena where many of the forces of American political life converge—ambitious politicians, cabinet members, lowly bureaucrats, and lobbyists both powerful and weak. The issues they voice on Capitol Hill affect the well-being of all.

This Congress is more than a collection of its members at any given time. It is a mature institution with a complex network of rules, structures, and traditions. These norms mark the boundaries of the legislative playing field and define the rules by which the game is played. Individual members generally must accept Congress on its own terms and conform to its established ways of doing things. Paradoxically, the institution at once both resists change and invites change.

A second Congress also exists, and it is every bit as important as the Congress of the textbooks. This is the representative assembly of 540 individuals (100 senators, 435 representatives, 4 delegates, and 1 resident commissioner). It is composed of men and women of diverse ages, backgrounds, and routes to office. The electoral fortunes of its members depend less upon what Congress produces as an institution than upon the support and goodwill of voters hundreds or thousands of miles away. "As locally elected officials who make national policy," asserts Paul S. Herrnson, "members of Congress almost lead double lives."[4]

The two Congresses are in some ways widely separated. The tight-knit, complex world of Capitol Hill is a long way from most constituencies, in perspective and outlook as well as in miles. Moreover, the two Congresses are analytically distinct. Studies suggest that public officials and citizens view the twin functions of elected assemblies—lawmaking and representing—as separate, definable tasks.

Yet these two Congresses are closely bound together. What affects one sooner or later affects the other.

Legislators' Tasks

The dualism between institutional and individual duties surfaces in legislators' daily activities and roles. As Speaker Sam Rayburn, D-Texas, once remarked: "A congressman has two constituencies—he has his constituents at home, and his colleagues here in the House. To serve his constituents at home, he must also serve his colleagues here in the House."[5]

Senators and representatives suffer from a lack of time to accomplish what others expect of them. No problem vexes members more than that of juggling constituency and legislative tasks. Despite scheduled recesses for constituency business (called "district work periods" by the House, "nonlegislative periods" by the Senate), the pull of constituency business is relentless. The average representative spends 120 days a year in the home constituency; the average senator, 80 days.[6] Even in Washington, legislative and constituency demands clash. According to one study, less than 40 percent of a representative's Washington time is allotted to lawmaking duties on the floor of the House or in committee.[7]

Members of Congress, when asked to describe the functions they should perform in office, stress the twin roles of legislator and representative. Legislators vary in how they balance these roles, not to mention what time and resources they devote to them. With their longer terms, senators can stress voter outreach and fence-mending during the year or so before reelection and focus on legislative activities at other times. Yet senatorial contests normally are more competitive and costly than House races, and many senators now run flat out for reelection all the time—like most of their House colleagues.[8]

Legislators must choose between the demands of these two roles. A congressionally sponsored survey asked members about how they spent their time and what they would like to do ideally as a member of Congress. By a wide margin the senators and representatives said they would devote extra time to lawmaking and other Capitol Hill duties instead of to constituency demands.[9]

Congress's dual nature—the unresolved dichotomy between its lawmaking and representative functions—is dictated by the U.S. Constitution, validated by historical experience, and reinforced by the inclinations of voters and legislators alike. Yet Congress is one body, not two. The same members who shape bills in committee and vote on the floor must rush to catch planes back to their districts, where they are plunged into a different world, one of local problems and personalities. And the same candidates who must sell themselves at shopping center rallies must in the nation's capital help shape the federal budget or military weapons systems. The unique character of Congress arises directly from its dual role as a representative assembly and a lawmaking body.

Popular Images

The notion of the two Congresses also conforms with the perceptions of the average citizen. Opinion studies reveal that people view the U.S. Congress through lenses different from those through which they see their individual senators and representatives. Congress as an institution is perceived primarily as a lawmaking body. It is judged mainly on the basis of citizens' overall attitudes about politics, policies, and the state of the union. Do people like the way things are going, or do they not? Are they optimistic or pessimistic about the nation's future? Do they subscribe to Mark Twain's cynical view that Congress is "a distinctly native criminal class"?

Citizens view their own legislators as agents of local concerns. People judge their legislators by such yardsticks as service to the district, communication with constituents, and home style (the way officeholders deal with the home folks). In judging their senators or representative, voters are likely to ponder questions such as these: Is the legislator trustworthy? Does the legislator communicate well with the state (or district) by answering mail promptly and offering timely help to constituents? Does the legislator listen to the state (or district) and its concerns? [10]

The public's divergent expectations of Congress and its members often send conflicting signals to senators and representatives. Congress as a whole is judged by policies and results, however vaguely voters understand them. Individual legislators are more apt to be elected, and returned to office, because of personal qualities and constituent service. For many legislators, this incongruity dictates a strategy of opening as much space as possible between them and the politicians back in Washington—even sometimes their party's leaders.

The Historical Basis

The dual character of Congress is rooted in history. Congress's mandate to write the nation's laws is found in Article I of the Constitution which details the powers of government as set forth by the founders in 1787. It was no accident that the Constitution's drafters devoted the first article to the legislature and that most of the government's powers were enumerated there. Familiar with the British Parliament's prolonged struggles with the Crown, the authors assumed the legislature would be the chief policy-making body and the bulwark against arbitrary executives. "In republican government, the legislative authority necessarily predominates," observed James Madison in *The Federalist Papers.*[11]

Although in the ensuing years the initiative for policy making has shifted many times between the legislative and executive branches, the U.S. Congress remains virtually the only national assembly in the world that drafts in detail the laws it passes, instead of simply debating and ratifying measures prepared by the government in power.

As a representative body, Congress must respond to the insistent demands of voters and constituents. Although not specifically spelled out in the Constitution, these duties inevitably flow from constitutional provisions for electing representatives and senators.

The House of Representatives was intended to be the most representative element of the U.S. government. Representatives are elected directly by the people for two-year terms to ensure that they do not stray too far from popular opinion. As Madison explained, the House should have "an immediate dependence on, and an intimate sympathy with, the people."[12] For most members of the House, this two-year cycle means nonstop campaigning, visiting, looking after constituents, and errand running. For some the job is simpler than for others; yet no elected official is immune to electoral defeat.

The Senate originally was intended to be one step removed from popular voting to temper the House's popular passions: State legislatures selected senators. But the founders ultimately were overruled. In 1913 the people's voice was assured with the ratification of the Seventeenth Amendment, which provided for direct election of senators. Although elected for six-year terms, senators must stay in close touch with the electorate. Like their House colleagues, senators typically regard themselves as servants of their constituents. Most have transformed their office staffs into veritable cottage industries for generating publicity and handling constituents' inquiries.

Thus the Constitution and subsequent historical developments affirm Congress's dual functions of lawmaker and representative assembly. Although the roles are tightly bound together, they nonetheless impose separate duties and functions.

Back to Burke

On November 3, 1774, in Bristol, England, the British statesman and philosopher Edmund Burke set forth for his constituents the dual character of a national legislature. The constituent-oriented parliament, or Congress, he described as

> a Congress of ambassadors from different and hostile interests, which interests each must maintain, as an agent and advocate, against other agents and advocates.

The parliament of substantive lawmaking he portrayed in different terms. It is

> a deliberative assembly of one nation, with one interest, that of the whole—where not local purposes, not local prejudices, ought to guide, but the general good, resulting from the general reason of the whole.[13]

Burke preferred the second concept and did not hesitate to let his voters know it. He would give local opinion a hearing, but his judgment and conscience would prevail in all cases. "Your faithful friend, your devoted servant, I shall be to the end of my life," he declared; "flatterer you do not wish for."[14]

Burke's Bristol speech is an enduring statement of the dilemma confronting members of representative assemblies. Burke was an inspired lawmaker. (He even sympathized with the cause of the American colonists.) But, as might be said today, he suffered from an inept home style. His candor earned him no thanks from his constituents, who turned him out of office at the first opportunity.

Burke's dilemma applies equally on this side of the Atlantic. From colonial times to the present, American voters have tended to prefer their lawmakers to be delegates, who listen carefully to constituents and follow their guidance.

During an encounter in Borger, Texas, an irate Baptist minister shouted at then-representative Bill Sarpalius, D-Texas, "We didn't send you to Washington to make intelligent decisions. We sent you to represent us."[15] Sarpalius subsequently was defeated for reelection. The authors of the Constitution expected intimate bonds between voters and lawmakers (at least in the House), ensuring them by providing frequent elections.

So it does no violence on constitutional theory to assume that election, or reelection, is the paramount operational goal of individual office seekers. As a former representative put it: "All members of Congress have a primary interest in getting reelected. Some members have no other interest."[16] After all, politicians are (like other people) self-interested, and winning elections is the prerequisite for achieving long-range political goals. "[Reelection] has to be the *proximate* goal of everyone, the goal that must be achieved over and over if other ends are to be entertained" writes David R. Mayhew in his noted essay *Congress: The Electoral Connection.*[17]

The reelection imperative is by no means the whole story. Burke's idea that legislators are trustees of the nation's common good is still extolled. In a 1995 decision, U.S. Supreme Court justice John Paul Stevens noted that, once elected, members of Congress become "servants of the people of the United States. They are not merely delegates appointed by separate, sovereign states; they occupy offices that are integral and essential components of a single national Government."[18]

Furthermore, legislators do not always engage in self-interested bidding for local constituents' votes. Politicians harbor a range of ultimate goals (health, wealth, fame, family, religious faith). Among the most prominent is promoting what they view as the public interest. A reasonable assumption, therefore, is that elected officials "make an honest effort to achieve good public policy."[19]

Burke posed the tension between the two Congresses so vividly that we have adopted his language to describe the conceptual distinction that forms the crux of this book. From Burke, we have also drawn the titles for Part 2, "A Congress of Ambassadors," and Part 3, "A Deliberative Assembly of One Nation." Every legislator sooner or later must come to terms with Burke's dichotomous Congress; citizens and voters will have to form their own answers.

DIVERGENT VIEWS OF CONGRESS

Congress has been the subject of a huge array of books, monographs, and articles. Many of its features make Congress a favorite object of scholarly scrutiny. It is open and accessible. It can be approached by traditional means—journalistic stories, case studies, and normative or historical accounts. It is amenable to scientific analysis, whether empirical, mathematical, or theoretical. Its work can be measured by statistical indicators (floor votes, for example) that permit elaborate comparative analyses. And Congress is, above all, a fascinating place—the very best site from which to view the varied actors in the American political drama.

Writers of an interpretive book on the U.S. Congress thus can draw on a multitude of sources, an embarrassment of riches. Studies of Congress constitute a vast body of political literature. This is a mixed blessing because all this information must be integrated into something resembling a coherent whole. Moreover, much of the writing is highly specialized, technical, or theoretical. We have tried to put such material into perspective, make it accessible to all interested readers, and use illustrative examples wherever possible.

A gaping chasm exists between this rich scholarly literature and the caricature of Congress often prevalent in the popular culture. Pundits and humorists from Mark Twain and Will Rogers to Jay Leno and David Letterman have found Congress an inexhaustible source of raw material. The other branches of government have nothing like the cartoon image of lawmakers as corrupt, pompous windbags. Citizens tend to share this disdain toward the legislative branch—especially at moments of furor over, say, congressional pay raises or ethics scandals.

The picture of Congress conveyed in the media is scarcely more flattering. Journalistic hit-and-run specialists, especially news magazines, editorial writers, and talk-show hosts, perpetuate a cartoon-like stereotype: an irresponsible and somewhat sleazy gang resembling Woodrow Wilson's caustic description of the House as "a disintegrated mass of jarring elements."[20] Legislators in their home states or districts often contribute to Congress's poor image by portraying themselves as escapees from the funny farm on Capitol Hill. As Richard F. Fenno Jr. puts it, they "run *for* Congress by running *against* Congress."[21]

Citizens' ambivalence toward the popular branch of government—which, by the way, goes back to the beginnings of the Republic—says something of the milieu in which public policy is made. To comprehend how the two Congresses function—both the institution and individual members—popular stereotypes must be abandoned and the complex realities examined. This book is intended to fill in the details left unexamined in popular accounts. We believe we know our subject well enough to appreciate Congress's foibles and understand why it works the way it does. Yet we try to maintain a professional—yes, scholarly—distance from it.

According to an old saying, two things should never be viewed up close: making sausage and making laws. Despite this warning, we urge readers to take a good look and form their own opinions about Congress's effectiveness. Some may recoil from what they discover. Numerous flaws can be identified in members' personal or public behavior, in their priorities (incentive structures), and in their lawmaking practices. But careful observers also will discover much behavior in Congress that is purposeful and principled, many policies that are reasonable and workable. We invite students and colleagues to examine with us what Congress has done thus far and consider what prospects lie ahead.

SUGGESTED READINGS

Bianco, William, ed. *Congress on Display, Congress at Work.* Ann Arbor: University of Michigan Press, 2000.

Hamilton, Lee H. *How Congress Works, and Why You Should Care.* Bloomington: Indiana University Press, 2004.

Hibbing, John R., and Elizabeth Theiss-Morse. *Congress as Public Enemy.* Cambridge, United Kingdom: Cambridge University Press, 1995.

Mayhew, David R. *Congress: The Electoral Connection.* 2d ed. New Haven: Yale University Press, 2004.

"A woman's place is in the House—and the Senate": Left, the seven women members of the 71st Congress (1929–1931) pose on the Capitol steps less than a decade after passage of the Nineteenth Amendment, ratified in 1920, granting women the right to vote. Below, the fourteen women senators serving in the 109th Congress (2005–2007) meet for a "power coffee." Sixty-nine women serve in the House of Representatives.

chapter 2

Evolution of the Modern Congress

The first Congress met in New York City, the seat of government, in the spring of 1789. Business was delayed until a majority of members arrived to make a quorum. On April 1 the thirtieth of the fifty-nine elected representatives reached New York; Frederick A. C. Muhlenberg of Pennsylvania was chosen Speaker of the House. Five days later the Senate achieved its quorum, although its presiding officer, Vice President John Adams, did not arrive for another two weeks.

New York City was then a bustling port on the southern tip of Manhattan Island. Congress met in Federal Hall at the corner of Broad and Wall Streets. The House of Representatives occupied a large chamber on the first floor and the Senate a more intimate chamber upstairs. The new chief executive, George Washington, was still en route from his home at Mount Vernon, Virginia, his trip having become a triumphal procession with crowds and celebrations at every stop. To most of his countrymen, Washington—austere, dignified, the soul of propriety—embodied a government that was otherwise no more than a plan on paper.

The two houses of Congress did not wait for Washington's arrival. The House began debating tariffs, a perennially popular legislative topic. In the Senate, Vice President Adams, a brilliant but self-important man, prodded his colleagues to decide upon proper titles for addressing the president and himself. Adams was dubbed "His Rotundity" by a colleague who thought the whole discussion absurd.

On inaugural day, April 30, Adams was still worrying about how to address the president when the representatives, led by Speaker Muhlenberg, burst into the Senate chamber and seated themselves. Meanwhile, a special committee was dispatched to escort Washington to the chamber for the ceremony. The swearing-in was conducted on an outside balcony in front of thousands of assembled citizens. The nervous Washington haltingly read his speech. Then everyone adjourned to St. Paul's Chapel for a special prayer service. Thus the U.S. Congress became part of a functioning government.[1]

ANTECEDENTS OF CONGRESS

The legislative branch of the new government was untried and unknown, searching for procedures and precedents. And yet it grew out of a rich history of development—stretching back more than five hundred years in Great Britain, no less than a century and a half in North America. If the architects of the U.S. Constitution of 1787 were unsure how well their new design would work, they had firm ideas about what they intended.

The English Heritage

From the time of the English king Edward the Confessor in the eleventh century, the central problem of political theory and practice was the relationship of the Crown to its subjects. Out of prolonged struggles, a strong, representative parliament emerged that rivaled and eventually eclipsed the power of the Crown. The evolution of representative institutions on a national scale began in medieval Europe. Monarchs gained power over large territories where inhabitants were divided into social groupings, called "estates of the realm"—among them the nobility, clergy, landed gentry, and town officials. The monarchs brought together leaders of these estates, not to create representative government but to fill the royal coffers.

These assemblies—parliaments, as they later came to be called—evolved over the centuries into the representative assemblies of today. Four distinct stages of their development have been identified. At first the parliaments, representing the various estates, met to vote taxes for the royal treasury, engaging in little discussion. Next, these tax-voting bodies evolved into lawmaking bodies that presented the king with petitions for redressing grievances. Third, by a gradual process that culminated in the revolutions of the seventeenth and eighteenth centuries, parliaments wrested lawmaking and tax-voting powers from the king, transforming themselves into truly sovereign bodies. In the nineteenth century, finally, parliamentary representation expanded beyond the older privileged groups to embrace the masses, eventually every adult man and woman.[2]

By the time the New World colonies were founded in the 1600s, the struggle for parliamentary rights was well advanced into the third stage, at least in England. Bloody conflicts, culminating in the beheading of Charles I in 1649 and the dethroning of James II in 1688 (the Glorious Revolution), established parliamentary influence over the Crown. Out of such struggles flowed a remarkable body of political and philosophic writings. By the eighteenth century, works by James Harrington (1611–1677), John Locke (1632–1704), and others were the common heritage of educated people—including the leaders of the American Revolution.

The Colonial Experience

This tradition of representative government migrated to the New World. As early as 1619 the thousand or so Virginia colonists elected twenty-two burgesses, or delegates, to a General Assembly. In 1630 the Massachusetts Bay Company established itself as the governing body for the Bay Colony, subject to annual elections. The other colonies, some of them virtually self-governing, followed suit.

Representative government took firm root in the colonies. The broad expanse of ocean shielding America fostered self-reliance and autonomy on the part of colonial assemblies. Claiming prerogatives similar to those of the British House of Commons, these assemblies exercised the full range of law-making powers—levying taxes, issuing money, and providing for colonial defense. Legislation could be vetoed by colonial governors (appointed by the Crown in the eight royal colonies), but the governors, cut off from the home government and depending on local assemblies for revenues and even for their own salaries, usually preferred to reach agreement with the locals. Royal vetoes could emanate from London, but these took time and were infrequent.[3]

Other elements nourished the tree of liberty. Many of the colonists were free spirits, dissidents set on resisting all authority, especially that of the Crown. Readily available land, harsh frontier life, and—by the eighteenth century—a robust economy fed the colonists' self-confidence. The town meeting form of government in New England and the separatists' church assemblies helped cultivate habits of self-government. Newspapers, unfettered by royal licenses or government taxes, stimulated lively exchanges of opinions.

When Britain decided in the 1760s to tighten its rein upon the American colonies, the restraint was met, not surprisingly, with stubborn opposition. Did not the colonists enjoy the same rights as Englishmen? Were not the colonial assemblies the legitimate governments, with authority derived from popular elections? As British enactments grew increasingly unpopular, along with the governors who tried to enforce them, the locally based colonial legislatures took up the cause of their constituents.

The colonists especially resented the Stamp Act of 1765 (later repealed) and the import duties imposed in 1767. From these inflated customs receipts the home government began paying the salaries of royal governors and other officials, thus freeing those officials from the grasp of colonial assemblies. The crisis worsened in the winter of 1773–1774, when a group of colonists staged a revolt, the Boston Tea Party, to protest the Tea Act. In retaliation, the House of Commons closed the port of Boston and passed a series of Intolerable Acts, further tightening royal control.

National representative assemblies in America were born on September 5, 1774, when the First Continental Congress convened in Philadelphia, Pennsylvania. Every colony except Georgia sent delegates, a varied group that included peaceable loyalists, moderates such as John Dickinson, and firebrands such as Samuel Adams and Paul Revere. Gradually anti–British sentiment congealed, and Congress passed a series of declarations and resolutions (each colony casting one vote) amounting to a declaration of war against the mother country.[4] After Congress adjourned on October 22, King George III declared that the colonies were "now in a state of rebellion; blows must decide whether they are to be subject to this country or independent." [5]

The First Continental Congress gave colonists a taste of collective decision making, and the Second Continental Congress proclaimed their independence from Britain. When the Second Continental Congress convened on May 10, 1775, many still thought war might be avoided. A petition to King George asking for "happy and permanent reconciliation" was even approved. The British responded by proclaiming a state of rebellion and launching efforts to crush it. Sentiment in the colonies swung increasingly toward independence, and by the middle of 1776 Congress was debating Thomas Jefferson's draft resolution that "these united colonies are, and of right ought to be, free and independent states." [6]

The two Continental Congresses gave birth to national politics in America. Riding the wave of patriotism unleashed by the British indignities of 1773–1774, the Congresses succeeded in pushing the sentiments of leaders and the general public toward confrontation and away from accommodation with the mother country. They did so by defining issues one by one and by reaching compromises acceptable to both moderates and radicals—no small accomplishment. Shared legislative experience, in other words, moved the delegates to the threshold of independence. Their achievement was all the more remarkable in light of what historian Jack N. Rakove describes as the "peculiar status" of the Continental Congress, "an extra-legal body whose authority would obviously depend on its ability to maintain a broad range of support." [7]

More than five years of bloody conflict ensued before the colonies won their independence. Meanwhile, the former colonies hastened to form new governments and draft constitutions. Unlike the English constitution, these charters were written documents. All included some sort of bill of rights, and all paid lip service to the doctrine of separating powers among legislative, executive, and judicial branches of government. But earlier conflicts with the Crown and the royal governors had instilled a fear of executive authority. So equal branches were not created. Nearly all the constitutions gave the bulk of powers to their legislatures, effectively creating what one historian termed "legislative omnipotence." [8]

The national government was likewise, as James Sterling Young put it, "born with a legislative body and no head." [9] Strictly speaking, no national executive existed between 1776 and 1789—the years of the Revolutionary War and the Articles of Confederation (adopted in 1781). On its own, Congress struggled to wage war against the world's most powerful nation, enlist diplomatic allies, and manage internal affairs. As the war progressed and legislative direction proved unwieldy, Congress tended to delegate authority to its own committees and to permanent (executive) agencies. Strictly military affairs were placed in the hands of a designated leader: George Washington, who at the war's end returned his commission to Congress in a public ceremony. Considering the obstacles it faced, congressional government was far from a failure. Yet the mounting inability of all-powerful legislative bodies, state and national, to deal with postwar problems spurred demands for change.

At the state level, Massachusetts and New York rewrote their constitutions, adding provisions for potentially stronger executives. At the national level, the Confederation's frailty led many to advocate what Alexander Hamilton called a more "energetic" government—one with enough authority to implement laws, control currency, levy taxes, dispose of war debts, and, if necessary, put down rebellion. Legislative prerogatives, it was argued, should be counterbalanced with a vigorous, independent executive.

In this spirit, delegates from the states convened in Philadelphia on May 25, 1787, intending to strengthen the Articles of Confederation. Instead, they drew up a wholly new governmental charter.

CONGRESS IN THE CONSTITUTION

The structure and powers of Congress formed the core of the Constitutional Convention's deliberations. On these questions, the fifty-five delegates at the Philadelphia convention were divided, and more than three months passed before they completed their work. A tripartite governmental system was outlined, with Congress named first in the Constitution. The plan, agreed upon and signed September 17, 1787, was a bundle of compromises. Nationalist and states' rights interests—large and small states, northern and southern states—had to be placated. The result was a singular blend of national and federal features based on republican principles of representation and limited government. The Constitution served the nationalists' goal of an energetic central government that could function independently of the states. It also conceded the states' rights principle of limited powers shared by the various branches.

Powers of Congress

The federal government's powers are shared by three branches: legislative, executive, and judicial. Although considered one of the Constitution's most innovative features, separation of powers arose from English and colonial experience, which argued for dispersing governmental functions. It was advocated by philosophers Harrington, Locke, and the baron de Montesquieu. The Articles of Confederation's failure to separate these functions was widely regarded as a mistake.

Legislators have unfettered authority to organize the chambers as they see fit and are accorded latitude in performing their duties. To prevent intimidation, they cannot be arrested during sessions or while traveling to and from sessions (except for treason, felony, or breach of the peace). Members in their deliberations enjoy immunity from any punitive action: In speech and debate, "they shall not be questioned in any other place" (Article I, Section 6).

Despite their worries over all-powerful legislatures, the founders laid down an expansive mandate for the new Congress. Mindful of the achievements of

New World assemblies, not to mention the British Parliament's age-long struggles with the Crown, they viewed the legislature as the chief repository of governmental powers. Locke had observed that "the legislative is not only the supreme power, but is sacred and unalterable in the hands where the community have placed it."[10] Locke's doctrine found expression in Article I, Section 8, which enumerates Congress's impressive array of powers. Here is laid out virtually the entire scope of governmental authority as the eighteenth-century founders understood it. This portion of the Constitution reflects the founders' vision of a vigorous legislature as the engine of an energetic government.

Raising and spending money for governmental purposes lies at the heart of Congress's prerogatives. The power of the purse was the lever by which parliaments historically gained bargaining advantages over kings and queens. The Constitution's authors, well aware of this, gave Congress full powers over taxing and spending.

Financing the government is carried out under Congress's broad mandate to "lay and collect taxes, duties, imposts and excises, to pay the debts and provide for the common defense and general welfare of the United States" (Article 1, Section 8). Although this wording covered almost all known forms of taxing, there were limitations. Taxes had to be uniform throughout the country; duties were prohibited on goods traveling between states; and "capitation . . . or other direct" taxes were prohibited, unless levied according to population (Article I, Section 9). This last provision proved troublesome when the U.S. Supreme Court held in 1895 (*Pollock v. Farmers' Loan and Trust Co.*) that it applied to taxes on incomes. To overcome this confusion, the Sixteenth Amendment, ratified eighteen years later, explicitly conferred the power to levy income taxes.

Congressional power over government spending is no less sweeping. Congress is to provide for the "common defense and general welfare" of the country (Article I, Section 8). Furthermore, "No money shall be drawn from the Treasury, but in consequence of appropriations made by law" (Article I, Section 9). This provision is one of the legislature's most potent weapons in overseeing the executive branch.

Congress possesses potentially broad powers to promote the nation's economic well-being and political security. It has the power to regulate interstate and foreign commerce, and it has used this power to regulate not only trade but also transportation, communications, and such disparate subjects as labor practices, civil rights, and crime. This power is not unlimited and historically has been legally and politically contentious. Congress may also coin money, incur debts, establish post offices, build post roads, issue patents and copyrights, provide for a militia, and call forth the militia to repel invasions or suppress rebellions.

Although the three branches supposedly are coequal, the legislature takes the lead in formulating the structure and duties of the other two. Although the Constitution mentions executive departments and officers, it does not specify their structure or duties, aside from those of the president. Thus the design of the executive branch, including cabinet departments and other agencies, is spelled out in laws passed by Congress and signed by the president.

The judiciary, too, is largely a statutory creation. It consists of a Supreme Court and "such inferior courts as the Congress may from time to time ordain and establish" (Article III, Section 1). Although the courts' jurisdiction is delineated, the Supreme Court's appellate jurisdiction is subject to "such exceptions" and "such regulations as the Congress shall make" (Article III, Section 2).

Congress's powers within the federal system were greatly enlarged by the Civil War amendments—the Thirteenth (1865), Fourteenth (1868), and Fifteenth (1870). The Radical Republicans, who had supported the war and controlled Congress in its aftermath, feared that former Confederate states would ignore the rights of blacks—the cause over which the war had been waged. Thus these amendments nationalized such citizens' rights as voting, due process, and equal protection of the laws. By implication—eventually recognized through a series of Court rulings—citizens were protected against state actions that violated a number of other core Bill of Rights guarantees. To underscore such a basic change in the federal bargain, the three amendments' authors gave Congress the powers of enforcement by "appropriate legislation."

Congress is a full partner in foreign relations with its power to declare war, ratify treaties, raise and support armies, provide and maintain a navy, and make rules governing the military forces. Finally, Congress is vested with the power "to make all laws which shall be necessary and proper for carrying into execution the foregoing powers" (Article I, Section 8). This Elastic Clause, undoubtedly added to give Congress the means to implement its enumerated powers, has provoked far-reaching debates over the scope and reach of governmental activity.

Limits on Legislative Power

Congress's enumerated powers—those "herein granted"—are not boundless. The very act of listing the powers was intended to limit government, for by implication those powers not listed are prohibited. The Tenth Amendment reserves to the states or to the people all those powers neither explicitly delegated nor prohibited by the Constitution. This guarantee is a rallying point for those who take exception to particular federal policies or who wish broadly to curtail federal powers.

Eight specific limitations on Congress's powers are noted in Article I, Section 9. The most important bans are against bills of attainder, which pronounce a particular individual guilty of a crime without trial or conviction and impose a sentence, and ex post facto laws, which make an action a crime after it has been committed or otherwise alter the legal consequences of some past action. Such laws are traditional tools of authoritarian regimes.

The original Constitution contained no bill of rights or list of guarantees for citizens or states. Pressed by opponents during the ratification debate, supporters of the Constitution promised early enactment of amendments to remedy this omission. The resulting ten amendments, drawn up by the First Congress and ratified December 15, 1791, are a basic charter of liberties that limits the reach of government. The First Amendment prohibits Congress from establishing a national religion, preventing the free exercise of religion, or abridging the freedoms of speech, press, peaceable assembly, and petition. Other amendments secure the rights of personal property and fair trial and prohibit arbitrary arrest, questioning, or punishment.

Rights not enumerated in the Bill of Rights are not necessarily denied (Ninth Amendment). In fact, subsequent amendments, legislative enactments, judicial rulings, and states' actions have enlarged citizens' rights to include the rights of citizenship, of voting, of privacy, and of "equal protection of the laws."

Separate Branches, Shared Powers

The Constitution not only lists Congress's powers but also sets them apart from those of the other two branches. Senators and representatives, while in office, are prohibited from serving in other federal posts; those who serve in such posts are in turn forbidden from serving in Congress (Article I, Section 6). This restriction forecloses any form of parliamentary government, in which leading members of the dominant parliamentary party or coalition form a cabinet to direct the ministries and other executive agencies.

Legislative Interdependence. Because the branches are separated, some people presume that the powers they exert should also be isolated. In practice, however, governmental powers are interwoven, even if the branches are separate. James Madison explained that the Constitution created not a system of separate institutions performing separate functions but separate institutions that share functions so that "these departments be so far connected and blended as to give each a constitutional control over the others."[11]

Congress cannot act alone, even in lawmaking. Although the Constitution vests Congress with "all legislative powers," these powers cannot be exercised without involvement by the president and by the courts. This same interdependency applies to executive and judicial powers. The president is a key figure in lawmaking. According to Article II, the president can convene one or both houses of Congress in special session. Although unable to introduce legislation directly, the president "shall from time to time give to the Congress information on the state of the Union, and recommend to their consideration such measures as he shall judge necessary and expedient." The president also has the power to veto congressional enactments. After a bill or resolution has passed both houses of Congress and been delivered to the White House, the president must sign it or return it within ten days (excluding Sundays). Overruling a presidential veto requires a two-thirds vote in each house.

Carrying out laws is the duty of the president, who is enjoined by the Constitution to take care that laws are faithfully executed. As head of the executive branch, the president has the power to appoint "officers of the United States," with the Senate's advice and consent. Although Congress sets up the executive departments and agencies, outlining their missions by statute, chief executives and their appointees manage the character and pace of executive activity.

In diplomacy and national defense, traditional domains of royal prerogative, the Constitution apportions powers between the executive and legislative branches. Following tradition, presidents are given wide discretion in such matters. They appoint ambassadors and other envoys, they negotiate treaties, and they command the country's armed forces. However, like other high-ranking presidential appointees, ambassadors and envoys must be approved by the Senate. Treaties do not become the law of the land until they are ratified by a two-thirds vote of the Senate. Although the president may dispatch troops, only Congress has the power of formally declaring war. Reacting to the Vietnam War, Congress in 1973 passed the War Powers Resolution, intended to restrain presidents from making war without congessional approval.

Historically, presidents and Congresses (and courts) have reached accommodations to exercise the powers they share. As Justice Joseph Story once wrote, the authors of the Constitution sought to "prove that rigid adherence to [separation of powers] in all cases would be subversive to the efficiency of government and result in the destruction of the public liberties." Justice Robert Jackson noted in 1952 that "while the Constitution diffuses power the better to secure liberty, it also contemplates that practice will integrate the dispersed powers into a workable government."[12]

Impeachment. Congress has the power to impeach and remove the president, the vice president, and other "civil officers of the United States" for serious breaches of the public trust: treason, bribery, or "other high crimes and misdemeanors." The House of Representatives has the sole authority to draw up and adopt (by majority vote) articles of impeachment, which are charges that the individual has engaged in one of the named forms of misconduct. The Senate is the final judge of whether to convict on any of the articles of impeachment. A two-thirds majority is required to remove the individual from office or to remove and also bar the individual from any future "offices of public trust."

Three attributes of impeachment fix it within the separation of powers framework. First, it is exclusively the domain of Congress. (Even though the chief justice presides over Senate trials of the president, his rulings may be overturned by majority vote.) The two chambers are free to devise their own procedures for reaching their decisions. The Supreme Court refused to review the Senate's procedures when a former federal judge, Walter L. Nixon Jr., objected that, although he had been convicted by the full Senate, the evidence in his case had been taken by a committee, not the full Senate.[13]

Second, impeachment is a legislative proceeding that is essentially political in character. The structure may appear judicial—the House a grand jury, the Senate a trial court—but lawmakers decide whether and how to proceed, which evidence to consider, and even what constitutes an impeachable offense.

Treason is defined by the Constitution, and bribery by statute; but the words "high crimes and misdemeanors" are open to interpretation. They are usually defined (in Alexander Hamilton's words) as "abuse or violation of some public trust"—on-the-job offenses against the state, the political order, or the society at large.[14] This means they can be either more or less than garden-variety criminal offenses. Both presidential impeachment trials (Andrew Johnson, 1868; Bill Clinton, 1998–1999) were fiercely partisan affairs, in which combatants disputed not only the facts but also the appropriate grounds for impeachment.

Finally, impeachment is a clumsy instrument for punishing officials for the gravest of offenses. Congress has many lesser ways of reining in wayward officials. As for presidents and vice presidents, their terms are already limited. Although impeachments are often threatened, only fifteen Senate trials have taken place, and only seven individuals have been convicted. Significantly, all seven who were removed from office were judges—who, unlike executive officers, enjoy open-ended terms of office.[15]

Judicial Review

The third of the separated branches, the judiciary, has assumed a leading role in interpreting laws and determining their constitutionality. Whether the founders anticipated this function of judicial review is open to question. Probably they expected each branch to reach its own judgments on constitutional questions, especially those pertaining to its own powers. This reading of the founders' intent is called the doctrine of coordinate construction.

Whatever the original intent, Chief Justice John Marshall soon preempted the other two branches with his Court's unanimous assertion of judicial review in *Marbury v. Madison* (1803). Judicial review involves both interpretation and judgment. First, "it is emphatically the province and duty of the judicial department to say what the law is." Second, the Supreme Court has the duty of weighing laws against the Constitution, the "supreme law of the land," and invalidating those that are inconsistent—in the *Marbury* case a minor provision of the Judiciary Act of 1789.[16] Yet Congress, not the Court, remained the primary forum for weighty constitutional debates throughout the nineteenth century. Until the Civil War only one other law, the Missouri Compromise, had been declared unconstitutional by the Court (*Dred Scott v. Sandford*, 1857). Since the Civil War, however, the Court has been more aggressive in interpreting and judging congressional handiwork.

For the record, the Supreme Court has invalidated 160 congressional statutes, in whole or in part, in the two hundred years since *Marbury*.[17] This count does not include lower court holdings that have not been reviewed by the Supreme Court. Nor does it cover laws whose validity has been impaired because a similar law was struck down.

The justices' political leanings have historically worked either to expand or to contract the powers of Congress. Judges are said to exercise judicial restraint when using their power of judicial review sparingly, deferring to the judgments of the legislature (and executive) and intervening only in cases flagrantly at odds with the Constitution. Judicial activism involves more aggressive patrolling of the limits of the two elective branches' powers.

Judges are commonly labeled as practitioners of activism or restraint, but this is a false distinction. Ideology drives judges toward activity on some subjects and passivity on others. As Associate Justice Antonin Scalia observed, "Conservatives are willing to grow the Constitution to cover their favorite causes, just as liberals are."[18] Conservative courts from the Civil War to the late 1930s, for example, fashioned the concept of "economic due process" to shield businesses from state and federal attempts at regulating the economy. At the same time, they generally deferred to legislative interpretations of civil rights and civil liberties, even when those actions fell far short of what was required by the Bill of Rights or the Civil War amendments. Court liberals of the 1950s and 1960s (Chief Justice Earl Warren's era) pushed far ahead of Congress to remedy long-standing violations of individual liberties and rights, but they rarely challenged congressional regulation of the economy.

Recent conservative court majorities, buoyed by Republican appointees, have been more aggressive than their recent predecessors in setting limits upon federal regulatory powers over the states. At the same time they have tended to uphold government claims in dealing with public safety or national security policies—for example, post–September 11, 2001, laws or procedures. Conservative judges, in other words, may be activists restricting socioeconomic laws but cast a more benign eye on security actions. Liberal judges, by contrast, shy away from challenges to socioeconomic powers but question invasions of civil rights or liberties. (The labels "conservative" and "liberal," though commonly used to describe the Court's factions, are shorthand terms. Regarding the sitting justices, the liberals might better be termed centrists, along with at least two in the conservative wing—and all the justices harbor individual views, sometimes at variance with their ideological leanings.)

The Supreme Court does not necessarily have the last word in saying what the law is. Its interpretations of laws may be questioned and even reversed. If the congressional sponsors or supporters of a law disagree with the justices' readings of the text, they may clarify or modify the language in subsequent enactments. One study found that 121 of the Court's interpretive decisions had been overridden in the 1967–1990 period, an average of ten per Congress. The author of the study concluded that "congressional committees in fact carefully monitor Supreme Court decisions." Congress was most apt to override decisions of a closely divided Court, decisions that rely on the law's plain meaning, and decisions that clash with positions taken by federal, state, and local governments.[19]

Nor is the Court the sole arbiter of what is or is not constitutional. Courts routinely accept customs and practices developed by the other two branches. Likewise, they usually decline to decide sensitive political questions within the province of Congress and the executive. When courts strike down an enactment, Congress may turn around and pass laws that meet the courts' objections or achieve the same goal by different means.

Congress sometimes reacts to judicial holdings by trying to impede, modify, or reverse them or by simply ignoring them. The *Dred Scott* decision helped bring about the Civil War. Reconstruction laws and constitutional amendments after the war explicitly nullified the Court's holding. And despite *Immigration and Naturalization Service v. Chadha* (1983), Congress continues to enact legislative veto provisions, which were in large part outlawed but which administrators often feel obliged to honor out of political prudence.

The courts play a leading but not exclusive role in interpreting laws and the regulations emanating from them. When Congress passes a law, the policy-making process has just begun. Courts and administrative agencies then assume the task of refining the policy, but they do so under Congress's watchful eye. "What is 'final' at one stage of our political development," Louis Fisher observes, "may be reopened at some later date, leading to revisions, fresh interpretations, and reversals of Court doctrines. Through this never-ending dialogue, all three branches are able to expose weaknesses, hold excesses in check, and gradually forge a consensus on constitutional issues." [20]

Bicameralism

Although "the Congress" is discussed as if it were a single entity, Congress is divided internally into two very different, virtually autonomous, chambers. Following the pattern initiated by the British Parliament and imitated by most of the states, the Constitution outlines a bicameral legislature. If tradition recommended the two-house formula, the politics of the early Republic commanded it. Large states preferred the "nationalist" principle of popularly based representation, but the smaller states insisted on a "federal" principle also ensuring representation by states.

The first branch—as the House was termed by Madison and Gouverneur Morris, among others—rests on the nationalist idea that the legislature should answer to the people instead of the states. As George Mason put it, the House "was to be the grand depository of the democratic principles of the government." [21] Many years later the Supreme Court ruled (in *Wesberry v. Sanders*, 1964) that these principles demanded that congressional districts within each state be essentially equal in population.

In contrast, the Senate embodied the federal idea. Each state would have two seats, the occupants to be chosen by the state legislatures and not by popular vote. The Senate would serve to curb the excesses of popular government. "The use of the Senate," explained Madison, "is to consist in its proceeding with more coolness, with more system, and with more wisdom, than the popular branch." [22]

Historical evolution overran the founders' intentions. In most cases, senators tended to voice dominant economic interests and shun the general public.

British commentator Lord Bryce once remarked that the Senate seemed to care more for its "collective self-esteem" than it did for public opinion.[23] Yet state legislators often instructed their senators how to vote on vital issues. In some states legislative elections turned into statewide canvasses focusing on senatorial candidates. Such was the famous 1858 Illinois contest between Sen. Stephen A. Douglas and challenger Abraham Lincoln. The Democrats captured the legislature and sent Douglas back to Washington, but Lincoln's eloquent arguments against extending slavery to the territories west of the Mississippi River vaulted him into national prominence.

Direct election of senators came with the Seventeenth Amendment, ratified in 1913. A by-product of the Progressive movement, the new arrangement was designed to broaden citizens' participation and blunt the power of shadowy special interests, such as party bosses and business trusts. Thus the Senate became directly subject to popular will.

Bicameralism is the most obvious organizational feature of the U.S. Congress. Each chamber has a distinct process for handling legislation. According to the Constitution, each house sets its own rules, keeps a journal of its proceedings, and serves as final judge of its members' elections and qualifications. In addition, the Constitution assigns unique duties to each of the two chambers. The Senate ratifies treaties and approves presidential appointments. The House must originate all revenue measures; by tradition, it also originates appropriations bills. In impeachments, the House prepares and tries the case, and the Senate serves as the court.

The two houses jealously guard their prerogatives and resist intrusions by the other body. Despite claims that one or the other chamber is more important—for instance, that the Senate has more prestige or that the House pays more attention to legislative details—the two houses staunchly defend their equal places. On Capitol Hill there is no "upper" or "lower" chamber.

INSTITUTIONAL EVOLUTION

Written constitutions, even those as farsighted as the 1787 one, go only a short way in explaining how real-life governmental institutions work. On many questions such documents are inevitably silent or ambiguous. Issues that lie between the lines must be resolved in the course of later events.

In adapting to demands far removed from those of eighteenth-century America, Congress has evolved dramatically. Many of these changes can be subsumed under the term *institutionalization*—the process whereby structures and procedures take shape and become regularized. Instead of being unformed and unpredictable, the institution becomes structured and predictable, following settled traditions and widely held expectations about how it should perform. Institutionalization has shaped the two Congresses—Congress as deliberative body and Congress as individual representatives.

The Size of Congress

Looking at the government of 1789 through modern lenses, one is struck by the relatively small circles of people involved. The House of Representatives, that "impetuous council," was composed of sixty-five members—when all of them showed up. The aristocratic Senate boasted only twenty-six members, two from each of the thirteen original states.

As new states were added, the Senate grew. There were thirty-two senators in 1800, sixty-two in 1850, ninety by 1900, and one hundred today. (Since 1912 only the states of Alaska and Hawaii have been added.)

As for the House, the Constitution (Article I, Section 2) sets forth the method of apportioning its members—a decennial census. When the first census was taken in 1790, the nation's population count was fewer than four million—smaller than that of an average state today. "I take it for granted," Madison wrote in *The Federalist Papers* No. 55, "that the number of representatives will be augmented from time to time in the manner provided by the Constitution." [24] The House was raised to 104 members after the first census, and throughout the nineteenth century there were steady enlargements. The 1910 census, which counted ninety-two million people, led to a final expansion to 435 members. But following the 1920 census Congress declined to enlarge the House further. And that is the way things stand to this day.

Enlarging the House is periodically urged—especially by states losing seats after a census. More seriously, some worry that congressional districts are too populous (only those in India are larger) to permit meaningful ties between citizens and their representatives.[25] The framers contemplated House districts of no more than thirty thousand people—huge by 1789 standards. Following that guideline would now require a House of some ninety-four hundred members. Modest enlargement would only marginally alleviate the problem. Most observers concur with Speaker Sam Rayburn, who served in Congress from 1913 to 1961, that the House is already at or above its optimum size for lawmaking.

Size profoundly affects an organization's work. Growth compelled the House to develop strong leaders, to rely heavily on its committees, to impose strict limits on floor debate, and to devise elaborate ways of channeling the flow of floor business. It is no accident that strong leaders emerged during the House's periods of rapid growth. After the initial growth spurt in the first two decades of the Republic, vigorous leadership appeared in the person of Henry Clay, whose speakerships (1811–1814, 1815–1820, and 1823–1825) demonstrated the potentialities of that office. Similarly, post–Civil War expansion was met with an era of forceful Speakers that lasted from the 1870s until 1910. Size is not the only impetus for strong leadership, but it also inevitably works to centralize procedural control.

In the smaller and more intimate Senate, vigorous leadership has been the exception rather than the rule. The relative informality of Senate procedures, not to mention the long-cherished right of unlimited debate, testifies to looser reins of leadership. Compared with the House's complex rules and voluminous precedents, the Senate's rules are brief and simple. Informal negotiations among senators interested in a given measure prevail, and debate typically is governed by unanimous consent agreements—agreed-upon ways of proceeding, brokered by the parties' floor leaders. Although too large for its members to draw their chairs around the fireplace on a chilly winter morning—as they did in the early years—the Senate today retains a clubby atmosphere that the House lacks.

The congressional establishment itself has changed in scale, with staffs added gradually. In 1891 a grand total of 142 clerks, 62 for the House and 80 for the Senate, were on hand to serve members of Congress. Many senators and all representatives handled their own correspondence. Keeping records and counting votes were the duties of committee clerks. After the turn of the twentieth century, House and Senate members, their clerks, and their committees moved into two ornate office buildings, one for each house. Today the legislative branch embraces some twenty-three thousand staff members. Housed in nearly a dozen Capitol Hill buildings, they include experts in virtually every area of government policy and constitute a distinct Washington subculture.

The Legislative Workload

During the Republic's early days, the government in Washington was "at a distance and out of sight."[26] Lawmaking was a part-time occupation. As President John F. Kennedy was fond of remarking, the Clays, Calhouns, and Websters of the nineteenth century could afford to devote a whole generation or more to debating and refining the few great controversies at hand. Rep. Joseph W. Martin, R-Mass., who entered the House in 1925 and went on to become Speaker (1947–1949, 1953–1955), described the leisurely atmosphere of earlier days and the workload changes during his service.

> From one end of a session to another Congress would scarcely have three or four issues of consequence besides appropriations bills. And the issues themselves were fundamentally simpler than those that surge in upon us today in such a torrent that the individual member cannot analyze all of them adequately before he is compelled to vote. In my early years in Congress the main issues were few enough so that almost any conscientious member could with application make himself a quasi-expert at least. In the complexity and volume of today's legislation, however, most members have to trust somebody else's word or the recommendation of a committee. Nowadays bills, which thirty years ago would have been thrashed out for hours or days, go through in ten minutes.[27]

The most pressing issue considered by the Foreign Affairs Committee during one session, Martin related, was a $20,000 authorization for an international poultry show in Tulsa, Oklahoma.

Congress's workload—once limited in scope, small in volume, and simple in content—has burgeoned since 1789. Some ten thousand bills and resolutions are introduced in the span of each two-year Congress; perhaps five hundred or so are enacted into law. By most measures—hours in session, committee meetings, floor votes—the congressional workload has about doubled over the past half century.

Legislative business has expanded in scope and complexity as well as in sheer volume. Today's Congress grapples with many issues that once were left to states or localities or were considered entirely outside the purview of governmental activity. Moreover, legislation tends to be more complex than it used to be. The average public bill of the late 1940s was two and a half pages long; by the late 1990s it ran to more than eighteen pages.[28]

For most of its history Congress was a part-time institution. Well into the twentieth century Congress remained in session for only nine of every twenty-four months, the members spending the rest of their time at home attending to private business. In recent decades legislative business has kept the House and Senate almost perpetually in session—punctuated by constituency work periods. During the average two-year Congress the Senate is in session nearly three hundred eight-hour days; the more efficient House gets by on somewhat less time.[29] The average senator or representative works an eleven-hour day when Congress is in session.[30]

Structures and Procedures

A mature institution not only exhibits the professionalism of its members but also is reflected in the number and complexity of its structures and procedures.

No trait illustrates Congress's institutional growth more dramatically than the division of labor through the committee system. Although fashioned gradually and seemingly inexorably, the committee system rests on precedents drawn from the British House of Commons, the colonial assemblies, and the Continental Congresses.[31] The first House standing committee (Elections) was created in 1789, but legislative business in both houses tended to be handled by temporary committees or on the floor. By the third decade of the nineteenth century, however, standing committees were firmly established.

The creation and, occasionally, abolition of committees parallel important historical events and shifting perceptions of public problems.[32] As novel policy problems arose, new committees were added. The House, for example, established Commerce and Manufactures in 1795, Public Lands in 1805, Freedmen's Affairs in 1866, Roads in 1913, Science and Astronautics in 1958, Standards of Official Conduct in 1967, Small Business in 1975, and Homeland Security in 2003. Numerous committees have existed at one time or another—as many as sixty-one in the House and seventy-four in the Senate.

Today the Senate has sixteen standing committees and the House has twenty. These committees are only the tip of the iceberg, however. House committees now have nearly one hundred subcommittees; Senate committees, nearly seventy subcommittees. Four joint House–Senate committees have been retained. This adds up to some two hundred work groups, plus an abundance of task forces, party committees, voting blocs, informal caucuses, and the like.

The number of formal and informal leaders in Congress has grown as a function of proliferating work groups. Every committee and subcommittee has a chairman and a ranking minority member. The formal party leaders help organize the two chambers, assign members to committees, schedule business, and devise parliamentary strategy. Supplementing formal leadership posts in Congress are a host of informal leaders who represent factions, regions, economic interests, or issue positions. Thus formal leaders are obliged to adopt what Barbara Sinclair calls a "strategy of inclusion"; that is, "drawing into the leadership's orbit and including in leadership efforts as many [partisans] as possible." [33] The result is ever more complex networks of give-and-take relationships in which less-informed members seek cues from better-informed colleagues, issue by issue. Today's Congress, in other words, abounds in leaders of every stripe.

In the early days, proceedings at the Capitol were disorderly, especially in the crowded, noisy, and badly ventilated chambers. "Debate has been rough and tumble, no holds barred, bruising, taunting, raucous, sometimes brutal," one historian related. "The floor of the House has been no place for the timid or the craven." [34] Before the Civil War, duels between quarreling legislators were not uncommon. One celebrated incident occurred in 1856, when Rep. Preston Brooks, a southern Democrat, stalked Sen. Charles Sumner, a Massachusetts Republican, and beat him senseless with a cane on the Senate floor for his views on slavery in the new territories.

As Congress matured, decorum by and large replaced chaos, and stricter rules of order came to govern the proceedings. Today there are formidable rules and precedents as well as numerous informal norms and traditions. Altering the rules is not a casual matter. (The House adopts its rules anew with each new Congress; as a continuing body the Senate has ongoing rules.) Most rules changes result from concerted effort by the leadership, party caucuses, or the respective rules committees. When major rules changes or committee realignments are considered, select committees may be established to make recommendations.

Despite institutional inertia the Senate and House repeatedly shift and adapt their ways of doing things—partly in response to changes in public and workload demands, partly in reaction to altered partisan or factional alignments, partly to accommodate shifts in membership. Just as physical anthropologists believe the earth's history is marked by periods of intense, even cataclysmic, change—punctuated equilibrium—so historians of Congress have identified several eras of extensive institutional change. "Reconstitutive change" is what Elaine K. Swift calls these instances of "rapid, marked, and enduring shift[s] in the fundamental dimensions of the institution." [35] During one such period (1809–1829), Swift argues, the Senate was transformed from an elitist, insulated "American House of Lords" into an active, powerful institution whose debates stirred the public and attracted the most talented politicians of the time. Another such period was the Progressive Era (roughly the first two decades of the twentieth century), when House leaders were toppled and the Senate became an elective body. The so-called reform era of the 1960s and 1970s qualifies as a third time of wide-ranging change, ushering in a period of heightened partisanship.

Not all institutional changes are so concentrated. Incremental changes of one kind or another are always unfolding. For example, the House in 1999 streamlined and codified its rules, and hardly anyone noticed. In a detailed examination of changes in committee jurisdictions, David C. King showed that periodic, large-scale jurisdictional "reform acts" were mainly compilations of gradually accumulated precedents created as novel bills were introduced.[36]

In short, Congress is no longer an informal institution. It bristles with norms and traditions, rules and procedures, committees and subcommittees. The modern Congress is highly institutionalized. How different from the First Congress, personified by fussy John Adams worrying about what forms of address to use. The institutional complexity of today's Congress enables it to cope with a staggering workload while for the most part containing personal conflict. Institutional complexity, however, carries its own costs—in rigidity and the cumbersome administrative apparatus needed to keep the system afloat.

EVOLUTION OF THE LEGISLATOR'S JOB

What is it like to be a member of Congress? The legislator's job, like the institution of Congress, has evolved since 1789. During the early Congresses being a senator or representative was a part-time occupation. Few members regarded congressional service as a career, and from most accounts the rewards were slim. Since then the lawmakers' exposure to constituents' demands, their career expectations, and their factional loyalties have changed dramatically. Electoral units, too, have grown very large. After the 2000 census, which counted 282 million citizens, the average House constituency contained 680,000 people; the average state, almost 6 million.

Constituency Demands

American legislators have been expected to remain close to their voters. From the very first, representatives reported to their constituents through circular letters, communications passed around throughout their districts.[37] In an era of limited government, however, there was little constituent errand running. "It was a pretty nice job that a member of Congress had in those days," recalled Rep. Robert Ramspeck, D-Ga. (1929–1945), describing the Washington of 1911, when he came to take a staff job:

> At that time the government affected the people directly in only a minor way. . . . It was an entirely different job from the job we have to do today. It was primarily a legislative job, as the Constitution intended it to be.[38]

In those days a member's mail was confined mainly to awarding rural mail routes, arranging for Spanish War pensions, sending out free seed, and only occasionally explaining legislation. At most, a single clerk was required to handle correspondence. Members from one-party areas often did little personal constituency work. It was said that Democratic Speaker John Nance Garner, who entered the House in 1903 and ended his career as vice president (1933–1941), "for thirty years did not canvass his [south Texas] district and franked no speeches home."[39] His major constituency outreach consisted of barbecues given at his home in Uvalde, Texas.

This unhurried pace has long since vanished. Reflecting on his forty years on Capitol Hill, Representative Martin remarked on the dramatic upsurge of constituent awareness.

> Today the federal government is far more complex, as is every phase of national life. People have to turn to their Representative for aid. I used to think ten letters a day was a big batch; now I get several hundred a day. In earlier times, constituents didn't know their Congressman's views. With better communications, their knowledge has increased along with their expectations of what he must know.[40]

Even people of Martin's era (he left the House in 1967) would be astonished at the volume of constituency work now handled by House and Senate offices. Not only are constituents more numerous than ever before, but they are also better educated, served by faster communication and transportation, and mobilized by lobby organizations. Public opinion surveys show that voters expect legislators to dispense federal services and to communicate frequently with the home folks. Even though the crasser forms of pork-barrel politics have come under attack, constituents' demands are unlikely to ebb in the future.

The Congressional Career

During its early years Congress was an institution composed of transients. The nation's capital was an unsightly place, its culture was provincial, and its summers were humid and mosquito-ridden. Members remained in Washington only a few months, spending their unpleasant sojourns in boardinghouses. "While there were a few for whom the Hill was more than a way station in the pursuit of a career," James Sterling Young observes, "affiliation with the congressional community tended to be brief."[41]

The early Congresses failed to command the loyalty needed to keep members in office. Congressional service was regarded more as odious duty than as rewarding work. "My dear friend," wrote a North Carolina representative to his constituents in 1796, "there is nothing in this service, exclusive of the confidence and gratitude of my constituents, worth the sacrifice. . . . Having secured this, I could freely give place to any fellow citizen, that others too might obtain the consolation due to faithful service."[42] Of the ninety-four senators who served between 1789 and 1801, thirty-three resigned before completing their terms, only six to take other federal posts.[43] In the House almost 6 percent of all early nineteenth-century members resigned during each Congress. Citizen legislators, not professional politicians, characterized that era.

Careerism mounted toward the end of the nineteenth century. As late as the 1870s more than half the House members at any given time were freshmen, and the mean length of service for members was barely two terms. By the end of the century, however, the proportion of newcomers had fallen to 30 percent, and average House tenure reached three terms, or six years. About the same time, senators' mean term of service topped six years, or one full term.[44] Today the average senator has served nearly sixteen years (almost three terms); the

TABLE 2-1 **Length of Service in House and Senate, 1789–2007**

	Congress			
Chamber and terms	*1st–56th (1789–1901)*	*57th–103d (1901–1995)*	*104th–108th (1995–2005)*	*109th (2005–2007)*
House				
One (up to 2 years)	44.0%	23.3%	13.6%	8.5%
Two to six (3–12 years)	53.4	49.7	56.4	52.2
Seven or more (12+ years)	2.6	27.0	30.1	39.3
Mean number of terms[a]	2.1	4.8	5.3	6.2
Senate				
One (up to 6 years)	65.6	45.6	33.8	31.0
Two (7–12 years)	23.4	22.4	27.4	26.0
Three or more (12+ years)	11.0	32.0	38.8	43.0
Mean number of terms[a]	1.5	2.2	2.6	3.0

Source: Adapted from David C. Huckabee, *Length of Service for Representatives and Senators: 1st–103d Congresses,* Congressional Research Service Report No. 95–426GOV, March 27, 1995. Authors' calculations for the 104th through 109th Congresses.

[a] Figures are derived from the total number of terms claimed by members whether or not those terms were served out. For example, members in their initial year of service are counted as having one full term, and so on. Thus the figures cannot be equated precisely with years of service.

average representative, about twelve (six terms). The data in Table 2-1 show changes since 1789 in the percentages of new and veteran members and the mean number of terms claimed by incumbents.

Rising careerism had a number of causes. The increase in one-party states and districts following the Civil War, and especially after the partisan realignment of 1896, made possible repeated reelection of a dominant party's candidates—Democrats in the core cities and the South, Republicans in the Midwest and the rural Northeast. Vigorous state and local party organizations dominated the recruitment process and tended to select party careerists to fill safe seats.[45] Around the turn of the twentieth century, however, electoral reforms—for example, direct primaries and the so-called Australian ballot (a uniform, secret, government-printed ballot)—blunted party control at the polling booth and encouraged candidates to appeal directly to their followers.

At the same time the power of the legislative branch, expressed in Woodrow Wilson's phrase "congressional government," made federal service ever more attractive and rewarding.[46] The government's subsequent growth enhanced the excitement and glamour of the national political scene, especially compared with state or local politics. Moreover, the physical environment of the nation's capital eventually improved. As Representative Martin related:

> The installation of air conditioning in the 1930s did more, I believe, than cool the Capitol: it prolonged the session. The members were no longer in such a hurry to flee Washington in July. The southerners especially had no place else to go that was half as comfortable.[47]

The rise of careerism, aided by turn-of-the-century political warfare between Progressives and the Old Guard (mainly within the dominant Republican Party), established the seniority rule to reward lengthy service. As long as senior members were scarce, they led their chambers and relied more on party loyalty than longevity in naming committees or chairmen. With careerists more numerous, greater respect had to be paid to seniority in distributing favored committee posts.

Seniority triumphed in both chambers at about the same time. In the Senate there was no decisive event. Seniority was largely unchallenged after 1877.[48] In the House strong post–Civil War Speakers, struggling to control the unruly chamber, sometimes bypassed seniority to appoint loyal lieutenants to major committees. But in 1910, when Speaker Joseph G. Cannon passed over senior members for assignments and behaved arbitrarily in other ways, the House revolted, divesting the Speaker of committee assignment power. With the Speaker's clout diminished, David W. Brady relates, "seniority came to be the most important criterion for committee assignments and chairmanships, and committees rather than parties became the major policy actors."[49]

Adherence to seniority fostered career patterns within the two houses. New members found themselves at the bottom of internal career ladders that they could ascend only through continued service. In recent decades seniority barriers have been lowered. After taking over the House in 1995, Republican leaders passed over several senior members in naming committee chairs. At the same time the GOP Conference limited chairs' terms to three years. The Committee on Committees holds interviews and selects chairs for committees and Appropriations subcommittees. Some of their choices depart from seniority, but all contenders are experienced members. Extended service, if not always strict seniority, remains a prerequisite for top party and committee posts.

Parties and Factions

Political parties had no place in the constitutional blueprint, which was deliberately fashioned to divide and dilute factional interests. However, when Treasury secretary Alexander Hamilton unveiled his financial program in 1790, a genuine partisan spirit swept Capitol Hill. The Federalists, with Hamilton as their intellectual leader, espoused energetic government to deal forcefully with national problems and foster economic growth. The rival Republicans, who looked to Thomas Jefferson and James Madison for leadership, rallied opponents of Federalist policies and championed local autonomy, weaker national government, and programs favoring rural, lower-class, or debtor interests.

When war broke out in Europe between revolutionary France and a coalition of old regimes, the Federalists sided with the dependable (and commercially profitable) British, while the Republicans tended to admire "French principles." By 1794 Sen. John Taylor of Virginia could write:

> The existence of two parties in Congress is apparent. The fact is disclosed almost upon every important question. Whether the subject be foreign or domestic—relative to war or peace—navigation or commerce—the magnetism of opposite views draws them wide as the poles asunder.[50]

U.S. House Speakers have always been political officers, and so they quickly came to reflect partisan divisions in wielding their powers. The other partisan institution in those early days was the congressional nominating caucus that selected a faction's presidential candidates. Not all members professed clear-cut partisan or factional affiliations, however. During the so-called Era of Good Feelings (roughly 1815–1825), party voting was the exception rather than the rule. With the conspicuous exception of the nominating caucuses, no formal party apparatus existed. Between the quadrennial caucuses, Young explains, "the party had no officers, even of figurehead importance, for the guidance or management of legislative processes."[51] The nominating caucus collapsed after 1824, and the Jacksonians laid the foundation for something approaching a stable party system based on grassroots support.

Parties flourished in the years following the Civil War. Regional conflicts, along with economic upheavals produced by rapid industrialization, nurtured partisan differences. The Civil War and World War I mark the boundaries of the era of militant partisanship on Capitol Hill and in the country at large. At the grassroots level the parties were divided along class, occupational, and regional lines to a degree unimaginable today. Grassroots party organizations were massive and militant by American standards. Strong Speakers tamed the unruly House, and a coterie of statewide party bosses dominated the Senate. Even after the demise of the strong speakership (1910) and direct election of senators (1913), party caucuses or committees assumed responsibility for assigning members to committees and sometimes even for formulating policy.

Today the parties' formal apparatus is extensive. There are policy committees, campaign committees, research committees, elaborate whip systems, and numerous task forces. Some four hundred staff aides are employed by party leaders and perhaps an equal number by assorted party committees.[52] Party-oriented voting bloc groups (such as the conservative House Democrats' Blue Dogs or the Republicans' Mainstreet Coalition), class clubs (such as the Republican Freshman Class or the Democratic First Term Class), and social groups complement and reinforce partisan ties.

Partisanship and factionalism are very much alive on Capitol Hill. The first thing a visitor to the House or Senate chamber notices is that the seats or desks are divided along partisan lines—Democrats to the left facing the dais, Republicans to the right. Seating arrangements betoken the parties' role in organizing the legislative branch. By means of party mechanisms, leaders are selected, committee assignments made, and floor debates scheduled. Parties also supply members with voting cues. Recent Congresses have seen modern-day peaks of party-line voting.

Partisanship has been underscored by recent events. Despite the American public's professed antipathy toward partisanship (and toward the two major parties in particular), recent elections have had distinctly partisan effects. Robust partisanship has led to congressional party platforms designed to attract voters and validate the party's bid for power. With gaping policy differences and bitter personal battles, Capitol Hill political alignments are more rigid, and appeals to partisan loyalty more shrill, than at any time in nearly a century.

CONCLUSION

At its birth the U.S. Congress was an unstructured body. Although the founders understood the guiding principles of representative assemblies, they could not have foreseen what sort of institution they had created. They wrote into the Constitution legislative powers as they understood them and left the details to future generations. During its rich and eventful history, Congress has developed into a mature organization with highly articulated structures, procedures, routines, and traditions. In a word, it became institutionalized.

This fact must be taken into account by anyone who seeks to understand Congress. Capitol Hill newcomers—even those who vow to shake things up—confront not an unformed, pliable institution but an established, traditional one that must be approached largely on its own terms. This institutionalization has a number of important consequences, some good and some bad.

Institutionalization enables Congress to cope with its contemporary workload. Division of labor, primarily through standing committees, permits the two houses to process a wide variety of issues simultaneously. In tandem with staff resources, this specialization allows Congress to compete with the executive branch in absorbing information and applying expertise to public issues. Division of labor also serves the personal and political diversity of Congress. At the same time, careerism encourages legislators to develop skills and expertise in specific areas. Procedures and traditions can contain and channel the political conflicts that converge upon the lawmaking process.

The danger of institutionalization is organizational rigidity. Institutions that are too brittle can frustrate policy making, especially in periods of rapid social or political change. Structures that are too complex can tie people in knots, producing inaction, delays, and confusion. Despite its size and complexity, however, today's Congress continues to adapt and change. Institutional changes since 1995, when Republicans became the majority in both chambers for the first time in forty years, show vividly that Congress's evolution has by no means run its full course.

The broad historical process of institutionalization by no means explains the full range of change on Capitol Hill. Five collective motivations for change are identified by Eric Schickler in his study of congressional innovations over the last century: (1) incumbents' efforts to heighten their electoral advantage; (2) efforts to defend and preserve Congress's power; (3) individual members' desire to gain access to power bases; (4) members' political party stakes—majority party prerogatives versus minority rights; and (5) the search for policy-based advantages.[53]

In a careful survey of forty-two major institutional innovations, Schickler concludes that no single theory can explain congressional change. "[L]egislative institutions are historical composites, full of tensions and contradictions."[54] Planned reforms inevitably fall short of their sponsors' objectives. Instead of achieving stable, effective arrangements, what results is "a set of institutions that often work at cross-purposes."[55] Inescapable change is thus a product of the dual Congress—driven by both electoral and institutional goals.

SUGGESTED READINGS

Binder, Sarah A. *Minority Rights, Majority Rule: Partisanship and the Development of Congress.* Cambridge, United Kingdom: Cambridge University Press, 1997.

MacNeil, Neil. *Forge of Democracy: The House of Representatives.* New York: McKay, 1963.

Polsby, Nelson W. *How Congress Evolves: Social Bases of Institutional Change.* New York: Oxford University Press, 2004.

Rakove, Jack N. *Original Meanings: Politics and Ideas in the Making of the Constitution.* New York: Vintage, 1997.

Schickler, Eric. *Disjointed Pluralism: Institutional Innovation and the Development of the U.S. Congress.* Princeton: Princeton University Press, 2001.

Swift, Elaine K. *The Making of an American Senate: Reconstitutive Change in Congress, 1787–1841.* Ann Arbor: University of Michigan Press, 1996.

Wirls, Daniel, and Stephen Wirls. *The Invention of the United States Senate.* Baltimore: Johns Hopkins University Press, 2004.

Young, James S. *The Washington Community, 1800–1828.* New York: Columbia University Press, 1966.

Elected representatives reach Congress through a series of hurdles erected by laws, customs, party groups, and voter preferences: Although minority membership in Congress lags proportionally behind the minority population at large, minority candidates are increasingly winning seats. Among the twenty-nine Hispanics serving in the 109th Congress (2005–2007) are two sets of siblings. Above, (left to right) House members Linda T. and Loretta Sanchez, Democrats from Los Angeles and Anaheim, California, respectively, celebrate on election night 2002. Below, (left to right) Sen. Ken Salazar and Rep. John Salazar, Democrats from Colorado, tour their family homestead in Manassa, a small community in the south-central part of the state, in 2004. Right, Sen. Jim Bunning, R-Ky., who won a closely fought reelection in 2004, belongs to another kind of minority: He is Capitol Hill's only member of the Baseball Hall of Fame.

chapter 3

Going for It: Recruitment and Candidacy

In the Senate chamber, on the first day of the 109th Congress (2005–2007), men and women who were formerly a lobbyist, a Rhodes Scholar, a kitchen appliance salesman, an ice cream shop owner, a cabinet member, a stockbroker, a farmer, and a major league baseball player waited expectantly for their names to be called. They were born in such places as Alamosa, Colorado; Pierre, South Dakota; Helena, Arkansas; Brooklyn, New York; Las Vegas, Nevada; and Sagua La Grande, Cuba. The sergeant at arms called them forward alphabetically in groups of four. Colleagues from their states escorted them to the front of the chamber, where the vice president, the Senate's constitutionally designated presiding officer, administered the oath of office. Newly elected or reelected, the senators were now officially members of "the world's greatest deliberative body," as the Senate likes to call itself. Over in the House chamber, all the elected or reelected members were just sworn in as well.

How did these people get to Congress? The question has no simple answer. In the broadest sense all incumbent legislators are products of recruitment, the social and political process through which people achieve leadership posts. Social analysts agree that recruitment is a key to the effective functioning of all institutions, including legislatures. The first great book about politics, Plato's *Republic,* addressed the question of finding and enlisting the ablest individuals to lead their community. Conservatives, following Plato, believe that societies should be ruled by the most talented people—in John Adams's phrase, the "rich and the wise and the well-born." Marxists believe recruitment reflects a society's class structure, with the most privileged people landing in the ranks of leadership. Contemporary political scientists, whatever their ideology, eagerly chart the paths individuals travel to posts in Congress and other institutions of government.

Any recruitment process has both formal and informal elements. As for Congress, formal elements include the constitutional framework and state and federal laws governing nominations and elections. Equally important are informal, often unwritten, rules of the game. Ambitions, skills, and resources favor certain aspirants over others; popular attitudes lead citizens to support certain aspirants and reject others. Taken together, such elements add up to a series of filters or screens. The recruitment process is a mix of rules, probabilities, chance, and timing. Its biases, both overt and hidden, affect the day-to-day operation of the House and Senate, not to mention the quality of representation and decision making.

FORMAL RULES OF THE GAME

The constitutional qualifications for holding congressional office are few and simple, though specific. The three are age (twenty-five years of age for the House, thirty for the Senate); citizenship (seven years for the House, nine years for the Senate); and residency (in the state from which the officeholder is elected). Thus the constitutional gateways to congressional officeholding are fairly wide.

These qualifications cannot be augmented by the states (or by Congress, for that matter) without altering the Constitution itself, as the U.S. Supreme Court ruled in a 1995 case involving term limits.[1] By the early 1990s, twenty-three states had adopted restrictions on the number of terms their members of Congress could serve. The state of Arkansas, whose law the Court reviewed, argued that its scheme did not create an additional "qualification" for holding office (Article I, Sections 2 and 3) but had been written as a ballot-access measure within the state's power to regulate the "times, places, and manner of holding elections" (Article I, Section 4). Speaking for the Court, Justice John Paul Stevens spurned this subterfuge as "an indirect attempt to accomplish what the Constitution prohibits Arkansas from accomplishing directly." (State laws limiting the terms of state or local officials were unaffected by the ruling.)

As the term limits controversy showed, even the three simple requirements for holding congressional office can arouse controversy. The authors of the Constitution considered but eventually rejected several other proposed qualifications, such as property ownership and term limits. Trusting comments made by the framers (especially by the authors of *The Federalist Papers*), reelection of senators and representatives was left unrestricted because the framers did not wish to limit electors' choices; they regarded the reelection option as a powerful incentive for faithful service by officeholders; and they valued the expertise that experienced lawmakers could bring to legislative deliberations.

The residency requirement is traditionally stricter in practice than the Constitution prescribes. Voters tend to prefer candidates with long-standing ties to their states or districts and to shun carpetbaggers (historically, outsiders who move into a state to seek public office). The issue is sure to be raised when the candidate is an outsider. In New York's 2000 Senate contest, Republican representative Rick A. Lazio of Long Island leveled this charge at his opponent, first lady Hillary Rodham Clinton. Only by crisscrossing the state and learning about the issues affecting the Empire State was Clinton able to prove her qualifications. (A Long Islander, Lazio himself was something of an outsider to upstate voters.)

Americans' high geographical mobility has swollen the "carpetbagger caucus" on Capitol Hill. In the 109th Congress about a third of the members of both chambers were born outside the states they represented. Especially in fast-growing areas, shrewd candidates can overcome objections to their outsider status. Barely a year after he settled in the state, Sen. John McCain, R-Ariz., a career navy officer, combat hero, and six-year prisoner of war in North Vietnam, beat three established politicians for a congressional nomination. He stifled carpetbagging charges by explaining that, as a navy officer and the son of one, he had never been able to put down roots: "The longest place I ever lived was Hanoi."

Senate Apportionment

The Senate was intended to add stability, wisdom, and forbearance to the actions of the popularly elected House. The founders stipulated that senators be chosen by the respective state legislatures, not by the voters themselves. This distinction between the two houses was eroded by the Seventeenth Amendment, which, in 1913, provided for the direct popular election of senators.

The states' equal representation in that body was the price for adoption of the Constitution and is virtually unamendable (Article V assures that no state can be deprived of its equal voice in the Senate without its own consent). Because states vary wildly in population, the Senate is the one legislative body in the nation where "one person, one vote" emphatically does not apply. By this measure "the Senate is the most malapportioned legislature in the world."[2]

The Senate's representative character has been further undermined by widening disparities in state populations. After the first census in 1790, the spread of House seats between the most populous state (Virginia) and the least populous one (Delaware) was nineteen to one. Today the spread between the most populous state (California) and each of the seven least populous states (Alaska, Delaware, Montana, North Dakota, South Dakota, Vermont, Wyoming) is fifty-three to one. Almost a third of U.S. citizens live in four megastates (California, Texas, New York, and Florida), represented by only eight senators. Large urban states complain that they are shortchanged in the federal bargain: Compared with lightly populated states, they contribute more revenue and receive fewer benefits.[3] Thus in spite of constitutional barriers, the late senator Daniel Patrick Moynihan, D-N.Y. (1977–2001), warned that "sometime in the twenty-first century the United States is going to have to address the question of apportionment in the Senate."[4]

The Senate's design has historically affected party control and policy outcomes. When senators were chosen indirectly and states were less populous, the Senate tended to be a collection of promoters for dominant regional interests such as cotton, railroads, or tobacco. Today, many states boast economic, racial, ethnic, and social diversity. Thus Senate seats are more competitive than House seats—a state of affairs that would surely have confounded the framers. Still, demography bestows power. In the 109th Congress, for example, the forty-four

Senate Democrats represented more people than the fifty-five Republicans—a result of the divergent political landscapes of large versus small states.[5]

House Apportionment

The 435 House seats are apportioned among the states by population—now averaging 680,000 people per district. This apportionment process excludes the four delegates (American Samoa, the District of Columbia, Guam, and the Virgin Islands) and one resident commissioner (Puerto Rico). They speak for populations ranging from 70,000 (Samoa) to 3.8 million (Puerto Rico).

To allocate House seats among the states, a census of population—mandated by the Constitution—is taken every ten years by the Commerce Department's Bureau of the Census. Once the census figures are gathered, apportionment is derived by a mathematical formula called the method of equal proportions.[6] The idea is that proportional differences in the number of persons per representative for any pair of states should be kept to a minimum. The first fifty seats are taken because the Constitution allots to each state at least one representative. The question then becomes: Which state deserves the fifty-first seat, the fifty-second, and so forth? The mathematical formula yields a priority value for each seat, up to any desired number.

Because the House's size has remained fixed since 1910, states may lose as well as gain congressional seats as the nation's population shifts. One state's gain means another's loss. For some decades now, older industrial and farm states of the Northeast and Midwest have lost ground to fast-growing states of the South and West—the declining Rust Belt versus the booming Sun Belt. Within states, people have shifted from rural areas to cities and then to suburbs.

The 2000 census showed what a difference ten years can make. Although all states added people, growth was slower in northeastern and midwestern states (only 5.5 percent in New York, for example). The South and West grew more rapidly. Nevada's growth rate, 66 percent, was the nation's highest, and its Second District (Las Vegas) was the nation's most populous (1.06 million). Arizona and six other western states all boasted gains of 20 percent or more. Figure 3-1 shows the current allocation along with projected gains and losses from the 2010 census—with trends similar to those of the 1990s.

Census figures also govern how legislative seats are apportioned within the states. Moreover, the federal government uses population numbers and other census data to distribute funds—involving an estimated $185 billion—to states and other entities. Business firms, marketers, and researchers also rely upon these data.

Because population figures determine seats and affect power, controversy surrounds nearly every aspect of apportionment and districting. The Census Bureau's statisticians, who are civil servants, are regarded as able and nonpartisan. But the bureau is part of the Commerce Department, a highly politicized entity whose political managers respond to White House pressures. And fol-

FIGURE 3-1 **House Apportionment in the 2000s and Estimates for the 2010s**

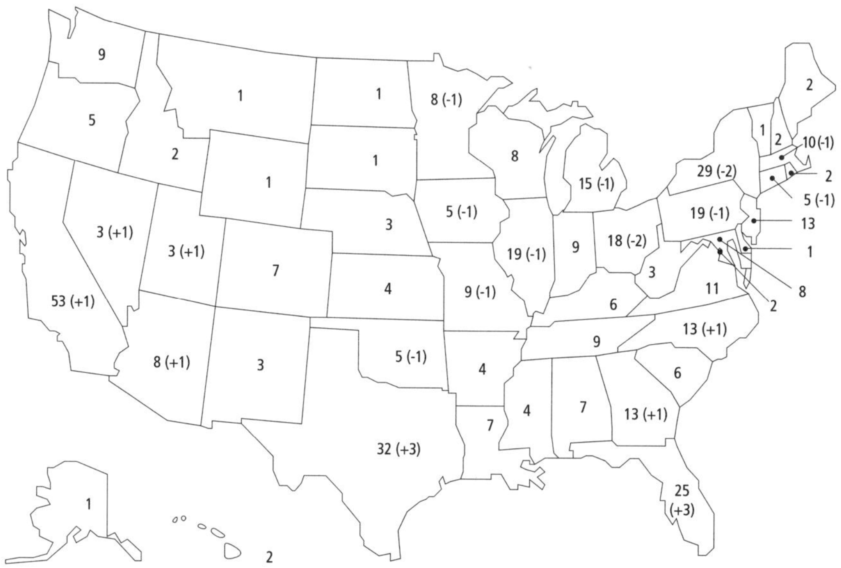

Sources: Apportionment figures derived from the 2000 census are found in: David R. Tarr, ed., *Congressional Districts in the 2000s: A Portrait of America* (Washington, DC: CQ Press, 2003), 5. Projections for the 2010s are from: Clark Benson, "Possible Changes in the House: Apportionment in 2010," Polidata Political Data Analysis (press release, January 10, 2004).

Note: Numbers in parentheses show estimated gains and losses following the 2010 census, based on Census Bureau population projections. These projections mirror states' gain-and-loss trends over recent decades, although the numbers may not all be borne out by the 2010 count.

lowing the last two counts, diverse political forces—among them lawmakers, state and local officials, party strategists, minority groups, and courts—have waged battles over census numbers.

The decennial census is described as an "actual enumeration" (Article I, Section 2). But counting such a large and diverse population is logistically and methodologically daunting. Certain hard-to-contact groupings—transients, the homeless, renters, immigrants (legal or not), children, and poorer people generally—elude census takers and are undercounted. (Some groups, such as college students living away from home, can be double-counted.)

After the 1990 count, representatives of areas where the hard-to-count were concentrated prevailed on the Census Bureau to undertake a recount. Using statistical projections, the bureau estimated that their original count had missed more than five million residents, or 2.1 percent of the total. Those missed were disproportionately minorities, mainly Latinos and African Americans. The undercount of non–Latino whites was negligible.[7] The Republican secretary of commerce chose the original figures amid cries from Democrats that both counts had been politically biased. The Supreme Court upheld his decision.

The issue of statistical sampling became the pivot for partisan and regional conflict over the 2000 census. The parties took predictable positions.

> Because Hispanics and African Americans—who in sheer numbers are the ones most undercounted—tend to be Democrats, Democrats almost universally see the wisdom in sampling and adjusting the totals, while Republicans, with very few exceptions[,] . . . do not.[8]

Census Bureau statisticians proposed using statistical samples and surveys to determine the rest. But Rep. Dave Weldon, R-Fla., chairman of the House Reform Committee's census panel, complained that any use of adjusted data "would be as flawed as the data itself."[9]

Although the 2000 count was more accurate than the prior one, the bureau analyzed a sample of households and projected that it had still missed at least 6.4 million people and double-counted at least 3.1 million—a net undercount of some 3.3 million. As in 1990, blacks and Latinos tended to be undercounted. (Of the estimated half million Californians who were missed, three-fifths were Latinos.)[10] Non–Hispanic whites were more apt to be overcounted. But the bureau was unsure that a statistical fix would be more accurate than the earlier numbers. As did his predecessor ten years earlier, the Republican commerce secretary embraced the original count.[11]

Because of population disparities between the states, reapportionment does not yield equal districts. (Congressional districts cannot cross state lines.) After the 2001 apportionment, Montana, with one representative for nearly a million people, was the nation's most populous district. Neighboring Wyoming, with barely half a million, was the least populous.

DISTRICTING IN THE HOUSE

Once congressional seats are apportioned, those states entitled to more than one seat must create districts—each represented by a single member. A 1967 statute prohibits at-large or multimember elections in these states. Districts must be nearly equal in population within states—a standard rigorously enforced by the courts—and they must not dilute representation of racial minorities, an outgrowth of amendments to the Voting Rights Act of 1965.

Redistricting is a fiercely political process upon which hinges the fortunes of the Republican and Democratic parties, not to mention other intensely interested people—state legislators, governors, incumbent House members, lobbyists, and leaders of racial and ethnic causes. (Six states have turned the job over to nonpartisan overseers.) Even in California, where redistricting would seem a slam-dunk given that Democrats then controlled the state, the party and its consultants were buffeted by clashing interests: nervous incumbents who sought safer reelection margins; term-limited state legislators, who set their sights on Washington, D.C.; minority groups demanding more representation (especially Latinos, who account for much of the state's population growth); and national party leaders counting on California to help Democrats retake the House by offsetting GOP districting gains elsewhere in the country.[12]

Both political parties poured money into statehouse elections in 2000 and into postcensus lobbying efforts. An Albany, New York, lobbyist hired to represent an upstate House member during the 2001 remapping put it bluntly: "No matter how successful [incumbents] are as lawmakers, nothing prepares them for the intensity and raw politics of the reapportionment process."[13]

In the redistricting wars no weapons are left untouched. Creating districts for elections from 2002 through 2010 thus hinged on how the contending parties utilized their array of national and state resources. Going into the redistricting cycle, the parties were well matched. Democrats controlled (that is, held the governorships and legislatures) in states with 135 seats; Republicans controlled states with 98 seats.[14] The rest of the states had divided party control.

If a state's politicians become deadlocked on redistricting, or if they fail to observe legal guidelines, judges may step in to finish the job—sometimes awarding victory to parties that lost out earlier in the political fracas. Both parties engage in forum shopping, seeking the friendliest court to aid them in the remapping process. Republicans during both Bush administrations could rely on the Justice Department and a federal bench composed of a majority of GOP appointees. State courts can also become engaged in these battles. The Supreme Court has ruled that they should normally be preferred over federal courts in redistricting cases.[15]

Because congressional seats are political prizes, districting is a tool for partisan, factional, or even personal advantage. Two historical anomalies of districting are malapportionment and gerrymandering.

Malapportionment

Before 1964 districts of grossly unequal populations often existed side by side. Within a single state, districts varied by as much as eight to one. As metropolitan areas expanded in population and political clout, their representation lagged in Congress and even more in state legislatures. Sometimes malapportionment resulted from explicit actions. More often rurally dominated legislatures simply refused to redistrict, letting population movements and demographic trends do the job for them. This failure to act was called the silent gerrymander.

The courts were slow to venture into this political thicket. By the 1960s, however, the problem of unequal representation cried out for resolution. An activist Supreme Court, led by Chief Justice Earl Warren, ruled that state districting schemes that fell short of standards of equality violated the Fourteenth

Amendment's Equal Protection Clause (*Reynolds v. Sims*, 1964). Writing for the Court, Warren held that state legislative seats must be apportioned "substantially on population"—even in bicameral arrangements.[16]

That same year, the Court applied the "one person, one vote" principle directly to the U.S. House of Representatives. An Atlantan who served in the Georgia senate, James P. Wesberry Jr., charged that the state's congressional districting violated equal protection of the laws. The Supreme Court upheld his challenge (*Wesberry v. Sanders*, 1964). The decision, however, was based not on the Fourteenth Amendment but on Article I, Section 2, of the Constitution, which directs that representatives be apportioned among the states according to their respective numbers and that they be chosen by the people of the several states. This language, argued Justice Hugo Black, means that "as nearly as is practicable, one person's vote in a congressional election is to be worth as much as another's."

How much equality of population is "practicable" within the states? The Supreme Court has adopted rigid mathematical equality as the underlying standard. In a 1983 case (*Karcher v. Daggett,*) a 5–4 majority voided a New Jersey plan in which districts varied by no more than one-seventh of 1 percent. "Adopting any standard other than population equality would subtly erode the Constitution's ideal of equal representation," wrote Justice William J. Brennan for the majority.[17]

Population equality has been achieved at the expense of other goals. To attain strict parity in numbers of residents, district mapmakers must often violate political divisions, crossing city and county lines. It is not easy to follow economic, social, or geographic boundaries. The congressional district, therefore, tends to be an artificial creation, often bearing little relationship to real communities of interest—economic or geographic or political. "The main casualty of the tortuous redistricting process now under way," remarked journalist Alan Ehrenhalt, "is the erosion of geographical community—of place—as the basis of political representation."[18]

The congressional district's isolation from other natural or political boundaries forces candidates to forge their own unique factions and alliances. It also aids candidates (incumbents especially) who have ways of reaching voters beyond relying on costly commercial media.

Traditional Gerrymandering

Most districting is gerrymandering in the sense that single-member, winner-take-all districts normally favor the local majority party. But the term *gerrymander* usually refers to conscious line drawing that maximizes seats for one's party or voting bloc. The gerrymander takes its name from Gov. Elbridge Gerry of Massachusetts, who in 1811 created a peculiar salamander-shaped district north of Boston to benefit his Democratic Party. Gerrymandering is used not only to gain partisan advantage but also to protect (and occasionally punish) incumbents, boost aspirants' political prospects, and help or hinder racial or ethnic groups.

From the mid-nineteenth to the early twentieth century, congressional statutes usually required that districts be equal in population and contiguous in territory. However, a 1911 law specifying "contiguous and compact territory" lapsed and has not been replaced, despite attempts to enact congressional districting standards. For most of its history, Congress has regarded gerrymandering as part of the spoils of partisan warfare.

Two gerrymandering techniques are cracking and packing. Cracking a district splits an area of partisan strength among two or more districts, thus diluting that party's voting leverage. Packing a district draws the lines to encircle as many of one party's voters as possible, thus rendering the district safe—either to make one party's representatives more secure or to confine its opponents' seats. Whatever the motivation, packed districts waste votes because the majority party wins with far more votes than it needs.

Partisan Gerrymandering. The most common form of gerrymandering, partisan districting, occurs in states in which one political party clearly controls the process. In the 2001–2002 cycle, GOP-controlled Florida added three seats for the party—two new districts and defeat for one Democrat in a redrawn district. In Pennsylvania the controlling Republicans committed "a brilliant and legal manslaughter" that threw together three pairs of incumbents to yield a net gain of four seats.[19] Remapping in Democratic Maryland yielded two seats—both swing areas redrawn to favor Democrats.

Redistricting politics continued even after the maps were in place for 2002. The next year, Texas Republicans—controlling both legislative houses for the first time since Reconstruction—pushed through a partisan redistricting plan over frantic opposition. (Democratic lawmakers staged quorum-busting walkouts to Oklahoma and then New Mexico.) The new map "reflects the fact that Texas is an increasingly Republican state," argued House majority leader Tom DeLay, R-Texas, who instigated the plan.[20] Democrats, along with black and Latino advocates, countered that a second postcensus remapping was impermissible (though such mid-decade revisions were common in the late nineteenth century) and that it deprived them of fair and equal representation. Declining to rule on the Texas scheme's wisdom, a federal circuit court panel upheld the Republicans' actions. The Supreme Court declined to ban the new map's use for the 2004 balloting, in which four Democratic members went down to defeat.

On the issue of partisan gerrymandering the Supreme Court, like Congress, has thus far chosen to look the other way. In a 1986 case involving Indiana state legislative districts, a Court majority held that gerrymandering was a justiciable issue—that is, it could be properly raised in court (*Davis v. Bandemer*).[21] If the gerrymandering were substantial, long-standing, and truly harmful to the political minority, it could violate the Constitution's Equal Protection Clause. At the same time, the Court's majority was not convinced the Indiana gerrymander met those tests. Although the Court invited legal challenges to partisan districting schemes, it has never confronted the problem of measuring inequities. And by 1999 the Court was ready explicitly to embrace a state's right to engage in "constitutional political gerrymandering"—whatever that means (*Hunt v. Cromartie*).[22]

The issue of whether extreme partisan gerrymandering might deny equal protection of the laws remains unresolved. In a 2004 case, the Supreme Court reviewed Pennsylvania's Republican congressional districting of 2001. By a 5–4 margin the Court upheld the state's plan. Four conservative justices, led by Antonin Scalia, held that districting was a highly political issue that rested in legislatures, not courts. They were joined by Anthony M. Kennedy, who in a concurring opinion admitted the difficulty of measuring the inequality caused by such gerrymandering but held that "the rights of fair and effective representation" remained a justiciable matter.

Four liberal justices, led by John Paul Stevens, would have invalidated the Pennsylvania map. States that "discriminate against a political minority for the sole and unadorned purpose of maximizing the power of the majority plainly violate" the Constitution's guarantee of equal rights.[23] Relatedly, the Court later, in a one-line order, instructed the relevant lower court to reconsider whether the 2003 Texas redistricting was constitutional.

Pro-incumbent Gerrymandering. Bipartisan or sweetheart gerrymanders are those with lines drawn to protect incumbents. Any gains or losses in the number of seats are shared by the two parties. These gerrymanders are often by-products of divided party control—within the legislature or between the legislature and the governor. Such was the case in New York, which lost two seats after the 2000 count. In the end two pairs of incumbents (one from each party) were thrown together, resulting in two retirements. The remaining twenty-seven districts were drawn for incumbents.

The big story of the post–2000 redistricting was the number of populous states—California, Illinois, Michigan, New York, Ohio, and initially Texas—that chose in the main to hoard their parties' existing assets. "Neither party [wanted] to lose its hard-won gains," election analyst Rhodes Cook explained. "With the partisan balance almost even, every seat counts."

> Incumbent protection [was] the path of least resistance for state legislatures redrawing the lines. Unlike in 1992, there were comparatively few retirements this time that would naturally create competitive, open-seat districts. And there were fewer districts that [were] competitive by virtue of their internal contradictions—for example, voting for one party's candidate for president and the other party's for Congress. In 2000, the number of such "split-ticket" districts was at its lowest level in nearly 50 years.[24]

Less than 10 percent of the post–2000 House races were truly competitive, even fewer of them in the large states. In California, home of 12 percent of all

House members, the dominant Democrats opted to play it safe and claim only the added seat awarded by the census. This minimalist remapping dismayed the party's national strategists and angered Latino leaders who had counted on gaining more seats. The redrawn map eliminated one swing district (its Republican incumbent retired) to craft a new Latino district in Los Angeles County, created a new GOP seat in the Central Valley, and shored up several swing-district members. (The snake-shaped Twenty-fourth District, for example, spans some 250 miles of coastland to corral liberal votes for Democratic incumbent Lois Capps. See Figure 3-2.) The result was that, in 101 races (2002, 2004), every single incumbent who ran was reelected, only six of them drawing less than 60 percent of the vote.

Because both parties and members prefer safe seats, gerrymandering has been blamed for contributing to incumbents' rising electoral fortunes. But

FIGURE 3-2 **Bipartisan Gerrymandering: California 2001**

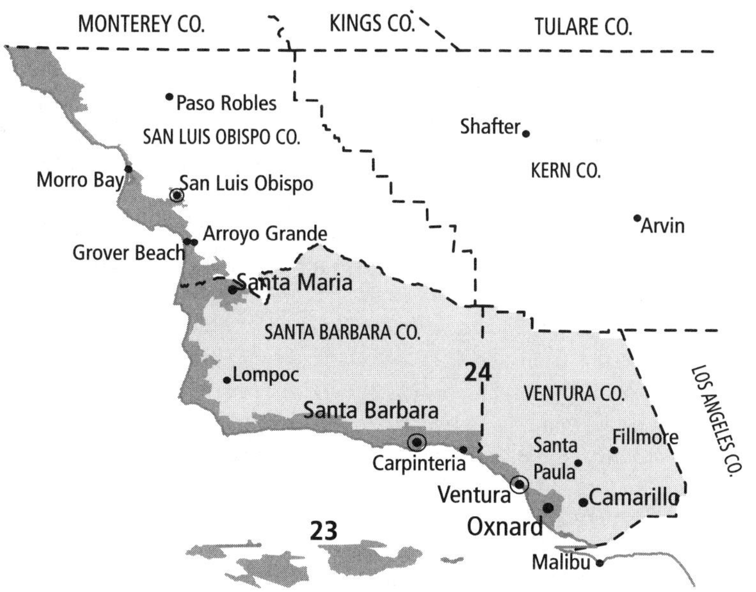

Source: Map adapted from Map Resources.

Note: In the 2001 redistricting, California Democrats opted for a bipartisan protection plan. Dividing central and south coast voters, the Twenty-third District stretched over some 250 miles of coast—from the San Luis Obispo county line to Oxnard in Ventura County—to enhance the fortunes of Democrat Lois Capps. The more conservative inland voters in two of the counties were grouped into Republican Elton Gallegly's Twenty-fourth District.

incumbents enjoy multiple advantages, even when they do not have the luxury (as critics put it) of choosing their own constituents. More visible and better financed than most challengers, incumbents tend to be as successful in unredistricted areas as in redistricted ones. As an example, Iowa's five districts were drawn in 2001 by a nonpartisan panel to be competitive. Incumbents who ran in the next two elections—some considered vulnerable—were all returned to office. The same thing happened in Arizona, which has a similar districting process.

Another cause of safe districts is purely demographic. "The problem is not who draws the legislative lines, it's where people live," one observer notes.[25] As Bruce Oppenheimer of Vanderbilt University puts it, "Democrats tend to live next to Democrats. Republicans tend to live next to Republicans."[26]Although such population mobility is recorded in census-taking and redistricting, it apparently occurs between those decennial events, not in the wake of partisan gerrymandering. Emory University's Alan Abramowitz tested this proposition by measuring the post-redistricting jump in noncompetitive districts (those that were more than 10 percentage points above or below the presidential margin in the nation as a whole). He confirmed that imbalances occurred not so much from newly redrawn districts as from population shifts over the intervening years.

The state of California illustrates this insight. Although regarded as a "blue" (Democratic) state, California has a deep political fault line readily visible on electoral maps. Democratic voters tend to center in populous and mainly coastal counties, whereas Republicans are strongest in mostly inland counties. (Even the strung-out coastal district of Figure 3-2 might be regarded as a community of political interests.) Creating truly competitive districts would mean, to put it simply, linking together disparate coastal and inland communities—an exercise that could itself require extensive gerrymandering. Such geographic patterns are by no means peculiar to this one state.

Combating partisan and incumbent-friendly districting has nonetheless become a reformist cause. California governor Arnold Schwarzenegger, for example, revived a ballot initiative that would remove districting from the legislature to a panel of retired judges. A number of states may consider similar proposals. Whether such remedies can address the root causes of safe districts is another matter. Some reformers hold that the ultimate solution lies in some form of proportional representation, involving multimember districts, which are now prohibited in federal elections.

Racial Gerrymandering

Another form of gerrymandering is intended to promote the election of racial minorities. The Voting Rights Act, enacted in 1965 to ensure the right of blacks to vote in elections, is credited with drastically curtailing voting discrimination. Coverage of language minorities was added in 1975. Amendments in 1982 barred election laws having the intent or effect of reducing minority voting power (Section 2). Sixteen states (mainly southern) that historically discriminated against minorities are required (under Section 5 of the act) to "pre-clear" changes in election rules with federal authorities to ensure that the changes do not have the purpose or effect of "denying or abridging the right to vote on account of race or color."

Under cover of the 1982 provisions, states not only were restrained from diluting (cracking) minority votes, but also were encouraged to pack districts to elect minority officeholders (majority-minority districts). In a 1986 decision the Supreme Court enunciated tests for determining whether a racial minority's representation had been compromised. Is the group large enough and located in a compact enough area to elect a representative if grouped into a single district? Is the group politically cohesive? Is there evidence of racially polarized voting by the majority against candidates of that group? [27]

After the 1990 census a number of states set about creating majority-minority black or Latino districts. The decade thus saw the creation of fifteen new African American districts, thirteen of them in the South (for a total of thirty-two nationwide, seventeen of them in the South), and nine new Latino districts (totaling twenty). Many of these were artfully contrived to concentrate minority voters, making Governor Gerry's 1811 creation look innocent by comparison.

Racial redistricting contributed to the Democratic Party's southern meltdown in the 1990s. It was not lost on Republican Party strategists that confining minority (mostly Democratic) voters into safe (mainly urban) districts would strengthen the GOP in outlying suburban areas. Political scientist Charles S. Bullock noted that "all districts held by Democrats in 1991 in which redistricting reduced the black percentage by more than 10 points have now fallen to the Republicans." [28] The GOP captured and held four of these districts in 1992 and three more in subsequent elections. Bullock summarized the impact of racial gerrymandering in the South:

> After 1994, Republicans received handsome rewards while black Democrats were becoming an increasing numerical force within the minority party. The replacement of moderate white Democrats with conservative Republicans, even with the addition of a few African American legislative seats, bodes ill for the ability of African American legislators to find the allies they need to achieve their policy goals.[29]

Political scientist David Lublin termed the outcome a "paradox of representation": Packed districts yielded more minority lawmakers but also led to a more conservative House and thus reduced minorities' leverage over legislative outcomes.[30]

Minority officeholders and groups supporting them view racially gerrymandered districts as "the political equivalent to the ethnically homogeneous neighborhood," in the words of law professor Lani Guinier. "They are a safe haven for members of that group, a bit of turf that one ethnic grouping controls, a place where their voice is pre-eminent."[31] But categorizing voters by race and ethnicity troubles critics. It creates majority-minority enclaves while further bleaching nonminority districts. "Racial districting is a vision of America deeply at odds with that upon which the civil rights revolution was built," warns Abigail M. Thernstrom, a leading opponent. "Race-based districting has been unprincipled, unnecessary—and (to top it off) a gross distortion of the law."[32] In Supreme Court Justice Sandra Day O'Connor's words, racial districting conveys "the belief . . . that individuals should be judged by the color of their skin."[33]

Others doubt that packing districts is the best way to advance minorities' interests. Concentrating minorities in their own districts wastes their votes by producing outsized electoral majorities for the winning candidates. In doing so, minority voters, along with whatever leverage they have, are drained from areas surrounding the new districts. Even if the number of minority officeholders rises, "the number of white legislators who have any political need to respond to minority concerns goes down as their minority constituents are peeled off to form the new black and Hispanic districts."[34]

Another strategy for maximizing the political influence of minorities would thus be to maintain substantial minorities, say 40 percent or so, in a larger number of districts (termed "influence districts") to expand the ranks of officeholders responsive to minority needs.[35] So it was no surprise that in the wake of the 2000 census Democratic strategists, concluding that racial gerrymandering had hurt their party, set about unpacking some of the minority districts—an effort that was in the main unsuccessful.[36]

The Court Enters the Quagmire

Since the 1960s the Supreme Court has repeatedly ruled against districts drawn deliberately to disadvantage a racial or ethnic group. In 1960 the Court declared unconstitutional the "obscene, 28-sided" boundaries of Tuskegee, Alabama, that disfranchised blacks by excluding them from the city (*Gomillion v. Lightfoot*).[37] Courts upheld the Voting Rights Act of 1965 and its later amendments, which forbid electoral arrangements that dilute the voting power of racial or language minorities. But would districting aimed at increasing minority officeholders pass constitutional muster?

Wading its way through cases over more than a decade, the Supreme Court established a pair of guidelines for states to follow.

Race-Based Districting. First, race cannot be the predominant factor in drawing districts, unless the state can show a compelling reason for it. Moreover, states must not violate the Fourteenth Amendment's Equal Protection Clause by drawing irregularly shaped districts based solely or primarily upon racial considerations.

In a 1993 case, *Shaw v. Reno*, the Court recoiled at two oddly shaped North Carolina congressional districts, the First and Twelfth. White citizens contended that such blatant gerrymandering violated their right to equal protection under the law by diluting their votes. By a narrow 5–4 majority, the Court agreed that nonminority citizens (whites, in this case) had standing to sue the state over racial gerrymandering. Although conceding that race-conscious districting might be permissible, the Court's majority expressed shock at the bizarre boundaries of the Twelfth District. Writing for the majority, Justice O'Connor questioned "districting so highly irregular that, on its face, it rationally cannot be understood as anything other than an effort to segregate voters . . . on the basis of race." [38]

In *Miller v. Johnson* (1995), the Supreme Court took a giant step along the path it began in *Shaw* by rejecting two Georgia districts drawn with race as the "predominant factor." [39] "To challenge a districting scheme as violating the equal protection clause," wrote Justice Anthony M. Kennedy for a 5–4 majority, a plaintiff must prove that "race was the predominant factor motivating the legislature's decision to place a significant number of voters within or without a particular district." To prove racial predominance, it must be shown that "the legislature subordinated to racial considerations traditional race-neutral districting principles, including but not limited to compactness, contiguity, and respect for political subdivisions of communities defined by actual shared interests."

In the next five years federal courts ruled on districting plans in several states—most notably, California, Florida, Georgia, Louisiana, South Carolina, Texas, and North Carolina (four times). By the decade's end several states had drawn new district maps in response to the Court's ruling in *Miller.* Affected majority-minority districts were in Texas (two of thirteen redrawn districts), Georgia (two), North Carolina (two), and Florida, Louisiana, and Virginia (one each). North Carolina's shoestring Twelfth District remained under a legal cloud after two remappings (see Figure 3-3).

Virtually all the minority members running in their new districts won subsequent elections, some with widened margins. Foes of racial gerrymandering seized on the results as vindication. "The idea that minorities have to have a super-majority of black voters to win in their districts, that's history now," declared the lawyer who had challenged the Georgia districts. Black officeholders credited their success to incumbency, which they argued was made possible by racial gerrymandering. They won reelection by combining overwhelming black support with 20 percent or more of the white vote.[40]

Taking Race into Account. A second Court-adopted principle softens this stance against racial districting: If race is simply one of many factors considered in drawing a district, then the state may surmount the constitutional barrier against race-based districting.

The Supreme Court, like outside commentators, was ideologically torn. Individual justices' views on racial districting, however, seem inconsistent with—and even the opposite of—their approaches to partisan gerrymandering. For example, the five conservative justices who comprised the majority in *Shaw* and *Miller* saw racial gerrymandering as a brand of political affirmative

FIGURE 3-3 **Racial Gerrymandering in the 1990s and 2000s: North Carolina's First and Twelfth Congressional Districts**

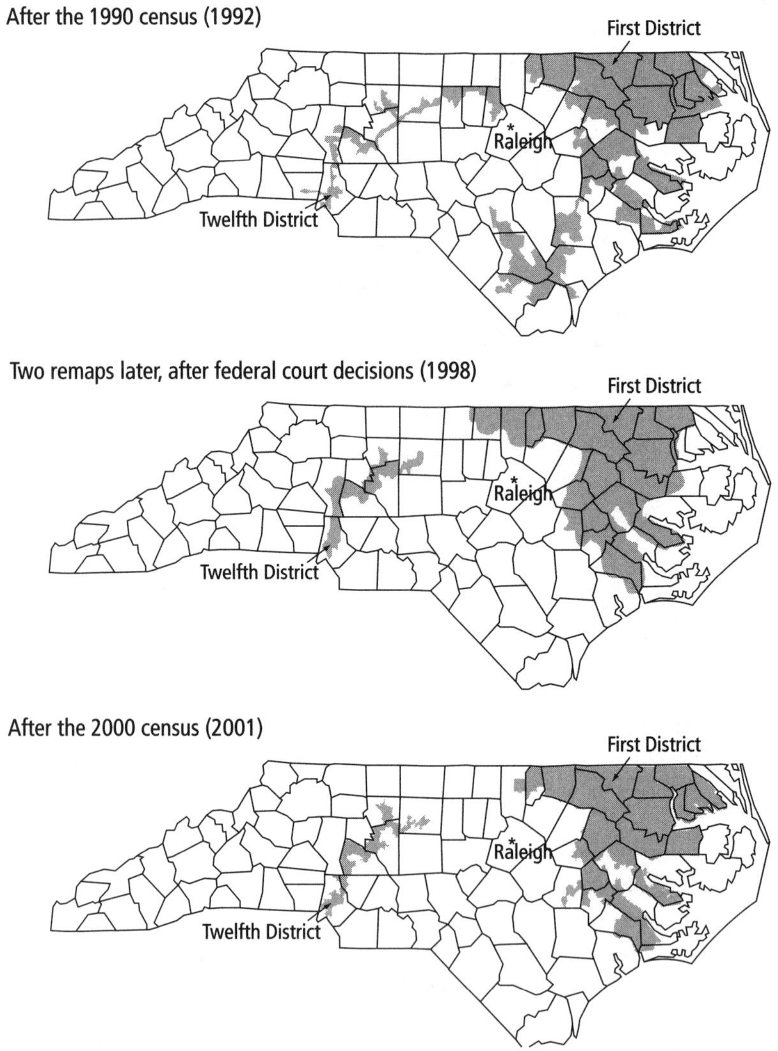

Sources: Congressional Districts in the 1990s: A Portrait of America (Washington D.C.: Congressional Quarterly, 1993), 548. *Congressional Districts in the 2000s: A Portrait of America* (Washington, D.C.: CQ Press, 2003), 673.

Note: North Carolina's First and Twelfth Districts were drawn to give the state its first black representatives in ninety-three years. First elected in 1992, the two African American representatives were subsequently reelected; after the First District representative retired in 2003, she was replaced by another African American.

action repugnant to the Constitution—a departure from race-neutral standards that courts had a duty to review.

The four Court liberals, in contrast, regarded race-based districting as just a new variant of a venerable political practice. The Court's minority in *Miller*, speaking through Justice Ruth Bader Ginsburg, noted that "legislative districting is a highly political business" and that "apportionment schemes, by their very nature, assemble people in groups." Historically, many ethnic groups sought and gained power through their own voting districts. "Until now, no constitutional infirmity has been seen in districting Irish or Italian voters together, for example." Why, she asked, shouldn't African Americans be accorded the same right? Courts should intervene only to protect the rights of minorities. In Ginsburg's words: "Special circumstances justify vigilant judicial inspection to protect minority voters—circumstances that do not apply to majority voters."

This argument offered a path for the Court to beat a strategic retreat from its hard-line stance on racial gerrymandering. The final decisions on 1990s redistricting involved the much litigated North Carolina Twelfth District, whose black population had been whittled from 57 to 47 percent after two remappings. A group of the district's white voters had persuaded a lower court that the newly remapped district was still racially gerrymandered. The state, for its part, argued that it simply wanted to create a district of loyal Democrats, many of whom happened to be black. A unanimous Court sent the case back to the district court, which was instructed to take into account the state's point of view (*Hunt v. Cromartie,* 1999). Writing for the Court, Justice Clarence Thomas declared:

> A jurisdiction may engage in constitutional political gerrymandering, even if it so happens that the most loyal Democrats happen to be black Democrats and even if the state were conscious of that fact. Evidence that blacks constitute even a supermajority in one Congressional district while amounting to less than a plurality in a neighboring district will not, by itself, suffice to prove that a jurisdiction was motivated by race in drawing its district lines when the evidence also shows a high correlation between race and party preference.[41]

All nine judges agreed with the decision, although the four liberal dissenters from earlier cases declined to sign Justice Thomas's opinion. In a concurring opinion written by Justice Stevens, they held that the evidence of race-based districting in this instance was weak. At the very least, the guideposts erected in *Hunt* gave the states "very significant breathing room" in the post–2000 round of redistricting.

Two years later—just as states were beginning their next round of redistricting—the Court moved in the direction indicated by Justice Thomas (*Easley v. Cromartie*, 2001). Weighing the final challenge to North Carolina's redrawn Twelfth District, a three-judge district court had ruled that the districting was driven by race. By yet another 5–4 vote, the Court disagreed, describing as "clearly erroneous" the district court's findings. "The evidence taken together," wrote Justice Stephen G. Breyer, "does not show that racial considerations predominated in the drawing of District 12's boundaries. That is because race closely correlates with political behavior." [42] Justice Thomas, now writing for the minority, did not dispute the facts but simply held that the Court should have deferred to the lower court's factual findings.

More to Come. Race-conscious districting is likely to be contested well beyond the 2000 census. As a North Carolina state senator in charge of his chamber's redistricting efforts quipped to a reporter: "If the Lord God Almighty threw down lightening bolts and carved plans into the side of Mount Mitchell, and we adopted them, there would still be challenges to redistricting under every legal theory devised." [43]

In 2003 the Court held in *Georgia v. Ashcroft* that states can consider a variety of factors to promote minority influence in the electoral process—for example, creating minority "influence districts" instead of "packed" districts. "The state may choose," Justice O'Connor wrote for another 5–4 majority, "that it is better to risk having fewer minority representatives in order to achieve greater overall representation of a minority group by increasing the number of representatives sympathetic to the interests of minority voters." [44]

On the one hand, courts can be expected to protect minority voting power from being unconstitutionally diluted—in Justice Kennedy's words, "eradicating invidious discrimination from the electoral process." But states have a good deal of leeway in making such political arrangements. Nonminority voters challenging such plans, Justice Breyer explained, must show how the state legislature "could have achieved its legitimate political objectives" in another way.

On the other hand, Justice Breyer noted, judges should be reluctant to second-guess state legislators on such intensely political matters. Majority-minority districts can be valid if they are properly drafted by the states to serve compelling state governmental interests and adhere to what the judges regard as traditional principles.[45]

The leading question is whether the Supreme Court means to back away from its initial activist stance toward gerrymandering. After all, the Court has never defined what districting would be allowable. Apparently the justices have adopted a version of the late Justice Potter Stewart's test for identifying obscenity: You know it when you see it. And given the closeness of its past decisions—every major case on this question has turned on a 5–4 vote—the Court could again shift its direction in response to, say, a change in its membership.

BECOMING A CANDIDATE

Very few of those who are eligible for Congress vie for a seat. Candidates who meet the legal qualifications must weigh a variety of considerations—some practical and rational, others personal and emotional. Candidacy decisions are often the pivotal moments in the entire recruitment process, although students of politics have only recently given them the attention they deserve. "The decision to run obviously structures everything else that goes on in the primary process," writes L. Sandy Maisel. "Who runs, who does not run, how many candidates run. These questions set the stage for the campaigns themselves."[46]

Called or Chosen?

In their heyday—roughly from the time of Andrew Jackson in the 1830s to the decline of big-city machines in the 1960s—local party organizations customarily enlisted and sponsored candidates. Then, as such organizations withered, the initiative passed to the candidates themselves: self-starters who pulled their own bandwagons. "The boys in the back room aren't going to decide who stays in this race," one representative remarked. "There are no boys anymore."[47] "The skills that work in American politics at this point in history," wrote Alan Ehrenhalt, "are those of entrepreneurship. At all levels of the political system, from local boards and councils up to and including the presidency, it is unusual for parties to nominate people. People nominate themselves."[48]

Although typically launching their own careers, aspirants for Congress soon encounter national networks of party committees and their allied interest groups. At the heart of these networks are the two major parties' House and Senate campaign committees, now active in nearly all phases of congressional elections.[49] They seek out and encourage promising candidates at the local level, sometimes even taking sides to help ensure their nomination. Once nominated, candidates receive help in nearly every phase of the campaign, from fund raising to finding seasoned campaign managers to digging up dirt on opponents. Filing deadlines must be met, backers lined up, and financing sought. Candidates may be free to keep their national party at arm's length, but few nonincumbents can turn their backs on party sponsorship. Most would-be officeholders seek advancement within the two major parties, which boast not only the brand loyalties of a majority of voters but also extensive financial and logistical resources.

During the recruiting season (beginning in early 2005 for the 2006 contests, for example), the two major parties' leaders and campaign committee staffs "reach out across the country in search of political talent. Like college football coaching staffs in hot pursuit of high-school prospects, they are . . . putting together the lineups of the future."[50] Prospects can expect calls from the president, former presidents, governors, high-profile financial backers, and other notables. The run-ups to recent elections all began with fierce recruiting seasons, as both parties sought lineups that could win them House and Senate majorities.

Not all recruiting takes place on the road. Because open seats—newly created districts or those in which incumbents have died or retired—are less secure, party leaders strive also to discourage their incumbent colleagues from retiring.

In light of citizens' professed coolness toward the two major parties, independents and minor-party candidates not surprisingly are entering congressional contests. Some thirty-nine party labels appeared on ballots somewhere in 2004. But only seven minor-party candidates that year broke the 20 percent mark, providing alternatives where only one major party fielded a candidate. Occasionally such candidates draw enough votes to swing the election results. Only two Independents currently serve in Congress: Vermonters Sen. James M. Jeffords and Rep. Bernard Sanders.

Nonparty groups also sponsor congressional candidates. The leading small business lobby, the National Federation of Independent Business (NFIB), has been a major contributor to the GOP cause. In the 1995–1996 cycle the NFIB began to pick potential candidates from its own membership, train them, and help them run for office. "We're trying to develop a farm team for down the road," explained the federation's national political director, "so we can work in more of a proactive instead of a reactive way," fielding, not just endorsing, candidates who support the small business agenda.[51] Other organizations with strong grassroots networks now pursue the same course.

Amateurs and Pros

How do would-be candidates, whether self-starters or anointed by party leaders, make up their minds to run? The answer depends on whether the individual is an amateur or a strategic politician.

Amateurs. These candidates by definition lack previous political experience. Despite their usual liabilities—inexperience and low name recognition—many amateurs run for Congress; few of them manage to win. Some amateurs are serious political strategists whose behavior resembles that of experienced politicians. Others run to bring a specific issue before the public; they are less interested in winning than in advancing a cause.

Amateurs with highly visible nonpolitical careers may be nicely positioned to move into politics. Astronauts, war heroes, entertainers, and athletes are in big demand as candidates. Local or statewide television personalities also make attractive contenders. Only occasionally do other nonpolitical careers have such visibility. First elected to the Senate in 1988, Democrat Herb Kohl was familiar throughout Wisconsin from his family's food stores long before he wrote an $18.5 million check in 1985 to keep the Milwaukee Bucks basketball team from moving elsewhere—not a bad advertisement for a would-be senator. And in 2000 Republican Tom Osborne captured 80 percent of the vote in Nebraska's open Third District even though he wholly lacked political experience. But everyone in the state knew him as a twenty-five-year football coach of the University of Nebraska's Cornhuskers.[52]

Most amateurs, however, are what David T. Canon calls "hopeless amateurs"—people with little or no chance of winning.[53] A long-shot bid is their only way of becoming a candidate. They run because "it was something they knew they were going to do sometime and for whatever reasons it appeared to be the right time."[54] "I think his chances have gone from absolutely out of the question to extremely remote," remarked the wife of one hopeless contender. "But he's learning a lot, and I think he has enjoyed it."[55]

Strategic Politicians. Unlike all but the savviest amateurs, these contenders painstakingly weigh the pros and cons of launching a campaign. A strategic politician asks himself: Do the rewards exceed the drawbacks of the office, especially compared with what I am doing now? What are the chances of success, and what will it cost to succeed? If there is an incumbent, what are his weaknesses? What are my strengths and weaknesses in campaigning, voter appeal, and fund raising? What local or national trends will boost or impede my chances?

Most successful candidates are seasoned politicians long before they run for Congress. Grassroots organizations and movements are a breeding ground for a number of candidates—for example, environmental activists in the 1970s, religious conservatives and antiregulation businesspeople in the 1990s. More often, elective offices are the springboards: mayors, district attorneys, or state legislators for the House; and governors, lieutenant governors, and attorneys general—who have already faced a statewide electorate—for the Senate. House members, especially from smaller states, are also strategically positioned. A majority of senators in the 109th Congress had moved over from the House.

The circle of people pondering a candidacy (the challenger pool) may be large or small, depending on the office and the circumstances.[56] Any number of elected officials—state legislators (especially if subject to term limits), county officers, mayors, city council members, even governors—are weighing a race for Congress.

Finding the Quality Candidates

The quality of candidates and the vigor of their campaigns are critical factors in many battles for congressional seats.[57] The parties' November triumphs hinge on their efforts during the recruitment season. Often races turn on bids that are not made.

Two elements of candidate quality emerged from an extensive study of candidate recruitment conducted by Maisel and his colleagues. These are strategic resources, indicating that an individual can mount a successful campaign, and personal attributes, predicting leadership in the campaign and in public office.[58]

Strategic Resources. Quality challengers are people who are attractive to voters, skilled in presenting themselves as candidates, and able to contribute or raise funds. Attractiveness typically means having gained experience in public office, which implies visibility among, and credibility with, the voters. Simply having a familiar political name is increasingly a ticket to candidacy.

Alternatively, fame or notoriety may overcome lack of relevant background or experience. Attributes include physical appearance, personality, speaking ability, and a talent for organizing or motivating others.

Fund-raising ability or potential is an essential attribute of quality challengers. When a vacancy suddenly occurred in Ohio's Second District (Cincinnati) early in 2005, several serious primary hopefuls were on hand within the GOP-controlled area. One of them, a county commissioner, was described thusly: "He's going to be able to raise a whole lot of money in a short period of time."[59] An opponent's war chest is also appraised—often as revealed in the Federal Election Commission (FEC) reports issued sixteen months before the election. When the incumbent in Virginia's Eleventh District reported less than $25,000 on hand in 1993, Republican Thomas M. Davis III decided to take the plunge. "If she would have had $250,000, I would not have gotten into the race."[60] Davis won the seat.

Personal Attributes. Personal qualities also determine who is urged to run, and who decides to run, for Congress. Stamina, leadership potential, personal style, and even physical appearance determine whether someone has "the right stuff" for campaigning. Ambition and a keen desire for public life and congressional perquisites lead people to become candidates and help them to succeed.[61]

No matter how talented or principled, aspirants for public office must be physically and emotionally ready to face the rigors of campaigning. They must be willing to hit the road nonstop, meet new people, attend gatherings, sell themselves, ask for money, and endure verbal abuse—all the while appearing to enjoy it. "People who do not like to knock on strangers' doors or who find it tedious to repeat the same 30-second introduction thousands of times," explains Ehrenhalt, "are at a severe disadvantage in running for office."[62]

No-Shows. High-caliber potential candidates apparently abound in America's communities—even among minority-party circles within noncompetitive districts.[63] But all too often these individuals prefer to remain on the sidelines. The road to public office is increasingly arduous and costly, and the odds are often long, especially when running against a dominant party or an entrenched incumbent. Therefore, quality challengers often fail to surface. Low-quality challengers raise less money and are less successful than the handful of blue-ribbon contenders. The dynamic works in Senate as well as House elections.

Raising the money needed to run an effective race is a major deterrent to would-be candidates. This stumbling block was cited twice as often as any other factor by the potential contenders in two hundred districts surveyed by Maisel and Walter J. Stone.[64] Other candidates reject campaigns because of the cost to their personal lives, incomes, and families.

The benefits side of the ledger may not outweigh the costs of gaining and holding public office. Rep. Thomas M. Davis III, R-Va., former House GOP campaign chair, describes the drill:

> We'd get them here under the Capitol dome, have their wife take a picture, have the Speaker of the House tell how important they'll be. You're not selling the lifestyle. You're not selling the salary. You're selling relevance.[65]

More often than not, prospective candidates decide that their interests lie elsewhere—in state or local politics, in nonprofit community service, or in family and profession.

From the number of successful politicians who complain about such impediments, however, one can only conclude that many misjudge the costs before taking the plunge. Many simply indulge in self-delusion. Maisel, a political scientist who wrote candidly of his unsuccessful congressional primary campaign, described politicians' "incredible ability to delude themselves about their own chances."[66]

The Incumbency Factor

Of all the inducements for launching a candidacy, the odds of winning stand at the top. A seat that is clearly winnable seldom lacks for candidates eager to capture it. Open seats especially attract contenders; races without an incumbent candidate are more likely to be competitive and to shift in party control than those with an incumbent. Party strategies thus pinpoint those races.

In most House and Senate contests, however, incumbents will be running, and most of them will be reelected. As Gary C. Jacobson writes, "Nearly everything pertaining to candidates and campaigns for Congress is profoundly influenced by whether the candidate is an incumbent, challenging an incumbent, or pursuing an open seat."[67] With somewhat less force, the same could be said of the Senate.

Anyone contemplating a congressional race would do well to study Table 3-1 with care. Since World War II, on average, 93 percent of all incumbent representatives and 80 percent of incumbent senators running for reelection have been returned to office. Historically, incumbents' reelection rates have always been robust, whereas voluntary turnover declined in the late nineteenth century and has remained low ever since. In 2004, winners included 98 percent of all representatives and 96 percent of senators who ran. Sixty-four of those incumbents faced no major-party opponent in the general election.

Higher than normal casualty rates occur periodically: for example, a post–World War II generational shift (1946–1948), a midterm recession (1958), Barry Goldwater's failed presidential candidacy (1964), the Watergate burglary fallout (1974), and a combination of generational shift and partisan realignment (1978–1980). During the early 1990s, political unrest, Capitol Hill scandals, an economic recession (in 1992), and voter anger at those in charge (the Democrats and President Bill Clinton in 1994) and further partisan shifts conspired to produce the largest turnover in two generations. But subsequent

TABLE 3-1 **Reelection Rates in the House and Senate, by Decade, 1950–2000**

	House					Senate				
Decade	Sought reelection	Faced no opponent	Lost primary	Lost general election	Percent reelected	Sought reelection	Faced no opponent	Lost primary	Lost general election	Percent elected
1950s	402	85	6	25	93.2	30	4	1	6	77.3
1960s	404	52	8	26	91.5	32	1	2	4	80.8
1970s	289	57	2	23	92.3	27	1	2	6	67.7
1980s	403	67	13	15	95.7	29	1	0	3	88.0º
1990s	385	36	8	18	93.6	26	0	0	3	87.4
Fifty-year average	376.6	59.4	7.4	21.4	93.3	28.9	1.4	1.0	4.4	80.2
2000s	390	70	5	8	96.8	27	3	1	2	90.7

Source: Congressional Quarterly Weekly Report, April 5, 1980, 908; November 8, 1980, 3302, 3320–3321; July 31, 1982, 1870; November 6, 1982, 2781; November 10, 1984, 2897, 2901; November 12, 1988, 3264, 3270; November 10, 1990, 3796–3805; November 7, 1992, 3557–3564, 3570–3576; November 12, 1994, 329ff; February 15, 1997, 447–455; November 7, 1998, 3027–3035; November 11, 2000, 2694–2706; December 14, 2002, 3289–3297; and November 6, 2004, 2653–2660; and *Roll Call,* November 4, 2004, 25.

Note: Statistics for each decade are election-year averages for the five elections conducted under that decade's apportionment of House districts. For example, the 1950s include the five elections 1952 through 1960. Percent reelected includes both primary and general election defeats. Figures for the 2000s are derived from the 2002 and 2004 elections.

elections favored incumbents. Decennial redistricting also produces a flurry of retirements and defeats.

Nowadays defeating a House incumbent is an uphill struggle, short of a major scandal or misstep. This is a relatively recent phenomenon. Although incumbents have been fattening their margins of victory for some time, through the 1970s they were just as vulnerable to defeat as they had been earlier. That is, incumbents were, on average, just as apt to lose any given election as before; but when they won, it was by higher margins.[68] By the 1980s, however, incumbents had erected imposing barriers against defeat by amassing campaign war chests and aggressively exploiting the perquisites of office. Therefore, competition for their House seats dropped to exceedingly low levels. Incumbent advantage fell perceptibly in the early 1990s. The anti-incumbent atmosphere emboldened many strategically minded nonincumbents to try for House or Senate seats. Even so, turnover resulted less from electoral defeats than from retirements (some of them involuntary, to be sure). In those years of upheaval (1990 to 1994), 194 members retired and 112 were defeated for reelection.[69]

Senate races tend to be closer, and so challengers—more often well known and generously financed—have a stronger chance of unseating incumbents than do those seeking House seats. Still, four of five Senate incumbents win the contests they enter. The proportion of marginal elections (candidates winning by less than 60 percent) has dropped somewhat. About half of all winning Senate candidates receive more than 60 percent of the votes.

In Senate contests, the size of the state affects all elections, not just those in which an incumbent is running. Frances E. Lee and Bruce I. Oppenheimer find that "Senate elections in more populous states tend to be decided by much closer margins than Senate elections in less populous states"—mainly because larger states are more diverse and tend to be more competitive.[70] Yet small-state senators reap no real incumbency advantage. Although they are better known and tend to enjoy higher public approval than their big-state colleagues, their challengers, too, can more easily win visibility and support. The sole Senate casualty in 2004 occurred in South Dakota, where Democratic leader Tom Daschle was defeated by someone who had shared the same statewide constituency: former representative John Thune.

Why are incumbents so formidable? Political scientists have launched a veritable cottage industry to answer this question. It is no secret that incumbents have built-in methods of promoting support—through speeches, press coverage, newsletters, staff assistance, and constituent service. The average House member enjoys perquisites valued at about $2.5 million over a two-year term; senators, with six-year terms, command between about $15 million and $25 million in resources.

Everyone concedes the value of incumbents' perquisites, but scholars differ sharply on how they affect electoral success. One view is that incumbents exploit their resources to ensure reelection, seizing upon their ability to assist constituents in dealing with the bureaucracy to build electoral credit. Others counter that legislators simply are responding to constituents' demands, aided by technological advances in communications. Still others question whether incumbents' resources are directly translatable into votes. However these questions are resolved, incumbents and their staffs spend much of their time and effort forging links with their voters, and these links typically hold fast on election day.[71]

An incumbent's most effective electoral strategy is to scare off serious opposition. "If an incumbent can convince potentially formidable opponents and people who control campaign resources that he or she is invincible," Jacobson observes, "he or she is very likely to avoid a serious challenge and so will be invincible—as long as the impression lasts."[72] Any sign of weakness may invite opponents the next time around. That is why wise incumbents try to sustain wide electoral margins, show unbroken strength, keep up constituency ties, and build giant war chests of funds. If these tactics fail, there is always the option of retiring more or less gracefully.

NOMINATING POLITICS

Nominating procedures, set forth in state laws and conditioned by party customs, help to shape the potential pool of candidates. Historically, they have expanded to ever wider circles of participants—a development that has diminished party leaders' power and thrust more initiative upon the candidates themselves. In most states the direct primary is the formal mechanism for nominating congressional candidates.

Rules of the Nominating Game

Who should be permitted to vote in a party's primary? The states have adopted varying answers. Party leaders naturally prefer strict rules that reward party loyalty, discourage outsider candidates, and maximize the leaders' influence upon the outcome. States with strong party traditions therefore tend to have closed primaries. This arrangement, found in twenty-six states, requires voters to declare party affiliation to vote on their parties' nominees. (Their affiliation is considered permanent until they take steps to change it.) In open primaries, conducted in twenty states, voters can vote in the primary of either party (but not in both) simply by requesting or selecting the party's ballot at the polling place.

Four states have experimented with a scheme that diminishes the parties' role even further. In blanket primaries (politicians call them jungle primaries), voters (in Alaska, California, and Washington) received a single ballot listing all candidates running for office, regardless of party affiliation. People voted for one candidate for each office, moving back and forth between parties if they wish. More people would come to the polls, California's lawyers told the Supreme Court, "because candidates will be more representative of the electorate and more broadly reflect the views of the voters."[73] Louisiana employs a nonpartisan primary variant held on election day, when all candidates appear on one ballot. If a candidate receives a majority, he is elected; if no one gains a majority, the top two vote-getters, regardless of party, move to a runoff election.

The California scheme, a voter initiative, was adopted overwhelmingly in 1996. Four California parties (Democrats, Republicans, Libertarians, Peace and Freedom) challenged the initiative in court as a violation of their First Amendment right to free association. The U.S. Supreme Court upheld their challenge by a 7–2 vote.[74] Calling the blanket primary a "stark repudiation of freedom of political association," Justice Scalia argued that it invited nonparty members to raid the primary and select a candidate who did not share the party's core beliefs. "In no area is the political association's right to exclude more important than in the process of selecting its candidates." In dissent, Justice Stevens noted that, while a party's internal governance was a private matter, "an election, unlike a convention or a caucus, is a public affair." (Early civil rights cases established that parties could not arbitrarily exclude classes of persons from their nominating processes.)

The 2000 ruling served to invalidate primaries in the three blanket primary states, though advocates of the device vowed to try and devise a Court-proof version. (The Court explicitly excluded nonpartisan primaries, such as Louisiana's, from its decision.) Some observers speculated that the Court's ruling cast constitutional doubt on all open primaries, though that seemed unlikely.

Not all primaries are competitive races. In the 1982–1996 period, nearly 70 percent of representatives and 60 percent of senators faced no challenge at all for renomination. Only twelve incumbents faced closely contested primaries; only 30 percent had any contests at all.[75]

Contests usually occur in both parties if the House or Senate seat is open and within the challenging party if the seat is deemed competitive. The level of competition depends on the party's prospects in the general election. "If a district party is without an incumbent, and has a fighting chance in November," Harvey L. Schantz writes, "there is a strong possibility of a public contest for the U.S. House nomination."[76] In one-party areas the dominant party's nomination is tantamount to election. Within that party, open seats are virtually certain to be contested, and in some states runoff primaries are held when no one receives a majority. Contests also are likely in two-party competitive areas.

Parties and Nominations

Despite the prevalence of primaries, party organizations at all levels are not without leverage in nominations. Party organizations play no formal role in the primary process in the majority of states.[77] But in nine states, parties have conventions that influence candidates' access to the primary ballot—for example, by conferring preprimary endorsements.

Party organizations mostly influence nominations indirectly—by contacting promising prospects, offering support, endorsing them, and assisting in other ways. Of the hundreds of prospective candidates identified in a recent canvass, about two out of five had been contacted by one or more party organizations—local, state, or national.[78] Parties are most active in districts regarded as winnable, and the people they seek out are the "usual suspects"—officeholders, prominent figures, high-income individuals, and so forth. "They go after the obvious candidates and leave some of the less obvious ones alone."[79]

National parties increasingly assert themselves in nominating contests. To regain the Senate in 2002 and keep it two years later, Republicans and the George W. Bush White House targeted seats that were open or held by retiring or vulnerable Democrats—recruiting promising GOP candidates, "clearing the field" by elbowing rivals aside to forestall divisive primaries, and channeling resources to the campaigns. Democrats were not far behind, convening a three-day retreat for its ten top Senate contenders.

In 2004 both parties persuaded "800-pound gorillas" to run in competitive states such as Alaska, Florida, North Carolina, and South Carolina. Florida's presumed GOP front-runner, Rep. Katherine Harris—who as secretary of state was at the vortex of the 2000 presidential voting maelstrom—was persuaded to postpone a Senate run to make way for Mel Martinez, a Bush cabinet member.[80] The White House actively promoted several other winners, including former representative Thune in South Dakota.

Party leaders tend to be pragmatists, above all bent upon finding winners. Thus Democrats occasionally court anti-abortion figures in swing states or districts; the GOP leans toward moderates over extremists in such areas. The ultra-right Club for Growth has backed conservative prospects in a number of intraparty contests, including 2004 senatorial primaries in Colorado (won by a centrist, Pete Coors, the brewery heir) and Pennsylvania, where more than $2 million was spent against Sen. Arlen Spector, a moderate, who won narrowly with help from the White House and the party establishment.[81]

Not all nationally sponsored choices win nomination. Democrats failed to find top-tier contenders in several potentially competitive states, including Georgia, Missouri, and Pennsylvania; Republicans fell short in such states as Indiana, North Dakota, and Washington. The Republicans' chief embarrassment in 2004 was Illinois' open Senate seat: The party's vulnerable incumbent retired, the preferred candidate shunned the race, the front-runner withdrew in the wake of a marriage scandal, and the final nominee was an out-of-state ideologue too extreme for the state. So Democrat Barack Obama won seven out of ten general election votes to become the third black senator in a hundred years. More often than not, however, the parties' estimates pan out; their choices normally prevail in primaries.[82]

Sizing Up the Primary System

The direct primary was one of the reforms adopted early in the twentieth century to overcome corrupt, boss-dominated conventions. It has certainly permitted more participation in selecting candidates. Yet primaries normally attract a narrower segment of voters than do general elections (except in one-party areas, where primaries dictate the outcomes). Primary contests have drawn less than 20 percent of eligible voters in recent years—less than half the number who voted in the general elections.[83] Less publicized than general elections, primaries tend to attract voters who are somewhat older, wealthier, better educated, more politically aware, and more ideologically committed than the electorate as a whole.[84]

Primaries also have hampered the political parties by encouraging would-be officeholders to appeal directly to the public and construct support networks apart from the party machinery. Still, leaders strive to influence who enters their primaries and who wins them. Displaying impressive resilience and adaptability, party organizations at all levels have recast themselves into organizations " 'in service' to [their] candidates and officeholders but not in control of them."[85]

Finally, primaries are a costly way of choosing candidates. Unless candidates begin with overwhelming advantages (such as incumbency), they must mount virtually the same kind of campaign in the primary that they must repeat later in the general election.

THE MONEY FACTOR

"Money is the mother's milk of politics," declared California's legendary boss Jess Unruh. Money is not everything in politics, but many candidates falter for lack of it, and many others squander valuable time and energy struggling to get it. Money attracts backers (who in turn give more money), it can frighten away rivals, and it can augment or lessen the gap between incumbents and challengers. Every candidate, writes Paul S. Herrnson, wages not one but two campaigns—a campaign for resources that precedes, and underwrites, the more visible campaign for votes.[86]

Campaigns in the United States are very costly. In the 2003–2004 electoral cycle, congressional candidates raised $1.2 billion and spent most of it. The average Senate race cost $2.6 million. House contests averaged $531,000.[87] Twenty-five years ago (when modern record keeping began) no House candidate spent that much.[88] Even controlling for inflation, expenditures for congressional campaigns have more than doubled over the last twenty-five years. And beyond what candidates spend, interest groups of all stripes throw untold millions of dollars into independent efforts aimed at changing election outcomes.

No mystery surrounds these skyrocketing costs. Inflation, population growth, and new campaign technologies—media ads, polling, and consultants of all kinds—account for much of the increase. Moreover, long-term changes in the campaign process itself have escalated costs. In old-style campaigns, party-anointed candidates could rely upon the party's legions of volunteers to mobilize loyal voters and to canvass precincts. Contrast that process with modern campaigns in which candidates must win their party's nominating primary and then face general election voters who can be reached most easily through direct mail, phone banks, or electronic media. Many campaign services once provided by well-oiled local parties must now be purchased on the open market. That is why today's costs of reaching voters are so high.

Campaign price tags also depend on the level of competition and other characteristics of the electoral unit. "Candidates for open seats tend to raise and spend the most money because when neither candidate enjoys the benefits of incumbency, both parties normally field strong candidates, and the election is usually close."[89] Costs in competitive races can be astronomical. In close House races (gaining less than 55 percent of the vote), the average winner in 2004 spent more than $1.5 million.

A district's demography also affects campaign costs. One study showed that suburban districts have the most expensive campaigns and urban districts the least expensive, with rural districts somewhere in between.[90] In the suburbs partisan loyalties are shifting and contests volatile. Where stable party organizations are lacking, candidates must advertise through paid media. In rural districts wide-open spaces keep costs high. Candidates must travel farther and advertise in many small media markets to get their messages across. In cities candidates shun media contests because of the huge cost and wasted effort of covering adjoining districts. Here, too, party organizations are strongest.

The Haves and Have-Nots

Although incumbents need less money than do challengers, they receive more—a double-barreled financial advantage (see Figure 3-4). Because they are better known and have government-subsidized ways of reaching constituents, incumbents usually can get their message across less expensively than challengers can. Incumbents tend to attract more money than challengers do because contributors see them as better investments. As Jacobson points out, "Incumbents can raise whatever they think they need. They are very likely to win, and even when they lose, it is almost always in a close contest."[91]

Challengers must raise a great deal of money to defeat an incumbent; the more they can raise, the more votes they are likely to receive. Every one of the 382 incumbents who won reelection in 2004 outspent their challengers—from as much as ten times as much (277 members) to as little as twice as much. In the seven districts where incumbents lost in the general election (including two where incumbents were pitted against one another), the candidates' financial resources were roughly equal.[92]

Many incumbents finish their campaigns with a surplus. After the 2003–2004 electoral cycle, the average returning House member had more than $400,000 on hand. This money can be hoarded for future races, dispensed to needier candidates, or used to buy constituency goodwill through outreach projects or charitable donations.

The incumbency advantage in fund raising, especially in House contests, is bipartisan. Prior to 1994, the advantage worked to the benefit of Democrats,

FIGURE 3-4 **Average Campaign Expenditures for Incumbents, Challengers, and Open-Seat Candidates, House and Senate (1974–2004)**

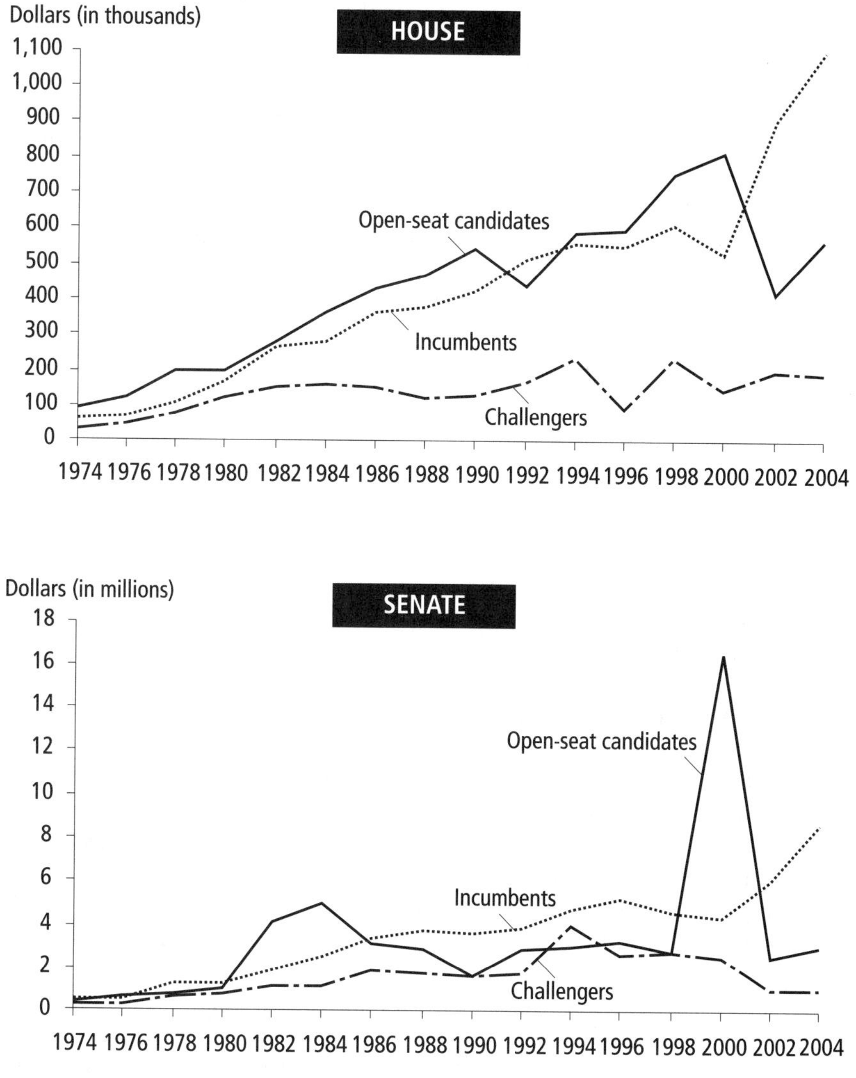

Sources: Federal Election Commission figures for campaigns through 2000 are compiled in Norman J. Ornstein, Thomas E. Mann, and Michael J. Malbin, *Vital Statistics on Congress 2001–2002* (Washington D.C.: AEI Press, 2002), 87–98. Figures through 2004, also derived from the FEC, are found in: Center for Responsive Politics, "Election Overview, Incumbent Advantage," accessed at www.opensecrets.org.

who had more incumbents than Republicans had. During the following decade, the parties achieved rough parity. As a party, the GOP has normally been more efficient than the Democrats in raising funds. As their majority has grown, Republicans have harvested a bounty from lobby groups, eager as always to back winners to gain access to the policy-making process.

Shaking the Money Tree

Raising money preoccupies all candidates. Incumbents need it to scare off opponents, challengers need it to gain visibility, and contenders for open seats need it to gain an edge. Fund raising is time-consuming, odious, and demeaning. "I'd rather wrestle a gorilla than ask anybody for another fifty cents," grumbled John Glenn, D-Ohio, as he retired after twenty-four years in the Senate.[93]

Funding sources include individuals (including the candidates and their families), party committees, and political action committees (PACs). Their motivations fall into two major categories. Consumers, usually individuals, want simply to show their support for a candidate or a cause, often responding to candidates most in need of funds. Investors—interest groups and PACs, for example—give or spend to gain personal or institutional benefits. Because they seek access or support from winning candidates, they tend to disregard the candidates' needs and support those (mainly incumbents) most likely to win.[94]

Federal law requires strict accounting by candidates and political committees. All contributions of $50 or more must be recorded; donors of more than $100 must be identified. Accounting of funds must be made by a single committee for each candidate, and receipts and expenditures must be reported regularly.

Individuals. More than half of the money raised by House and Senate candidates comes from individuals. Individuals may lawfully contribute up to $2,000 per candidate for primaries and $2,000 per candidate in the general elections (the figure will be indexed in the future), totaling no more than $37,500 in any given year. Primary, runoff, and general contests are regarded as separate elections. Individuals may contribute up to $20,000 a year to a political party committee and $5,000 to any PAC, and they may spend an unlimited amount independently to promote parties, causes, or candidates. Expenditures greater than $250 must be reported, and the individual must declare that the money was not spent in collusion with the candidate. Many individual donations are solicited by interest groups, which seek to magnify their influence by collecting and then forwarding these personal checks to the designated candidates, a practice known as bundling.

Congressional candidates are not restricted in how much they may contribute to their own cause. (Donations and loans from family members also are unrestricted.) The hope is that heavy spending may boost an underdog's chances of winning (usually futile in the absence of other resources) or help pad a front-runner's margin of victory. Sen. John D. Rockefeller IV, D-W.Va., spent about $10 million of his fortune to win his Senate seat in 1984—more than $27 for every vote he received. Especially in long-shot races, a candidate's ability to shoulder the financial burden may attract support from party or group leaders.

Party Committees. National, congressional, and state party campaign committees may contribute $5,000 apiece to each House candidate at each stage of the electoral process—primary, runoff, and general election. The national and senatorial committees can give a combined total of $17,500 to each Senate candidate in an election cycle, whereas state committees can give $5,000. Inflation has shrunk the buying power of these sums. Party funds do not begin to cover the costs of campaigns today. Party organizations of all types account for a relatively small portion of campaign funding—more often in the form of coordinated expenditures rather than direct contributions.

Political parties are also permitted to make coordinated expenditures, funds a party pays for services (polling, producing ads, or buying media time, for example) requested by a candidate who has a say in how they are spent. Coordinated funds apply to general elections but not to primaries. For Senate races, party committees may spend two cents (adjusted for inflation) for every person of voting age. Dollar limits restrict spending for House races (doubled for states with only one House seat).

Since its rebuilding effort after the post–Watergate electoral disaster of 1974, the Republican Party has had spectacular success in raising money—much of it from modest contributions solicited through targeted mailings and phone banks. In the 2003–2004 cycle, GOP House and Senate campaign committees raised $264.7 million, compared with $181.6 million for their two Democratic counterparts.[95] Especially in Senate contests, the parties can pump in huge sums of money by means of cooperative arrangements among state committees and the several national committees.

Funding patterns affect candidates' strategies and, on occasion, electoral outcomes. The Republican Party's fund-raising edge, some argue, has helped to swell victories in good years and to minimize losses in bad years.[96] In the decades before 1994, however, House Democrats relied on the funding advantages of their many incumbents to offset the GOP's national fund-raising superiority. But once in the majority, the Republicans' basic fund-raising superiority was augmented by the inevitable windfalls of incumbency. In the 2003–2004 cycle, Republican representatives raised an average of more than $647,000, compared with Democrats' $543,000.[97]

Interest Groups. Under existing law, corporations, federal contractors, and labor unions may not contribute funds directly to candidates, though individuals within those entities may do so on their own. Such groups may indulge in independent spending for or against candidates without the candidates' cooperation or consent. Corporations, labor unions, and membership organizations may recommend to their stockholders, personnel, or members the election or defeat of a candidate. Unions and corporations also may pay for nonpartisan voter registration or participation drives directed at their members, stockholders, or employees.

Other kinds of groups are embraced by existing finance laws. Multicandidate committees may give no more than $5,000 per election to a candidate. These committees must have more than fifty members and must support five or more candidates. Such committees also may contribute up to $15,000 per year to a political party.

PACs. Corporations, labor unions, membership groups, and even individuals may sponsor PACs and underwrite their administrative or fund-raising costs. PACs are the preferred method of channeling corporate or union energies into campaign war chests. Corporate executives contribute to PACs with such names as the Good Government Fund. Industry associations such as the National Association of Realtors and the American Medical Association donate millions of dollars, mostly through their PACs. Unions—both large and small—have PACs, most of which favor Democrats. Ostensibly, such donations are voluntary. However, it does not take a confirmed cynic to assume that subtle coercion and social pressure help pump money into the coffers.

Political action committees are thriving, in part because the finance laws encourage them. At the end of 1974 there were 608 PACs; by 2004, more than 4,000. All types of PACs grew in numbers, but business-related PACs grew most of all. The growth of PACs has changed the way campaigns are run. Candidates are forced to make the rounds of PACs to beg for funds. Nonincumbents win support by knocking on doors, filling out forms, being interviewed, and proving the viability of their candidacy.[98] Members attract PAC support by gaining a lucrative congressional committee assignment and compiling a favorable voting record.

PACs also have grown in financial clout. In 1972 they contributed $8.5 million to House and Senate candidates; in 2004 their contributions topped $250 million. PAC donations are especially significant in House races: They accounted for a third of House candidates' receipts in 2004 but less than half that for Senate candidates.

Because they are campaign investors, PACs favor incumbents and shun all but the most promising nonincumbents. Incumbents seeking reelection receive, on average, six times the PAC donations that their challengers receive.

Members themselves increasingly create so-called leadership PACs to exploit their prominence and fund-raising prowess. Although they trade on the name of their sponsors, such PACs are separate from their sponsors' own war chests. They are normally used to contribute to other candidates' campaigns as a way of gaining a party majority and earning their colleagues' gratitude. These PACs distributed some $27 million over the 2003–2004 cycle. Such PACs are especially popular among GOP ranks. Compared with their minority-party colleagues, Republican members' assets are more attractive to donors; their leaders—who have more rewards to give out—are more insistent that they spread their wealth to needier candidates. As a respected insider, Rep. J. Dennis

Hastert of Illinois, for example, collected $130,000 for his Keep Our Majority PAC during 1997–1998. As Speaker, Hastert was able to distribute six times that amount by 2003–2004[99]

After the GOP takeover, PAC giving naturally flowed to the victors. "The shift in PACs from the Democrats to the Republicans was dramatic and almost overnight," noted Larry Makinson of the Center for Responsive Politics, a non-profit reform group. "When the Republicans took over all these chairmanships and subcommittees, they reaped a whirlwind of money."[100] Still, with control of the House in doubt, many PACs hedged their bets in post–1994 campaigns. Business and banking interests traditionally support Republicans, whereas labor, law firms (especially trial lawyers), and the entertainment industry lean the opposite way.[101]

Pressure comes from both givers and recipients. PAC officers complain that they are dogged by incumbents, most of whom do not need the contributions, and that members keep mental accounts of contributors. "I've had congressmen open up the door and look down a list to see if we have contributed," one of them said. "And I've had them say, 'Well, I like your organization but you haven't given me a contribution.' "[102]

Candidate Funding: A Regulated Industry?

Financial inequalities—between incumbents and nonincumbents and between wealthy donors and average citizens—inevitably lead to demands for legal ways of monitoring or even controlling campaign finance. Laws have been passed not only to clean up campaigns but also to shift political influence from those who rely on financial contributions to those who depend on other resources. Several techniques have been employed. The primary ones thus far have been disclosure of campaign contributions and expenditures, limits on campaign contributions and expenditures, and (in presidential races) public financing of campaigns.

FECA, 1974, 1976. Reacting to campaign scandals of the early 1970s, Congress decided to erect regulatory standards for financing federal election campaigns. A broad-gauged campaign finance law, the Federal Election Campaign Act (FECA) Amendments of 1974, was signed into law by President Gerald R. Ford. Major features of the act included limits on individual contributions, limits on party and nonparty group contributions, and reporting requirements for all contributions.

The Supreme Court, ruling on a challenge to the law, held that Congress may limit contributions to congressional candidates but that it may not limit expenditures by candidates themselves, their campaign committees, or individuals or organizations independent of the candidate (*Buckley v. Valeo,* 1976). The reasoning was that, as a form of free expression protected by the First Amendment, spending to influence elections cannot be constrained. To end the confusion and meet the Court's constitutional objections, Congress quickly passed a revised act aimed at reconciling the Court's rulings with the original congressional intent.

The *Buckley* decision, experience has shown, undercut Congress's intentions and ultimately rendered the law unworkable. The Court's reasoning has been criticized as wrongheaded. First, it stretched the First Amendment to treat donations to federal campaigns as pure, protected speech. Such giving might better be treated as, say, economic activity—which can be regulated. As dissenting Justice Stevens put it: "Money is property; it is not speech."[103] "In fact," writes lawyer-novelist Scott Turow, "given *Buckley*'s rationale, I've never figured out why outright vote-buying isn't also protected by the First Amendment."[104]

Second, with no enforceable restrictions on campaign spending, politicians and interested groups were free to exploit creative ways of maximizing their financial leverage, in the process stripping from the law the one fig leaf the Court sanctioned: contribution limits. The free-for-all system that resulted, critics charge, has replaced the principle of "one person–one vote" with a "regime of one dollar–one vote," which "distorts the fundamental principle of political equality underlying the First Amendment itself."[105]

The law is enforced by the bipartisan Federal Election Commission, appointed by the president and confirmed by the Senate. The commission may issue regulations and advisory opinions, conduct investigations, and prosecute violations of the law. Most important, the FEC compiles and disseminates campaign finance data from the reports it receives. Disclosure of the sources and uses of campaign money is the one aspect of current regulations that everyone agrees is a success.

Campaign Finance Politics. Campaign financing laws have failed to limit the influence of big money in politics. Big money is alive and well in American elections, although now it flows through more issue and candidate groups than in the past. The best that can be said is that many of the best-funded PACs depend on large numbers of mail-solicited donations instead of on a few fat cats. The 1976 act, moreover, failed utterly to reduce inequalities between incumbents and challengers. The changes may even have helped incumbents and kept challengers from raising the money they need to win.[106] Finally, the reforms have blurred the distinction between interest groups and political parties. Labor unions, business and industry associations, consumer and environmental organizations, ideological movements, and a host of special issue groups have invaded the electoral arena as never before. By boosting and even recruiting candidates—and hindering others—they hope to win favorable treatment for their causes on Capitol Hill.

Campaign finance laws are so loosely drawn that money pours freely into congressional elections. Parties and PACs use tax-exempt foundations to take donations in excess of legal limits. Creative accounting and independent spending on behalf of candidates are used to skirt legal limits on what PACs can give directly to candidates. Bankers and other moneyed people can lend money or extend credit to candidates under permissive rules. And money is moving underground, thwarting federal enforcement and disclosure efforts. "You can do just about anything, as long as you take care," said one party official.[107]

In campaign financing debates, where you stand depends on where your money comes from. Change is resisted by those who thrive under existing rules. Republicans tend to shun monetary limits—for the very good reason that the party overall is very adept at fund raising. Many conservatives would abolish all limits on contributions to candidates and parties, relying solely upon better reporting through electronic filing and Internet dissemination.

BCRA, 2002. The Bipartisan Campaign Reform Act (BCRA) of 2002 was something of a political miracle, given the opposition to reform from across the political spectrum (see Box 3-1 on bipartisan campaign reform act). The drive to tighten up the 1974 law began in the mid-1980s and raged through four presidencies, multiple floor votes, a 1992 veto by President George Bush, and repeated parliamentary setbacks. In the mid-1990s the cause was taken up in the Senate by John McCain, R-Ariz., and Russell D. Feingold, D-Wis., and in the House by Christopher Shays, R-Conn., and Martin T. Meehan, D-Mass. Scandals associated with the 1996 and 2000 elections—and the growth of unregulated soft-money spending—kept the issue alive. And a final scandal in 2002—involving Enron, the energy firm whose political connections kept it in business despite its economic collapse—pushed the bill over the top. "What McCain said repeatedly was right," Senator Feingold remarked. "It would take a scandal—might take more than one scandal—but we would prevail."[108]

Court challenges to BCRA quickly surfaced. When the act reached the Supreme Court, its major provisions were upheld by a 5–4 majority. This majority upheld the act's core provision (Title I), which prohibited national parties and their committees from accepting "soft money"—the large, unlimited contributions that corporations, labor unions, and individuals gave to party committees outside of "hard-money" limits set by law. These totaled some $500 million in the 2001–2002 cycle. The opinion, written by Justices O'Connor and Stevens, accepted Congress's judgment on the issue:

> As the record demonstrates, it is the manner in which parties have sold access to federal candidates and officeholders that has given rise to the appearance of undue influence. It was not unwarranted for Congress to conclude that the selling of access gives rise to the appearance of corruption.[109]

The act's more problematic Title II, regulating "electioneering communications," was upheld by the majority with only a brief discussion.

The dissenters expressed a narrower view of corruption—limited to something close to bribery (trading votes for dollars). The majority saw this as a "crabbed view of corruption, and particularly of the appearance of corruption, that ignores precedent, common sense, and the realities of political fundraising." The minority also sought refuge in the *Buckley* view that campaign donors were simply exercising free speech. "This new definition of corruption,"

BOX 3-1 The Bipartisan Campaign Reform Act of 2002

The Bipartisan Campaign Reform Act (BCRA) of 2002, which took effect November 6 of that year, was the first major enactment since the advent of modern campaign finance regulations in 1974. More than ninety pages long, BCRA has a variety of provisions but was touted mainly for its ban on soft money and for regulating election-time issue advertising on radio and television by corporations, unions, and interest groups. Following are the major provisions of the law, known as McCain-Feingold for its principal Senate sponsors, John McCain, R-Ariz., and Russell D. Feingold, D-Wis.:

Hard-Money Contribution Limits. Individual contribution limits for House and Senate candidates are doubled to $2,000 per election, indexed to grow with inflation; aggregate contribution limits for individuals are $ 95,000—$37,500 to candidates and $ 57,500 to parties and political action committees (PACs). Contribution limits for PACs are unchanged: $5,000 per candidate per election, plus $15,000 to a national party committee and $5,000 combined to state and local party committees.

Soft Money. National party committees cannot accept or spend soft money—unregulated contributions from corporations, labor unions, and wealthy individuals ostensibly intended for party-building activities, such as voter registration, but often used for campaign-related purposes.

State and Local Parties. Non-national political parties cannot spend soft money on federal election activities. They may spend soft money for voter registration and mobilization under certain conditions.

Independent and Coordinated Expenditures. The Federal Election Commission (FEC) must issue new rules covering coordination between candidates or parties and outside

Justice Kennedy held, "sweeps away all protections of speech that lie in its path." The Court's decision "leaves us less free than before."

Skeptics argued that the new law would do little to halt the overall flow of money into political campaigns. "This law will not remove one dime from politics," predicted Sen. Mitch McConnell, R-Ky., the leading GOP opponent of the measure.[110] His prediction was borne out by political scientist David Magleby, who has recorded "a surge in individual giving to the political parties and the candidates, which more than replaced the old soft money." [111]

The soft-money ban does, however, favor those who are best equipped to attract hard-money donations—including Republican party committees and individual candidates with hordes of dedicated followers, most notably President Bush and Democratic contender Howard Dean in 2004.

The other growth sector in campaign finance is the explosion in third-party nonprofit advocacy groups (that is, not formally associated with either parties or candidates). Many register as PACs; others are so-called 527 groups (from the relevant tax code section). They are free to collect money—much of groups. The rules cannot require formal evidence of coordination to treat spending by outside groups as a regulated contribution instead of an unregulated independent expenditure.

Tax-Exempt Organizations. National, state, and local parties may neither solicit money from nor contribute to any nonprofit group that spends money on federal elections. They also may not contribute to or solicit money from so-called 527 organizations that intervene in campaigns but do not expressly advocate any candidate's election or directly subsidize federal campaigns.

Electioneering Communications. Broadcast, cable, or satellite communications that name candidates for federal office or show their likeness and are targeted at candidates' states or districts—known as electioneering communications—may not be issued within sixty days of a general election or thirty days of a primary.

Unions and Corporations. Labor unions and corporations remain banned from directly funding electioneering communications and can pay for such advertising only through political action committees with regulated hard money.

Nonprofits and 527s. Tax-exempt groups, including those covered under Section 527 of the Internal Revenue Code, raise unregulated (soft) money for political activities: voter registration, issue advocacy, and the like. They may operate through PACs, and they may even contribute to candidates (under hard-money rules).

Sources: Revised and reprinted from *CQ Researcher*, November 22, 2002, 974; and Center for Responsive Politics, "Types of Advocacy Groups," www.opensecrets.org.

it unlimited soft money—and, ironically, may contribute a portion to parties or candidates according to hard-money limits. But their energies are typically devoted to influencing elections through voter mobilization and issue ads, often with strong partisan or candidate messages. Such efforts added hundreds of millions of dollars to the 2004 presidential contest, but many such groups, such as the Club for Growth (conservative Republican) and EMILY'S List (pro-choice Democratic women), focus on congressional contests.

Reformers and Skeptics. Some critics advocate public funding of Senate and House campaigns. As for presidential campaigns, the 1974 act included an optional public financing scheme that was intended to provide sufficient resources for presidential candidates who agreed to use it. But that has not stopped candidates and parties from raising money over and above the public funds, in violation of both the spirit and the letter of the law. In any event, Congress declined to extend public financing to its own elections. The public funding option, moreover, runs afoul of public antipathy toward spending more tax dollars on politicians.

Perhaps the most promising way to level the playing field, at least for incumbents and challengers, would be to provide the latter with subsidized mailings and free radio and TV time. This option, predictably, is fiercely opposed by broadcasters—a potent lobby because politicians crave the exposure their outlets provide. Even the innocuous provision that broadcasters offer time for political messages at the lowest prevailing rates has drawn opposition.

Reform commands public support, but for voters it rarely seems a salient issue—a fact not lost on those who benefit from the current state of affairs. The Court's notion that spending money is protected speech is another huge obstacle. That interpretation has its critics, but few public figures want to campaign publicly for a narrower reading of the First Amendment.

Conceding that further controls are desirable, most political scientists nonetheless are skeptical about the benefits of many of the proposed changes in campaign financing. Overall spending limits must be approached cautiously. Challengers need to be able to spend money to offset incumbents' advantages, and because they start from behind they get more value for every dollar they spend. As for PAC contributions, they are easily stigmatized, but they are nonetheless a lawful way for interested groups to give money—gifts that at least are recorded and scrutinized. Independent campaign activities of individuals or groups are forms of free expression that should be accorded wide elbowroom. Even the much-maligned soft money served in part to underwrite party activities. Abolishing it will surely force interest groups to shun the parties and spend the money on their own.

Finally, there is what journalist Chuck Alston calls the "whack-a-mole" problem. In the arcade game "the mole pops up in one hole, and you whack him down. But then he pops up somewhere else. Similarly, campaign spending, whenever it is suppressed in one form, always pops up elsewhere."[112] That fate will surely confound any reform that is adopted.

CONCLUSION

The rules of the game that narrow the potential field of congressional contenders can be thought of as a series of gates, each narrower than the one before. First are the constitutional qualifications for holding office. Then there are complex rules of apportionment and districting. Beyond these are nominating procedures (usually primaries) and financial requirements. These gates cut down sharply the number of people who are likely to become real contenders.

Equally important, individuals must make up their own minds about running for the House or Senate. Such choices embrace a range of considerations—many personal and emotional but all based on some estimate of the likely benefits and costs of their candidacy. This winnowing process presents voters with a limited choice on election day: two, sometimes more, preselected candidates. From this restricted circle senators and representatives are chosen.

SUGGESTED READINGS

Canon, David T. *Race, Redistricting, and Representation.* Chicago: University of Chicago Press, 1999.

Ehrenhalt, Alan. *The United States of Ambition.* New York: Random House, 1991.

Fowler, Linda L., and Robert D. McClure. *Political Ambition: Who Decides to Run for Congress.* New Haven: Yale University Press, 1989.

Giroux, Gregory L., et al., "Special Report, The New Congressional Demograpic: Suburbs Rule." *CQ Weekly,* June 27, 2005, 1713–1738.

Kazee, Thomas A., ed. *Who Runs for Congress? Ambition, Context, and Candidate Emergence.* Washington, D.C.: Congressional Quarterly, 1994.

Loomis, Burdett. *The New American Politician.* New York: Basic Books, 1988.

Magleby, David B., and J. Quin Monson, eds. *The Last Hurrah?* Washington D.C.: Brookings Institution Press, 2004.

Monmonier, Mark. *Bushmanders and Bullwinkles: How Politicians Manipulate Electronic Maps and Census Data to Win Elections.* Chicago: University of Chicago Press, 2001.

Scenes of campaigns and elections: Above, Republican senatorial candidate John Thune makes a campaign stop in Presho, South Dakota, a week before the 2004 balloting. Thune defeated Senate Democratic leader Tom Daschle by some 4,500 votes. Left, senator-elect Barack Obama, D-I with his wife and two daughters, braves a blizzard confetti as supporters celebrate his 2004 election a the third African American senator since Reconstruction. Below left, Rep. John D. Dingell, D-Mich., rides in a campaign parade. First elected in 1955, Dingell is dean of the House; he won his twenty-fifth term in 2004. Below right, a West Pal Beach resident uses a new voting machine, part of Florida's efforts to improve its election manageme

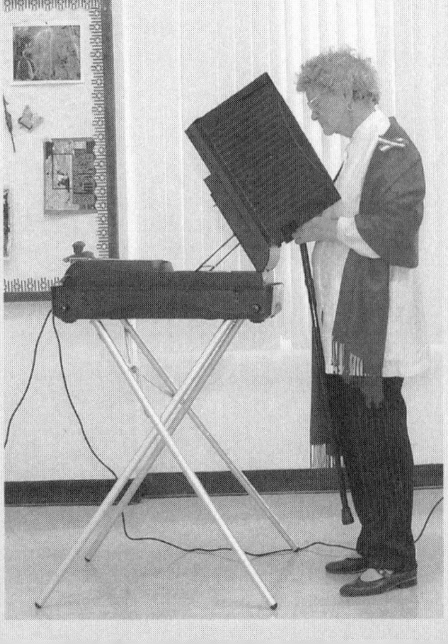

chapter 4

Making It: The Electoral Game

John Thune's silver campaign bus stopped at DeSmet, a small South Dakota farming town made famous by the books of Laura Ingalls Wilder. Addressing one of his "pancake feeds," he scorned Senate Democrats' efforts to block judicial nominees labeled as outside the mainstream. "That's code," he said, "for these judges [who] are pro-life." [1]

Thune, a telegenic former representative, was recruited by the White House two years earlier to challenge the state's junior Democratic senator, Tim Johnson, losing by only 524 votes. Now he was back, again with White House blessing, to take on a more formidable incumbent: Tom Daschle, Senate Democratic leader and national political figure. For Congress-watchers, this race was 2004's big kahuna.

Daschle, a veteran of twenty-six years on Capitol Hill, eighteen of them in the Senate, commanded all the resources he needed from his allies throughout the nation. He raised $21.1 million—90 percent of it from outside the state. Thune also had ample cash, $16.1 million; and GOP heavyweights such as Senate majority leader Bill Frist, R-Tenn., came to the state to campaign with him. Out-of-state conservative groups spent millions on ads blasting Daschle as an obstructionist, and worse. (A renegade group, disavowed by Thune, sent out bumper stickers saying that a vote for Daschle was a vote for sodomy.) Daschle responded with thirty-second ads saying that "Daschle cuts taxes for the middle-class; Thune cuts taxes for the rich."

When Daschle's own silver campaign bus rolled through the main streets of dusty South Dakota towns, nearly everyone knew who was on board. Every year he had driven across the state, visiting all sixty-six counties. People here know the candidates as "Tom" and "John." Daschle hardly ever mentioned Senate politics or procedures, stressing instead how his power enriched South Dakota—for example, federal drought aid, highway funding, and subsidies for corn-based ethanol fuel.

In the end, Thune's message overcame Daschle's by some forty-five hundred votes. This was in a presidential year, in a red state that gave incumbent GOP president George W. Bush 63 percent of the vote. "Daschle has been powerful," one voter explained, "and that has been an asset to the state. But I feel he no longer represents the state, the small-town beliefs of the state."

The South Dakota contest was singular but not unique. The average Senate victor in 2004 raised $7.85 million; none raised less than $2.4 million.[2] One challenger's campaign, a write-in affair, came in at $13,000. (History's costliest Senate race occurred four years earlier: the New York contest between first lady Hillary Rodham Clinton and former New York City mayor Rudolph W. Giuliani, who dropped out, and finally Rep. Rick A. Lazio, which cost a total of $91.3 million.) These campaigns are waged in the new-fashioned way—through seasoned campaign specialists underwritten by truckloads of money. The South Dakota race, for example, cost $95 for every voter who turned out, and that was only what the candidates themselves spent.

CAMPAIGN STRATEGIES

Campaigns are volatile mixtures of personal contacts, fund raising, speech making, advertising, and symbolic appeals. As acts of communication, campaigns are designed to convey messages to potential voters. The goal is to win over a plurality of those who cast ballots on election day.

Asking the Right Questions

Candidates, whether incumbents or challengers, strive to set the basic tone or thrust of their campaign. To map out a successful strategy, a candidate must ask himself: What sort of constituency do I have? Are my name, face, and career familiar to voters, or am I relatively unknown? What resources—money, group support, volunteers—can I attract? What leaders and groups are pivotal to a winning campaign? What issues or moods are uppermost in potential voters' minds? How can I reach those voters most effectively with my message? When should my campaign begin and how should it be paced? And what are my chances for victory? The answers to such questions define the campaign strategy.

The constituency (its demography as well as its partisan balance) shapes candidates' campaign strategies. In populous states, Senate aspirants must appeal to diverse economic and social groups, scattered over wide areas and multiple media markets. In fast-growing states, even Senate incumbents must introduce themselves to hordes of new voters who have arrived in the intervening six years. Only small-state Senate candidates can know their states as intimately as House candidates know their districts. House districts often fit no natural geographic, community, media market, or political divisions.[3] In such situations, candidates and their managers must find the most suitable forums, media outlets, and local organizations.

Because incumbents are usually tough to beat, the presence or absence of an incumbent colors the entire electoral undertaking. Also critical is the partisan slant of the electorate. The dominant party's candidates stress party loyalty, underscore long-standing partisan values (called valence issues), and sponsor get-out-the-vote (GOTV) drives, because high voter turnout usually aids their cause. Minority-party campaigns strive to highlight personalities, obscure partisan differences, and exploit factional splits within the majority party, perhaps by invoking issues that can pry voters away from their majority-party home (called wedge issues).

The perceptions and attitudes of voters, finally, must be reflected in campaign planning. Through sample surveys, focus groups, or informal pulse taking, strategists try to detect what is on voters' minds and what, if anything, they know or think about the candidate. Well-known candidates try to capitalize on their visibility; lesser-known ones run ads that repeat their names over and over again. Candidates with a reputation for openness and geniality highlight those qualities in ads. Those who are more introverted (yes, there are such politicians) stress experience and competence, at the same time displaying photos or film clips reminding voters that they, too, are human. Candidates who have made tough, unpopular decisions are touted as courageous leaders. And so it goes.

As popular moods change, so do the self-images candidates try to project. Candidates' appearances, speeches, advertising, and appeals are designed to exploit such voter preferences. In the wake of scandals, honesty and openness are on display. Thus in the early 1990s, challengers sold themselves as outsiders (even if they were political veterans). Incumbents of both parties countered by portraying themselves as independent-minded apostles of change. Political experience soon came back in fashion, however. The Capitol dome and its marble halls reappeared in campaign ads. In crisis times, moreover, voters prefer experience, competence, and continuity.

Choosing the Message

The average citizen is barraged with media messages of all kinds—an hour of television commercials per day, among other things. The candidate's overarching challenge is how to project an image through this morass of media appeals, including those from other candidates. "The only way to cut through this communication clutter," a political marketing executive points out, "is to adopt the strategy proven effective by successful businesses. Create a brand. And manage the message with discipline and impact."[4]

Framing the Voters' Choice. In other words, forge a message that will stand out from all the competing messages in the media marketplace. A candidate's message is usually distilled into a single theme or slogan that is repeated on radio, TV, and billboards and in campaign literature. "A good message . . . is a credible statement that can be summed up in a few sentences and frequently ends with a kicker slogan. . . . In most races, messages define campaigns."[5]

Strategists use these messages to frame the campaign, that is, to pose the election's core issue in such a way that voters respond favorably to their candidate or negatively to the opponent. "There's only three or four plots," explained Carter Eskew, a Democratic consultant. Plots for incumbents are Representative X is different from the rest; X can deliver; X stands with you.

And the perennial plot for challengers is (fill in the blank) years are long enough; it is time for a change.[6]

Campaign messages usually appear in the form of slogans attempting to frame the voter's choice. In her 2004 race for the South Carolina Senate seat, Democrat Inez Tenenbaum relentlessly repeated a theme that arose from her party's minority status in the state: "It's not whose team you're on, it's whose side you're on." The message of her victorious opponent, Republican representative Jim DeMint, was expressed by the shouts of his backers: "Jim DeMint, George Bush!"[7]

Vulnerable Incumbents. Incumbency can have its liabilities. An extensive public record gives enterprising opponents many potential openings to exploit. Votes or positions may be highlighted, and sometimes twisted, to discredit the officeholder. Incumbents may be shackled to unpopular issues, such as nuclear waste dumps or Medicare premium hikes, or to unpopular personalities on the national scene.

Or incumbents become careless, taking for granted their voters' loyalty. One of only six candidates to topple an incumbent in 2000 was Republican Rob Simmons in Connecticut's Second District. His theme was "Rob Simmons is a perfect fit for the district. [Sam] Gejdenson [the ten-term Democratic incumbent] is out of touch with the district, and it is time for a change." One TV spot began with a picture of an iron gate and an announcer who said: "Living outside our district in a gated community, Sam Gejdenson no longer shares our values. Rob Simmons does."[8]

Simmons won narrowly and has hung on in a Democratic state. One campaign consultant summed up the lesson of such races: "You have to earn that support every two years. A lot of members of Congress forget how to run. . . . Voters will change members of Congress like they change shoes if they think it makes the outfit look better."[9]

CAMPAIGN RESOURCES

Campaigns require resources to play out the strategy that has been devised. The cleverest strategy in the world is of no avail without the wherewithal to bring its message to voters. The type of state or district, incumbency status, candidate visibility, and party margin matter little if the candidate lacks two essential resources: a budget that can be met or exceeded, and an organization that can get the message across to voters.

Allocating Resources

The importance of money in campaigns cannot be overemphasized. Virtually any kind of campaign can be mounted with enough money. Old-fashioned alternatives, such as door-to-door canvassing or use of volunteer organizations, have proved effective, although they eat up time and resources that might be used to reach larger numbers of voters. Candidates facing tough contests in both primary and general elections and lacking personal wealth have an especially vexing dilemma. Should they ration their outflow of funds and risk losing the primary, or should they wage an expensive primary campaign and risk running out of money later on?

Especially useful is early money—funds on hand at the outset of the campaign, or even earlier. EMILY's List—Early Money Is Like Yeast ("It makes the 'dough' rise")—a group begun in 1985, was formed on this premise. EMILY's List collects (bundles) individuals' donations for Democratic women candidates who support abortion rights. In 2004 it raised $43.8 million from its members, $10.7 of which went directly to candidates. The group claims to have helped some forty-four women (five of them newcomers) win seats in the 109th Congress (2005–2007).[10] The Republican counterpart is Women in the Senate and House (WISH).

Late blitz money also can turn the tide, although money alone rarely makes the difference. The final weeks of a hard-fought race are tough because both sides are trying to reach undecided voters. "You've got to move that 10 or 15 percent, many of whom are not paying much attention," a Democratic consultant explained. "Unfortunately, the way to do that is with negative or comparative ads."[11] Late in the game, opponents frantically attack and—despite the scant time—counterattack.

Incumbents' Money. Incumbents raise more money and also spend more on their campaigns than challengers do (see Figure 4-1). Because incumbents are better known than challengers, their spending often has strategic purposes. Preemptive spending involves constant fund raising, which, along with surpluses from previous campaigns, can dissuade serious opponents. "If you look like a 900-pound gorilla, people won't want to take you on," remarked a GOP campaign aide.[12] The current champion fund-raiser is New York Democratic senator Clinton, who early in 2005 had $8.7 million in campaign funds for her 2006 reelection effort—with no big-foot Republican challenger in sight.[13]

If a strong, well-financed challenger surfaces, incumbents can spend reactively to stave off defeat. The 1990s found incumbents spending more than ever to counter challengers (who were better financed than usual). Facing fewer such challengers, House incumbents in 2004 still raised on average more than $1 million to defend their seats—more than five times what their opponents could muster.[14]

New incumbents tend to invest heavily in preemptive and reactive spending because they are more likely than longtime veterans to face vigorous challenges. More senior members raise and spend less than junior members, especially in the early campaign stages (before July of an election year). Incumbents who are sure-fire vote-getters over the long haul—with five or more terms—may establish such commanding positions that they rarely face serious challenges.

Sometimes established incumbents deliberately overspend for reasons beyond the race at hand. Decisive victories can establish claims for higher

FIGURE 4-1 **Average House Campaign Expenditures by Incumbency and Party, 1980–2004**

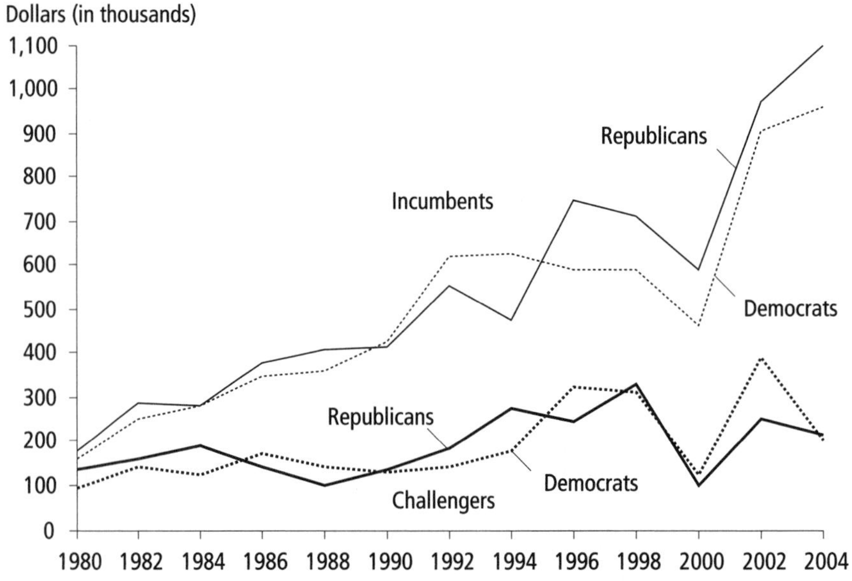

Sources: Norman J. Ornstein, Thomas E. Mann, and Michael J. Malbin, *Vital Statistics on Congress, 2001–2002* (Washington D.C.: American Enterprise Institute, 2002), 87–88; and Federal Election Commission figures reported by the Center for Responsive Politics at www.opensecrets.org.

office: Many House members yearn for a Senate seat; some senators harbor presidential ambitions. Others strive to impress colleagues or interest groups with their electoral prowess. They are encouraged to distribute unused funds to needier candidates, who may repay in the future—perhaps with support in a leadership contest. Or they may simply bid for freedom to concentrate on Capitol Hill business or other pursuits.

Incumbents' overspending is motivated, finally, by a sense of uncertainty and risk. "Because of uncertainty," Gary C. Jacobson explains, "members tend to exaggerate electoral threats and overreact to them. They are inspired by worst-case scenarios—what would they have to do to win if everything went wrong?—rather than objective probabilities."[15]

Challengers' Money. Challengers and open-seat candidates raise money to gain visibility, win credibility, and get a head start over other contenders. (For one open-seat candidate's fund-raising efforts, see Table 4-1.) "Failure to raise enough money creates a vicious spiral," explains political analyst Thomas B. Edsall. "Some donors become reluctant to invest their cash, and then state and national parties are less likely to target their unlimited 'soft money' for party building and get out the vote drives in those races."[16]

Challengers, for their part, spend all the money they can raise to make their names and faces known to voters. And, because normally they start far behind, their campaign dollars tend to be more cost-effective than those of incumbents. As Jacobson has demonstrated, the more a challenger spends, the more votes he is likely to attract.[17] The five challengers who toppled incumbents in 2004 were all adequately financed, though none of them matched their opponents' resources.

Spending Campaign Funds

As exercises in communication, campaigns are driven, and their budgets shaped, by the need to find a cost-effective way of reaching citizens and getting them to vote. Spending patterns vary widely between the House and the Senate, among congressional districts and states, and between incumbents and challengers.

TABLE 4-1 **See How He Ran: Candidate Brian Baird's Time Budget, July–October 1998**

Activity	Hours and minutes spent[a]	Percentage of time
Fund-raising call time	397:30	32
Other fund raising	36:00	3
Meeting with individuals, groups, politicians	146:00	12
Public events	96:00	8
Meeting with media	31:00	2
Voter contact	89:15	7
Meeting with staff	58:45	5
Travel	203:15	16
Personal time	201:30	16
Total hours	1,259:15	101[b]
Average hours per day	10:12	

Source: Baird for Congress Campaign, 1998; and James A. Thurber and Carolyn Long, "Brian Baird's 'Ring of Fire': The Quest for Funds and Votes in Washington's Third District," in *The Battle for Congress,* ed. James A. Thurber (Washington, D.C.: Brookings Institution, 2001), 188.

[a]Excludes the three days of campaigning in November: 33 hours, 15 minutes, mostly in voter contact.
[b]Does not add to 100 percent because of rounding.

As a rule, statewide Senate races are mass media contests with messages conveyed mainly through radio and television. Costs are especially high in densely populated states with numerous metropolitan media markets. Senate candidates spend far more on media advertising and fund raising than do their House counterparts, who spend correspondingly more on traditional means of voter contact. The most expensive House contests are in states where the population is small and spread out.[18] Consider central and western Nebraska's Third District, which spans 85 percent of the state's land area and is served by nine media markets in six states (only three of them within Nebraska).

Despite its astronomic costs, television advertising is popular because candidates find it cost-effective, and they believe it works. They are probably right. Political scientist Thomas Patterson estimated that as early as the 1980s it cost only about one-half cent to get to a single television viewer, compared with one and a half cents to reach a newspaper reader and twenty-five cents to reach a direct-mail recipient.[19]

The character of candidates and their party organizations also affects the media mix and budgeting. Confident incumbents can channel their money into telephone or door-to-door appeals that direct their messages to activists, partisans, and supporters. Lesser-known candidates must turn to broad-scale media, such as television or billboards, to promote name recognition.[20] Both House and Senate challengers spend more on media and less on traditional campaigning than do incumbents. And, although challengers presumably need more money to get their messages across, they spend less in fund raising than incumbents do.

Incumbents also spend more on constituent gifts and entertainment and donations to local causes. Since 1989 campaign funds have been barred from personal use, and in 1995 the Federal Election Commission (FEC) tightened its definition of permissible uses—though the issue remains a thorny one. The FEC still allows gifts of nominal value to constituents. Spending reports from members' campaigns and their related political action committees (PACs) disclose a surprising array of activities, such as buying flowers and tickets to sports events, organizing athletic teams, sponsoring contests and prizes, and subsidizing travel and entertainment.[21]

Organizing the Campaign

Implementing the campaign strategy is the job of the candidates and their organizations. Waging a campaign is not for the fainthearted. Take the case of psychology professor Brian Baird, a Democrat who won Washington's Third District seat in 1998. Having lost to the incumbent by a mere 887 votes two years earlier, Baird vowed to run full tilt the second time, when the incumbent bowed out to run for the Senate. His campaign schedule is summarized in Table 4-1. Baird spent nearly all his waking hours on the campaign during the peak months (July through October)—more than ten hours a day for 123 days. By far the largest block of time—more than one-third—was spent raising the $1.3 million he needed to win the open seat. Most of those hours he sat in a tiny room he called his bunker, wearing a headset and phoning potential contributors. Many of his meetings with individuals, groups, or other politicians were also related to fund raising. Travel ate up many valuable hours in the average-size Third District (Olympia and southwest Washington). His days of hard campaigning are by no means over. Although he won reelection three times by widening margins, his district will continue to be targeted by both parties.

Few localities today boast tight party organizations. In some strong party areas, voter contact is the job of ward, precinct, and block captains. Candidates in some such areas still dispense "walking-around money" to encourage precinct captains to get out the vote and provide small financial rewards for voting.

Such traditional local parties have often been replaced by hybrid organizations—partnered with state and national parties and their allied interest groups. In one California metropolitan area of some 350,000 people, the Democratic Service Club of Santa Barbara claims about two thousand supporters, more than half of them active volunteers. In 2004 the organization produced 100,000 brochures featuring the party's slate of twenty-two candidates, fielded one hundred poll watchers, and raised money to fly thirty volunteers to the swing state of New Mexico the last week of the campaign.[22]

When they can pay the price, today's candidates can purchase campaign services from political consulting firms. Some companies offer a wide array of services; others specialize in survey research, direct-mail appeals, phone banks, advertising, purchase of media time, coordinating volunteer efforts, fund raising, or financial management and accounting. Despite the hype they often receive, consultants rarely turn a campaign around. At best they can make the most of a candidate's resources and help combat opponents' attacks. They cannot compensate for an unskilled or lazy candidate or for a candidate's staff that does not follow through on details.

Reliance upon professional firms raises its own set of problems. Not all firms are scrupulous in adhering to professional or ethical standards. One example is opposition research, the purpose of which is "to get the skinny on the client's opponents and, if all goes well, expose them as hypocrites, liars, thieves, or just plain unsavory characters."[23] Most campaigns invest in opposition research. Some of them go too far, straying beyond the public record into private-eye snooping into personal matters. Another debatable form of campaigning is the push poll. This is a survey instrument that features questions intended to change opinions of the contacted voters. Negative information—often false or misleading—is divulged with the hope of pushing the voter away from the opponent and toward the candidate paying for the polling.

CAMPAIGN TECHNIQUES

Campaigns are designed to convey candidates' messages to people who will lend support and vote in the election. Campaigns are not necessarily directed at all voters. Often narrower groups are targeted, mainly those most likely to vote for the candidate—most notably, the political parties' core supporters. Campaign techniques are distinguished by the breadth and kind of audiences they seek to reach.

The Air War: Media and Other Mass Appeals

Candidates reach the largest numbers of voters by running ads and making televised appearances. Especially in statewide elections, media efforts may be the only way for candidates to get their messages to the mass of voters. Television is the broadest spectrum medium and often the most cost-effective. But its costs eat up the largest chunk of most campaign budgets.

Media efforts vary in the degree to which candidates control their preparation and distribution. Paradoxically, some of the most effective appeals—news coverage and endorsements, for example—are determined by persons other than the candidate. But because journalists can raise unwanted or hostile questions, many politicians seek out the friendlier environments of talk shows hosted by nonjournalists. Even more congenial are appeals the candidates themselves buy and pay for—newsletters, media ads, and direct mail. The drawback is that self-promotion is seen as less credible than information from independent sources.

Three-fourths of all voters in 2004 received campaign news from television—network, cable, or local. Nearly half also relied on newspapers, and more than a fifth cited Internet communications.[24] Yet the electronic media largely ignore congressional campaign coverage. In the weeks preceding the 2004 elections, 92 percent of the scheduled half-hour local news programs in eleven select media markets offered no coverage at all of local candidate races, including U.S. House races. In the ten markets with statewide Senate races, the blackout rate was 94 percent.[25] Most candidates must thus pay to reach out to voters: Local TV stations nationwide took in $2.6 billion from candidate advertising in 2004.

Positive Advertising. Most campaign themes call for promotions that evoke positive responses from citizens. Little-known candidates must initially boost name familiarity. Their ads introduce the candidates to voters, underscore their personal and public qualities, and tell of their accomplishments. Running in California's Twenty-second (now Twenty-third) District following her husband's sudden death, Democrat Lois Capps introduced herself by stressing her local ties and associating herself with popular issues.

> ***Capps:*** For thirty-three years I've lived and raised my family here. My husband, Walter, had the honor of representing you, and now I'm

running to finish his term. As a teacher and a mother, I'll make improving our schools a top priority. I'll use my experience as a nurse to fight for health care that protects seniors and the right to choose our own doctor, and I'll support tax reform and tax relief for working families.

Announcer: The experience of a lifetime makes Lois Capps the qualified choice for Congress.[26]

Between January and November 1998, Capps ran and outpolled her opponents in four separate contests—the special election and subsequent runoff for the partial term and then the primary and general election for a full term. Ads such as hers present candidates in warm, human terms to which citizens can relate. Democrat Dennis Moore, a 1998 challenger in Kansas's Third District (northeast; Kansas City suburbs) had a superb résumé, but it was his talent as an amateur singer and guitar player that enabled him to connect with voters on a personal level. Moore had to be coaxed into making a hokey TV spot entitled "Guitar Lessons." After mentioning a style of music (country, rock, blues), he would play a short tune and then apply it to an issue. Example: "Rock: We need to make Social Security solid as a rock."[27] Moore captured the seat, a feat he repeated three times.

If skillfully done, TV ads can be artful as well as effective in bringing home the candidates' themes. A case in point was the series of brilliant, funny—and inexpensive—television ads that helped a little-known Wisconsin state legislator, Russell D. Feingold, win the Democratic primary over better-known and better-financed rivals and then to defeat a two-term incumbent senator.[28] As his opponents battered each other with negative ads, Feingold ran clever, personal spots describing himself as the "underdog candidate." One showed Elvis, alive and endorsing Feingold. Another showed Feingold walking through his modest home, opening up a closet and saying, "No skeletons." In another he posted his three key pledges on his garage door. Although outspent in both the primary and the general election, Feingold became one of five successful challengers in the 1992 Senate races.

Some media appeals are coordinated with field operations. Trolling for the student vote in Madison, Wisconsin, Democratic candidate Tammy Baldwin ran what her staff called the "Bucky" ad (for the University of Wisconsin mascot "Bucky Badger"). It ran on MTV and youth-oriented shows. The ad said that "there is one candidate who understands our issues" and ended with a pitch to get out and vote, with phone number and Baldwin's Web site. Every time the ad ran, all the headquarters phone lines would light up.[29]

Negative Ads. Different from positive ads are those known as contrast ads, which separate the candidate from the opponent, and attack (truly negative) ads, which strike at the opponent's views or behavior. The line between contrast ads and negative ads is not always clear. Dennis Moore's gun control spot was a contrast ad. The message was delivered by a seedy-looking gunman prowling outside a school playground, and the "this could happen here" theme was played off against the incumbent's votes and positions on gun control. The ad was a hit with women in focus groups, but the wary campaign managers decided to use it only at the end of the campaign and only during nonprime hours.[30] Ads slide into negativism when they mainly attack the opponent.

In many races, voters' opinions are tracked throughout the campaign, and damaging opposition tactics are countered at once. More than one politician has lost by hesitating to counter opponents' thrusts. Technology now enables reactive ads to be produced and distributed in a few hours. They can be sent by satellite to television stations on the campaign trail. Numerous attack and response ads may be produced in the course of a hard-fought campaign.

Attack ads are common in modern campaigning because politicians believe they work. Recent experiments by two noted communications researchers tend to confirm this intuition. Negative ads, the scholars found, do lift voters' information levels, even if the information conveyed is distorted or trivial. Neither positive nor negative ads have much effect on partisans. Ads tend to reinforce previously held views and only slightly raise (or lower) their predisposition to vote. But negative ads can work powerfully on citizens who have little information to begin with and on those with little or no party allegiance.[31]

These provocative findings have been challenged by other researchers. "We should not necessarily see negative ads as a harmful part of our electoral system," contends Kenneth Goldstein, head of the University of Wisconsin's political advertising project. "They are much more likely [than positive ads] to be about policy, to use supporting information, and to be reliable. Few negative ads are on personal issues." [32] One study of 189 different Senate campaigns found that "negative campaigning . . . generally *mobilizes*, rather than *de*mobilizes, the electorate." [33] But people react differently: Political independents, for example, were turned off by all forms of negative advertising.

Distortions and Dirty Tricks. Like other forms of product promotion, political ads often stretch or distort the truth to make their point. Sometimes the disinformation is so blatant that the term *dirty tricks* applies. This includes not only spreading falsehoods but also using doctored photographs or faking news reports or news headlines. An especially sinister tactic is blaming an opponent for bad events over which the person had no control. For example, several candidates were slammed in 2004 by ads that morphed their portraits into Osama bin Laden or Saddam Hussein.

Candidates who are victims of smear tactics have some weapons of defense. The campaign can respond promptly, at least accusing the offender of mudslinging. Formal complaints can sometimes persuade local broadcasters to kill the offending ads. Media outlets find themselves in the unwanted role of arbitrating between contending candidates. (The legal situation is murky. Courts have held that candidates have a right to buy ads even if their content is challenged, but broadcasters are not legally required to air ads from party organizations or advocacy groups.)[34]

The Bipartisan Campaign Finance Act (BCRA) of 2002 requires that candidates personally appear and vouch for their advertisements. Some have proposed tighter controls on campaign advertising—for example, requiring candidates to appear in all ads that talk about their opponents.

Formal or legal remedies against misrepresentations raise thorny constitutional questions, not to mention the specter of excessive regulation and litigation. Instead, citizens are probably better off trusting that "the give-and-take of campaign thrust-and-parry and the activity of a free and skeptical press create a balance" between contenders.[35]

Mass Media Shortcomings. Media campaigns increasingly display what political scientist Darrell West describes as a law of diminishing returns. "It becomes difficult to break through the clutter," he observes, "and at this point there is a lot of clutter out there."[36] Burgeoning media outlets—cable TV channels, specialized publications, and Web-based sources—are crowded with ads, most of them nonpolitical. Some 1.5 million thirty-second spots were aired in the 2002 campaign season. That year, the two candidates in lightly populated South Dakota's competitive Senate race ran some twenty-one thousand commercials. "When the people are sick to death of ads," Rep. Don Sherwood, R-Pa., said of that contest, "it doesn't do much good to do more."[37]

"We are moving into a new world," said former House Democratic leader Richard A. Gephardt of Missouri (1977–2005), "and I think the traditional model we have gone on for 30 years, jamming millions of dollars into a television set and driving enough folks to the polls on Election Day, is a passing method."[38] In short, politicians have rediscovered the virtues of retail as opposed to wholesale campaigning: personal appeals to voters.

The Ground War: Pressing the Flesh and Other Forms of Close Contact

Direct appeals to voters through personal appearances by candidates or their surrogates—at shopping centers, factory gates, or even door to door—are part of every campaign. In his first Senate campaign in 1948, Lyndon B. Johnson swooped out of the sky in a helicopter to visit small Texas towns, grandly pitching his Stetson from the chopper for a bold entrance. (An aide was assigned to retrieve the hat for use at the next stop.)[39] Other candidates, preferring to stay closer to the ground, stage walking tours or other events to attract attention. Few elected officials get by without doing a great deal of what is inelegantly called pressing the flesh.

Personal appeals remain the best way to gather votes. Although not as cost-effective as media campaigns in reaching masses of people, personalized techniques can target those most apt to go to the polling booth: loyalists within the parties' core constituency groups. As political reporter David S. Broder put it: "More and more political strategists are coming to believe that the high-tech tools that have dominated campaigns for the past four decades—TV spots, mass mailings and professionally staffed phone banks—are far less effective [in motivating voters] than the old-fashioned way of turning out the vote."[40]

An obvious advantage of so-called shoe-leather campaigning is cost, at least when compared with mass media appeals. "Door-to-door canvassing is the tactic of choice among candidates and campaigns that are short on cash," explain Yale political scientists Donald P. Green and Alan S. Gerber. "Precinct walking is often described as the weapon of underdogs."[41] Former representative Dan Glickman, D-Kan. (1977–1995), then a thirty-one-year-old and now the motion picture industry's chief lobbyist, describes his first House campaign:

> I walked door-to-door to 35,000 homes over an eight-month period. I walked from 10:30 a.m. to 2 p.m. and again from 5:30 to 8 p.m. I lost 35 pounds and learned to be very realistic about dogs. I met a woman my father had lent $100 or $150 to 30 years before. She embraced me and said, "You saved us." I won by three percentage points.[42]

Face-to-face campaigning is obligatory in smaller communities, where people expect politicians to show up at festivals, parades, or annual county fairs. "If you ain't seen at the county fair, you're preached about on Sunday," remarked a politician as he led his party's Senate candidate around the hog and sheep barns in Ada, Oklahoma.[43] In small states, first-name relationships are often valued. Of Vermont's voters, political scientist Garrison Nelson remarks, "They want to know you." The state's Independent representative Bernard Sanders's bumper stickers simply say, "Bernie."[44] In Bristol, on Rhode Island's coast, the Fourth of July parade—the oldest in the country—is "the first and perhaps biggest event of the campaign season."[45] Candidates are expected. By town decree, only public officials may march in the parade; all others must work the crowd from the sidelines.

One-on-one campaigning is physically and emotionally challenging, and the payoff is often elusive. "The hardest doorbell for a candidate to ring is the first one," campaign specialist Ron Faucheux recalls of his canvassing days. "Canvassing takes an enormous amount of time and a serious commitment."[46] At best, he cautions, canvassers reach only about 30 percent of an area's voters. Only about 60 percent of the people will be home, and the person who comes to the door may represent only half the household's eligible voters. To reach more voters per visit, candidates seek out shopping malls, organized groups, fairs, or rallies. Leafleting or targeted mailings reach even more voters.

Personal encounters by candidates or their surrogates are essential for GOTV: making sure constituents are registered and getting voters to the polls. All these tasks (employing phone banks or canvassing) can be hired for a price, but they are most effective when carried out by someone who can connect with the potential voter. According to Green and Gerber, face-to-face canvassing raises turnout by 7 to 12 percentage points and in the end is more cost-effective than alternative media-based campaigns.[47]

Some campaigns make a point of mobilizing cadres of volunteers. Rep. Tammy Baldwin's winning run in 1998 for an open seat in Wisconsin's Second District (Madison) was boosted by some three thousand volunteers, seventeen hundred of them University of Wisconsin (UW) students. Most of these helpers did a literature drop or two, or they worked the phones for an evening. Some—thirty-five during the general election race—worked full time. Much of the volunteer effort targeted Madison's forty thousand UW students, notoriously indifferent voters who make up 10 percent of the district's potential electorate. The volunteer effort paid off. Baldwin topped 70 percent of the vote in the six wards with the highest concentration of UW students.[48]

Other groups can similarly be goaded to the polls by personal appeals. Disenchanted with the payoffs from heavy media spending, labor unions and the Democratic National Committee (DNC) boosted their party turnout by some 4 percent in 1998 and 2000, thanks to vote-pulling operations in the campaigns' final days. In 2002 the Democratic National Committee together with labor unions spent nearly $35 million on such activities. "In most states union members will be contacted between fourteen and twenty-four times by other union members in some fashion," AFL-CIO's political director reported.[49]

Republicans struck back that year with a "72-hour Plan" (masterminded by White House strategist Karl Rove and Georgia party chair Ralph Reed). After testing it in off-year elections, they rolled it out in thirty-one states in 2002. The party recruited more volunteers, made more phone calls, rang more doorbells, and pulled out more votes from Republican households than ever before. In Georgia, for example, volunteers at telephone banks—"neighbors calling neighbors"—spoke in the final weeks with thousands of people who had voted in GOP primaries. "And those were live phone calls, not recorded messages," explained victorious Senate candidate Saxby Chambliss's campaign manager. "In the last election cycle [the money] would've been spent on TV. This cycle, it went into manpower."[50] This revamped ground game was credited with the party's Georgia successes that year.

In 2004 both parties, cooperating with their allied groups, made unprecedented GOTV efforts. Taking its cue from the 72-hour Plan, the National Republican Campaign Committee (NRCC) expanded its grassroots project, STOMP (Strategic Taskforce for Organizing and Mobilizing People). It was set up as a pyramid: House members assured of reelection would each recruit others, who in turn would identify grassroots leaders, and so on. The party's GOTV targeted friendly precincts, where hordes of voters were mobilized not only by party workers but also by churches, local business alliances, and advocacy groups, among others. Party officials claimed after the balloting to have amassed "a corps of roughly 1.4 million party stalwarts who have proved they can offset the traditional Democratic advantages at the grassroots level."[51]

Heartened by their past successes, Democrats also mounted massive GOTV efforts, registering many thousands of new voters, mainly young people. The party was aided by such traditional allies as labor unions and the Sierra Club as well as by a clutch of new, independent organizations—for example, Americans Coming Together (ACT), the New Voters Project, and something called Voter Virgin. However, observers faulted the Democrats' efforts as lacking the local touch that pervaded the Republicans' efforts (and earlier labor-to-neighbor programs). Before he became chair of the Democratic National Committee, former Vermont governor and presidential contender Howard Dean remarked on *Meet the Press* about the November 2004 election:

> [The Democrats] ran the best grassroots campaign that I've seen in my lifetime. They [the Republicans] ran a better one. Why? Because we sent 14,000 people into Ohio from elsewhere. They had 14,000 people from Ohio talking to their neighbors, and that's how you win in rural states and rural America. If we don't learn to do these things, we aren't going to win. We have to learn to do those things.[52]

Both parties are sure to expand their ground-war troops in future elections. Their computers are crammed with exhaustive precinct-by-precinct, even block-by-block, data defining targeted residents. Also in their computers are the names of millions of volunteers who will be called upon to wage campaigns in 2006 and beyond.

THE PARALLEL CAMPAIGNS

The scene is set in a boardroom. Staff aide says to business executive: "Tom has too many people in his department." Executive says to aide: "We have one too many Democrats around here, and that's not a good thing." Then he bellows, "You're fired!"—mimicking Donald Trump's reality show, *The Apprentice.* The target of the ad was Senator Daschle. Radio ads echoed the same theme. The sponsor of the $150,000 ad campaign in 2004 was an out-of-state businessman and his wife operating in South Dakota as the "You're Fired Committee."[53]

The big story about recent congressional campaigns is the soaring activity of groups not formally affiliated with the candidates or the parties. Campaigns no longer resemble boxing matches between two combatants. They are more like mud-wrestling contests in which anyone can take part.

Groups interested in congressional election outcomes have every reason to mount their own campaigns. Individual donations to candidates by themselves have limited impact: Legal limits on contributions mean that they are tiny drops in the bucket. And since passage of BCRA in 2002, individuals and groups are barred from donating soft money to the parties for organizational and GOTV purposes.

Private groups themselves, however, can indulge in unlimited independent spending for or against candidates, as long as it is reported to the Federal

Election Commission and not coordinated with the candidates' own fund raising. Better yet is issue advocacy—messages aimed at influencing voters' choices without explicitly advocating the election or defeat of specific candidates. Such efforts are clearly designed to sway federal elections; most are indistinguishable from candidate advertising. Courts have on First Amendment grounds rebuffed the FEC's attempts to limit such ads, but in upholding BCRA's Title II, the U.S. Supreme Court endorsed certain restrictions upon "electioneering communications"—television advertising that refers to specific candidates for federal office sixty days before a general election (and thirty days before a primary).[54]

There are several categories of groups, some known by sections of the Internal Revenue Code. PACs raise and spend limited hard-money contributions to elect or defeat candidates. Tax-exempt groups under Section 527 of the tax code raise money for political activities, including issue advocacy and GOTV efforts. Nonprofit, tax-exempt groups under several parts of Section 501(c) can engage in certain activities, mainly not directed at specific candidates.

Right-wing groups such as the Christian Coalition, the National Rifle Association, and the small business lobby helped propel the Republicans' takeover of Congress in the 1994 elections and sustain it since then. Democrats and their allies mobilized to retake Congress—a goal that eluded them (and may be unattainable in the near term, barring unforeseen events).

Republicans can count on support from business and industry, whose PACs and other groups have the deepest pockets. One power center is the Business Industry Political Action Committee (BIPAC), a group that advises and coordinates election activities of businesses and industry associations. Another group, spearheaded by the U.S. Chamber of Commerce, embraces a wide spectrum of business groups such as the National Federation of Independent Business (NFIB), which has 600,000 members from small companies. Besides mobilizing these members, the NFIB in 2002 rolled out a GOTV drive aimed at some twenty House races and eight Senate-race states.[55]

Another GOP power cluster is made up of right-wing ideological groups—those opposed to taxes, gun control, abortion, and gay rights, and those favoring term limits, prayer in schools, and homeschooling. These include such familiar names as the Partnership for American Families, the National Rifle Association, and the Club for Growth, along with conservative religious organizations.

On the left side of the spectrum, the AFL-CIO, the umbrella organization for seventy-seven labor unions, began with media campaigning but increasingly pours its money and personnel into GOTV efforts. "Magically, we have learned that when we talk to union members on the phone or face to face in the workplace and get them information, they vote—and they vote for the candidates and positions we have endorsed," explained the AFL-CIO's political chief.[56]

Liberal ideological groups compose the Progressive Network, described as "a progressive political coffee klatch where . . . information, gossip, hearsay and innuendo" are exchanged.[57] It is an alliance of environmental, feminist, gay, and lesbian organizations. Key players include the Sierra Club, the League of Conservation Voters, the Natural Resources Defense Council, the National Abortion and Reproductive Rights Action League, and the Human Rights Campaign.

Interest group involvement in elections resembles an arms race. Hundreds of organizations engage in congressional campaigning, most of them in league with one or the other major political party. Such groups poured more than $400 million into the 2004 federal elections, over and above what candidates and parties spent.

WHO VOTES?

Although Congress is supposed to be the people's branch of government, less than half of voting-age citizens take part in House elections in presidential years, less than 40 percent vote in off-years. In 2004, a presidential year, 120 million citizens cast ballots—a record number, but only 55 percent of the voting-age population, or VAP (all residents age eighteen and over, estimated in 2004 at 221.3 million).[58] As Figure 4-2 indicates, voting participation in national elections has declined since 1960.

Reasons for Not Voting. Political analysts disagree over the reasons for the anemic voting levels in the United States, near the bottom among established democratic countries. Several explanations—not all of them compatible—have been suggested.[59]

One explanation for nonvoting is demographic. Certain sizable (and growing) segments of the population—such as jailed felons (thirteen million), barred from voting in all but two states, and undocumented aliens (twelve million or more)—are formally excluded. And today's populace embraces expanding categories of people with traditionally low voting rates, for example, young voters, African Americans, and Latinos.

Young people (ages eighteen through twenty-nine) are traditional no-shows, perhaps because they claim fewer of those life events (mortgages, taxes, school-age children, community ties) that propel older people toward activism. But in 2004 some 21 million young people, 52 percent of the age group, showed up at the polls. Maybe this happened because of targeted GOTV drives by both parties and many other groups, such as Rock the Vote, MTV's "Choose or Lose," and hip-hop entrepreneur Sean P. "Diddy" Combs's Citizen Change (which sold "Vote or Die" T-shirts).

Paradoxically, other demographic trends ought to raise turnout. For example, the single factor most closely linked with political engagement of virtually all kinds—education level—has been on the rise among the population.[60]

FIGURE 4-2 **Turnout in Presidential and House Elections, 1944–2004**

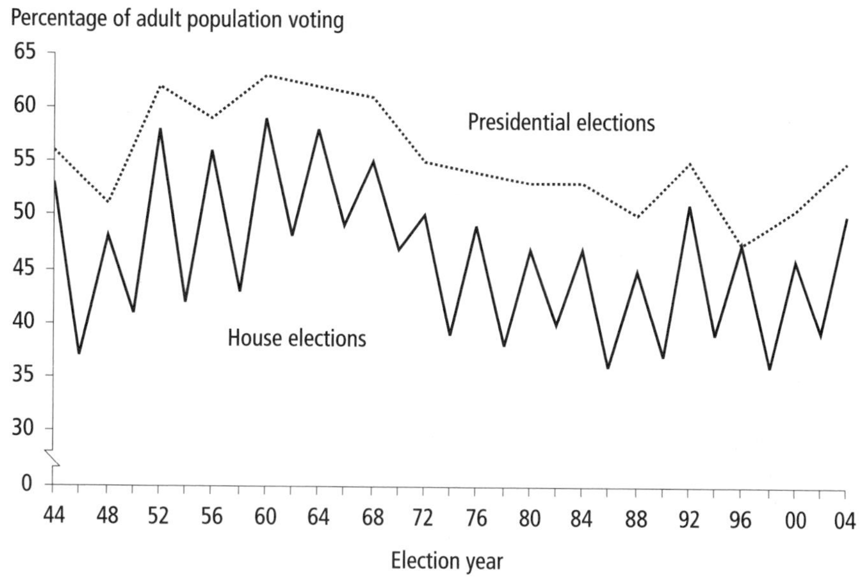

Sources: U.S. Bureau of the Census, Statistical Abstract of the United States: 2001 (Washington D.C.: U.S. Government Printing Office, 2001), Tables 401–404; Norman J. Ornstein, Thomas E. Mann, and Michael J. Malbin, *Vital Statistics on Congress, 2001–2002* (Washington D.C.: American Enterprise Institute, 2002), Table 2-1; and Martin P. Wattenberg, "Turnout in the 2004 Presidential Election," *Presidential Studies Quarterly* 35 (March 2005): 138–146.

A second explanation stresses legal barriers to voting. Only about 70 percent of the VAP are registered to vote. Many democracies automatically register all adults; some even require that people vote. In contrast, U.S. citizens must take the initiative to register and vote. The National Voter Registration Act of 1993 (the so-called motor voter law) links voter registration to motor vehicle licensing. Registration of eligible voters soon rose about 3.8 percent nationwide, but that did not substantially raise voting levels, especially among the young and the poor, who were the targets of the measure.[61] "Motor Voter is a howling success as a registration tool," remarked Kentucky's chief election officer, "but turnout is still a dog."[62]

Other disincentives can be blamed on the electoral arrangements. Citizens are asked to vote far more often than people in parliamentary regimes; and election days are not holidays. State laws govern most aspects of voting, which localities carry out with dizzying diversity. Careless or biased election administration can turn away voters or miscount their ballots—as uncovered in voting scandals in Florida (2000), Ohio (2004), and many other locales. Yet many states and localities have modernized their election processes, lowering barriers to registering and voting. Absentee balloting is common. Some states permit ballots to be submitted over a period of time. Oregon citizens may vote by telephone. And, prompted by the 2000 fiasco, the Bipartisan Campaign Reform Act of 2002 (P.L. 107-252) raised federal election standards and promised money to help states meet those standards.

A third explanation is citizen disaffection. Poor candidates and contentious or negative campaigning supposedly keep people away from the polling booths. Apathy and cynicism are, to be sure, part of the picture. Surveys sponsored by Harvard University's *Vanishing Voters* project found that four out of ten nonvoters in 2000 claimed to care little about politics and public affairs. A quarter were dismayed or confused by the barrage of campaign messages. And another quarter were simply angry or cynical about politics.[63]

Fourth, citizens may rationally abstain from voting in favor of other forms of participation, including membership in political groups and activism on issues. Even in competitive presidential years, few congressional races are truly competitive. With so many electoral outcomes a foregone conclusion, citizens may prefer to participate elsewhere. Or they may simply want to spend their time doing something else. One study of a recent presidential election found that one in five people who registered but did not vote said they were too busy or could not take time off from work.[64]

Finally, even conceding all these disincentives, the level of nonvoting may be seriously exaggerated. For one thing, VAP measuring has become so unreliable that, according to Samuel L. Popkin and Michael P. McDonald, "it significantly overstates the size of the eligible electorate, and therefore artificially depresses the turnout rate." Recalculating the VAP for every national election since World War II, the two political scientists estimated turnout ranging from 52.7 to 60.6 percent—still nothing to be proud of, but "a lot less dismal than is generally believed."[65]

Biases of Voting. Although voting is the simplest, most accessible form of political involvement, it is still biased in favor of people at the higher rungs of the social and generational ladders—those who are more mature, more affluent, better educated, and more in touch with political events. Eight of ten people whose annual incomes exceed $50,000 vote in a typical election. This is twice the voting rate of the poor, defined as people with incomes of less than $15,000. Moreover, this gap has been widening over the past decade or so. In one recent election year poor people—who are nearly 20 percent of the voting-age population—accounted for only 7.7 percent of voters.[66]

Alternative forms of political participation are even more sharply biased. For example, giving money is mainly an elite activity. In the sample Sidney Verba and his colleagues examined, 35 percent of all political money flowed from the 4 percent of people making more than $125,000 a year. Poor people, who were 19 percent of the sample, made only 2 percent of political donations.[67]

Turnout varies according to whether the election is held in a presidential or a midterm year (even in presidential years votes for lesser offices typically lag about 5 percent below presidential votes). Midterm races often lack the intense publicity and stimulus to vote provided by presidential contests. Since the 1930s, turnout in midterm congressional elections has averaged about 12 percent below that of the preceding presidential election. Midterm electorates include proportionately more people who are interested in politics and, incidentally, who are more affluent and better educated.[68] Turnout also varies by region. Less than 20 percent of the voters turn out in certain one-party areas; in competitive states turnout far above 50 percent is common.

HOW VOTERS DECIDE

What induces voters to cast their ballots for one candidate and not another? As a general rule, voters reach their decisions on the basis of three considerations: mainly party loyalties, but also candidate assessments, as well as salient issues—overall judgments about the state of the nation and what are perceived as its most pressing issues. The relative strength of these forces varies over time and among specific races.

Although American voters are often uninformed—or even indifferent—about political issues and candidates, they employ what is called low-information rationality, or gut reasoning, to make voting-booth decisions. As Popkin explains, people "triangulate and validate their opinions in conversations with people they trust and according to the opinions of national figures whose judgments and positions they have come to know."[69] Thus voters work through imperfect information to make sensible choices, resembling the choices they would have made with perfect information.

Party Loyalties

Party identification is the single most powerful factor in determining voters' choices. It remains the strongest single correlate of voting in congressional elections. In 2004, at least nine of every ten Democrats and Republicans voted for their parties' nominees. Independents split their votes more evenly.[70]

The 2004 campaign season found registered voters divided roughly in thirds among Republicans (29 percent), Democrats (33 percent), and independents (38 percent).[71] These preferences, measured by indexes of party identification, have remained relatively stable over the past several elections, despite short-term fluctuations.

According to surveys, most people who claim to be independents are in fact closet partisans who lean toward one party or the other. These independent leaners—about a quarter of the total electorate—hold attitudes similar to those of partisans. Not only do they favor one party over the other, but they also share many (though not necessarily all) of the party's values and say they will vote for the party's candidates—if they bestir themselves to vote.

Only a small percentage of citizens (5 to 10 percent) are true independents, that is, they are unpredictable and have dismal turnout rates. "I would encourage candidates not to play to them," advises David Magleby of Brigham Young University, "because they tend to jump on bandwagons, to follow tides. You're better off [working] on getting your weak partisans and your leaners."[72]

Party Decline and Surge. Partisan loyalty declined among the American electorate from the 1950s through the 1980s. In that era, when the party lines were in flux, voting cues may simply have conveyed less meaning. As Jacobson put it, "The party label became less informative and thus less useful to voters as a shorthand cue for predicting what elected officials would do once in office. Information about individual candidates became more important."[73]

Weakened party ties led to an epidemic of split-ticket voting—in which voters supported presidential candidates of one party and congressional candidates of another. A certain level of ticket splitting—by perhaps one in ten voters—can be expected in every election. But the number of voters in surveys between 1952 and 1988 who reported that they split their ticket between presidential and House candidates increased from 12 percent to 25 percent. Those who split their ballots between different parties' House and Senate candidates grew from 9 percent to 27 percent.[74]

Most ticket splitters were in the throes of moving from one party to another. Some were so-called Reagan Democrats—favoring the GOP's national tickets while backing Democrats in other races. Many of these were white southern conservatives embarking on a slow but steady trek from their Democratic roots toward their new home with the Republicans. Targeted by the GOP's southern strategy, these voters were attracted to such candidates as Dwight D. Eisenhower, Barry Goldwater, and Ronald Reagan. They kept backing Democrats in congressional and state races because the party put up conservative candidates and because it controlled legislative chambers and could deliver the most benefits to constituents. The same phenomenon occurred to a lesser degree in the Northeast, where voters were drawn to the Democrats' national policies and candidates, which were compatible with moderate to liberal Republican representatives or senators.[75] In short, the bulge in split-ticket voting was a by-product of gradual partisan realignment.

Over the past four presidential elections, therefore, ticket splitting plummeted to less than 10 percent—exactly the level of fifty years ago. By the same token, the number of congressional districts voting for one party's presidential candidate and the other party's House candidate—which had spiked dramatically—fell back in recent elections. In 2004 only fifty-nine House members (forty-one Democrats and eighteen Republicans) won in districts carried by the opposite party's presidential candidate—the lowest number of split districts since the 1950s.[76]

Recent party realignment has brought party affiliation into sync with policy and ideological preferences. Although the process extended over many years, the long Republican courtship of southern conservatives was consummated in 1994. Merle Black of Emory University estimates that more than 80 percent of white conservatives in the South are Republicans; only 10 percent are Democrats.[77] A parallel trend, though less dramatic, has been the Democratic Party's absorption of GOP moderates and liberals. Finding acceptable candidates up and down the ballot, these voters have less need to pick and choose—hence, revived partisanship and dwindling split tickets.

Politicians have long talked about coattails: how House and Senate candidates could be pulled into office by the strength of a popular presidential candidate of the same party. Ronald Reagan, for example, boosted his party's congressional votes by 2 to 3 percent in 1980 and 4 to 5 percent in 1984.[78] In 1992 and 2000, defections were evenly balanced, although President Bill Clinton's reelection in 1996 added about 2.6 percentage points to House and Senate totals. In 2004 George W. Bush's popularity undoubtedly aided several Senate and House winners in contested southern and midwestern races.

Midterm Elections. Historically, partisan forces have operated differently in presidential years and midterm years. Until about 1960, presidential-year races displayed a high correlation between votes cast for president and votes cast for House members on a district-by-district basis. Although the correlation declined as more voters split their tickets in the 1950s–1980s period, it has been robust in recent elections.

What happens when presidential candidates are not on the ballot? The midterm electorate is both smaller than and different from the presidential-year electorate. Normally, midterm elections result in losses for the party that captured the White House two years earlier (see Table 4-2). In midterm elections during recent decades the presidential party lost an average of twenty-eight House seats and almost four Senate seats. In 1994 the Democrats lost a net of fifty-two seats in the House and eight in the Senate, a result that was certainly related to President Clinton's unpopularity at the time.

The surge and decline theory held that the shrunken electorate of midterm years explained the normal falloff in the presidential party's votes. That is, a presidential surge, swollen by less motivated voters attracted by presidential campaigns, is followed two years later by a decline as those voters drop out of the electorate. But other studies suggested that midterm voters are no more or less partisan than those in presidential years and share most of their demographic characteristics.[79]

Another theory argues that midterm elections serve in part as a referendum on the president's popularity and performance in office during the previous two years.[80] Voters may hold the president's party responsible for the nation's economic health or its political or moral climate. This provides plausible explanations for such outcomes as the Democrats' 1974 post–Watergate bonus of fifty-two representatives and four senators, their 1982 recession harvest of twenty-six House seats, and the Republicans' 1994 bonanza. Yet in other years the referendum aspect of midterm elections is harder to discern.

TABLE 4-2 **Midterm Fortunes of Presidential Parties, 1934–2002**

		Seats gained or lost	
Year	President	House	Senate
1934	Franklin D. Roosevelt (D)	+9	+10
1938	Roosevelt (D)	–71	–6
1942	Roosevelt (D)	–55	–9
1946	Roosevelt and Harry S. Truman (D)	–45	–12
1950	Truman (D)	–29	–6
1954	Dwight D. Eisenhower (R)	–18	–1
1958	Eisenhower (R)	–48	–13
1962	John F. Kennedy (D)	–4	+3
1966	Lyndon B. Johnson (D)	–47	–4
1970	Richard M. Nixon (R)	–12	+2
1974	Nixon and Gerald R. Ford (R)	–48	–5
1978	Jimmy Carter (D)	–15	–3
1982	Ronald Reagan (R)	–26	+1
1986	Reagan (R)	–5	–8
1990	George H. W. Bush (R)	–8	–1
1994	Bill Clinton (D)	–52	–8
1998	Clinton (D)	+5	0
2002	George W. Bush (R)	+7	+2
Average seats lost (18 elections)		–25.7	–3.2

Source: Compiled by the authors.

The 1998 and 2002 results were surprises, however. President Clinton's Democrats gained five seats in the House and held their own in the Senate in 1998, in the midst of an impeachment scandal. Four years later President Bush's GOP gained seven House and two Senate seats, despite a lagging economy. (The only other anomaly occurred in 1934, when President Franklin D. Roosevelt's popularity strengthened the Democrats' hold in both chambers.)

What explains the president's party's gain in the last two midterm elections, defying historical precedents? In the 1998 case, off-year contests confronted a mostly satisfied public that expressed confidence in the high-flying U.S. economy and, by a margin of two to one, opposed impeaching the president. To energize its loyalists, the House Republican campaign committee aired hard-edged last-minute ads in key districts that only confirmed the public's view of the GOP as "the impeachment party." "The Republicans' drive to turn the election into a referendum on President Clinton," analysts concluded, "ran head-on into an electorate less interested in the Monica S. Lewinsky scandal than in maintaining the status quo of a healthy economy." [81]

The 2002 midterm elections were equally intriguing. Most pundits predicted Democratic gains, based not only on the historical record (forgetting 1998, however) but also on surveys showing that the faltering economy was the No. 1 issue on the voters' minds. These factors were balanced, however, by positive feelings toward President Bush—his leadership after the September 11 terrorist attacks and his talk of waging war against Iraq. Thus, he was not blamed for the economic woes. The scales were also tipped in the Republicans' favor by superior efforts in recruiting candidates, supporting them, and mustering core voters in swing areas. In races where Bush appeared in the final two weeks of the campaign, Republicans elected thirteen of eighteen senators and sixty of sixty-nine representatives.[82] Having framed the elections in terms of a likely Bush loss, media commentators then rushed to call the outcome a major victory.

"In any election," notes Curtis Gans, "the outcome is not determined by turnout, but by *who* turns out." [83] Recent off-year elections have been no exception. Having learned that lesson all too well, Democratic and Republican strategists and their interest group allies were targeting their core voters in elections of the 2000s.

The Appeal of Candidates

"My theory on politics is ultimately that people vote for the person they like most," declared the revered former senator David Pryor, D-Ark. (1979–1997).[84] Apart from partisan loyalties, the appeal of given candidates is the strongest force in congressional voting. Not surprisingly, candidate appeal normally tilts toward incumbents. When voters abandon their party to vote for House or Senate candidates, they usually vote for incumbents.

Incumbency, Again. Over the past generation the incumbency factor has strengthened to the point that it rivals and sometimes eclipses partisanship. Scholars estimate the incumbency advantage in House and Senate races rose from about 2 percent of the vote totals during the 1954–1960 period to as much as 7 percent after 1960 (after controlling for national trends and district partisanship).[85] The proportion of marginal incumbents (those winning by less than 60 percent) fell by more than one-fourth. According to Jacobson, the proportion of marginal incumbents remained at this lower plateau (about 30 percent), dropping still further for a period in the late 1980s.[86] But wider reelection margins did not prevent incumbents from losing office at traditional rates—except for the late 1980s and late 1990s, bonanza periods for incumbents (see Table 3-1, p. 62). However its effects are measured, incumbency confers powerful advantages upon officeholders who work to build and maintain support and who shrewdly exploit the resources available to them.

Incumbents are better known than their opponents. Even if voters cannot recall officeholders' names in an interview, they can recognize and express opinions about them when the names are presented to them—as in the voting booth. In National Election Study (NES) surveys extending over more than twenty years, nearly all respondents were able to recognize and rate Senate and House incumbents running for reelection (means of 97 percent and 92 percent, respectively). Senate challengers were recognized and rated by 77 percent of the respondents, House challengers by only 53 percent. Open-seat candidates fell somewhere between incumbents and challengers in visibility. Thus most voters can recognize and express views about congressional candidates, except for House challengers. The unequal visibility of candidates is a key context for voting decisions.[87]

In evaluating candidates, voters normally favor incumbents over challengers. On the eve of the 2004 balloting, 69 percent of likely voters agreed that their member of Congress deserved reelection; only 19 percent said no.[88] Voters in the NES surveys tend to evaluate incumbents according to personal characteristics and such noncontroversial activities as casework and constituent outreach. Even on the issues, references to incumbents were overwhelmingly positive. More than two-thirds of those voters claimed to have agreed with their legislator's votes, although only one in ten could cite how the representative had voted on a piece of legislation during the preceding two years.

Incumbents' popularity depends in large part upon their success in shaping information that constituents receive about them and their performance—through advertising, credit claiming, and position taking.[89] Not surprisingly, high levels of contact are reported with House and Senate incumbents. The more contact voters have with their legislators, the more positive their evaluations are likely to be. According to NES surveys, at least nine out of ten voters said they had some form of contact with their representative. A fifth of them reported having met the lawmaker in person. Many constituents receive mail from their representatives or read about them in newspapers. Virtually all voters reported some contacts with their senators, but most were through mailings, TV appearances, or other media coverage.

The visibility gap between incumbents and challengers is wider in House races than in Senate races. Half of the voters, at best, report contact with House challengers, but as many as 85 percent of voters report contacts with Senate challengers (mostly through media coverage or candidate mailings). Senate voters are more likely to be reached by both incumbent and challenger. In open seats the gap is narrower. Senate candidates for seats with no incumbent are able to reach nearly all potential voters; House hopefuls reach at least three-quarters of them.

Senate and House. These findings help explain why senators are more vulnerable at the polls than are their House counterparts. First, surveys indicate that representatives are more warmly regarded than senators—probably because they are judged more on positive actions, such as personal contacts or constituent service, whereas senators are more closely linked to divisive national issues.

Second, Senate challengers are far more conspicuous than House challengers. Senate contests are more widely reported by the media, and challengers can gain almost as much exposure as incumbents. Media coverage of House races is more fragmentary than that of Senate races, throwing more weight to incumbents' techniques of contacting voters.

Third, senators cannot manipulate voter contacts as much as representatives do. Voters get their information about Senate races largely through organized media, which senators do not control. Representatives gain exposure through focused means—personal appearances, mailings, and newsletters—which they fashion to their own advantage. "Somewhat ironically," observed Michael J. Robinson, "powerful senators are less able to control their images than 'invisible' House members."[90] Finally, senatorial elections are simply more competitive than House elections. That is, one-party states are rarer, proportionately, than one-party congressional districts.

Among senators, constituency size is a crucial variable in elections. Small-state senators in many respects resemble representatives. Compared with their large-state colleagues, they are more visible, more accessible, and more able to raise the campaign money they need. But they are not electorally safer—probably because their challengers, too, have an easier time mounting their campaigns and gaining visibility.[91] (Recall former representative John Thune's two competitive races against Democratic incumbents in South Dakota.)

Incumbents' Risks. Although incumbency bestows numerous advantages (such as name recognition and media coverage), it also can be a curse for personal failings (inattentiveness, ineffectiveness, and even physical disabilities). But Jacobson surely captured the normal state of affairs when he observed that "most incumbents face obscure, politically inexperienced opponents whose resources fall far short of what is necessary to mount a formidable campaign."[92]

Still, challengers can and do win—with luck, timing, and attention to certain basic principles. Run for an open seat or against an incumbent whose support is slipping, or run in a year of voter restlessness. Be a credible, forceful candidate. Be prepared to spend money to erase the incumbent's visibility advantage. Exploit the incumbent's weaknesses—or at least blame the incumbent for the "mess in Washington." In some years (1992 and 1994, for example) this strategy works for many challengers. But even in years of political quiescence, as in more recent elections, a handful of challengers win by following these rules. That handful is usually enough to keep other incumbents on their guard.[93]

Issue Voting

Issue preferences and even ideological beliefs figure prominently in congressional campaigns. A significant number of voters are attuned to issues and base their choices on a specific issue or cluster of issues. Issues matter especially to committed core voters as well as to undecided voters. Not a few elections turn on those margins. Party realignment over the last generation has brought on a convergence of issue or ideological preferences and party identification.

Congressional Party Platforms. One by-product has been efforts by parties (and other groups) to forge nationwide platforms and to market them as templates for congressional campaigns. The most notable example was the Contract with America, signed by more than three hundred Republican candidates on the steps of the Capitol's West Front in September 1994.[94] It was a set of ten proposals that included a balanced-budget amendment, a presidential line-item veto, internal House reforms, term limits for lawmakers, and policy proposals on crime, welfare, business regulation, and tax cuts. If a GOP majority were elected, the candidates pledged that they would put the measures to a House floor vote within the first hundred days of the new Congress.

Flush with victory that November, Republican leaders quickly claimed a popular mandate to enact the Contract with America. However, what we know about issues in elections—and about the contract in particular—leads us to skepticism about its impact upon voting choice. Candidates' embrace of the contract in their campaigns varied widely. Some used it to underscore themes they had already been employing. Others rarely mentioned it. "I didn't use the contract that much," reported a typical GOP candidate. "I made very limited reference to it and the voters didn't know much about it. . . . I did talk about things that were in the Contract, but that's not the same as using the Contract per se." Most voters, moreover, denied having heard about the contract. At best, no more than three in ten voters were acquainted with it. "Almost all the GOP candidates admitted that few voters, aside from a few 'C-SPAN groupies,' could recognize what the contract was by election day."[95]

Such manifestos are regularly showcased by congressional parties. House Democrats issued a 2004 pamphlet, "New Partnership for America's Future," which laid out six "core values" (prosperity, national security, fairness, opportunity, community, and accountability). Republicans ridiculed what they saw as platitudes: "I could agree on their package," remarked GOP chief whip Tom DeLay, R-Texas, who promised instead "an agenda of deeds, not words."[96]

Issues and Partisanship. Voters' responses to political issues show up in the different patterns of choice displayed by demographic groups. Many Americans sort themselves out politically according to their sex, their income or social class, their race or ethnicity, their age, their region, even their habits of religious devotion. True, these differences are typically reflected in people's long-term party loyalties, but issues can exert an independent force. Consider abortion. Although this issue cuts across party lines, the Democratic Party's generally pro-choice stance has cost it support from its traditional cadres of voters—for example, southern white evangelicals, traditional Catholics, and devout blacks and Latinos. The Republican Party's record (strongly anti-abortion) has conversely hurt its standing among middle- and upper-class women who might otherwise prefer the party's candidates. Abortion is an example of wedge issues—concerns that can overpower long-standing party loyalties, perhaps even displacing those party loyalties over time.

A demographic snapshot of the two parties' voters would start at the much-discussed gender gap, which is the difference between the way men and women vote. This gap was a mere 4 percent in 2004, although it has amounted to as much as 10 percent in recent elections—women leaning toward Democratic candidates, men toward Republicans.[97] Gender gaps appear in virtually all recent contests. As pollster Celinda Lake remarked, "You'll get [a gender gap] in a race for dogcatcher in Montana, if it's a Republican against a Democrat."[98] The presence of a female candidate affects but does not remove the phenomenon. The explanation for the gender gap probably lies in men's and women's differing responses to political and social issues. Men are more attracted to issues such as military preparedness, tough anticrime laws, and restrictions on welfare recipients and immigrants. Women seem to respond more positively than men to social equality issues such as government-sponsored health benefits, job training, child care, and welfare aid.[99]

A host of similar patterns is found among congressional voters. "There's a family gap, a generation gap, a gender gap," said GOP pollster Neil Newhouse of the fissures among the voting population. "They're all alive and well."[100] Many of the patterns are familiar. Republicans attract upper-income, conservative, well-educated voters who are not racial or ethnic minorities; Democrats draw in voters with opposite characteristics. Republicans draw upon married people, Protestants, and churchgoers; Democrats attract singles, mainstream Catholics, Jews, and occasional churchgoers. Such loyalties are built on issues and themes adopted by parties and candidates over the years.

Issues and Campaigns. Regardless of what nationwide surveys may show, therefore, legislators and their advisers are highly sensitive to voters' expected reactions to stands on issues. Much energy is devoted to framing positions, communicating them (sometimes in deliberately obscure words), and assessing their effect. Moreover, every professional politician can relate instances in which issues tipped an election one way or another. Frequently cited is the electoral influence of single-interest groups. Some citizens vote according to a single issue they regard as paramount, such as gun control, abortion, or gay marriage. Even if small in numbers, such voters can decide close contests. That is why legislators often shrink from taking positions on issues that evoke extreme responses, issues that prompt certain voters to oppose them regardless of their overall record.

Public policy issues also have powerful indirect effects upon election outcomes. For one thing, issues motivate those voters who are opinion leaders, who can lend or withhold support far beyond their single vote. Issues are carefully monitored by organized interests and their PACs, which are in a position to channel funds, publicity, and volunteer workers to the candidate's cause. Legislators devote time and attention to promoting and explaining issues to attentive publics because it pays them to do so.

ELECTION OUTCOMES

The process by which representatives and senators reach Capitol Hill is an essential aspect of the two Congresses notion. House and Senate contests are waged one by one on local turf. At the same time, local contests are waged against a backdrop of national events, issues, and partisan alignments.

Top-down trends in 2004 included economic concerns, certain social issues, uneasiness over terrorist threats, and seemingly positive assessments of President Bush, especially his post–September 11 leadership. The increasing involvement of national party entities and their allied interest groups has imposed a large measure of national coordination upon congressional campaigns, especially those in marginal states and districts. The result is that a mix of local and national forces converge on congressional elections to shape their content and their results.

Party Balance

Of the thirty-nine parties that appeared on ballots somewhere in the United States in 2004, only two parties are in a position to govern. Despite the oft-claimed independence of candidates and voters, virtually all races are run with these party labels, fought on playing fields sloped toward one party or the other, and aimed mainly at citizens who are likely to turn out for the parties' candidates.

Shifting Majorities. As in many congressional elections, the overall partisan outcomes of the 2004 contests were largely fixed months and even years before the actual balloting. First, the parties' successes or failures over the recruitment season determined whether quality candidates (mostly incumbents) or long-shot contenders were on the ballots. Second, partisan gerrymandering shaped many House districts, most of them safe for one party or the other. Republicans benefited from both trends, according to election analysts. Less than 10 percent of all House districts and no more than a third of Senate seats were truly in play that year.

Election forecasters thus regard a Democratic recapture of Congress as unlikely, at least before the post–2010 census elections (barring some major economic or national security upheaval). Even then, the census will likely reflect further population shifts from traditionally Democratic areas to Republican ones.

The Democrats or the Republicans have controlled Congress since 1855. (Appendix A lists the partisan majorities in the House and Senate since 1901.) Between 1896 and 1920 the two parties had approximately equal numbers of partisans in the electorate, but lower participation rates in Democratic areas favored the Republicans. The GOP's relative position improved further after 1920, when women received the vote.

The New Deal realignment of the 1930s shifted the balance to the Democrats. After that the Democrats became virtually a perennial majority and the Republicans a permanent minority on Capitol Hill. In all that time the Republicans controlled both chambers simultaneously for only four years (1947–1949, 1953–1955) and the Senate alone for only six years (1981–1987). Democratic sweeps in 1958, 1964, and 1974 padded their majorities. Republicans eventually recovered from these setbacks, but Democratic dominance, especially in the House, was hard to overcome because incumbents learned how to exploit their reelection assets successfully.

In 1994, for the first time in forty years, Republicans won control of both houses of Congress. Not one Republican incumbent was defeated that year, while thirty-four Democratic representatives and two senators lost their seats. In succeeding elections Republicans clung to their narrow majority in the House, with Democrats gaining ten (1996), then five (1998) and two (2000). The Senate had a Republican majority until 2000, when Democrats pulled even by gaining five seats. In 2002 and 2004, however, the Republicans added to their majorities in both chambers.

Recent elections have confirmed long-term shifts in the two parties' power bases. Historically, the Grand Old Party was dominant in the populous states of the Northeast and Midwest. "The Democracy," by contrast, owned the solid South from the Civil War era through the 1970s, as well as the large urban political machines. The tectonic plates of political alliances move slowly, but they sometimes produce results of earthquake proportions.

Regional Patterns. The 1994 earthquake signaled the Republicans' conquest of the South. For the first time in history, the GOP claimed a majority of the South's seats in the two chambers as nineteen House seats and four Senate seats moved into the party's fold. The party's grip on the region tightened in the ensuing decade. It now claims nearly two-thirds of the House seats and all but four senators in the eleven southern states. The GOP is the party of choice for conservative white southerners and unquestionably their true philosophic home. Breaking the Democrats' historic stranglehold in the southern states, with their rapidly growing population, was the step that gave the Republicans majorities on Capitol Hill. The 2004 elections virtually completed this process, adding five GOP seats in each chamber.

Regionally, the South and the Great Plains and Rocky Mountain states (all but one of which went for Bush in 2004) form the backbone of the congressional GOP. In the plains and mountain states the party claims two-thirds of the representatives and nearly three-quarters of the senators. The Upper

Midwest, from Ohio to Wisconsin, is a competitive region, with three states leaning Democratic and two leaning Republican.

Democrats are strongest in the edges of the national map—the two coasts and parts of the Upper Midwest. The eleven states of the eastern Amtrak corridor, from Boston to the nation's capital, are increasingly Democratic (though some have lost population and thus House seats). In these states (all were in the party's presidential column in 2000 and 2004) the party has 65 percent of the House seats and a nine-seat Senate margin. Similarly, the left-hand coast—the four Pacific-rim states (excluding Alaska), again all won by Democratic presidential candidates in 2000 and 2004—has a Democratic margin of twenty-one House seats and seven of eight Senate seats.

Looking beyond such regional patterns, the two parties tend to represent different kinds of districts. Democratic strength lies in cities and inner suburbs (and majority-minority districts), even in the South and Midwest. Republicans dominate rural, small town, and outer suburban areas. One result is that Democratic districts are more packed than Republican areas, meaning that their candidates win by larger majorities than Republican winners normally do. Put another way, more Democratic votes are wasted (that is, inefficiently distributed), which gives the GOP another structural advantage.

Polarized Parties, Polarized Voters? Underlying this geographic distribution is what might be called a cultural divide between the two parties. Democrats tend to represent urban interests, economic intervention by the government, environmental protection, and acceptance of racial, ethnic, and sexual minorities. Republicans tend to be traditionalists—economic and cultural conservatives who promote businesses large and small, advocate certain religious causes, and generously support military and security agencies but favor limited federal activity in most other sectors. Such long-standing commitments give the lie to those who claim that there is scant difference between the two parties.

How pervasive are these partisan differences within the electorate? Political elites—candidates, officeholders, activists, and strong party identifiers—have long been found to inhabit the extremes of the ideological spectrum: Democrats to the left, Republicans to the right.[101] Such activists do not necessarily represent the majority of citizens, of average voters, or even of average party identifiers who tend to occupy the middle of the spectrum.[102] If recent surveys are to be believed, however, rank-and-file party identifiers have become more polarized than in past elections.[103] Many of them, after all, heed the partisan rhetoric dispensed by congressional leaders and other sources, including media, cable, and Internet outlets that are blatantly biased. Moreover, these loyal voters increasingly make up the U.S. electorate. Thus they are ardently wooed by parties and candidates—who seek reliable supporters (not waverers) to turn out at the polls.

Party Alignment and Realignment

Historically, political upheavals have shifted party control in the House or Senate with decisive results. Political scientists talk of "critical elections" or "critical periods," in which one party yields preeminence to another, or major voting groups alter the shape of the parties' coalitions, or both. Such watershed eras include the Civil War, the turbulent 1890s, the New Deal of the 1930s, and the unrest of the mid-1990s. Each of these upheavals brought to Capitol Hill new lawmakers, new voting patterns, and new legislative priorities.[104]

Recent trends clarify that post–New Deal realignment has occurred, at least from a congressional perspective. First, the Democratic Party's supremacy, established in the Roosevelt era of the 1930s, has been superceded, first by a competitive balance between the two parties, and then by a seemingly entrenched Republican regime. Second, the parties' infrastructures have shifted. The Democrats, long split by divisions between conservative southerners and liberal urban-dwellers, have consolidated their liberal base, in the process pushing away many white southerners but widening their reach to include blacks and other minorities. Republicans, for their part, have achieved ideological consistency by co-opting southern and rural conservatives and by shedding most of their moderate wing—especially those from Northeastern, Mid-Atlantic, and Pacific states.

Meaningful changes can occur even without an underlying party realignment. The Wilson-era Democratic dominance (1913–1919), the Johnson-era Great Society's high-water mark (1965–1967), the post–Watergate Democratic landslide (1974), the Reagan juggernaut (1981–1982), and even the Republican "revolution" of 1994–1995 involved changes in partisan strength on Capitol Hill that for one reason or another went far beyond any underlying shifts in attitudes or voting habits within the electorate as a whole. Elected officeholders, like most political activists, tend to be more committed to ideology or policy than are most voters, even those of the officeholder's own party. Congress turned leftward in the 1960s and 1970s and rightward in the 1990s as voters shifted their electoral choices but not necessarily their underlying attitudes.

Turnover and Representation

Reelection rates should not be confused with turnover rates. Even in years when few members are turned out of office by the voters, many leave Capitol Hill voluntarily—to retire, to run for another office, or to follow other pursuits. In 2002, a year of moderate turnover, eleven senators and sixty-one representatives did not return to office.

In other words, a natural process of membership change is continuous though fluctuating. When the 109th Congress convened in January 2005, a majority of senators and representatives had been elected in the previous five elections. The recent past, when most current House members came to Capitol Hill, began with a period of uncommonly low turnover (1984–1990) that brought only 162 newcomers to the House—an average of 9 percent per election, compared with a normal rate of 15 percent or more. In the early 1990s, however, high electoral turnover left the chamber significantly younger and more junior than it was when the decade began. These members have recently tended to remain in office, thus raising the chamber's average age and seniority. The Senate's membership has been altered to a lesser degree by recent elections. Despite respectable turnovers, however, the average age and seniority of senators have recently crept upward.

For Congress to be a responsive institution, constant turnover of members is a given—whether by steady increments or by sudden, massive partisan realignments. Even when few lawmakers are turned out of office, all of them are keenly aware of the threat of defeat. Most take steps to prevent that eventuality by heightened attentiveness to constituents' needs through personal visits, speeches, newsletters, and polls. But are voters' views accurately reflected by the representatives they elect to Congress? This question is not easily answered. Popular control of policy makers is not the same thing as popular control of policies. Constituents' views are not precisely mirrored by legislators' voting behavior and the laws passed by the legislature.

CONCLUSION

What link exists between voters' attitudes and members' voting on issues? Miller and Stokes found that constituency attitudes correlated differently according to the kind of policy.[105] In foreign affairs a negative correlation existed between constituents' attitudes and legislators' votes (a gap that persists today); in social and economic welfare issues the correlation was moderate; in civil rights issues the correlation was very high. In other words, in at least one and possibly in two major policy areas the linkage was weak enough to cast some doubt on constituency control.

Political scientists explain the absence of strong linkages by noting how difficult it is to meet all the conditions needed for popular control of policies. Voters would have to identify the candidates' positions on issues, and they would have to vote by referring to those positions. Differences among candidates would have to be transparent, and winners would have to vote in accord with their preelection attitudes. These conditions are not routinely met. Candidates' stands are not always clear, and candidates do not invariably differentiate themselves on issues.

Political scientists John L. Sullivan and Robert E. O'Connor tried to test these conditions by submitting to all House candidates a questionnaire covering three issue areas—foreign affairs, civil rights, and domestic policies—and then following the successful candidates' voting records in the House.[106] Their findings suggest that elements of popular control are present. First, according to their inquiries, voters had meaningful choices among candidates. Second, winning candidates generally voted according to their preelection stands.

Third, candidates were ideologically distinct, with Democrats invariably more liberal than Republicans. To these pieces of evidence we can add another: According to recent surveys, most congressional voters can rank their representative on a liberal–conservative scale, and most of these voters claim an affinity with their representative's ranking.[107] In other words, voters' attitudes and legislators' views are roughly parallel, even though they may diverge on numerous specific points.

If ideological or attitudinal links between voters and their representatives are rough and variable, actual contacts between constituents and individual legislators are numerous and palpable. Individual legislators do not necessarily mirror their constituents, much less the nation as a whole, in terms of demographic characteristics. Yet much of their time and effort while in office is devoted to dealing with the folks back home. Constituency politics are ever present in the daily lives of senators and representatives.

SUGGESTED READINGS

Cain, Bruce, John Ferejohn, and Morris Fiorina. *The Personal Vote: Constituency Service and Electoral Independence.* Cambridge: Harvard University Press, 1987.

Dolan, Kathy. *Voting for Women: How the Public Evaluates Women Candidates.* Boulder, Colo.: Westview Press, 2003.

Herrnson, Paul S. *Congressional Elections: Campaigning at Home and in Washington.* 3d ed. Washington, D.C.: CQ Press, 2004.

Jacobson, Gary C. *The Politics of Congressional Elections.* 6th ed. New York: Pearson Longman, 2004.

Krasno, Jonathan S. *Challengers, Competition, and Reelection.* New Haven: Yale University Press, 1994.

Thurber, James A., ed. *The Battle for Congress: Consultants, Candidates, and Voters.* Washington, D.C.: Brookings Institution, 2001.

The two worlds of a congressional leader: Above, (second from left) House Republican whip Roy Blunt works on a Habitat for Humanity project in his southwestern Missouri district. Right, at a Washington press conference, Blunt studies a chart of GOP goals for the 109th Congress (2005–2007). Below, Rep. Sander M. Levin, D-Mich., reviews the daily schedule with his chief of staff, Hilarie Chambers.

chapter 5

Being There: Hill Styles and Home Styles

Rep. Roy Blunt, R-Mo., exhibits two qualities essential to a successful political career: He manages to be in the right place at the right time, and he knows how to count votes. These traits led him early into public office in his home state and have made him a House leader and Republican star.

As a twenty-two-year-old, Blunt drove his 1958 Ford pickup truck to Republican congressional candidate John Ashcroft's campaign headquarters in Springfield. "Have you got gas in this truck?" Ashcroft asked. Blunt said yes and became the candidate's driver.[1] Ashcroft lost his bid for Congress but went on to become governor, senator, and U.S. attorney general. The next year, 1973, Blunt's father (who had served in the state legislature) urged the young man to seek his first public post, the vacant Greene County clerkship. He was appointed by Gov. Christopher S. Bond (now the state's senior U.S. senator) and reelected twice. Although he later lost a couple of races, he became Missouri secretary of state in 1985 and was elected to the House from Missouri's Seventh District in 1996.

On Capitol Hill the new representative immediately made his mark. Republican Party chairman Ken Mehlman, who had worked for one of Blunt's freshman colleagues, remembers him as "the one person every single member of his class felt like they could [consult] to solve a problem."[2]

Blunt soon hitched his wagon to a powerful engine: Majority Whip Tom DeLay, R-Texas, known to friends and foes alike as "The Hammer." After only three years in the House, Blunt became DeLay's chief deputy whip. After another three years, Blunt succeeded his mentor as majority whip (DeLay became majority leader). "We decide big things," he explains. "I go to the floor every day to win. My job is to advance what I am for."[3]

Blunt's talent for listening to his colleagues and recording their preferences came to the fore in his duties as majority whip. Less controversial than DeLay, Blunt is nonetheless quietly effective. His style mirrors that of Speaker J. Dennis Hastert, R-Ill. "Roy is more of the velvet glove [than DeLay], almost a confessor figure," explains a GOP lobbyist.[4] Blunt's meteoric rise might someday take him to the Speaker's chair—if Hastert were to retire, and if DeLay were thought too politically controversial for the post.

At home, Blunt typifies his southwestern Missouri district, which has been historically Republican since it resisted secession in 1861. He raises cattle and a few horses on his farm near Springfield. His father was a dairy farmer. Born, raised, and educated in the Ozarks region, Blunt returns to meet with constituents, appear in public forums, and conduct annual tours of the district's farms and ranches with foreign trade officials in tow. His record on Capitol Hill abounds with actions aimed at benefiting his rural and small-town constituents.

Local booster and congressional leader, Roy Blunt personifies the two Congresses. All members live and work in these two worlds: one on Capitol Hill and the other back home in their states or districts.

HILL STYLES

Members of Congress, as Richard F. Fenno Jr. says, spend their lives "moving between two contexts, Washington and home, and between two activities, governing and campaigning."[5] The two contexts and the two activities are interwoven. How members govern is deeply affected by their campaign experience, especially that of the most recent election. In turn, their Capitol Hill activities affect all their subsequent contacts with people back home.

Who Are the Legislators?

The Constitution names only three criteria for individuals serving in Congress: age, citizenship, and residency. However, entrance requirements are far more restrictive. Aristotle first observed that elections are essentially oligarchic affairs that involve few active participants.

By almost any measure, senators and representatives constitute an economic and social elite. They are well educated. They come from a small number of prestigious occupations. The pay of senators and representatives ($158,100 in 2005) puts them in the top 1 percent of the nation's wage earners. Many possess or attain material wealth, but those who come from state or local posts boost their salaries when they arrive in Congress. And expenses are high, especially for members who maintain a residence in the nation's capital as well as one back home. A federal pay commission reported that "most members of Congress find it difficult to live on their current salaries."[6] Most of them have outside sources of income, although several such income sources have been shut down—including gifts, travel, and honoraria (fees provided by interest groups for speeches or other appearances).

Occupation. Historically, law and politics have been closely linked in the United States. A humorist once quipped that the U.S. government "of laws and not men" is really "of lawyers and not men." When the 109th Congress convened in January 2005, 168 representatives and 58 senators were lawyers.[7]

Many lawyers view forays into electoral politics as a form of professional advancement. The legal profession stresses personal skills, such as verbalization, advocacy, and negotiation, that are useful in gaining and holding public office. Important, too, is lawyers' monopoly over offices that serve as stepping-stones to Congress—especially elected law enforcement and judicial posts.[8] Unlike many other high-status professionals, lawyers can move in and out of their jobs without hurting their careers.

The historical dominance of lawyers on Capitol Hill has declined in recent decades. Lawyers are now outnumbered by members with other careers. Public service/politics and business are the next most prevalent occupations, the latter on the rise since the Republican takeover in the mid-1990s. As for prior public service, the 109th Congress included ten former governors, three former cabinet secretaries, a federal judge, two state supreme court judges, and 274 former state legislators. No less than 125 members had once served as congressional or White House staffers.

War heroes have often found their way to Capitol Hill. Following World War II, returning veterans surged into Congress. Among them were Reps. John F. Kennedy, D-Mass.; Richard M. Nixon, R-Calif.; Gerald R. Ford, R-Mich.; and Bob Dole, R-Kan. By the 1970s more than seven of ten members were veterans. Since then the veterans' ranks have thinned, as World War II faded from view and draftees were replaced by volunteer forces. Only about a quarter of the 109th Congress's members served in the military. The dwindling of the veterans' bloc, however, does not seem to have dimmed congressional enthusiasm for military programs.[9]

Today's media-centered campaigns have spawned a few celebrity legislators. Several astronauts, including Sen. Bill Nelson, D-Fla., have served. Former athletes and coaches in the 109th Congress included a member of the Baseball Hall of Fame: Sen. Jim Bunning, R-Ky., who once pitched a perfect game for the Philadelphia Phillies.

Many occupations are, and always have been, drastically underrepresented in Congress. Low-status occupations, including farm labor, service trades, manual and skilled labor, and domestic service, are rare on Capitol Hill. One blue-collar worker elected in recent years quit after one term in part because he was unhappy and self-conscious about his social status.

Education and Religion. By every measure, Congress is a highly educated body. More than nine out of ten members have college degrees. Three-quarters have graduate degrees, which are required in such heavily represented professions as law. Seventeen have medical degrees. Eight members were Rhodes scholars.

Virtually every member of the 109th Congress professed a formal religious affiliation, compared with about seven of ten Americans in surveys.[10] More than one-quarter of all House and Senate members are Roman Catholics, the largest single contingent. Most other legislators are Protestants, either from mainline denominations—Methodists, Episcopalians, Presbyterians, and Baptists—or from evangelical groups. Jews, who make up 2.6 percent of the total U.S. population, accounted for 7 percent of the 109th Congress. Catholics, evangelical Protestants, and Jews have enlarged their share of Congress's membership, while mainline Protestants have declined in numbers.

Sex and Sexual Orientation. Neither chamber accurately reflects the nation in terms of sex or sexual identity. Congress historically has been a male bastion. Diversity has developed slowly.

Unable to vote until 1920, women have always been underrepresented in Congress. Beginning in 1916 with Jeannette Rankin, elected as a Republican from Montana, 199 women have been elected or appointed to Congress. In the 109th Congress a record number of women served—sixty-eight representatives (nineteen of them in the California delegation) and fourteen senators (two each from California, Maine, and Washington), including two committee chairs and several party leaders.[11]

The advent of a critical mass of women has changed both chambers. Aside from obvious details (installing a Senate women's restroom, opening the gymnasiums to both sexes), the influx of women has brought adjustments in political agendas and ways of doing things.

Policy concerns once labeled "women's issues"—which in truth affect everyone—began to receive respectful hearing. For the first time, workplace and women's health issues—gender discrimination and drive-by mastectomies, for example—had to be seriously addressed. Rep. Nita M. Lowey, D-N.Y., whose mother died of breast cancer, asked for increased funding for research on the disease. During debate over family leave policy, Sen. Patty Murray, D-Wash., talked about having to quit a secretarial job sixteen years earlier when she was pregnant with her first child. At a hearing on Social Security taxes for household help, Rep. Carrie P. Meek, D-Fla. (1993–2003), a granddaughter of slaves, brought her own vivid experiences to the proceedings. "I was once a domestic worker," she told her colleagues. "My mother was a domestic worker. All my sisters were domestic workers."[12] Referring to the women serving in the Senate, Senator Murray declared, "We've made it okay for men to talk about these [women's] issues, too."[13]

Women legislators soon moved beyond the so-called women's issues. As chair of the Senate Homeland Security and Governmental Affairs Committee, Sen. Susan Collins, R-Maine, steered the complex 2004 intelligence reform bill through fierce turf battles. "You enjoyed it," said the panel's ranking Democrat, "because the old bulls couldn't push her around." Said Collins of her experience: "There now is recognition that every issue is a woman's issue."[14]

Gays and lesbians passed a milestone in 1998 when Tammy Baldwin, D-Wis., became the first lesbian representative whose sexual orientation was known before her initial election. The two gay men who also serve in the House (and several former representatives) revealed their sexuality or were outed after they had served for some time. Baldwin, who served six years in the state legislature, did not shy away from the issue. Her campaign slogan was "A different kind of candidate." Still, as Rep. Barney Frank, D-Mass., observed, the hardest part of running as a gay is "convincing voters that you will not disproportionately focus on that minority's issues."[15] That lesson applies to all candidates contending in districts where they are in the minority—for example, blacks running in majority-white areas.

Race. African Americans, who make up 12 percent of the nation's population, account for 8 percent of Congress's members. In 2005, forty-two African Americans (including two delegates) served in the House and one in the Senate, all Democrats. In all U.S. history only 115 blacks have served in Congress, five of them in the Senate and the rest in the House. Some served during the Reconstruction era after the Civil War—all of them Republicans, loyal to the party of Abraham Lincoln. No blacks served in Congress from 1900 to 1928, when Rep. Oscar De Priest, a Republican, was elected from a heavily black district on Chicago's South Side. In the next twenty-five years only three more blacks entered Congress, but after the 1960s African American representation rose steadily. All but four of the post–Reconstruction black legislators were Democrats.

Other minorities are represented in smaller numbers. Latinos make up 12 percent of the population but only 5 percent on Capitol Hill. Of the twenty-six Latino representatives and two senators, most are Mexican Americans, four are Cuban Americans, and three are of Puerto Rican descent. Twenty-one are Democrats and seven are Republicans. Asians and Pacific Islanders claim five representatives and two senators—all Democrats. There are two Native Americans.

Most minority members of the House represent majority-minority districts, a number of them created since the 1990s. The goal of boosting minority representation through redistricting succeeded. All but one of these districts elected minority lawmakers. Only a handful of African Americans and Latinos are now elected from areas with less than 50 percent minority population, however. The ranks of such members must grow if minorities are to gain anything approaching proportionate representation.

Age and Tenure. When the 109th Congress convened in 2005, the average age of members was the highest in history: fifty-five for representatives, sixty for senators.[16] Tenure as well as age has risen since the early days. "Few die, and none retire," it was said as the twentieth century began. A century later, the average representative had served nearly twelve years, or six House terms. The average senator had served about sixteen years, or nearly three Senate terms (a figure that understates their congressional experience, inasmuch as fifty-two senators had prior House service).[17]

Age and tenure levels fluctuate over time. Periods of relatively low turnover (the 1980s, for example) are punctuated by dramatic changing-of-the-guard periods, as in the 1970s and the 1990s, involving both senior and junior members of Congress.[18] Electoral defeats play some role, but the majority of members leave voluntarily. During the political upheavals of the early 1990s, older members wearied of the frantic pace and occasionally were dogged by scandal. Younger members wanted to earn more money and see more of their families.

A certain balance between new blood and stable membership is undoubtedly desirable for legislative bodies. The rapid turnover of the early 1990s heightened the generational conflict. Many newly elected members had indulged in Congress-bashing in their campaigns and wanted to shake up the institution; not a few of them shunned the idea of making a career of public service. As the twenty-first century began, however, many of the firebrands had second thoughts; incumbency was no longer a dirty word. Some two dozen members reconsidered their original three-term pledges, and most of them were reelected.[19]

Representation. Must Congress demographically mirror the populace to be a representative institution? The question is hotly debated. Hannah Finichel Pitkin distinguishes between two types of representation: substantive and descriptive.[20] To represent a category of people substantively, a legislator must consciously act for people and their interests, whether a member of that grouping or not. Legislators from farming districts can voice farmers' concerns even though they have never plowed a field; whites can champion equal opportunities for minorities. Few Asian Americans serve in Congress, but their proportion in a district affects a member's support of issues advocated by that group.[21] Conversely, white representatives from districts that lost black voters in gerrymandering after the 1990s became more conservative and less supportive of policies preferred by African Americans.[22]

By and large, Congress is a body of transplanted locals who naturally speak up for their constituents. Most members keep in touch with the home folks without even thinking about it. A majority of representatives in one survey agreed with the statement: "I seldom have to sound out my constituents because I think so much like them that I know how to react to almost any proposal." [23]

Yet descriptive, or symbolic, representation can be as important as substantive representation. Symbolically, no real substitute exists for having a member of one's own grouping in a position of influence. "Even controlling for party membership," Katherine Tate found from surveying black constituents, "black legislators received significantly higher ratings on average than their white counterparts." [24] Moreover, tangible gains can be seen in the quality of representation. Studies indicate, for example, that women members of Congress are more likely than men to introduce, sponsor, and press for bills of special concern to women and children.[25]

Nor is representation restrained by state or district boundaries. When a member of an ethnic or racial minority goes to Congress, it is a badge of legitimacy for the entire grouping. Such legislators speak for people like them throughout the nation. Other, less obvious constituencies are likewise represented. One member who suffers from epilepsy defends job rights for other sufferers of the disease; another whose grandson was born prematurely champions funds for medical research into birth defects; a third, who fled the Nazis as a child in the 1940s, has sworn to perpetuate awareness of the Holocaust; members who are openly gay speak out for the rights of homosexuals. Such causes are close to members' hearts, even though they often pay scant political dividends and are rarely noticed by the press and the public.

How Do Legislators Describe Their Jobs?

In the late 1970s the House Commission on Administrative Review asked 153 representatives to list "the major kinds of jobs, duties, or functions that you feel you are expected to perform as an individual member of Congress." This question elicited not so much the members' own priorities as their diverse perceptions of what colleagues, constituents, lobbyists, and others expect of them. The responses, summarized in Table 5-1, form a snapshot of members' views of their jobs. Alas, this survey has not been repeated, but it remains a reasonably accurate representation of members' jobs as they see them.

Legislator. The rules, procedures, and traditions of the House and Senate impose many constraints on members' behavior. To be effective, new members must learn their way through the institutional maze. Legislators therefore stress the formal aspects of Capitol Hill duties and routines: legislative work, investigation, and committee specialization. Charles E. Schumer, D-N.Y., in elective

TABLE 5-1 **House Members' Views on the Jobs Expected of Them**

Volunteered responses	Percentage
Legislator	87
Constituency servant	79
Mentor or communicator	43
Representative	26
Politico	11
Overseer	9
Institutional broker	7
Office manager	6
Jack-of-all-trades	6
All other roles	4

Source: House Commission on Administrative Review, *Final Report,* 2 vols., H. Doc. 95–272, 95th Cong., 1st sess., December 31, 1977, 2:874–875.

Note: In total, 146 members took part in the survey. All responses were volunteered. Many members mentioned two or more jobs.

office for more than half his life (he was elected to the state assembly at age twenty-three and served nine terms in the U.S. House), explained his commitment as a professional legislator during his successful 1998 Senate campaign:

> I love to legislate. Taking an idea—often not original with me—shaping it, molding it. Building a coalition of people who might not completely agree with it. Passing it and making the country a little bit of a better place. I love doing that.[26]

Most legislators pursue information and expertise on issues, not only because it is the way to shape public policy but also because it sways others in the chamber.

The legislator's role dovetails with that of representing constituents. Most members seek committee assignments that will serve the needs of their states or districts. One House member related how his interest in flood control and water resource development impelled him to ask for a seat on the committee responsible for those issues. "The interests of my district dictated my field of specialization," he explained, "but the decision to specialize in some legislative field is automatic for the member who wants to exercise any influence."[27]

Members soon learn the norms, or folkways, that expedite legislative bargaining and maximize productivity. Examining the post–World War II Senate, Donald R. Matthews identified six folkways governing behavior that were enforced informally. Senators should (1) serve an apprenticeship (exercising restraint and deference to elders in the early years); (2) concentrate on Senate work instead of on gaining publicity; (3) specialize in issues within their committees or affecting their home states; (4) act courteously to colleagues; (5) extend reciprocity to colleagues—that is, provide willing assistance with the expectation that it will be repaid in kind one day; and (6) loyally defend the Senate, "the greatest legislative and deliberative body in the world."[28]

In recent years certain Senate folkways have faded in importance. New senators now actively take part in most aspects of the chamber's work, ignoring the apprenticeship norm. Many senators, especially those with an eye on higher office, work tirelessly to attract national publicity and personal attention. Committee specialization, although still common, is less rigid than it once was. Senators now have many overlapping committee assignments and are expected to express views on a wide range of issues. The norms of courtesy and reciprocity are still invoked, but institutional loyalty wears thin in an era of harsh partisanship and cynicism about government.

The House relies more on formal channels of power than on informal norms. From interviews, however, Herbert B. Asher uncovered seven norms: (1) friendly relationships are desirable; (2) the important work of the House is done in committee; (3) procedural rules of the House are essential; (4) members should not personally criticize a colleague on the House floor; (5) members should be prepared to trade votes; (6) members should be specialists; and (7) freshmen should serve apprenticeships.[29]

Even this loose network of norms has come unraveled. New members, impatient to make their mark, assert themselves more quickly. "I can't imagine why you would want to waste a single minute after you got here," exclaimed Rep. Marilyn Musgrave, R-Colo. "I do believe you should hit the ground running."[30] Leadership comes earlier to members than it used to. Specialization is still attractive—more so than in the Senate—but many members branch out into unrelated issues. No longer are committees the sole forums for influencing legislation. Today's members, more partisan and ideologically driven than their predecessors, shun norms such as specialization, reciprocity, and compromise.

Legislatively minded members have countered by championing the decaying norms and decrying the rancorous outbursts that have marked recent Congresses. Reassertions of the importance of civility and a spirit of reciprocity suggest that traditional institutional norms are not dead. Asked to compare the House with his earlier career (as an economics professor), former majority leader Dick Armey, R-Texas (1985–2003), remarked, "Here you're working with a more pleasant group of people. There isn't the petty meanness in Congress that you find in university politics."[31] So even in an era of high partisanship, reciprocity and compromise are acknowledged as necessary if members' disparate goals are to be reconciled into legislation that can be passed.

Constituency Servant. Nearly eight of ten respondents in the House survey mentioned the role of constituency servant. The constituency servant attempts to give voice to citizens' concerns and solve their problems. This role was cited by half the House members. Typically, the task is performed by legislators and their staffs as casework—individual cases triggered by constituent letters or visits. Even though mostly delegated to staff aides, this is a chore that weighs heavily on members. The philosophy of most legislators is expressed by one House member like this:

> Constituent work: that's something I feel very strongly about. The American people, with the growth of the bureaucracy, feel nobody cares. The only conduit a taxpayer has with the government is a congressional office.[32]

Sometimes members stress their constituency service to gain breathing room for legislative stands that stray from district norms.

Constituency servants typically make sure their states or districts get their fair share of federal money and assistance. "It's a big pie down in Washington," Michael "Ozzie" Myers, then a Democratic representative from Pennsylvania, told Federal Bureau of Investigation (FBI) agents posing as aides of an Arab sheik during the so-called Abscam probe of influence peddling in the late 1970s:

> Each member's sent there to bring a piece of that pie back home. And if you go down there and you don't—you come back without milkin' it after a few terms . . . you don't go . . . back.[33]

The words are inelegant and the context sleazy, but they characterize members' traditional view of constituency advocacy, even if they also rail against pork-barrel spending in other people's areas.

There is no reason to think that pork has vanished from the congressional diet. Particularized benefits still normally trump collective benefits. When budgets are lean, fewer discretionary dollars are available to distribute to localities. Government programs with highly visible local benefits—highway and mass transit grants, for example, or homeland security contracts—are smothered with attention. If members are unable to win earmarked funds for their constituents, however, they can nonetheless seek nonfiscal benefits—for example, favorable regulatory rules or trade concessions for local industries.[34] An Arkansas lobbyist tells the story of going to visit one of his state's Republican members known for his anti-pork speeches. "I know you're anti-pork," the lobbyist began, "but I have to tell you about our needs and how to position yourself." "What do you mean?" the representative retorted. "As far as I can tell, it's not pork if it's for Arkansas."[35]

Mentor-Communicator and Representative. The mentor-communicator role is linked both to legislating and to constituency errand running. Most members who stress this role view it in connection with issues that must be debated and voted on. Another aspect of the mentor-communicator role is the act of keeping in touch with constituents by mail, by personal appearances, and by print and electronic media. Rep. Barber B. Conable Jr., R-N.Y., conducted what he called a "dialogue of representation" by means of 254 newsletters to his Rochester, New York, constituents during his twenty-year tenure in the House. "Conable never campaigned," a local professor explained, "he just conducted seminars every other year" (actually, a majority of his newsletters went out during nonelection years).[36]

Closely allied is the role of the issue emissary (representative), articulated by a quarter of the House members. Constituents expect their representatives to understand and express their views in Washington. This role is the essence of elective office, both in theory and in practice, and incumbents take it very seriously.

Other Roles. Some members pose as outsiders who adopt a maverick posture; others act as Capitol Hill insiders. Some stress party leadership duties, others their social obligations, still others institutional brokerage—dealing with the executive branch, interest groups, and state and local governments. And, yes, a few members of Congress focus merely on campaigning and gaining reelection. One former member placed this goal in perspective: "All members of Congress have a primary interest in being reelected. Some members have no other interest."[37]

How Do Legislators Spend Their Time?

Time is the most precious commodity for senators and representatives. The lack of it is their most frequent complaint about their jobs.[38] Allocating time requires exceedingly tough personal and political choices.

According to a 1993 congressional survey, members' daily priorities are roughly as follows: (1) meeting on legislative issues with constituents, either at home or in Washington; (2) attending committee hearings, markups, and other committee meetings; (3) meeting with government officials and lobbyists on legislative issues; (4) studying pending legislation or discussing legislation with other members or staff; (5) working with informal caucus groups of colleagues; (6) attending floor debate or watching the debate on television; (7) doing nonlegislative work (casework) for constituents in Washington; (8) managing personal office operations and staffs; (9) raising funds for the next campaign, for others' campaigns, or for the political party; (10) working with party leaders to build legislative coalitions; (11) overseeing how agencies are carrying out laws or policies; and (12) making appearances on legislation outside the state or district (see Table 5-2).[39] Staff members usually prepare daily schedules for members of Congress to consult as they whirl through a busy day on Capitol Hill.

Scheduling is complicated by the large number of formal work groups—mainly committees and subcommittees, but also joint, party, and ad hoc panels. Despite downsizing in recent Congresses, the average senator sits on three full committees and seven subcommittees; representatives average two committees and four subcommittees.

With so many assignments, lawmakers are hard-pressed to control their crowded schedules. Committee quorums are difficult to achieve, and members' attention is often focused elsewhere. All too often working sessions are composed of the chairman, the ranking minority member, perhaps one or two colleagues, and staff aides. Recent House rules tightening quorum requirements have only made scheduling problems worse.

Repeated floor votes, which lawmakers fear to miss, are another time-consuming duty. In a typical Congress more than one thousand recorded votes may be taken in the House chamber and perhaps six hundred in the Senate. "We're like automatons," one senator complained. "We spend our time walking in tunnels to go to the floor to vote."[40]

Lawmakers' daily schedules in Washington are "long, fragmented, and unpredictable," according to a study based on time logs kept by senators' appointment secretaries.[41] "In Congress you are a total juggler," recalls former representative Patricia Schroeder, D-Colo. (1973–1997), now a trade association executive. "You have always got seventeen things pulling on your sleeve."[42] Members' schedules are splintered into so many tiny bits and pieces that effective pursuit of lawmaking, oversight, and constituent service is hampered. According to a management study of several senators' offices, an event occurs

TABLE 5-2 **Activities of Members of Congress: Actual and Ideal (in percentages)**

Activity	Members actually spending time: *Great deal*	*Moderate amount*	*A little*	*Almost none*	Members preferring to spend more time
Representation					
Meet with citizens in state or district	68%	30%	1%	0%	17%
Meet in Washington, D.C., with constituents	45	50	5	0	17
Manage office	6	45	39	10	13
Raise funds for next campaign, for others, for party	6	33	45	16	7
Lawmaking					
Attend committee hearings, markups, other meetings	48	46	6	0	43
Meet in Washington on legislative issues	37	56	6	0	31
Study, read, discuss pending legislation	25	56	17	2	78
Work with informal caucuses	8	43	36	13	25
Attend floor debate, follow it on television	7	37	44	12	59
Work with party leaders to build coalitions	6	33	43	18	42
Oversee how agencies are carrying out policies and programs	5	22	43	29	53
Give speeches about legislation outside state or district	5	23	49	23	16

Source: U.S. Congress, Joint Committee on the Organization of Congress, *Organization of Congress, Final Report,* H. Rept. 103–413, 103d Congress, 1st sess., December 1993, 2:231–232, 275–287.

Note: A total of 161 members of Congress (136 representatives, 25 senators) responded to this survey, conducted in early 1993 under the auspices of the Joint Committee on the Organization of Congress. This series of questions elicited responses from 152 to 155 members.

every five minutes, on average, to which the senator or the chief aide must respond personally.[43] Often members have scant notice that their presence is required at a meeting or a hearing. Carefully developed schedules can be disrupted by changes in meeting hours, by unforeseen events, or by sessions that run longer than expected. (After the terrorist attacks in 2001, members were issued BlackBerry pagers so they could keep track of developments.)

Political scientists may pretend that Congress runs in harmony with members' needs, but the members know otherwise. In a survey of 114 House and Senate members, "inefficiency" was the thing that most surprised them about Congress (45 percent gave this response).[44] "[Congress] is a good job for someone with no family, no life of their own, no desire to do anything but get up, go to work, and live and die by their own press releases," quipped former representative Fred Grandy, an Iowa Republican who left Congress in 1995. "It is a great job for deviant human beings."[45]

Nearly half the respondents in a 1987 survey agreed that they had "no personal time after work"; a third said they had "no time for family."[46] When they came to power in 1995, Republican leaders promised a "family friendly schedule," but the frantic pace of the next two years was anything but that. Subsequent Congresses took a more leisurely pace. House members and their families even held several weekend retreats to get to know one another better.

The dilemma legislators face in allocating their time is far more than a matter of scheduling. It is a case of conflicting role expectations. Look again at Table 5-2, where lawmakers' activities are arrayed to illustrate the tensions inherent in the two Congresses, from the representative Congress (at the top of the list) to the legislative Congress (at the bottom). More members want to devote extra time to legislative duties than would choose to spend more time on constituency and political chores. According to the 1993 survey, an average of 43 percent of the members would like to spend more time on the eight legislative tasks, whereas on average only 14 percent of them would give more time to the four representation items. Eight of ten members would study more thoroughly the legislation they vote on; six of ten would follow floor debate more closely.[47] The two Congresses pull members in different directions. As a retiring House committee chairman remarked:

> One problem is that you're damned if you do and damned if you don't. If you do your work here, you're accused of neglecting your district. And if you spend too much time in your district, you're accused of neglecting your work here.[48]

The Shape of the Washington Career

Once a short-term activity, congressional service has become a career. Accompanying this careerism, or longevity, is a distinctive pattern of Washington activity: The longer members remain in office, the more they sponsor bills, deliver floor speeches, and offer amendments. Despite the democratizing trends of the reform era (1960s and 1970s), senior lawmakers continue to lead in all these categories. "The *apprenticeship norm* may or may not be dead, but *apprenticeship* is stronger than it has been in decades," John R. Hibbing concluded from his painstaking study of four cohorts of members who entered the House between 1957 and 1971.[49]

Long tenure also tends to pull members toward legislative specialization. Members settle into their committee slots, cultivate expertise in a distinct policy field, and spend their time managing legislation and conducting oversight in that field. Seniority tends to boost legislative achievement. Veterans usually enjoy more success than do freshmen in getting their bills passed.

The correlation between members' service and effectiveness reflects the indispensable role careerists play in the legislative process. As Hibbing observed:

> Senior members are the heart and soul of the legislative side of congressional service. . . . Relatively junior members can be given a subcommittee chairmanship, but it is not nearly so easy to give them an active, focused legislative agenda and the political savvy to enact it. Some things take time and experience, and successful participation in the legislative process appears to be one of those things.[50]

The wisdom of this statement is repeatedly borne out. The newcomers elected in the 1990s brought with them zeal, energy, and fresh approaches. At the same time, many of them lacked patience, bargaining skills, institutional memory, and respect for the lawmaking process. Not a few of them demanded overnight reversals of long-standing policies and practices and vowed to retire voluntarily after a few terms.

LOOKING HOMEWARD

Not all of a representative's or a senator's duties lie in Washington, D.C. Legislators not only fashion policy for the nation's welfare, but they also act as emissaries from their home states or districts.

What Is Representation?

Although found in virtually every political system, representation is the hallmark of democratic regimes dedicated to sharing power among citizens. In small communities decisions can be reached by face-to-face discussion, but in populous societies this sort of personalized consultation is impossible. Thus, according to traditional democratic theory, citizens can exert control by choosing "fiduciary agents" to act on their behalf, deliberating on legislation just as their principals, the voters, would do if they could be on hand themselves.[51] As Pitkin explains:

> The representative must act in such a way that, although he is independent, and his constituents are capable of action and judgment, no conflict arises between them. He must act in their interest, and this means he must not normally come into conflict with their wishes.[52]

Some recent opinion surveys seem to echo Pitkin's formulation. As one analyst puts it, "[T]he public seems to want elected officials to internalize the majority's values and then try to assess how those values come to bear on an issue." No less than 85 percent agreed with the statement: "The goal of Congress should be to make the decisions that a majority of Americans would make if they had the information and time to think things over that Congress has."[53]

Incumbent legislators give high priority to representation. Four of five House members interviewed in 1977 saw themselves as constituency servants. Many were mentor-communicators; others, issue spokespersons. In an earlier survey of eighty-seven members, the role most often expressed was called the tribune: the discoverer, reflector, or advocate of popular needs and wants.[54]

Although legislators agree on the importance of representation, they interpret it differently. One point of departure is Edmund Burke's dictum that legislators should voice the "general reason of the whole," not speak merely for "local purposes" and "local prejudices."[55] This conception of the legislator as Burkean trustee has always had its admirers. Speaking to a group of newly elected House members, Rep. Henry J. Hyde, R-Ill., voiced the Burkean ideal:

> If you are here simply as a tote board registering the current state of opinion in your district, you are not going to serve either your constituents or the Congress well. . . . You must take, at times, a national view, even if you risk the displeasure of your neighbors and friends back home. . . . If you don't know the principle, or the policy, for which you are willing to lose your office, then you are going to do damage here.[56]

Representative Hyde followed his own precepts as chairman of the Judiciary Committee that in 1998 voted to impeach President Bill Clinton. Defying the weight of expert opinion, national opinion polls, and even some within his own party, he carried his committee's articles of impeachment to the full House, which adopted two of them, and then to the Senate, which rejected them.

Nearly every member can point to conscience votes cast on deeply felt issues. A few, such as Rep. Mike Synar, D-Okla. (1979–1995), compile a contrarian record, challenging voters to admire their independence if not their policies. Synar was an unabashed liberal Democrat from a state that now elects mostly conservative Republicans. "I want to be a U.S. congressman from Oklahoma, not an Oklahoman congressman," Synar declared when he arrived in the capital.[57] If turned out of office by hostile sentiment (as Synar later was), the Burkean can at least hope for history's vindication.

Electoral realities imperil the Burkean ideal. Burke himself was ousted from office for his candor. Modern electorates, motivated by self-interest and schooled in democratic norms, prefer instructed delegates—lawmakers who follow instructions rather than exercise independent judgments. However, a recent study revealed that citizens' expectations (and hence their "instructions") for representatives can vary widely. "Some citizens desire assistance in dealing with government; others want their representative to focus on national policy concerns. Still others want their member[s] to devote most of their time to local policy concerns." [58]

In practice, legislators assume different representational styles according to the occasion. They ponder factors such as the nation's welfare, their personal convictions, and constituency opinions. "The weight assigned to each factor," writes Thomas E. Cavanagh, "varies according to the nature of the issue at hand, the availability of the information necessary for a decision, and the intensity of preference of the people concerned about the issue." [59]

Members of Congress are called upon to explain their choices to constituents—no matter how many or how few people truly care about the matter.[60] The anticipated need to explain oneself shapes a member's decisions and is part of the dilemma of choice. A cynical saying among lawmakers asserts that "a vote on anything [is] a wrong vote if you cannot explain it in a 30-second TV ad."[61] Votes to increase congressional pay and perquisites, for example, often fail simply because members fear having to defend their stand in front of skeptical constituents.

What Are Constituencies?

No senator or representative is elected by, interacts with, or responds to all the people in a given state or district. The constituencies fixed in lawmakers' minds as they campaign or vote may be quite different from the boundaries found on maps. Fenno describes a "nest" of constituencies, ranging from the widest (geographic constituency) to the narrowest (personal constituency), which is made up of supporters, loyalists, and intimates.[62]

Geographic and Demographic Constituencies. The average House district today numbers more than 680,000 people. As for senators, fourteen represent states with only one House district; the rest represent multidistrict states with as many as thirty-seven million people.[63] Such constituencies differ sharply from one another. More than half (57 percent) of the people in Manhattan's Upper East Side (New York's Fourteenth District) have college degrees, compared with only 6 percent in California's central valley (Twentieth District). Median family income ranges from $92,000 (New Jersey's Eleventh District, Morris County) to less than $21,000 in New York's Sixteenth District in the South Bronx, where 40 percent of the families live in poverty.[64] Such disparities among districts animate their representatives' outlooks.

There is also the political equivalent of microclimates. Democrat Nydia M. Velázquez's Twelfth District in New York begins in a Hispanic area of Brooklyn, jumps across the East River to take in Manhattan's Chinatown, Little Italy, and the Lower East Side, and doubles back again to encompass neighborhoods in north Brooklyn and Queens. Republican Mary Bono's sprawling southern California Forty-fifth District embraces smog-ridden suburbs east of Riverside, irrigated farmland of the Coachella Valley, and wealthy desert oases of Palm Springs and Palm Desert, where retired Hollywood stars reside. Even these geographical distinctions grossly simplify the complex and subtle mixtures of ethnic, economic, and social categories that make up these communities.

Demographically, constituencies may be homogeneous or heterogeneous.[65] Some constituencies, even a few whole states, remain uniform and one-dimensional—mostly wheat farmers or urban ghetto dwellers or small-town citizens. Because of rising population, economic complexity, and educational levels, however, virtually all constituencies, House as well as Senate, have become more heterogeneous than they used to be. The more heterogeneous a constituency, the more challenging is the representative's task.

Another attribute of constituencies is electoral balance, especially as manifested in the incumbent's reelection chances. Heterogeneous districts tend to be more competitive than uniform ones. Incumbents predictably prefer safe districts—those with a high proportion of groups sympathetic to their partisan or ideological stance. Not only do safe districts favor reelection, but they also imply that voters will be easier to please.[66]

Truly competitive districts are not the norm, especially in the House of Representatives. Three out of four House victors in 2004 boasted margins of 60 percent or more; nearly one in ten faced no major party foe. Less than 10 percent of the seats were truly competitive (won by 55 percent or less). As Table 5-3 shows, competitiveness varies over time. The mid-1990s elections, for example, were unusually competitive because short-term factors (retirements, scandals, and voter unrest) put more seats into play. Since then, competition has plummeted. Senate seats are more likely to be closely contested than House races, but many senators still win in a walk.

Whatever the numbers show, few incumbents regard themselves as truly safe. The threat of losing is very real. Most lawmakers have a close call at some time in their congressional careers, and many of them eventually suffer defeat.[67] Incumbents worry not only about winning or losing but also about their margins of safety. Downturns in normal electoral support narrow the member's breathing space in the job, may invite challengers for future contests, and could block chances for advancement.[68]

Political and Personal Constituencies. As candidates or incumbents analyze their electoral base, three narrower constituencies can be discerned: supporters (the reelection constituency), loyalists (the primary constituency), and intimates (the personal constituency).[69] Supporters are expected to vote for them on election day, but some do not. Candidates and their advisers repeatedly monitor these voters, reassessing precinct-level political demography—registration figures, survey data, and recent electoral trends. The more elections incumbents have survived, the more precisely they can identify supporters. Areas and groups with the biggest payoff are usually targeted.

Loyalists are the politician's staunchest supporters. They may be from preelectoral ventures—racial, environmental, or anti-abortion activism, for example. They may be concentrated in religious or ethnic groups, or political or

TABLE 5-3 **House and Senate Margins of Victory, 1974–2004**

Chamber and election year	Percentage of vote				Number of seats
	Under 55	*55–59.9*	*60 plus*	*Unopposed*	
House					
1974	24	16	46	14	435
1976	17	14	56	12	435
1978	17	14	53	16	435
1980	18	14	60	8	435
1982	16	16	63	6	435
1984	12	13	61	14	435
1986	9	10	64	17	435
1988	6	9	67	18	435
1990	11	16	58	15	435
1992	20	18	58	3	435
1994	22	17	52	9	435
1996	22	18	57	3	435
1998	10	17	63	10	435
2000	23	12	59	15	435
2002	10	10	80	18	435
2004	7	14	64	15	435
Senate					
1974	41	18	35	6	34
1976	30	33	30	6	33
1978	24	33	36	6	33
1980	58	18	21	3	34
1982	30	27	43	—	33
1984	18	21	58	3	33
1986	38	15	47	—	34
1988	33	15	52	—	33
1990	26	11	49	14	34
1992	34	34	32	—	35
1994	32	34	34	—	35
1996	59	18	24	—	34
1998	29	9	62	—	34
2000	29	15	55	—	34
2002	38	18	44	4	34
2004	32	15	50	3	34

Source: CQ Weekly and authors' calculations.
Note: Percentages may not add to 100 because of rounding. "Unopposed" includes districts or states where only one major-party candidate was on the ballot.

civic clubs. They may be friends and neighbors. They are willing volunteers who can be counted on to lend a hand in reelection campaigns.

Candidates dare not ignore these loyalists. A favorite story of House Speaker Thomas P. "Tip" O'Neill Jr., D-Mass. (1953–1987), came from his first, losing, campaign for city council. A neighbor told him, "Tom, I'm going to vote for you even though you didn't ask me." "Mrs. O'Brien," replied a surprised O'Neill, "I've lived across the street from you for 18 years. I shovel your walk in the winter. I cut your grass in the summer. I didn't think I had to ask you for your vote." To this the lady replied, "Tom, I want you to know something: people like to be asked." [70] Expressions of gratitude are equally important. The Bush family, for example, is noted for personal thank-you notes to supporters. The elder George Bush reportedly "always carried a box of note cards with him on the campaign trail and penned a personal note immediately following each event to the volunteers and hosts." [71] Such catering to core supporters helped send both Bushes, father and son, to the White House.

Even entrenched officeholders worry about keeping their core supporters energized. Loyalists are also a politician's defenders in times of adversity. "There's a big difference between the people who are for you and the people who are excitedly for you," an Iowa politician told Fenno, "between those who will vote if they feel like it and those for whom the only election is [your] election. You need as many of that group as you can get." An inadequate base of core support, the informant explained, spelled the downfall of two one-term Democratic senators. One had a base that was a mile wide and an inch deep; the other's support was an inch wide and a mile deep.[72]

Intimates are close friends who supply political advice and emotional support. Nearly every candidate or incumbent knows a few of them. They may be members of the candidate's family, trusted staff members, political mentors, or individuals who shared decisive experiences early in the candidate's career. The setting and the players differ from state to state and from district to district. Tip O'Neill's inner circle was made up of the "boys" of Barry's Corner, a local clubhouse in Cambridge, Massachusetts, whose families O'Neill had known intimately over more than fifty years of political life. When Rep. David E. Price, D-N.C., first decided to run for Congress, he relied on what he called the "Wednesday night group," which he described as "an inner circle without whom the effort would never have gotten off the ground." [73] Such intimates play an indispensable role. They provide unvarnished advice on political matters and serve as sounding boards for ideas and strategies.

Home Styles

Legislators evolve distinctive ways of presenting or projecting themselves and their records to their constituents—what Fenno calls their home styles. These styles are exhibited in members' personal appearances, mailings, newsletters, press releases, telephone conversations, radio and television spots, and Internet Web site pages. Little is known about how home styles coalesce, but they are linked to members' personalities, backgrounds, constituency features, and resources. The concept of home style shifts the focus of constituency linkage from representation to presentation. As Fenno states, "It is the style, not the issue content, that counts most in the reelection constituency."[74]

Presentation of Self. The core ingredient of a successful home style is trust—constituents' faith that legislators are what they claim to be and will do what they promise.[75] Winning voters' trust does not happen overnight; it takes time. Three major ingredients of trust are qualification, the belief that legislators are capable of handling the job, a critical threshold that nonincumbents especially must cross; identification, the impression that legislators resemble their constituents, that they are part of the state or region; and empathy, the sense that legislators understand constituents' problems and care about them.

Given variations among legislators and constituencies, countless available home styles can effectively build the trust relationship. The legendary Speaker "Mr. Sam" Rayburn represented his East Texas district for nearly fifty years (1913–1961) as a plain dirt farmer. Once back in his hometown of Bonham, his drawl thickened; his tailored suits were exchanged for khakis, an old shirt, and slouch hat; and he traveled not in the Speaker's limousine but in a well-dented pickup truck. A biographer relates:

> If Rayburn ever chewed tobacco in Washington, a long-time aide could not recall it, but in Bonham he always seemed to have a plug in his cheek. He made certain always to spit in the fireplace at his home when constituents were visiting, so that if nothing else, they would take away the idea that Mr. Sam was just a plain fellow.[76]

Today's legislators are no less inventive in fashioning home styles. Representative A's direct style features face-to-face contacts with people in his primary constituency. He rarely mentions issues because most people in his district agree on them. Representative B, a popular local athlete, uses national defense issues to symbolize his oneness with a district supportive of the military. Representative C displays himself as a verbal, issue-oriented activist, an outsider ill at ease with conventional politicians. Senator D, articulate and personable, comes across as "a mom in tennis shoes." And so on. The repertoire of home styles is limitless.

Voters are likely to remember style long after they forget issue pronouncements or voting records. Even so, legislators know full well that they must explain their decisions to others.[77]

Explaining Washington Activity. Explaining is an integral part of decision making. In home district forums, constituents expect members to be able to describe, interpret, and justify their actions. If they do not agree with the member's conclusions, they may at least respect the decision-making style.

> They don't know much about my votes. Most of what they know is what I tell them. They know more of what kind of a guy I am. It comes through in my letters: "You care about the little guy."[78]

Although few incumbents fear that a single vote can defeat them, all realize that voters' disenchantment with their total record can be fatal—more so these days when lobby groups publicize voting records. Members stockpile reasons for virtually every position they take, and often more than are needed. Facing especially thorny choices (for example, on abortion policy or Social Security reform), they might find an independent stance to be the best defense. More often, they huddle under the umbrella of their party's line. Whichever course they choose, they will find that inconsistency is mentally and politically costly. While the issues may vary, politicians thus give much the same account of themselves, no matter what group they are talking to (contrary to the popular belief that politicians talk out of both sides of their mouths).

Constituency Careers. Constituency ties evolve over the course of a senator's or representative's career. Constituency careers have at least two recognizable stages: expansionism and protectionism. In the first stage the member constructs a reelection constituency by solidifying the help of hard-core supporters and reaching out to attract added blocs of support. This aggressive expansionism—plus exploitation of the perquisites of incumbency, such as fund-raising and an election-year avalanche of communications to constituents—accounts for the "sophomore surge," in which newcomers typically boost their margin in their first reelection bid.[79] In the second stage the member ceases to expand the base of support, content with protecting already won support. Once established, a successful style is rarely altered.

Certain developments, however, can lead to a change in a member's constituency style. One is a demographic change in the constituency, as a population shift or redistricting forces a member to cope with unfamiliar voters or territory. A second cause is a strategic reaction, as a fresh challenger or a novel issue threatens established voting patterns. Because coalitions may shift over time, members and their advisers scrutinize the results of the past election (and survey findings, if available).

Finally, home styles may change with new personal goals and ambitions. Growing responsibilities in Washington can divert attention from home state business, from family responsibilities, and from amassing wealth. Faced with new aspirations or shifting constituency demands, not a few members decide to retire. Others struggle ineffectively and are defeated. Still others rejuvenate their constituency base and survive.

OFFICE OF THE MEMBER INC.

Home style is more than a philosophy for weighing constituents' claims. It affects the way a member answers day-to-day questions: How much attention should I devote to state or district needs? How much time should I spend in the state or district? How should I maintain contact with my constituents? How should I deploy my staff aides to deal with constituents' concerns? One of the most vexing problems is how to balance demands for being in Washington with the need to be back home with constituents.

Road Tripping

During the nineteenth century legislators spent much of their time at home, traveling to Washington only when Congress was in session. After World War II (and the advent of air conditioning), however, congressional sessions lengthened until they spanned virtually the entire year. Legislators began to set up permanent residence in the nation's capital, a practice that in earlier times would have struck citizens as arrogant. By the 1970s both houses had adopted parallel schedules of sessions punctuated with brief district work periods (House) or nonlegislative periods (Senate).

At the same time, the two houses authorized members to make more paid trips to states or districts. Today senators and representatives are allowed as many trips home as they want, subject to the limits of their official expense allowances.

Currently fashionable home styles entail frequent commutes. Although travel has increased for all members, the more time-consuming the trip home, the less often it is made. (Members from Alaska and Hawaii make about a dozen round-trips a year—each requiring an elapsed twenty-four hours and spanning four or five time zones.)[80] When their families remain at home, members are more inclined to travel. They tend to avoid their districts during periods of congressional unpopularity, but they spend more time there during periods of adverse economic conditions. As election day approaches, representatives stay close to their districts.[81]

Seniority is also a factor. Senior members tend to make fewer trips to their districts than do junior members, perhaps reflecting junior members' greater attentiveness to their districts. Finally, members' decisions to retire voluntarily are usually accompanied by large drops in trips home. "There was no reason to go back," one member told Hibbing. "My engagement calendar used to be booked up for seven or eight months in advance; after I announced, no one seemed anxious to have me. I stayed in town and found out that Washington was not as bad as I had thought all those years."[82]

Constituency Casework

"All God's chillun got problems," exclaimed Rep. Billy Matthews, D-Fla. (1953–1967), as he pondered mail from his constituents.[83] In the early days lawmakers lacked staff aides and wrote personally to executive agencies for help in such matters as pension or land claims and appointments to military academies. The Legislative Reorganization Act of 1946 provided de facto authority for hiring caseworkers, first in Senate offices and later in the House.

What are these cases all about? As respondents in a nationwide survey reported, the most frequent reason for contacting a member's office (16 percent of all cases) is to express views or obtain information on legislative issues.

Requests for help in finding government jobs form the next largest category, followed by cases dealing with government services such as Social Security, veterans' benefits, or unemployment compensation. Military cases (for example, transfers, discharges, personal hardships) are numerous, as are tax, legal, and immigration problems. Constituents often ask for government publications. And there are requests for flags that have flown over the U.S. Capitol.

Many citizen appeals, moreover, betray a hazy understanding of the officeholder's duties. Rep. Luis V. Gutierrez, D-Ill., reports being barraged with all manner of complaints and requests when he shops in his North Side Chicago neighborhood. Examples of what he has heard are: "They haven't picked up my trash!" (city responsibility); "Can you get my son a scholarship to the state university?" (a state matter); or "I can't pay my child support" (personal). Representative Gutierrez's personal favorite is: "I own property in Puerto Rico and someone is blocking my driveway."[84]

Cases come to legislators' offices by letter, phone, e-mails, faxes, or walk-ins at district or mobile offices. Occasionally, members themselves pick up cases from talking to constituents. Many hold office hours in their districts for this purpose. When a constituent's request is received, it is usually acknowledged immediately by a letter that either fills the request or promises that an answer will be forthcoming.

Keeping up with incoming communications is a priority for all congressional offices. All representatives and senators now have Internet e-mail addresses and home pages, some of them interactive. A handful have blogs—online diaries with commentary.[85]

The volume of Internet communications has, to all accounts, swamped congressional offices. House and Senate offices received an estimated eighty million messages in 2000, and the rate is rising by a million messages each month.[86] Representatives' offices may receive as many as eight thousand e-mails a month; for senators the figure is fifty-five thousand or more.

If the constituent's request requires contacting a federal agency, caseworkers communicate by e-mail, phone, letter, or buckslip (a preprinted referral form).[87] Usually, the contact in the executive agency is a liaison officer, although some caseworkers prefer to deal directly with line officers or regional officials. Once the problem has been conveyed, it is a matter of time before a decision is reached and a reply forwarded to the congressional office. The reply is then sent along to the constituent, perhaps with a cover letter signed by the member. If the agency's reply is deemed faulty, the caseworker may challenge it and ask for reconsideration; in some cases the member may intervene in person to lend weight to the appeal.

Casework loads vary from state to state and from district to district. In both chambers senior legislators receive proportionately more casework requests than do junior members.[88] Perhaps senior legislators are considered more powerful and better equipped to resolve constituents' problems. Legislators themselves certainly cultivate this image in seeking reelection.

Demographic variations among electorates can affect casework volume. Some citizens simply are more likely than others to have contact with government agencies.

Comparing senators and representatives, casework loads depend mainly on constituency size. Frances E. Lee and Bruce I. Oppenheimer found that

> [s]enators as a group are not different from House members in the amount of contact they have with constituents. Instead, senators who represent constituencies that are similar in size to House districts have contact levels that mirror or exceed those of House members.[89]

Thus large-state senators would draw proportionately fewer requests than small-state senators. "As state population decreases . . . House members and senators look increasingly similar in accessibility and responsiveness."[90] As for clout, however, senators win hands down (they are 1 out of 100 instead of 1 out of 435). So constituents in small states are more than twice as likely to contact their senator than people in larger states, who tend to rely on their House member.

From all accounts, casework pays off in citizens' support for individual legislators. In one National Election Study (NES) survey, 17 percent of all adults reported that they or members of their families had requested help from their own representatives. Eighty-five percent of them said they were satisfied with the response they received; seven in ten felt the representative would be helpful if asked in the future.[91] "Casework is all profit," contends Morris P. Fiorina. If so, the profit statements may be written in disappearing ink. Only 16 percent of all citizens in the NES survey could remember anything specific the representative had done for the people of the district while in office.[92] A sensible middle-ground view holds that "service responsiveness has an electoral payoff for incumbents regardless of issue positions or other factors. Casework does not operate to supplant issue positions, however."[93]

Some criticize constituency casework as unfair or biased in practice. Citizens may not enjoy equal access to senators' or representatives' offices. Political supporters or cronies may get favored treatment at others' expense. But in the great bulk of cases, help is universally dispensed.

Personal Staff

Legislators head sizable office enterprises that reflect their two-Congresses responsibilities within the institution and toward their constituents. In 2005 each House member was entitled to an annual staff allowance covering no more than eighteen full-time and four part-time employees. The average House member's full-time staff numbers about fourteen. Representatives also are entitled to an annual office allowance, used for travel, telecommunications, district office rental, office equipment, stationery, computer services, and mail.[94]

Senators' personal staffs range in size from thirteen to seventy-one; the average is about thirty-four full-time employees. Unlike the House, the Senate places no limits on the number of staff a senator may employ from their two personnel accounts: an administrative and clerical account (which varies according to a state's population) and an account for hiring legislative assistants. A senator's office expense account depends upon factors such as the state's population and its distance from Washington, D.C. Separate categories for mailing, stationery, local offices, and furniture can be shifted within the overall financial allotments.

Members' offices always seem crowded and overburdened, but freezes on staff size have been partially offset by computerization, shifting to state and district offices, and use of volunteers. These offices depend heavily on unpaid help, mainly college-age interns. On average, each House and Senate office uses about nine interns every year (see Appendix B for information on internships).

Staff Organization. No two congressional offices are exactly alike. Each is shaped by the personality, interests, constituency, and politics of the individual legislator. State and district needs also influence staff composition. A senator from a farm state likely will employ at least one specialist in agricultural problems; an urban representative might hire a consumer affairs or housing expert. Traditions are important. If a legislator's predecessor had an enviable reputation for a certain kind of service, the new incumbent will dare not let it lapse.

The member's institutional position also affects staff organization. Committee and subcommittee chairmen have committee staff at their disposal. Members without such aides rely heavily on personal staff for committee work.

Staff Functions. Most personal aides in the House and Senate are young, well educated, and transient. Senate and House aides have served on average less than four years in their posts. Their salaries, although somewhat above the average for full-time workers in the United States, fall well below those for comparably educated workers.[95]

The mix of personal staff functions is decided by each member. Most hire administrative assistants, legislative assistants, caseworkers, and press aides as well as a few people from the home state or district. Administrative assistants supervise the office and impart political and legislative advice. Often they function as the legislator's alter ego, negotiating with colleagues, constituents, and lobbyists. Legislative assistants work with members in committees, draft bills, write speeches, suggest policy initiatives, analyze legislation, and prepare position papers. They also monitor committee sessions that the member is unable to attend.

To emphasize the personal touch, many members have moved casework staff to their home districts or states. Virtually all House and Senate members have home district offices in post offices or federal buildings. Some members have as many as five or six. With the decline of party workers to assist local citizens, members' district staffs fill this need and, simultaneously, enhance members' reelection prospects. Senators have an average of four home state offices and deploy a third of their staff there. Representatives have an average of 2.3 offices and deploy almost half of their aides in their districts.[96]

Other reasons are cited for decentralizing constituent functions. Congressional office buildings on Capitol Hill are crowded. Field offices have lower staff salaries and lower overhead. They also are more convenient for constituents, local and state officials, and regional federal officers. Computers and fax machines make it easy for Washington offices and district offices to communicate. This decentralizing trend, which is likely to persist, implies a heightened division between legislative functions based on Capitol Hill and constituency functions based in field offices. In other words, "Office of the Member Inc." is increasingly split into headquarters and branch divisions—with the Capitol Hill office dealing with legislative duties and the state or district office dealing with constituents.

Congressional staff aides are not supposed to engage in campaign duties—a cloudy distinction, inasmuch as members' offices are suffused with electoral concerns. (Aides may go on leave and transfer to the campaign organization's payroll for the duration of the campaign season.) Members' families are also barred from the congressional payroll (some of them work without pay). The campaign apparatus can serve as a loophole: A recent study found that thirty-nine House members had family members on their campaign payrolls—totaling $3 million in salaries over the last two election cycles (2002–2004).[97]

MEMBERS AND THE MEDIA

Office allowances in both chambers amply support lawmakers' unceasing struggle for media attention. A member's office bears some resemblance to the communications division of a medium-size business. Nearly every day, stacks of printed matter and electronic messages are released for wide distribution. In addition to turning out press releases, newsletters, and individual and mass mailings, members communicate through telephone calls, interviews, radio and TV programs, videotapes, and e-mail messages. Most of the time, these publicity barrages are aimed not at the national media but at individual media outlets back in the home state or district.

Direct Mail

The traditional cornerstone of congressional publicity is the franking privilege—the right of members to send out mail at no cost to them with their signature (the frank) instead of a stamp. The practice, which in the United States dates from the First Continental Congress in 1775, is intended to facilitate official communication between elected officials and the people they represent (a rationale accepted by federal courts in upholding the practice). In recent times members found that aggressive use of the frank could aid reelection. Rep. Bill Frenzel, R-Minn. (1971–1991), noted that both parties teach newcomers three rules for getting reelected: "Use the frank. Use the frank. Use the frank."[98]

Critics point out that franked mail is largely unsolicited and politically motivated. First, outgoing mail costs are much higher in election years than in nonelection years. Second, most items are mass mailings, not individual letters. These mass mailings are either general-purpose newsletters blanketing home states or districts, or special messages targeted to certain categories of voters. Recipients are urged to share their views or contact local offices for help. Sometimes the newsletter may feature an opinion poll asking for citizens' views on selected issues. Whatever the results, the underlying message is that the legislator cares what folks back home think.

The current franking law confers wide mailing privileges but forbids use of the frank for mail "unrelated to the official business, activities, and duties of members." It also bars the frank for a "matter which specifically solicits political support for the sender or any other person or any political party, or a vote or financial assistance for any candidate for any political office." In addition, chamber rules forbid mass mailings (five hundred or more pieces) sixty days (Senate) or ninety days (House) before a primary, runoff, or general election. In the two months before the beginning of each cutoff period, streams of U.S. Postal Service trucks are seen pulling away from loading docks of the congressional office buildings.

Criticisms of such abuses led both houses to impose new franking restrictions in the 1990s. Most important, mailing costs have been integrated into members' office allowances, which forces trade-offs between mail and other expenditures, such as travel or staff. Caps have been placed on newsletters and on total outgoing mail—one piece for each address in the state for senators, three pieces for each address in the district for representatives. Rules governing newsletters curb their advertising features, for example, personal references or pictures of the member.

The reforms have reversed the upward spiral of congressional mail costs.[99] Members have turned toward discounted bulk mailings and away from mass newsletters and first-class letters. Although it can still be abused, the franking privilege is essential to sustain communications between lawmakers and their constituents. A former chairman of a House oversight commission posed the issue: "How do you write rules and regulations that distinguish between a thoughtful discussion of some important public issue and a self-promoting thing with the photograph of a member on every other page?"[100]

The advent of e-mail poses the problem of whether, or how, the much-debated franking restrictions should apply. The Senate has generally applied the franking rules to electronic mail. The House, however, has declined to adopt such strict rules. As Rep. Vernon J. Ehlers, R-Mich., says,

> It is not partisan, it is just simply an informational summary of these bills that were taken up, this is the result of the bills. My constituents are finding that useful, the e-mail list is growing. I think my constituents . . . will find it a bit strange to suddenly, three months before

> the election, they are not allowed to hear from me about what the Congress has done in a nonpartisan way.[101]

Feeding the Local Press

News outlets in North America are highly decentralized and dispersed. About 1,500 daily newspapers and 6,500 weeklies are published in the United States. There are also more than 13,000 radio stations, 1,700 TV stations, and 11,800 cable systems throughout the country.[102] Virtually all these media outlets are locally based because of the vitality of local issues and local advertising.

Taken as a whole, local media outlets have inadequate resources for covering what their congressional delegations are doing in the nation's capital. Few of them have their own Washington reporters. Most rely on syndicated or chain services that rarely follow individual members consistently. "If they report national news it is usually because it involves local personalities, affects local outcomes, or relates directly to local concerns," stated a Senate report.[103]

Relations with the press receive careful attention from members. Most legislators have at least one staffer who serves as a press aide; some have two or three. Their job is to generate coverage highlighting the member's work. Executive agencies often help by letting incumbents announce federal grants or contracts awarded in the state or district. Even if the member had nothing to do with procuring the funds, the press statement proclaims, "Senator So-and-So announced today that a federal contract has been awarded to XYZ Company in Jonesville." Many offices also prepare weekly or biweekly columns that small-town newspapers can reprint under the lawmaker's byline.

The House, the Senate, and the four Capitol Hill parties (House and Senate Republicans and Democrats) have fully equipped studios and satellite links where audio or video programs or excerpted statements (called actualities) can be produced for a fraction of the commercial cost.[104] Some incumbents produce regular programs that are picked up by local radio or television outlets. More often, these outlets insert brief audio or TV clips on current issues into regular news broadcasts—to give the impression that their reporters have gone out and obtained the story. Members also create their own news reports and beam them directly to hometown stations, often without ever talking to a reporter. With direct satellite feeds to local stations, members regularly go "live at five" before local audiences.

Some members invite controversy as a way of showing their accessibility. For example, Rep. Mark Souder, R-Ind., tapes five-minute reports every weekday for local airing and hosts an hour-long call-in show every Sunday—unofficially dubbed "Bark at Mark"—on a popular talk radio station in Fort Wayne.[105]

Like printed communications, radio and TV broadcasts pose ethical questions. House and Senate recording studios are supposed to be used only for communicating about legislation and other policy issues, but the distinction between legitimate constituent outreach and political advertising remains blurred. (The well-equipped studios run by the parties have no such limits.) Some radio and television news editors have qualms about using members' programs. "It's just this side of self-serving," said one television editor of the biweekly "Alaska Delegation Report."[106] Others claim to see little difference between these electronic communications and old-fashioned press releases. Local editors and producers still have to decide whether to use the material, edit it, or toss it.

Local Press Boosterism?

In the eyes of home district media outlets, incumbents fare splendidly. Michael J. Robinson cited the case of "Congressman Press," a midlevel House member, untouched by scandal, who had an average press operation. One year Congressman Press issued 144 press releases, about three a week. That year the major paper in his district ran 120 stories featuring or mentioning him. More than half the stories drew heavily on the press releases. "On average, every other week, Congressman Press was featured in a story virtually written in his own office."[107]

Even when local stories are not drawn from press releases, they tend to be respectful if not downright laudatory. A detailed study of the local press corps in eighty-two contested races highlighted the journalists' tendency toward "safety and timidity." Incumbents were rendered respectful coverage based on their experience; in contested open seats, journalists tended to keep their distance.[108]

Electronic media are even more benign than print media. As one legislator said, "TV people need thirty seconds of sound and video at the airport when I arrive—that's all they want."[109] Most local reporters for radio and TV are on general assignment and do little preparation for interviews. Their primary goal is to get the newsmaker on tape. This is especially true of outlets in smaller markets, few of which have access to a Washington bureau.

Local radio and television's weakness for congressionally initiated communications magnifies the advantages incumbents enjoy. ABC-TV correspondent Cokie Roberts concludes, "The emergence of local TV has made some members media stars in the home towns and, I would argue, done more to protect incumbency than any franking privilege or newsletter ever could, simply because television is a more pervasive medium than print."[110] "I've been treated very fairly back home by the media, who have been content to just report the facts," concedes Rep. Kenny Hulshof, R-Mo.[111]

Reports on Congress from the national press corps are far more critical than those from local news organizations. Following the canons of investigative journalism, many national reporters are on the lookout for scandals or evidence of wrongdoing. The national press reports primarily on the institution of Congress, whereas the local press is interested mostly in local senators and representatives. Individual members tend to be reported on far more favorably than the institution. The content and quality of press coverage underscore the two Congresses. Congress as collective policy maker, covered mainly by the national press, appears in a different light from the politicians who make up the Congress covered mainly by local news outlets.

CONCLUSION

How members of Congress manage the two Congresses dilemma is reflected in their daily tasks on Capitol Hill and in their home states or districts. Election is a prerequisite to congressional service. Incumbent legislators allocate much of their time and energy, and even more of their staff and office resources, to the care and cultivation of voters. Their Hill styles and home styles are adopted with this end in mind.

Yet senators and representatives do not live by reelection alone. Not a few turn their backs on reelection to pursue other careers or interests. For those who remain in office, reelection is not usually viewed as an end in itself, but rather as a lever for pursuing other goals—policy making or career advancement, for example. Fenno challenged one of the representatives whose constituency career he had followed, remarking that "sometimes it must be hard to connect what you do here with what you do in Washington." "Oh no," the lawmaker replied, "I do what I do here so I can do what I want to do there." [112]

SUGGESTED READINGS

Baker, Ross K. *Friend and Foe in the U.S. Senate.* New York: Free Press, 1980.

______. *House and Senate.* 3d ed. New York: Norton, 2001.

Davidson, Roger H. *The Role of the Congressman.* Indianapolis: Bobbs-Merrill, 1969.

Fenno, Richard F., Jr. *Home Style: House Members in Their Districts.* Boston: Little, Brown, 1978.

Fiorina, Morris P. *Congress: Keystone of the Washington Establishment.* 2d ed. New Haven: Yale University Press, 1989.

Hibbing, John R. *Congressional Careers: Contours of Life in the U.S. House of Representatives.* Chapel Hill: University of North Carolina Press, 1991.

Price, David E. *The Congressional Experience: A View from the Hill.* 2d ed. Boulder, Colo.: Westview Press, 2004.

Swers, Michele L. *The Difference Women Make: The Policy Impact of Women in Congress.* Chicago: University of Chicago Press, 2002.

Parties and leaders on Capitol Hill: Above, (far left) Senate Republican leader Bill Frist of Tennessee and (far right) Republican whip Mitch McConnell of Kentucky meet with circuit court nominees (center, left to right) Janice Roberts Brown and Priscilla Owen to show support for them during Senate debate over President George W. Bush's judicial nominations. Left, House Speaker J. Dennis Hastert, R-Ill., leads a House GOP delegation to meet with war veterans. Immediately behind him are (left) Majority Leader Tom DeLay of Texas and (right) Majority Whip Roy Blunt of Missouri. Below, Democratic floor leaders Sen. Harry Reid of Nevada and Rep. Nancy Pelosi of California walk to a Capitol news conference on Bush's judicial nominees.

chapter 6

Leaders and Parties in Congress

Do congressional leaders matter? Reflecting on Newt Gingrich, R-Ga., who at the time was House Speaker and was widely credited with ending forty years of Democratic control of the House in the November 1994 elections, Rep. Sherwood Boehlert, R-N.Y., said: "Gingrich is the one responsible for leading the Republican Party out of the wilderness of the minority . . . to the promised land of the majority. He is singularly responsible for us being where we are now."[1] Four years after that electoral triumph Gingrich was out as Speaker and subsequently resigned as a member of Congress, the victim of personal scandals and his party's poor showing in the 1998 midterm elections.

After Gingrich's presumptive successor, Appropriations chairman Robert Livingston of Louisiana, announced his resignation from the House after admitting to adultery, Republicans turned to J. Dennis Hastert of Illinois, the GOP's chief deputy whip since 1995. A respected and well-liked lawmaker, he so quickly locked up the support of his partisan colleagues that he headed off any potential challengers.[2] On January 6, 1999, the opening day of the 106th Congress, Hastert was elected Speaker. Dubbed the "accidental Speaker" by the press, his GOP colleagues recognized that he was the right person for the job. "We needed somebody who was not nuclear," said Majority Leader Tom DeLay, R-Texas, "that was not controversial, that members trusted."[3]

Hastert soon demonstrated that he was no caretaker Speaker. His talent for unifying his party, devising effective legislative strategies, and forging compromises all helped Republicans hold off strong Democratic election challenges in November 2000, 2002, and 2004 to maintain or expand their House majority. The popular Hastert emerged a stronger and more formidable Speaker after each election. For example, after the GOP won control of the House in 2004 for the fifth straight election, a feat not accomplished since 1922, the *New York Times* ran a front-page story with a headline highlighting what Capitol Hill insiders already knew: "Quietly, but Firmly, Hastert Asserts His Power."[4]

These references to the relationship between leaders and followers parallel the constant interaction between the two Congresses—between the lawmaking institution and the representative assembly. In their inside role, party leaders guide institutional activities and influence policy. Leaders also must find ways of persuading members who represent different constituencies, regions, ideologies, values, and interests to support legislation that addresses national concerns. "The only thing that counts is 218 votes, and nothing else is real," explained a House Democratic leader. "You have to be able [to attract a majority of the House] to pass a bill."[5]

Implicit in this party leader's statement is recognition that mobilizing winning coalitions is not easy. Party leaders encounter what scholars call a "collective action" dilemma.[6] How can leaders mobilize a majority to pass legislation (for the collective or public good) when it is often in the self-interest of many lawmakers to do little or nothing to secure the measure's enactment, even if they favor it, because the bill's advocates will invest whatever time and effort are required to achieve the collective result? Thus, many lawmakers may take a free ride on the efforts of their colleagues and then claim credit and receive benefits from the bill's enactment. Too many free riders and little lawmaking may be the result.

Congressional leaders usually resolve the collective action problem in two main ways: devising sufficient incentives (political, policy, or procedural, for example) to attract majority support and coordinating the work of the bill's champions to win desired objectives. Leadership in legislatures, then, "can be seen as having been instituted to ameliorate the problems of collective action. . . . [P]arty leaders are seen as agents of the members who select them and charge them" with acting on their behalf to achieve a number of goals, including the production of collective goods.[7] This scholarly view of party leadership is sometimes called the principal-agent model. Party leaders (the agents) are selected by the partisan rank-and-file (the principals) to advance policy and electoral goals.

In their outside role, party leaders formulate and publicize issue agendas designed to galvanize the support of partisans and swing voters nationally. They help recruit candidates for Congress and assist in their campaigns. Leaders also must serve as the party's link to the president, the press, the public, and the partisan faithful. In 2004 Speaker Hastert was heavily involved in both House electoral races and the reelection campaign of President George W. Bush. The House and presidential elections were interconnected, he told a reporter. "I see us all in this together," Hastert said. "It is important for us to go and run a good campaign for our own survival and that's good for the president. If the president does well and he gets people excited positively, that helps us. There is a cumulative effect here."[8]

The leaders' inside and outside roles interact constantly. For example, party leaders calculate how their actions on the House or Senate floor can give a boost to their party's candidates in the next election. Today, in a period of relative party parity, ideological polarization, and intense electoral competition, the line between campaigning and governing on the major issues that divide the two parties has all but disappeared. The permanent campaign approach to lawmaking aims to generate public support and momentum to force legislative action on party priorities. "The reality is, to get something done in this town you've got to deal with the policy and the politics," exclaimed former Rep. Rob

Portman, R-Ohio (now U.S. Trade Representative).[9] Congress is a partisan body. Stated differently, legislative organization is partisan organization. The majority party in the House or the Senate controls not only the top leadership posts and each chamber's agenda of activities but also the chairmanships and majorities on committees and subcommittees.

LEADERS OF THE HOUSE

House rules permit a determined majority to achieve its policy objectives. During much of the nineteenth century, the struggle between majority rights and minority rights was paramount until the majoritarian principle became embedded in House procedures by the turn of the twentieth century. Stalling tactics by the minority during the pre– and post–Civil War House often prevented action. Finally, Republican Speaker Thomas "Czar" Reed of Maine broke the minority's capacity to frustrate House decision making. The House adopted new rules (the famous Reed Rules) to facilitate majority rule and action. "No dilatory motion shall be entertained by the Speaker" is an 1890 House rule that remains in effect today.

The Speaker

No other member of the House possesses the visibility and authority of the Speaker of the House. The Constitution states that the House "shall choose their Speaker." Although the Constitution does not require the Speaker to be a House member, all of them have been. Under the Presidential Succession Act of 1947, the Speaker is second in line behind the vice president to succeed to the presidency.

For a time in the mid-1990s House Speaker Gingrich was a virtual rival to the White House in setting the nation's course. In an unprecedented event mirroring what presidents often do, Gingrich made a prime-time, nationally televised address on April 17, 1995, highlighting the accomplishments of Congress and outlining the country's future direction. Not since the early 1800s when Speaker Henry Clay put forward an agenda (titled "The American System") for strengthening the nation's infrastructure had a Speaker so exploited the position's bully pulpit. Under Gingrich, the speakership became a platform for focusing public debate on crucial issues of national governance. Speaker Hastert, by contrast, maintains a lower public profile and shares with other Republicans the national spokesman's role. As Hastert said: "I don't think I have to be [at] the head of every news release or press conference . . . and . . . on every Sunday talk show."[10] Hastert, noted one account, "is not known for the pithy sound bites that modern politics demands."[11]

The office of Speaker combines procedural and political prerogatives with policy and partisan leadership. Speakers preside over the House, rule on points of order, announce the results of votes, refer legislation to the committees, name lawmakers to serve on conference committees and select committees, and maintain order and decorum in the House chamber. In addition to these procedural prerogatives, they exercise important political powers. They set the House's agenda of activities, control the Rules Committee, chair their party's committee assignment panel, bestow or withhold various tangible and intangible rewards, coordinate policy making with Senate counterparts, and, in this age of videopolitics, present party and House positions to the public at large.

Before 1899 it was not uncommon for Speakers to have only a few years of service as representatives. Whig Henry Clay of Kentucky was elected to the speakership on November 4, 1811—his first day in the House. Speakers elected since 1899 have served, on average, more than twenty years before their election to the post. Hastert served a dozen years before becoming Speaker in 1999.

Once in position, Speakers traditionally have been reelected as long as their party controlled the House. Not since 1923 has there been a floor battle over the speakership, because one party has always had a clear majority. Typically, members vote for the speakership along straight party lines, although there have been a few recent cases in which, for example, lawmakers have voted for individuals who were not members of the House (1997) or for a lawmaker who was not their party's official nominee (2005, for instance). As chief parliamentary officer and leader of the majority party (see Figure 6-1), the Speaker enjoys unique powers in scheduling floor business and in recognizing members during sessions. Occasionally, Speakers will relinquish the gavel to join in floor debate. They usually vote only in case of a tie.

The Speaker is also in charge of administrative matters. When Speaker Gingrich took office, he revamped the administrative structure and management of the House. Administrative units and positions were abolished, management was streamlined and modernized, an outside independent audit of the accounting systems was undertaken, and a new chief administrative officer—elected by the House at the start of each Congress—was assigned overall responsibility for running the House's administrative operations in a professional manner.[12] Speaker Hastert retained this administrative structure.

Cannon and Rayburn. During the Republic's first 120 years, Speakers gradually accrued power. By 1910 Speaker Joseph G. Cannon, R-Ill., dominated the House. He assigned members to committees, appointed and removed committee chairmen, regulated the flow of bills to the House floor as chairman of the Rules Committee, referred bills to committee, and controlled floor debate. Taken individually, Cannon's powers were little different from those of his immediate predecessors, but taken together and exercised to their limits they bordered on the dictatorial. The result was a revolt against Cannon. Progressive Republicans combined with discontented minority Democrats to reduce the Speaker's authority.

The House forced Cannon to step down from the Rules Committee in 1910 and required the House to elect its members. The next year, when Democrats took control of the House, the new Speaker (James B. "Champ" Clark of Missouri) was denied the authority to make committee assignments

FIGURE 6-1 **Organization of the House of Representatives, 109th Congress (2005–2007)**

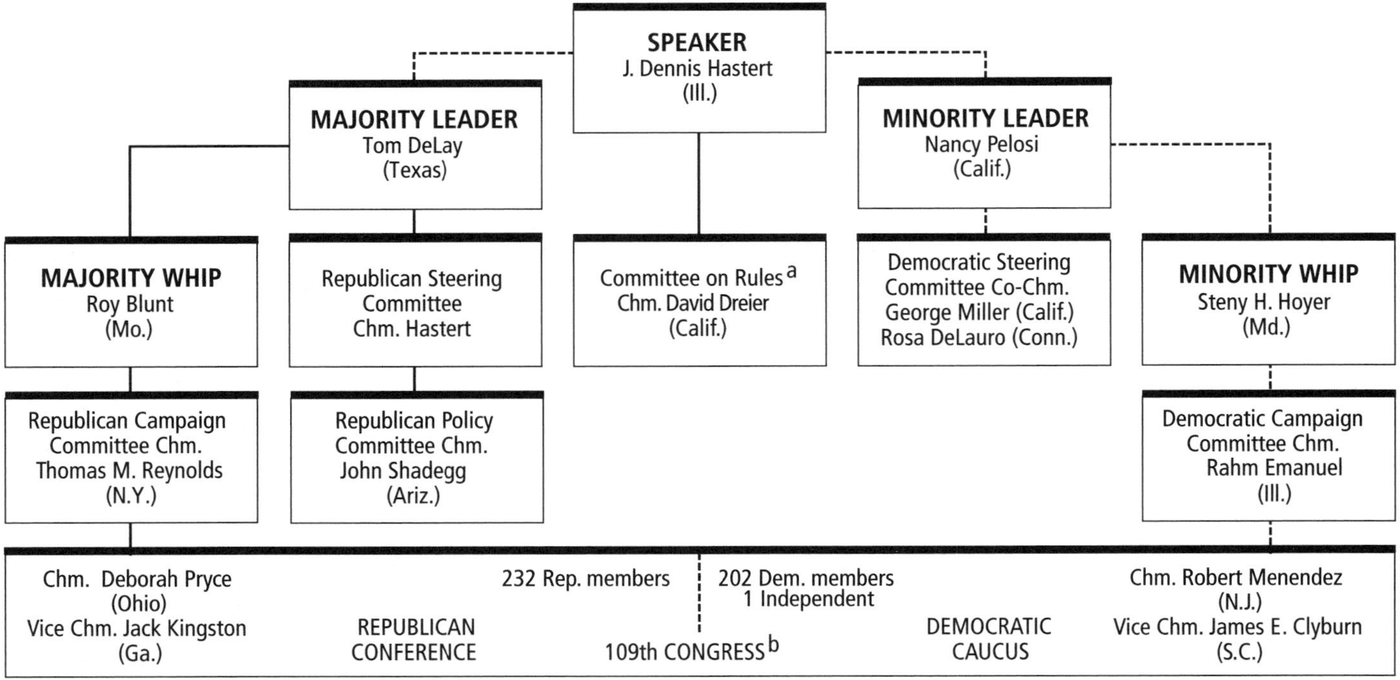

[a] Although not strictly a party panel, the Rules Committee in modern times functions largely as an arm of the majority leadership.

[b] As of February 2005.

(all standing committees were elected by the House) and his power of recognition was curtailed. The speakership then went into long-term eclipse. Power flowed to the majority leader, to the committee chairmen, and for a while to party caucuses.

Speakers after Cannon exhibited various leadership styles that reflected their personalities, the historical context in which they operated, and the partisan divisions and level of conflict within the chamber. Democrat Sam Rayburn of Texas (Speaker, 1940–1947, 1949–1953, 1955–1961) was a formidable leader because of his personal prestige as well as his long political experience and immense parliamentary skills. As he explained, "The old day of pounding on the desk and giving people hell is gone. . . . A man's got to lead by persuasion and kindness and the best reason—that's the only way he can lead people."[13] Rayburn lent coherence to a House in which power was diffused among a relatively small number of powerful committee chairmen who were often called the "dukes" and "barons" of Capitol Hill. However, the rise of committee authority in the decades following the 1910 revolt—triggered in part by a near inviolable seniority system that elevated conservative southern Democrats from safe seats to top committee posts—meant that Rayburn functioned as a broker or mediator, negotiating with and persuading the powerful chairs to report out legislation supported by the Democratic majority.

The relationship between these two centers of institutional power—committee and party—provides a useful analytical framework for evaluating the extent of centralized (party dominance) versus decentralized (committee autonomy) authority in the legislature. The Cannon era was plainly a time of party power. Much of the twentieth century, with the seniority principle exercising primacy in the selection of House and Senate committee chairmen, was a period in which the balance of power tilted toward committee leaders. Today, it is not that committees are unimportant but that party leaders are more important in influencing action on the major issues of the day. Both power centers, meanwhile, can be fettered by majority vote of the chamber's membership.

Revival of the Speakership. The distribution of internal power changed fundamentally after Rayburn. To curb the power of the committee barons, activist and liberal-oriented lawmakers elected during the Vietnam War and the Watergate era combined forces with longtime members disgruntled with the status quo. The majority Democrats used a two-pronged reform approach. The first aimed at infusing accountability into the rigid custom of seniority and dispersing power to subcommittees. For example, the new party rules required that committee chairs be elected by secret ballot of the Democratic Caucus. Committee chairs were also obligated to share power with subcommittee chairs. At the same time the reformers in the late 1960s and 1970s strengthened the hand of the party leadership. The Speaker, for example, gained the right to name all the majority party members of the Rules Committee, including the chair, and House rules were amended to permit the

Speaker to refer measures to more than one committee. By the late 1970s, majority Democrats recognized that dispersing power to more subcommittees jeopardized their ability to accomplish policy and political goals. Accordingly, rank-and-file Democrats encouraged their party leaders to use their new powers to overcome institutional fragmentation and to curb minority Republicans' ability to obstruct action on the floor.

Three Democratic Speakers—Thomas P. "Tip" O'Neill Jr. of Massachusetts (1977–1987), Jim Wright of Texas (1987–1989), and Thomas S. Foley of Washington (1989–1995)—were the beneficiaries of these various changes, which strengthened their persuasive powers and ability to assemble winning coalitions. O'Neill held the speakership for ten consecutive years, the longest uninterrupted service of any Speaker. Using a strategy of inclusion to draw Democratic rank-and-file into the leadership orbit, he expanded the whip structure and encouraged junior Democrats to back partisan priorities by appointing them to leadership task forces.[14] During the first six years of the Reagan presidency, when the Senate was also in Republican hands, O'Neill became the Democratic Party's national spokesman. In the process he transformed the speakership into an office of high national visibility.

O'Neill's successor was Jim Wright, who pushed the prerogatives of the office even further. In domestic and foreign policy, Wright took bold risks. Whereas O'Neill strived for consensus, Wright laid out an agenda and then worked diligently, by himself if necessary, to mobilize support. "The Congress," declared Wright, "should not simply react, passively, to recommendations from the president but should come forward with initiatives of its own."[15] His unyielding personal style and knack for making "minority status more painful," as one House GOP leader put it, embittered Republicans (and even some of his own party).[16]

"If Wright consolidates his power, he will be a very, very formidable man," warned Representative Gingrich. "We have to take him on early to prevent that."[17] Gingrich brought ethics charges against the Speaker, and they were investigated by the Committee on Standards of Official Conduct. That panel eventually charged Wright with violating House rules by accepting gifts from a close business associate and circumventing limits on members' outside income through bulk sales of his 1984 book *Reflections of a Public Man* to lobbyists and interest groups. Wright did not survive these ethical and political challenges and left the House in June 1989. Eight years later—as political payback—many House Democrats tried to force Gingrich from the speakership for ethical violations.

End of an Era: Foley (1989–1995). Next in line to succeed Wright as Speaker was Majority Leader Foley. Elected to the House in November 1964, Foley had risen through the ranks to become Speaker during an era of sharp partisan, political, and personal infighting. The new Speaker had a reputation for being a judicious, low-key, and consensus-oriented leader. His initial objectives as Speaker were to restore civility, integrity, and bipartisan cooperation to the House and to provide policy direction. Although Republicans found Foley easier to deal with than Wright, they soon lamented the Speaker's willingness to use procedural rules to frustrate GOP objectives. When Democrat Bill Clinton was elected president in 1992, Foley's instincts for conciliation became an asset as he worked to foster harmony among House Democrats and good ties with the Clinton White House. However, problems that afflicted the Wright speakership—scandals (revelations in the early 1990s of check bouncing at the House bank by nearly three hundred members) and intraparty divisions—continued under Foley. Republicans targeted Foley for defeat in November 1994 and hammered him for not supporting term limits for lawmakers, a big issue at the time. After a thirty-year congressional career, Speaker Foley lost his reelection bid and Democrats lost the House

Gingrich: A New Style of Speaker (1995–1999). Newt Gingrich was a unique Speaker. His Democratic predecessors, he once said, were "essentially legislative leaders speaking to the press about legislative matters." He went on to say, "I, on the other hand, was essentially a political leader of a grassroots movement seeking to do nothing less than reshape the federal government along with the political culture of the nation." [18] Gingrich, summarized a commentator, was "first a leader of a national movement, then a Republican spokesman and, only third, Speaker of the House." [19]

As his party's unanimous choice for Speaker, Gingrich took the office to new heights. His ten-point party platform titled the Contract with America, which the House acted upon within the promised first hundred days of the 104th Congress, set the agenda for Congress and the nation during that period. Three factors help explain his influence: recognition on the part of most GOP lawmakers in the House that they owed their majority status to him; broad commitment on their part to the GOP's agenda, especially cutting spending and balancing the budget; and the new majority's need to succeed at governance after forty years in the minority.

A centralizing aspect of Gingrich's speakership was his influence over committees. Not only did Gingrich personally select certain Republicans to chair several standing committees, ignoring seniority in the process, but he also required the GOP members of the Appropriations Committee to sign a written pledge that they would heed the Republican leadership's directives for spending reductions. He often bypassed committees entirely by establishing leadership task forces to process legislation. Most significantly, he changed House rules to impose term limits of six years on all committee and subcommittee chairs so no chairperson could accumulate over time the influence to challenge the central party leaders. Party power during this period dominated committee power.

Gingrich's speakership went through four main phases prior to his departure from the House. The first was characterized by the triumphalism of the first hundred days: Everything in the ten-point contract passed the House except term limits for lawmakers. As an aggressive and strong-willed Speaker,

Gingrich for a time reversed the principal-agent leadership model. Instead of acting as the agent of the GOP rank-and-file, he dictated to them a common agenda that was in their best interest to pass. It was a different story in the GOP-controlled Senate, where bipartisan opponents stalled action on many contract items.

In the second phase, Gingrich's confrontational strategy with the White House produced political disaster for Republicans. In a face-off with President Clinton, Republicans were publicly blamed for twice shutting down the government in late 1995 and early 1996. Further, their revolutionary plans for downsizing government by eliminating cabinet departments and reducing spending for education, environment, and health programs were successfully characterized by Democrats as extreme. Gingrich's public popularity plummeted, and the Speaker became a campaign issue in many 1996 congressional races.

The lead-up to the November 1996 campaign ushered in the third phase of Gingrich's speakership. Worried that President Clinton would campaign against a do-nothing Congress, congressional Republicans and the White House cooperated and passed health, minimum wage, and welfare reform legislation. Each side wanted something positive to campaign on. The result was that Clinton won reelection to a second term, and the Republicans—although they lost nine House seats—held majority control of Congress.

A narrower majority was not Gingrich's only problem when the House convened in the 105th Congress (1997–1999). A few weeks earlier, on December 21, 1996, Gingrich admitted that he had provided inaccurate and incomplete information to the House ethics committee regarding his solicitation of tax-deductible contributions, which were used for partisan purposes contrary to federal law. Two weeks after Gingrich's reelection as Speaker, the House voted 395–28 to reprimand him for ethical misconduct and to fine him $300,000. He became the first Speaker formally disciplined by the House for ethical wrongdoing.

Weakened by the ethics charge, Gingrich no longer dominated the House as he once did. In the 105th Congress, the final phase of his leadership, he decided on a modest agenda (keeping the House in session the fewest number of days in two decades) and focused on hot-button issues (late-term or "partial-birth" abortion, education vouchers, tax cuts) designed to energize the GOP electorate for the 1998 midterm elections. Rank-and-file Republicans and his top leadership lieutenants became frustrated with Gingrich's impulsive leadership style. Rep. Peter T. King, R-N.Y., recommended that Gingrich step aside as Speaker because his low popular standing (below 30 percent job approval) made him unable to boost Republican priorities. "As roadkill on the highway of American politics," wrote King, "Newt Gingrich cannot sell the Republican agenda."[20] *Time* magazine's 1995 "Man of the Year" had fallen far. Top GOP leaders and a small band of ideologically hard-line junior conservatives complained that Gingrich compromised too much with the Democrats.

As a result, a coup plot in the summer of 1997 was hatched by the hard-liners with the encouragement of some in the leadership. The plan to depose Gingrich was uncovered and averted, but it exposed the deep frustration with the Speaker within Republican ranks.[21]

On the eve of the November 3, 1998, elections, the Speaker took a high-risk political gamble. Despite polls showing the public was sick of hearing about President Clinton's sexual relationship with White House intern Monica S. Lewinsky, Gingrich gave the order to GOP campaign officials to blanket selected House districts with multimillion-dollar TV ads highlighting the scandal. When the House adjourned two weeks before the election, Clinton-preoccupied Republicans had no coherent agenda to promote. Furthermore, they had allowed the president to win large spending increases in an omnibus appropriations bill nearly four thousand pages in length, which no one had time to read and which was filled with pork. Many Republicans and conservative voters were angry with the Speaker about this end-of-session budget deal.

When the midterm results came in, Republicans were shell-shocked at their poor showing. Scores of Republicans blamed Gingrich for another election in which they lost seats despite the early predictions, including those of the Speaker, that their party would gain seats and coast to victory. The traditional principal-agent model had returned: A leader who fails to fulfill or jeopardizes the needs, expectations, and preferences of his partisan colleagues soon loses their support. Gingrich became an early casualty of the election. He abruptly departed the race for the speakership and resigned from the House. A skillful insurgent leader as a minority lawmaker, Gingrich had difficulty adjusting to the formidable job of governing the House.

The Coach as Speaker: Dennis Hastert (1999–). A former high school wrestling coach and Illinois state legislator, Hastert took office in the aftermath of the contentious House impeachment proceedings against President Clinton. The new Speaker promised to restore some semblance of bipartisanship between Democrats and Republicans and to unite his often fractious and divided party. Known as a patient, congenial, behind-the-scenes workhorse, Hastert excelled at counting votes as then chief deputy whip to Majority Whip DeLay and at crafting compromises and winning coalitions. Employing the coaching metaphor, Hastert explained his leadership role. "A good coach knows when to step back and let others shine in the spotlight," he said. "A coach worth his salt will instill in his team a sense of fair play, camaraderie, respect of the game and for the opposition. Without those, victory is hollow."[22] He added, "They call me speaker, but they probably ought to call me the listener because I just do a lot of it."[23]

A strong conservative, Hastert became Speaker without having served in an elective leadership post—something that had not occurred since the 1919–1925 period, when Frederick Gillett, R-Mass., was Speaker. For much of the 106th Congress, Hastert's speakership was a work in progress as he developed new relationships with the other GOP leaders, the committee chairs, and the factional groups in the House. Among Hastert's new departures was "ceding substantial authority to committee chairmen, delegating his role as party spokesman to a variety of Members, hiring seasoned staff who work well with the other leadership offices and playing a more active role in the day-to-day gruntwork of legislating."[24]

Subsequently, Hastert acted to consolidate power in a trio of leaders—himself (as Speaker), the majority leader, and the majority whip. This leadership team was not reluctant to inform rank-and-file members or committee chairmen that they needed to toe the line on issues of importance to Republicans. For example, during a GOP Conference meeting, Veterans' Affairs chairman Christopher H. Smith, N.J., criticized the Republicans' budget resolution and the White House's spending proposals for veterans. Speaker Hastert "got up and shut him down," said a witness to the tongue-lashing. "That was off the charts. I've never seen anything like that. . . . It was scathing."[25] In a precedent-setting action at the start of the 109th Congress (2005–2007), GOP leaders removed Smith as Veterans chair after serving only four of the six years allowed. He refused to curb his advocacy of more spending for veterans, contrary to the wishes of Republican leaders and the Bush administration. Smith was also removed as a member of the panel. In brief, Hastert's style of leadership was different from Gingrich's because each operated in a different legislative context and with different personal skills. (See Box 6-1 for a summary comparison of some of the differences between Gingrich and Hastert.)

Hastert's leadership role also changed when Republican George W. Bush was inaugurated president on January 20, 2001, and then again in 2005. No longer did Hastert need to develop agendas and strategies to counter the plans of a Democratic president. With his party in control of all three elective branches—only until June 2001 in the 107th Senate because of Vermont senator James M. Jeffords's party switch; unified control returned with the 108th Congress for effectively the first time since the 83d Congress (1953–1955)—Speaker Hastert worked with President Bush to coordinate communications strategies and to move the administration's priorities through Congress. "It's my job to make sure that we can pass bills the president can sign," stated Hastert, "and if we [pass] bills the president can't support, then I'm derelict in my duty."[26] Sometimes this means that Hastert opposes the president, as he did in November 2004 on a bill overhauling the nation's intelligence community. Bush was demanding action on the bill, but many GOP lawmakers opposed the legislation. "The bill had enough support to pass, but Hastert held it back until the White House made concessions to the Republicans who believed it undercut the Pentagon and those who wanted to add new immigration restrictions."[27]

The Speaker's Influence: Style and Context. Congressional analysts suggest a number of ways to study the primary determinants of the Speaker's influence. (See Box 6-2 for a brief review of the principal scholarly theories about congressional leadership.) Analysts generally emphasize context over

BOX 6-1 **A Comparison of the Speakerships of Gingrich and Hastert**

Newt Gingrich, R-Ga. *(Speaker 1995–1999)*	**J. Dennis Hastert, R-Ill.** *(Speaker 1999–)*
▸ A visionary leader who often set aside traditional legislative procedures	▸ A pragmatic leader who emphasized the regular order of lawmaking
▸ Decreased power of committees	▸ Restored committees' prerogatives but exercised leadership control on priority issues
▸ Set aside seniority in naming several committee chairs	▸ Employed interview process in naming committee chairs
▸ Delegated floor management duties to the majority leader	▸ Managed the floor schedule in consultation with other GOP leaders
▸ Increased use of party task forces	▸ Limited use of party task forces
▸ Assumed large public spokesman role	▸ Played relatively small role as public spokesman
▸ Contributed to partisan rancor	▸ Somewhat eased partisan tension in the House
▸ Relished national spotlight	▸ Operated behind-the-scenes
▸ Exercised confrontational style of leadership	▸ Exercised accommodating style of leadership
▸ Bypassed committees on occasion to achieve his party's legislative ends	▸ Relied on committee chairs

personal style as the main factor affecting the Speaker's institutional clout. Personal style refers to the skills, abilities, and qualities of the Speaker, such as intelligence, talent for coalition building, or political acumen. Advocates of the individualist school of leadership stress that personally adroit and forceful Speakers can lead by molding circumstances and opportunities to their own objectives.[28] Here is how one analyst viewed Newt Gingrich's impact on the House: "If Newt Gingrich had been run over by a truck in 1993, it is almost certain that there would not be a Republican majority in the House. Few other congressional politicians have made such a difference in partisan history."[29] Speakers' personal capacities, in short, allow them to exercise that elusive quality called leadership—persuading others to follow their lead even if they disagree with their leaders' views. For example, a committee chairman during the Contract with America period stated why he voted for a Gingrich-advocated policy that he opposed. "At times like these," he said, "many of us subordinate our preferences to the greater good of the team."[30]

Consider the assertive styles of Speakers Wright and Gingrich. Both were willing to dictate to committee chairmen; advance party agendas; take procedural actions, as circumstances warranted, to hamstring the minority party; and challenge the White House. Wright and Gingrich had the advantage of serving with a president of the opposite party, reducing their need to carry out his programs. Their personal talents were augmented by formal and informal procedural changes that allowed them to accomplish more of their objectives than if they lacked these powers. For example, whether a Democrat or a Republican occupies the speakership today, he chairs his party's committee that makes committee assignments (known generally as the committee on committees), a significant resource that the Speaker can employ strategically when appointing colleagues to coveted panels. On expected close floor votes, which the Speaker needs to win, he may remind wavering lawmakers of how they won their preferred committee position. Different personal styles, as in the "nice guy" Speakers who succeeded Wright (Foley) and Gingrich (Hastert) and who retained the same formal powers as their predecessors, can produce a leader less likely to exert intense pressure on colleagues to vote a certain way, to utilize the full range of his parliamentary prerogatives to achieve party objectives, or to advance political and policy positions independent of any consensus within his party caucus or conference.

An important explanation that accounts for such variance among individual Speakers is context.[31] Context refers to the House's external and internal environment, both of which overlap and change over time. External elements include whether the Speaker's party controls the White House, the public's demand for legislation, the complexity of national problems, the popularity of the president, the electoral environment, and the strength of partisan identification within the voting public. As the electoral constituencies of the two parties predominantly select either a liberal Democrat or a conservative Republican, a pattern of the last few decades, the Speaker can set an agenda that enjoys wide support among partisans. Internal elements that condition the Speaker's influence are the configuration of forces within the House, such as the size and cohesiveness of the majority party, the diffusion of power among members, and the autonomy of committees.

A prominent scholarly theory that applies the principal-agent model, called conditional party government, suggests that if rank-and-file partisans share common policy views and confront an opposition party with sharply different substantive perspectives, then these dual conditions favor strong centralized leadership. Rank-and-file partisans empower their party leaders to advance an agenda that nearly all of them support and, conversely, oppose conflicting policies advocated by the other party. As the two leading proponents of the theory state:

> These two considerations—preference homogeneity [or policy agreement within parties] and preference conflict [or policy disagreement

BOX 6-2 Theories of Congressional Leadership

Political scientists have developed different theories to explain why congressional leaders appear to be stronger during some eras than others. The most prominent is called conditional party government.[a] A competing theory—the pivotal voter theory—suggests that the influence of party leaders is marginal with respect to their ability to shift policy outcomes away from what a majority of the chamber prefers toward the policy preferences of the majority party.[b]

Proponents of each theory view party leaders as agents of their principals—their rank-and-file partisans. Members want their party leaders to help them accomplish their fundamental goals: getting reelected, making good policy, and gaining—or maintaining—power in the House or Senate. A correspondence in leader-member views means that party leaders will work to advance the majority preferences of the rank-and-file. After all, party leaders hold their positions at the sufferance of their partisan colleagues, and they usually want to be reelected to those leadership posts.

Conditional Party Government Theory

- The power of congressional leaders hinges on the degree of homogeneity within the majority party concerning policy and on the extent of interparty conflict between Democrats and Republicans.
- With both conditions in play, rank-and-file party members are supportive of changes that strengthen their party leaders, such as the Speaker. Thus, a cohesive majority party can pass legislation without any support from the minority party.
- Conversely, when parties' policy goals are fragmented, partisan lawmakers have little incentive to give their leaders more authority. They may use their power against the political and policy interests of many in the rank-and-file.

Pivotal Voter Theory

- Suggests that policy outcomes on the floor rarely diverge from what is acceptable to the pivotal voter—the member who casts the 218th vote in the House.
- Rarely does everyone in the majority party support a particular policy. Why, then, should majority members change their policy views to back a party position with which they disagree? Instead, they will join with members of the other party to form the winning coalition. According to this theory, these pivotal voters determine chamber outcomes.
- If each party is internally united in its policy preferences, as the conditional party government theory states, there will be no difference between what the majority party wants and what the chamber membership will agree to.
- Simply observing party leaders engaged in frenetic activity—often seeking pivotal votes—does not mean they can skew legislative outcomes beyond what is acceptable to a majority of the entire membership.

---

[a] See, for example, John H. Aldrich and David W. Rohde, "The Transition to Republican Rule in the House: Implications for Theories of Congressional Politics," *Political Science Quarterly* 112, no. 4, (Winter 1997–1998): 541–567.

[b] See Keith Krehbiel, *Pivotal Politics: A Theory of U.S. Lawmaking* (Chicago: University of Chicago Press, 1998).

> between parties]—together form the "condition" in the theory of conditional party government. As they increase, the theory predicts that party members will be progressively more willing to create strong powers for leaders and to support the exercise of those powers in specific instances. But when diversity grows within parties, or the differences between parties are reduced, members will be reluctant to grant greater powers to leaders. This is the central prediction of [conditional party government].[32]

A dynamic interaction exists between context and style that is often hard to untangle. Both factors shape to varying degrees the limits and possibilities of leadership.

Floor Leaders

The Speaker's principal deputy—the majority leader—is the party's floor leader. As Majority Leader DeLay said of his relationship with Speaker Hastert: "I see it that Hastert is the chairman of the board and I am the chief executive officer."[33] Elected every two years by secret ballot of the party caucus, the floor leader is not to be confused with a floor manager. The floor managers, usually two for each bill, are frequently the chairman and ranking minority member of the committee that reported the bill. They try to steer the bill to a final decision.

The House majority leader is usually an experienced legislator. When Tom DeLay took the post at the start of the 108th Congress (2003–2005), he had served in the House for eighteen consecutive years. He was elected majority whip when Republicans took control of the House following the November 1994 elections. As majority whip, DeLay established himself as perhaps the most effective party whip in the House's history and the chamber's most influential Republican, except for Gingrich. When Gingrich departed the House, DeLay mobilized his formidable whip organization to line up speakership support first for Livingston and then for Hastert—DeLay's chief deputy whip. He later secured top leadership posts for two proteges: Roy Blunt of Missouri as majority whip and Deborah Pryce of Ohio as chair of the GOP Conference, the fourth-ranking party position and the highest leadership position ever occupied by a woman in the majority party. As one conservative analyst exclaimed, "Everyone now in leadership basically was put there by [DeLay]."[34]

Nicknamed "The Hammer" by colleagues for his combative style, DeLay is an accomplished vote counter and enforcer, an aggressive fund-raiser, a skillful coordinator of the party's connections on K Street (a street in the District of Columbia where numerous lobbying firms have their offices), and a shrewd campaign and legislative strategist. One of his most significant but controversial political achievements was to orchestrate a re-redistricting of House seats in Texas after Republicans—with DeLay's help—captured control of the state legislature in the November 2002 elections. Five targeted Democratic incumbents were forced to run in new redrawn GOP-leaning districts in the November 2004 elections. The result was that four of the five lost their seats, expanding the GOP's majority in the House.

DeLay's aggressive actions in this case and several others prompted the bipartisan House ethics committee to chastise him on three issues in 2004 for unbecoming conduct. DeLay accepted the panel's judgments but contended that "Democrats have hurled relentless personal attacks at me, hoping to tie my hands and smear my name. All have fallen short, not because of insufficient venom, but because of insufficient merit."[35] Many Republicans closed ranks behind DeLay—"Redistricting in Texas is something [GOP] members feel very grateful about," said a GOP lawmaker—but they also wondered whether or how DeLay's ethical troubles might weaken his leadership role within and outside the House.[36]

DeLay encountered further problems when allegations surfaced in spring 2005 that lobbyists—such as Jack Abramoff, a friend of DeLay's who was under federal investigation—paid for overseas trips by the GOP leader contrary to House rules. Because the congressional travel rules are not entirely clear, other lawmakers became concerned that they, too, may have been in technical violation of them. As a result, DeLay asked the ethics committee "to look at this problem for the institution, and hopefully they will make recommendations that will clear up this situation."[37] Speaker Hastert also requested the ethics committee to clarify and strengthen regulations regarding privately sponsored trips.[38] Hastert's request likely was aimed at heading off an ethics war on Capitol Hill as "opposition researchers for both parties plunge into member [travel] disclosure forms in search of lapses."[39]

By modern custom, neither the Speaker nor the Democratic or Republican floor leader chairs committees. Sometimes exceptions are made. During the 107th Congress (2001–2003), Majority Leader Dick Armey, R-Texas, chaired the Select Committee on Homeland Security, which reported the bill signed into law by President Bush creating the Department of Homeland Security. The majority and minority leaders, as well as the Speaker, may serve on formal or informal task forces or panels. For example, the Speaker and minority leader are ex officio members of the Permanent Select Intelligence Committee.

House and party rules are largely silent about the majority leader's duties. By tradition, the primary duties are to be principal floor defender, negotiator, strategist, and spokesperson for the party. "The role of the majority leader puts you in a spokesman role, but I won't be a show horse," declared Majority Leader DeLay.[40] DeLay also has assumed the roles of coordinating the work of the committee chairmen and enforcing party discipline. The majority leader helps to plan the daily, weekly, and annual legislative agendas; consults with members to gauge sentiment on legislation; coordinates chamber action with the majority party floor manager and other party leaders; confers with the president about administrative proposals, particularly when the president is of the same party;

urges colleagues to support or defeat measures; and, in general, works to advance the purposes and programs of the majority party. As one majority leader said: "The Majority Leader has prime responsibility for the day-to-day working of the House, the schedule, working with the committees to keep an eye out for what bills are coming, getting them scheduled, getting the work of the House done, making the place function correctly." He added: "[Y]ou are also compelled to try to articulate to the outside world what [your party stands] for, what [your party is] fighting for, what [your party is] doing."[41]

The minority leader is the floor leader of the loyal opposition. Like the Speaker, these party leaders bring different styles to their roles. In general, the minority leader promotes unity among party colleagues, monitors the progress of bills through committees and subcommittees, and forges coalitions with like-minded members of the opposition party. Bertrand Snell, R-N.Y., minority leader from 1931 to 1939, thus described the duties:

> He is spokesman for his party and enunciates its policies. He is required to be alert and vigilant in defense of the minority's rights. It is his function and duty to criticize constructively the policies and program of the majority, and to this end employ parliamentary tactics and give close attention to all proposed legislation.[42]

Perhaps the most important task of the minority leader is to work to win back majority control of the House. For example, Minority Leader Richard A. Gephardt, D-Mo. (1995–2003), campaigned for scores of partisan colleagues, raised millions of dollars for Democrats, persuaded senior Democrats not to retire but to run again, stymied GOP initiatives in the House, and worked to inspire his partisan troops. He even "appeared before [the Democratic] caucus in the war paint and breastplate of the Scottish freedom fighter William Wallace, highlighted in the movie 'Braveheart.' "[43] His efforts fell short. Thus, after the November 2002 elections, when Democrats lost seats, Gephardt chose not to seek reelection as minority leader and instead began to focus on running for president.

In his place, Democrats promoted their minority whip, Nancy Pelosi of California, to be their party leader.[44] An eight-term veteran of the House, her election made congressional history. She became the highest-ranking female in either the House or Senate ever to lead a political party. An exceptional fundraiser, tireless campaigner, shrewd party strategist, and telegenic personality, Pelosi is well known as a San Francisco liberal. Some analysts suggested that her selection would allow Republicans to cast her in a negative light as a poster child for liberal orthodoxy (gun control, for example) among swing voters. She responded: "I don't think [my Democratic colleagues] chose me as an outspoken San Francisco liberal. I think they chose me as a person who can lead the caucus to victory, as a person who can build coalitions among various segments of our caucus and as a person who represents various points of view within the caucus."[45]

Pelosi, to be sure, reflects mainstream Democratic views. As the conditional party model suggests, a conservative Nancy Pelosi could no more be elected party leader by the liberal-oriented Democratic Caucus than a liberal Republican could be chosen Speaker by the conservative-dominated GOP Conference. Her victory underscores that colleagues believe she can accomplish the principal functions of any minority leader: party spokesperson, fund-raiser, coalition builder, and deviser of a party agenda to catapult Democrats into the majority. Although her hopes of winning back the House in November 2004 did not materialize, her Democratic colleagues reelected her without opposition and expressed confidence in her leadership performance. Some Democratic members and aides suggest that to remain as party leader Pelosi "will have to prove her mettle by continuing to keep the Caucus in line on votes, showing she can help orchestrate an electoral success by gaining seats in 2006, and proving her influence reaches beyond her progressive allies by reaching out to Members representing more conservative districts."[46]

The Whips

Another top elective party post is the whip. As the term implies, the duties of a whip are to encourage party discipline, count votes, and, in general, mobilize winning coalitions on behalf of partisan priorities. These objectives are accomplished primarily through persuasion and hard work and with the assistance of an efficient whip organization.

In recent years both parties have expanded their whip systems to include a variety of deputy, regional, or assistant whips who meet regularly to discuss issues and strategy. Naming more members as whips involves them in leadership decision making and gives them additional incentives to back their top leaders. With about a sixty-person GOP whip organization in the 109th Congress, headed by Majority Whip Blunt, it is feasible "to reach everybody in the [Republican] conference and deliver their votes when it counts."[47] Having more whips also ensures leadership representation for important party groups and broadens the party's appeal to outside constituencies.

For example, Blunt named Eric Cantor of Virginia as his chief deputy whip—a once obscure position that has become a stepping-stone to higher party office. Cantor was the only Jewish Republican in the 108th House, and he brought both geographical balance and credibility in reaching out to a constituency that generally votes against Republicans. "We have a great opportunity to reach out to Jewish voters, and Eric's been doing that already," remarked Blunt.[48] The majority whip also names the assistant whips.

Majority Whip Blunt and his chief deputy whip meet weekly with their deputy and assistant whips to count votes, share intelligence, and ensure that everything is being done to marshal support for GOP proposals. Blunt's main mission is to "grow the vote," working with lobbyists, trade associations, the White House, and others to plan strategy on how best to reinforce the support of colleagues on key votes and to persuade reluctant lawmakers to vote for legislation they may not support. As Blunt explained his job:

> What the whip needs to understand is what members want to accomplish while they're here, what things about their district define the way they do their job here, what things about their philosophy define the way they do their job here. The whip should know the members better than anybody else in the leadership and know the whole [GOP] conference better than anybody else in the building.[49]

To win colleagues' votes, Blunt has mobilized the support of business and trade lobbyists "to help negotiate deals with individual House members to produce majorities on important issues."[50]

Minority Whip Steny H. Hoyer of Maryland—who had failed twice in his quest to be party whip, including a 2001 loss to Nancy Pelosi—heads a large whip organization composed of about one-third of the Democratic members of the House. They assist Hoyer in vote counting, preparing alternatives to GOP programs, monitoring the interests and needs of party members, tracking the views of informal party groups, and devising party strategy. A centrist member skilled in consensus building, Hoyer assists Minority Leader Pelosi in developing a Democratic message that resonates with the party's base supporters and swing voters. He asserts, too, that Democrats need to be more aggressive in challenging the agenda of the Bush White House.

Hoyer understands that Democratic victories are hard to achieve in a House noted for the sharp ideological divide between the two parties. "In many instances, as the minority whip, it's how much you lose by" that measures success, he said. "But there are opportunities to prevail. There are opportunities to reach across the aisle" and attract votes for Democratic issues.[51]

Each party's whip prepares weekly whip notices advising members of the upcoming floor agenda. Because scheduling changes can occur frequently, Blunt issues "The Whipping Post," a one-page daily bulletin. It identifies the time when the House is to convene and when the last vote is expected; it spells out what action is to take place that day on the floor, in the Senate, and in selective committees; and it forecasts the next day's schedule of floor business.

LEADERS OF THE SENATE

Today's Senate, more than the House, is an institution that tolerates and even promotes individualism. Candidate-centered elections, the proliferation of policy- and ideologically oriented interest groups, the large role of money in campaigns, and the huge influence of the press and media in political life are among the factors that have led to today's individualistic Senate. Senators cherish their independence, which exacerbates the challenges faced by those elected to lead them. Unlike House leaders, Senate leaders lack the buttress of rules designed to expedite business and so must rely heavily on personal skills and negotiation with their colleagues.

Presiding Officers

The House majority's highest elected leader, the Speaker, presides over the House. By contrast, the Senate majority leader, the majority party's highest leader, almost never presides in the Senate chamber.

The Senate has three kinds of presiding officers. First, the constitutional president of the Senate is the vice president of the United States (see Figure 6-2). Except for ceremonial occasions, the vice president seldom presides over Senate sessions, and he can vote only to break—not make—a tie. When votes on major issues are expected to be close, party leaders make sure that the vice president is presiding so that he can break tie votes. Vice presidents experienced in the ways of Congress, such as former senators Al Gore (Bill Clinton), Dan Quayle (George Bush), and Walter F. Mondale (Jimmy Carter), can help bridge the gap between Capitol Hill and the White House.

Vice President Dick Cheney's congressional role looms especially large for President George W. Bush's administration. A former House Republican whip, chief of staff to President Gerald R. Ford, and defense secretary, Cheney is widely respected among lawmakers. He meets regularly with House and Senate Republicans and exercises significant influence in shaping legislation and developing floor strategy to move Bush's priorities through Congress. The real possibility of tie votes in the Senate underscores Cheney's position as the "101st senator" and means close coordination between Senate Republicans and the GOP-controlled executive branch. In an unprecedented action, Speaker Hastert provided Cheney with office space near the House chamber—the first time a vice president "has ever had space on both sides of the Capitol."[52] Another sign of Cheney's elevated Capitol Hill role is his establishment of a legislative liaison team focused on the House and Senate that is separate from the White House's congressional affairs office.[53] Both liaison operations coordinate and consult with each other. Cheney is also kept well informed by the numerous policy experts on his staff.

Second, the Constitution provides for a president pro tempore to preside in the vice president's absence. In modern practice this constitutional officer is the majority party senator with the longest continuous service. Sen. Ted Stevens of Alaska, for example, became president pro tempore of the Republican-controlled 109th Senate. By passing a simple resolution, the Senate sometimes appoints a deputy president pro tempore. This majority party official presides over the Senate in the absence of the vice president and president pro tempore.

Third, a dozen or so senators of the majority party, typically junior members, serve approximately one-hour stints each day as the presiding officer. The opportunity to preside helps newcomers become familiar with Senate rules and procedures.

FIGURE 6-2 **Organization of the Senate, 109th Congress (2005–2007)**

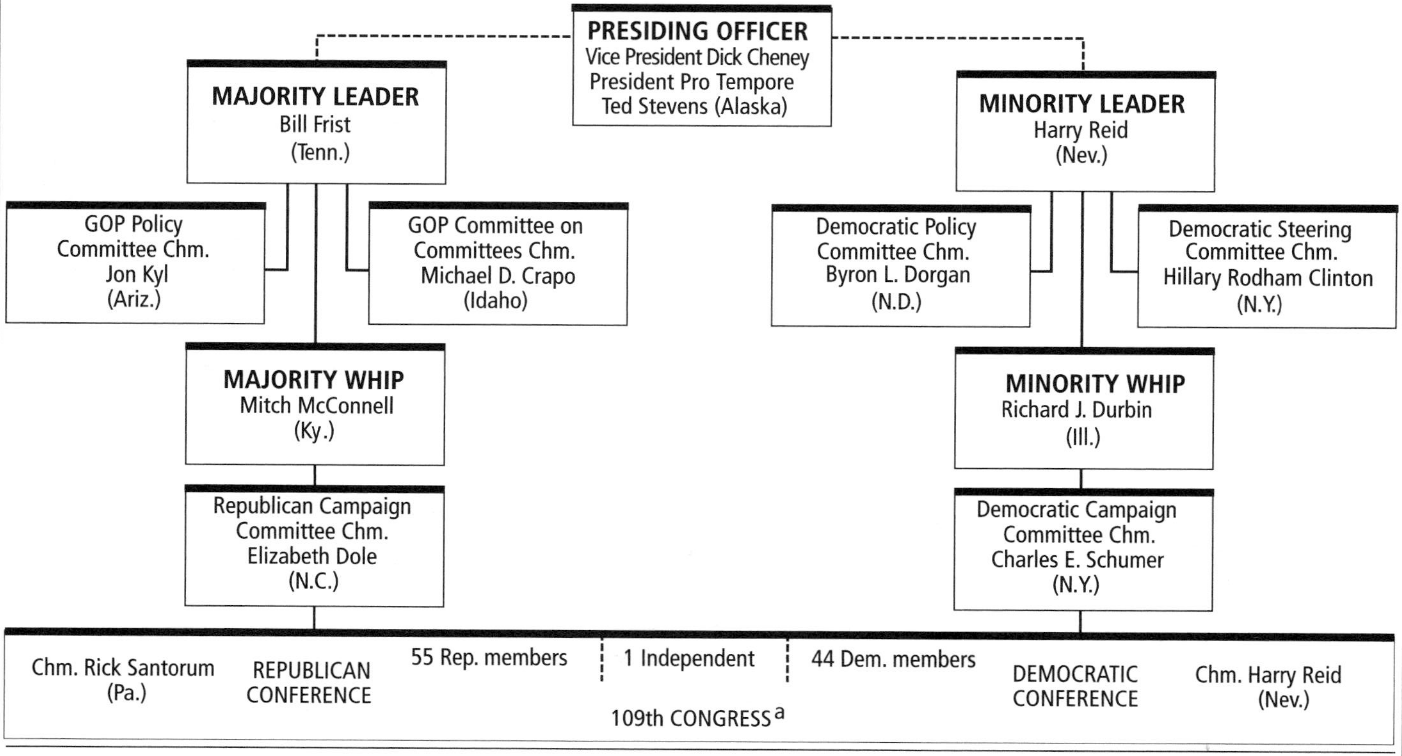

[a] As of February 2005.

Floor Leaders

The majority leader is the head of the majority party in the Senate, its leader on the floor, and the leader of the Senate. Similarly, the minority leader heads the Senate's minority party. (Nowadays, minority leaders prefer to be called "Republican leader" or "Democratic leader," as the case may be.) The majority and minority leaders are elected biennially by secret ballot of their party colleagues. Neither position is mentioned in the Constitution, and each is a relatively recent creation that dates from the early 1900s.

The Emergence of the Floor Leader. Historically, the Senate has always had leaders, but no single senator exercised central management of the legislative process in the fashion of today's floor leader. During the Senate's first century or so—especially in the 1790s and early 1800s, when there was no system of permanent standing committees or organized senatorial parties—leadership flowed from the personal talents and abilities of individual legislators. The small size of the early Senate and its tradition of viewing members as ambassadors from sovereign states promoted an informal and personal style of leadership.

Throughout the nineteenth century scores of prominent senators were called "leaders" by scholars and other observers. Some were sectional or factional leaders; others headed important committees (by the mid- to late 1840s committees and their chairmen had become centers of power); and still others (such as Henry Clay, John C. Calhoun, and Daniel Webster) exercised wide influence because of their special political, oratorical, or intellectual gifts. Even as late as 1885, however, Woodrow Wilson could write, "No one is *the Senator*. . . . No one exercises the special trust of acknowledged leadership." [54]

By the turn of the twentieth century the political landscape had changed. Party structures and leaders emerged as clearly identifiable forces in organizing and managing the Senate's proceedings. This important development occurred, according to a historian of the Senate, because of the influx of a "new breed" of senator who valued party unity and "the machinery of [party] organization," especially the party caucus.[55] Soon those senators who chaired their respective party caucuses acquired levers of authority over senatorial affairs. They chaired important party panels, shaped the Senate's agenda of business, and mobilized party majorities behind important issues. From the caucus chairmanship, scholars agree, the position of majority leader had informally emerged by 1913.[56]

Not until Lyndon B. Johnson (LBJ) became majority leader in 1955 was the post transformed into one of immense authority and prestige.[57] Considered by many analysts to be the most influential majority leader ever, the Texas Democrat had an extensive network of trusted aides and colleagues who gave him better information about more issues than any other senator. Opposition party control of the White House gave the aggressive Johnson the luxury of choosing which policies to support and which strategies to employ to get them enacted. And his pragmatic outlook, domineering style, and arm-twisting abilities made him the premier vote gatherer in the Senate. The majority leader's awesome display of face-to-face persuasion was called the Johnson Treatment.

> The Treatment could last ten minutes or four hours. It came, enveloping its target, at the LBJ Ranch swimming pool, in one of LBJ's offices, in the Senate cloakroom, on the floor of the Senate itself. . . . Its tone could be supplication, accusation, cajolery, exuberance, scorn, tears, complaint, the hint of threat. It was all of these together. It ran the gamut of human emotions. Its velocity was breathtaking, and it was all in one direction. Interjections from the target were rare. Johnson anticipated them before they could be spoken. He moved in close, his face a scant millimeter from his target, his eyes widening and narrowing, and his eyebrows rising and falling. From his pockets poured clippings, memos, statistics. Mimicry, humor, and the genius of analogy made The Treatment an almost hypnotic experience and rendered the target stunned and helpless.[58]

Buttressing Johnson was an inner club, a bipartisan group of senior senators, mainly southern Democrats such as Richard B. Russell of Georgia, who was their leader. (The Russell Senate Office Building on Capitol Hill is named after the Georgia senator, a lawmaker of immense influence who endorsed Johnson as Democratic leader.) The club, observers said, wielded the real power in the Senate through its control of chairmanships and committee assignments.[59] Furthermore, unwritten rules of behavior (for example, junior members should be seen and not heard) encouraged new senators to defer to the establishment.

Every successor to Johnson as majority leader encounters a much different Senate from the one led by Johnson. Gone was the seniority-ruled, club-like, relatively closed Senate of old, ended largely by three key developments: (1) the influx of independent-minded and activist senators who wanted and expected to be major policy participants; (2) internal senatorial changes that promoted egalitarianism, such as the provision of staff resources to all members; and (3) external developments in the broader political environment (the twenty-four-hour news cycle, for instance).

Together, these developments led to an individualistic Senate where leaders are expected to serve members' personal needs and advance their individual agendas. As former majority leader Robert C. Byrd, D-W.Va. (1977–1981; 1987–1989) once remarked about the egalitarian, individualistic, assertive, independent, and C-SPAN-covered Senate, "Circumstances don't permit the Lyndon Johnson style. What I am saying is that times and things have changed. Younger Senators come into the Senate. They are more independent. The 'establishment' is a bad word. Each wants to do his 'own thing.' "[60] Unlike the demanding and aggressive Johnson, Byrd as majority leader referred to himself as "slave" to the needs of his senatorial colleagues.

Limits on Today's Leadership: Individualism and Partisanship. If individualism characterizes the post–Johnson Senate where activist members, under the Senate's permissive rules, can engage in extended debate, offer scores of amendments, and participate in any policy domain, another development added to the leader's difficulties in managing and processing the Senate's business: escalating partisanship. Why the uptick in partisanship? Because the conditional party government model discussed in the context of the House also marks the Senate. The two Senate parties have become, wrote journalist David S. Broder, "more cohesive internally and further apart from each other philosophically."[61] Or as Sen. Orrin G. Hatch, R-Utah, phrased it: "Today, most Democrats are far left; most Republicans are to the right; and there are very few in between."[62] The two Congresses theme is also in play as Democratic senators initiate and support policies backed by their core national constituencies (environmentalists, single women, gays, minorities, and union members, for instance) and Republican lawmakers do the same for their constituency base (the religious right, business owners, white males, rural Americans, gun owners, and pro-life advocates, for example).

Good indicators of heightened partisanship are the large number of party-line votes (a majority of Democrats facing off against a majority of Republicans) and the increase in party cohesion on those votes. For example, the percentage of party-line votes went from 39 percent in the 1970s to 58 percent in the 1990s. Even more striking is the growth in cohesion—call it discipline or philosophical agreement—within both party caucuses. In the 1970s, on partisan roll calls, the average member of Congress backed the party position 65 percent of the time. In the 1980s, the average degree of partisan loyalty rose to 73 percent; and in the 1990s to 81 percent. In 2001 and 2002, it has been 87 percent.[63] Two years later Republicans voted to support the party position on average 90 percent of the time and Democrats [with Senators John Kerry and John Edwards missing most roll-call votes because they were campaigning for the Democratic presidential nomination and then, as running mates, for the White House] lined up behind the party position 83 percent of the time.[64] Other factors, too, contributed to more partisanship in the Senate, such as a decline in the number of centrists who acted as bridge-builders between the two parties.

What all this means for the majority leader is extraordinary difficulty in achieving consensus to enact legislation and approve nominations. Any senator has awesome parliamentary powers to stymie action, which puts a premium on the leader's skill in deal making, negotiating, and compromising. Absent formidable leadership tools to exert tight control over chamber proceedings, leaders rely heavily on patience, perseverance, personal ties, and, on occasion, procedural hardball to move legislation. Yet if one or more senators decide to filibuster (extended debate) a matter, the leader needs sixty votes to invoke a procedure called cloture (closure of debate) if he is to provide the Senate with an opportunity to vote on the measure or matter. As former majority leader Trent Lott, R-Miss. (1996–2002), stated:

> It's a tough job [being majority leader], and it has gotten tougher and tougher. Part of it is that now you don't need 50 votes—you've got to have 60 votes. The filibuster and cloture used to be used occasionally for big issues. [In more recent years], it has become an instrument used on almost every bill. You can have 51 votes, you can have 55 votes, but if you don't get 60 votes, [the bill] can die. And it is very hard to dredge up 60 votes.[65]

Dredging up sixty votes is especially taxing given the close partisan divide within the Senate and in the country at large. With intense electoral competition the order of the day, each party carefully assesses how legislative actions—or inactions—may affect the next election and majority control of the chamber. One party, for instance, may block action on a bill to prevent the other from claiming a legislative victory. The tenuousness of party control in the 107th Congress (2001–2003) produced a number of unexpected developments, several of which affected the 108th Congress.

When the 107th Senate convened on January 3, 2001, it was equally divided between Democrats and Republicans. For its first seventeen days, Democrat Tom Daschle of South Dakota was the majority leader. With Vice President Al Gore, as president of the Senate, still presiding and able to break tie votes until Republican Dick Cheney took the oath of office on January 20—the constitutional date set for the inauguration of the president and vice president—Daschle was in charge of running the Senate.

With Cheney in office, Republican Lott became the majority leader. He and Daschle then negotiated a historic 50–50 power-sharing agreement. Among other things, the agreement provided for an equal number of Democrats and Republicans on all Senate committees; an equal division of office space and staff; and a commitment by the two leaders to schedule measures of prime importance to each party.[66]

On May 24, 2001, moderate senator James Jeffords of Vermont announced that he was changing his party affiliation from Republican to Independent and caucusing with the Democrats for organizational purposes. Jeffords was unhappy with the conservative direction of GOP policy. Officially, Democrats became the majority party on June 5, with Daschle back as majority leader and Lott as minority leader. The shift in party control ended the power-sharing agreement, and another arrangement was negotiated between the two party leaders. Consented to on June 29, it stated, for example, that Democrats would have a one-seat majority on all Senate committees except Ethics, which is always divided equally between the parties. Majority Leader Daschle said of the Jeffords switch: "We have just witnessed something that has never happened before in all of Senate history—the change of power during a session of

Congress."[67] An angry Lott blamed Jeffords for staging a "coup of one" to give Democrats control of the Senate.[68]

Republicans returned to power following the November 2002 elections. On November 13, 2002, Trent Lott was unanimously reelected by his GOP colleagues to be majority leader of the 108th Senate, which would be composed of fifty-one Republicans, forty-eight Democrats, and Independent Jeffords. Three weeks later, on December 5, Lott made racially charged comments at retiring GOP South Carolina senator Strom Thurmond's one hundredth birthday party. Lott praised Thurmond's 1948 run for the presidency on a segregationist Dixiecrat platform. A political firestorm developed as Lott's remarks were denounced by many in his party, including President Bush (who, many believe, quietly orchestrated Lott's eventual ouster). In a case of an agent (Lott) damaging the political expectations and legislative goals of the principals (rank-and-file Republicans), momentum built for Lott to step down as party leader even though he apologized five times for his comments. Lott had become a liability to his party. On December 20, Lott announced his resignation as majority leader. (To ease his fall from power, Republicans elected Lott to chair the Committee on Rules and Administration.)

Three days after Lott's resignation, Senate Republicans elected, by acclamation, Tennessee senator Bill Frist as the new majority leader. In another history-making event, Frist became the first majority leader to be elected via a telephone conference call. GOP senators were scattered across the country and unable to convene quickly in Washington. The Senate's only physician at the time (a practicing heart surgeon), Frist enjoyed close relations with the White House and received help from President Bush to succeed Lott. As chair of the GOP senatorial campaign committee, Frist worked closely with White House political strategist Karl Rove to devise the electoral game plan that led to the Republican senatorial victory in November 2002.

Majority Leader Frist's job in leading a narrowly divided Senate was not easy. He was an untested party leader with limited procedural and senatorial experience, first winning election in 1994 and promising to serve only two terms in the Senate. Frist noted: "The frustration here of needing 60 votes" to get action on almost anything that becomes controversial "requires collaboration, reaching out, negotiation."[69] A low-key, inclusive leader who works well with committee chairs and colleagues, Frist had his share of successes and failures as "leader-manager," as he describes himself, of an acrimonious and often unruly 108th Senate.[70]

Much to Frist's satisfaction, Republicans in the November 2004 elections picked up four additional Senate seats, including the one held by Democratic leader Tom Daschle. In a rare event and indicative of the sharper partisanship enveloping the Senate, Frist went to South Dakota to personally campaign against Daschle as an "obstructionist." Although fifty-five Republicans in the 109th Senate is not sixty, Frist faced a somewhat easier task forging consensus on various measures and matters, in part because the seven newly elected

Republicans are more conservative than the lawmakers they replaced. Still, Frist confronted formidable goals and hurdles in directing the Senate during his final two years. He faced a feisty Democratic minority armed with ample parliamentary means to frustrate action and a diverse political constituency he wants to serve: Senate Republicans, the Bush White House, and outside party activists who could influence his opportunity for a 2008 run for the White House. Frist's frustration in trying to win approval of several of President Bush's controversial circuit court judicial nominees, which were blocked by Democratic-led filibusters, prompted him to consider changing the Senate's tradition of extended debate by an unusual parliamentary maneuver dubbed the "nuclear option" (see Chapters 8 and 12). The nuclear option would change Senate practice by permitting fifty-one senators, instead of sixty, to end filibusters on judicial nominations.

Minority Leader. The Senate minority leader consults continually with the majority leader, because the Senate usually operates by consensus. "We work well together," said Minority Leader Harry Reid, D-Nev., of his relationship with Frist.[71] To get things done typically requires cooperation across party lines. If a member of the president's party, the minority leader has the traditional duties of trying to carry out the administration's program and answering partisan criticisms of the president. If a member of the opposite party, the minority leader has to calculate when to cooperate and when to confront the president.

As minority leader, Reid, who was the unanimous choice of his party colleagues to replace Daschle, meets regularly with Senate Democrats and with his House counterpart to develop and communicate a party agenda (assignments made harder without the bully pulpit of the White House), coordinate strategy, craft policy alternatives, devise tactics to block or modify Republican initiatives, and promote his party's political interests. Senator Reid, for example, built on efforts by Daschle to develop a formal and ongoing relationship with Democratic lobbyists as a way to spread the party message more broadly and to enlist their assistance in moving the party's legislative goals.[72] The minority leader is always searching for ways to win back control of the Senate.

Party Whips. The Senate's whip system carries out functions that are similar to those of the House's system, such as counting noses before crucial votes, monitoring floor activity, and fostering party consensus. When Mitch McConnell, R-Ky., became majority whip at the start of the 108th Congress, he brought energy, organization, and coordination to the GOP's whip system of deputy and regional whips. A seasoned parliamentary tactician who for years almost single-handedly blocked Senate action on campaign finance reform, McConnell's focus is on day-to-day floor operations. "I'll be on the floor a lot," he said, "trying to make the trains run on time, which is always difficult in the Senate, as well as handling the traditional role of the whip, which is trying to win votes. And that means not only Republicans, but Democrats as well." [73] If Republicans hold onto the Senate following the November 2006 elections, McConnell is a likely successor to Frist as majority leader.

Richard J. Durbin of Illinois is the Democrats' second in command. He heads a whip structure that includes a chief deputy whip and four regionally appointed deputy minority whips. A skilled debater and public spokesperson, Durbin will be one of several key Democrats who will deal with the press and media. Another part of Durbin's job will be to work "with ranking members and chairmen to sort through dozens of amendments offered to pending legislation."[74]

SELECTION OF LEADERS

Before the beginning of each new Congress, senators and representatives elect their top leaders by secret ballot in their party caucuses. Although the whole House votes for the Speaker, the election is pro forma. With straight party voting the modern unspoken rule on this and other organizational matters, the majority party has always elected the Speaker.

Candidates for party leadership positions usually wage elaborate campaigns to win support from their partisan colleagues. Occasionally, last-minute entrants successfully bid for leadership positions. But whether short or long, campaigns for party leadership positions are intense. Members understand that a party leadership post can be a "career launching pad . . . either within the [Congress] or outside it."[75]

The two parties treat their hierarchies differently in the House: the Democrats as something like a ladder and the Republicans as a slippery slope. Democrats have a history of elevating their next-in-line officer—from whip to majority leader to Speaker—as vacancies occur. Republicans have a history of pushing people off the leadership track because of turmoil in their ranks. For example, in 1959 Charles A. Halleck of Illinois ousted Joseph W. Martin Jr. of Massachusetts as the GOP leader; in 1965 Gerald R. Ford of Michigan turned the tables on Halleck; in 1980 John J. Rhodes of Arizona was persuaded by his colleagues to step down as party leader; and in 1994 Robert H. Michel of Illinois retired in the face of Gingrich's stated intention to challenge him.

Seniority in Congress is only one of many criteria that influence the election of party leaders. Other considerations are ideological or geographical balance within the leadership; parliamentary expertise; competency in organizational matters; skill in forging winning coalitions; fund-raising prowess; communication skills; sensitivity to the mood of the membership; and personal attributes, such as intelligence, fairness, persuasiveness, political shrewdness, and media savvy.

Serving as a party leader in the House is typically a full-time position, although top party leaders sometimes serve ex officio or in some other capacity on committees. By contrast, every party leader in the Senate sits on several committees. The smaller size of the Senate allows leaders to participate in committee work while discharging their leadership duties. For example, in the

109th Senate, Frist, McConnell, Reid, and Durbin each served on several standing committees.

LEADERSHIP ACTIVITIES

House and Senate leaders have basically the same job: to bring coherence, direction, and efficiency to a largely decentralized and individualistic legislative body. Leadership duties can be described in terms of institutional maintenance (ensuring that Congress and its members perform their lawmaking and oversight duties effectively and preserving Congress's reputation and integrity) and party maintenance (crafting winning coalitions among partisan colleagues and providing assistance to their members).[76] Both kinds of general functions point toward the parties' objectives of influencing policy making in conformity with their political leanings. Leaders, too, are expected to boost their partisan colleagues electorally through strategic and tactical actions designed to win them majority control of their chamber. As journalist David Broder said about Speaker Hastert: "[He] has gained stature among his colleagues because he has managed the agenda to their benefit and because he has been assiduous in campaigning for them in their districts."[77] Hastert regularly visits more than one hundred districts each election cycle to campaign for GOP candidates.[78]

Institutional Tasks

From an institutional perspective, party leaders have a number of obligations associated with their positions. They are provided with extra staff resources beyond those accorded individual lawmakers to assist in carrying out these diverse responsibilities.

Organizing the Chamber. Party leaders influence congressional organization and procedure. They select the chief administrative officers of the House or Senate, oversee committee jurisdictional revisions, and revise congressional rules. In 1995 Speaker Gingrich backed the abolition of three standing committees. In 1999 Speaker Hastert supported a major recodification of House rules, the first since 1880. Four years later he supported creation of a new Select Committee on Homeland Security to oversee the newest cabinet department. In 2005, this panel was transformed into a permanent committee.

At the start of the 109th Congress, Frist and Reid had to hammer out an accord over how to divide committee funds between Republicans and Democrats and how to allocate committee space between the parties. In light of the GOP's 2004 election gains, Frist argued that a Senate precedent dating from the 1970s entitled them to two-thirds of committee funds, space, and staff with minority Democrats receiving one-third. Reid insisted, however, that committee resources in the 109th Congress track the party division (55% to 45%) in the chamber, as occurred in the two previous Congresses. Lacking control of any elective branch, Democrats need the extra staff and financial resources to challenge the majority Republicans and the Bush White House.

They could also filibuster any committee organizing resolution offered on the floor by Frist. In the end, Frist and Reid agreed that Republicans would control 60 percent of committee resources and Democrats 40 percent.[79]

Scheduling Floor Business. "The power of the Speaker of the House is the power of scheduling," Speaker O'Neill once declared.[80] Or, as Newt Gingrich put it, "When you are Speaker you get to set the agenda. . . . [Y]ou get to decide what legislation is up."[81] After consulting with committee leaders, interested members, the president, and others, House and Senate party leaders decide what, when, and in which order measures should come up for debate. Setting the chamber's agenda and schedule is perhaps the single most important prerogative of the Speaker and Senate majority leader.

Once a bill is scheduled for action, the leaders' job is to see that members vote—a task more difficult than merely herding bodies into the chamber. Party leaders may seek out certain members to speak on an issue because their endorsement can persuade other legislators to support it. Or they may delay action until the bill's sponsors are present. "The leadership must have the right members at the right place at the right time," said Byrd when he was the Senate majority whip.[82] In short, the leaders' scheduling prerogatives mold policy; arranging the time that bills reach the floor can seal their fate. A week's delay in scheduling a controversial White House initiative, for instance, gives the president, lobbying groups, and others additional time to mobilize votes for the proposal.

Legislative business is also scheduled with forthcoming elections in mind. Measures are postponed to avoid an electorally embarrassing defeat, or, alternatively they are brought to the floor to satisfy groups allied with each party. What better time to take up legislation revamping the Internal Revenue Service or a constitutional amendment affecting the internal revenue code than on or around April 15, the filing deadline for federal income taxes? The period close to July 4 is also popular for scheduling consideration of constitutional amendments banning the desecration of the American flag. Both parties commonly use the floor as an election platform to raise issues that appeal to their outside partisans. When it passes measures advocated by its electoral base, a party can say, "Look what we did for you." Conversely, a party that fails to pass a measure can say to its bedrock supporters, "Look what we tried to do."

Influencing Colleagues. Party leaders also have the task of persuading members to support their legislation. In the modern Congress arm-twisting means pleading and cajoling to coax votes. "If you have no sense of what other people's judgments, values or goals are," stated Representative Foley, who served as Speaker from 1989 to 1995, about the negotiating process, "you're in a very poor position to evaluate how you might accommodate them."[83] Although leaders generally seek to influence members of their own party and chamber, they also try to win cooperation from the other chamber and from the opposition party. Senate GOP leader Frist and Speaker Hastert, and their top aides, meet regularly to coordinate agendas, priorities, and strategies.

Frequent meetings between Pelosi and Reid, the two Democratic leaders, to coordinate political, policy, and public relations strategies are more important than ever because they lack the megaphone of a Democratic president. The two leaders, for example, agreed to a coordinated campaign "to paint Republicans as an out-of-control ruling party that's willing to flaunt its privileged status to appease the GOP base and to protect itself from ethical scrutiny."[84]

Party leaders do not have to rely solely on their powers of persuasion, however. Informal political networks and access to strategic information give them an edge in influencing colleagues.

> Because of an improved whip system and because members will respond more candidly to leadership polls than to lobbyist or White House polls, [leaders] have perhaps the most important information in a legislative struggle—information on where the votes are and (sometimes) what it will take to win certain people over.[85]

Top leaders also can bestow or withhold a variety of tangible and intangible rewards, such as naming legislators to special or select committees, influencing assignments to standing committees, aiding reelection campaigns, and smoothing access to the White House or executive agencies.

Consulting the President. A traditional duty of party leaders is to meet with the president to discuss the administration's goals and to convey legislative sentiment about what the executive branch is doing or not doing. This consultative duty is performed mainly by leaders of the president's party. Presidents also consult with opposition leaders and the joint bipartisan leadership of the House and Senate. President George W. Bush, for instance, periodically has the joint bipartisan leadership to the White House to discuss issues such as the global war on terrorism and his domestic policy plans.

Party Tasks

From a party perspective, congressional party leaders have a number of formal and informal responsibilities. Formally, the rules of each party specify certain roles and responsibilities for their leaders. Parliamentary precedents and chamber rules also assign certain duties to party leaders. Informally, party leaders have assumed a wide range of duties, such as devising and implementing strategic decisions.

Organizing the Party. Congressional leaders help to organize their party by selecting partisan colleagues for standing committees, revising party rules, choosing other party leaders, appointing party committees, and influencing policy formation. Three examples serve as illustrations. First, House minority leader Pelosi named Rahm Emanuel of Illinois, a former Clinton White House aide, to chair the Democratic Congressional Campaign Committee, and Juanita Millender-McDonald of California to be the top Democrat on the House Administration Committee. Second, House majority leader DeLay was instrumental in winning the chairmanship of the House Resources Committee for Richard W. Pombo of California, who leapfrogged over several more senior Republicans on the panel to gain the post. "This is the guy DeLay wanted," said Rep. Joel Hefley, R-Colo.[86] Third, Hefley was replaced in the 109th Congress as chairman of the Ethics Committee in part because he "angered GOP leaders and rank-and-file lawmakers for his handling of an ethics complaint filed against" Majority Leader DeLay. "Republicans were privately furious at [Hefley], saying he gave in to a political witch hunt by Democrats and government watchdog groups when he supported public admonishment of the powerful Majority Leader."[87]

Promoting Party Unity. Another leadership assignment is to encourage party unity in Congress on priority legislation. Everett Dirksen (minority leader, 1959–1969) used social gatherings to accomplish this goal.

> Dirksen brought party members together in a series of social affairs. He held cocktail parties at a Washington country club, inviting all Republican senators and sometimes their wives too. These were calculated by Dirksen to improve party harmony and to build a friendly feeling for himself with the Republican senators.[88]

Party leaders' assistance to the rank-and-file goes far beyond extending them social invitations. Leaders schedule members' bills, provide them with timely political information, advise them on electoral issues, visit with their constituents, help them obtain good committee assignments, and work with them to forge policy agendas. "You really have to make people feel part of the process, and I guess it is a little bit like a shepherd," remarked a Senate Democratic leader. "You really want to keep as much as you can the flock together, and that takes different approaches with different people."[89] Periodically, leaders organize partisan retreats where members discuss party and policy goals, consider specific legislative initiatives, air differences, and resolve disputes. House and Senate minority leaders typically emphasize party unity as a way to maximize their advantage as the loyal opposition and, with an eye toward the next election, to better contrast their views and positions with the majority party's.

Publicizing Party Views. Leaders are expected to publicize their party's policies and achievements. They give speeches in various forums, appear on radio and television talk shows, write newspaper and journal articles, hold press conferences, organize town meetings around the country, and establish Web sites that highlight party issues and images. Leaders are also expected to develop public relations strategies that neutralize the opposition's arguments and proposals. The spokesperson's role has increased in importance in recent years in part because of the political effect of the twenty-four-hour news cycle. "We've created a situation," noted a scholar, "where the real way you drive the legislative process is by influencing public opinion, rather than by trading for votes."[90]

The House Republican Conference, like the other party caucuses on Capitol Hill, provides its members with talking points for meetings with journalists or constituents. (The Bush White House also provides House and Senate Republicans with talking points and themes so party members are all sending a unified public message.) These party units often create communications teams that meet regularly to discuss message and delivery and to recommend their more telegenic members to present party positions on television. "We're focused on making sure we deliver the [party] message both here in Washington and out in the hinterlands," said Sen. Rick Santorum of Pennsylvania, chairman of the Senate Republican Conference.[91] For example, President Bush's top domestic priority in his second term is to overhaul Social Security (see Chapter 14) by, among other things, allowing workers to invest some of their payroll taxes in stocks and bonds. To sell the idea to the general public, a confidential plan was developed with the advice of pollsters, marketing experts, and communications consultants. Congressional Republicans and the president started out using the terms "private accounts" and "privatizing" and then realized "personal accounts" tested better with focus groups, so they changed their language to avoid any implication that the proposal implied a corporate takeover of the retirement system. Minority Leader Pelosi enlisted several informal Democratic groups (the Congressional Black Caucus and the Congressional Hispanic Caucus, for example) to fire away rhetorically at the GOP plan by using the word "privatization." In one letter to President Bush, a Democratic group used the words "privatization" and "private accounts" six times.[92]

Providing Campaign Assistance. Leaders must be energetic campaigners and fund-raisers on behalf of their partisan colleagues. They assist party incumbents and challengers in raising campaign funds. They establish their own leadership political action committees (PACs) to raise money and donate it to candidates of their party. They help to raise large sums of money so issue ads can be run on television in the months leading up to the November elections. They travel to numerous House districts or states to campaign with either incumbents or challengers of their party. They encourage outside groups to raise money for the party. They also develop ways to boost the reelection chances of their partisan colleagues, such as creating working groups to provide members running for reelection with greater public exposure.[93]

Members anticipating a run for a leadership post distribute campaign funds as standard operating practice. As one account noted about a party leader's ability to raise money, "It seems that the job of fundraiser is becoming more important to senators' expectations of what a majority leader should do. The candidates [for this leadership position] thus are not trying to buy votes so much as to demonstrate how well they can fulfill that role."[94] The ability to raise funds for colleagues is an increasingly important criterion for judging prospective party leaders and another reminder that leaders stand at the conjunction of the two Congresses: the representative assembly, where money is needed to join, and the lawmaking body, where power calls the shots.

PARTY CAUCUSES, COMMITTEES, AND INFORMAL GROUPS

House and Senate leaders operate in different institutional contexts. In the larger, more impersonal House, majority party leaders sometimes ignore the wishes of the minority party. This seldom happens in the Senate, which emphasizes individualism, minority rights, reciprocity, and mutual accommodation. Despite these differences between parties in the House and Senate, they are organized into the same three components: caucuses, committees, and informal party groups.

Party Caucuses

The organization of all partisans in a chamber is called the conference or (in the case of House Democrats) the caucus. Party conferences or caucuses elect leaders, approve committee assignments, provide members with services, debate party and legislative policies, encourage party unity, appoint task forces or issue teams, develop themes to keep members on message, enable members to vent their frustrations, and discuss outreach programs that appeal to voters. House GOP Conference chair Pryce is heavily involved in devising public relations campaigns to promote Republican initiatives. "We're going to operate more like a Madison Avenue public relations firm—more emphasis on benchmark polling, more direct-to-constituent contact, editorial placement and town hall meetings," she said.[95] In an explanation that applies equally well to how the caucus in both parties and chambers can serve to promote consensus on issues, a senior House Democrat said:

> The caucus is the place where a great deal of freewheeling debate over an issue takes place and where sometimes a consensus develops. . . . Most of the discussions, although they have taken place at leadership meetings and at chairmen's meetings and in whips' meetings, have ended up in the broader forum of the caucus where every member of the Democratic party participates. You don't take a vote, but you try to develop a consensus and make concessions where they're necessary and develop the strongest possible position that can be supported by the maximum number of Democrats.[96]

In brief, party caucuses are useful forums where party members and leaders can assess and sway sentiment on substantive or procedural issues. On rare occasions, party caucuses vote to strip members of their committee seniority or to oust committee leaders. Committee leaders are removed from their posts when legal action is taken against them (for example, if they are indicted). Sometimes presidents attend their party's House or Senate caucus to rally the troops as President George W. Bush did on several occasions. In an unprecedented action, Bush spoke at retreats of House and Senate Democrats to win backing for his agenda and to promote productive relationships.[97]

TABLE 6-1 **Party Committees in the Senate and House**

Committee	Approximate number of Members	Function
Senate Democratic		
Policy	18	Considers party positions on specific measures and assists the party leader in scheduling bills
Steering and Coordination	17	Assigns Democrats to committees and works to coordinate policy, legislative, and message issues for the Democratic Conference
Campaign	20	Works to elect Democrats to the Senate
Senate Republican		
Policy	40	Provides summaries of GOP positions on specific issues; researches procedural and substantive issues; drafts policy alternatives
Committee on Committees	9	Assigns Republicans to committees
Campaign	6	Works to elect Republicans to the Senate
House Democratic		
Steering	50	Assists the leadership and Democratic Caucus in establishing, implementing, researching, and communicating party priorities; assigns Democrats to committees
Campaign	16	Aids in electing Democrats to the House
House Republican		
Policy	47	Considers majority party proposals and works for consensus among Republican members
Steering	29	Assigns Republicans to standing committees
Campaign	40	Seeks to elect Republicans to the House

Note: The official names of the parties' campaign committees are as follows: Democratic Senatorial Campaign Committee, National Republican Senatorial Committee, Democratic Congressional Campaign Committee, and National Republican Congressional Committee. The sizes of these panels vary over time.

Party Committees

Each of the four congressional parties—Senate and House Democrats, Senate and House Republicans—establishes committees to serve partisan needs and objectives (see Table 6-1). Three of the four parties on Capitol Hill have policy committees, for example. House Democrats disbanded their policy committee at the direction of Minority Leader Pelosi. In its place, she established a revamped Steering Committee, which has a policy part (headed by George Miller of California) and a committee assignment component (chaired by Rosa DeLauro of Connecticut).[98] The committees do not make policy, but they provide advice on scheduling, encourage party unity, research substantive and political issues, distribute policy papers, track party votes on issues, and discuss and implement party policy. Their influence has varied over the years, assuming greater importance when the party does not control the White House and thus needs policy guidance. To counter President Bush's claim that an immediate fiscal crisis confronts Social Security and requires remedial action by the 109th Congress, the Senate Democratic Policy Committee held an oversight hearing to present competing information and analysis. The two Senate and House GOP policy committees maintain Web sites that party members and staff can access at any time for pertinent information. Other important party panels are the campaign and committee assignment committees.

Informal Party Groups

In addition to party committees, a variety of informal groups operate on Capitol Hill. House and Senate leaders also employ party task forces to devise policy alternatives, formulate strategy, and coordinate floor action. Informal groups on Capitol Hill numbered more than three hundred in 2005. They may be unicameral or bicameral in composition. Many have a policy focus, such as the boating, steel, mining, soybean, rural health, electricity, automotive, children's, bicycle, or Internet caucus. They strive to promote specific policies and heighten congressional and public awareness of their importance. There are also partisan and bipartisan groups. The House, for instance, has such party groups as the moderate Republican Tuesday Group, the conservative Republican Study Committee, the centrist New Democrat Coalition, and the Blue Dog coalition (fiscally conservative Democrats). Representative Mike Pence, R-Ind., the leader of the one-hundred-member Republican Study Group for the 109th Congress, worked to "create a broader network between House and Senate conservatives and with like-minded policy groups outside the Capitol" to advance conservative issues and values in Congress.[99]

PARTY CONTINUITY AND CHANGE

Several features of the contemporary party system on Capitol Hill stand out. Among these are the vigor of the congressional parties, the persistence of the two-party system, and the advent of new coalition-building practices.

Vigorous Congressional Parties

By any test one can use, the four Capitol Hill parties are flourishing. The organizational elements are healthy and active, leaders are increasingly prominent, and party voting is at relatively high levels. The congressional parties are assisted by well-staffed and professional congressional campaign committees whose ultimate task is either to win or to keep majority control of the House or Senate.[100] These campaign panels recruit and train candidates, raise money, engage in research on the opposition party, target competitive districts, furnish polling advice and services, develop election strategies, and, in general, do everything they can to support congressional campaigns by their party's candidates.[101]

Demographic factors also contribute to the vigorous partisanship on Capitol Hill. Constituency changes in the South have led to the election of Democrats who are more ideologically compatible with their party colleagues from the rest of the country. The once prominent conservative coalition of Republicans and southern Democrats no longer is an important voting bloc in Congress. The South, as recent elections have shown, is now largely in the GOP camp. For the first time since Reconstruction, more lawmakers from the South are Republicans than Democrats. Meanwhile, the disappearance of liberal "Rockefeller Republicans" from GOP ranks has led to the dominance of conservative lawmakers in that party. (House redistricting also plays a role in heightened partisanship as many lawmakers represent constituencies filled predominately with Democratic or GOP voters.)

In addition, the electoral element triggers trench warfare between the two parties. Recent highly competitive elections have demonstrated that neither party has been able to solidify its hold on the House or Senate. Both legislative parties jockey to win public credit for their agenda and issue positions and to block the goals and aims of the opposition. As one congressional scholar put it:

> We can no longer try to understand congressional behavior simply as the pursuit of individual goals [such as reelection, gaining power, or making good policy]. Instead, we must also see how Republicans and Democrats seek the collective goal of majority status. In this sense, they resemble armies, which try to get their troops to subordinate their narrow self-interest to the good of the whole. [Thus, a key job of party leaders is] to rally the troops for electoral ground war.[102]

Lawmakers from each party also face an electorate whose political views are more coherent, which "ratchets up the intensity of conflict," and that is prone to vote straight down the line for Democrats or Republicans rather than engage in split-ticket voting.[103] One consequence is that legislators are more beholden to activists who vote in the primary and general elections. (Harvard professor David King found that, between 1996 and 2002, "turnout in congressional primaries halved from 34 percent to 16.8 percent.")[104]

As a result, lawmakers are often reluctant to work for bipartisan compromises that antagonize the vocal concerns of well-organized groups, such as the Christian Coalition, the National Rifle Association, or labor unions. As one analyst observed, moderate members of Congress in the Republican Party today,

> even popular incumbents who would win a general election by overwhelming margins, are hostage to the party's right wing. With few exceptions, they are vulnerable because of low turnouts in the primary elections, in which a relative handful of determined conservatives could oust the most popular incumbent while most voters are not paying attention.[105]

The heightened partisanship in Congress—fomented by the legislative and electoral prevalence of attack politics—motivates party leaders to demand, and often get, party loyalty on various votes. "Procedure is always a party vote," declared House GOP leader DeLay.[106] To reinforce that view, DeLay and Speaker Hastert have told GOP whips that "any lawmaker who votes against the leadership on a procedural matter will be booted from the whip team."[107] Further, one of Hastert's governing principles, shared by DeLay, is that the right kind of House majority must pass bills. That overall majority must be composed of the "majority of the majority party," otherwise the legislation is unlikely to be called up. As Rep. Michael N. Castle, R-Del., a leader of the relatively small band of moderate Republicans, noted with respect to the majority leader: "It is Tom DeLay's adamant belief . . . that what is done in the House is done by the Republican party. That leaves little room for Democrats."[108] Compromise may be a traditional hallmark of legislative decision making, but in today's House the majority party usually prefers to win by party-centered votes. The two parties are not "just opponents or rivals now. [They] are enemies, with every fight being zero-sum," exclaimed a senior GOP lawmaker. "Compromise is seen as weakness by many of your constituents, and by all your potential opponents in the next primary."[109]

The rancorous partisan atmosphere got so bad in the House (in the mid-1990s Speaker Gingrich and Minority Leader Gephardt, for instance, refused to speak to each other for a year) that a bipartisan group of lawmakers organized a weekend retreat in March 1997 for all members and their families. The so-called civility retreat was designed to allow members with different partisan viewpoints to get to know each other better. This result might then encourage them to work together on a bipartisan basis to resolve the nation's problems. Only marginal improvements flowed from this event. Three other civility retreats were held—in March 1999, March 2001, and March 2003—with similar limited improvements in comity among the members and between the parties, in part because of fundamental policy and ideological disagreements that often spark angry clashes and personal attacks. No civility retreat occurred in March 2005 for lack of interest and because these events had limited impact in changing a partisan environment where even party leaders discourage their colleagues from working with members of the opposing party. Nonetheless, bipartisan interest still exists in overcoming interparty hostility in the House, as shown by the 2005 formation of the Congressional Civility Caucus.[110]

Episodes of sharp partisanship occur even in the usually sedate Senate, in part because so many House members have been elected to that body (a record fifty-two former House members serve in the 109th Senate). Many bring with them to the Senate the hard-edged partisanship that they learned in the House. As part of the orientation program for the nine newly elected senators to the 109th Senate, a workshop on how to work across party lines was conducted for the newcomers.[111] Still, as Sen. Olympia J. Snowe, R-Maine, remarked, "The whole Congress has become far more polarized and partisan so it makes it difficult to reach bipartisan agreements. The more significant the issue, the more partisan it becomes."[112]

The call for bipartisanship is a common refrain among many lawmakers and pundits. An important issue, however, is who defines bipartisanship. There are at least two versions. First, there is the bipartisanship in which, as Senate majority whip McConnell stated, "some Democrats join Republicans to do things that Republicans would like to do."[113] Or as House majority leader DeLay phrased it: "We'll write conservative bills and ask the Democrats to participate" by providing votes. The other type requires the two parties to work together with the White House so that legislation reflects the views of both Democrats and Republicans. As a conservative House Democrat said: "We want to be involved on the front end, not just be counted on for votes after the legislation is written" by Republicans.[114]

There are virtues in sharp partisanship. For one, it enables voters to better comprehend the different views, values, and principles of the two parties. For another, party leaders sometimes prefer confrontation over bipartisan compromise as a way to minimize the need to make concessions to the other party and to underscore interparty differences. "Confrontation fits our strategy," stated Dick Cheney when he was in the House (1979–1989). "Polarization often has very beneficial results. If everything is handled through compromise and conciliation, if there are no real issues dividing us from Democrats, why should the country change and make us the majority?"[115] Partisanship, too, can either be policy- or process-oriented. Policy partisanship is when one of the two congressional parties advances substantive measures—so-called wedge issues or wedgislation (abortion rights or affirmative action, for instance)—to unite their own and to foment political divisions within the other party. Process partisanship involves efforts by party leaders to structure the procedural playing field to advance their own agenda and to stymie the other party's goals.[116] Process partisanship is easier to invoke in the majority-run House (assuming unity within the majority party) than in the Senate, where power is more evenly divided among all senators.

The Two-Party System

The Democratic and Republican parties have dominated American politics and Congress since the mid-nineteenth century. Scholars have posited various theories for the dualistic national politics of a country as diverse as the United States. Some trace the origins of the national two-party system to early conflicts between Federalists (advocates of a strong national government) and Antifederalists (advocates of limited national government). This dualism continued in subsequent splits: North versus South, East versus West, agricultural versus financial interests, and rural versus urban areas.[117] Constitutional, political, and legal arrangements are other bases of the two-party system. Plurality elections in single-member congressional districts encouraged the creation and maintenance of two major parties. Under the winner-take-all principle, the person who wins the most votes in a state or district is elected to the Senate or House. This principle discourages the formation of third parties. In addition, many states have laws that make it difficult to create new parties.

Whatever mix of causes produced the two-party system, one thing is clear: Few third-party or independent legislators have been elected to Congress during the last century. The high-water mark was the 63d Congress (1913–1915), which had one Progressive senator and nineteen representatives elected as Progressives, Progressive-Republicans, or independents. Since the post–World War II period, only a handful of lawmakers have been elected from minor parties or as independents.[118] Most legislators convert to one of the major parties or vote with them on procedural and substantive matters. The 109th Congress has two independents: Progressive representative Bernie Sanders of Vermont aligns with the Democrats and Independent senator Jeffords of Vermont caucuses with the Democrats. (When Jeffords announced that he would retire from the Senate at the end of the 109th Congress, Representative Sanders stated he would seek to replace Jeffords in the Senate.) Third-party members have no institutional status. Their participation in Democratic or Republican matters is by invitation only.

Advances in Coalition Building

To get the legislative results they desire, party leaders increasingly use media strategies, omnibus bills, and strategic planning. Procedural innovations also are important elements in the arsenal of the party leaders, such as multiple referrals, ad hoc task forces, creative rules from the House Rules Committee, and unanimous consent agreements in the Senate.

Media Strategies. Party leaders understand that media strategies (the use of the press, television, radio, polls, the Internet, speeches, and so on) are essential to move or block legislation. They form issue teams, message groups, or theme teams to orchestrate, organize, and coordinate political events and communications strategies that promote the party's message to the general public. No longer is the inside game—working behind-the-scenes to line up votes—

sufficient to pass major, controversial measures. Also necessary is the outside game—influencing public opinion, coordinating with advocacy groups, and creating grassroots support for policy initiatives. Today, media and parliamentary strategies are complementary processes that both parties use to, among other things, raise issues, communicate with voters, define and frame priorities, or respond to partisan criticisms. For example, members of the House GOP theme team "remain close to the chamber during difficult votes, ready to stand up and either object or simply respond to Democratic charges" that Republicans are pushing costly or ineffective economic or foreign policies.[119] Dueling news conferences may follow with each party blaming the other for irresponsible behavior.

Both congressional parties understand the importance of words as political weapons. GOP consultants found, for example, that characterizing the estate tax as the "death tax"—and having GOP officeholders repeat it again and again over several years—aroused public ire against the tax. This sentiment was instrumental in accomplishing the temporary repeal of the inheritance tax as part of President Bush's successful 2001 tax cut plan. Bush advocates the permanent demise of the "death tax." At a time when the nation is engaged in a war on terrorism, both parties employ "national security" as a way to advance their agenda. Congressional Republicans, for example, frame the debate over drilling for oil and gas in the Arctic National Wildlife Refuge (ANWR) as a way to reduce the nation's dependency on oil from the volatile Middle East and add that Bush's tax-cutting initiative is a way to strengthen "economic security." Democrats castigate Republicans for not spending more on homeland (recast as "home town") security, such as "border security," "port security," or "nuclear power plant security." And with changes to Social Security a priority of the 109th Congress, both parties have devised a "message strategy" to convince constituents of the rightness of their point of view.[120]

With President Bush having the megaphone of the White House to advance GOP initiatives, congressional Democrats understand that they lack a single messenger who can focus the nation's attention in the same manner as the president. As a result, they use the House and Senate floor and a wide variety of communications techniques to shape national debate. The two Democratic leaders—Pelosi and Reid—hold press conferences, appear on diverse media outlets, organize town meetings, prepare talking points for the press (and their own members), develop party themes (bashing corporate corruption, for instance), write newspaper editorials, circulate data and statistics that skewer Republican proposals, organize policy forums, and engage in a variety of other actions to promote their legislative agenda to the public and to challenge GOP initiatives. Because it is hard for Democrats to attract news coverage and public attention, "they have had few opportunities to explain what they are for, only what they are against."[121]

Omnibus Bills. A phenomenon of modern lawmaking is the rise of megabills—legislation that is hundreds or thousands of pages in length and which encompasses disparate policy topics. Many of Congress's most significant policy enactments are sometimes folded into four or five omnibus bills. Many reasons account for the use of these packages. For instance, some initiatives are incorporated into megabills to improve their chances of enactment. Bundling popular programs with painful spending cuts increases the chances of enacting megabills. This tactic limits the number of difficult votes lawmakers cast and provides them with political cover. Members can explain to angry constituents or groups that they had to support the indivisible whole because its discrete parts were not open to separate votes.

Joining several bills may increase the chances of garnering more support. (The reverse concern is that a megabill may attract a coalition of minorities with the votes needed to reject the measure.) Sweeteners can be added to woo supporters, or provisions that are unable to win majority support in stand-alone bills can be buried in megabills. Megabills can also strengthen Congress's leverage with the executive branch. Measures that presidents might veto if presented to them separately can be folded into megabills and be enacted in that fashion.

Party leaders command the resources and authority to exercise coordinative and substantive influence over the packaging process. "Omnibus bills place a huge amount of power in the hands of a few key leaders and their staffs," remarked one House member.[122] Rank-and-file members look to party leaders to formulate a package acceptable to at least a majority of members. However, these megabills sometimes arouse the ire of lawmakers. As one member said about their increasing prevalence, "These omnibus bills—often gauged more by weight than the number of pages—are abominations. No one member of Congress has a chance to read much of them, let alone understand them, before they are voted on."[123] Late in the 108th Congress, lawmakers were compelled to vote on an omnibus appropriations bill more than three thousand pages long and with less than twenty-four hours to review it.

Strategic Planning and Coordination. On major policy issues, strategic planning and coordination are crucial to the leadership's ability to forge successful coalitions. House and Senate leaders meet regularly with their partisan allies to craft their plans, to anticipate the legislative moves of the opposition, and to develop their countermoves. For example, party leaders employ defensive messages as a way to protect their members from political attack. The objective is to appropriate the other party's popular issues by blurring the distinctions between congressional Democrats and Republicans. For example, on an immigration reform issue, Democrats called their package the Latino and Immigrant Fairness Act; Republicans dubbed their initiative the Legal Immigration Family Equity Act.[124]

Congressional GOP leaders calculate whether the House or Senate should take the lead on passing much of President Bush's legislative agenda. As Senate GOP Policy Committee chairman Jon Kyl, R-Ariz., stated: "The House has to initiate some things, like money bills, and because the Republican leadership in the House can control things better than the Republican leadership in the

Senate, it will be the first to act on the president's agenda in some circumstances."[125] House Republican leaders call this strategy "willful triangulation." They plan to push some of Bush's policies beyond what he suggests—"compromising up," in the words of a GOP leadership aide—to ensure that legislation emerging from a House-Senate conference closely tracks the president's original recommendation. "We set the bar high to pass ambitious, bold legislation," the aide said, noting: "In the final analysis, we want to work down to the president's proposal and don't want [Bush's] plan to be watered down."[126] House GOP leaders also prefer that the Senate act first on overhauling Social Security, otherwise House Republicans "might have to cast a potentially politically damaging vote only to see the bill go up in flames in the Senate."[127]

CONCLUSION

Congressional parties have elaborate organizations, and their leaders fulfill a multiplicity of roles and duties. The Senate majority leader, explained Byrd when he held that post, "facilitates, he constructs, he programs, he schedules, he takes an active part in the development of legislation, he steps in at crucial moments on the floor, offers amendments, speaks on behalf of legislation and helps to shape the outcome of the legislation."[128] Party leaders can do many things, but they cannot command their colleagues. Their leadership rests chiefly on their skill in providing others with reasons to follow them.

The party principle organizes Congress.[129] The committee principle, however, shapes the measures Congress acts upon. These two principles are often in conflict. The first emphasizes aggregation, the second fragmentation. Party leaders struggle to manage an institution that disperses policy-making authority to numerous work groups. In short, leaders provide the centripetal force to offset committees' centrifugal influence.

SUGGESTED READINGS

Aldrich, John H. *Why Parties? The Origins and Transformation of Party Politics in America.* Chicago: University of Chicago Press, 1995.

Baker, Richard A., and Roger H. Davidson, eds. *First among Equals: Outstanding Senate Leaders of the Twentieth Century.* Washington, D.C.: Congressional Quarterly, 1991.

Cox, Gary W., and Mathew D. McCubbins. *Legislative Leviathan: Party Government in the House.* Berkeley: University of California Press, 1993.

Davidson, Roger H., Susan Webb Hammond, and Raymond W. Smock, eds. *Masters of the House: Congressional Leaders over Two Centuries.* Boulder, Colo.: Westview Press, 1998.

Peters, Ronald M., Jr. *The American Speakership: The Office in Historical Perspective.* 2d ed. Baltimore: Johns Hopkins University Press, 1997.

Rohde, David W. *Parties and Leaders in the Postreform House.* Chicago: University of Chicago Press, 1991.

Sinclair, Barbara. *Legislators, Leaders, and Lawmaking: The U.S. House of Representatives in the Postreform Era.* Baltimore: Johns Hopkins University Press, 1995.

______. *The Transformation of the U.S. Senate.* Baltimore: Johns Hopkins University Press, 1989.

Three public faces of committee work: Left, the Senate Foreign Relations Committee meets in April 2005 to consider the nomination of John R. Bolton as U.S. ambassador to the United Nations. Middle, Sen. Olympia J. Snowe, R-Maine, consults with Sen. John B. Breaux, D-La., during a Finance Committee markup. Bottom, NASA administrator Sean O'Keefe hands a document to an aide during a joint House-Senate hearing on the Columbia space shuttle accident.

chapter 7

Committees: Workshops of Congress

Committees serve two broad purposes: individual and institutional. Individually, lawmakers look for ways from their committee perches to benefit their constituents. "As far as I can see, there is really only one basic reason to be on a public works committee," admitted a House member. "Intellectual stimulation" is not it. "Most of all, I want to be able to bring home projects to my district."[1] With scores of representatives seeking assignment to the Transportation and Infrastructure Committee, it has grown to be the largest (seventy-five members in the 109th Congress (2005–2007)) in congressional history. Members of Congress understand the reelection connection between their committee assignments and their electoral opportunities.

Committees also enable legislators to utilize or develop expertise in areas that interest them. A former teacher, for instance, may seek assignment to the committee overseeing education policy. And some panels, such as the tax and appropriations committees, enable members to wield personal influence among their colleagues. Members ask to be on the House Appropriations Committee, explained a GOP leader, because "instantaneously . . . they have a host of new friends, and we all know why"—that panel controls the distribution of discretionary federal money.[2]

Institutionally, committees are the centers of policy making, oversight of federal agencies, and public education (largely through the hearings they hold). By dividing their membership into a number of "little legislatures," the House and Senate are able to consider dozens of proposed laws simultaneously.[3] Without committees a legislative body of 100 senators and 440 House members could not handle roughly 10,000 bills and nearly 100,000 nominations biennially, a national budget over $2 trillion, and a limitless array of controversial issues. Although floor actions often refine legislation, committees are the means by which Congress sifts through an otherwise impossible jumble of bills, proposals, and issues.

Congressional committees serve another important institutional function in the political system. They act as safety valves, or outlets for national debates and controversies. Military and economic responsibilities, demographic shifts, trade agreements, global environmental concerns, the drug war, the social dislocations caused by technological advances, and the rising cost of health care place enormous strains on the political system. As forums for public debates, congressional committees help to vent, absorb, and resolve these strains. Moreover, the safety-valve function gives the citizenry a greater sense of participation in national decision making and helps educate members about public problems.

The individual and institutional purposes of the committee system can conflict. Because members tend to gravitate to committees for constituency or career reasons, they are not the most impartial judges of the policies they authorize. "It's one of the weaknesses of the system that those attracted to a committee like Agriculture are those whose constituents benefit from farm programs," acknowledged Sen. Charles E. Schumer, a Democrat from New York. "And so they're going to support those programs and they're not going to want to cut them, even the ones that are wasteful."[4]

THE PURPOSES OF COMMITTEES

Senator Schumer's comment highlights an ongoing debate about the development and fundamental purposes of the committee system. To explain the organization of legislatures and the behavior of their committees, scholars have advanced the distributional, informational, and party hypotheses.

The distributional hypothesis suggests that legislatures create committees to give lawmakers policy influence in areas critical to their reelection. Members seek committee assignments to "bring home the bacon" (public goods and services) to their constituents. Because lawmakers self-select these kinds of committees, the committees become filled with what scholars call preference outliers—members whose homogeneous preferences for benefits to their constituents put them out of step with the heterogeneous views of the membership as a whole. Chamber majorities, in brief, may need to rein in overreaching committees by rejecting or amending their recommended actions.[5]

The informational hypothesis proposes that legislative bodies establish committees to provide lawmakers with the specialized expertise required to make informed judgments in a complex world. Furthermore, the division of labor under the committee system augments Congress's role in relation to the executive branch. Instead of being composed primarily of preference outliers, committees under this model will consist of a diverse membership with wide-ranging perspectives. The basic goal of committees, then, is to formulate policies that resolve national problems.[6]

The party hypothesis views committee members as agents of their party caucuses. According to this perspective, committee members are expected to support their party's programs.

The committee system in fact encompasses aspects of all three models. Lawmakers are concerned with local issues, but every district and state is also affected by broad national concerns—the condition of the economy and the environment, for example. Issues may lend themselves on occasion more to the distributional than to the informational or party theory of policy making.

Because good public policy may be impeded by the parochial orientations of individual members, Congress has a small number of control, or centralizing, committees that promote institutional and policy integration over committee and programmatic particularism. For example, each house has a Budget Committee, which proposes limits on how much Congress can spend for designated functional areas.[7] However committees are characterized, they focus and concentrate the policy and oversight activities of individual lawmakers.

EVOLUTION OF THE COMMITTEE SYSTEM

Committees in the early Congresses generally were temporary panels created for specific tasks. Proposals were considered on the House or Senate floor and then were referred to specially created panels that worked out the details—the reverse order of today's system. The Senate, for example, would "debate a subject at length on the floor and, after the majority's desires had been crystallized, might appoint a committee to put those desires into bill form."[8] About 350 ad hoc committees were formed during the Third Congress (1793–1795) alone.[9] The parent chamber closely controlled these temporary committees. It assigned them clear-cut tasks, required them to report back favorably or unfavorably, and dissolved them when they had completed their work.

The Senate by about 1816—and the House a bit later—had developed a system of permanent, or standing, committees, some of which are still in existence. Standing committees, as historian DeAlva Stanwood Alexander explained, were better suited than ad hoc groups to cope with the larger membership and wider scope of congressional business. Another scholar, George H. Haynes, pointed out that the "needless inconvenience of the frequent choice of select committees" taxed congressional patience. Lawmakers recognized that debating bills one at a time before the whole chamber was an inefficient way of processing Congress's legislative business. Perhaps, too, legislators came to value standing committees as counterweights to presidential influence in setting the legislative agenda.[10] Permanent committees changed the way Congress made policy and allocated authority. The House and Senate now reviewed and voted upon recommendations made by specialized, experienced committees. Standing committees also encouraged oversight of the executive branch. Members have called them "the eye, the ear, the hand, and very often the brain" of Congress.[11]

As committees acquired expertise and authority, they became increasingly self-reliant and resistant to chamber and party control. After the House revolt against domineering Speaker Joseph G. Cannon, R-Ill., in 1910, power flowed to the committee chairmen, who took on substantial powers. Along with a few strong party leaders, they held sway over House and Senate policy making during much of the twentieth century. In rare instances committee members rebelled and diminished the chairman's authority. But most members heeded the advice that Speaker John W. McCormack, D-Mass. (1962–1971), gave to freshmen: "Whenever you pass a committee chairman in the House, you bow from the waist. I do." [12]

The chairmen's authority was buttressed by the custom of seniority that flourished with the rise of congressional careerism. The majority party member with the most years of continuous service on a committee virtually always became its chairman. There were no other qualifications, such as ability or party loyalty. As a result, committee chairmen owed little or nothing to party leaders, much less to presidents. This automatic selection process produced experienced, independent chairmen but concentrated authority in a few hands. The have-nots wanted a piece of the action and objected that seniority promoted the competent and incompetent alike. They objected, too, that the system promoted members from safe one-party areas—especially conservative southern Democrats and midwestern Republicans—who could ignore party policies or national sentiments.

The late 1960s and 1970s saw a rapid influx of new members, many from the cities and suburbs, who opposed the conservative status quo. Allying themselves with more senior members seeking a stronger voice in Congress, they pushed through changes that diffused power and shattered seniority as an absolute criterion for leadership posts. Today, House and Senate committee chairmen (and ranking minority members) must be elected by their party colleagues. No longer free to wield arbitrary authority, they must abide by committee and party rules and be sensitive to majority sentiment within their party's caucus or conference. For example, the House Republican Conference adopted party rules for the 109th Congress that state, "The Chairman on each committee has an obligation to ensure that each measure on which the Republican Conference has taken a position is managed in accordance with such position on the Floor of the House of Representatives."

TYPES OF COMMITTEES

Congress today has a shopper's bazaar of committees—standing, select, joint, and conference—and within each of these general types there are variations. Standing committees, for example, can be characterized as authorizing or appropriating panels. Authorizing committees (such as Agriculture, Armed Services, and Judiciary) are the policy-making centers on Capitol Hill. As substantive committees, they propose solutions to public problems and advocate what they believe to be the necessary levels of spending for the programs under their jurisdictions. The House and Senate Appropriations Committees recommend how much money agencies and programs will receive. Continuing conflict not surprisingly exists between the two types of panels. Typically, authorizers press for full funding for their recommendations, while appropriators are in the habit of recommending lower spending levels.

Standing Committees

A standing committee is a permanent entity created by public law or House or Senate rules. Standing committees continue from Congress to Congress, except in those infrequent instances when they are eliminated or new ones are created. Table 7-1 compares the standing committees in the 109th Congress in terms of their sizes, party ratios, and number of subcommittees.

Standing committees process the bulk of Congress's daily and annual agenda of business. Typically, measures are considered on the House or Senate floor after first being referred to, and approved by, the appropriate committees. Put negatively, committees are the burial ground for most legislation. Stated positively, committees select from the thousands of measures introduced in each Congress those that merit floor debate. Of the hundreds of bills that clear committees, fewer still are enacted into law.

Sizes and Ratios. Biennial election results frame the party negotiations that establish committee sizes and ratios (the number of majority and minority members on a panel). At the beginning of each new Congress, each chamber adopts separate resolutions, offered by Democrats and Republicans, that elect party members to the committees and thus set their sizes and ratios. In practice, committee sizes and ratios are established in the House by the majority leadership. Because the majority party has the votes, it can be the final arbiter if the minority protests its allotment of seats. By contrast, minority senators have significant influence in setting committee sizes and ratios. If they believe they are being unfairly treated, they can filibuster the resolution assigning senators to committees.

With a net gain of three House seats after the November 2004 elections, the GOP's share of seats in the chamber increased from 52.6 percent to 53.3 percent. At the start of the 109th Congress, Speaker J. Dennis Hastert, R-Ill., after consultation with Minority Leader Nancy Pelosi, D-Calif., increased the size of certain committees, reduced others, kept the same size for several highly sought-after panels (Ways and Means and Energy and Commerce, for example), and left the party ratios on fifteen committees the same as in the previous Congress. "We tried to be as fair as possible and work with the Democrats," said Hastert's spokesman. "There has been no protest from them."[13] Hastert's decision to largely maintain the status quo on ratios avoided partisan charges common at the start of a new Congress that the majority was stacking the deck and robbing the minority of its rightful number of committee seats. Some committees, such as Rules and Ways and Means, traditionally have disproportionate ratios to ensure firm majority party control.

In the Senate, sizes and ratios are negotiated by the majority and minority leaders. Once it became clear after the November 2004 elections by what margin the Republicans had taken control of the 109th Congress, the two party leaders considered two basic options. Because Republicans held fifty-five seats compared with fifty-one in the preceding Congress, one option was to provide

TABLE 7-1 **Standing Committees of the House and Senate, 109th Congress (2005–2007)**

Committee	Size and party ratio	Number of subcommittees
House		
Agriculture	46 (R 25; D 21)	5
Appropriations	66 (R 37; D 29)	10
Armed Services	62 (R 34; D 28)	5
Budget	39 (R 22; D 17	—
Education and the Workforce	49 (R 27; D 22)	5
Energy and Commerce	57 (R 31; D 26)	6
Financial Services	70 (R 37; D 33)	5
Government Reform	41 (R 23; D 18)	7
Homeland Security	34 (R 19; D 15)	5
House Administration	9 (R 6; D 3)	—
International Relations	50 (R 27; D 23)	7
Judiciary	40 (R 23; D 17)	5
Resources	49 (R 27; D 22)	5
Rules	13 (R 9; D 4)	2
Science	44 (R 24; D 20)	4
Small Business	36 (R 19; D 17)	4
Standards of Official Conduct	10 (R 5; D 5)	—
Transportation and Infrastructure	75 (R 41; D 34)	6
Veterans' Affairs	28 (R 16; D 12)	4
Ways and Means	41 (R 24; D 17)	6

a two-seat GOP majority on all major committees, as occurred in the 106th Congress (1999–2001) when Republicans had fifty-five seats. The other option was to make the ratio "determination on a committee-by-committee basis," as occurred in the 101st Congress (1989–1991) when Democrats controlled fifty-five seats.[14] Majority Leader Bill Frist, R-Tenn., and Minority Leader Harry Reid, D-Nev., opted for the two-seat GOP margin on all committees except Ethics, which always has an equal number of Republicans and Democrats.

Party leaders often enlarge panels to accommodate lawmakers competing for membership on the same committees. They recognize that party harmony

Committee	Size and party ratio	Number of subcommittees
Senate		
Agriculture, Nutrition, and Forestry	20 (R 11; D 9)	4
Appropriations	28 (R 15; D 13)	13
Armed Services	24 (R 13; D 11)	6
Banking, Housing, and Urban Affairs	20 (R 11; D 9)	5
Budget	22 (R 12; D 10)	—
Commerce, Science, and Transportation	22 (R 12; D 10)	10
Energy and Natural Resources	22 (R 12; D 10)	4
Environment and Public Works	18 (R 10; D 8)	4
Finance	20 (R 11; D 9)	5
Foreign Relations	18 (R 10; D 8)	7
Health, Education, Labor, and Pensions	20 (R 11; D 9)	4
Homeland Security and Governmental Affairs	16 (R 9; D 7)	3
Judiciary	18 (R 10; D 8)	6
Rules and Administration	18 (R 10; D 8)	—
Small Business and Entrepreneurship	18 (R 10; D 8)	—
Veterans' Affairs	14 (R 8; D 6)	—

Source: House and Senate committee Web pages, www.house.gov/committee and www.senate.gov/committees, accessed February 18, 2005.

can be maintained by boosting the number of committee seats. Or members may be granted waivers from chamber or party rules limiting their service on standing committees. Waivers are sometimes granted to permit members to sit on an extra major committee that they deem important to their reelection prospects. This is another example of the two Congresses, the institution bending to suit individual preferences.

Subcommittees. Subcommittees perform much of the day-to-day lawmaking and oversight work of Congress. Like standing committees, these subunits of committees vary widely in rules and procedures, staff arrangements, modes of operations, and relationships with other subcommittees and the full committee. They are created for various reasons, such as lawmakers' need to subdivide a committee's wide-ranging policy domain into manageable pieces, their desire to chair these panels and to have a platform to shape the legislative agenda, and their wish to respond to the policy claims of specialized constituencies.

In an important restructuring during the 108th Congress (2003–2005) on the House Appropriations Committee, Chairman C. W. Bill Young, R-Fla., created a new Homeland Security Subcommittee while keeping the total number of subcommittees at the panel's traditional thirteen. "Eight subcommittees have jurisdiction over facets of the new department under the current committee structure," said Chairman Young. "Creating one subcommittee will allow us to focus our attention and resources on the unique challenges confronting the new department."[15] The Senate Appropriations Committee followed suit and also created an Appropriations subcommittee on homeland security.[16] (A major overhaul of Appropriations subcommittees took place early in 2005; see the section below on committee change.)

Under House rules adopted in 2005, Republicans limited most standing committees to no more than five subcommittees. Committees bound by the limit of five may create a sixth subcommittee if it is devoted to oversight. This requirement, championed by Speaker Hastert, was intended to encourage his GOP-run committees to emphasize programmatic oversight (evaluating agency and program performance). Committees permitted to have more than five subcommittees are Appropriations (ten), Armed Services (six), Transportation and Infrastructure (six), and International Relations (seven). Various reasons account for committees having more than five subcommittees, such as long-standing custom, the acquisition of additional jurisdiction, accommodation of a lawmaker, and bicameral considerations.

Another House rule limits members to no more than four subcommittees. These limits on the number of subcommittees for each standing committee and subcommittee assignment restrictions for each member are designed to make Congress "more deliberative, participatory, and manageable by reducing scheduling conflicts and jurisdictional overlap."[17] In contrast to the practice when Democrats ran the House, GOP committee chairmen manage their committees without having to contend with independent subcommittee chairmen. GOP party rules stipulate that the selection of subcommittee chairmen "shall be at the discretion of the full Committee Chairman."

House minority leader Pelosi won adoption of a new party rule in March 2004 designed to encourage party loyalty among her top subcommittee leaders. The change came about after sixteen Democrats voted with the Republican majority in November 2003 to pass a controversial bill expanding Medicare. Speaker Hastert, in an unprecedented action, kept the vote open nearly three hours (from about 3:00 a.m. to 6:00 a.m.), until GOP leaders rounded up enough votes to pass the legislation.[18] Under the Pelosi-instigated change, Democrats on the "exclusive" standing committees would continue to select the ranking member of each of their panel's subcommittees, but these Democrats are now subject to approval by the Steering and Policy Committee as well as the Democratic Caucus. (Under party rules, the exclusive committees are Appropriations, Energy and Commerce, Financial Services, Rules, and Ways and Means. Democrats who serve on these panels may serve on no other standing committee unless they are granted an exemption, or waiver, from this requirement.) According to Democratic aides, the new party rule is designed to discourage members from voting against the Democratic Caucus "out of fear they could get passed over for subcommittee leadership."[19]

Although silent on the number of subcommittees that standing committees may establish, Senate and party rules set subcommittee assignment limits for senators and prohibit them from chairing more than one subcommittee on any given committee. The number of subcommittees not surprisingly often equals the number of majority party members on a committee eligible to chair a subcommittee. For example, despite Arizona Republican senator John McCain's high seniority rank on the Commerce Committee, he was not eligible to chair a Commerce subcommittee in the 109th Congress. The reason was that he chairs the Indian Affairs Committee as well as a subcommittee on the Armed Services Committee. Under GOP rules, a senator who heads a full committee "may not serve as chair of more than one subcommittee." Subcommittee chairmen and assignments are determined in one of two ways: by the full chair in consultation with the ranking member or by senators' order of seniority on the full committee.

Select, or Special, Committees

Select, or special, committees (the terms are interchangeable) are usually temporary panels that go out of business after the two-year life of the Congress in which they were created. But some select committees take on the attributes of permanent committees. The House, for example, has a Permanent Select Intelligence Committee. Select committees usually do not have legislative authority (the right to receive and report out measures); they can only study, investigate, and make recommendations.

Select panels are created for several reasons. First, they accommodate the concerns of individual members. The chairmen of these panels may attract publicity that enhances their political careers. For example, Democrat Harry S Truman of Missouri came to the public's (and President Franklin D. Roosevelt's) attention as head of a special Senate committee investigating World War II military procurement practices. Second, special panels can be a point of access for interest groups, such as the elderly and owners of small businesses. Third, select committees supplement the standing committee system by overseeing and investigating issues that the permanent panels lack time for or prefer to ignore. Finally, select committees can be set up to coordinate consideration of issues that overlap the jurisdictions of several standing committees. A good example occurred at the start of the 108th Congress when the House created a Select Committee on Homeland Security with both legislative and oversight jurisdiction.

Scores of House standing committees have jurisdiction over various issues pertaining to homeland security. For example, Agriculture has jurisdiction over animal and plant health; Energy and Commerce over public health; Financial Services over terrorist financing; Judiciary over the Federal Bureau of Investigation (FBI); Science over computer security; Transportation and Infrastructure over transportation security; and Ways and Means over the Customs Service. To strengthen supervision of the new Department of Homeland Security, formed from the merger of twenty-two agencies with around 180,000 employees, Speaker Hastert and other lawmakers wanted "a single point of oversight for the massive new department."[20] The select committee also had the responsibility to recommend to the Committee on Rules, by September 30, 2004, "possible changes in committee jurisdiction with respect to homeland security."[21] (The section below on committee change discusses the transformation of the select homeland security committee into a standing committee by the 109th House.)

Joint Committees

Joint committees, which include members from both chambers, have been used since the First Congress for study, investigation, oversight, and routine activities. Unless their composition is prescribed in statute, House members of joint committees are appointed by the Speaker, and senators are appointed by that chamber's presiding officer. The chairmanship of joint committees rotates each Congress between House and Senate members. In the 109th Congress there were four joint committees: Economic, Library, Printing, and Taxation. The Joint Library Committee and the Joint Printing Committee oversee, respectively, the Library of Congress and the Government Printing Office. The Joint Taxation Committee is essentially a holding company for staff who work closely with the tax-writing committees of each house. The Joint Economic Committee conducts studies and hearings on a wide range of domestic and international economic issues.

Conference Committees

Before legislation can be sent to the president to be signed, it must pass both the House and the Senate in identical form. Conference committees, sometimes called the third house of Congress, reconcile differences between similar measures passed by both chambers. They are composed of members from each house. A representative highlighted their importance:

> When I came to Congress I had no comprehension of the importance of the conference committees which actually write legislation. We all knew that important laws are drafted there, but I don't think one person in a million has any appreciation of their importance and the

process by which they work. Part of the explanation, of course, is that there never is a printed record of what goes on in conference.[22]

Conference bargaining roughly can be classified in four ways: traditional, offer-counteroffer, subconference, and pro forma. Traditional conferences are those in which the participants meet face to face, haggle among themselves about the items in bicameral disagreement, and then reach an accord. The bulk of conferences are of this type. In offer-counteroffer conferences, often used by the tax-writing committees, one side suggests a compromise proposal; the other side recesses to discuss it in private and then returns to present a counteroffer. Conferences with numerous participants (on omnibus bills, for example) usually break into small units, or subconferences, to reconcile particular matters or to address special topics. Pro forma conferences are those in which issues are resolved informally—by preconference negotiations between conferee leaders or their staffs. The conference itself then ratifies the earlier decisions.[23]

Some scholars argue that congressional committees are influential because they possess unilateral authority at the conference stage to veto or negotiate alterations in legislation. Others dispute this contention and claim that the "ex post veto is not a significant institutional foundation of congressional committee power."[24] Another model suggests that conferees serve as agents of their respective chamber majorities and advocate their policy positions instead of committee viewpoints.[25] Increasingly, the top party leaders in each chamber are taking a more direct and active role in determining who should (or should not) be a conferee. The top leaders, such as Senate majority leader Frist and House majority leader Tom DeLay, R-Texas, serve sometimes as conferees on priority measures to increase their leverage in the bicameral bargaining process.

THE ASSIGNMENT PROCESS

Every congressional election sets off a scramble for committee seats. Legislators understand the linkage between winning desirable assignments and winning elections. Newly elected representatives and senators quickly make their preferences known to party leaders, to members of the panels that make committee assignments, and to others. At the same time, incumbents may be trying to move to more prestigious panels.

The Pecking Order

The most powerful, and so most desirable, standing committees are House Ways and Means and Senate Finance, which pass on tax, trade, Social Security, and Medicare measures, and the House and Senate Appropriations Committees, which hold the federal purse strings. The Budget Committees, established in 1974, have become sought-after assignments because of their important role in economic and fiscal matters and their guardianship of the congressional budgeting process. The House and Senate Commerce Committees are also influential panels for two main reasons: their significant jurisdictional mandate and the campaign cash that committee members can raise from the many interest groups affected by the panel's decisions.

Among those that seldom have waiting lists are the Senate Ethics and House Standards of Official Conduct Committees. The House and Senate ethics panels are required to have an equal number of Democrats and Republicans. These committees in both chambers are unpopular because legislators are reluctant to sit in judgment of their colleagues. "Members have never competed for the privilege of serving on the ethics committee, and I am no exception," remarked Rep. Howard L. Berman, D-Calif., after the Democratic leader prevailed on him to join the ethics panel. Or as a GOP member said after serving as ethics chairman, "I've paid my debt to society. It's time for me to be paroled."[26] Sometimes an ethics chair is not paroled but simply replaced. This occurred a month after the 109th Congress convened when the Speaker named party loyalist Doc Hastings, R-Wash., to replace the independent-minded Joel Hefley, R-Colo. Although Hefley had served the term-limit maximum of six years, Speaker Hastert chose not to exercise his authority to waive the rule and grant the lawmaker an additional two years as ethics chair. Hefley had aroused the ire of many Republicans for supporting three public rebukes of Majority Leader DeLay.[27]

Ethical allegations against DeLay contributed to an impasse in organizing the ethics committee when the 109th Congress began. House Republicans, on a party-line vote, unilaterally changed several ethics rules. Democrats on the evenly divided panel were outraged by the changes and refused to participate in committee meetings. As a result of the partisan deadlock, the ethics committee was unable to function for months. Democrats insisted that Republicans repeal the new ethics rules. On April 27, 2005, the House voted 406 to 20 to revoke the new rules and return to those used in the 108th Congress. Speaker Hastert defended the new rules but said that DeLay "needs to have the [ethics] process move forward so he can clear his name—right now, we can't clear his name. The media wants to talk about ethics, and as long as we're at a stalemate," that is all the press will focus on. "We need to get this behind us."[28] Staff's hiring conflicts further delayed the panel's organization.

The attractiveness of committees can change. For instance, the Senate Foreign Relations Committee, long a panel that elicited great interest among members (especially during the Vietnam War era), often has had trouble since the end of the cold war in filling vacancies. Senators viewed it as largely a debating society without much influence either within or outside the Senate. Today, given heightened public concern about the global war on terrorism and a large array of other important international issues, Foreign Relations chairman Richard G. Lugar, R-Ind., has worked tirelessly to make the panel a force to be reckoned with in influencing international decision making. A foreign policy expert underscored the renewed importance of the panel: "Yeah, they've got clout. You control money, you control nominations, you control treaties, and you control the microphone" to discuss an array of global issues. "That's a lot of power in Washington."[29]

Preferences and Politicking

In an analysis of six House committees, Richard F. Fenno Jr. found that three basic goals of lawmakers—reelection, influence within the House, and good public policy—affect the committee assignments that members seek. Reelection-oriented members were attracted to committees such as Resources (then called the Interior Committee). Appropriations and Ways and Means attracted influence-oriented members. Policy-oriented members sought membership on what are now called the Education and the Workforce Committee and the International Relations Committee. Members with similar goals find themselves on the same committees, Fenno concluded. This homogeneity of perspectives may result in harmonious but biased committees.[30]

Since Fenno's study, scholars have elaborated on the relationship between members' goals and committee assignments. They have divided House committees into reelection (or constituency), policy, and power panels and concur that some mix of the three goals motivates most activity on the committees. They agree, too, that members' goals "are less easily characterized in the Senate than in the House."[31] Almost every senator has the opportunity to serve on one of the top committees, such as Appropriations, Armed Services, Commerce, and Finance. Hence, the power associated with a particular committee assignment is less important for senators than for representatives (see Table 7-2).

In the weeks after an election, members campaign vigorously for the committees they prefer. When Rep. Robert B. Aderholt, R-Ala., was a freshman, he set out to win a coveted spot on the Appropriations Committee. He solicited the help of the majority leader and lobbied each member who sat on the GOP's committee assignment panel. "It was almost like this was another congressional campaign," Aderholt explained. "While a lot of [new] members were driving around house hunting and interviewing staff members, I was working" to win appointment to Appropriations.[32] Rep. Jennifer Dunn, R-Wash. (1993–2005), provided all incoming GOP freshmen with a how-to booklet on securing committee assignments. She devised a three-part strategy emphasizing personal, political, and geographical factors. For example, Dunn suggested face-to-face meetings with members of the Steering Committee, letters and phone calls to committee chairmen, and personal contact with party leaders. "Do not be afraid to go to each Member of the Leadership to let them know of your political needs. Leadership has proven . . . open to placing freshmen Members on key committees," she advised the newcomers. Dunn also urged freshmen to seek help from key GOP members in their state or region.[33] Sometimes party leaders recruit stellar candidates by promising them favorable committee assignments should they win; they may also entice former House members to

TABLE 7-2 **House and Senate Committee Comparison**

Category	House	Senate
Number of standing committees	20	16
Committee/subcommittee assignments per member	About 6	About 11
Power or prestige committees	Appropriations, Budget, Commerce, Financial Services, Rules, Ways and Means	Appropriations, Armed Services, Commerce, Finance, Foreign Relations [a]
Treaties and nominations submitted by the president	No authority	Committees review
Floor debate	Representatives' activity is somewhat confined to the bills reported from the panels on which they serve	Senators can choose to influence any policy area regardless of their committee assignments
Committee consideration of legislation	More difficult to bypass	Easier to bypass [b]
Committee chairs	Subject to party and speakership influence that limits their discretionary authority over committee operations	Freer rein to manage committees
Committee staff	Often assertive in advocating ideas and proposals	More aggressive in shaping the legislative agenda
Subcommittee chairmanships	Representatives of the majority party usually must wait at least one term	Majority senators, regardless of their seniority, usually chair subcommittees

[a] Almost every senator is assigned to one of these committees.
[b] For example, by allowing riders—unrelated policy proposals—to measures pending on the floor.

run again by pledging to restore their previous seniority on their old committees.

Although both parties try to accommodate assignment preferences, some members inevitably receive unwelcome assignments. A classic case involved Democratic representative Shirley Chisholm of Brooklyn (1969–1983), the first African American woman elected to Congress. She was assigned to the House Agriculture Committee her first year in the House. "I think it would be hard to imagine an assignment that is less relevant to my background or to the needs of the predominantly black and Puerto Rican people who elected me, she said. Chisholm's protests won her a seat on the Veterans' Affairs Committee. "There are a lot more veterans in my district than there are trees," she later observed.[34] Yet some urban lawmakers welcome service on the Agriculture Committee, where they can fuse metropolitan issues with rural issues through food stamp, consumer, and other legislation.

How Assignments Are Made

Each party in each house has its own panel to review members' committee requests and hand out assignments (the Steering Committee for House Republicans, the Steering Committee for House Democrats, the Republican Committee on Committees for Senate Republicans, and the Steering and Coordination Committee for Senate Democrats.) The decisions of these panels are the first and most important acts in a three-step procedure. The second step involves approval of the assignment lists by each party's caucus. Finally, there is pro forma election by the full House or Senate.

Formal Criteria. Both formal and informal criteria guide the assignment panels in choosing committee members. Formal criteria are designed to ensure that each member is treated equitably in committee assignments. For example, the House Republican Conference divides committees into three classes: exclusive, nonexclusive, and exempt. A member assigned to an exclusive panel (Appropriations, Budget, Energy and Commerce, Rules, and Ways and Means) may not serve on any other standing committee unless the GOP Conference waives this party rule for certain members. Republicans may serve on only two of the nonexclusive panels: Agriculture, Armed Services, Budget, Education and the Workforce, Financial Services, Government Reform, International Relations, Judiciary, Resources, Science, Small Business, Transportation and Infrastructure, and Veterans' Affairs. The exempt committees are House Administration, Select Intelligence, and Standards of Official Conduct. House minority leader Pelosi enforces Democratic Caucus rules that limit ranking members from serving on certain other committees without a waiver as a way to distribute more choice assignments to her party colleagues. For instance, Pelosi declined to grant a waiver to Barney Frank, D-Mass., to remain on the Judiciary Committee when he became ranking member on the Financial Services Committee.[35]

Since 1953, when Senate Democratic leader Lyndon B. Johnson of Texas announced his "Johnson rule," all Senate Democrats are assigned one major committee before any party member receives a second major assignment. In 1965 Senate Republicans followed suit. Senate rules also classify committees into different categories, which are popularly called "A," "B," and "C." There is even a separate category in the A group informally called "Super A." Senators may serve on only one of the four Super A panels (Appropriations, Armed Services, Finance, and Foreign Relations) unless the rule is waived for them. Senate rules state that members must serve on no more than two committees in the A category, which includes the four Super A panels; one in the

B grouping (Budget, Rules and Administration, and Small Business, for example); and any number of C committees (Ethics, Indian Affairs, Joint Library, Joint Printing, and Joint Taxation).

Informal Criteria. Many informal criteria affect committee assignments, such as party loyalty, geography, expertise, or ideology. House Democrats have guidelines in their party rules instructing the Steering Committee to consider "merit, length of service, degree of commitment to the Democratic agenda, and Caucus diversity" in granting committee assignments.[36] Members' own wishes are another criterion. Lawmakers who represent districts or states with large military installations may seek assignment to the Armed Services Committee. Or lawmakers with a specific policy interest (education, health, and so on) may strive to win appointment to panels that deal with those topics.

Worth underscoring is the reality of the two Congresses in assignment decisions. Each party seeks through the appointments process to give electoral advantage to lawmakers of their party. House GOP and Democratic leaders, for instance, sometimes grant their electorally vulnerable freshmen an extra committee assignment to broaden their appeal as they head into the November elections. "All of these committees have constituents," said Democratic whip Steny H. Hoyer of Maryland. "And all of these [freshmen Democratic appointees] have people in their districts who are members of these constituencies."[37]

More seasoned members who could face tough electoral competition may seek plum assignments to boost their influence and capacity for fund-raising. Three-term representative Melissa A. Hart, R-Pa., launched a successful campaign in 2005 to win assignment to the tax-writing Ways and Means Committee. Well-versed in revenue matters as chair of the Finance Committee when she served in the Pennsylvania Senate, her appointment enhanced her campaign fund-raising. Hart easily beat her Democratic opponents in prior House elections, but subsequent elections might see the emergence of a potentially more formidable challenger. For example, Chris Heinz, the stepson of Senator John Kerry, D-Mass., and son of Teresa Heinz and the late Pennsylvania Republican senator (1977–1991) John Heinz, might be harder for Hart to defeat. "The family home where Heinz was raised is in Fox Chapel, in Hart's district."[38] Party leaders also award coveted committees to members who may be thinking of retiring or running for statewide office as a way to keep to a minimum the number of open—and, therefore, usually more competitive—seats they must defend.

Seniority. Normally, the assignment panels observe seniority when preparing committee membership lists. The member of the majority party with the longest continuous committee service is usually listed first. Senate Republicans, unlike House Republicans and House and Senate Democrats, apply seniority rigidly when two or more GOP senators compete for either a committee vacancy or chairmanship. As a senator noted: "When I first came to the Senate, I was skeptical [of the seniority tradition]. But as I've become more senior, I've grown more fond of it."[39] (The Senate GOP leader fills half of all vacancies on the "A" committees; seniority determines the other half.) By contrast, the two House parties do not observe seniority as strictly as Senate Republicans. House GOP Conference rules even state that the member designated as chair by the party's committee on committees (the Steering Committee) "need not be the Member with the longest consecutive service on the Committee." (See Box 7-1 on party assignment committees.)

When Newt Gingrich, R-Ga., was Speaker, he bypassed the seniority custom on several occasions to give chairmanships to Republicans who could move the party's agenda despite their having less committee longevity than some others on those panels. Further, in 1995 the House imposed a six-year term limit on committee and subcommittee chairmen, which both promotes party direction of committees and triggers a round of musical chairmanships every new Congress. Although various GOP chairs have tried to repeal the rule so they could continue in their position beyond six years, they were unsuccessful in making the change. (At the start of the 109th Congress, David Dreier, R-Calif., was granted a waiver by Speaker Hastert to serve an extra two years as chairman of the Rules Committee.) To settle the highly competitive contests among Republicans competing to chair the various committees, Speaker Hastert took a new approach to settle these bouts.

Hastert decided upon an unprecedented interview procedure by which the Steering Committee would make its recommendations for chairman to the full Republican Conference, which votes to approve each nominee. In a letter to GOP members, Speaker Hastert explained several basic features of the interview process. "The candidates will be given an opportunity to discuss their legislative agenda, oversight agenda, how they intend to organize the committees, and their communication strategy," he wrote.[40] Fund-raising prowess was another consideration. "You can't tell me a Member who raises $1 million for the party and visits 50 districts is not going to have an advantage over someone who sits back and thinks he's entitled to a chairmanship. Those days are gone," said a top GOP leadership aide.[41] Minority Leader Pelosi emulated Hastert's interview technique in the 109th Congress. She directed the Steering Committee to interview most ranking committee members before they could be reappointed by the Democratic Caucus. For example, Collin C. Peterson, D-Minn., was chosen to be ranking member on the Agriculture Committee but faced tough questioning by the Steering Committee as to his party loyalty, financial and electoral contributions to the party, and his voting record.[42]

Many of the criteria employed to designate GOP chairmen (or ranking minority members) are comparable to those that top party leaders must possess: coalition-building skills, fund-raising ability, and talent for media advocacy. (Party loyalty, too, is an important criterion.) Like party leaders, GOP candidates for vacant chairmanships launch their own campaigns to influence, in this case, the Hastert-led Steering Committee. Some enlist the support of outside groups, others make PowerPoint presentations to the panel, several may

BOX 7-1 Party Assignment Committees

House Republicans. Before the 104th Congress began in 1995, incoming Speaker Newt Gingrich, R-Ga., revamped his party's committee on committees, which he would chair. Gingrich renamed it the Steering Committee; transformed it into a twenty-nine-member, leadership-dominated panel; eliminated a weighted voting system wherein a GOP member of the assignment panel cast as many votes as there were Republicans in his state delegation; and granted the Speaker control over about one-fourth of the total votes on the panel with the Speaker personally casting the most votes (five). These reforms continued in the subsequent Congresses. The Speaker also appoints all GOP members of the Rules, House Administration, and Standards of Official Conduct Committees.

House Democrats. Democrats on the House Ways and Means Committee functioned as their party's committee on committees from 1911 until 1974, when the Democratic Caucus voted to transfer this duty to the Steering and Policy Committee. Renamed the Steering Committee at the beginning of the 104th Congress, the fifty-member assignment panel in the 109th Congress was chaired by Rosa DeLauro of Connecticut.

Senate Republicans. The chairman of the Republican Conference appoints the assignment panel of about eight members. In addition, the floor leader is an ex officio member. Idaho senator Michael D. Crapo chaired the panel during the 109th Congress.

Senate Democrats. The Steering and Coordination Committee makes assignments for Democrats. Its size (about twenty-five members) is set by the party conference and may fluctuate from Congress to Congress. The party's floor leader appoints the members of this panel and its chair (Sen. Hillary Rodham Clinton of New York, for the 109th Congress).

develop memorandums or briefing books to highlight their plans as chairman, and still others hand out home-state products, such as peanuts or raisins, to the Steering members.

The most-watched recent contest in the lead-up to the 109th Congress was who among three experienced GOP Appropriations members—Ralph Regula, Ohio; Jerry Lewis, Calif., and Harold Rogers, Ky.—would succeed the term-limited Bill Young of Florida. Regula had more seniority on the panel than either Lewis, who was second, or Rogers, but more than seniority decided this race. All three were grilled individually behind closed doors by the Steering Committee (as well as by conservative and moderate House GOP groups), and each had to answer questions about their campaign fund-raising history, commitment to spending restraint, responsiveness to GOP leaders, and willingness to reform the appropriations process. In the end, Lewis won the post for a variety of reasons: his long record of fund-raising for the party (during the 2004 election cycle he distributed $1.35 million to GOP candidates compared with $1.3 million for Regula and $1.15 million for Rogers); the support he had from other influential California chairs, such as Ways and Means chairman Bill Thomas and Rules Committee chairman

David Dreier; and recognition by GOP leaders that Lewis is "a capable appropriator as well as a team player." [43]

The contest for the Appropriations chair largely overshadowed press attention on a precedent-making event for House Republicans. GOP leaders, for the first time since Republicans won control of the House in the mid-1990s, stripped a colleague of a chairmanship. Veterans' Affairs chairman Christopher H. Smith of New Jersey, who was in the fourth year of his six-year term, was both ousted as chair and removed from the panel. Smith had the strong backing of veterans' organizations, but his outspoken advocacy for more spending on veterans' benefits angered the Speaker and other party leaders. A senior Republican who supported Smith's removal said: "If [GOP leaders] don't do what they did, they send a message to others that you just thumb your nose at the team and you still get rewarded." [44] GOP leaders chose Steve Buyer of Indiana to replace Smith as chair of the Veterans panel.

Senate Republicans followed the House regarding term limits by adopting a party rule, effective in 1997, restricting committee chairmen (or ranking members) to six years of service. "The whole thrust behind this," said the Senate author of the term-limit change, "is to try to get greater participation, so new members of the Senate don't have to wait until they've been here 18 years to play a role." [45] However, in the lead-up to the November 2002 elections, Senate Republicans modified their party rule on term limits. With Vermont senator James M. Jeffords's midsession 2001 party switch, which put Democrats in charge of all Senate committees, concern arose about how to count the interrupted service of the GOP chairs. Some GOP senators wanted a strict six-year limit, counting service as both chair and ranking member, which would have produced large turnover in chairmanships after Republicans recaptured control of the 108th Senate. Other senators wanted to abolish the six-year limit entirely. In the end, Senate Republicans adopted a complex compromise that reaffirmed and clarified the six-year ban. Under the compromise,

> Republicans will be allowed to serve a total of six years as chairman and six as ranking Republican. But anyone who has served six years as chairman can no longer serve as ranking member. On the other hand, a senator who has served six years as chairman can no longer serve as a ranking member but less than that as chairman could finish out a six-year tenure as chairman. [46]

Under the change, Republicans who served as chairmen in the 107th Senate until the Jeffords switch still had two years left to chair their committee. For example, Sen. Ted Stevens, R-Alaska, who chaired the Appropriations Committee since 1997 until the June 2001 change in party control of the Senate, was back for two more years as chair of Appropriations in the 108th Congress. "Once he hits that six-year total as chairman, he can no longer chair the [Appropriations] committee or serve as ranking member," but he was not prohibited from seeking the chairmanship of another committee.[47] In fact, Stevens became chair of the Commerce Committee in the 109th Congress as Thad Cochran, R-Miss., took the reins of the Appropriations Committee. A number of other musical-chair changes took place as several other GOP senators hit their party-imposed, six-year term limit for chairmanships. The most controversial changeover concerned the Judiciary Committee. The six-year term of Orrin G. Hatch of Utah was at an end and, by the party's seniority practices, Arlen Specter of Pennsylvania was next in line to be chair. Because he made remarks following the November 2004 election that aroused the ire of social conservatives (they tried to block his elevation), Specter had to launch a campaign to persuade his GOP colleagues to make him Judiciary chair. His campaign was successful.[48]

Biases. The decisions made by the assignment panels inevitably determine the geographical and ideological composition of the standing committees. Committees can easily become biased toward one position or another. Farm areas are overrepresented on the Agriculture Committees and small business interests on the Small Business Committees. No wonder committees are policy advocates. They propose laws that reflect the interests of their members and the outside groups and agencies that gravitate toward them.

Who gets on a panel or who is left off affects committee policy making. Committees that are carefully balanced between liberal and conservative interests can be tilted one way or the other by new members. A committee's political philosophy influences its success on the House or Senate floor. Committees ideologically out of step with the House or Senate as a whole are more likely than others to have legislation defeated or significantly revised by floor amendments.

Approval by Party Caucuses and the Chamber

For most of the twentieth century each chamber's party caucuses either ratified the assignment decisions of their committees on committees or took no action on them at all. Beginning in the 1970s, however, party caucuses became major participants in the assignment process. Chairmen and ranking minority members were subjected to election by secret ballot of their partisan colleagues. Clearly, committee leadership is no longer an automatic right.

Although seniority still encourages continuity on committees, the seniority system has now become more flexible and is under caucus control. House GOP rules for the 109th Congress stated that the "Conference shall vote by secret ballot on each recommendation of the . . . Steering Committee for the position of Chairman. If the Republican Conference fails to approve a recommendation . . . the matter shall be automatically recommitted without instruction to [the Steering] Committee." In the Senate the parties can exercise control over committees but nearly always defer to the seniority rankings of lawmakers in determining who heads a committee or subcommittee.

Each chamber's rules require that all members of standing committees, including chairmen, be elected by the entire House or Senate. The practice, however, is for each party's leaders to offer the caucus-approved assignment lists to the full chamber. Normally, these are approved quickly by voice vote.

COMMITTEE LEADERSHIP

Committee leaders are usually the chairmen and the ranking minority members. Committee chairmen call meetings and establish agendas, hire and fire committee staff, arrange hearings, recommend conferees, act as floor managers, allocate committee funds and rooms, develop legislative strategies, chair hearings and markups, and regulate the internal affairs and organization of the committee.

The procedural advantages of a chairman are hard for even the most forceful minority members to overcome. The chairman may be able to kill a bill simply by refusing to schedule it for a hearing. Or a chairman may convene meetings when proponents or opponents of the legislation are unavoidably absent. The chairman's authority derives from the support of a committee majority and a variety of formal and informal resources, such as substantive and parliamentary experience and control over the agenda, communications, and financial resources of the committee. When told by a committee colleague that he lacked the votes on an issue, then House Energy and Commerce chairman John D. Dingell, D-Mich., replied, "Yeah, but I've got the gavel."[49] Dingell banged his gavel, adjourned the meeting, and the majority had no chance to work its will before the legislative session ended.

The Dingell example highlights the formidable ability of chairs to stymie action on legislation they oppose. However, committee chairs are also among the most substantively and strategically knowledgeable members on their panel and in the chamber. They are advantageously positioned to advance ideas into law. Ways and Means chairman Bill Thomas is widely regarded by lawmakers of both parties as a talented, hard-working, assertive, and shrewd member. On numerous controversial issues (tax, trade, and health), he has demonstrated skill in mobilizing winning coalitions in committee, in the chamber, and in conference with the Senate. Thomas even seeks out senatorial advice on how to move legislation in the House in a way that maximizes its chances in the Senate. "[H]e will venture to the Senate floor to run options by key senators of both parties, or to stop in Senate leadership offices, before returning to the House to brief appropriate leaders on the latest state of play."[50]

The top minority party member on a committee is also an influential figure. Among his powers on various committees are nominating minority conferees, hiring and firing minority staff, sitting ex officio on all subcommittees, assisting in setting the committee's agenda, managing legislation on the floor, and acting as committee spokesperson for his party. For example, Ways and

Means ranking member Charles B. Rangel, D-N.Y., an experienced and knowledgeable lawmaker, presents Democratic alternatives to Chairman Thomas's proposals, challenges the chairman on procedural and policy matters, develops tactics and strategies to foil GOP plans, and highlights party goals and views to the attentive public.

POLICY MAKING IN COMMITTEE

Committees foster deliberate, collegial, fragmented decisions. They encourage bargaining and accommodation among members. To move bills through Congress's numerous decision points from subcommittee to committee, authors of bills and resolutions typically make compromises in response to important committee members. These gatekeepers may exact alterations in a bill's substance. The proliferation of committees also multiplies the points of access for outside interests.

Overlapping Jurisdictions

The formal responsibilities of a standing committee are defined by the rules of each house, various public laws, and precedents. Committees with overlapping jurisdictions sometimes formulate a written memorandum of understanding that informally outlines how policy topics are to be referred among them.[51] Committees do not have watertight jurisdictional compartments. Any broad subject overlaps numerous committees. The Senate has an Environment and Public Works Committee, but other panels also consider environmental legislation; the same is true in the House. These House bodies, along with a brief sketch of some of their environmental responsibilities, are as follows:

Agriculture: pesticides; soil conservation; some water programs

Appropriations: funding for environmental programs and agencies

Energy and Commerce: health effects of the environment; environmental regulations; solid waste disposal; clean air; safe drinking water

Financial Services: open space acquisition in urban areas

Government Reform: federal executive branch agencies for the environment

International Relations: international environmental cooperation

Resources: water resources; power resources; land management; wildlife conservation; national parks; nuclear waste; fisheries; endangered species

Science: environmental research and development

Small Business: effects of environmental regulations on business

Transportation and Infrastructure: water pollution; sludge management

Ways and Means: environmental tax expenditures

Jurisdictional overlaps can have positive results. They can enable members to develop expertise in several policy fields, prevent any one group from dominating a topic, and promote healthy competition among committees. However, healthy competition can quickly turn to intercommittee warfare.

Various House and Senate committees periodically clash over issues that do not fit neatly into any single panel's area of responsibility (energy and environmental issues, for instance). Committees' formal jurisdictional mandates have not kept pace with change—nor can they, given the constant emergence of new issues (genetic discrimination and cloning, for instance). Another trigger of turf battles is forum shopping by outside interests who want their carefully drafted bills referred to sympathetic committees. The expansionist tendency of some committees also can create intercommittee tussles. The "bold jurisdictional power grab" by the House Energy and Commerce Committee for an intellectual copyright bill will not stand, declared the bipartisan leaders of the Judiciary Committee. "Rest assured, we will wholeheartedly oppose this move in a bipartisan fashion, as we would expect Energy and Commerce leaders to do if we attempted to write energy legislation."[52]

Multiple Referrals

When a bill is introduced in the House, it usually is referred to a single committee. Until 1975 House rules made no provision for multiple referrals, although informally occasions arose when more than one panel reviewed the same bill. In that year, however, the rules were changed to permit several types of multiple referrals. This change augmented the Speaker's authority and granted him additional flexibility in referring measures to various committees.

When Republicans assumed control of the House in 1995, they streamlined multiple referrals and placed them firmly under the Speaker's control. The Speaker must "designate a committee of primary jurisdiction upon the initial referral of a measure to a committee." The primary committee concept is designed to increase accountability for legislation while retaining for the Speaker flexibility in determining whether, when, and for how long other panels can receive the measure.

At the time of initial referral, the Speaker identifies the primary committee. It has predominant responsibility for shepherding the legislation to final passage. The Speaker may also send the measure to secondary panels. The House parliamentarian calls this practice an additional initial referral. In the following example of referral language, the Energy and Commerce Committee is the primary committee and Judiciary is the additional initial panel.

> H.R. 650. A bill to establish reasonable legal reforms that will facilitate the manufacture of vital, life-saving vaccines, and for other purposes; to the Committee on Energy and Commerce, and in addition to the Committee on the Judiciary, for a period to be subsequently deter-

mined by the Speaker, in each case for consideration of such provisions as fall within the jurisdiction of the committee concerned.

At the start of the 108th Congress, Republicans again modified the House rule on multiple referrals. Because of jurisdictional difficulties in determining which committee is primary in matters of health—Energy and Commerce or Ways and Means—Republicans authorized the use of joint referrals, a practice utilized by Democrats when they controlled the House. Rules chairman David Dreier explained the intent of the new rule: "This change is meant only as a minor deviation from the normal requirement under the rules for the designation of one committee of primary jurisdiction and should be exercised only in extraordinary jurisdictionally deserving instances."[53] This rule remains in effect.

Multiple referrals may promote integrated policy making, broader public discussion of issues, wide access to the legislative process, and consideration of alternative approaches. They also enhance the Speaker's scheduling prerogatives. The Speaker can use the referral power to intervene more directly in committee activities and even to set deadlines for committees to report multiply referred legislation. The reverse is also possible: The Speaker can delay action on measures by referring them to other committees. Thus, multiple referrals can be employed to slow down legislative decision making.

The Senate usually sends measures to a single committee—the committee with jurisdiction over the subject matter that predominates in the legislation. Although multiple referrals have long been permitted by unanimous consent, they are infrequently used, mainly because senators have many opportunities to influence policy making on the floor.

Where Bills Go

Many bills referred to committee are sent by the chairman to a subcommittee. Others are retained for review by the full committee. In the end, committees and subcommittees select the measures they want to consider and ignore the rest. Committee consideration usually consists of three standard steps: public hearings, markups, and reports.

Hearings. When committees or subcommittees conduct hearings on a bill, they listen to a wide variety of witnesses. These include the bill's sponsors, federal officials, pressure group representatives, public officials, and private citizens—sometimes even celebrities. Movie-star witnesses can help give a bill national visibility. When Elizabeth Taylor appeared before a Senate panel to testify on acquired immune deficiency syndrome (AIDS), the chairman said of the press coverage, "I haven't seen anything like this in the 30 days we have had hearings."[54] Or as Sen. Arlen Specter put it, "Quite candidly, when Hollywood speaks, the world listens. Sometimes when Washington speaks, the world snoozes."[55]

Equally important are witnesses who can add drama to hearings because of their first-hand experience with an issue or problem. The Senate Finance

Committee, for example, attracted national headlines with its hearings on alleged wrongdoings by the Internal Revenue Service (IRS). Taxpayers recounted their horrendous experiences, and IRS agents donned black hoods to tell about the organization's mistreatment of taxpayers.[56] Testimony by employees who lost their retirement savings because of corporate scandals (Enron Corp. and WorldCom Inc., for example) helped to galvanize congressional enactment of corporate accounting and accountability laws. Hearings, in brief, are often orchestrated as a form of political theater where witnesses who put a human face on a public problem tell a story that may generate public momentum for legislation.

Hearings provide opportunities for committee members to be heard on the issues. Frequently, lawmakers present their views on legislation in their opening statements and in the guise of asking questions of witnesses. Most hearings follow a traditional format. Each witness reads a prepared statement. Then each committee member has a limited time (often five minutes) to ask questions before the next witness is called. To save time and promote give-and-take, committees occasionally use a panel format in which witnesses sit together and briefly summarize their statements.

After 1997 new House rules were adopted to promote opportunities for longer exchanges between lawmakers and witnesses. The majority and minority on a committee now can designate one of their panel members or committee staff aides to question a witness for up to one hour.

Gradually, committees are beginning to harness contemporary technology to conduct Capitol Hill hearings. Several House and Senate panels have used interactive video, teleconferencing, and other technology to collect testimony from witnesses who may be located in other parts of the nation or world. The Internet has been used to transmit testimony, and cable television viewers have e-mailed or faxed questions to witnesses.[57] The House Agriculture Committee became "the first congressional panel to broadcast its proceedings in live audio format over the internet."[58]

Among the overlapping purposes served by hearings are

- to explore the need for legislation;
- to build a public record in support of legislation;
- to publicize the role of committee chairmen;
- to stake out committee jurisdictions;
- to review executive implementation of public laws;
- to provide a forum for citizens' grievances and frustrations;
- to educate lawmakers and the attentive public on complex issues; and
- to raise the visibility of an issue.

With Senate Democrats in the minority following the November 2004 elections, they lacked the ability to schedule hearings, issue subpoenas, or initiate investigations of the Republican administration. As a result, they sometimes scheduled informal hearings (policy forums with outside experts, for instance) to air their criticisms of the Bush administration and to highlight their own alternatives. For example, the Senate Democratic Policy Committee held a hearing to criticize President Bush's plan to change the Social Security system, "part of an increasingly sharp Democratic attack on his proposal."[59] Sometimes committees conduct field hearings around the country to generate and assess public support for measures or hold joint hearings with other House or Senate panels. For example, the House and Senate Intelligence Committees conducted joint hearings in the aftermath of the September 11, 2001, terrorist attacks to assess why the intelligence agencies failed to detect and prevent the assault on the United States.

Hearings are shaped mainly by the chairman and staff, with varying degrees of input from party leaders, the ranking minority member, and others. By revealing patterns of support or opposition and by airing substantive problems, hearings indicate to members whether a bill is worth taking to the full chamber. Chairmen who favor bills can expedite the hearings process; conversely, they can kill with kindness legislation they oppose by holding endless hearings. When a bill is not sent to the full chamber, the printed hearings are the end product of the committee's work. Committee chairmen can also use hearings to try and win reelection by addressing issues that appeal to various voting groups in their state or district.

Markups. After hearings have been held, committee members decide the bill's actual language; that is, the bill is marked up or amended (see Box 7-2 on committee decision making). The chair may circulate his mark to committee colleagues via e-mail and solicit their comments and suggestions. Just as committees and the hearings process differ one from the other, so do markups vary among committees. Some panels adhere closely to parliamentary rules during this committee amending phase, others operate by consensus with few or no votes taken on the issues, and still others have "conceptual markups". Sen. Rick Santorum, R-Pa., explained that Finance Committee markups "are not about legislative language. There are concept documents that are then put into legislative language and brought to the floor."[60] Concepts may include, for instance, whether going to school counts as work for welfare recipients or what kind of tax plan best fosters economic growth.

Proponents try to craft a bill that will muster the backing of their colleagues, the other chamber, lobbyists, and the White House. This process can be arduous because members often face the two Congresses dilemma: whether to support a bill that might be good for the nation or oppose it because of the opposition of their constituents. Not surprisingly, the bill that emerges from markup is usually the one that can attract the support of the most members. As Rep. Dan Rostenkowski, D-Ill. (1959–1995), said when he chaired the House Ways and Means Committee, "We have not written perfect law; perhaps a faculty of scholars could do a better job. A group of ideologues could have produced greater consistency. But politics is an imperfect process."[61] Or as

Senate Intelligence Committee chairman Pat Roberts, R-Kan., said about a bill revamping the intelligence community: "While this is not the best possible bill, it is the best bill possible." [62]

Outside pressures are often intense during markup deliberations. Under House and Senate sunshine rules, markups must be conducted in public, except on national security or related issues. Compromises can be difficult to achieve in markup rooms filled with lobbyists watching how each member will vote. Hence, committees sometimes conduct pre-markups in private to work out their positions on various issues.

After conducting hearings and markups, a subcommittee sends its recommendations to the full committee. The full committee may conduct hearings and markups on its own, ratify the subcommittee's decision, take no action, or return the matter to the subcommittee for further study.

Reports. If the full committee votes to send the bill to the House or Senate, the staff prepares a report, subject to committee approval, describing the purposes and provisions of the legislation. Reports emphasize arguments favorable to the bill, summarizing selectively the results of staff research and hearings. Reports are noteworthy documents. The bill itself may be long, highly technical, and confusing to most readers. "A good report, therefore, does more than explain—it also persuades," commented a congressional staff aide.[63] Furthermore, reports may guide executive agencies and federal courts in interpreting ambiguous or complex legislative language.

The Policy Environment

Executive agencies, pressure groups, party leaders and caucuses, and the entire House or Senate form the backdrop against which a committee makes policy. These environments may be consensual or conflictual. Some policy questions are settled fairly easily, while others are bitterly controversial. Environments also may be monolithic or pluralistic. Some committees have a single dominant source of outside influence, while others face numerous competing groups or agencies.

Environmental factors influence committees in at least four ways. First, they shape the content of public policies and thus the likelihood that these policies will be accepted by the full House or Senate. The Judiciary Committees are buffeted by diverse and competing pressure groups that feel passionately on volatile issues such as abortion, school prayer, and gun control. The committees' chances for achieving agreement among their members or on the floor depend to a large extent on their ability to deflect such issues altogether or to accommodate diverse groups through artful legislative drafting.

Second, policy environments foster mutual alliances among committees, federal departments, and pressure groups—the "iron triangles". The House and Senate Veterans' Affairs Committees, for example, regularly advocate legislation to benefit veterans groups, the second point in the triangle. This effort is backed by the Department of Veterans Affairs. At the very least, issue networks

BOX 7-2 Committee Decision Making: A Formal Model

Political scientists use a variety of sophisticated techniques to understand legislative decision making. Employing concepts from economics such as rational choice—the notion that individuals (or lawmakers) have preferences or desires and that they will act in their self-interest to achieve their goals—these scholars utilize a number of analytical tools to consider how lawmakers devise strategies to accomplish their policy objectives. One such analytical approach is called spatial theory. The term *spatial* refers to a mathematical idea that theorists rely on called a policy space. An easy-to-understand example is that certain policy preferences can all be arrayed along a straight line, or unidimensional continuum. So, for example, one end of the line might be labeled "more spending" and the other "less spending." Different spending preferences could be placed at different points, or spaces, along the line.

In employing spatial theory to model legislative decision making, scholars make a number of assumptions. Two are especially important: (1) lawmakers hold consistent preferences and (2) members have an ideal policy outcome that they prefer. Put differently, lawmakers will vote for policy alternatives that bring them closer to their policy ideal and oppose those that do the reverse. The work of these scholars highlights the importance of institutional rules and procedures in determining which of several policy alternatives will prevail. Analysts have also found that the median voter—the midpoint lawmaker with an equal number of other members to his left or right—is the ultimate determiner of outcomes in unidimensional cases. Another way to view the median voter is the 218th vote in the House, the Supreme Court justice who casts the fifth vote in a 5 to 4 decision, or the member who casts the sixth vote in a committee of eleven members.

To depict this graphically, assume that a House Appropriations subcommittee has sent to the floor a spending bill that reflects its committee median (CM). The subcommittee also must take into account a floor median (FM) if it wants its majority position to carry the day on the floor. The current policy status quo (Q) means that, if the bill does not pass, last year's funding level remains in force. If the subcommittee's bill is brought to the floor under a no-amendment rule, then the House membership can either accept or reject the panel's position. If the House rejects the subcommittee's policy recommendation, it has agreed to retain the status quo. Whether the subcommittee's position prevails on the floor can be depicted using these two examples.

If the subcommittee's position is to win on the House floor, it must devise a strategy that takes account of the majority preferences of the membership. Furthermore, the subcommittee

emerge. These are fluid and amorphous groups of policy experts who try to influence any committee that deals with their subject area.[64]

Third, policy environments establish decision-making objectives and guidelines for committees. Clientele-oriented committees, such as the House and Senate Small Business Committees, try to promote the policy views of their clientele groups, small business enterprises. Alliances between committees and federal departments also shape decisions.

must have some way to acquire information about the policy options likely to be accepted by at least a majority of the House. These types of considerations are commonplace in the real world of Capitol Hill policy making.

Example 1

More Spending — Less Spending

FM CM Q

In Example 1, the preferences of a majority of the House clearly are closer to the committee's position than the status quo. Hence, the committee's position prevails.

Example 2

More Spending — Less Spending

FM CM Q

In Example 2, a majority of the House clearly favors the policy status quo instead of the committee's position, which loses in an up-or-down floor vote.

Most bills concern not a single dimension, such as more or less spending, but a multitude of dimensions. For example, a bill might be close to a member's ideal point on the spending dimension but be far away on another dimension, such as which governmental level (federal or state) should handle the issue. The introduction of additional dimensions (multidimensionality) produces greater difficulty in analyzing legislative decision making. By employing spatial theory and other analytical approaches, political scientists strive to better understand and explain congressional politics and decision making.[a]

[a] See, for example, Kenneth Shepsle and Mark Boncheck, *Analyzing Politics* (New York: W. W. Norton, 1977); Charles Stewart, *Analyzing Congress* (New York: W. W. Norton, 2001); and Gerald Strom, *The Logic of Lawmaking: A Spatial Theory Approach* (Baltimore: Johns Hopkins University Press, 1990).

Finally, environmental factors influence the level of partisanship on committees. Some committees are relatively free of party infighting, but other committees consider contentious social issues such as poverty and welfare that often divide the two parties. The House Judiciary Committee is filled with conservative Republican and liberal Democratic firebrands. Their sharp ideological clashes got wide publicity during the panel's nationally televised impeachment proceedings against President Bill Clinton.[65]

COMMITTEE STAFF

Throughout the three principal stages of committee policy making—hearings, markup, and report—staff aides play an active part. Representatives and senators (to a greater degree because there are fewer of them) cannot handle the large workload on their own and so must rely heavily on the unelected lawmakers. Part of the Senate Democratic motivation for seeking nearly equal committee budgets in the 109th Senate is their need to counter the expertise lodged in the Bush-controlled executive branch. In the House, committee resources are generally divided between the majority and minority parties on a two-thirds to one-third basis. Informally, congressional Democrats rely on a network of outside experts to help them scrutinize and evaluate proposals from the GOP administration and to forge their own proposals. For example, retired general Wesley Clark, a 2004 Democratic presidential hopeful, consulted with senior House Democrats on crafting "a strengthened message [and national security policy] on Iraq."[66]

The discretionary agenda of Congress and its committees is powerfully shaped by the congressional staff. Their influence can be direct or indirect, substantive or procedural, visible or invisible. In the judgment of one former senator, "most of the work and most of the ideas come from the staffers. They are predominantly young men and women, fresh out of college and professional schools. They are ambitious, idealistic, and abounding with ideas."[67] However, staff tenure is short. According to a 2004 study by the Congressional Management Foundation, "Over 60% of House staff have two or less years of experience in their current position, including 39% of Chiefs of Staff, 64% of Legislative Directors, and 66% of Press Secretaries."[68] The average tenure for Senate aides is about 5.3 years. Many committee, personal, and leadership aides use their experience as a stepping-stone to other jobs, such as lobbying.

Policy proposals emanate from many sources—the White House, administrative agencies, interest groups, state and local officials, scholars, and citizens—but staff aides are strategically positioned to advance or hinder these proposals. As one Senate committee staff director recounted, "Usually, you draw up proposals for the year's agenda, lay out the alternatives. You can put in some stuff you like and leave out some you don't. I recommend ideas that the [chairman's] interested in and also that I'm interested in."[69] Many committee staff are active in outside communications and issue networks (health or environment, for example) that enhance lawmakers' ability to make informed decisions.[70]

Staff aides negotiate with legislators, lobbyists, and executive officials on issues, legislative language, and political strategy. Sometimes they travel to foreign countries to conduct investigations. Congress's investigative power undergirds its ability to make informed judgments on policy matters. And staff members are the ones who do the essential spadework that can lead to changes in policy or new laws. For example, a "team totaling 20 [Senate Governmental

Affairs] aides, including detailees from the FBI and [Central Intelligence Agency]," drafted the 2004 bill that reorganized the nation's intelligence community.[71] Staff aides sometimes make policy decisions. Consider their crucial role on a defense appropriations bill.

> The dollar figures in the huge piece of legislation [were] so immense that House-Senate conferees, negotiating their differences . . . , relegated almost every item less than $100 million to staff aides on grounds that the members themselves did not have time to deal with such items, which Sen. Ted Stevens (R-Alaska) called "small potatoes."[72]

During hearings, aides recruit witnesses, on their own or at the specific direction of the chairman, and plan when and in what order they appear. In addition, staff aides commonly accompany committee members to the floor to give advice, draft amendments, and negotiate compromises. The number of aides who can be present on the floor is limited, however, by House and Senate regulations.

For information, analyses, policy options, and research projects, committee staff can turn to the three legislative support agencies: the Congressional Research Service, established in 1914; the Government Accountability Office, established in 1921 (as the General Accounting Office and renamed in 2004); and the Congressional Budget Office, established in 1974. The Office of Technology Assessment, a support agency created in 1972 to assist lawmakers in making scientific and technological policy, was abolished by the Republican-controlled Congress in 1995. One factor in the office's demise was the perception that its research duplicated that performed by other public and private organizations.[73] Unlike committee or personal aides, the Congressional Research Service, the Government Accountability Office, and the Congressional Budget Office operate under strict rules of nonpartisanship and objectivity. Staffed with experts, they provide Congress with analytical talent matching that in executive agencies, universities, and specialized groups.

Staffing reflects members' dual roles in the two Congresses: individual policy maker and constituency representative. It can be a controversial process. A New Jersey senator, for example, was criticized by African American clergy in his state for "failing to appoint blacks to important positions on his personal staff" as he had promised when running for office. The senator responded that he had hired professional black staffers and "defended his efforts to hire members of racial minorities."[74]

COMMITTEE REFORM AND CHANGE

Since passage of the Legislative Reorganization Act of 1946, Congress has made numerous attempts to reform the committee system but has only rarely succeeded. In 1973 and 1974 the Select Committee on Committees, headed by

Rep. Richard Bolling, D-Mo. (1949–1983), tried to eliminate several standing committees and make extensive changes in the jurisdiction of other committees. Instead, because of strong opposition from members who stood to surrender subcommittee chairmanships or favored jurisdictions, the House adopted a watered-down version of the committee proposal. In 1977 a Senate select committee, chaired by Adlai E. Stevenson, D-Ill. (1970–1981), tried committee reform with somewhat greater success.

Given the mixed results of these earlier efforts, Congress has since moved gingerly to restructure committees. A House select committee proposal in 1979 to create a standing committee on energy failed, and a Senate select panel, created in 1984 to address committee reform and assignment limitations, had few of its recommendations acted upon by the full Senate.

Many witnesses who appeared before the 1993 Joint Committee on the Organization of Congress urged a major overhaul of the House and Senate committee systems. Others argued for modest changes: reducing committee sizes, eliminating subcommittees, or restricting the use of multiple referrals. Neither the House nor the Senate acted during the 103d Congress on the reform recommendations of the joint committee.[75] Then came the electoral earthquake of November 1994, and Republicans took control of the Congress. Three standing committees with Democratic constituencies—District of Columbia, Merchant Marine and Fisheries, and Post Office and Civil Service—were abolished and their functions assigned to other standing committees. In addition, there were a number of other formal (amendments to House rules) changes—six-year term limits for committee and subcommittee chairs, for instance—and informal (the Speaker selects chairs of key committees, ignoring seniority) developments.

Since the mid-1990s, two noteworthy initiatives were put forth to change certain features of the committee system; both occurred during the 2004–2005 period. One revision created a homeland security panel in each chamber; the other involved reducing and reorganizing the number of appropriating subcommittees in the House and the Senate.

Homeland Security Committees

The National Commission on Terrorist Attacks Upon the United States (the 9/11 Commission) urged the House and Senate to each create a single authorizing committee for homeland security. Its report stated that at least eighty-eight committees and subcommittees in Congress had some jurisdiction over the Department of Homeland Security (DHS). The formation of House and Senate homeland security panels would minimize turf conflicts, reduce the number of panels top DHS officials had to appear before as witnesses, and strengthen congressional oversight of the new department. Both chambers responded to the commission's suggestion, but in different ways.

In the Senate, the GOP and Democratic leaders created in August 2004 a twenty-two-person working group (headed by Sens. Mitch McConnell, R-Ky., and Harry Reid, D-Nev.) to review the commission's recommendations for improving oversight of intelligence and homeland security. Two months later, the Senate debated the McConnell-Reid plan (S. Res. 445), which called for renaming the Governmental Affairs Committee the Homeland Security and Governmental Affairs Committee and assigning it broad authority for overseeing domestic security and DHS. To achieve that objective, however, required ten standing committees to give up some of their jurisdiction to the renamed Governmental Affairs panel.

During floor action on S. Res. 445, several amendments were successfully offered by committee chairs and ranking members that reclaimed the jurisdiction that would have been lost to the renamed Governmental Affairs Committee if the resolution was adopted unchanged. "We're creating a shell," lamented Joseph I. Lieberman of Connecticut, the ranking Democrat on the Governmental Affairs Committee. "We're calling a committee a homeland security committee. But if you pick up the shell, there's not much homeland security under it."[76] The chair of the Governmental Affairs Committee, Susan Collins, R-Maine, said the changes made to S. Res. 445 left her newly renamed panel with "less than 38 percent of the Department of Homeland Security's budget and 8 percent of its personnel."[77] Dismayed by these events, both Collins and Lieberman voted against S. Res. 445, which was agreed to on October 9 by a 79–6 vote. S. Res. 445 also called for the creation of a Senate Appropriations Subcommittee on Intelligence, but that proposal was not acted upon in the 109th Congress by the Appropriations panel. "Since it would be difficult to create an intelligence subcommittee with a classified budget [the 9/11 Commission recommended public disclosure of the nation's budget for intelligence, which Congress rejected], it may not be possible to do so at this time," said Senator Specter, a member of the Appropriations Committee.[78]

At the opening of the 109th Congress, the House replaced its temporary panel on homeland security with a standing committee. The new permanent panel was granted, among other matters, jurisdiction over overall homeland security policy and the organization and administration of the Department of Homeland Security. The new committee also was assigned broad oversight authority over all government "activities relating to homeland security, including the interaction of all departments and agencies with the Department of Homeland Security." Even with creation of the new panel, oversight of homeland security is still spread among nine other authorizing committees.

The turf-conscious committee chairs negotiated with the GOP leadership to preserve some portion of their panels' jurisdiction that was given to the new standing committee. Two of the chairs are members of the new standing committee, well positioned to defend their own committee's prerogatives. A detailed analysis of how homeland security legislation is to be referred among all the committees with homeland security jurisdiction was included in the *Congressional Record*.[79] To illustrate, the Homeland Security Committee is to receive bills dealing with "transportation security"; the Transportation and

Infrastructure Committee retains its jurisdiction over measures dealing with "transportation safety." As Rules chairman Dreier, one of the authors of the jurisdictional revision, said during January 4, 2005, floor debate, "We envision a system of purposeful redundancy. By that, we mean more than one level of oversight and an atmosphere in which the competition of ideas is encouraged."

Realignment of Appropriations Subcommittees

After the November 2004 elections, House majority leader DeLay floated a plan to reduce to ten from thirteen the number of Appropriations subcommittees, redistributing their jurisdiction among the remaining subcommittees or assigning some to the full committee. DeLay's idea was discussed during a bicameral GOP retreat in January 2005 between the new chairs of the House (Jerry Lewis of California) and Senate (Thad Cochran of Mississippi) Appropriations Committees along with the top GOP leaders of each chamber. (One of the criteria for being chosen Appropriations chair in the 109th House was a commitment to revamp the panel.)

Traditionally, the House has taken the lead in reshuffling Appropriations subcommittees and jurisdictions, as when the House created in 2003 a homeland security appropriations subcommittee and then the Senate panel established a similar subcommittee. The proposed elimination of three subcommittees (District of Columbia, Legislative Branch, and VA-HUD) required intense discussions between Lewis and Cochran, in part because three chairs in the House and Senate would lose their posts. Rearranging jurisdictions among the ten new subcommittees was also controversial.

Many Republicans on Senate Appropriations opposed the DeLay-driven proposal. In general, they were displeased that the House was trying to impose its plan on the Senate. As Sen. Kay Bailey Hutchison, R-Texas, who faced the prospect of losing her chairmanship of the Military Construction Subcommittee, stated: "It was a unanimous view of our Republicans on the Senate Appropriations Committee that we would not accept the House's organization as our own. Obviously, the House has the right to organize as it wants to. So does the Senate."[80] In mid-February 2005, the House Appropriations Committee acted unilaterally to establish ten subcommittees.

A few weeks later, Senate Appropriations chairman Cochran won the support of his GOP colleagues on the panel for his subcommittee reorganization plan. The committee went from thirteen to twelve subcommittees. The panel retained its District of Columbia and Legislative Branch subcommittees, but, like the House, it eliminated the VA-HUD subcommittee and transferred its jurisdiction to other relevant subcommittees. To ensure that the "cardinals" serving in the previous Congress chaired an Appropriations subcommittee, which facilitated member agreement to the reshuffling, Cochran gave up his chairmanship of the Homeland Security Subcommittee. (The Appropriations subcommittee chairs are informally called "cardinals" because of their major role in shaping spending measures.) Whether omnibus bills will be avoided by the reorganization is not clear. Given the "structural differences that remain between the House and Senate subcommittees, an omnibus or small package of [appropriations] bills, dubbed minibuses, may be necessary."[81]

DeLay pushed his plan for at least four key reasons. First, he sought to promote a more efficient appropriations process by minimizing the need for massive, end-of-year omnibus appropriations bills. Nine times since 1995 Congress has been unable to pass all thirteen annual appropriations bills—one bill is reported from each of the thirteen subcommittees—by the end of the fiscal year. As a result, the outstanding measures were forced into an omnibus bill often hundreds or thousands of pages in length with few lawmakers knowing what these omnibus bills contain. (See Chapter 14 for a discussion of Congress's budget process.) For example, a controversial tax provision (allowing Appropriations staff to review any person's tax returns) made its way into a three-thousand-page omnibus bill that Congress approved in December 2004. The bipartisan and public outcry against the provision caused it to be removed by Congress. "No omnibus," declared DeLay. "We ain't doing an omnibus. Never again."[82] Cochran added: The Senate will "modernize [the process] in terms of [the] organizational structure of the committee to avoid the big omnibus bills . . . [of] the past."[83] However, lacking jurisdictional similarity among each chamber's appropriating subcommittees, such a mismatch is likely to compound the bicameral bargaining process in conference and promote continuing use of omnibus bills.

Second, DeLay wanted to change the titles and jurisdictions of the subcommittees to reflect GOP priorities. As a GOP leadership aide put it: "It makes a difference in whether we have a Congress that's organized to fund the New Deal or organized in a way to fund a conservative world view."[84] (See Box 7-3 on the new House and Senate Appropriations subcommittee alignment.) Third, more effective oversight of the executive branch is expected from a ten-subcommittee structure. As Appropriations chairman Lewis noted, "This structure will allow us to spend less time on the floor and in committee and more time doing oversight over the expenditure of taxpayer funds."[85]

Fourth, with an eye on the two Congresses, DeLay backed jurisdictional restructuring to protect jobs in his Houston-area district. He was particularly upset with the VA-HUD Subcommittee in 2004 for reducing spending for the National Aeronautics and Space Administration (NASA), the largest employer in his district, below what President Bush requested for the agency. DeLay preferred that NASA be covered in another subcommittee where it did not have to compete for funds with veterans. "I think especially VA-HUD is a committee that has shown it creates a lot of confusion and a lot of competition that is I think unnecessary," stated DeLay.[86] David R. Obey of Wisconsin, the ranking Democrat on the Appropriations Committee, had another interpretation for DeLay's displeasure with the subcommittee: "The originating purpose [of the reorganization] was to engage in payback to the subcommittee that tried to squeeze NASA."[87]

BOX 7-3 **House and Senate Appropriations Subcommittees**

House (13)	Senate (13)
2003	
Agriculture, Rural Development, FDA, and Related Agencies	Agriculture, Rural Development, and Related Agencies
Commerce, Justice, State, the Judiciary, and Related Agencies	Commerce, Justice, State, and the Judiciary
Defense	Defense
District of Columbia	District of Columbia
Energy and Water Development	Energy and Water Development
Foreign Operations, Export Financing, and Related Programs	Foreign Operations
Homeland Security	Homeland Security
Interior and Related Agencies	Interior
Labor, Health and Human Services, Education, and Related Agencies	Labor, Health and Human Services, and Education
Legislative Branch	Legislative Branch
Military Construction	Military Construction
Transportation, Treasury, and Independent Agencies	Transportation, Treasury, and General Government
Veterans Affairs, Housing and Urban Development, and Independent Agencies	Veterans Affairs, HUD, and Independent Agencies

Committees are remarkably durable, resilient, and stable institutions despite the periodic forces for change (public criticism of Congress, reformist sentiment among institutionally minded lawmakers, and so on) that buffet them. Major committee restructuring plans, as the several committee reform efforts since the post–World War II period attest, almost always fail or produce only marginal adjustments in committees' jurisdictional mandates, policy-making influence, or method of operation. Scholars and lawmakers posit various theories to explain why it is difficult to accomplish major jurisdictional realignment. For example, given that the control of jurisdictional turf is viewed as power, Speaker Thomas P. "Tip" O'Neill Jr., D-Mass., explained the House's rejection of a major 1973–1974 committee realignment plan in this succinct manner: "The name of the game is power, and the boys don't want to give it up."[88] A political scientist offered an electoral explanation, which embodies the two Congresses concept, for the demise of committee reshuffling plans.

House (10)	Senate (12)
2005	
Agriculture, Rural Development, FDA, and Related Agencies	Agriculture, Rural Development, and Related Agencies
—	Commerce, Justice, and Science
Defense	Defense
—	District of Columbia
Energy and Water Development and Related Agencies	Energy and Water
Foreign Operations, Export Financing, and Related Programs	—
Homeland Security	Homeland Security
Interior, Environment, and Related Agencies	Interior and Related Agencies
Labor, Health and Human Services, Education, and Related Agencies	Labor, Health and Human Services, Education, and Related Agencies
—	Legislative Branch
Military Quality of Life and Veterans Affairs and Related Agencies	Military Construction and Veterans Affairs
Science, State, Justice, Commerce, and Related Agencies	State, Foreign Operations, and Related Programs
Transportation, Treasury, and Housing and Urban Development, the Judiciary,	Transportation, Treasury, the Judiciary, Housing and Urban Development, and Related Agencies

Note: FDA = Food and Drug Administration; HUD = Housing and Urban Development.

> [A] primary and constant force hindering committee restructuring movements has been the electoral objectives of members of Congress. Under pressure to bolster their reelection prospects in order to achieve long-term legislative and personal goals, rational politicians with the ability to shape legislative structures utilize the arrangement of rules and procedures to secure targeted government benefits for needy constituents and voting blocs. Any widespread change in the established order of policy deliberation—particularly its centerpiece—the committee system—would create far too much uncertainty in members' electoral strategies and therefore would be broadly opposed from the start.[89]

Whatever variety of other factors (interest group, party leadership, or committee member and staff opposition, for instance) impedes major committee overhaul, these workshops of Congress evolve in response to new events and circumstances. Several recent developments highlight the dynamic quality of the committee system. These include ebbs and flows in the authority of committee chairs, the use of task forces, and the circumvention of the committee process.

Constricting the Authority of Committee Chairmen

When Republicans took control of both houses of Congress in the mid-1990s, many GOP committee chairmen had to take more direction from their top leaders, especially in the House. Committee chairmen "have been at the mercy of top House and Senate Republicans leaders," wrote two congressional analysts, "who—given the high level of partisanship and the small size of their majorities—have resorted to dictating legislation from the top down in order to maintain some semblance of control."[90] Centralized control over committees was particularly pronounced during the speakership of Gingrich (1995–1999), who sometimes circumvented committee consideration of legislation, dictated legislative changes to committees, used the Rules Committee to redraft committee-reported measures, and engaged in other actions that undermined the committee system, such as creating partisan task forces. Speaker Hastert, by contrast, has encouraged committees to reclaim their prerogatives. "You are now beginning to see the committees re-establish themselves," said Ways and Means chairman Thomas.[91] The enhancement of the chairmen's authority comports with Speaker Hastert's general leadership style of involving and delegating responsibility to chairmen and others for implementing the GOP agenda hammered out in discussions among the members, in leadership circles, and with the George W. Bush administration.

However, Speaker Hastert and the GOP leadership are not reluctant to rein in committee chairs. The removal of the Veterans' chair and the leadership's tight control over the Appropriations Committee illustrate their large influence. After Hastert and DeLay won adoption in 2003 of a party rules change requiring the Appropriations subcommittee chairs to be approved by the Steering Committee, one of the subcommittee leaders said, "Now the leadership gets to have the Cardinals come in and grovel before them."[92] Two years later, the Steering Committee warned Rep. Charles H. Taylor, R-N.C., that he could lose the chairmanship of his Appropriations subcommittee if he "does not raise or donate more money to Republicans."[93] The competition among Republicans to succeed chairs vacated because of term limits, combined with the Steering Committee's ability to approve or reject the subcommittee chairs of the Appropriations Committee, fosters party loyalty among GOP lawmakers and heightens partisanship on various committees, such as Appropriations. "Ten years ago it would have been impossible for an outside observer to know who was a Republican or Democrat on the Appropriations Committee except for which side members sat on," remarked Representative Hoyer, a longtime Appropriations member before he became minority whip. "It was one of the most bipartisan committees in the House. Unfortunately, the committee is much more partisan now."[94]

Occasions also arise when Senate committee chairs are subject to party leadership direction. For example, toward the late 1990s when political momentum began to build for a patients' bill of rights bill, the majority leader took the issue away from the chairman of the Health, Education, Labor, and Pension Committee and "created a [party] task force . . . to write the GOP version of the bill."[95] When Sen. Tom Daschle, D-S.D., was majority leader, he gave the Finance Committee a deadline to report a priority bill or else he would call up the proposal that he favored. "I told the Finance Committee they have a window, and I'd love to have them pass out a bill and give it to us and then we'll take it up," said Daschle. "If that fails, we'll have to go to the floor with another vehicle."[96] The point is that, on measures of utmost party importance, congressional leaders will override the prerogatives of committee chairs to take control of crucial agenda items.

The ability of today's party leaders, particularly in the House, to exercise significant control over committee leaders represents a major change in how today's Congress works. Term limits, by design, have reduced the ability of GOP chairs to create independent fiefdoms, as occurred during the four decades (1955–1995) of Democratic control of the House. GOP chairs are subject to centralized leadership direction and may face sanctions if their performance does not comport with party expectations. On the one hand, this development ensures that the chairs (and ranking minority members) are ultimately accountable for their actions to the Democratic Caucus or Republican Conference. On the other hand, tight leadership control, combined with term limits, could gradually diminish the traditional role of committees as the policy specialization system for the legislative branch. Why bother to devote years of effort to become substantive experts, some committee members might say, if policy on major issues is decided at the top and committee leaders are forced to relinquish their posts after six years (if not sooner)?

Task Forces

Speaker Gingrich created numerous party task forces in part because he could determine their mandate and timetable, appoint the chair and members, and assign a deadline for drafting a product. Many of these task forces did little, but some wrote legislation. Task forces, in sum, can forge consensus, draft legislation, coordinate strategy, promote intraparty communication, and involve noncommittee members and junior members in issue areas.

Gingrich's use of task forces provides a practical look at the three theories of legislative organization: the distributional hypothesis, the informational hypothesis, and the party hypothesis. The Speaker's Task Force on California was established in large measure to ensure that the politically important state of California received its fair share of federal funds from the GOP-controlled House. This panel's formation buttressed the committee autonomy or distributive politics view of congressional organization: Committees are designed to accommodate important constituencies. The Task Force on Immigration underscored the chamber-dominated, or informational, perspective. Its work enhanced the expertise of all members by providing them with specialized information on the complexities of immigration policy. Finally, the Task Force on the Environment was formed in part to promote the GOP's deregulatory agenda. A partisan perspective shaped much of its work.

Speaker Hastert has deemphasized the use of party task forces, but they are still occasionally employed to address issues of importance to the party. Hastert, for instance, created task forces to deal with health and terrorism issues. Minority Leader Nancy Pelosi has employed task forces to mobilize support behind party priorities. For example, mindful that faith and values were important factors influencing many November 2004 voters, Pelosi established a faith-based working group to convince Democrats to use religious references "when debating issues involving Medicare, a higher minimum wage, universal health care and additional funding for education."[97]

Senate Republican leaders also form party task forces to showcase GOP senators up for reelection and to promote Republican priorities. GOP Conference chairman Santorum heads a Social Security Communications Working Group "to motivate the base and persuade key political constituencies" to back President Bush's initiative to revamp Social Security.[98] Democratic leaders, too, employ task forces selectively. For example, a Homeland Security Task Force was formed to monitor the government's antiterrorism efforts, including the activities of the Department of Homeland Security. On occasion, leaders establish bipartisan task forces or working groups.

Bypassing Committees

Sen. Robert C. Byrd, D-W.Va., and other senators were upset with the Budget chairman when he decided in 2001 to forgo committee markup of a concurrent budget resolution, which largely tracked the administration's budget recommendations. With the likelihood of deadlock on the Budget Committee, the chair decided to avoid a contentious markup and call up the resolution in the Senate. "[C]ircumventing a committee markup of the budget resolution is unprecedented and has never been done in the history of the Senate Budget Committee," declaimed Senator Byrd.[99] On another occasion, Sen. Barbara A. Milkulski, D-Md., contended that "legislative malpractice" occurred during Senate debate on a medical liability bill. "First of all, the procedure for considering this bill is seriously flawed. The bill was brought to the full Senate without hearings, without consideration by the Judiciary Committee."[100]

Circumventing committees is not unique to the Senate. On the same day that Senator Byrd was urging that a markup go forward, a House member was upset that a bill had been called up on the floor that had not been the subject of consideration by the House committee of jurisdiction. "I was flabbergasted," he said, "when I found out . . . that [this bill] was coming to the floor of the House without hearings, without committee deliberation, without the ability to offer amendments."[101] When Minority Whip Hoyer asked Majority Leader DeLay if a Senate-passed, class action bill sent to the House would first be considered in committee, DeLay responded that the measure would go "straight to the floor . . . without committee action."[102]

These examples highlight the tendency of party leaders to bypass some or all of the stages of committee consideration of legislation. In general, the circumvention of committees reflects the dominance of party power over committee power. Other specific reasons are also noteworthy. For instance, heightened partisanship in certain committees encourages party leaders to take charge of priority measures to avoid negative media coverage of committee markups. Or factional disputes within committees may prevent committees from reaching agreement on measures deemed important to party leaders. Party leaders, too, may believe insufficient time exists for committees to hold hearings and markups on major bills that they want to consider within a specific time period. Some analysts contend that "there are few consequences if [committees are bypassed] because nobody outside Congress cares whether a bill went through committee or not."[103] Today, committee review of major legislation can sometimes be problematic.

CONCLUSION

Several generalizations can be made about congressional committees today. First, they shape the House and Senate agendas. Not only do they have negative power—pigeonholing legislation referred to them—but they have positive power as well. The bills they report largely determine what each chamber will debate and in what form. As one House chairman stated in his testimony before the Joint Committee on the Organization of Congress,

> [Committees] provide Congress with the expertise, skill, and organizational structure necessary to cope with the increasingly complex and technical questions in both the domestic and international arenas. They also ensure a forum for the broadest possible participation of diverse interests and constituencies in the formative stages of the legislative process. They are, in short, the window through which much of the democratic participation in lawmaking is made possible.[104]

Second, committees differ in their policy-making environments, mix of members, decision-making objectives, and ability to fulfill individual members' goals. Recruitment methods reinforce the committees' autonomy. Committees frequently are imbalanced ideologically or geographically. They are likely to advocate policies espoused by agencies and outside groups interested in their work.

Third, committees often develop an esprit de corps that flows across party lines. Committee members usually will defend their panels against criticisms, jurisdictional trespassing, or any attempt to bypass them.

Fourth, committees typically operate independently of one another. This longtime custom fosters an attitude of mutual noninterference in the work of other committees. However, multiple referrals of bills spawn broader interrelationships among committees.

Fifth, the committee system contributes fundamentally to policy fragmentation, although a few committees—Rules and Budget, for example—act as policy coordinators for Congress. "This is one of the anomalies here," remarked a House member. "In order to attain legislative efficiency, we say that we have to break down into committees with specialized jurisdictions. When you do that, you lose your ability to grapple with the big problems."[105] Party leaders, as a result, are more involved than ever in coordinating policy making and forging winning coalitions in committees and on the floor.

Finally, committee autonomy is increasingly under pressure from assertive party leaders who strive to move the party's agenda forward and enforce party discipline—with or without the committee leaders' cooperation. In theoretical terms, it may be seen as a shift in committee roles from distributional purposes to partisan-programmatic goals.

SUGGESTED READINGS

Deering, Christopher J., and Steven S. Smith. *Committees in Congress.* 3d ed. Washington, D.C.: CQ Press, 1997.

Evans, C. Lawrence. *Leadership in Committee: A Comparative Analysis of Leadership Behavior in the U.S. Senate.* Ann Arbor: University of Michigan Press, 1991.

Fenno, Richard F., Jr. *Congressmen in Committees.* Boston: Little, Brown, 1973.

Hall, Richard L. *Participation in Congress.* New Haven: Yale University Press, 1996.

King, David C. *Turf Wars: How Congressional Committees Claim Jurisdiction.* Chicago: University of Chicago Press, 1997.

Krehbiel, Keith. *Information and Legislative Organization.* Ann Arbor: University of Michigan Press, 1991.

Maltzman, Forrest. *Competing Principals: Committees, Parties, and the Organization of Congress.* Ann Arbor: University of Michigan Press, 1997.

Wilson, Woodrow. *Congressional Government.* Reprint of 1885 ed. Baltimore: Johns Hopkins University Press, 1981.

A view from the back of the House chamber spotlights the Speaker's rostrum, gallery, and lawmakers' seats. Unlike the Senate, House members do not have assigned seats.

chapter 8

Congressional Rules and Procedures

Congress needs written rules to do its work. Compiling the Senate's first parliamentary manual, Thomas Jefferson stressed the importance of a known system of rules.

> It is much more material that there should be a rule to go by, than what the rule is; that there may be uniformity of proceeding in business not subject to the caprice of the Speaker or captiousness of the members. It is very material that order, decency, and regularity be preserved in a dignified public body.[1]

Jefferson understood that how Congress operates affects what it does. Thus Congress's rules protect majority and minority rights, divide the workload, help contain conflict, ensure fair play, and distribute power among members. Because formal rules cannot cover every contingency, precedents—accumulated decisions of House Speakers and Senate presiding officers—fill in the gaps. These precedents are codified by House and Senate parliamentarians, printed, and distributed. There are also informal, unwritten codes of conduct such as courtesy to other members. These folkways are transmitted from incumbent members to newcomers.[2]

Before bills become laws, they typically pass successfully through several stages in each house (see Figure 8-1). Bills that fail to attract majority support at any critical juncture may never be passed. Congress, in short, is a procedural obstacle course that favors opponents of legislation and hinders proponents. This defensive advantage promotes bargaining and compromise at each decision point.

Congressional rules are not independent of the policy and power struggles that lie behind them. There is very little that the House and Senate cannot do under the rules so long as the action is backed by votes and inclination. Yet votes and inclination are not easily obtained, and the rules persistently challenge the proponents of legislation to demonstrate that they have both resources at their command. Little prevents obstruction at every turn except the tacit understanding that the business of the House and Senate must go on. Members recognize that the rules can be redefined and prerogatives taken away or modified. Rules can also be employed against those who use them abusive-

FIGURE 8-1 **How a Bill Becomes Law**

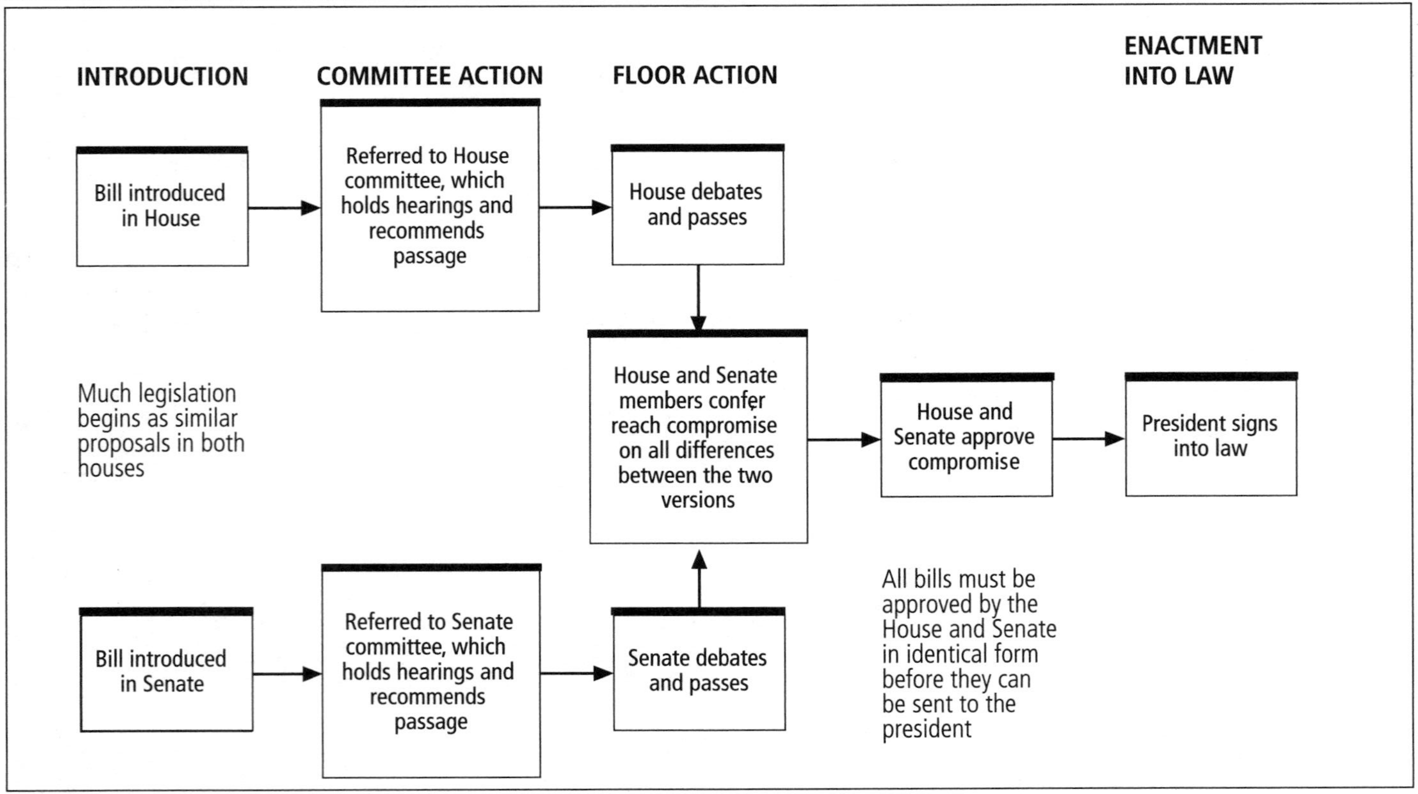

ly. In brief, rules can be employed to block or advance actions in either chamber, and proponents or opponents of measures or matters do not look on them as neutral devices.

INTRODUCTION OF BILLS

Only members of Congress can introduce legislation. Often embedded in these measures are a number of assumptions—for example, that a problem exists; that it can best be resolved through enactment of a federal law instead of allowing administrative agencies or state and local governments to handle it; and that the proposed solution contained in the bill ameliorates the problem rather than makes it worse. The reasons that lawmakers introduce the bills they do are fascinating and numerous.

> Lawmakers are led to their choice of legislation by many factors: parochial interest, party preference, and crass calculation connected to campaign fund raising. But there is a motivator that is rarely discussed that can be just as potent: a personal brush with adversity. Congress is an intensely human place where personal experience sometimes has powerful repercussions.[3]

As Sen. Gordon H. Smith, R-Ore., stated: "Each of us, as United States senators, comes to . . . this public place with the sum of our beliefs, our personal experience and our values, and none of us checks them at the door."[4] For example, Sen. Pete V. Domenici, R-N.M., whose daughter suffers from mental illness, is Congress's acknowledged champion for the mentally ill. "In the field of mental health," said a Democratic House member, "I think it's possible that nothing at all would have been done by Congress if it weren't for legislators like Domenici who were galvanized by personal experience."[5] Personal experience, however, is not the only source of legislative proposals. Often members get ideas for bills from the executive branch, interest groups, scholars, state and local officials, constituents, the press and media, and their own staff.

A member who introduces a bill becomes its sponsor. This member may seek cosponsors to demonstrate wide support for the legislation. Outside groups also may urge members to cosponsor measures. "We were not assured of a hearing," said a lobbyist of a bill that his group was pushing. "There was more hostility to the idea, so it was very important to line up a lot of cosponsors to show the over-all concern."[6] As important as the number of cosponsors is their leadership status and ideological stance. Cosponsors are not always like-minded politically. Massachusetts senator Edward M. Kennedy, a liberal Democrat, once said of South Carolina senator Strom Thurmond, a conservative Republican (1954–2003), "Whenever Strom and I introduce a bill together, it is either an idea whose time has come, or one of us has not read the bill."[7]

Although identifying a bill's sponsors is easy, pinpointing its real initiators may be difficult. Legislation is "an aggregate, not a simple production," wrote

Woodrow Wilson. "It is impossible to tell how many persons, opinions, and influences have entered into its composition."[8] President John F. Kennedy, for example, usually is given credit for initiating the Peace Corps. But Theodore Sorensen, Kennedy's special counsel, recalled that the Peace Corps was

> Based on the Mormon and other voluntary religious service efforts, on an editorial Kennedy had read years earlier, on a speech by General [James] Gavin, on a luncheon I had with Philadelphia businessmen, on the suggestions of [Kennedy's] academic advisers, on legislation previously introduced and on the written response to a spontaneous late-night challenge he issued to Michigan students.[9]

In short, the ideas behind many bills have tangled histories.

Required legislation, particularly funding measures, makes up much of Congress's annual agenda. Bills that authorize programs and specify how much money can be spent on them (authorization bills) and bills that provide the money (appropriation bills) appear on Congress's schedule at about the same time each year. Other matters recur at less frequent intervals, every five years perhaps. Emergency issues require Congress's immediate attention. Activist legislators also push proposals onto Congress's program. Bills not acted upon die automatically at the end of each two-year Congress. "Anybody can drop a bill into the hopper [a mahogany box near the Speaker's podium where members place their proposed bills]," said a House GOP leader. "The question is, Can you make something happen with it?"[10]

Drafting

"As a sculptor works in stone or clay, the legislator works in words," observed one member.[11] Words are the building blocks of policy, and legislators frequently battle over adding, deleting, or modifying terms and phrases. Members increasingly give their bills eye-catching titles. The Republicans' celebrated Contract with America bristled with items such as the American Dream Restoration Act (tax code reform), the Common Sense Legal Reforms Act (tort and product liability changes), and the Taking Back Our Streets Act (crime control). Lawmakers sometimes use the names of famous sports figures to gain publicity and support for their ideas, such as the Muhammad Ali Boxing Reform Act, or they affix popular phrases to legislation, such as the patients' bill of rights. As Sen. Trent Lott, R-Miss., pointed out: "If you ask [voters], 'Are you for the Bill of Rights?' Yeah, they're for the Bill of Rights. 'Bill of Rights' is a great term. It's the new term. It may even be supplanting reform."[12] Instead of proposals to reduce estate taxes, they are called bills to end death taxes. Conversely, opponents of measures try to attach unattractive labels to them. Critics of an energy bill dubbed it the "Hooters and Polluters Bill" because the legislation contained a provision benefiting a Hooters restaurant in Louisiana. How measures are framed influences how they are viewed by the public. "Whoever controls the language controls the debate," asserted one commentator.[13]

BOX 8-1 **Types of Legislation**

Bill

- Most legislative proposals before Congress are in a bill form.
- Bills are designated H.R. (House of Representatives) or S. (Senate) according to where they originate, followed by a number assigned in the order in which they were introduced, from the beginning of each two-year congressional term.
- *Public bills* deal with general questions and become public laws if approved by Congress and signed by the president.
- *Private bills* deal with individual matters, such as claims against the government, immigration and naturalization cases, and land titles. They become private laws if approved and signed by the president.

Joint Resolution

- A joint resolution, designated H. J. Res. or S. J. Res., requires the approval of both houses and the president's signature, just as a bill does, and has the force of law.
- No significant difference exists between a bill and a joint resolution. The latter generally deals with limited matters, such as a single appropriation for a specific purpose.
- Joint resolutions are used to propose constitutional amendments, which do not require presidential signatures but become a part of the Constitution when three-fourths of the states have ratified them.

Concurrent Resolution

- A concurrent resolution, designated H. Con. Res. or S. Con. Res., must be passed by both houses but does not require the president's signature and does not have the force of law.
- Concurrent resolutions generally are used to make or amend rules applicable to both houses or to express their joint sentiment. A concurrent resolution, for example, is used to fix the time for adjournment of a Congress and to express Congress's annual budgeting plan. It might also be used to convey the congratulations of Congress to another country on the anniversary of its independence.

Resolution

- A simple resolution, designated H. Res. or S. Res., deals with matters entirely within the prerogatives of one house.
- It requires neither passage by the other chamber nor approval by the president and does not have the force of law.
- Most resolutions deal with the rules of one house. They also are used to express the sentiments of a single house, to extend condolences to the family of a deceased member, or to give advice on foreign policy or other executive business.

Although bills are introduced only by members, anyone may draft them.[14] Expert drafters in the House and Senate offices of legislative counsel assist members and committees in writing legislation. Executive agencies and lobby groups often prepare measures for introduction by friendly legislators. Many home-state industries, for instance, draft narrowly tailored tariff or regulatory measures that enhance their business prospects. These proposals are then introduced by the local lawmakers—another instance of the two Congresses linkage. As a senatorial aide said, the senator "just introduces it as a courtesy to his constituents."[15] (See Box 8-1 outlining the four basic types of legislation: bills, joint resolutions, concurrent resolutions, and simple resolutions.)

Nowadays, Congress frequently acts on comprehensive or omnibus bills or resolutions (called packages or megabills by the press). Packages contain an array of issues that once were handled as separate pieces of legislation. Their increasing use stems in part from members' reluctance to make hard political decisions without a package arrangement. A House Budget Committee chairman once explained their attractiveness:

> You can use large bills as a way to hide legislation that otherwise might be more controversial, as a way to be able to slam-dunk issues that otherwise might be torn apart, as a way to avoid hard votes that Members would have to account for at election time, as a way to avoid angering special-interest groups that use votes [to decide] contributions to campaigns and as a way to guarantee that the President will have to accept it.[16]

Sometimes Congress has little choice but to use the omnibus approach. Months overdue in passing nine regular appropriations bills, Congress in late 2004 packaged the unfinished measures into one huge three-thousand-page bill. In this way, procedural action on the outstanding measures was expedited by GOP congressional leaders, who minimized opportunities for further delay if each bill had been taken up separately.

Timing

"Everything in politics is timing," Speaker Thomas P. "Tip" O'Neill Jr., D-Mass., used to say. A bill's success or failure often hinges on when it is introduced or brought to the floor. A bill that might succeed early in a session could fail as adjournment nears. However, controversial legislation sometimes could be rushed through during the last hectic days of a Congress.

Elections greatly influence the timing of legislation. Policy issues can be taken off or kept on Congress's agenda because of electoral circumstances—a good illustration of how the two Congresses are inextricably connected. For example, coming off a major success in the 2004 elections, congressional Republicans moved to capitalize on their momentum by acting quickly early in 2005 to enact into law one of their top priority measures: moving class action lawsuits from state courts to federal courts.

BOX 8-2 **Rules and Referral Strategy**

Sometimes, the Senate's rules can be so arcane that it takes major strategy sessions to get even the most routine bills through the legislature.

That was the case when Sen. Bob Graham, D-Fla. (1987–2005), drafted a bill (targeted only at Florida) to permit the Forest Service to sell eighteen tracts of land and use the proceeds to buy up patches of private lands within the Apalachicola National Forest. To ensure that such a low-profile bill moved, Graham wanted it to go through the Energy and Natural Resources Committee, on which he sat.

Instead, Parliamentarian Alan S. Frumin told Graham's aides that the bill, which was soon to be introduced, would be referred to the Agriculture, Nutrition, and Forestry Committee. Because Graham was not a member, such a move could have guaranteed the bill a quiet death.

Why the Agriculture Committee? For at least three decades, the jurisdiction over land bills was split between the two committees. Bills affecting land east of the 100th Meridian—which runs through North Dakota and South Dakota and the middle of Texas—are assigned to Agriculture, while bills that affect lands west of it go to Energy.

Graham's bill dealt with the wrong side of the country. To change Frumin's mind, Graham's aides needed to turn the rules to their advantage.

They found their opportunity by uncovering the roots behind the 100th Meridian rule. The idea was to divide jurisdiction between public lands and privately owned lands. Because most land on the East Coast is privately owned, that side of the country went to Agriculture, which had jurisdiction over private lands. Everything in the West fell to Energy, which had jurisdiction over public lands.

Graham's aides, however, found out that a majority of tracts in Florida were always public lands. That persuaded Frumin that the bill belonged to the Energy panel.

Source: Adapted from David Nather, "Graham Turns Rules to His Advantage," *CQ Weekly,* June 8, 2002, 1494.

REFERRAL OF BILLS

After bills are introduced, they are referred formally to appropriate standing committees by the Senate presiding officer or the House Speaker. (In practice, the reference of measures is done by the Senate or House parliamentarian, who is the official procedural adviser to each chamber's presiding officer.) A bill's phraseology can affect its referral and hence its chances of passage. This political fact of life means that members use words artfully when drafting legislation. The objective is to encourage the referral of their measures to sympathetic, not hostile, committees. If a bill mentions taxes, for example, it invariably is referred to the tax panels. To sidestep these committees, Senator Domenici avoided the word *tax* in a bill proposing a charge on waterborne freight.

> If the waterway fee were considered a tax—which it was, basically, because it would raise revenues for the federal treasury—the rules would place it under the dominion of the Senate's tax-writing arm, the Finance Committee. But Finance was chaired by Russell B. Long, of Louisiana, whose state included two of the world's biggest barge ports and who was, accordingly, an implacable foe of waterway charges in any form. Domenici knew that Long could find several years' worth of bills to consider before he would voluntarily schedule a hearing on S. 790 [the Domenici bill]. For this reason, [Domenici staff aides] had been careful to avoid the word *tax* in writing the bill, employing such terms as *charge* and *fee* instead.[17]

Domenici's drafting strategy worked. His bill was jointly referred to the Commerce Comittee and the Environment Committee, on which he served. Because committees' jurisdictional mandates are ambiguous or overlap, it is not unusual for legislation to be referred to two or more Senate or House committees—the concept of "one bill, many committees." (See the Box 8-2 illustrating that parliamentary convention affects the reference of legislation.)

Of the thousands of bills introduced annually, Congress takes up relatively few. During the 108th Congress (2003–2005), 8,623 public bills and joint resolutions were introduced; of these only 430 became public laws (see Table 8-1). Many reasons can be cited for the general decline in the enactment of laws, such as legislative interest in limiting the size of the national government, an emphasis on community and private action for resolving problems, the complexity of issues, the use of omnibus or megabills, the intensity of partisanship, legislative-executive conflicts, the narrow party divisions in Congress, and significant sentiment in both chambers that more laws may not be the answer to the nation's problems.

Lawmaking, too, is an arduous and intricate process. As a Senate GOP leader noted, "That's the way Congress works. You work for two years and finally you get to the end and either it all collapses in a puddle or you get a breakthrough."[18] Or as John D. Dingell, D-Mich., the most senior House member, phrased it: "Legislation is hard, pick-and-shovel work," and it often "takes a long time to do it."[19] For example, advocates of bankruptcy reform tried for nine years to get Congress to pass legislation and finally succeeded in 2005.

Once committees complete action on the bills referred to them, House and Senate rules require a majority of the full committee to be physically present to report out any measure. If this rule is violated and neither waived nor ignored, a point of order can be made against the proposal on the floor. (A point of order is a parliamentary objection that halts the proceedings until the chamber's presiding officer decides whether the contention is valid.)

Bills reported from committee have passed a critical stage in the lawmaking process. The next major step is to reach the House or Senate floor for debate and amendment. The discussion below begins with the House because

TABLE 8-1 **Bills Introduced and Legislation Enacted, 91st–108th Congresses**

Congress and years		Bills and joint resolutions introduced			Laws enacted	
		Total	House	Senate	Public	Private
91st	(1969–1971)	26,303	21,436	4,867	695	246
92d	(1971–1973)	22,969	18,561	4,408	607	161
93d	(1973–1975)	23,396	18,872	4,524	649	123
94th	(1975–1977)	21,096	16,982	4,114	588	141
95th	(1977–1979)	19,387	15,587	3,800	634	170
96th	(1979–1981)	12,583	9,103	3,480	613	123
97th	(1981–1983)	11,490	8,094	3,396	473	56
98th	(1983–1985)	10,559	7,105	3,454	623	52
99th	(1985–1987)	9,885	6,499	3,386	664	24
100th	(1987–1989)	9,588	6,263	3,325	713	48
101st	(1989–1991)	10,352	6,683	3,669	650	16
102d	(1991–1993)	10,513	6,775	3,738	590	20
103d	(1993–1995)	8,544	5,739	2,805	465	8
104th	(1995–1997)	6,808	4,542	2,266	333	4
105th	(1997–1999)	7,732	5,014	2,718	394	10
106th	(1999–2001)	9,158	5,815	3,343	580	24
107th	(2001–2003)	7,439	5,115	2,284	377	5
108th	(2003–2005)	8,623	5,812	2,811	430	5

Sources: Rozanne M. Barry, *Bills Introduced and Laws Enacted: Selected Legislative Statistics, 1947–1992,* Congressional Research Service Report, January 15, 1993, 2. See also U.S. Congress, *Congressional Record,* daily ed., 106th Cong., 1st sess., January 19, 1997, D29; U.S. Congress, *Congressional Record,* daily ed., 107th Cong., 1st sess., January 30, 2001, D45; U.S. Congress, *Congressional Record,* daily ed., 107th Cong., 2d sess., December 16, 2002, D1193; and U.S. Congress, *Congressional Record,* daily ed., 108th Cong., 2d sess., December 20, 2004, D1135.

tax and appropriation bills originate there—the former under the Constitution, the latter by custom.

SCHEDULING IN THE HOUSE

All bills reported from committee are listed in chronological order on one of several calendars—lists that enable the House to put measures into convenient categories. Bills that raise or spend money are assigned to the Union Calendar. The House Calendar contains all other major public measures. Private bills, such as immigration requests or claims against the government, are assigned to the Private Calendar. There is no guarantee that the House will debate legislation placed on any of these calendars. The Speaker, in consultation with other party and committee leaders, largely determines if, when, how, and in what order bills come up. The power to set the House's agenda constitutes the essence of the Speaker's institutional authority. His agenda-setting authority is bolstered by rules and precedents biased toward the principle of majority rule.

Shortcuts for Minor Bills

Whether a bill is major or minor, controversial or noncontroversial, influences the procedure employed to bring it before the House. Most bills are relatively minor and are taken up and passed through various shortcut procedures.

One shortcut is the designation of special days for considering minor or relatively noncontroversial measures. An especially important routine and time-saving procedure is suspension of the rules. It is in order Monday, Tuesday, and Wednesday of each week. The procedure is controlled by the Speaker through his power of recognizing who may speak. Most public laws enacted by the House are accomplished through this procedure. A study by Donald Wolfensberger, former staff director of the House Rules Committee, determined that in the 107th Congress (2001–2003) nearly three-quarters of bills enacted into public law came to the floor via this procedure, compared with around 33 percent two decades ago. During the 108th Congress, suspension procedure was used 65 percent of the time to enact measures into law.[20] Legislation considered under suspension of the rules does not have to be reported from committee before the full House takes it up. The procedure permits only forty minutes of debate, allows no amendments, and requires a two-thirds vote for passage. The procedure is often favored by bill managers who want to avoid unfriendly amendments and points of order against their legislation.

The heightened partisanship in the closely divided House raises the question, Why is the suspension procedure, which requires bipartisanship to attract the two-thirds vote, increasingly employed in such a polarized institution? The answer seems to involve a trade-off. "As members are increasingly being denied opportunities in special rules to offer amendments to more substantive bills on the floor," explained Wolfensberger, "the leadership is providing alternative mechanisms to satisfy members' policy influence and reelection needs through the relatively non-controversial and bipartisan suspension process."[21] Thus, greater use of suspensions serves two prime purposes: providing an outlet for members to achieve their policy and political goals and keeping the lid on members' frustration with limited or closed amendment procedures.

The current rules of the House Republican Conference establish some guidelines for using suspension procedure. Under Conference Rule 28, a measure is not to be scheduled for consideration via suspension that "creates a new program, extends an authorization whose originating statute contained a sunset provision, or authorizes more than a 10% increase in authorization, appropriations, or direct spending in any given year."

Another expedited procedure is unanimous consent. However, the Speaker will recognize a lawmaker to call up bills or resolutions by unanimous consent "only when assured that the majority and minority floor leadership and committee chairmen and ranking minority members have no objection." [22] Without these clearances, unanimous consent is not a viable avenue to the floor.

Major measures reach the floor by different procedures. Budget, appropriation, and a limited number of other measures are considered privileged—the House rulebook grants them a "ticket," or privileged access, to the floor—and may be called up from the appropriate calendar for debate at almost any time. Most major bills, however, do not have an automatic green light to the floor. Before they reach the floor they are assigned a rule (a procedural resolution) by the Rules Committee.

The Strategic Role of the Rules Committee

A House Rules Committee has existed since the First Congress. During its early years the committee prepared or ratified a biennial set of House rules and then dissolved. As House procedures became more complex with increases in membership and workload, the committee became more important. In 1858 the Speaker became a member of the committee and the next year its chairman. In 1880 Rules became a permanent standing committee. Three years later the committee launched a procedural revolution. It began to issue rules (sometimes called special rules), which are privileged resolutions that grant priority for floor consideration to virtually all major bills.

Arm of the Majority Leadership. In 1910 the House rebelled against the arbitrary decisions of Speaker Joseph G. Cannon, R-Ill., and removed him from the Rules Committee. During the subsequent decades, as the committee became an independent power, it extracted substantive concessions in bills in exchange for rules, blocked measures it opposed, and advanced those it favored, often reflecting the wishes of the House's conservative coalition of Republicans and southern Democrats.

The chairman of the Rules Committee from 1955 to 1967, Howard W. "Judge" Smith, D-Va., was a diehard conservative and a master at devising delaying tactics. He might abruptly adjourn meetings for lack of a quorum, allow requests for rules to languish, or refuse to schedule meetings. House consideration of the 1957 civil rights bill was temporarily delayed because Smith absented himself from the Capitol. His committee could not meet without him. Smith claimed he was seeing about a barn that had burned on his Virginia farm. Retorted Speaker Sam Rayburn, D-Texas, "I knew Howard Smith would do most anything to block a civil rights bill, but I never knew he would resort to arson." [23]

Liberals' frustration with the coalition of conservatives who dominated the committee boiled over. After John F. Kennedy was elected president in 1960, Speaker Rayburn realized he needed greater control over the Rules Committee if the House was to advance the president's activist New Frontier program. Rayburn proposed enlarging the committee from twelve members to fifteen. This proposal led to a titanic struggle between Rayburn and the arch-conservative Rules chairman.

> Superficially, the Representatives seemed to be quarreling about next to nothing: the membership of the committee. In reality, however, the question raised had grave import for the House and for the United States. The House's answer to it affected the tenuous balance of power between the great conservative and liberal blocs within the House. And, doing so, the House's answer seriously affected the response of Congress to the sweeping legislative proposals of the newly elected President, John Kennedy.[24]

In a dramatic vote the House agreed to expand the Rules Committee. Two new Democrats and one Republican were added, which loosened the conservative coalition's grip on the panel.

During the 1970s the Rules Committee came under even greater majority party control. In 1975 the Democratic Caucus authorized the Speaker to appoint, subject to party ratification, all Democratic members of the committee. (Thirteen years later Republicans authorized their leader to name the GOP members of the Rules Committee.) The majority party maintains a disproportionate ratio on the panel (nine Republicans and four Democrats in the 109th Congress). The Rules Committee, in short, has become the Speaker's committee. As a GOP Rules member said about the panel's relationship with the Speaker, "How much is the Rules Committee the handmaiden of the Speaker? The answer is, totally."[25] Rep. David Dreier, R-Calif., chaired the panel in the 109th Congress.

The Speaker's influence over the Rules Committee ensures that he can both bring measures to the floor and shape their procedural consideration. Because House rules require bills to be taken up in the chronological order listed on the calendars, many substantial bills would never reach the floor before Congress adjourned. The Rules Committee can put major bills first in line. Equally important, a rule from the committee sets the conditions for debate and amendment.

A request for a rule usually is made by the chairman of the committee reporting the bill. The Rules Committee conducts hearings on the request in the same way that other committees consider legislation, except that only members testify. The House parliamentarian usually drafts the rule after consulting with committee leaders and staff. The rule is considered on the House floor and is voted on in the same manner as regular bills (see Box 8-3 for an example of a structured rule from the Rules Committee).

BOX 8-3 Example of a Rule from the Rules Committee

The following structured rule (H. Res. 126) set the terms for debating and amending the Job Training and Improvement Act of 2005. A structured rule limits the number of amendments and specifies who may offer them and how they will be considered.

Resolved, That at any time after the adoption of this resolution the Speaker may, pursuant to clause 2(b) of rule XVIII, declare the House resolved into the Committee of the Whole House on the state of the Union for consideration of the bill (H.R. 27) to enhance the workforce investment system of the Nation by strengthening one-stop career centers, providing for more effective governance arrangements, promoting access to a more comprehensive array of employment, training, and related services, establishing a targeted approach to serving youth, and improving performance accountability, and for other purposes. The first reading of the bill shall be dispensed with. General debate shall be confined to the bill and shall not exceed one hour equally divided and controlled by the chairman and ranking minority member of the Committee on Education and the Workforce. After general debate the bill shall be considered for amendment under the five-minute rule. It shall be in order to consider as an original bill for the purpose of amendment under the five-minute rule the amendment in the nature of a substitute recommended by the Committee on Education and the Workforce now printed in the bill. The committee amendment in the nature of a substitute shall be considered as read. No amendment to the committee amendment in the nature of a substitute shall be in order except those printed in the report of the Committee on Rules accompanying this resolution. Each such amendment may be offered only in the order printed in the report, may be offered only by a Member designated in the report, shall be considered as read, shall be debatable for the time specified in the report equally divided and controlled by the proponent and an opponent, shall not be subject to amendment, and shall not be subject to a demand for division of the question in the House or in the Committee of the Whole. All points of order against such amendments are waived. At the conclusion of consideration of the bill for amendment the Committee shall rise and report the bill to the House with such amendments as may have been adopted. Any Member may demand a separate vote in the House on any amendment adopted in the Committee of the Whole to the bill or to the committee amendment in the nature of a substitute. The previous question shall be considered as ordered on the bill and amendments thereto to final passage without intervening motion except one motion to recommit with or without instructions.

Source: House Rules Committee, March 1, 2005, www.house.gov/rules.

Types of Rules. Traditionally, the Rules Committee has granted open, closed, or modified rules as well as waivers. An open rule means that any germane amendments can be proposed. A closed rule prohibits the offering of amendments. A modified rule comes in two forms: modified open and modified closed. The distinction hinges on the number of amendments made in order by the Rules Committee—few under modified closed, more under modified open. Waivers of points of order set aside technical violations of House rules to allow bills to reach the floor. Waivers are commonly included in the different types of rules.

Whether Democrats or Republicans control the House, their majority on the Rules Committee displays procedural creativity and imagination.

> Instead of choosing from among a few patterns the Rules Committee has demonstrated a willingness to create unique designs by recombining an increasingly wide array of elements, or by creating new ones as the need arises, to help leaders, committees, and members manage the heightened uncertainties of decision making on the House floor.[26]

The trend toward creative use of complex rules reflected several developments: the desire of majority party leaders to exert greater control over floor procedures, members' restlessness with dilatory floor challenges to committee-reported bills, the rise of megabills hundreds of pages in length, and efforts by committee leaders either to limit the number of amendments or to keep unfriendly amendments off the floor. The sharp rise in partisanship also triggered an increase in restrictive rules.

When Republicans took control of the House, they remembered their bitter experience with rules that restricted their right to offer amendments. They promised more openness and greater opportunities for all lawmakers to offer floor amendments to pending legislation. Republicans did work to provide more open amendment procedures when they first took control of the House in 1995, although Democrats contended that the Republicans fell short of meeting their claims that about 70 percent of special rules would be open. (Republicans exceeded the 70 percent target by taking up 16 of 22 Contract with America measures under open or modified open rules.) However, as Republican majorities dropped from 235 in the 104th Congress (1995–1997) to 222 in the 107th (2001–2003), the Rules Committee moved away from open rules. Open and modified open rules declined from 57 percent in the 104th Congress to only 37 percent in the 107th Congress. The 108th Congress saw a further decline (27 percent) in the number of open and modified open rules (see Table 8-2).

This downturn underscores that open rules sometimes clash with a fundamental objective of any majority party: passage of priority legislation even at the cost of restricting members' amending opportunities. Under an open rule, minority Democrats could offer scores of dilatory amendments to stall action on the GOP's agenda. Such actions prompted a Rules chairman to say, "It looks like we're going to have to increasingly restrict rules if the Democrats won't cooperate."[27]

The Republicans not only have used most of the known creative rules (see Box 8-4 on examples of creative rules), but they also have devised new rules of their own. When they were in the minority, Republicans opposed the so-called king-of-the-hill rules crafted by the Democrats. These rules made in order a limited number of major amendments but stipulated that only the last alternative voted on is the one that counts for purposes of accepting or rejecting

TABLE 8-2 **Open and Restrictive Rules, 95th–108th Congresses**

Congress and years		Total rules granted	Open rules		Restrictive rules	
			Number	Percent	Number	Percent
95th	(1977–1979)	211	179	85	32	15
96th	(1979–1981)	214	161	75	53	25
97th	(1981–1983)	120	90	75	30	25
98th	(1983–1985)	155	105	68	50	32
99th	(1985–1987)	115	65	57	50	43
100th	(1987–1989)	123	66	54	57	46
101st	(1989–1991)	104	47	45	57	55
102d	(1991–1993)	109	37	34	72	66
103d	(1993–1995)	104	31	30	73	70
104th	(1995–1997)	151	86	57	65	43
105th	(1997–1999)	142	72	51	70	49
106th	(1999–2001)	184	93	51	91	49
107th	(2001–2003)	112	71	37	71	63
108th	(2003–2005)	128	33	26	95	74

Sources: U.S. Congress, *Congressional Record,* daily ed., 103d Cong., 2d sess., October 7, 1994, H11278. For the 104th Congress, see House Rules Committee, press release, December 10, 1996. For the 105th Congress, the Rules Committee issued a total of 207 rules, but many did not directly involve bills and resolutions. As a result, the authors selected 142 as the number of rules granted for bills and resolutions. Minority Democrats have made their own calculation of the kinds of rules granted by the committee. They identify a total of 163 rules of which 38 are open (23 percent) and 115 (77 percent) are restrictive. See *Survey of Activities of the House Committee on Rules* (Washington, D.C.: U.S. Government Printing Office, 1999). For the 106th Congress, the Rules Committee issued 267 rules with 184 directly affecting the amending process on the floor. Hence, the authors employ the 184 figure instead of 267, which included rules, for example, that permitted the House to go to conference with the Senate. See *Survey of Activities of the House Committee on Rules* (Washington, D.C.: U.S. Government Printing Office, 2001). For the 107th Congress, the panel issued 191 rules with 112 directly related to the amendment process for the consideration of bills and resolutions. See *Survey of Activities of the House Committee on Rules* (Washington, D.C.: U.S. Government Printing Office, 2003). During the 108th Congress, the panel issued 192 rules with 128 either open (28), modified open (5), structured or modified closed (59), or closed (36). See Survey of Activities of the House Committee on Rules *(Washington, D.C.: U.S. Government Printing Office, 2005).*

national policy. The yeas and nays on the other amendments were free votes; that is, they provided political cover to lawmakers who could explain them however they wished. Republicans argued that these rules "violated the democratic principle that the position with the strongest support should prevail."[28]

BOX 8-4 **Examples of Creative Rules**

Queen-of-the-Hill Rule

- Under this special rule, a number of major alternative amendments—each the functional equivalent of a bill—are made in order to the underlying legislation, with the proviso that the substitute that receives the most votes is the winner.
- If two or more alternatives receive an identical number of votes, the last one voted upon is considered as finally adopted by the membership.

Self-Executing Rule

- This special rule provides that when the House adopts a rule it has also agreed simultaneously to pass another measure or matter.
- Adoption of a self-executing rule means that the House has passed one or more other proposals at the same time it agrees to the rule.
- Whether this rule is controversial or not usually depends on the nature of the policy being agreed to in the two-for-one vote.

Restrictive Rule

- The essential feature of the restrictive rule is that it limits the freedom of members to offer germane amendments to the bills made in order by those rules.
- The number of restrictive rules has increased since the 1980s.
- Rank-and-file members often rail against these rules because they restrict their opportunities to amend committee-reported measures or majority party initiatives.

Multiple-Step Rule

- This type of rule facilitates an orderly amendment process.
- One variation is for the Rules Committee to report a rule that regulates the debating and amending process for specific portions of a bill and then report another follow-on rule to govern the remainder of the measure and amendments to it.
- Another variation is for the Rules Committee to state publicly that, if a measure encounters difficulties on the floor, the panel will report a subsequent rule that limits time for further debate or further amendments.

Anticipatory Rule

- To expedite decision making on the floor, the Rules Committee may grant a rule even before the measure or matter to which it would apply has been reported by a House committee or conference committee.

The GOP-controlled Rules Committee now issues queen-of-the-hill rules, by which the major amendment that wins the most votes among all the amendments voted upon in the Committee of the Whole is forwarded to the full House for a vote on final passage.

Another GOP innovation, the time-structured rule, allows lawmakers to offer their amendments but only within specified time limits set by the Rules Committee. A ten-hour cap for debating and voting on amendments is an example of such a rule. Democrats criticize this type of rule as not being genuinely open. They argue, for instance, that a ten-hour cap may leave only seven hours for amendments because the time for voting is counted against the overall time restriction. Republicans reply that it is up to the Democratic leadership to decide which amendments have priority over others. These and other kinds of creative rules enable the majority party to advance its policy and political agenda and to cope effectively with today's substantive and procedural complexities.

In summary, rules establish the conditions under which most major bills are debated and amended. They determine the length of general debate, permit or prohibit amendments, and may waive points of order. Writing the rules is the majority party's way of ensuring that measures reach the floor under terms favorable to the party's preferred outcomes on bills and amendments. Put differently, the majority party limits and structures the votes to get the results they intend. For their part, minority Democrats object strongly to the wider use of restrictive rules that block them from offering and getting votes on their policy alternatives. "We don't expect to win," said Democratic representative Obey, "but we do expect to be able to at least offer amendments so the two parties can define their differences." [29] Special rules are often as important to a bill's fate as a favorable vote out of committee.

Dislodging a Bill from Committee

Committees do not necessarily reflect the point of view of the full chamber. What happens when a standing committee refuses to report a bill or when the Rules Committee does not grant a rule? To circumvent committees, members have three options, but they are extraordinary actions and are seldom successful: the discharge petition, the Calendar Wednesday rule, and the ability of the Rules Committee to extract a bill from committee.

The discharge petition permits the House to relieve a committee from jurisdiction over a stalled measure. This procedure also provides a way for the rank-and-file to force a bill to the floor even if the majority leadership, the committee chairman, and the Rules Committee oppose it. If a committee does not report a bill within thirty legislative days after the bill was referred to it, any member may file a discharge motion (petition) requiring the signature of 218 members, a majority of the House. Once the signatures are obtained, the discharge motion is placed on the Discharge Calendar for seven days. It can then be called up on the second and fourth Mondays of the month by any member who signed the petition. If the discharge motion is agreed to, the bill is taken up right away. Since 1910, when the discharge rule was adopted, only three discharged measures ever have become law. Its threatened or actual use, particularly as the number of signatures close in on 218, may stimulate a committee to act on a bill and the majority leadership to schedule it for floor action.

The minority party also uses discharge petitions to spotlight the two Congresses. For example, Democrats identify their high-priority issues and circulate discharge petitions "in an attempt to force House votes—and provide a contrast with Republicans in an election year."[30] Outside groups also may run ads in selected lawmakers' districts to discourage them from signing discharge petitions on legislation they oppose.

The discharge rule also applies to the Rules Committee. A motion to discharge a rule is in order after seven legislative days, instead of thirty days, as long as the bill made in order by the rule has been in committee for thirty days. Any member may enter a discharge motion, but majority members seldom break ranks with their party leaders to sign the petition. When Rep. Christopher Shays, R-Conn., signed a successful discharge petition to force House action on a major campaign finance reform bill (the Bipartisan Campaign Reform Act of 2002) opposed by the GOP leadership, there were charges of treason against Shays and rumblings that he might face a GOP challenger in the Republican primary. Signing discharge petitions, "along with other kinds of procedural betrayals, are being considered and discussed by members" of the GOP's committee on committees, remarked the GOP Conference chair.[31] Shays was subsequently passed over as chair of the Government Reform Committee, even though he had more seniority than the two other Republicans in contention.

Adopted in 1909, the Calendar Wednesday rule provides that on Wednesdays committees may bring up from the House Calendar or Union Calendar their measures that have not received a rule from the Rules Committee. Calendar Wednesday is cumbersome to employ, seldom used, and generally dispensed with by unanimous consent. Since 1943 fewer than fifteen measures have been enacted into law under this procedure.[32]

Finally, the Rules Committee has the power of extraction. The committee can propose rules that make bills in order for House debate even if the bills have been neither introduced nor reported by standing committees. Based on an 1895 precedent, this procedure is akin to discharging committees without the required 218 signatures. It stirs bitter controversy among members who think it usurps the rights of the other committees and is seldom used.

HOUSE FLOOR PROCEDURES

The House meets Monday through Friday, often convening at noon. In practice, it conducts the bulk of its committee and floor business during the middle of the week (the so-called Tuesday to Thursday Club). This scheduling pattern helps representatives juggle legislative business with weekend trips to their districts—weekly testimony to the two Congresses.

At the beginning of each day's session, bells ring throughout the Capitol and the House office buildings, summoning representatives to the floor. The bells also notify members of votes, quorum calls, recesses, and adjournments.

Typically, the opening activities include a daily prayer; recitation of the Pledge of Allegiance; approval of the *Journal* (a constitutionally required record of the previous day's proceedings); receipt of messages from the president (such as a veto message) or the Senate; announcements, if any, by the Speaker; and one-minute speeches by members on any topic. A period of morning hour debate, on Mondays and Tuesdays, takes place after the opening preliminaries but before the start of formal legislative business.

After these preliminaries, the House generally begins considering legislation. For a major bill, a set pattern is observed: adopting the rule, convening in Committee of the Whole, allotting time for general debate, amending, voting, and moving the bill to final passage.

Adoption of the Rule

The Speaker, after consulting other majority party leaders and affected committee chairmen, generally decides when the House will debate a bill and under what kind of rule. When the scheduled day arrives, the Speaker recognizes a majority member of the Rules Committee for one hour to explain the rule's contents. By custom, the majority member yields half the time for debate to a minority member of the Rules Committee. At the end of the debate, which may take less than the allotted hour, the House votes on the previous question motion. Its approval brings the House to an immediate vote on the rule; its rejection (a rare occurrence) allows the minority party to amend the rule—and then to vote on the rule.

Opponents of a bill can try to defeat the rule and avert House action on the bill itself. But rules seldom are defeated because they are viewed by majority party members as party-line votes and the Rules Committee is sensitive to the wishes of the House. Since 1999, when J. Dennis Hastert, R-Ill., became Speaker, the House has rejected only three rules offered by the Rules Committee. Splits within the majority party account for the defeats. Once the rule is adopted, the House is governed by its provisions. Most rules state that "at any time after the adoption of [the rule] the Speaker may declare the House resolved into the Committee of the Whole."

Committee of the Whole

The Committee of the Whole House on the state of the Union is a parliamentary artifice designed to expedite consideration of legislation. It is simply the House in another form with different rules. For example, a quorum in the Committee of the Whole is only 100 members, compared with 218 for the full House. The Speaker appoints a majority party colleague to preside over the committee, which then begins general debate of a bill.

General Debate

A rule from the Rules Committee specifies the amount of time, usually one to two hours, for a general discussion of the bill under consideration.

Controversial bills will require more time, perhaps four to ten hours. Control of the time is divided equally between the majority and minority floor managers—usually the chairman and ranking minority member of the committee that reported the legislation. (When bills are referred to more than one committee, a more complex division of debate time is allotted among the committees that had jurisdiction over the legislation.) The majority floor manager's job is to guide the bill to final passage; the minority floor manager may seek to amend or kill the bill.

After the floor managers have made their opening statements, they parcel out several minutes to colleagues on their side of the aisle who wish to speak. General debate rarely lives up to its name. Most legislators read prepared speeches. Give-and-take exchange occurs infrequently at this stage of the proceedings.

The Amending Phase

The amending process is the heart of decision making on the floor of the House. Amendments determine the final shape of bills and often dominate public discussion. Illinois Republican Henry J. Hyde, for example, repeatedly and successfully proposed amendments barring the use of federal funds for abortions.

An amendment in the Committee of the Whole is considered under the five-minute rule, which gives the sponsor five minutes to defend it and an opponent five minutes to speak against it. The amendment then may be brought to a vote. Amendments are routinely debated for more than ten minutes, however. Legislators gain the floor by saying, "I move to strike the last word" or "I move to strike the requisite number of words." These pro forma amendments, which make no alteration in the pending matter, simply serve to give members five minutes of debate time.

If there is an open rule, opponents may try to load a bill with so many objectionable amendments that it will sink of its own weight. The reverse strategy is to propose sweetener amendments that attract support from other members. Offering many amendments is an effective dilatory tactic because each amendment must be read in full, debated for at least five to ten minutes, and then voted on.

In this amending phase the interconnection of the two Congresses is evident: Amendments can have electoral as well as legislative consequences. Floor amendments enable lawmakers to take positions that enhance their reputations with the folks back home, put opponents on record, and shape national policy. For example, "put-them-on-the-spot amendments," as one representative dubbed them, can be artfully fashioned by minority lawmakers to force the majority Republicans to vote on issues (such as increasing veterans' benefits) that can be used against them in the next campaign.[33] The majority party's control of the Rules Committee minimizes the use of this tactic because the panel commonly "scripts" the amendment process. For example, only the amendments made in order by Rules can be offered, often in a set order, and only by a specific member.

The minority guards the floor to demand explanations or votes on amendments brought up by the majority. When Republicans were in the minority, one of their floor guardians wrote, "So long as a floor watchdog exists all members of the House are afforded some additional protection from precipitous actions."[34] With Democrats in the minority since the mid-1990s, Rep. Barney Frank, D-Mass., and others assumed this role for their party.

Voting

Before the 1970 Legislative Reorganization Act was passed, the Committee of the Whole adopted or rejected amendments by voice votes or other votes with no public record of who voted and how. Today, any legislator supported by twenty-five colleagues can obtain a recorded vote. (The member who requested a recorded vote is counted as one of the twenty-five who rise to be counted by the chair.)

Since the installation of an electronic voting system in 1973, members can insert their personalized cards (about the size of a credit card) into one of more than forty voting stations on the floor and press the Yea, Nay, or Present button. A large electronic display board behind the press gallery provides a running tally of the total votes for or against a motion. The voting tally, said a representative, is watched carefully by many members.

> I find that a lot of times, people walk in, and the first thing they do is look at the board, and they have key people they check out, and if those people have voted "aye," they go to the machine and vote "aye" and walk off the floor.
>
> But I will look at the board and see how [members of the state delegation] vote, because they are in districts right next to me, and they have constituencies just like mine. I will vote the way I am going to vote except that if they are both different, I will go up and say "Why did you vote that way? Let me know if there is something I am missing."[35]

After all pending amendments have been voted on, the Committee of the Whole rises. The chairman hands the gavel back to the Speaker, and a quorum once again becomes 218 members.

Final Passage

As specified in the rule, the full House must review the actions of its agent, the Committee of the Whole. The Speaker announces that under the rule the previous question has been ordered, which means in this context that no further debate is permitted on the bill or its amendments. The Speaker then asks whether any representative wants a separate vote on any amendment. If not, all the amendments agreed to in the committee will be approved.

The next important step is the recommittal motion, which provides a way for the House to return, or recommit, the bill to the committee that reported it. By precedent, the request is always made by a minority party member who opposes the legislation. Recommittal motions are seldom successful because they are so heavily identified as an opposition party prerogative, but they do serve to protect the rights of the minority. When Republicans won majority control, they amended House rules to guarantee the minority leader or his designee the right to offer a recommittal motion with instructions (the instructions embody the minority's policy alternative).

After the recommittal motion is defeated, the Speaker then declares, "The question is on passage of the bill." Final passage is usually by recorded vote. Passage of the bill, by the House in this case, marks about the halfway point in the lawmaking process. The Senate must also approve the bill, and its procedures are strikingly different from those of the House.

SCHEDULING IN THE SENATE

Compared with the larger and more clamorous House, which needs and follows well-defined rules and precedents, the Senate operates more informally. And, unlike the House, where the rules permit a determined majority to make decisions, the Senate's rules emphasize individual prerogatives (unlimited freedom to debate and to offer amendments, including nonrelevant amendments) and minority rights (those of the minority party, a faction, or even a single senator). "The Senate," said one member, "is run for the convenience of one Senator to the inconvenience of 99." [36] No wonder some commentators say the Senate has only two rules (unanimous consent and exhaustion) and three speeds (slow, slower, and slowest). As Sen. Byron L. Dorgan, D-N.D., said, "The only thing it's easy to do in the Senate is slow things down. The Senate is 100 human brake pads." [37]

The scheduling system for the Senate is relatively simple. The Calendar of Business is used for all public and private bills and the Executive Calendar for treaties and nominations. The Senate has nothing comparable to the scheduling duties of the House Rules Committee, and the majority and minority leadership actively consult about scheduling. The Senate majority leader is responsible for setting the agenda and is aided in controlling the scheduling by the priority given him when he seeks recognition on the floor. Despite the Senate's smaller size, establishing a firm agenda of business is harder in the Senate than in the House. As a former majority leader once said:

> The ability of any Senator to speak without limitations makes it impossible to establish total certainty with respect to scheduling. When there is added to that the difficulty and very demanding schedules of 100 Senators, it is very hard to organize business in a way that meets the convenience of everybody.[38]

BOX 8-5 Examples of Unanimous Consent Agreements

S. 384

Ordered, That on Wednesday, February 16., 2005, at 11:00 a.m., the Senate proceed to the consideration of S. 384, a bill to Extend the Existence of the Nazi War Crime Working Group; *provided,* that there be 90 minutes of debate equally divided between the Majority leader, or his designee, and the Democratic Leader, or his designee; *provided further,* that no amendment be in order, and that following the use or yielding back of time, the bill be read a third time and the Senate proceed to a vote on passage, without any intervening action or debate.

S. 306

Ordered, That on Thursday, February 17, 2005, at 3:00 p.m., the Senate resume consideration of S. 306, a bill to prohibit discrimination on the basis of genetic information with respect to health insurance and employment; provided that the Senate immediately proceed to a vote on passage without intervening action or debate.

S. 256

Ordered, That on Monday, February 28, 2005, at 2:00 p.m., the Senate proceed to the consideration of S. 256, a bill to amend title 11 of the United States Code, and for other purposes; provided that consideration of the bill during Monday's session be for the purposes of debate only.

Source: U.S. Senate, Calendar of Business, 109th Cong., 1st sess., February 28, 2005, 2, 10, 17.

Legislation typically reaches the Senate floor in two ways: by unanimous consent or by motion. Senators, too, can offer nonrelevant amendments to pending business and force Senate consideration of their proposals. Unanimous consent agreements, however, are of utmost importance to the smooth functioning of the Senate.

Unanimous Consent Agreements

The Senate frequently dispenses with its formal rules and instead follows negotiated agreements submitted to the Senate for its unanimous approval (see Box 8-5 on unanimous consent agreement). The objective is to expedite work in an institution known for extended debate, to impose some measure of predictability on floor action, and to minimize dilatory activities. As a party floor leader observed:

> We aren't bringing [measures] to the floor unless we have [a unanimous consent] agreement. We could bring child-care legislation to the floor right now, but that would mean two months of fighting. We want to maximize productive time by trying to work out as much as we can in advance [of floor action].[39]

It is not uncommon for party leaders to negotiate piecemeal unanimous consent agreements—limiting debate on a specific amendment, for example—and to hammer them out in public on the Senate floor.

Unanimous consent agreements (also called time-limitation agreements) limit debate on the bill, any amendments, and various motions. In effect, these accords are a form of voluntary cloture. Occasionally, they specify the time for the vote on final passage and typically impose constraints on the amendment process. For example, to facilitate enactment of an omnibus crime package that contained provisions with widespread Senate support, senators agreed to a unanimous consent request barring floor amendments on controversial issues such as gun control or the death penalty.[40]

The Senate's unanimous consent agreements are functional equivalents of special rules from the House Rules Committee. They waive the rules of their respective chambers, and each must be approved by the members—in one case by majority vote and in the other by unanimous consent. These accords are binding contracts and can be terminated or modified only by another unanimous consent agreement. Senators and aides often negotiate and draft unanimous consent agreements privately, whereas the Rules Committee hears requests for special orders in public session.

Ways to Extract Bills from Committee

If a bill is blocked in committee, the Senate can do one of several things to obtain floor action. It can add the bill as a nonrelevant floor amendment to another bill, bypass the committee stage by placing the bill directly on the calendar, suspend the rules, or discharge the bill from committee. Only the first two procedures are effective; the other two are somewhat difficult to employ and seldom succeed.[41]

Because the Senate has no general germaneness (or relevancy) rule, senators can take an agriculture bill that is stuck in committee and add it as a nonrelevant floor amendment to a pending health bill. "Amendments may be made," Thomas Jefferson noted long ago, "so as to totally alter the nature of the proposition." It is not uncommon, however, for unanimous consent agreements to limit or prohibit nonrelevant amendments.

Bypassing committees also occurs when senators invoke one of its formal rules (Rule XIV). Typically, when senators introduce bills or joint resolutions (or when bills or joint resolutions are passed by the House and sent to the Senate), they are referred to the appropriate committee of jurisdiction. Rule XIV specifies that those measures are to be read twice by title on different legislative days before they are referred. If a senator interposes an objection after the first reading and again after the second reading, the bill or joint resolution is automatically placed on the Senate's calendar of business. Although not used for the vast majority of measures, Rule XIV is often invoked on party issues of high priority. The majority leader, for example, may employ it to circumvent committees because no time is available for lengthy committee review, or he wants an issue ready to be called up at his discretion.

SENATE FLOOR PROCEDURES

The Senate, like the House, often convenes at noon, sometimes earlier, to keep pace with the workload. Typically, it opens with a prayer. This is followed by the Pledge of Allegiance and then leaders' time (usually ten minutes each to the majority leader and the minority leader to discuss various issues). If neither leader wants any time, the Senate typically either permits members who have requested time to make statements or resumes consideration of old or new business under terms of a unanimous consent agreement. The Senate, too, must keep and approve the *Journal* of the previous day's activities. Commonly, the *Journal* is "deemed approved to date" by unanimous consent when the Senate adjourns or recesses at the end of each day.

Normal Routine

For most bills the Senate follows four steps:

1. The majority leader secures the unanimous consent of the Senate to an arrangement that specifies when a bill will be brought to the floor and the conditions for debating it.
2. The presiding officer recognizes the majority and minority floor managers for opening statements.
3. Amendments are then in order, with debate regulated by the terms of the unanimous consent agreement.
4. A roll call vote takes place on final passage.

As in the House, amendments in the Senate serve various purposes. For example, floor managers might accept "as many amendments as they can without undermining the purposes of the bill, in order to build the broadest possible consensus behind it."[42] Some amendments highlight the two Congresses and bestow benefits to the electorate or embarrass members who must vote against them. "My amendment can be characterized as a 'November amendment,' " remarked a Republican senator, "because the vote . . . will provide an opportunity for Senators to go home and say, 'I voted to reduce Federal taxes' and 'I voted to cut Federal spending.' "[43] As another example, Senate Democrats make "vigorous use of amendments to strike a contrast with Republican policies."[44] Unless constrained by some previous unanimous consent agreement, senators generally have the right to offer an unlimited number of floor amendments.

A bill is brought to a final vote whenever senators stop talking. This can be a long process, particularly in the absence of a unanimous consent agreement. (A number of laws restrict a senator's right to prolong debate, such as trade or reconciliation measures. As a former Senate parliamentarian noted: "We have on the books probably a couple hundred laws that set up specific legislative vehicles that cannot be filibustered or only amended in a very restricted way.")[45] On some bills unanimous consent agreements are foreclosed because of deliberate obstructive tactics, particularly the filibuster. In these instances, bills cannot be voted upon until the filibuster has ended.

Holds, Filibusters, and Cloture

The old-style filibuster has long been associated with the 1939 movie *Mr. Smith Goes to Washington,* which featured Jimmy Stewart conducting a dramatic solo talkathon to inform the public about political wrongdoing. In its new incarnation the filibuster is usually threatened more than invoked to gain bargaining power and negotiating leverage.

Filibusters involve many blocking tactics besides extended debate in which senators hold the floor for hours of endless speeches. Many contemporary filibusters are waged by those who skillfully use Senate rules. For example, senators might offer scores of amendments, raise points of order, or demand numerous and consecutive roll-call votes. Holds also function as a form of silent filibuster.

Holds. A hold permits one or more senators to block floor action on measures or matters by asking their party leaders not to schedule them. A hold, explained Sen. Charles E. Grassley, R-Iowa, is "a notice by a Senator to his or her party leader of an intention to object to bringing a bill or nomination to the floor for consideration."[46] Neither Senate rules nor precedents make provision for holds; they are an informal custom. The majority leader decides whether, or for how long, he will honor a colleague's hold. The power of holds is grounded in the implicit threat of senators to conduct filibusters or to object to unanimous consent agreements.

Holds have come under criticism because they often lead to delays or even the death (choke holds) of measures or nominations. Originally intended as a way for senators to get information about when the majority leader planned action on a measure, holds have become devices to kill measures by delaying them indefinitely or to gain bargaining leverage by, for instance, stalling action on presidential nominations. On one occasion, so many holds on nominations were pending before the Senate that a Democratic leader felt left out. As he explained: "I'm going to have to pick out a nominee to get to know him or her a lot better because it works that way. I mean, it's 'Hello, I'm your holder . . . come dance with me.' "[47] Periodically, proposals are made to reform the practice, such as ending secret holds, but such initiatives have been neither easy to accomplish nor easy to enforce.[48]

Filibusters and Cloture. The right of extended debate is unique to the Senate. Any senator or group of senators can talk continuously in the hope of delaying, modifying, or defeating legislation. In 1957 South Carolina senator Strom Thurmond, then a Democrat, set the record for the Senate's longest solo performance—twenty-four hours and eighteen minutes—trying to kill a civil rights bill.

The success of a filibuster depends not only on how long it takes but also on when it is waged. A filibuster can be most effective late in a session because there is insufficient time to break it.[49] Even the threat of a filibuster can encourage accommodations or compromises between proponents and opponents of legislation.

Defenders of the filibuster say it protects minority rights, permits thorough consideration of bills, and dramatizes issues. "In many ways," noted Sen. Robert C. Byrd, D-W.Va., "the filibuster is the single most important device ever employed to ensure that the Senate remains truly the unique protector of the rights of our people."[50] Critics contend that talkathons enable minorities to extort unwanted concessions. During most of its history, the Senate had no way to terminate debate except by unanimous consent, exhaustion, or compromise. In 1917 the Senate adopted Rule XXII, its first cloture (debate-ending) rule. After several revisions, Rule XXII now permits three-fifths of the Senate (sixty members) to shut off debate on substantive issues or procedural motions. (A two-thirds vote is required to invoke cloture on a proposal to change the rules of the Senate.) Once cloture is invoked, thirty hours of debate time remain before the final vote.

Senators complain about the frequent use of filibusters and cloture attempts. In the past, filibusters generally occurred on issues of great national importance; today they occur on a wide range of less momentous topics. As one majority leader pointed out:

> Not long ago the filibuster or threat of a filibuster was rarely undertaken in the Senate, being reserved for matters of grave national importance. That is no longer the case. . . . The threat of a filibuster is now a regular event in the Senate, weekly at least, sometimes daily. It is invoked by minorities of as few as one or two Senators and for reasons as trivial as a Senator's travel schedule.[51]

Unsurprisingly, many commentators call it the "sixty-vote Senate."

Attempts to invoke cloture also have increased. For example, in the decade from 1961 to 1971, there were 5.2 cloture votes per Congress; during the 108th Congress (2003–2005), there were 50 cloture votes (there were 14 other cloture motions filed but they were not voted upon).[52] Moreover, the norm of one cloture vote per measure has changed. The modern Senate reached a record of eight cloture votes (all unsuccessful) on a controversial campaign financing measure during the 100th Congress (1987–1989).

This upward trend reflects the willingness of senators today to employ their procedural prerogatives to gain concessions, delay the consideration of legislation and nominations, or accomplish other objectives through greater use of filibusters and threatened filibusters (as well as holds and nonrelevant amendments). Two examples illustrate the point. First, the majority leader usually requests and receives unanimous consent to bring legislation to the Senate floor. If senators object to that request, perhaps signaling that blocking

BOX 8-6 The Path to a "Nuclear" Showdown on Judicial Nominations: A Step-by-Step Choreography of the Procedure

1. Majority Leader Bill Frist, R-Tenn., will make a motion to "proceed to executive session for consideration of" the nomination of [a controversial Supreme or Circuit Court nominee]. Under Senate Rule XXII, a motion to proceed to nomination cannot be filibustered. Such motions are normally adopted by voice vote. Democrats could object. If they do and a roll-call vote is necessary, a simple majority of senators present and voting would be needed to proceed to the nomination.

2. Debate will officially begin and continue for an unspecified amount of time.

3. Later, Frist will file a motion to invoke cloture, or limit additional debate on the nomination.

4. The Senate will vote on Frist's cloture motion two legislative days after it is filed, with sixty votes required for its adoption.

5. If the cloture motion is adopted, further debate on the nomination will be limited to thirty hours in total, with no single senator allowed to speak for more than one hour. At the end of that period, the Senate will proceed to a vote on the nominee, with a simple majority needed for confirmation.

(The process ends here.)

OR

If there are fewer than sixty votes to invoke cloture, debate on the nomination can continue indefinitely. Additional cloture motions can be filed, but Frist has something else in mind.

Priscilla Owen, a Texas Supreme Court Justice, was blocked by Senate Democrats for appointment to the federal circuit court on the ground that she was too conservative or out of the mainstream in her judicial philosophy. She was first nominated for the bench in May 2001 by President George W. Bush. Senate consideration of her nomination began on May 18, 2005. She was confirmed a week later by a 55–43 vote.

actions will be taken on the measure, the majority leader may then offer a debatable motion to take up the legislation. Recent Congresses have witnessed an increase in the number of cloture petitions filed on the leader's motion to take up measures. From only two cloture motions filed during the 96th Congress (1979–1981), the 1990s and early 2000s regularly saw cloture motions in the double digits on the leader's motion to bring legislation to the floor. The high-water mark was thirty-five cloture petitions filed during the 102d Congress (1991–1993) on the leader's motion to take up legislation.

Second, cloture is employed for purposes unrelated to ending a filibuster. The purposes are usually twofold: to expedite the Senate's business by limiting

6. If the cloture motion fails, as is expected, Frist will later make a point of order that no more than a certain number of hours or days of debate should be allowed on appellate court and Supreme Court nominations.

7. The presiding officer—probably Vice President Dick Cheney—will rule in Frist's favor.

8. Democrats will appeal that decision.

9. Frist will make a motion to table, or kill, the appeal. A tabling motion is not debatable, and requires a simple majority for adoption.

10. The Senate will vote on the tabling motion.

11. If the motion to table the Democratic appeal is agreed to, debate on the judicial nomination will continue until the time specified in Frist's point of order has been exhausted. Then, the Senate will vote on the nominee, with a simple majority of those present and voting required for confirmation.

OR

If the tabling motion is defeated, the Republicans would be unable to bring the nomination to a vote with a simple majority.

Source: Adapted from Keith Perine and Daphne Retter, "Judicial Showdown Starts with Owen," *CQ Today,* May 18, 2005, 33.

debate and to impose a germaneness, or relevancy, requirement on all amendments. (If invoked Rule XXII requires all amendments to be germane to the clotured measure.) Majority party leaders sometimes file cloture on the first day the Senate takes up a measure. Their objective in trying to invoke cloture is to prevent minority Democrats from offering their agenda priorities as non-relevant amendments to the pending legislation and thus protect electorally vulnerable Republicans from casting votes on difficult issues.

The GOP majority was particularly incensed when Democrats employed extended debate to prevent Senate votes during President George W. Bush's first term on ten of his federal appellate court nominations. Majority Leader Bill Frist,

R-Tenn., threatened to employ a "nuclear option" (or "constitutional option" as Republicans prefer to call it) in the 109th Congress to end filibusters against judicial nominees. (See Box 8-6 on the Senate showdown on judicial nominations.) One form of nuclear option would be to have a GOP senator raise a point of order that further debate on a judgeship nominee is dilatory and out of order. The president of the Senate (the vice president—currently Republican Dick Cheney) would then issue a parliamentary ruling sustaining the point of order, thereby setting aside and disregarding the existing Rule XXII (or sixty-vote) procedure for ending a talkathon. If a Democratic senator appeals the ruling of the presiding officer, a Republican would move to table (or kill) the appeal, establishing a new, majority-vote precedent for Senate approval of judicial nominations. (The motion to table is nondebatable and subject to simple majority approval.)

Senate Democrats have promised that the parliamentary fallout from using the nuclear option would be so severe as to produce gridlock and stalemate in senatorial decisionmaking. When asked about the parliamentary steps Democrats could take if Republicans employed the nuclear option, former Senate Democratic leader Tom Daschle of South Dakota noted:

> The Senate runs on "unanimous consent." It takes unanimous consent to stop the reading of bills, the reading of every amendment. On any given day, there are fifteen or twenty nominations and a half-dozen bills that have been signed off for unanimous consent. The vast majority of the work of the Senate is done that way. But any individual senator can insist that every bill be read, every vote be taken, and bring the whole place to a stop.[53]

Or as Senate Judiciary chairman Arlen Specter, R-Pa., put it: "If we have a nuclear option, the Senate will be in turmoil, and the Judiciary Committee will be hell."54 (See Chapter 12 for discussion of how use of the nuclear option was temporarily averted.)

These actions and issues reflect the Senate's shift away from its norms of collegiality, civility, and accommodation. The various explanations for this development include the election to the Senate of House members who have brought with them the aggressive partisanship common to the lower house, heightened demands placed on senators by constituents and lobbyists, and the escalating costs of campaigns. "Daily priorities [are] shaped more by personal agendas—campaign needs, interest-group demands, personal staff, obligations to meet constituents, and off-the-Hill speeches—and less by the expectations of colleagues and the needs of Senate colleagues," wrote Steven S. Smith. "Pressed by constituencies and lobbyists and more strongly motivated to grab a headline, senators now more routinely and more fully exploit their procedural prerogatives than at any other time in the Senate's history."[55] The upshot of these developments is a more individualistic and partisan Senate, which means that compromises and accommodations are harder to achieve on significant substantive issues.

RESOLVING HOUSE-SENATE DIFFERENCES

Before bills can be sent to the president, they must be passed by the House and the Senate in identical form. One way this occurs is if one chamber simply accepts the other body's bill. Another approach is to ping-pong House and Senate amendments between the chambers until each chamber is satisfied with the product. If neither chamber will accept the other's changes, a House–Senate conference committee is usually appointed to reconcile the differences.

Most public laws are approved without conferences. Either they pass each chamber without any changes (roughly 70 percent) or the House and Senate amends a bill in turn until both chambers agree on the wording (about 20 percent of laws follow this shuttle route). Only about 10 percent of the measures passed by Congress—usually the most important and controversial—are subject to bicameral reconciliation by conference committees.

Under each chamber's rules and precedents, conference committees meet to resolve the matters in bicameral dispute; they are not to reconsider provisions already agreed to, and they are not to write new law by inserting matter that neither house may have considered. However, parliamentary rules are not self-enforcing, and either chamber can waive or ignore them. It is not unusual for conference reports to contain new matter that neither chamber debated nor amended in committee or on the floor. No wonder conference committees are called the third house of Congress. As Senator Specter stated,

> [Conference committees] are when the work is concluded. Everything else which is done is really of much less significance than the conferences, where the final touches are put on legislation which constitutes the laws of the country.[56]

Selection of Conferees

Conferees usually are named from the committee or committees that reported the legislation. Congressional rules state that the Speaker and the Senate presiding officer select conferees. In fact, that decision typically is made by the relevant committee chairmen and the ranking minority members. House and Senate party leaders commonly get involved in naming conferees on major legislation. For example, when Newt Gingrich, R-Ga., was Speaker, he took a strong role in the selection of House conferees. In precedent-setting action for the modern House, Gingrich several times even named conservative minority Democrats (in part to woo them to convert to the Republican Party) to serve as conferees on the House Republican conference delegation. Speaker Hastert, too, has not hesitated to designate GOP conferees for the party's priority bills.

Knowing that the GOP leadership opposed many provisions in the landmark campaign finance reform bill passed by the Senate early in the 107th Congress and long championed by Sen. John McCain, R-Ariz., then Senate

Democratic leader Tom Daschle offered to appoint McCain as a conferee on the bill if Republicans refused to do so.[57] (The so-called McCain-Feingold bill, named for McCain and Sen. Russell D. Feingold, D-Wis., would ban soft money. In 2002 it was signed into law as the Bipartisan Campaign Reform Act.) Daschle made the same offer to moderate GOP senator Lincoln Chafee of Rhode Island on a bill of which he was a prime sponsor. The GOP leader made it clear that Chafee was unlikely to be chosen a conferee. (Both McCain and Chafee were viewed by Democrats as possible party switchers, as in the case of James M. Jeffords of Vermont.)

Each chamber may name as many conferees as it wants, and in recent years some conference delegations have grown large. The 1981 omnibus reconciliation conference set the record, with more than 250 House and Senate conferees working in fifty-eight subconferences to resolve more than three hundred matters in bicameral disagreement. The ratio of Republicans to Democrats on a conference committee generally reflects the proportion of the two parties in the House and Senate.

Today's conference committees represent a sharp departure in size and composition from the pre-1980 era, when conference delegations generally ranged from five to twelve conferees from each house. And before the mid-1970s conferees nearly always were the most senior lawmakers from the committees that reported the legislation. Although seniority frequently determines who the conferees will be, it is not unusual for junior and even first-term members to be conferees. Further, conferees today commonly are chosen from many standing committees and sometimes reflect intricate selection arrangements. For example, House conferees may be named to negotiate only certain items in disagreement instead of the entire bill. Multiple referrals and megabills are the driving forces behind these two developments.

In conference each chamber has a single vote determined by a majority of its conferees, who are expected generally to support the legislation as it passed their house. But, a senator confessed, as conference committees drag on, the "individual attitudes of the various members begin to show."[58] House conferees on some occasions have a "knowledge advantage" over Senate conferees. Because representatives serve on fewer committees than do senators, they have greater opportunities to specialize in various policy areas. This means that representatives on conference committees often find that they are "arguing with Senate staff. For a House member, that's a frustrating experience."[59]

For minority Democrats, a recent annoying development is their exclusion from conferences on major legislation. One outcome is that Senate Democrats, given their ability to filibuster the naming of conferees, have sometimes blocked the appointment of conferees until the majority party provides assurances that Democratic conferees will be full conference participants. Otherwise, the bargaining in these House-Senate forums occurs only between and among GOP conferees, who also receive advice and counsel from the

Republican Bush White House. (The House minority, sometimes also barred from conferences on major legislation, has no such recourse.)

Openness

Secret conference meetings were the norm for most of Congress's history. In 1975 both houses adopted rules requiring open meetings unless the conferees from each chamber voted in public to close the sessions. Two years later the House went further, requiring open conference meetings unless the full House agreed to secret sessions. Sometimes the Cable-Satellite Public Affairs Network (C-SPAN) will televise conference proceedings.

The open conference is yet another instance of individual-institutional cleavage. Under the watchful eye of lobbyists, conferees fight harder for provisions they might have dropped quietly in the interest of bicameral agreement. Private bargaining sessions still permeate conference negotiations. As one senator noted:

> When we started the openness thing we found it more and more difficult to get something agreed to in the conferences; it seemed to take forever. So what did we do? We would break up into smaller groups and then we would ask our [conference] chairman . . . to see if he could find his opposite number on the House side and discuss this matter and come back and tell us what the chances would be of working out various and sundry possibilities.[60]

Senators and representatives expect certain bills to go to conference and plan their strategy accordingly. For example, whether to have a recorded vote on amendments can influence conference bargaining. In the absence of a recorded vote, amendments may be easier to drop in conference. Conference committees are where the final version of the law is often written, sometimes making changes or additions to legislation that neither chamber ever reviewed or considered in committee or on the floor.

The Conference Report

A conference ends when its report (the compromise bill) is signed by a majority of the conferees from each chamber. House and Senate staff then prepare the conference report and the accompanying joint explanatory statement, which summarizes the conferees' recommendations. The House and Senate then vote on the conference report without further amendment. If either chamber rejects the conference report—an infrequent occurrence—a new conference may be called or another bill introduced. Once passed, the compromise bill is sent to the president for approval or disapproval.

CONCLUSION

The philosophical bias of House and Senate rules reflects the character of each institution. Individual rights are stressed in the Senate, majority rule in the House. In both chambers, however, members who know the rules and precedents have an advantage over procedural novices in affecting policy outcomes. Senator Byrd is an acknowledged procedural expert in the Senate. Byrd understands that passing measures often involves unorthodox processes and procedures (for example, forgoing committee hearings or markups or even floor debate).[61]

In addition to congressional rules, persistence, strategy, timing, compromise, and pure chance are important elements in the lawmaking process. To make public policy requires building majority coalitions at successive stages where pressure groups and other parties can advance their claims. Political, procedural, personal, and policy considerations shape the final outcome. Passing laws, as one former representative said, is like the "weaving of a web, bringing a lot of strands together in a pattern of support which won't have the kind of weak spots which could cause the whole fabric to fall apart."[62]

SUGGESTED READINGS

Binder, Sarah A., and Steven S. Smith. *Politics or Principle? Filibustering in the United States Senate.* Washington, D.C.: Brookings Institution, 1997.

_____. *Stalemate: Causes and Consequences of Legislative Gridlock.* Washington, D.C.: Brookings Institution, 2003.

Evans, Diana. *Greasing the Wheels: Using Pork Barrel Projects to Build Majority Coalitions in Congress.* Cambridge, U.K.: Cambridge University Press, 2004.

Krehbiel, Keith. *Pivotal Politics: A Theory of U.S. Lawmaking.* Chicago: University of Chicago Press, 1998.

Krutz, Glen. *Omnibus Legislating in the U.S. Congress.* Columbus: Ohio State University Press, 2001.

Longley, Lawrence D., and Walter J. Oleszek. *Bicameral Politics: Conference Committees in Congress.* New Haven: Yale University Press, 1989.

Loomis, Burdett, ed. *Esteemed Colleagues: Civility and Deliberation in the U.S. Senate.* Washington, D.C.: Brookings Institution, 2000.

Oleszek, Walter J. *Congressional Procedures and the Policy Process.* 6th ed. Washington, D.C.: CQ Press, 2004.

Sinclair, Barbara. *Unorthodox Lawmaking: New Legislative Processes in the U.S. Congress.* 2d ed. Washington, D.C.: CQ Press, 2000.

Smith, Steven S. *Call to Order: Floor Politics in the House and Senate.* Washington, D.C.: Brookings Institution, 1989.

Congressional decision making (clockwise from top): Top right, in the Senate Foreign Relations Committee, (center) Sen. George V. Voinovich, R-Ohio, is congratulated by ranking Democrat Joseph R. Biden Jr. of Delaware, an opponent of the nomination of John R. Bolton as U.S. ambassador to the United Nations, after Voinovich requests a delay in voting on the appointment. Committee chairman Richard G. Lugar, R-Ind., prepares to leave. Center right, the House employs an electronic system to record members' floor votes. Members insert plastic cards into voting boxes throughout the chamber and vote "yea," "nay," or "present." Bottom right, vote totals by party, along with the time remaining to vote, are displayed on C-SPAN. The image here is from the 1998 vote on the fourth article of impeachment against President Bill Clinton. Bottom left, votes are scrutinized and rated by hundreds of interest groups, including by state PIRGs (public interest research groups) in their congressional scorecards.

chapter 9

Deliberation in Congress

It was a typical week in the busy first session of the 109th Congress (2005–2007). The Senate was roiled by a looming showdown on the president's judicial nominations. The so-called nuclear option was a proposed parliamentary move to change Senate rules to forbid filibusters on court nominees. Democrats all fiercely opposed it. While most Republicans backed the idea, GOP leaders struggled to line up a simple majority to vote for the rules change. Two Republicans had already announced their opposition, so pressure was applied to seven others, whose decisions would determine the outcome.

Another quarrel erupted in the Senate Foreign Relations Committee, which was scrutinizing a controversial nominee for ambassador to the United Nations. Again, decisions had to be made: Some senior Republicans joined Democrats questioning the nominee's fitness, but Sen. George V. Voinovich, R-Ohio, surprised everyone by requesting that the vote be postponed to allow further review of the question. With a majority vote in doubt, Chairman Richard G. Lugar, R-Ind., agreed to a delay

That same week Congress adopted a $2.56 trillion budget resolution. The focus was again on the Senate, inasmuch as the more tightly led House was expected to uphold the GOP leadership's bill, including its severe cuts in Medicaid funds. Sen. Gordon H. Smith, R-Ore., speaking for a small group of Republican moderates, was able to pare by four-fifths the projected reductions and to demand a bipartisan commission to study Medicaid's future. House leaders then mustered enough votes to pass the measure, even though some Republicans voted with Democrats to exclude a provision for oil drilling in the Arctic National Wildlife Refuge (ANWR).

Meanwhile, Sen. Charles E. Grassley, R-Iowa, Senate Finance Committee chair, reluctantly opened hearings on President George W. Bush's Social Security reform ideas. Although the president had launched a needed debate on the program's economic future, his solution—partial privatization of the program—proved unpopular with members and the public and, in any event, would not assure the program's long-term solvency. Lawmakers were left to sift through the evidence in search of a workable legislative solution.

All of these questions (and hundreds more) required that lawmakers make policy choices—through discussion, debate, compromise, and problem solving. Legislative assemblies are by definition deliberative bodies. Individual members confront thousands of choices: how and when to participate, how to decide, how to find allies, and how to explain their actions.

THE POWER TO CHOOSE

Although not all members' decisions command public or media attention, every one of them has the potential power of shaping public policy. In both chambers every legislator has the right, indeed the obligation, to vote. Legislators cast their own votes; no colleague or staff aide may do it for them. To exchange their votes for money or for any other thing of value would be to accept a bribe, which is a federal crime.

Furthermore, no legal grounds exist for attacking legislators for performing their duties, at least in legislative deliberations and votes. Anxious to prevent reprisals against legislators in the conduct of office, the U.S. Constitution's authors specified in Article I, Section 6, that "for any speech or debate in either House, they shall not be questioned in any other place."

Much of Congress's decision making is a matter of public record: voting as well as taking part in formal meetings, markups, debates, and amending activities. But equally important are the complex informal negotiations that surround nearly every enactment—away from the prying eyes of reporters and lobbyists and often conducted by staff aides. From his study of members' committee activity, Richard L. Hall distinguishes between formal and informal modes of participation.[1]

A full accounting of lawmakers' performance, then, would embrace not only how members participate in floor and committee deliberations but also how much effort they expend overall. How much attention do they pay to issues, how do they gain expertise on them, and how do they discharge party or caucus affairs? How do they allocate time between legislative and constituent duties? How do they hire, deploy, and supervise their staff? Countless such decisions—some reached with the solemnity of, say, a vote to commit troops abroad, others made hastily or inadvertently—define what it means to be a member of Congress.

Capitol Hill norms strongly underscore lawmakers' individual responsibility for their decisions. Although party leaders may plead, coax, or warn, using roughhouse tactics against members can backfire. Exhibit A would be Sen. James M. Jeffords of Vermont—a liberal Republican from a liberal state—who endured a series of petty snubs by Senate leaders and the White House after he balked at President George W. Bush's tax and education initiatives. In mid-2001, Jeffords resigned from the party, becoming an independent and voting with the Democrats on organizational matters, thus shifting Senate control from Republican to Democratic hands. "The party establishment . . . has to understand it is nonproductive for them to threaten retaliation on people who don't vote their way," declared John McCain of Arizona, another Republican senator who had risked the wrath of his party's leaders.[2]

"It's déjà vu all over again," quipped political scientist Norman J. Ornstein. He recalled that the Clinton administration had employed hardball tactics against Alabama senator Richard C. Shelby, a conservative Democrat who opposed the Clinton-Gore economic package. With each White House confrontation, Shelby's popularity soared in his home state, and nobody was surprised when he switched to the GOP.[3]

The issues of members' independence came up again in 2005 as the Senate considered President Bush's appointees—several of them highly controversial—and such White House priorities as Social Security reform and new tax reductions. Again the White House tried a full-court press on several wavering senators, including presidential speeches in the members' home states and coordinated lobby group ads. Support for the president is high, especially in the Senate and especially among his own partisans. But even though Republicans control both chambers, majority votes have to be won, not assumed.

TYPES OF DECISIONS

One basic decision facing legislators is how much time to spend in the nation's capital. Members within air-commuting range often remain at their home bases, commuting to Washington, D.C., for midweek sessions. Many of these Tuesday-to-Thursday Club members rarely if ever spend a weekend in Washington. Others, with varying degrees of enthusiasm, plunge into the capital's social and political life. Such individuals rarely "go back to Pocatello," as the saying goes. Between these two extremes are many variations.

A more subtle question is how lawmakers will spend their time and energy while in the nation's capital. Some try to digest the mountains of studies and reports that cross their desks. They "do their homework," in Capitol Hill parlance. Others seem to know or care little about legislative matters. They pursue other duties—communication, outreach, visits with constituents or lobby groups, and fund-raising. Such members rarely contribute to committee or floor deliberations. Their votes usually follow cues from party colleagues, staff aides, the White House, or interest groups. Some are found in the ranks of the Obscure Caucus, a list of unnoticed members compiled periodically by *Roll Call,* a Capitol Hill newspaper. "These members kept their noses down for the most part, made the welfare of their district their number one priority, and largely avoided joining any contentious national debates."[4]

Either of these strategies can be successfully pursued, and distressingly few voters can tell the difference. Still, most legislators claim to prefer legislative tasks. They strive to make time for their legislative duties, regardless of distractions.

Specializing

Within the legislative realm, members may dig deeply in a particular area or range widely across issues and policies. Senators are more apt to be generalists, while representatives are inclined to cultivate a few specialties. Sen. Jim DeMint, R-S.C., then head of the House GOP's class of '98 caucus, explained why members should specialize:

> If you've got twenty things you want to do, see where everything is. You'll find that maybe ten of those are already being worked on by people, and that while you may be supportive in that role, you don't need to carry the ball. But you can find those two or three things that are important to you that no one seems to be taking the lead on. But if you try to play the lead on everything, you'll be wasting your time and recreating work that's already going on.[5]

In both houses key policy-making roles are played by those whom Rep. David E. Price, D-N.C., a political scientist, calls policy entrepreneurs—those recognized for "stimulating more than . . . responding" to outside political forces in a given field.[6] Often nearly invisible to the mass of citizens, these legislators are known to specialized publics for their contributions to specific policies—for example, Rep. Charlie Norwood, R-Ga., on health care; Sen. Mitch McConnell, R-Ky., on campaign finance; Rep. C. W. Bill Young, R-Fla., on bone-marrow transplant programs; and Sen. Tom Harkin, D-Iowa, on policies for the disabled.

Legislative specialties are often dictated by constituency concerns. Alaska lawmakers focus on the policies toward the state's federally controlled lands, while the delegation from Washington State (home of thousands of Boeing and Microsoft employees) must be attuned to the needs of the aerospace and software industries. A pair of Senate liberals, Christopher J. Dodd, D-Conn., and Charles E. Schumer, D-N.Y., have honed their reputations as effective voices for, respectively, the insurance industry (Hartford, Connecticut, is the nation's insurance capital) and the banking industry (New York City is the world's financial center).

Committee assignments themselves may shape members' interests. Senate Foreign Relations chairman Lugar and his colleagues Joseph R. Biden Jr., D-Del., and Chuck Hagel, R-Neb., use their positions to express thoughtful, independent views on foreign affairs. Such specialties may not excite home-state voters, but the assignments challenge the senators to undertake serious legislative work.

Specializations may also reflect personal interests nurtured by background or experience. As former senator Warren B. Rudman, R-N.H. (1980–1993), explained:

> Who are we when we're elected to the Senate? . . . We are men and women. We are not bland, neutral, blank-slate people who never suf-

fered, and never were happy. You tend to be influenced by the sum total of life's experiences.[7]

Personal life stories impel members to specialize in particular issues. Gun control laws, for example, are a natural passion for Rep. Carolyn McCarthy, D-N.Y., whose husband was one of six people killed by a gunman on a Long Island commuter train, and Rep. Jim Langevin, D-R.I., a paraplegic injured in a freak gun accident.

Shared experiences sometimes forge unusual alliances. Sens. Pete V. Domenici, R-N.M., and Paul Wellstone, D-Minn. (1991–2002), both of whom had family members suffering from mental illness, led a 1996 fight to require health plans to offer the same coverage for severe mental disorders as for physical disorders. They agreed on so little else that they were dubbed the "odd couple of health care." Wellstone and House Speaker J. Dennis Hastert, R-Ill., both former school wrestlers, formed another unexpected team. They came together to support provisions of higher education bills that bolster the place of "non-revenue-producing sports" such as wrestling, gymnastics, tennis, and track.[8]

Members' policy reach can go beyond their committee assignments—through speeches, floor amendments, caucuses, and task forces, to name a few. When only in his second term, and not a member of the Armed Services Committee, Rep. Dick Armey, R-Texas (1985–2003), devised an ingenious scheme (employing an outside commission) for closing unneeded military bases. His proposal smoothed political sensitivities and won bipartisan support for passage in 1988. Such feats are not everyday occurrences, but the fluidity of today's procedures makes even the most junior member a potential policy entrepreneur.

Whatever a member's specialty, the ability to influence the decision-making process is what counts. As Sen. Edmund S. Muskie, D-Maine (1959–1980), once explained:

> People have all sorts of conspiratorial theories on what constitutes power in the Senate. It has little to do with the size of the state you come from. Or the source of your money. Or committee chairmanships, although that certainly gives you a kind of power. But real power up there comes from doing your work and knowing what you're talking about. Power is the ability to change someone's mind. . . . The most important thing in the Senate is credibility. Credibility! That is power.[9]

Staking Out Positions

Lawmakers do more than specialize in a particular policy field. They are constantly forced to adopt positions or take stands, which often reveal themselves in what Richard F. Fenno Jr. has called the "politics of timing."[10]

From his study of a 1981 vote on selling AWACS (airborne warning and control system) reconnaissance planes to Saudi Arabia, Fenno identified three types of decision makers: early deciders, active players, and late deciders.

Early deciders are fervent supporters who want to get out front in the debate. "I'd rather come out early and be part of the fight," said Rep. Peter T. King, R-N.Y., of his ready support for fast-track trade authority.[11] These members are buoyed by friendly lobbyists but ignored by others—because their commitments are known at the outset from declarations, bill sponsorship, or prior voting records.

Active players, in contrast, delay their commitments, inviting bids from various sides of the issue at hand and often gaining them leverage over the final language of legislation.

Late deciders delay their decision (or reconsider an earlier commitment) until the very last moment. They forfeit influence over the basic framework of the measure. Chiding colleagues who resisted supporting President George W. Bush's tax cut, then GOP whip Don Nickles of Oklahoma (1981–2005) warned, "People that don't support [the budget] won't have very much impact on how it's put together."[12] But late deciders are eagerly courted by all sides and may gain specific concessions. "I love a 50–50 tie," confided Sen. John B. Breaux, D-La. (1987–2005), who was a frequent endgame bargainer. "This is the kind of thing you dream about being involved in. It's a mandate for getting things done."[13] Such members are concerned not only about political payoffs and their need for political cover but also about their reputation for independence.

Individual senators and representatives differ widely in the rate at which they introduce and sponsor bills. Some lawmakers are inveterate initiators of bills and resolutions; others shy away from sponsoring measures. A Senate study by Wendy Schiller found that bills are most likely to be introduced by senior senators, those who are chairs or ranking members of high-volume committees (such as Commerce), and those who represent large, diverse states.[14]

Senate and House rules do not limit the number of members who can cosponsor bills or resolutions. Thus cosponsorship has become common. One survey found that a majority of bills introduced in both chambers were cosponsored; the average such bill had 7.2 cosponsors in the Senate and 22.2 cosponsors in the House.[15] Authors of measures often circulate a "Dear Colleague" letter detailing the virtues of the bill and soliciting cosponsors to demonstrate broad support and force committee action. According to another study, House members circulated no fewer than fifty-four hundred "Dear Colleague" letters over a year's time—an average of more than twelve letters per member.[16]

Cosponsorship, no less than sponsorship, is politically motivated, as freshman senator Dan Quayle, R-Ind. (1981–1989), understood when he asked the Senate's preeminent liberal, Edward M. Kennedy, D-Mass., to cosponsor his first major bill, the 1982 Job Training Partnership Act. Soliciting Kennedy's cooperation was a daring move for a young conservative embarking on his first subcommittee chairmanship. "The decision to travel the bipartisan route . . . was his earliest strategic decision," wrote Fenno of Quayle's eventual legislative success. "It caused him a lot of trouble, but he never looked back."[17] Despite right-wing opposition and stonewalling from President Ronald Reagan's administration, Quayle's decision helped win passage of the job training act. It was his greatest Senate achievement—and a notable entry in his résumé when he was later tapped for the vice presidency by George Bush.

Occasionally, however, cosponsors are shunned. Introducing his waterway users' fee bill, Senator Domenici decided against seeking cosponsors for several reasons.[18] First, as ranking Republican on the subcommittee, he could arrange for hearings without the support of cosponsors. Second, single sponsorship would be easier. ("If you've got cosponsors you have to clear every little change with them.") Third, if by chance he found no cosponsors, his effort might suffer a devastating initial setback. And, finally, if the bill became law, he would get full, undiluted credit. Thus, for a time, Domenici fought alone for his bill. In the end it was signed into law by President Jimmy Carter at a Democratic rally crowded with politicians who initially had opposed it. Domenici's role was barely mentioned. Such are the ironies of politics.

Do legislators favor the bills and resolutions they introduce? Normally they do, but as Sportin' Life, the *Porgy and Bess* character, said, "It ain't necessarily so." Members may introduce a measure to stake out jurisdiction for their committee or to pave the way for hearings and deliberations that will air a public problem. Or they may introduce measures they do not personally favor to oblige an executive agency or to placate an important interest group.

Taking Part

As those in any organization, some members of Congress take a passionate interest in what goes on; others pay selective attention to issues; a few seem just to be going through the motions. In his detailed study of three House committees, Richard L. Hall uncovered varying levels of participation among members, among committees and subcommittees, and among types of involvement.

Although members' attendance at committee and subcommittee sessions was respectable (about three-quarters of the members showed up for at least part of each session), active participation—taking part in markup debate, offering amendments, and the like—was far less common. Perhaps half a subcommittee's members could be considered players, by a generous counting. The rest are nonplayers. As a subcommittee staffer remarked, "On a good day half of [the members] know what's going on. Most of the time it's only five or six who actually mark a bill up."[19]

Constituency interests, as might be predicted, strongly propel members to participate in committee business. This is true even when the negotiations are informal and out of the public's sight. In formal subcommittee markup sessions, "the public forum has the benefit of allowing members to at once promote—through their votes, arguments, amendments, obstructionism—constituency interests and be seen doing so."[20]

Constituency-driven activity is especially common in the House Agriculture Committee, a panel historically driven by regional and commodity pressures. That committee also witnessed the most biased participation in that active members were unrepresentative of the full committee (much less the full House). Decisions on programs for dairy farmers and peanut growers, for example, were strongly tilted toward producers in those agricultural areas. Not even full committee or floor deliberations muted the enthusiastic advocacy of the dozen or so lawmakers from districts that produced those commodities. In debates over job training legislation in another committee, participating members tended to represent areas with higher unemployment rates than those of nonparticipants. In three additional cases, where concentrated district benefits were not at stake, Hall found no participatory biases.

Casting Votes

Lawmakers' most visible choices are embodied in the votes they cast. Voting is a central ritual in any legislative body. Members place great stock in their voting records, under the assumption (sometimes borne out) that constituents will judge certain of their votes at reelection time. Outside groups are keen-eyed followers of the votes on specific measures. Scholars, too, have a longstanding love affair with legislative voting, no doubt because votes provide concrete, quantifiable indicators that lend themselves to statistical analysis.

Senators and representatives strive to be recorded on as many floor and committee votes as they can. The average member participates in about 95 percent of recorded votes on the floor. Members seek to compile a record of diligence to buttress their home styles and to forestall charges of absenteeism by opponents. House and Senate leaders make it easier for members to fulfill high expectations by avoiding votes on Mondays and Fridays, stacking votes back to back in midweek, and promising no votes several evenings each week.[21]

If members cannot vote in person, they can still be recorded on an issue. They may announce their views in floor statements or in press releases. Or they may pair themselves with someone on the opposite side of an issue. Pairing is a voluntary arrangement that allows members to go on record without voting or affecting the final tabulation.

The practice of allowing absent members to vote by proxy—entrusting their votes to an ally who is present at the session—has never been permissible in floor deliberations, and in 1995 it was suspended in House committees. During their forty years in the minority, House Republicans resented the fact that their members in attendance invariably were outvoted by chairmen voting the proxies they had collected beforehand from busy Democrats (though the tactic was used by both parties). By abolishing proxies, the new majority hoped to encourage members to attend their committee meetings, even though it made life more hectic for everyone.

Offering Amendments

A chief strategy for shaping legislation during committee and floor deliberations is to offer amendments. Sometimes amendments are intended to provide a test of strength. During a debate on reauthorizing the National Aeronautics and Space Administration, Rep. Tim Roemer, D-Ind. (1991–2003)—then a junior committee member—introduced an amendment to cancel the costly space station program. Instead of losing by a wide margin (as happened in previous years), the amendment failed by only a single vote. That signaled plunging support for not only the space station but other "big science" projects, such as the superconducting super collider.[22]

In the House, majority party leaders can shape outcomes by deciding which, if any, members' floor amendments will be in order. The outcome of the 1997 debate over funding for the National Endowment for the Arts (NEA) hinged on the single floor amendment permitted by the leadership. Conservatives urged GOP leaders to honor their commitment to ax the NEA and uphold the Appropriations Committee's bill, which in essence ended the agency's funding. But fearing defeat by a bipartisan pro-arts coalition, Republican leaders seized upon an amendment proposed by Rep. Vernon J. Ehlers, R-Mich., and incorporated it into the Rules Committee's rule for the debate. This amendment would have eliminated the agency and sent the funds (a paltry $80 million) directly to the states for arts and education grants. The amendment satisfied neither of the warring camps, which pleaded for an up-or-down vote on NEA. By twisting arms, the leaders eked out a victory for the rule by one vote, 217–216. But the next day the Ehlers amendment itself went down to defeat, 155–271. And the bill went to the Senate with no NEA funding at all.[23]

In the Senate, which cherishes individual senators' prerogatives, amendments are more freely offered and form a central part of floor debate. In a GOP-controlled Senate, with elections looming in 1996, Senator Kennedy won passage of two popular measures by vowing to introduce them as amendments for a variety of floor bills. These were a hike in the minimum wage and a provision that insurance companies could neither drop coverage when people switch jobs nor deny coverage for preexisting medical conditions. GOP leaders strongly opposed both measures but allowed floor votes to avoid having to face repeated embarrassments in an election year.

Amendments can also derail legislation. President Bill Clinton's 1993 economic stimulus package came unglued in the Senate under a barrage of hostile amendments. While the bill's Democratic managers labored to keep the measure intact, Republicans put forward amendments to drop what they claimed were pork projects. When Democrats shut off amendments by a parliamentary maneuver, the Republicans' opposition hardened, and cloture could not be invoked.

Some amendments are designed to force members to declare themselves on symbolic issues that command public attention. Amendments on abortion funding or balanced budgets are prime examples. Others are "killer amendments," or poison pills, intended to make a bill so unpalatable that it will fail. Senate and House sponsors of campaign finance reform faced opponents who offered what are called non-severability amendments, meaning that the entire act would fall if courts ruled against any portion of the measure. Advocates and opponents alike realized that any one of the bill's provisions—the soft-money ban, issue ad restrictions, or hard-money limits—could be struck down by the courts. Authors of the Senate bill, John McCain, R-Ariz., and Russell D. Feingold, D-Wis., beat back those amendments in close votes.

Although killer amendments upset the sponsors and managers of bills, such roadblocks rarely alter a measure's ultimate fate. Examining seventy-six such amendments considered in the mid-1990s, John D. Wilkerson concluded that they "rarely, if ever, cause bills to fail. . . . Most were easily defeated." Nor did these proposals tempt lawmakers to vote not on the amendment's policy substance but on its effect on future floor voting choices (so-called strategic voting).[24]

What Do Votes Mean?

Like other elements in the legislative process, voting is open to manifold interpretations. A vote may or may not be what it seems to be. Therefore, one must be cautious in analyzing legislative votes.

House and Senate floor votes are imperfect channels for registering members' views. Votes are frequently taken on procedural matters that evoke responses independent of the issue at hand. Or members may favor a measure but feel constrained to vote against the version presented on the floor. Conversely, as with the No Child Left Behind Act (P.L. 107-110), members may go along because on the whole they deem it a step forward, even though they dislike specific portions. Or they may vote for a questionable proposal to prevent enactment of something worse. Or they may support a harmful amendment expecting that the other chamber or the conference committee will kill it. Finally, they may accede to party leaders' wishes on measures so long as their actions do not adversely affect their constituencies.

In some cases recorded votes are wholly misleading. A favorable vote may be negative, or vice versa. In such cases legislators' votes must be decoded to reveal their real meaning.

Sometimes voting conceals a legislator's true position. Given the multiplicity of votes—procedural as well as substantive—on many measures, lawmakers can come out on more than one side of an issue, or at least appear to do so. For instance, members may vote for authorizing a program but against funding it. Or they may vote against final passage of a bill but for a substitute version. This tactic assures the bill's backers that a lawmaker favors the concept, while pleasing voters who oppose the bill. Such voting patterns may reflect either a deliberate attempt to obscure one's position or a thoughtful response to complex questions. As in so many aspects of human behavior, lawmakers' motivations can be judged fully only in light of specific cases.

Lawmakers' voting rationales are sometimes hard to explain to outsiders. In some cases members face a dilemma: Either vote their convictions and deal with the consequences or swallow their misgivings and vote for the sake of appearance. Rep. Mark Sanford, R-S.C. (1995–2001), chose the former course in 1998, when he joined fourteen other Republicans in voting against a popular bill authorizing U.S. sanctions against nations that persecute religious minorities—an appealing idea but fraught with problems. "This was an awfully awkward vote, and I know I'll hear from the folks back home," he explained. "But the devil was in the details."[25]

More often lawmakers decide to go with the crowd. Regarding a highly appealing constitutional amendment requiring a balanced budget, Sen. Ernest F. Hollings, D-S.C. (1967–2005), admitted that he planned to vote for it because he got "tired of explaining" its deficiencies. It was easier "just to say put it in."[26] Such was the case in the Homeland Security Act of 2002—a massive but deeply flawed bill that transferred some 180,000 federal workers to a new executive department. Members went along because they feared being labeled as against homeland security.

Scholars often mistakenly treat votes as if they were unambiguous indicators of legislators' views. Lobbyists and reporters, too, are prone to assess lawmakers on the basis of floor votes. Many groups construct voting indexes that label legislators as "friendly" or "unfriendly." Citizens should be cautioned to examine such indexes closely. How many votes does the index comprise? Are they a fair sample of the group's concerns? Does the index embody a partisan or ideological agenda, hidden or otherwise? The bottom line is: Beware of an interest group's voting scorecards, even if you agree with its policy leanings.

DETERMINANTS OF VOTING

Votes, particularly on single issues, should be examined, interpreted, and categorized with care. Several factors shape congressional voting: party affiliation, ideological leanings, constituents' views, and presidential leadership.

Party and Voting

The main way that members reach their voting decisions is to consult the views of their political party colleagues. Party affiliation is the strongest single correlate of members' voting decisions, and in recent years it has reached surprisingly high levels. Of all the floor votes cast by House and Senate members on articles of impeachment against President Clinton in 1998–1999, for example, 92 percent followed partisan battle lines—Republicans favoring impeachment, Democrats resisting it.

FIGURE 9-1 **Party Unity Votes in Congress, 1970–2004**

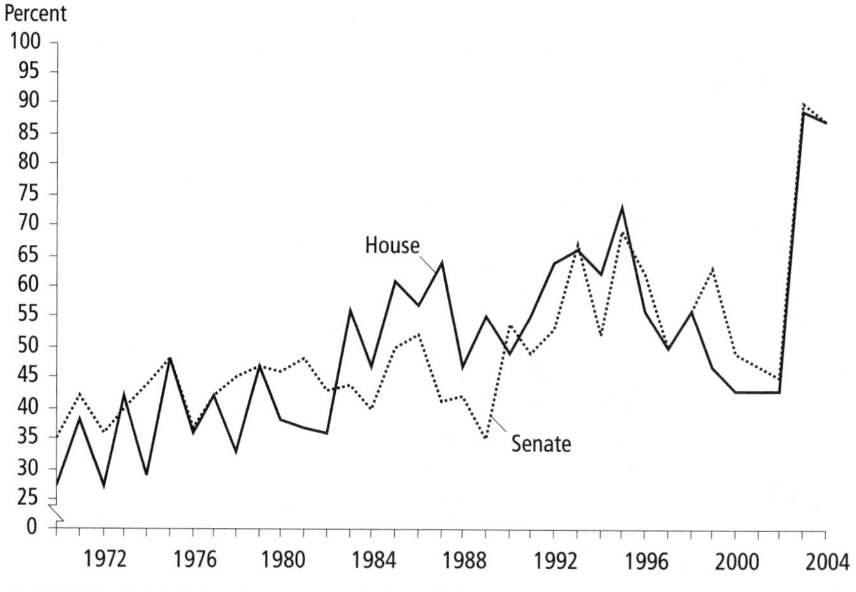

Source: "Party Unity History, *CQ Weekly,* December 11, 2004, 2953.

Note: Party unity votes are defined as the percentage of all House and Senate votes in which a majority of Democrats opposed a majority of Republicans.

In a typical year about two-thirds of all floor votes could be called party unity votes, defined by Congressional Quarterly as votes in which a majority of voting Republicans oppose a majority of voting Democrats. Figure 9-1 depicts such House and Senate party votes from 1970 through 2004. An upward trend since the early 1980s can be discerned. Today's revival of party voting recalls the militant parties era of a century ago.[27]

Party unity scores can be calculated for individual members—the percentage of party unity votes in which each member voted in agreement with the majority of his party colleagues. According to these scores, the average legislator now sticks with the party line on nearly nine out of ten votes. Aggregate party unity scores for Democrats and Republicans from 1970 through 2004 are displayed in Figure 9-2. Partisan voting blocs are evident also in many committees. From their painstaking study of voting in eight House committees as early as the mid-1970s, Glenn R. Parker and Suzanne L. Parker concluded that partisanship was a major factor in all of the panels except Foreign Affairs (now International Relations), which has a bipartisan tradition.[28]

Party voting levels in both houses have risen by at least 10 percent since the 1970s. Sharpened partisanship now dominates congressional politics, to the point that "partisan gridlock" has become a buzzword in recent campaigns.[29]

Partisan voting strength is rooted in several factors. Some students argue that party loyalty is mainly a shorthand term for constituency differences. That is, partisans vote together because they reflect the same kinds of political and demographic areas—for example, rural areas and outer suburbs for Republicans, inner cities and minority clusters for Democrats. In the House, these demographic divisions are sharpened by partisan and bipartisan redistricting schemes.

According to this reasoning, legislators stray from party ranks when they feel their constituents will not benefit from the party's policies. Today's few Democratic mavericks tend to be from nonminority southern districts, whose voters typically are to the right of the party's mainstream. (Thirteen of them—

FIGURE 9-2 **Levels of Party Voting in Congress, 1970–2004**

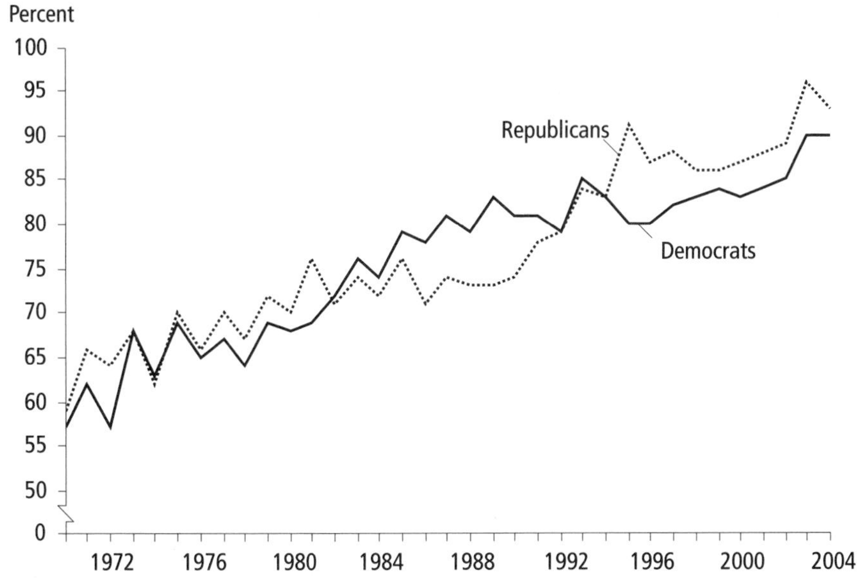

Sources: Derived from annual CQ voting studies reported in, for example, *CQ Weekly,* January 3, 2004, 48: and December 11, 2004, 2952.

Note: The graph shows the percentage of times the average Republican or Democrat in Congress voted with his party majority in partisan votes for the years listed. These composite party unity scores are based on votes that split the parties in the House and Senate—a majority of voting Republicans opposing a majority of voting Democrats. The scores have been recomputed to correct for absences.

ten representatives and three senators—decamped to the GOP over the last two decades.) Republican mavericks are mostly from New England and the Northeast corridor, where voters fall to the left of the party's center. To win in these areas, elected officials must lean away from their parties' main thrust. (However, only two such members left the GOP.)

Partisan realignment—in which constituencies sorted themselves out according to ideological and policy preferences—helps explain the recent upsurge in lawmakers' party loyalty. Among Democratic representatives, increasing numbers of their southern flank are African Americans. The dwindling number of Democrats representing conservative districts (including the self-named Blue Dog Democrats) try to put distance between themselves and their leaders. By the same token, the Republican congressional party is more uniformly conservative than it used to be. In the South, conservative areas now tend to elect Republicans, not Democrats. Elsewhere many areas once represented by GOP liberals have been captured by Democrats. The decline of conservative Democrats and moderate Republicans, especially in the House, underlies much of the ideological cohesion within, and chasm between, today's Capitol Hill parties.[30]

Party cohesion also flows from shared policy goals shaped early in a politician's career.[31] Those who entered politics through the civil rights, environmental, or antiwar movements gravitated toward the Democratic Party and displayed their shared values in voting. By contrast, individuals who became active to cut taxes, downsize the federal government, or promote conservative causes gathered under the GOP banner, strengthening and in some cases altering that party's historical approach to such issues. Long before taking their oath of office, today's candidates, and would-be candidates, receive an array of incentives and services from their parties' campaign committees.

Constituency and recruitment are not, however, the sole sources of Capitol Hill partisanship. Another source is institutional: the congressional parties and their activities to promote partisanship. New-member socialization is dominated by party organizations. Friendships cross party lines more rarely than they used to. Former senator Breaux, who was a habitual cross-party bargainer, blames social patterns for today's bitter partisan cleavages.

> If the only knowledge you have of "the other side of the aisle" is what you have read in an attack press release written by the party operatives, you wouldn't want to talk to them, and you certainly wouldn't want to be friends. With the House barely in town three days a week and members constantly rushing back to raise money and campaign, it leaves precious little time to "meet and greet" the folks you're supposed to work with.[32]

When seeking out voting cues, therefore, legislators usually turn to party colleagues as guides for their own behavior.

Party leaders are hardly shy about contacting members to solicit views and insist that they follow the party line. The more visible an issue, the harder leaders must compete against other pressures for members' votes. Rep. Mark Souder, R-Ind., described the exhortations of House Speaker Newt Gingrich, R-Ga. (1995–1999), and his lieutenants during the GOP's first year in power:

> They pull us into a room before almost every vote and yell at us. . . . They say, "This is a test of our ability to govern," or "This is a gut check," or "I got you here and you hired me as your coach to get you through, but if you want to change coaches, go ahead."[33]

Leaders are more likely to muster votes if the issue is defined in procedural terms than if the issue is presented substantively. Whatever the legislator's personal leanings, the institutional push toward partisan voting cannot be ignored.

Finally, party leaders exploit each chamber's rules and procedures to encourage favorable outcomes. David W. Rohde calls this "process partisanship," which means "the degree to which each institution is structured or operates in a partisan fashion."[34] House procedures and practices sharpen partisanship, inasmuch as a cohesive majority party can usually work its will. Through their control of key committees, their scheduling powers, and their use of special rules to structure floor debate and voting, majority party leaders can arrange for votes they are likely to win and avoid those they are apt to lose. Senate leaders have fewer opportunities to engineer victories because that chamber's rules and procedures distribute power more evenly between the parties and among individual members than does the House. Yet Senate floor leaders can regulate the timing of debates to their advantage and (through their right to be recognized first to speak or offer amendments on the floor) influence the order and content of floor deliberations.

"Conditional party government" is how political scientists describe today's legislative parties.[35] Considering the range of partisan influence, however, perhaps the word *conditional* could be dropped.

Ideology and Voting

Just as lawmakers are committed partisans, they also tend to harbor ideological views. Stable cleavages have been found along two dimensions (race and government intervention in the economy) by political scientists Keith T. Poole and Howard Rosenthal, who use roll-call votes to compile ideological scores for all members of Congress from 1789 to the present.[36]

When political scientists began to do serious voting analysis in the 1950s, party and ideology were distinct ingredients, despite measurable differences between the parties. The reason was deep ideological splits within the two parties. In the late 1930s a conservative coalition of Republicans and southern Democrats emerged in a reaction against the New Deal.[37] Historically, this coalition was stronger in the Senate than in the House, but its success rate was impressive in both chambers during the 1938–1964 period—no matter which party controlled the White House or Capitol Hill.

The conservative coalition surfaces so rarely these days that the respected *CQ Weekly* has stopped scoring it.[38] Bipartisan conservatism fell victim to the hardening ideological consistency of both political parties. The Republicans are more solidly conservative, and the Democrats more liberal, than they were in the period between the late 1930s and the mid-1980s. "Democrats are perched on the left, Republicans on the right, in both the House and the Senate as the ideological centers of the two parties have moved markedly apart," writes Sarah A. Binder.[39] In other words, the two parties are more cohesive internally and further apart externally than they were in the recent past.

Polarization on Capitol Hill—in which partisanship and ideology are closely intertwined—can be shown spatially on a left-right (liberal to conservative) continuum. See Figure 9-3. If one asks the American public to locate themselves at points along a left-right scale, the result roughly follows a normal bell-shaped curve (nowadays, perhaps slightly skewed to the right-hand side). Ideologically—and attitudinally, regarding many policy questions—citizens tend to cluster around the middle, their numbers declining toward the extreme ends of the scale (Panel A).[40]

In contrast, political elites—delegates to national political conventions, for example—are more opinionated than the public as a whole, and they cluster to the left or right of the median, nonetheless overlapping one another at the center. Ideological divisions in the House of Representatives, using data compiled by Sean M. Theriault, can be viewed at two historical points: before and after the recent partisan realignment (1968 and 1998). In the pre-realignment House (Panel B) ideological divisions look similar to those of the party elites. Democrats appeared in almost every ideological niche, from far left to far right; Republicans were more tightly clustered on the right, but a number spilled over to the liberal side of the scale.[41]

The contemporary Congress (represented by Panel C), however, is almost completely polarized. Only a handful of members fall at the midpoint; not a single Republican falls on the liberal side of the scale, and only a few Democrats stray into the mildest conservative category.

Although the diagrams in Panels B and C are based on ideological categories drawn from members' voting records (following the Poole-Rosenthal scale), they now virtually mirror partisan labels. (The figures are for the House; patterns in the Senate are similar though somewhat less dramatic.) This polarization, and the resulting collapse of the middle, is an outgrowth of realignment that has produced legislative battle lines of a clarity not seen in nearly a century.

The ideological center on Capitol Hill is thus a victim of partisan repositioning aided in the House by partisan gerrymandering. The proportion of political moderates—conservative Democrats or liberal Republicans—hovered at about 30 percent in the 1960s and 1970s. (Binder's definition of centrists is

FIGURE 9-3 **Ideological Divisions in Congress and the Public**

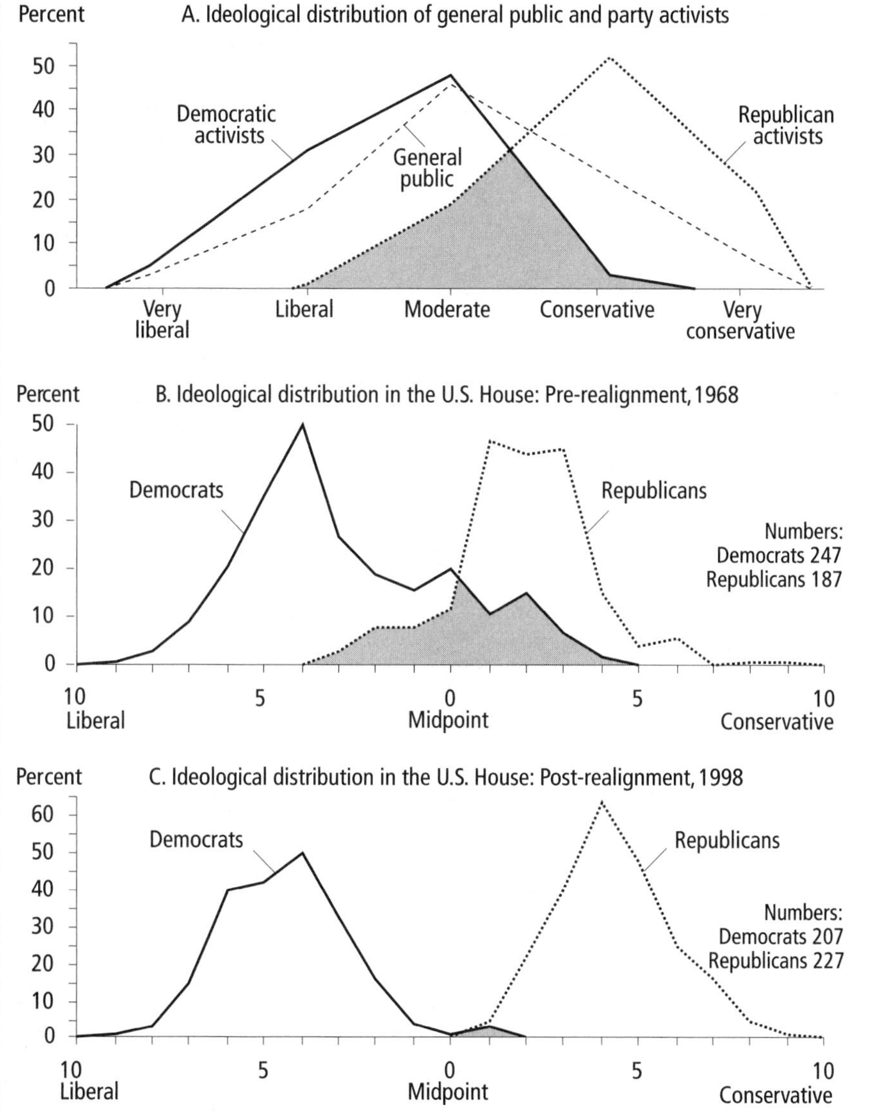

Sources: Panel A: *Washington Post*/ABC News survery, *Washington Post,* August 11, 1996, M8 and August 25, 1996, M4. Panels B and C: Adapted from Sean M. Theriault, "The Case of the Vanishing Moderates: Party Polarization in the Modern Congress," Paper presented at the Western Political Science Association, Denver, Colorado, March 2003, Figure 1. These data are derived from Keith T. Poole and Howard Rosenthal's DW-NOMINATE ideology scores. See Keith T. Poole and Howard Rosenthal, *Congress: A Political-Economic History of Roll-Call Voting* (New York: Oxford University Press, 1997). Scores for adjacent years (1969–1970 and 1999–2000) yield virtually identical results.

those members who are closer to the ideological midpoint between the two parties than to the ideological center of their own party.) Fewer than one in ten of today's lawmakers fall into this centrist category.[42] Conservative Democrats, the larger of the two centrist groupings, once represented a third of their party's members; today they could caucus in a small cloakroom. In the 108th Congress (2003–2005), they represented no more than 10 percent in the Senate and half that in the House. Most of these represented southern or border states. Even rarer were moderate to liberal Republicans, who accounted for no more than 3 percent of all House GOP members and 12 percent of senators.[43]

This "incredible shrinking middle" (former senator Breaux's term) on Capitol Hill, political scientist Binder concedes, "seems to substantially hamper the ability of Congress and the president to reach agreement on issues before them."[44]

Constituency and Voting

To illustrate the potency of constituency, consider how House members voted on an uncommonly partisan agenda: the Republicans' ten-point Contract with America in 1995. Fealty to the contract hinged mainly on partisanship and ideology, according to James G. Gimpel's multivariate analysis of the voting. Southern Democrats, for example, were more supportive than were nonsoutherners. Also significant were district characteristics: racial composition, median income, percentage of rural inhabitants, and percentage who voted for independent presidential candidate Ross Perot in 1992. Gimpel summarizes his findings:

> The plurality of legislators who found themselves on the losing side of these votes [on the contract] were from northern and western urban districts with significant minority and low-income populations. In this sense, the Contract with America was a legislative program supported most consistently by members from predominantly white, middle- and upper-income suburban and rural districts.[45]

The Pull of Constituencies

Constituencies control lawmakers' choices in two ways. First, people usually elect representatives whose views so mirror their own that floor votes automatically reflect the will of the constituents. In other words, representatives vote their constituency because they are simply transplanted locals. Certain constituency issues invariably override party or ideology—for example, farm subsidies, public lands management, and immigration.

Second, lawmakers are faced with the ever present threat of electoral defeat. Only rarely do politicians' careers hang on a single vote, but it happens. Pennsylvania Democrat Marjorie Margolies-Mezvinsky lost her swing district in 1994 because of her deciding vote that passed President Clinton's budget. Her constituents regarded her vote as a broken promise to oppose tax and spending increases. Naturally skittish in calculating voters' reactions, politicians usually play it safe. The choices they make, taken cumulatively, offer opportunities to expand or contract their electoral base of support.

Constituency concerns shape voting on Capitol Hill in ways both transparent and subtle. The most obvious examples are the pork-barrel measures that disperse benefits widely among regions and localities involving, for example, highway projects, farm commodity supports, and military bases. Less visible are constituency claims that occasionally run counter to partisan or ideological loyalties.

Despite their current ideological cohesion, the two major political parties remain broad coalitions cobbled together from diverse and not always compatible elements. The Republican Party, for example, embraces both economically conservative voters (higher-income cohorts who are often associated with businesses), along with those—called "Sam's Club" Republicans by one commentator—lower- or middle-income people who are drawn to the party's traditional social values and its hard line on crime and terrorism. In the Senate clash over judicial nominations in 2005, for example, social conservatives pushed senators to make way for "right-thinking" judges, whereas the business community worried that its legislative goals could be thwarted by procedural slowdowns.

The Democratic Party, for its part, is composed of both economic liberals (union members, for example) and those who adopt a liberal stance on social and international issues. Free-trade pacts, for example, split these two groups: Social liberals tend to welcome globalization, while union members fret about losing jobs to low-wage foreign labor. The near-term challenge to both parties' leaders, then, is to foster votes that will reflect their ideological unity while sidestepping these potential constituent fissures.

How politicians calculate the electoral effect of their decisions, R. Douglas Arnold argues, rests upon the long-standing distinction between attentive and inattentive publics. Attentive publics are those citizens who are aware of issues facing Congress and harbor decided opinions about what Congress should do. Such people usually, though not always, belong to interest groups that reinforce, mobilize, and voice their preferences. Politicians can easily determine who is paying attention to a given issue and estimate the electoral consequences. Their natural instinct is to yield to a group's strongly voiced preferences, unless the issue in question has mobilized two equally vociferous but opposing interests. Especially feared are single-interest groups that threaten to withhold electoral support if their preferences—for example, on abortion and gun control—are ignored. Happily for lawmakers, most citizens, even highly motivated ones, are interested in a range of issues. Thus politicians can cultivate support over the long haul and encourage voters to gloss over wrong votes on particular issues.

Inattentive publics are those who lack extensive knowledge or firm preferences about a specific issue. Frankly, this describes most people most of the time. People pay attention to only a small fraction of the issues before Congress. Yet a reelection-minded legislator dare not ignore those who seem indifferent to an issue. "Latent or unfocused opinions," Arnold cautions, "can quickly be transformed into intense and very real opinions with enormous political repercussions. Inattentiveness and lack of information today should not be confused with indifference tomorrow."[46]

Previously latent issues (such as a member's ethical lapses or failing health) may leap into the public spotlight, especially when prompted by aggressive media coverage or interest group activity. Legislators are well advised to approach even the most minor choices with this question in mind: Will my decision be defensible if it were to appear on the front pages of major newspapers in my state or district?

Calculating the electoral consequences of a lawmaker's multitude of daily decisions is no easy task. Arnold summarizes the components of such calculations:

> To reach a decision, then, a legislator needs to (1) identify all the attentive and inattentive publics who might care about a policy issue, (2) estimate the direction and intensity of their preferences and potential preferences, (3) estimate the probability that the potential preferences will be transformed into real preferences, (4) weight all these preferences according to the size of the various attentive and inattentive publics, and (5) give special weight to the preferences of the legislator's consistent supporters.[47]

Fortunately, lawmakers do not have to repeat these calculations every time they face a choice. Most issues have been around for some time. The preferences of attentive and even inattentive publics are fairly well known. Moreover, Congress is well structured to amass and assess information about individual and group preferences. And prominent officials—party leaders and acknowledged policy experts, for example—can often legitimize members' choices and give them cover in explaining those choices to voters.

The Presidency and Voting

Although Congress often pursues an independent course and members differ in their feelings toward the occupant of the White House, presidents do influence voting. Not only do presidents shape the legislative agenda, but they also can persuade members to lend support. Figure 9-4 depicts the percentage of times presidents from Dwight D. Eisenhower to George W. Bush have prevailed in congressional roll-call votes on which the president announced a position.

President Bush won 81 percent of the roll-call votes on which he took a position during his first four years in office. This was the best success record since President Lyndon B. Johnson's at the summit of his influence (1965).[48] Bush's record owed much to his strategy of focusing on a few core initiatives. Although his administration changed profoundly after the September 11,

2001, terrorist attacks, his legislative success level was fairly high in both of his first two years.

Presidential support votes—those on which presidents have taken an unambiguous stance—include a range of issues, from the momentous (dealing with tax cuts and the Iraqi war, in Bush's case) to large numbers of routine and noncontroversial matters (most Senate confirmations of executive nominations, for example). Still, the index roughly gauges presidents' standing on Capitol Hill and suggests several patterns.

First, modern presidents see their position prevail in two-thirds or more of House and Senate votes, though support levels can vary wildly from year to year. Many of their successes spring not so much from popularity or skill as from the routine nature of many of their initiatives. Yet some presidents—such as Eisenhower, John F. Kennedy, Lyndon Johnson, Reagan in his first year, and Clinton and George W. Bush in their first two years—enjoy extraordinary success in steering their proposals through Congress.

FIGURE 9-4 **Presidential Success History, 1953–2004**

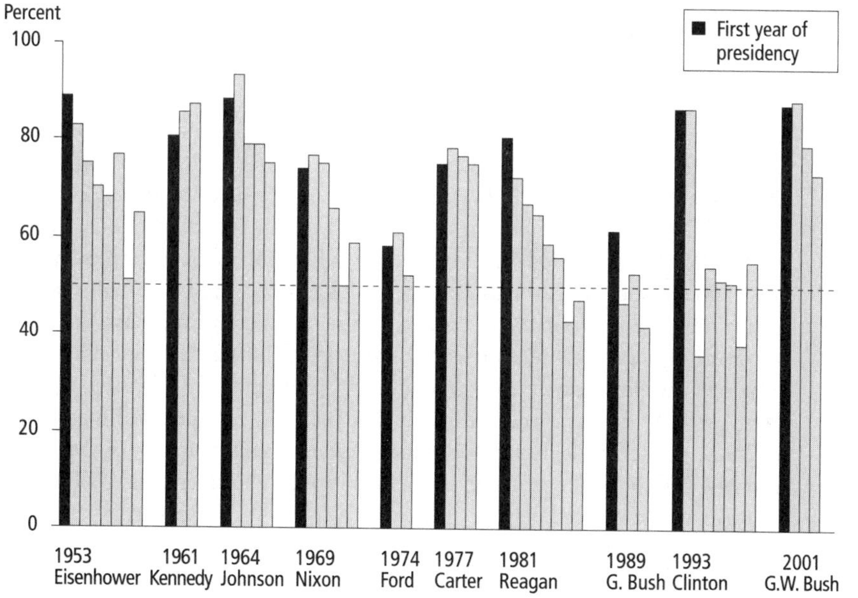

Source: CQ Weekly, December 11, 2004, 2901, 2946.

Note: Presidential success is defined as the percentage of the times the president won his way on roll-call votes on which he had taken a clear position.

Second, presidents do better with their own partisans than with those of the opposition party. Members of the president's party feel obliged to lend their support whenever they can. The party ratio that presidents confront in Congress is the single most important determinant of success or failure. "We don't live in a parliamentary system," observed Senator Jeffords as he departed the Republican Party, "but it is only natural to expect that people such as myself, who have been honored with positions of leadership, will largely support the president's agenda."[49] In 2004 the average House Republican supported President Bush 80 percent of the time; the average Senate Republican, 94 percent of the time. For Democrats, the figures were 30 percent for House members and 60 percent for senators.[50] (The disparity between the two chambers might seem counterintuitive but is explained by the Senate's numerous votes on the president's noncontroversial executive branch nominees.)

Third, partisan swings affect presidential success rates. As long as their party controls Congress, presidents win at least three of every four votes on which they have taken positions; when the government is divided, presidents fall well below that level. In his first two years in office, with Democrats controlling both chambers, President Clinton prevailed on 86.4 percent of all roll calls—comparable to his successor's numbers at the same stage of his tenure. Success smiled even upon Jimmy Carter, whose reputation on Capitol Hill was clouded by his stance as an outsider and the initial ineptness of his legislative liaison staff. With heavy partisan majorities in both chambers, however, Carter had a strong legislative record.[51]

When partisan control of the White House and Congress is divided, presidents' success levels are far less reliable. President Clinton's success rates on Capitol Hill plummeted to modern-day lows in 1995 and 1999 (36 percent and 37.8 percent, respectively).[52] President Eisenhower's success rate fell 24 percent after the Democrats' big victories in the 1958 congressional elections. Building on the 1964 Democratic landslide, President Johnson achieved a modern high of 93 percent success. (Johnson's success rate was boosted by his habit of sending up messages supporting measures he already knew would pass.)

Fourth, presidents tend to lose congressional support as their administrations age. Reagan's experience dramatically confirmed this finding. His support score fell thirteen points after his first year and dropped still further after the 1982 midterm elections boosted the Democrats' majority in the House. After the Democrats recaptured the Senate in the 1986 election and his administration was damaged by the Iran-contra revelations, Reagan's success rate sagged to 43.5 percent.

Finally, presidents have taken clear-cut stands on fewer issues over time.[53] In 2004 President Bush took a position on only thirty-four House and fifty Senate votes—about half the number of such votes in the 1980s. The White House weighed in on fewer than one of every ten votes; Eisenhower was taking positions on about three of five congressional votes at a comparable stage in his administration.

LEGISLATIVE BARGAINING

Legislators decide on a bewildering variety of matters, in relatively short periods of time, often with inadequate information. First, each legislator has unique and sometimes conflicting goals and information. Second, whatever the goals or information levels, every legislator ultimately has a single vote with which to affect the outcome.[54]

Such a state of affairs—disparate goals and widely scattered influence—is hazardous. Conflict may flare out of control if the contending policy objectives are not adequately met. However, stalemate is a constant threat. "Collective action problem" is how political scientists refer to the challenge of merging individual goals into group achievements. To overcome this predicament, members have to resort to politicking; that is, they must trade off goals and resources to get results. No wonder, then, that Congress is "an influence system in which bargain and exchange predominate."[55]

Implicit and Explicit Bargaining

Bargaining is a generic term that refers to several related types of behavior. In each case an exchange takes place. Goals or resources pass from a bargainer's hands in return for other goals or resources that he values. Bargains may be implicit or explicit.

Implicit Bargaining. Implicit bargaining occurs when legislators take actions designed to elicit certain reactions from others, even though no negotiation may have taken place. For example, legislators may introduce a bill or sponsor hearings not because they think the bill will pass but because they hope the action will prod someone else—an executive branch official, perhaps, or a committee chairman with broader jurisdiction on the question—into taking action on the problem. Or a bill's managers may accept a controversial amendment knowing full well that the objectionable provision will be dropped in the other chamber or in conference. These are examples of the so-called law of anticipated reactions.[56]

Another type of implicit bargaining occurs when legislators seek out or accept the judgments of colleagues with expertise on a given matter, expecting that the situation will be reversed in the future. Exchanges of voting cues are endemic in both chambers. What is being traded is information. The exchange not only saves the recipient the time and trouble of mastering the subject matter, but it may also provide a credible cover in defending the vote. A number of moderate House Republicans take cues from Sherwood Boehlert of New York on environmental issues. "I pay attention to how Sherry votes, and think other people do as well," said Christopher Shays, R-Conn. "He would not be in the mainstream of the Republican Party, but I think he's in the mainstream of American politics when it comes to the environment."[57]

Sen. John H. Chafee, R-R.I. (1977–1999)—while the Senate's most liberal Republican—served as cue-giver for his younger friend, Vermont's senator Jeffords, who said:

> I remember that if I ever had a question on how to vote or if I came in at the last minute and did not know what the issue was—I hate to admit that—I would first look to see how John voted. I knew, if nothing else, that if I voted as he did, I would probably not get in trouble.[58]

Exchanging cues is a key element in John W. Kingdon's model of representatives' decisions, derived from interviews with members immediately after their votes on specific issues.[59] Legislators have little difficulty making up their minds when they have strong personal convictions or when party leaders and interest groups agree and point them in the same direction. If all the actors in their field of vision concur, members operate in a consensus mode of decision making. Fellow members emerge as the most influential cue givers, with constituencies ranking second. As one lawmaker observed:

> I think that the other members are very influential, and we recognize it. And why are they influential? I think because they have exercised good judgment, have expertise in the area, and know what they are talking about.[60]

When members deviate from the consensus stance indicated by their cue givers, it is usually to follow their own consciences. Adding up these short-term forces, Kingdon in his model successfully predicted about 90 percent of the decisions.

Explicit Bargaining. Explicit bargains also take several forms. In making compromises legislators agree to split their differences. Compromises are straightforward in measures containing quantitative elements that can easily be adjusted upward or downward—for example, funding levels or eligibility criteria. Compromise on substance is also possible. For example, members who favor a major new program and members who oppose any program at all may agree to a two-year pilot project to test the idea.

"You cannot legislate without the ability to compromise," declared Sen. Alan K. Simpson, R-Wyo. (1979–1997), who often found fault with militant junior members of his own party. He recounted the following tale:

> On a recent bill, I went to [conservative House members] and said: "Here's what I'm doing. I've got six senators who will vote this far, and then the next time if you go any further, they will not be there." So [Sen.] Larry [E.] Craig [R-Idaho] and I delivered on this singular bill, and they said, "We want you to get more." And we said, "There is no more to get." Next vote on this bill, we lost six votes. Then they came in and said, "We are going to probably kill the whole thing." . . . [A]nd they got nothing.[61]

The lesson is that compromise is inevitable in crafting laws; those who are unwilling to give ground are bound to be disappointed.

Logrolling

Logrolling is bargaining in which the parties trade off support so that each may gain its goal. The term originated in the nineteenth century when neighbors helped each other roll logs into a pile for burning. In its most visible form, trading is embodied in a something-for-everyone enactment—known as pork barrel—in legislative areas such as public works, omnibus taxation, or tariffs and trade. Describing the classic logroll, former representative Edward J. Derwinski, R-Ill. (1959–1983), explained how the country's two million farmers put together a majority coalition every five years to pass the omnibus farm bill's basket of price supports, acreage allowances, and marketing agreements:

> What [the farmers] do is very interesting. The agriculture people from North Carolina, where agriculture means tobacco, discuss their problems with the man representing the rice growers in Arkansas or California. The sugar beet growers in Minnesota and sugar cane interests in Louisiana and Hawaii and the wheat and corn and soybean and other producers just gather together in one great big happy family to be sure there is a subsidy for every commodity. They put those numbers together again so that they have at least 218 supporters in the House and 51 in the Senate. A supporter of the tobacco subsidy automatically becomes a supporter of the wheat subsidy, or the sugar quota, or the soybean subsidy, or whatever else follows.[62]

One of the most successful logrolling achievements in farm policy is the food stamp program. It brought together farm lobbies that wanted to boost the agricultural market and urban welfare interests that wanted to feed low-income people. Environmentally minded lawmakers were lured to the farm bill because of subsidies linked to prudent land use. This logroll has proved inclusive and durable. In 1998, for example, a House-Senate agriculture conference report included a crop insurance provision for farmers and a provision restoring food stamps to a quarter-million immigrants who had lost them in the 1996 welfare overhaul. House Republican leaders decided to strip the food stamp provision from the agreement—a move calculated to please conservatives. The rule for debate was soundly defeated by an urban-rural coalition of 98 Republicans and 190 Democrats. "It was wrong to try to use procedure to amend a conference report that had such overwhelming bipartisan support," said Rep. Lincoln Diaz-Balart, R-Fla. "After today's vote, there is no doubt about food stamps."[63]

Logrolling draws individual lawmakers, at a personal level, into the finished legislative product by embracing (or anticipating) their special interests, proposals, or amendments. Henry M. "Scoop" Jackson, D-Wash. (House, 1941–1953; Senate, 1953–1983), when asked how he had assembled a majority for a new proposal, responded something like this: "Maggie said he talked to Russell, and Tom promised this if I would back him on Ed's amendment, and Mike owes me one for last year's help on Pete's bill."[64] Such reciprocity especially pervades the Senate, dominated as it is by individuals. Sponsors of a Senate bill often must placate most or all of the interested legislators to gain clearance to bring a bill to the floor.

Lawmakers who enter into, and stand to profit from, a logroll are expected to support the final package, regardless of what that package looks like. A broad-based logroll is hard to stop. "It's not a system of punishment. It's a system of rewards," explained Rep. Bill Frenzel, R-Minn. (1971–1991), about the House tax-writing process.[65] The House version of the 2005 transportation bill (self-advertised as the "Safe, Accountable, Flexible, and Efficient Transportation Equity Act"), crafted by House Transportation chairman Don Young, R-Alaska, embraced some four thousand specific highway and mass transit projects requested by lawmakers for their districts.

Fiscal constraints in recent years, however, have shifted the goal of logrolling. In a hostile fiscal environment, logrolling is often aimed at equalizing sacrifices instead of distributing rewards. Broad-spectrum bills—authorizations, omnibus tax measures, continuing resolutions, and budget resolutions—may include numerous less than optimal provisions, many of which would fail if voted on separately. Such a negative logroll enables lawmakers to support the measure as "the best deal we can get." In other words, members find it easier to accept hits to their favorite programs as long as they are sure that everyone else is taking their lumps through cutbacks or across-the-board formulas. Mark O. Hatfield, R-Ore., who served as chairman of the Senate Appropriations Committee (1981–1987; 1995–1997), explained that he would "hold my nose and do certain things here for the purpose of getting the job done, but certainly not with enthusiasm or anything other than recognizing that we are doing things under emergency."[66]

In times of fiscal stringency, legislators have fewer opportunities to claim credit for sponsoring new programs or obtaining added funding. Avoiding blame can displace claiming credit as a legislative objective, and these omnibus reverse logrolls are a result.[67] Aside from its political value, logrolling can have policy virtues. As R. Douglas Arnold notes,

> It can draw under a single umbrella coalition a whole series of programs, each of which targets funds according to need. Districts then receive substantial benefits where their needs are greatest and nothing where they are marginal.[68]

Logrolling, however, can turn narrowly targeted programs into broad-scale ones. In negotiating for passage of two high-priority measures—crime reduction and a national service corps—the Clinton administration had to scatter benefits so broadly that their effectiveness was severely impaired. The 1994 crime bill provided for 100,000 more police officers on the nation's streets, but it was diluted by spreading the funds throughout the entire country, not just in high-crime, inner-urban areas. Similarly, funds for Americorps were spread too thinly among too many sites for the volunteer program to be successful.[69]

In a time logroll, members agree to support one measure in exchange for later support for another measure. Sometimes the logroll specifies an exchange; at other times it is open-ended until the donor decides to call in the chips. That is why President Clinton failed to gain passage of fast-track trade negotiation authority late in 1997. Four years earlier, Clinton had won a narrow victory for the North American Free Trade Agreement (NAFTA) by promising wavering Democrats programs that would help workers and industries hurt by freer trade. In 1997 members complained that the bargains had not been carried out. Explained Rep. Xavier Becerra, D-Calif., "I was one of those opposed to NAFTA, and I gave the president the benefit of the doubt." Clinton had pledged to negotiate side agreements protecting labor and the environment. "There was an utter failure to implement those proposals."[70]

In a logroll with side payments, support is exchanged for benefits on an unrelated issue—for example, a federal project for the state or district, a better committee assignment, inclusion in an important conference, or access to the White House. Although such side payoffs often seem trivial or parochial, they may enable the member to achieve other valued goals.

An unsavory though futile attempt at a logroll of this type occurred during the House's consideration of the conference report on the 2003 Medicare drug bill, which was a high-priority item for the president's reelection strategy. In their frantic search for a majority, House Republican leaders kept the balloting open for nearly three hours (a modern record) over the night of November 21–22. One prime target was retiring representative Nick Smith, R-Mich. (1992–2005), who loathed the bill and had voted against it—but whose son was then running for his father's seat. Majority Leader Tom DeLay during the vote reportedly told Smith: "I will personally endorse your son. That's my final offer."[71] Other Republicans loudly berated Smith and made promises or threats aimed at his son (who later lost the GOP primary). Although Smith gamely held his ground (even after a 5:30 a.m. call from the president), the leaders squeezed out a 220–215 victory, after three members of each party switched their votes to "yes."

In the aftermath, DeLay and Rep. Candice S. Miller, R-Mich., were handed a "public admonishment" by the House's bipartisan Standards of Official Conduct Committee, which compiled a lengthy report of the events. The panel concluded that "it is improper for a member to offer to link support for the personal interest of another member as part of a quid pro quo to achieve a legislative goal."[72] The leadership was blamed for extending the vote overnight because it elevated "tensions on the House floor and contributed to an environment in which the usual traditions of civil discourse and decorum amongst members were not always followed."

Bargaining Strategy

For bargaining to take place, participants must be reasonably certain of each other's intentions and likely future actions. Rep. John P. Murtha, D-Pa., a master deal maker, cites two elements of power on Capitol Hill: "Develop expertise on an issue that makes you vital to colleagues, and keep your word."[73] Building on expertise in defense issues, Murtha often deals quietly in the back corner of the Democratic side of the House. His orbit includes the ultraconservative majority leader, Tom DeLay of Texas, whom he regards as an honest broker. When DeLay needs something, Murtha told a reporter, "He comes over to the corner and we work it out." On the Senate side of the Capitol, Majority Leader Bill Frist, R-Tenn., has not hesitated to do business with liberal icon Edward Kennedy. "He has always dealt straight with me," Frist said. "You know exactly where he's coming from."[74]

For bargaining to succeed, the participants must agree on the need for a legislative product. That is, the benefits of reaching a decision must exceed the costs of failing to do so. In the vast majority of cases—where there is sharp disagreement or concerted opposition—a negative political cost-benefit ratio results in no action at all. In other cases politicians may prefer a course of strategic disagreement, which John B. Gilmour describes as "efforts of politicians to avoid reaching an agreement when compromise might alienate supporters, damage their prospects in an upcoming election, or preclude getting a better deal in the future."[75]

Are there inherent limits to negotiation? According to bargaining theory, a measure's sponsors will yield only what they absolutely must to gain a majority of supporters. Under this size principle, a minimum winning coalition occurs in ideal legislative bargaining situations, that is, when the bargainers act rationally and with perfect information.[76] Recounting Senate majority leader Lyndon B. Johnson's meticulous vote counting before a floor fight, political scientist John G. Stewart concluded, "And once a sufficient majority had been counted, Johnson would seldom attempt to enlarge it: Why expend limited bargaining resources which might be needed to win future battles?"[77]

Most legislative strategists, however, lack Johnson's extraordinary skills. Uncertainty about outcomes leads them to line up more than a simple majority of supporters. Moreover, at many points in the legislative process supermajorities are required—for example, in voting under suspension of the rules, in overriding vetoes, or in ending Senate filibusters. Not surprisingly, therefore, minimum winning coalitions are not typical of Congress, even in the majoritarian House of Representatives.[78]

Yet coalition size is the crux of legislative strategy. Bargainers repeatedly face the dilemma of how broadly or how narrowly to frame their issues and how many concessions to yield in an effort to secure passage.

CONCLUSION

Congressional deliberation is today at risk. With parties unified and seemingly uninterested in debate or compromise, life on Capitol Hill has become, in Hobbes's words, "nasty and brutish" (though hardly "short"). Take-no-prisoners strategies are encouraged by today's competitive, polarized party system. As former senator Breaux observed,

> The pressure on congressional leaders both from interests in the party and from outside groups is severe. Many would rather fight and lose, rather than reach out and find common ground. Congress should not be like the Super Bowl, in which one team always has to win and the other team inevitably loses. There's nothing wrong with reaching legitimate compromise and getting something done for the American people[79]

Sarah Binder's findings echo this sentiment. "The decline of the political center," she writes, "has produced a political environment that more often than not gives legislators every incentive not to reach agreement."[80] The result is often legislative inaction—which can be interpreted as stalemate or gridlock.

Yet the enterprise of lawmaking rests on the premise that, at least where urgent matters are concerned, bargainers will normally prefer some sort of new outcome to none at all. As the legendary Senate Republican leader (1959–1969) Everett M. Dirksen, R-Ill., once remarked: "I am a man of fixed and unbending principle, and one of my principles is flexibility."[81] Especially is this the case with actions facing deadlines or imperiling government functions if not approved—reauthorizations, appropriations, debt ceiling adjustments, and the like. The alternative is stalemate, inaction, and in extreme cases actual shutdown of the federal government, which budget impasses have caused sixteen times in the last twenty-five years

Deliberation, which requires participation and bargaining, is a necessary part of the legislative way of life. It shapes the character of bills, resolutions, and other forms of congressional policy making. It also underlies many attributes of the legislative process—delay, obfuscation, compromise, and norms such as specialization and reciprocity.

Open deliberation produces better decisions than top-down or secretive processes. This means debate in which a diverse views are voiced, broad-based coalitions (preferably across party lines) are constructed, and a variety of members and interest groups participates. It is yet another point of contact and conflict between the two Congresses—the Congress of individual wills and the Congress of collective decisions.

SUGGESTED READINGS

Arnold, R. Douglas. *The Logic of Congressional Action.* New Haven: Yale University Press, 1990.

Baumgartner, Frank, and Bryan D. Jones. *Agendas and Instability in American Politics.* Chicago: University of Chicago Press, 1993.

Binder, Sarah A. *Stalemate: Causes and Consequences of Legislative Gridlock.* Washington, D.C.: Brookings Institution Press, 2003.

Edwards, George C. *At the Margins: Presidential Leadership of Congress.* New Haven: Yale University Press, 1989.

Kingdon, John W. *Congressmen's Voting Decisions.* 3d ed. Ann Arbor: University of Michigan Press, 1989.

Poole, Keith T., and Howard Rosenthal. *Congress: A Political-Economic History of Roll Call Voting.* New York: Oxford University Press, 1996.

The different roles of the president: Above, President George W. Bush greets congressional members following his 2005 State of the Union Address, which is delivered to a joint session of Congress in the chamber of the House of Representatives. Right, as commander in chief, Bush salutes U.S. military personnel after landing on the aircraft carrier USS *Abraham Lincoln* in May 2003 to proclaim the defeat of Saddam Hussein's Iraqi regime. Below, Bush plays golf and conducts business informally with GOP House members (left to right) Dan Burton of Indiana, Tom DeLay of Texas, and Michael G. Oxley of Ohio.

chapter 10

Congress and the President

The Social Security system is "headed toward bankruptcy," declared President George W. Bush in his 2005 State of the Union message. He urged Congress to act quickly to revamp Social Security in a way that he said would assure its long-term solvency. GOP lawmakers soon discovered scant Democratic support and significant public opposition to the president's top domestic priority, especially his key goal allowing younger and middle-age workers to divert part of their Social Security taxes into personal accounts where the money would be invested in stock and bond funds—a plan that the White House itself acknowledged would not address the solvency issue. Congressional Republicans, mindful of the two Congresses, worried that the president's overhaul ideas were politically risky. "It's fine for [Bush] to be bold on Social Security because he doesn't have to run again," said Rep. Mark Souder, R-Ind. "But we have the specter of a very tough reelection" in 2006 where "40 percent of the electorate in the midterm is 55 and older."[1] Little surprise that Speaker J. Dennis Hastert, R-Ill., warned that "you can't jam change down the American people's throat."[2] Or as Sen. Rick Santorum, R-Pa., chair of the Senate's GOP Conference, put it: "We have a lot of education to do, both internally with our members and staff, as well as externally with the American people."[3]

Tensions between the executive and legislative branches are inevitable. These two branches are organized differently; they have divergent responsibilities; they have different constituencies and terms of office; and they are jealous of their prerogatives. Executive officials see Congress as inefficient and meddlesome. Legislators perceive the executive branch as arrogant and arbitrary. At times these differences lead to conflicts that the media dramatize as "battles on the Potomac."

Yet day in and day out, Congress and the president work together. Even when their relationship is guarded or hostile, bills get passed and signed into law. Presidential appointments are approved by the Senate. Budgets are eventually enacted and the government is kept afloat. This necessary cooperation goes on even when control of the White House and the Capitol is divided between the two major parties. Conversely, as President Jimmy Carter sadly learned—and President Bill Clinton learned during his first two years in office—unified partisan control of both branches is no guarantee of harmony. President George W. Bush also confronted complaints from the GOP-controlled Congress. Many House Republicans, for instance, express strong disagreements with the president's immigration policy. "The White House is on a totally different wavelength than most House Republicans," remarked Rep. Ray LaHood, R-Ill. (referring to immigration policy).[4]

THE PRESIDENT AS LEGISLATOR

Presidents are sometimes called the chief legislators because they are closely involved in the decisions Congress makes. Article II, Section 3, of the Constitution directs the president from time to time to "give to the Congress Information of the State of the Union and recommend to their Consideration such Measures as he shall judge necessary and expedient." (Today, this means annually and during prime-time television.) Soon after delivering the annual State of the Union address, the president sends to Congress draft administration bills for introduction on his behalf. By enlarging the list of messages required from the president—the annual budget and economic reports, for example—Congress has further involved the chief executive in designing legislation. Congress often delegates authority to the president, because it appreciates the strengths of the White House, such as its capacity for coordination, and recognizes its own shortcomings, such as its decentralized committee structure, which inhibits swift and comprehensive policy making. Crises, partisan considerations, and public expectations all make the president an important participant in congressional decision making. And the president's constitutional veto power ensures that White House views will be listened to, if not always heeded, on Capitol Hill.

The concept of the legislative presidency did not become widespread until after World War II. Only then could it be said that the role was institutionalized, performed not because of some unique combination of personality and circumstance but because everyone—including Congress, the press, and the public—expected it.[5] This expectation could change, but there is no indication of it happening any time soon especially given the global terrorist threat.

To understand the chief executive's relations with Congress is no easy assignment. This appraisal is traceable in part to the founders, who did not clearly define legislative-executive relationships. From the country's earliest days, the relationship has always been a work in progress. Presidents bring their own style to the relationship, which Charles O. Jones characterizes as the "partnership model" or the "independent model." The partnership model means that presidents consult regularly with lawmakers and involve them directly in the policy and political affairs of the White House. The independent model states that presidents minimize their involvement with Congress and strive to accomplish their top priorities on their own.[6]

Scholars and others have long analyzed America's complex system of separate institutions sharing and competing for power. Different theories or models, such as Jones's, have been formulated to suggest what constitutes effective presidential leadership. Scholars have produced such an array of studies in recent decades that they have been marked by "a bewildering succession of new models of the presidency, each the product of an admixture of empirical and normative assessments."[7] Some studies focus on the person in the White House; others on the bureaucracy and institutional functions and structures of the presidency; and still others analyze discrete aspects of the relationship between Congress and the president, such as presidential spending power versus the legislative branch's power of the purse.[8] Here we employ five prominent presidential theories—persuasion, rhetoric, administrative, political time, and the "two presidencies"—as a way to illuminate important aspects of the chief executive's relations with Congress. To varying degrees, these analytical perspectives overlap one another and affect the activities of all presidents.

The Power to Persuade

Harvard professor Richard Neustadt (a former staff aide in the Truman White House and adviser to President-elect John F. Kennedy) wrote a classic study in 1960, read by President Kennedy and other presidents, that stated simply: "Presidential *power* is the power to persuade."[9] Power, according to Neustadt, meant more than the executive's ability to persuade Congress to enact a specific bill. "Strategically, the question is not how he masters Congress in a peculiar instance, but what he does to boost his chances for mastery in any instance."[10] To be successful, presidents must employ all their varied powers (constitutional, political, bureaucratic, personal, and more) to persuade Congress and others to do what they want. Setting Congress's agenda—determining the policies that the legislature pays attention to by taking them up in committee and on the floor—epitomizes the president's power to persuade. (The Office of Management and Budget has prime responsibility for central clearance, coordinating and sifting through departmental requests to Congress to ensure that they conform with the president's agenda.)

From the beginning, presidents have shaped Congress's agenda in varying degrees. The First Congress of "its own volition immediately turned to the executive branch for guidance and discovered in [Treasury secretary Alexander] Hamilton a personality to whom such leadership was congenial."[11] Two decades later (from 1811 to 1825) the "initiative in public affairs remained with [Speaker Henry] Clay and his associates in the House of Representatives" and not with the president.[12] Thus, dominance in national policy making may pass from one branch to the other. Strong presidents sometimes provoke efforts by Congress to reassert its own authority and to restrict that of the executive. Periods of presidential ascendancy often are followed by eras of congressional assertiveness. Still, Congress usually looks to the White House to outline its legislative program in the annual State of the Union message and in other formal and informal presidential messages.

Presidents follow different patterns in setting agendas. Two recent presidents—Ronald Reagan (1981–1989) and Jimmy Carter (1977–1981)—were opposites in their ability to persuade Congress to enact their policy priorities. Agenda control was the hallmark of Reagan's leadership during his first year in office. By limiting the number of legislative priorities, the president focused Congress's and the public's attention on one priority issue at a time. Most were encapsulated as Reaganomics—tax and spending cuts. He exploited the usual honeymoon period for new presidents by moving his agenda quickly and during a time of widespread anticipation of a new era of GOP national political dominance.

Reagan also dealt skillfully with Congress: meeting, negotiating, and socializing with lawmakers, including a private dinner for Democratic Speaker Thomas P. "Tip" O'Neill Jr. of Massachusetts and his wife. After the March 30, 1981, assassination attempt hospitalized the president, Reagan returned a month later and made a dramatic appeal for his economic program. "The White House shrewdly tied Reagan's return to action to the budget and tax debate, scheduling an April 28 comeback speech before a joint session of Congress. It was a triumph, and people began to call him the 'Great Communicator.' "[13] After only eight months in office, Reagan scored some of the biggest victories of his entire eight years in office. Later, when his control over the agenda slackened, Congress was still confined to a playing field largely demarcated by the president. It was forced to respond to, although not always accept, the positions the president had staked out on taxes, spending, defense, and social issues.

By contrast, Reagan's predecessor in the White House, Jimmy Carter, quickly overloaded Congress's agenda and never made clear what his priorities were. Three major consequences resulted:

> First . . . there was little clarity in the communication of priorities to the American public. Instead of galvanizing support for two or three major national needs, the Carter administration proceeded on a number of fronts. . . . Second, and perhaps more important, the lack of priorities meant unnecessary waste of the President's own time and energy. . . . Third, the lack of priorities needlessly compounded Carter's congressional problems. . . . Carter's limited political capital was squandered on a variety of agenda requests when it might have been concentrated on the top of the list.[14]

As for personal lobbying, Carter lacked the temperament for it. He met in formal sessions with a large number of members but shunned informal and personal contacts. He did not view informal discussions or negotiating meetings with members as a productive use of his time.

Most presidents recognize the importance of maintaining informal contacts with Congress, because they understand that it is not easy to persuade Congress to act in a certain way. As President Lyndon B. Johnson, who had served as Senate minority leader (1953–1955) and majority leader (1955–1961), once declared: "Merely placing a program before Congress is not enough. Without constant attention from the administration, most legislation moves through the congressional process at the speed of a glacier."[15] Johnson regularly (and sometimes crudely) admonished his aides and departmental officers to work closely with Congress. "[Get off] your ass and see how fast you can respond to a congressional request," he told his staff. "Challenge yourself to see how quickly you can get back to him or her with an answer, any kind of an answer, but goddamn it, an answer."[16] And at least since Harry S. Truman, presidents have maintained a formal White House legislative liaison office to promote the administration's program in Congress; to lobby outside groups, state officials, and others to do the same; to target members who could be coaxed for votes on certain issues; and, more generally, to foster a cooperative legislative-executive atmosphere.

In addition, to persuade members to support their programs, presidents commonly grant or withhold their patronage resources. Broadly conceived, patronage involves not only federal and judicial positions but also federal construction projects, location of government installations, campaign support, availability of strategic information, plane rides on *Air Force One,* White House access for important constituents, and countless other favors, large and small. Some presidents even keep records of the political favors they grant to lawmakers, IOUs that they can cash in later for needed support in Congress. Limits, however, do exist to the persuasive power of patronage. As one head of the White House congressional relations office said: "The problem with Congressional relations is that with every good intention, at the end of the day you can't accommodate all the requests that you get."[17] More significant, many factors influence how members vote on issues important to the White House. Although the persuasive skills of presidents are significant, other considerations—lawmakers' constituency interests, policy preferences, and ideological dispositions, as well as public opinion and the number of partisan seats in each chamber—usually are more important in shaping congressional outcomes.

Going Public: The Rhetorical President

"With public sentiment, nothing can fail; without it nothing can succeed," Abraham Lincoln once observed.[18] Lincoln's idea is the essence of the rhetorical presidency—how and when a chief executive strategically employs contemporary campaign techniques and the technology of the mass media to promote "himself and his policies in Washington by appealing to the American public."[19] The rhetorical president's ultimate objective is to produce an outpouring of public support that encourages lawmakers to push his ideas through the congressional obstacle course. Going public on an issue, however, is not without its risks. The president can raise expectations that cannot be met, make inept presentations, lose control over issues, infuriate legislators whose support he needs, or further stiffen the opposition. Furthermore, many legislators are more popular than the president in their districts or states. The president goes public to gather support, because "if he had the votes he would pass the measure first and go to the public only for the bill-signing ceremonies."[20]

President Reagan was an acknowledged master at using the electronic media to orchestrate public support. The Hollywood actor turned president was at home in front of cameras and microphones, and he had a keen sense of public ritual and symbolism as means of rallying support. Reagan's adroitness with the media, primarily during his first year in office, is where his legacy will loom large for future presidents and Congresses. He showed that "one man using the White House's immense powers of communication can lift the mood of the nation and alter the way it does business."[21]

President George H. W. Bush's public relations techniques "abandoned the elaborate, tightly controlled machinery developed in recent years to project, manipulate and polish a presidential image" in the television age.[22] Instead, the senior Bush used traditional methods—meeting with small groups of reporters, inviting journalists to lunch, or traveling outside Washington, D.C.—to build public support through communications.

President Clinton, by contrast, was innovative in using media technologies to reach voters and in employing campaign-style practices to generate public support for his programs. The April 1995 Oklahoma City bombing—and Clinton's empathetic response—reminded the public of the human face of the federal government, the very entity Republican "revolutionaries" were warring against. When Republicans added provisions to a flood relief bill that Clinton opposed, the president used the bully pulpit to paint the GOP position as "extreme" and generated a flurry of favorable publicity for his position. As one reporter noted:

> News accounts portrayed Republicans as, well, crazy extremists bent on playing games with flood victims. Rank-and-file Republicans writhed in political agony. Michigan Republican Fred Upton's mother watched the news accounts with alarm and warned her son, "You're getting killed." "When your mom tells you that, you know you're in trouble," said Upton.[23]

The White House also used "nightly tracking polls and weekly focus groups to help determine its daily message and the approach President Clinton should take to important national issues."[24]

George W. Bush was initially dubbed "the reticent president" by some analysts for several reasons: his preference not to seize the public spotlight and address every major event or issue that might arise; his determination to stay "on message" by sticking to prepared talking points; his predilection for carefully staged and scripted appearances; and his capacity to make verbal gaffes. Nonetheless, Bush worked diligently to win the battle for popular opinion and to mobilize public and political support for his policy and political objectives.[25] For example, he and his cabinet officers, in coordination with House and Senate GOP leaders, traveled across the country to promote broad public support for administration priorities. Bush also became the first president to deliver his weekly radio address in Spanish—political recognition of the electoral potential of the growing Hispanic population.

Bush came into his own as both communicator in chief and commander in chief in the aftermath of the terrorist attacks on the World Trade Center in New York City and the Pentagon. Several times he gave powerful and eloquent speeches in a variety of forums, such as before Congress and at the United Nations (UN), on the need to go after terrorists who threaten the United States and to disarm and (incidentally) to end Saddam Hussein's regime in Iraq. His direct and confident manner of speaking resonated with most Americans and boosted domestic and congressional support for his military and international campaign against terrorists and regimes deemed to be associated with them.

In addition, the Bush White House has gone to great lengths to use television to promote the president, employing many former network television aides who are expert at lighting, camera angles, and backdrops. For example, in a speech in Indianapolis urging public backing for one of his tax cut proposals, White House aides "went so far as to ask people in the crowd behind Mr. Bush to take off their ties . . . so they would seem more like the ordinary folk the president said would benefit from his tax cut."[26] Perhaps the most elaborate—and also criticized—event was Bush's flight to and speech on the aircraft carrier *Abraham Lincoln* announcing the end of major military combat in Iraq. White House aides "choreographed every aspect of the event, even down to the members of the Lincoln crew arrayed in coordinated shirt colors over Mr. Bush's right shoulder and the 'Mission Accomplished' banner placed to perfectly capture the president and the celebratory two words in a single shot."[27] The White House soon came to realize, however, that the struggle to produce stability and security in Iraq was far from accomplished.

During his "fly around" tours of various cities to drum up public support for revamping Social Security, the president held public conversations that were carefully planned and orchestrated. The panelists were carefully selected and the audience was filled solely with Bush supporters. "The night before the event, the chosen participants gathered for a rehearsal in the hall in which the president would appear the next day. An official dispatched by the White House played the president and asked questions. 'We ran through it five times before the president got here,' " remarked a White House aide about an event held in Memphis, Tennessee.[28] President Bush's administration, like others before his, also prepares and distributes laudatory "ready-to-serve news reports" that are often broadcast on local television stations "across the country without any acknowledgment of the government's role in their production."[29] The Government Accountability Office (GAO) viewed these government-funded prepackaged news reports as "covert propaganda"; the administration predictibly rejected this claim.[30]

The Administrative President

Presidents understand that getting Congress to pass legislation is an arduous process and, even when laws are enacted, bureaucratic indifference may hamper implementation of presidential initiatives. Thus, the core idea of the administrative strategy for presidents is to win policy goals by statute when that is feasible and, if not, to accomplish those aims through organizational or managerial techniques. A variety of methods are employed by administrative presidents, such as naming loyal political appointees to supervise and monitor agency activities, reorganizing executive departments to better accomplish presidential goals, using the budget process to reduce unwanted programs or increase favorite activities, and employing executive orders and rule-making authority to implement policies blocked by Congress.[31]

Stymied by the GOP-controlled Congress on issues such as antismoking legislation, a patients' bill of rights, and subsidies for school construction, President Clinton expanded the use of executive authority. Issuing executive orders—a form of administrative lawmaking to carry out authority delegated by the legislative branch—was a favorite technique of the president to bypass the Republican Congress. Presidents have long employed executive orders.[32] President Truman, for example, issued an executive order to integrate the armed services. But Clinton used them extensively. "His formula includes pressing the limits of his regulatory authority, signing executive orders and using other unilateral means to obtain his policy priorities when Congress fails to embrace them."[33] To dramatize the importance of trigger locks on guns, a proposal that stalled in Congress, Clinton issued an executive order requiring trigger safety locks on new guns purchased for federal law enforcement officers.[34] Congressional Republicans railed against Clinton's "go it alone" governing.

George W. Bush also exploited the techniques of the administrative president. First, not only did the president fill cabinet positions during his first term with seasoned Washington hands, such as Donald H. Rumsfeld (a former House member, White House chief of staff, and defense secretary during the Ford administration) as defense secretary, but he also named numerous conservatives to his White House staff and to high administration positions, burnishing his reputation with conservative activists. The most prominent example was the appointment of former Missouri senator John Ashcroft, a pro-life conservative, to be attorney general. Many conservatives said that the president surpassed even Ronald Reagan in the ideological commitment of his appointments.[35]

During his second term, Bush put a premium on loyalty in naming nine new cabinet secretaries while retaining six. (It is common for departmental secretaries to depart administrations starting their second term, in part because of exhaustion and the president's desire to shake things up.) Three examples of Bush's emphasis on loyalty in selecting new cabinet secretaries were: Condoleezza Rice, the president's national security adviser in the first term, to replace Colin Powell as secretary of state; Alberto Gonzales, previously the White House counsel, to be the first Hispanic attorney general, replacing John Ashcroft; and Margaret Spellings, a domestic policy adviser to the president during his first term, to be education secretary, replacing Rod Paige. Being either a "trusted team player or loyal steward in the first administration appears to be a common denominator of almost all of Bush's [cabinet secretaries] during his second four years."[36] These appointees work to ensure that bureaucratic intransigence does not hinder enforcement of Bush's policies.

Second, Bush quickly exercised executive authority to roll back, suspend, or challenge many Clinton-era regulations viewed as unnecessary, overly burdensome, or too costly. The president, too, moved with dispatch after September 11 to establish by executive order a White House Office of Homeland Security. Bush also was not reluctant to implement by executive fiat administration programs stalled in Congress. For example, when the Senate blocked action on Bush's faith-based initiative (assisting religious groups in winning government grants for charitable and social service work), the president ordered his administration to implement the program.

> Bit by bit, through executive orders and changes in agency regulations, the administration has been carrying out the initiative anyway. Its goal is to allow religious groups to compete more easily for federal funds to address under-served social needs, such as helping the homeless and the drug-addicted. Seven government departments now have faith-based offices, which steer religious groups toward billions of dollars in grant money. . . . The most controversial proposal to date has come out of the Department of Housing and Urban Development [HUD]: HUD has proposed a change in its rules to allow taxpayer money to be used for the construction, acquisition, or rehabilitation of houses of worship [so long as part of the building is used to provide social services].[37]

The president has employed executive authority on other matters blocked by Congress, such as permitting more logging in national forests and allowing industries more flexibility in meeting federal clean air regulations.[38] During Bush's second four years, administration officials would push for "more business-friendly environmental, health and safety rules."[39]

The President and Political Time

Political scientist Stephen Skowronek spotlights the importance of political time—the evolving array of social, economic, and partisan forces in play during diverse presidential eras or "regimes," using Skowronek's word—in assessing how chief executives interact with the broader political system of which they are a part. Painting in broad historical strokes, for example, there were eras when Republicans dominated national politics; at other times, Democrats were in charge; and in still other periods, both parties coexisted in rough parity until one broke out to establish itself as the nation's majority party.

Karl Rove, President George W. Bush's top political adviser and deputy chief of staff, has suggested that Bush's 2004 election may be equivalent politically and electorally to the 1896 presidential election of Republican William McKinley. During the two decades prior to McKinley's election, the two national parties were evenly balanced. McKinley's election, however, saw a large voter swing toward Republicans, who dominated nationally until the 1932 election of Franklin D. Roosevelt (FDR). FDR's victory began nearly four decades of national Democratic dominance.[40] Over the next few decades Republicans often won the White House while Democrats held onto one or both chambers of Congress until the elections of the early 2000s produced unified GOP control of the national elective branches, today's political era can be characterized as one of parity politics with a heavy dose of partisan polarization. Both parties eye each other carefully to prevent one from gaining a long-lasting political, policy, or electoral advantage over the other. Still, there is no denying that Republicans have made gains in the electorate (from 49 percent in the 2000 presidential election to 51 percent in the 2004 election) and in the House and Senate. In 2004, President Bush became the "first president since FDR to increase his party's number of House and Senate seats both at the mid-terms and in a presidential re-election year."[41] (See Appendix A for party control of the presidency, the House, and the Senate over time.)

Skowronek's point is that presidential leadership is shaped by whether a White House occupant begins his service at the start (waxing) or end (waning), or someplace in-between, of a specific political era or regime. Thus, presidents can be compared by whether they are affiliated with the dominate national coalition of the period (if there is one) as well as by how they perform within that historical context. "In the modern Democratic period" starting with FDR's election, "regime outsiders like Republicans Dwight D. Eisenhower and Richard Nixon faced different political problems from those confronted by regime insiders like John F. Kennedy and Lyndon B. Johnson."[42]

Leadership situations might also be differentiated according to political time; that is, when in a regime sequence the president engages the political-institutional order. Presidents Franklin Roosevelt, John Kennedy, and Jimmy Carter—all Democrats who enjoyed Democratic majorities in Congress—may be said to have faced different problems in leading the nation as they were arrayed along a sequence of political change that encompassed the generation and degeneration of the New Deal order.[43] More time needs to pass before informed judgment can be made about where Clinton or George W. Bush fit in Skowronek's theory. For example, was Clinton a deviant president during a Republican regime, or was he (like Carter) at the tail end of a fading

Democratic regime? Is George W. Bush a regime-creator at the start of a new national era of GOP dominance or a regime consolidator, completing the Reagan revolution?

The "Two Presidencies"

"The United States has one president, but it has two presidencies; one presidency is for domestic affairs, and the other is concerned with defense and foreign policy."[44] This formulation by political scientist Aaron Wildavsky stated that presidential proposals are likely to achieve more success in the international than the domestic arena, in part because Congress asserts itself more in domestic policy making than the foreign policy field. Wildavsky's thesis has sparked considerable controversy, such as how to measure success rates in the two arenas and whether the concept is relevant in today's world, when the international and domestic overlap constantly.[45] Whatever the strengths or weaknesses of the two presidencies idea as laid out by Wildavsky, the concept has some relevancy to the presidency of George W. Bush, considered before and after the September 11, 2001, terrorist attacks.

The Pre–9/11 Phase. Despite Bush's loss to Democratic candidate Vice President Al Gore in the popular vote tally, the absence of a clear mandate from the voters, public concern about the legitimacy of Bush's victory (which was determined on December 12, 2000, by the U.S. Supreme Court decision in *Bush v. Gore*), and the lack of any presidential coattails (the GOP lost seats in both chambers but held onto their majority in each), President Bush quickly advanced an ambitious agenda as if he had won a huge victory. He surprised many pundits who predicted that Bush would move slowly to implement his "compassionate conservative" campaign promises. "[T]his is the farthest thing from a caretaker administration you could get," declared a Brookings Institution analyst. "It's the farthest thing from a president saying I lost the popular vote, I'm here because of a 5 to 4 vote on the Supreme Court. I'd better [advance] some centrist positions."[46] That Bush could get off to a fast start was due in part to the public's favorable view of the new chief executive, especially in comparison to his predecessor, as an honest and trustworthy straight-shooter from Texas. And with a master's degree in business administration, Bush imposed a corporate model of governance at the White House, acting as chief executive officer who sets broad goals and policies and delegates responsibility for implementation to others. (See Box 10-1 for a comparison of Bush and Clinton.)

Strategically, Bush employed partisan and bipartisan models of governance to advance his agenda. He scored a major policy success early in his administration largely by staking out an assertive and partisan approach. When the government estimated in 2000 that it would run a projected surplus of $5.6 trillion over the next decade, the president soon after taking office sent a ten-year $1.6 trillion tax cut plan to Congress. As Bush said, "We recognize loud and clear the surplus is not the government's money—the surplus is the

BOX 10-1 **Differences between the Bush and Clinton Presidencies**

George W. Bush	Bill Clinton
Disciplined White House	Less disciplined White House
Scripted presidency	Unscripted presidency
Strict focus on a few key priorities	Wide-ranging policy focus
More reliance on vice president	Less reliance on vice president
Punctuality required for meetings with clear starting and ending times	Meetings start late and seldom end on time
Direct public communicator	Skillful public communicator
Frequent reliance on aides to provide policy overviews	Well informed on policy issues
Somewhat more attentive to Congress and its members	Less attentive to Congress and its members
Large responsibilities delegated to aides	Close supervisory role maintained over all top aides
Preference for executive summaries	Enamored of thick briefing books
Regular working days observed insofar as practicable	A "24/7" president

people's money, and we ought to trust them with their own money."[47] (Later, when the economy dipped downward, Bush added another argument for his tax cut: the need to stimulate a slowing economy by putting refund checks in the hands of consumers.) Despite Democratic complaints that the tax cut was too large and doubts that the huge projected surplus would ever materialize, Bush's determination to win combined with GOP control of Congress and lawmakers' hesitancy to vote against any tax reduction that benefitted their constituents produced the largest across-the-board tax cut since the presidency of Ronald Reagan.

Bush's tax cut plan first passed the House in several separate bills (repeal of the estate tax and income tax rate reductions, for instance)—all on a party-line vote. Bush's plan, however, faced a real challenge in the 50–50 Senate where moderates in both parties wanted to downsize the package. To generate support for his plan, Bush flew to several states that he carried, such as Montana, where ranking Finance Committee member Max Baucus was up for reelection in 2002, to pressure Democrats to back his proposal. Bush, too, refused to heed Democratic leadership calls to compromise, prompting then majority whip Harry Reid of Nevada to exclaim: "No one has talked more about bipartisanship and done less."[48] Bush's hardball approach carried the day. On June 7, 2001, the president signed a compromise $1.35 trillion tax cut into law, proclaiming victory for the centerpiece of his economic agenda. His victory came with political costs, "generating antagonism from Democrats and from some Republican moderates, including Sen. James Jeffords (Vt.), who quit the GOP and shifted leadership of the chamber to the Democrats."[49]

Bush chose a bipartisan approach to advance another major priority: the No Child Left Behind education bill. As Norman J. Ornstein explained:

> From the get-go, he aimed at negotiating an education package with liberal Democrats like Sen. Edward Kennedy (Mass.) and Rep. George Miller (Calif.). He dropped references to vouchers, to keep the most divisive issue off the table. He named Sandy Kress, a moderate Texas Democrat and close friend of the president, to head his negotiating team, underscoring his commitment to a bipartisan approach right down the middle of the ideological fairway. It took a bit longer, but the education bill also got enacted.[50]

The president's success in selectively using either a partisan or bipartisan approach to lawmaking kept both his electoral base happy and "the opposition party inside the tent."[51]

A different legislative dynamic emerged after May 2001 when Democrats suddenly became the majority party following Vermont Republican James M. Jeffords's switch of partisan affiliation. Jeffords became an Independent but caucused with the Democrats. Democratic control of the Senate produced significant problems for the Bush administration. Now the Democrats could initiate and force votes on their priorities, hold hearings to spotlight their agenda and critique Bush's, modify or block administration bills coming from the GOP House, disapprove the president's nominations, and require the White House to develop "a defensive strategy for responding to Democratic ideas."[52] The result was that Bush set bipartisanship aside and opted to emphasize the partisan model of governance. Given the choice "between making concessions that create a broader bipartisan majority and narrowly passing a bill that more closely tracks his preferences, Bush will choose the latter," said top White House aides.[53]

The president soon encountered serious opposition to many of his ideas in Congress and among the electorate. Furthermore, polls indicated public concern about the direction of the country. Economically, the expected surplus was falling behind earlier projections because of the weak economy and the tax cuts. On energy and environmental policy, polls suggested that the public preferred Democratic approaches to the GOP's. In June 2001, Bush's public standing had fallen "to a tepid 50% approval rating, the lowest presidential approval rating in more than five years."[54]

Thus, as Congress returned to Washington in early September 2001 after its traditional August recess, Democrats were blaming Bush for the sagging economy, squandering the declining surplus on tax cuts for the rich, and raiding the Social Security trust fund to pay for government expenses. On the day before the terrorist assault, a Gallup poll indicated a 51 percent approval rating for the president. A thicket of political and policy problems seemed to lie ahead for him.

The Post–9/11 Phase. The Bush presidency was transformed by the terrorist attacks. After the uncertainty of the first day, Bush became a confident, resolute, decisive, and strong commander in chief. Images of the president consoling firemen and others at the site of the World Trade Center, his calm and confident demeanor, and his eloquent statements to the public, including the September 20, 2001, national address before a joint session of Congress, rallied the nation to fight a global war against terrorists and those states that provide them safe haven. He called this global struggle "the first war of the 21st century," a war that could go on for years or decades as did the cold war.

Bush's public approval ratings soared to a record level 91 percent, breaking his father's previous record of 89 percent established during the 1991 Persian Gulf War.[55] The levels of bipartisanship on Capitol Hill were also remarkable in the initial weeks after the terrorist assaults. Congress moved quickly to enact a number of significant measures to strengthen homeland security and to combat terrorism.

The president, for instance, won congressional support to federalize security at airports, to grant larger law enforcement authority to the Justice Department (U.S.A. Patriot Act), and to assist in recovery efforts at the World Trade Center and the Pentagon. He was also authorized by Congress to employ "all necessary and appropriate force" against those groups or nations involved in the terrorist attacks. Subsequently, the president directed the military to oust the Taliban regime in Afghanistan, which had provided safe haven for Osama bin Laden, the al-Qaeda leader who organized the September 11 attacks. Later, in his January 29, 2002, State of the Union address, the president declared that three nations—Iraq, Iran, and North Korea—were part of an "axis of evil" that threatened the world. The president focused on the Saddam Hussein–led Iraq regime and persuaded Congress in October 2002 to enact a joint resolution granting him unilateral authority to launch a preemptive military strike against Iraq and remove Hussein from power, which successfully occurred early in 2003 after a three-week military campaign.

Beginning of Second Term. Two years later, as Bush commenced his second term, a violent insurgency continued in Iraq and claimed many lives. The administration's expectation that the removal of Saddam Hussein would quickly lead to a peaceful and stable regime that could eventually serve as a democratic model for other countries in the region are goals still to be realized. Despite the violence and security concerns, Iraq conducted an election on January 30, 2005—the first free election in fifty years—to select a 275-member transitional National Assembly. A principal function of the National Assembly is to draft a new constitution for Iraq, which is to be voted on by all Iraqis by mid-October 2005. If the constitution is approved, then another national election is to be held by December 15, 2005, for a permanent government. President Bush's objective of expanding "freedom all over the world," as he phrased it in his 2005 inauguration speech, was a laudable goal. It saw some success with the Iraqi election and in what appeared to be limited democratic openings in other Middle East nations (Egypt and Saudi Arabia, for example).

However, no one can predict how long it might take to achieve some form of durable democratic government in Iraq. The Iraqi election prompted calls from some lawmakers that it was time for the Bush administration to develop an exit strategy for withdrawing U.S. and foreign coalition troops from that nation. Bush disagreed, arguing that a fixed timetable would only encourage the insurgents (who are using Iraq as a terrorist training and recruiting ground). Congress remained supportive of the president's goals in Iraq and continued to provide funding for military operations and economic reconstruction. Still, a key objective of Congress and the White House is to eventually reduce the presence of foreign troops in Iraq by turning over the battle against the insurgents to Iraqi military and police forces once they are adequately trained and are up to the task of taking charge of their own nation's security. The continuing conflict in Iraq has presented Bush with a major, ongoing challenge, and it has required vigorous scrutiny by the House and Senate. "We're going to continue to have oversight hearings and be tough," said Sen. Chuck Hagel of Nebraska, the second-ranking Republican on the Foreign Relations Committee. "We don't work for the president," he added.[56]

In the domestic policy arena, some dismay with the president arose for his insistence that lawmakers do what he says. This administration "has the most executive-oriented view of government of any recent president," stated Thomas Mann of the Brookings Institution. "It believes that the president leads and Congress follows—that Republican members of Congress are there at his beck and call. That's not the way the constitutional system was designed."[57] Bush's assertive and partisan approach toward Congress sharpened legislative-executive tensions. Or as one senior Republican lawmaker characterized Bush's attitude toward Congress: "Come let us reason together—and do it my way."[58]

This sentiment seems certain to wane in the second term as Bush faces a new legislative and political environment. The president is a lame duck, unable to run for reelection like the scores of lawmakers who will seek to retain office in 2006 and beyond. His ambitious agenda (overhauling Social Security, revamping the tax code, reducing the deficit, and so on) means that it will be harder to mobilize winning coalitions from only within Republican ranks. Nervousness among congressional Republicans about the president's Social Security recommendations is a good example of the changed dynamic on Capitol Hill. "This does not have strong unanimity among Republicans in Congress or the rank-and-file," said a top GOP operative. "It is not an issue that galvanizes Republicans like tax cuts, that is for sure."[59]

As for the minority Democrats, they have been angered by Bush's penchant for either ignoring or attacking them. Cutting deals with Bush was something that many Democrats are not eager to do. They remember Bush's aggressiveness toward them on the campaign trail. A prime example

Democrats continue to cite was the defeat of incumbent senator Max Cleland, D-Ga., in the November 2002 election on the ground that he was "soft" on homeland security. "This is something that gnaws at us," said Sen. Richard J. Durbin, D-Ill. "A decorated and disabled Vietnam veteran [who lost three limbs in the war] would be discredited because of his stand in the homeland security debate."[60] Cleland favored civil service protections, opposed by Bush, for employees of the new Department of Homeland Security.

Thus, when Bush proposed a major revamping of the Social Security system, congressional Democrats united and aggressively challenged the president's plan to change this popular New Deal program. Democrats, too, suspected that much of Bush's second-term agenda aimed not only to overhaul public policy but also to make the GOP the nation's majority party for the next several decades. "When we push to save Social Security, we have an historic opportunity to bring more young Americans into our party," declared the GOP's national committee chairman.[61] Bush's plan to revamp immigration may appeal to the expanding number of Hispanic voters; school vouchers could attract African American voters whose children attend troubled public schools; limits on class-action lawsuits undermine trial lawyers, a major Democratic fund-raising group; and revisions in civil service regulations could weaken public employee unions' "reach into federal agencies, carving into union dues and, as a byproduct, into money for Democrats."[62] On issue after issue, noted a congressional journalist, "the White House is staking out positions that achieve a policy goal while expanding the GOP's appeal to new voters or undermining the Democrats' ability to compete."[63]

THE VETO POWER

Article I, Section 7, of the Constitution requires the president to approve or disapprove of bills passed by Congress. In the case of disapproval, the measure dies unless it "shall be repassed by two thirds of the Senate and House of Representatives." Because vetoes are so difficult to override, the veto power makes the president, in Woodrow Wilson's words, a "third branch of the legislature."[64] Presidents usually can attract one-third plus one of their supporters in Congress to sustain a veto, and so presidential vetoes are not often overridden.

The decision to veto is a collective administration judgment. Presidents seek advice from numerous sources, such as agency officials, the Office of Management and Budget, and White House aides. Five reasons commonly are given for vetoing a bill: (1) the bill is unconstitutional, (2) it encroaches on the president's independence, (3) it is unwise public policy, (4) it cannot be administered, and (5) it costs too much. Political considerations may permeate any or all of these reasons. The cost rationale is a favorite of recent presidents.

The veto is more than a negative power, however. Presidents also use it to advance their policy objectives. Veto threats, for example, often encourage legislators to accommodate executive preferences and objections. Presidents also practice the politics of differentiation in using their vetoes. A veto fight with Congress may suit presidents who want to underscore for voters how their views differ from the other party's. For its part, Congress can discourage vetoes by adding its desired items to must-pass legislation or to measures strongly favored by the president.

Veto Options

Once the president receives a bill from Congress, he has ten days (excluding Sundays) in which to exercise one of four options.

1. He can sign the bill. Most public and private bills presented to the president are signed into law. Presidents sometimes issue signing statements that express their interpretation of a new law's provisions.[65]
2. He can return the bill with his veto message to the originating house of Congress.
3. He can take no action, and the bill will become law without his signature. This option, seldom employed, is reserved for bills the president dislikes but not enough to veto (see Box 10-2 on how an unsigned bill becomes law).
4. He can pocket veto the bill. Under the Constitution, if a congressional adjournment prevents the return of a bill, the bill cannot become law without the president's signature.

The pocket veto has been a source of some controversy over the years. Article I, Section 7, of the Constitution states: "If any Bill shall not be returned by the President within ten Days (Sundays excepted) after it shall have been presented to him, the Same shall be a Law, in like manner as if he had signed it, unless Congress by the Adjournment prevents its Return, in which case it shall not be a Law." Several federal court decisions (see, for example, the 1974 case of *Kennedy v. Sampson*) have established the principle that pocket vetoes are not to be used during a congressional session.[66] Attorneys for Congress argued that during legislative recesses both chambers designate officials to receive executive communications, including veto messages. The issue that still arouses controversy is whether a president can pocket veto a bill between the first and second sessions. Until the Supreme Court makes a definitive ruling involving use of the pocket veto both during and between legislative sessions, it is likely that legislative-executive controversies over the pocket veto will occur periodically.

President Reagan, for instance, did pocket veto a measure in 1983 during the holiday season between the first and second session of the 98th Congress. Members of Congress brought suit but, by the time the case reached the Supreme Court in 1987, it was declared moot because the challenged law had already expired. Reagan's successor in the White House, George Bush, contended that he could pocket veto a measure any time Congress recesses for more

BOX 10-2 An Unsigned Bill Becomes Law

In November 1995 President Bill Clinton opposed legislation (S. 1322) that would relocate the U.S. embassy in Israel from Tel Aviv to Jerusalem. Clinton did not object in principle to moving the embassy to Jerusalem, which Israel has regarded as its capital since 1950. But he warned that ordering the shift would risk derailing the Middle East peace process because Arab nations strongly objected to the idea.

Both chambers of Congress approved S. 1322 by wide margins. Clinton decided not to veto the measure and face an almost certain override. Instead, he announced that he would allow the bill to become law without his signature and would make use of a provision added in the Senate after closed-door negotiations that would enable him to delay the move indefinitely for national security reasons.

Clinton's decision to distance himself from the embassy bill without vetoing it was by no means unprecedented, although it is an option rarely used by chief executives. S. 1322 was only the sixth bill to become law in this way since 1973.

Source: Adapted from Amy D. Burke, "An Unsigned Bill to Become Law Today," *CQ's Congressional Monitor,* November 7, 1995, 3.

than three days. (Article I, Section 5, of the Constitution states that neither house may adjourn without the consent of the other for more than three days.) Bush's interpretation has been criticized on several grounds, such as it does not comport with prevailing court precedents and "would allow pocket vetoes even during long weekends in the middle of a session."[67]

Veto Strategies

George Bush was among the most successful chief executives in employing the veto against an opposition Congress. He used it to block unwanted legislation and as a potent bargaining weapon to get concessions from the Democratic-controlled Congress. Not until his term was nearly over, and after thirty-five consecutive veto victories, did Congress, on October 5, 1992, manage to override a Bush veto of a popular bill—a measure to reregulate the cable television industry. Part of the explanation for Bush's veto successes was that he announced his intentions early and stuck by them unless the compromises he wanted were agreed to. Furthermore, he convinced congressional Republicans that their strength depended on sustaining the president's vetoes. (Of forty-six vetoes, Bush had only the cable bill overridden by Congress.) Frustrated by their inability to override presidential vetoes, congressional Democrats devised their own strategy: win by losing. To sharpen the policy differences between the two parties before the November 1992 election, they sent the president bills that he was certain to veto.

By contrast, President Clinton did not veto a single measure during his first two years in office—something that had not happened since the days of Millard Fillmore in the 1850s. Part of the explanation is that Congress was then controlled by Democrats. Clinton used his veto pen for the first time on June 7, 1995, rejecting an appropriations bill. Subsequently, the president either exercised or threatened to use the veto against numerous Republican-sponsored bills.

President George W. Bush stated that he would not hesitate to use his veto power to enforce his budgetary goals if Congress passed legislation he considered excessive. The threat of a veto, in short, often serves as a bargaining device that encourages lawmakers to accommodate the president's policy preferences. Bush did not exercise his veto during his first term.

One has to reach back all the way to James Garfield, the twentieth president, to find a veto-less president, and he did not even serve a full year before being assassinated. Partial-term presidents William Henry Harrison, Zachary Taylor, and Millard Fillmore never issued a veto, nor did one-termers John Adams and John Quincy Adams. Only Jefferson survived two terms without one.[68]

Several factors account for Bush's no-veto first term: unified GOP control of the House and Senate during most of the period; the refusal of top party leaders, such as Speaker Hastert, to send bills to the White House that Bush might veto; the desire of Republicans to demonstrate their capacity to govern with narrow majorities; and the ability of the White House and GOP congressional leaders to work out their disagreements.

Bush sometimes choreographed bill-signing ceremonies to reward supporters and send messages. For example, "Bush signed [a bill dealing with corporate corruption] on a table adorned with a sign saying 'Corporate Responsibility,' a technique used by the White House image-makers to associate the president's picture with the gist of his message."[69] Occasions did arise when bills were signed in virtual secrecy, such as a 2003 measure raising the federal debt ceiling by nearly $1 trillion. On the day he quietly signed that bill into law, Bush held a public bill-signing ceremony for his $350 billion tax-cut measure.

Post-Veto Action

Just as the president may feel strong pressure to veto or sign a bill, Congress may feel intense political heat after it receives a veto message. A week after President Nixon's 1970 televised veto of a bill funding welfare programs, House members received more than fifty-five thousand telegrams, most of them urging support for the veto. Congress upheld the veto, in part because of Nixon's televised appeal. However, despite a massive telephone campaign to congressional offices (as many as eighty thousand calls an hour) urging support for President Reagan's veto of a 1988 civil rights bill, the House and Senate easily overrode the veto.[70]

Congress need not act at all upon a vetoed bill. If party leaders believe they lack the votes to override, the chamber that receives a vetoed measure may refer it to committee or table it. Even if one house musters the votes to override, the other body may do nothing. No amendments can be made to a vetoed bill—it is all or nothing at this stage—and the Constitution requires votes on vetoed bills to be recorded.

The Line-Item Veto

Congress's habit of combining numerous items into a single measure puts the president in the position of having to accept or reject the entire package. Presidents and supporters of executive power have long touted the advantages of allowing the president to veto items selectively. Proponents argued that it would give the president an effective way to eliminate wasteful spending and reduce the federal deficit. Opponents countered that the item veto is about interbranch power and not fiscal restraint. Granting the item veto to the president, they said, would undermine Congress's power of the purse and give chief executives added bargaining leverage over lawmakers. "The president could say, 'I'm going to zap your dam, but I've got another piece of legislation coming around, and I won't be so inclined to do that [if you support me],' " said Rep. Jack Kingston, R-Ga.[71] After much debate, the 104th Congress expanded the president's rescission (cancellation of spending) authority. It eventually passed the line-item veto, as part of the Contract with America, despite some concern among congressional Republicans that President Clinton would use it against GOP-passed riders (extraneous policy provisos) in appropriations bills.

The Line-Item Veto Act of 1996 gave the president a fifth veto option. After a president signed a bill into law, he could exercise the line-item veto prerogative to cancel dollar amounts specified in any appropriations law or even in the accompanying House or Senate committee reports; strike new entitlement programs or expansions of existing programs; and delete tax breaks limited to one hundred or fewer beneficiaries. After using the line-item veto, the president was required to send a special message to Congress identifying what he had rescinded. To overturn his decisions, Congress would have to pass another bill that the president could then veto, requiring Congress to override it by a two-thirds vote of each chamber. Under the law the president could block something if he had the support of only one-third plus one of the members of each chamber. The act became effective January 1, 1997, and was to expire at the end of 2004.

Right after the bill took effect, a bipartisan group of lawmakers filed a lawsuit challenging the law's constitutionality. The group argued that the law allowed the president to repeal statutory provisions unilaterally and that it eroded Congress's constitutional power of the purse.[72] Without addressing the law's constitutionality, the Supreme Court ruled that members of Congress lacked legal standing to bring the suit. They had suffered no specific personal injury—a requirement if the Court is to decide cases or controversies—

because Clinton had never exercised the line-item act's cancellation authority. The Court's decision cleared the way for the president to exercise the line-item veto option, and he did so for the first time in August 1997.[73]

Contrary to the expectations of pundits, President Clinton exercised caution in his use of the line-item veto. Apparently, the president chose not to anger lawmakers whose support he might need later to enact administration priorities. As one account noted, the president "has deferred to Congress on the overwhelming majority of projects that members added to budget bills, even when the Administration could find no compelling public interest to justify them."[74]

Several lawmakers subsequently brought another suit challenging the president's use of the line-item veto. On June 25, 1998, in the case of *Clinton v. New York City,* the Supreme Court by a 6–3 vote declared the Line-Item Veto Act unconstitutional because it gave the president "unilateral authority to change the text of duly enacted statutes," wrote Justice John Paul Stevens for the majority.[75] The administration soon announced that it would release funding for projects that had been subject to the line-item veto. Subsequently, several lawmakers introduced line-item veto alternatives, including a constitutional amendment. As a chairman of the House Ways and Means Committee said, "I am deeply concerned that our commitment to fiscal discipline will be eaten away" unless Congress enacts a constitutional line-item veto amendment.[76] In light of today's record-setting deficits, there is some interest in further legislative action on the line-item veto. President George W. Bush recommended in his fiscal year 2006 budget submission that Congress revive the proposal. Bush corrected, he said, the constitutional flaw in the 1996 act by stating that spending items would be "deferred," not "rejected," and that all savings from the line-item veto "would be used for deficit reduction" and not used "to augment other spending."[77]

SOURCES OF LEGISLATIVE-EXECUTIVE COOPERATION

Unlike national assemblies where executive authority is lodged in the leader of parliament—called the prime minister or premier—Congress truly is separate from the executive branch. Yet the executive and legislative branches are mutually dependent in policy making. The 115 volumes of the *United States Statutes at Large* underscore the cooperative impulses of the two branches. Each volume contains the joint product of Congresses and presidents over the years, from the 108 public laws enacted by the First Congress (1789–1791) to the 430 enacted by the 108th Congress (2003–2005). These accomplishments are the result of party loyalties and public expectations, bargaining and compromise, and informal links between the president and lawmakers.

Party Loyalties and Public Expectations

Presidents and congressional leaders have met informally to discuss issues ever since the First Congress, when George Washington frequently sought the advice of Virginia representative James Madison. But meetings between the chief executive and House and Senate leaders did not become common until Theodore Roosevelt's administration (1901–1909). Today, congressional party leaders are two-way conduits who communicate legislative views to the president and inform members of executive preferences and intentions.

Presidents and members of their party are linked psychologically and ideologically. This means that "bargaining 'within the family' has a rather different quality than bargaining with members of the rival clan."[78] Congressional Republicans want President George W. Bush to succeed in moving his agenda even though they do not always share his priorities. "I think everyone on our side realizes that if the president does well, we do well," declaimed GOP representative Tom Latham of Iowa.[79]

It is not uncommon for presidents and their partisan colleagues on Capitol Hill to have divergent goals, especially when the president's party is in the minority. The need for legislative results impels presidents to deal with whichever is the majority party. As one Clinton adviser explained about the administration's dealings with the GOP-controlled Congress, the "president must present himself as a national leader, as opposed to a Democratic leader, to an electorate increasingly dominated by voters who feel no allegiance to either party."[80]

Bargaining and Compromise

The interdependence of the two branches provides each with the incentive to bargain. Legislators and presidents have in common at least three interests: shaping public policy, winning elections, and attaining influence within the legislature. In achieving these goals, members may be helped or hindered by executive officials. Agency personnel, for example, can heed legislators' advice in formulating policies, help them gain favorable publicity back home, and give them advance notice of executive actions. Executive officials, meanwhile, rely on legislators for help in pushing administrative proposals through the legislative process.

A classic illustration of effective presidential bargaining with Congress occurred on May 7, 1981, when the Democratic-controlled House adopted President Reagan's controversial budget package, intended to cut federal spending for social programs and to raise military spending. The plan easily passed the House because of Reagan's popularity and skill in dealing with representatives. The "greatest selling job I've ever seen," said Speaker O'Neill. Reagan, for instance, persuaded several governors to meet with members from their states who were opposing the program. He met or phoned conservative Democrats whose support was needed. Top executive officials were sent into targeted Democratic districts to drum up public support. Thus, on the key House vote all 191 GOP members and 63 Democrats backed the president's budget scheme.

Informal Links

Some presidents are able to deal with Congress more adeptly than others. Lyndon Johnson assiduously courted members. He summoned legislators to the White House for private meetings, danced with their wives at parties, telephoned greetings on their birthdays, and hosted them at his Texas ranch. He also knew how to twist arms to win support for his programs. Johnson's understanding of what moved members and energized Congress was awesome. "There is only one way for a President to deal with the Congress," he said, "and that is continuously, incessantly, and without interruption."[81]

After September 11, 2001, President Bush instituted a weekly breakfast with the bicameral leadership: the Speaker, House minority leader, Senate majority leader, and Senate minority leader. At the start of the 108th Congress, the White House added House majority leader DeLay "to the core group, giving him a voice in Washington's top-level Wednesday meeting."[82] Bush administration representatives are also "typically present at every key stage of a bill's development. When sticking points appear, the White House can work in 'real time' to resolve the issues, often through a quick phone call."[83] Presidential scholars suggest, however, that the chief executive's style and skills affect legislative success only "at the margins."[84] Far more important are contextual factors: the mood of the country, the state of the economy, the popularity of the president, the president's partisan strength in Congress, and so on. Even with the misgivings expressed by many Senate Republicans about the controversial nomination of John Bolton to be the U.S. ambassador to the United Nations, the Foreign Relations Committee still reported the nomination to the floor, albeit without recommendation. As a GOP strategist noted: "Republicans understand that George W. Bush has brought more Republicans [into Congress] . . . . and that means something. In a default position, Republicans are going to vote with him and stay with him."[85]

SOURCES OF LEGISLATIVE-EXECUTIVE CONFLICT

Legislative-executive conflicts were evident in 1789; they are present today; and they can be expected in the future for at least three reasons. First, the Constitution specifies neither the precise policy-making roles of Congress and the president nor the manner in which they are to deal with one another. Second, presidents and Congresses serve different constituencies. Third, important variations exist in the timetables under which the two branches operate.

Constitutional Ambiguities

Article I invests Congress with "all legislative powers," but it also authorizes the president to recommend and to veto legislation. In several specific areas the Constitution splits authority between the president and Congress. The Senate, for example, is the president's partner in treaty making and nominations under "advice and consent" clauses. And, before treaties can take effect, they require the concurrence of two-thirds of the Senate. The Constitution is silent, however, on how or when the Senate is to render its advice to the president.[86]

In 1919 and 1920 a historic confrontation occurred when the Senate vehemently opposed the Treaty of Versailles negotiated by President Wilson. The treaty contained an agreement binding the United States to the proposed League of Nations. Many senators had warned the president against including the league provision in the treaty, and during floor deliberations the Senate added several reservations that were strongly opposed by the president. Spurning compromise, Wilson launched a nationwide speaking tour to mobilize popular support for the treaty. Not to be outdone, senators opposed to the pact organized a "truth squad" that trailed the president and rebutted his arguments. During his tour Wilson suffered a stroke from which he never fully recovered. In the end the treaty was rejected. The Constitution, in short, intermingles presidential and congressional authority but also assigns each branch special duties.

Different Constituencies

Presidents and their vice presidents are the only public officials elected nationally. To win, they must create vastly broader electoral coalitions than is necessary for legislators, who represent either states or districts. Only presidents, then, can claim to speak for the nation at large. It is important to note, however, that

> there is no structural or institutional or theoretical reason why the representation of a "single" broader constituency by the President is necessarily better or worse than the representation of many "separate" constituencies by several hundred legislators. Some distortion is inevitable in either arrangement, and the question of the good or evil of either form of distortion simply leads one back to varying value judgments.[87]

Presidents and legislators tend to view policies and problems from different perspectives. Members often subscribe to the view that "what's good for Portland is good for the nation." Presidents are apt to say that "what's good for the nation is good for Portland." In other words, public officials may view common issues differently when they represent diverging interests.

For example, a president might wish to reduce international trade barriers. A representative from a district where a manufacturer is threatened by imported Japanese products is likely to oppose the president's policy, while importers and retailers of Italian shoes are likely to support the president. The challenge to national policy making is to forge consensus within an electorate that simultaneously holds membership in two or more competing constituencies.

Disparities in constituencies are underscored by differences in the ways voters judge presidents and members of Congress. Studies of presidential popularity ratings suggest that presidents are judged on the basis of general factors—economic boom or bust, the presence or absence of wars or other crises, the impact of policies on given groups.[88] The media, too, can affect the assessment of presidents. Legislators, by contrast, tend to be assessed on the basis of their personalities, their communication with constituents, and their service in material ways to the state or district. Not only do presidents and legislators serve different constituencies, but they also labor under divergent incentives.

Different Time Perspectives

Finally, Congress and the president operate on different timetables. Presidents have four years, at most eight, to win adoption of their programs. They are usually in a hurry to achieve all they can before they leave office. In practice, they have even less time—in view of the typical falloff of presidential support after the initial honeymoon. In reality, presidents and their advisers have a year, perhaps less, to sell their basic program to Congress and the public.

Lawmakers' attitudes toward the president are likewise influenced by election cycles. For instance, the George W. Bush administration announced a national energy strategy in May 2001 designed to ameliorate the country's energy problems over the next several years. Congressional Republicans, worried about rising gasoline prices, escalating natural gas prices, and rolling electricity blackouts in California, wanted immediate actions to address those problems. They were concerned about voter backlash against Republicans in the November 2002 midterm elections. Rep. Thomas M. Davis III of Virginia, chairman of the National Republican Congressional Committee, communicated these concerns to the White House. "Do they get the message?" a journalist asked Davis. "No," he said. "They think in four-year terms; we think in two."[89]

On major, long-standing issues, however, Congress typically moves slowly. Seldom does it pass presidential initiatives quickly. Moreover, many legislators are careerists. Once elected, House members are likely to be reelected, and senators serve six-year terms. Most members hold office a good deal longer than the presidents they deal with. Skeptical legislators, reluctant to follow the president, realize that if they resist long enough someone else will occupy the White House.

THE BALANCE OF POWER

"The relationship between the Congress and the presidency," wrote Arthur M. Schlesinger Jr., "has been one of the abiding mysteries of the American system of government."[90] Part of the mystery inheres in the Constitution, which enumerates many powers for Congress as well as those "necessary and proper" to carry them out, while leaving the president's powers largely ambiguous. Where does the balance of power lie? There is no easy answer, but at certain times the scale has tipped toward Congress and at other times toward the president. Scholars have even identified periods of "congressional government" or "presidential government."[91]

Four points need to be remembered about the ups and downs of Congress and the presidency. First, the power balance is in constant flux. The stature of either branch can be influenced by issues, events, partisan circumstances, personalities, or public opinion. Even during periods when one branch appears to dominate, actual relationships in specific policy areas may be far more complex.

The mid-1960s and early 1970s, for example, are cited as a time of "imperial presidents" and compliant Congresses.[92] But Congress was by no means passive during this period. While it enacted much of President Johnson's Great Society program, it also initiated scores of laws, including consumer, environmental, health, and civil rights legislation. Nor did executive actions go unchallenged. Nationally televised hearings conducted in 1966 by the Senate Foreign Relations Committee helped to mobilize congressional and public opposition to Johnson's Vietnam War policies.

Second, shifts of power occur within each branch. In Congress aggressive leaders may be followed by less assertive leaders. In the executive branch the forces for White House leadership regularly battle the forces for agency decentralization. These internal power fluctuations clearly affect policy making. As recently as the Eisenhower presidency in the 1950s, powerful committee and party leaders could normally deliver blocs of votes to pass legislation. Today, even with the resurgence of partisanship on Capitol Hill, the president can never be sure which of the 535 members will form a winning coalition.

Third, legislative-executive relationships are not zero-sum games. If one branch gains power, the other does not necessarily lose it. If one branch is up, the other need not be down. The expansion of the federal government since World War II has augmented the authority of both branches. Their growth rates were different, but each expanded its ability to address complex issues, initiate legislation, and frustrate proposals of the other. Conventional wisdom states that wars, crises, nuclear weapons, military expansion, and public demands fostered the imperial presidency. Such factors certainly enlarge the likelihood of executive dominance, but, for example, in the wars of 1812 and 1898, military action was encouraged in part by aggressive Congresses. Economic panics and depressions under Presidents James Monroe, James Buchanan, and Ulysses S. Grant did not lead to losses of congressional power.

Political scientist David Mayhew has asserted that it "does not seem to make all that much difference whether party control of the American government happens to be unified or divided" in influencing the productivity of laws and investigations.[93] Mayhew examined the period from 1946 to 1990, when the mobilization of cross-party majorities on Capitol Hill was commonplace. President Ronald Reagan, for instance, enjoyed large successes in 1981 on his policy priorities (tax cuts, defense hikes, and program reductions) when he won the support of conservative "Reagan Democrats" in the Democratically controlled House. Today, in an era of strong, closely divided, and ideologically distinct congressional parties—reflecting the conditional party government model—presidents may confront heightened potential for partisan impasses, especially in the Senate, regardless of whether the government is unified or divided.

Conflict between Congress and the president is embedded in the system of separation of powers and checks and balances. But the founders also expected their governmental arrangement to promote accommodation between the branches. Historical patterns have veered between these two extremes. The two branches worked together in the early days of Woodrow Wilson's progressive New Freedom (1913–1916), during the New Deal (1933–1937) and World War II (1941–1945), in the brief Great Society years (1964–1966) following John F. Kennedy's assassination (1963), for the even briefer "Reaganomics" juggernaut during Ronald Reagan's first year in office (1981), and for most of George W. Bush's first term in office (2001–2005). At other times they fought fiercely—during Wilson's second term (1919–1921); after 1937 during the Franklin Roosevelt administration; after 1966 during the Lyndon Johnson administration; and for much of Nixon's, Reagan's, George H.W. Bush's, and Clinton's tenures.[94]

More generally, President George W. Bush and Vice President Dick Cheney shared the view that the White House needed to reclaim power that they perceive it lost to Congress, especially during the Clinton presidency. "I've seen a constant, steady erosion of the power and the ability of the president to do his job," declared Cheney, "and time after time after time, administrations have traded away the authority of the president to do his job. We're not going to do that in this administration."[95] The Bush administration, for example, did not hesitate to minimize the public's access to information; to challenge the right of Congress's investigative arm, the Government Accountability Office, to gain access to records of a Cheney-led energy task force; or to refuse to cooperate with "even the most routine and basic congressional requests for information."[96] On many occasions, the Bush administration preferred acting unilaterally rather than collaboratively with Congress. While fierce interbranch conflicts in recent administrations (Reagan, George H.W Bush, Clinton) had thwarted many executive initiatives, the president continued to exercise broad and even growing authority in nonlegislative areas—for example, through executive orders, administrative rulemaking, and aggressive use of the war powers.

Finally, a wide gap often separates what presidents want from what they can get. Congress can influence what, when, how, or even whether executive recommendations are sent to Capitol Hill. White House agendas frequently are shaped by expectations of what will pass Congress. This indirect priority-setting power of the House and Senate can affect whether the president even transmits certain proposals to Congress. It also works in the other direction. Recommendations may be forwarded or endorsed because the White House knows they have broad legislative support. "The president proposes, Congress disposes" is an oversimplified adage.

Congress and the president are institutions shaped by diverging imperatives. Executive officials want flexibility, discretion, and long-range commitments from Congress. They prefer few controls and consultations with a limited number of legislators. The executive tends to be hierarchical in decision making, whereas Congress is collegial. One of the legislative branch's strengths, however, is to give voice and visibility to diverse viewpoints that the executive branch may have overlooked or ignored. The dispersion of power can slow down decision making, but it can also promote public acceptance of the nation's policies. Hence, what are often viewed as Congress's vices have genuine virtue.

CONCLUSION

Legislative-executive relations are characterized by accommodation, conflict, and flux. Of these, accommodation is the most important. Neither branch is monolithic. Presidents find supporters in Congress even when they are opposed by a majority of either house. Both branches seek support for their policy preferences from each other and from outside allies.

Furthermore, confrontation is a recurring element in dealings between Capitol Hill and the White House. The framers of the Constitution consciously distributed and mixed power among the three branches. They left it unclear how Congress or the president was to assert control over the bureaucracy and over policy making. No wonder these two branches tend to be adversaries even when they are controlled by the same party.

Lastly, legislative-executive relations are constantly evolving. Either branch may be active on an issue at one time and passive on the same or different issues at another time. So many circumstances affect how, when, what, or why changes are brought about in their relationship that it is impossible to predict the outlook.

However, over the past generation Congress clearly has equipped itself with a formidable arsenal of resources. As a result, it can play a more active role, initiating policies of its own and overseeing executive branch actions. This development need not be a formula for stalemate. "Our proper objective," counseled Sen. J. William Fulbright, D-Ark. (1945–1974), "is neither a dominant presidency nor an aggressive Congress but, within the strict limits of what the Constitution mandates, a shifting of the emphasis according to the needs of the time and the requirements of public policy."[97]

SUGGESTED READINGS

Binkley, Wilfred. *President and Congress.* New York: Knopf, 1947.

Bond, Jon R., and Richard Fleisher, eds. *Polarized Politics: Congress and the President in a Partisan Era.* Washington, D.C.: CQ Press, 2000.

Fisher, Louis. *Constitutional Conflicts between Congress and the President.* 4th ed. Lawrence: University Press of Kansas, 1997.

Gilmour, John B. *Strategic Disagreement: Stalemate in American Politics.* Pittsburgh: University of Pittsburgh Press, 1995.

Gregg, Gary L., II. *Considering the Bush Presidency.* New York: Oxford University Press, 2004.

Jones, Charles O. *Clinton & Congress 1993–1996.* Norman, Okla.: University of Oklahoma Press, 1999.

Mayhew, David R. *Divided We Govern: Party Control, Lawmaking, and Investigating, 1946–1990.* New Haven: Yale University Press, 1991.

A far-flung bureaucracy: Top, President George W. Bush congratulates lawmakers after signing the Medicare Prescription Drug and Modernization Act (P.L. 108-173) on December 8, 2003. The bill specifies who is covered and how much they must pay, but leaves the detailed rule-making concerning coverage (for example, which drugs insurers must cover) to the Center for Medicare and Medicaid Services within the Department of Health and Human Services. Center, in the aftermath of the attacks of September 11, 2001, federally directed security is tightened at Boston's Logan Airport. Bottom, former representative Lee H. Hamilton, D-Ind., vice chair of the 9/11 Commission, discusses a chart illustrating the number of congressional committees with which the Department of Homeland Security must work.

chapter 11

Congress and the Bureaucracy

In his 1981 inaugural address, President Ronald Reagan declared that "government is not the solution to our problem, government is the problem." Fifteen years later, in the State of the Union address, President Bill Clinton exclaimed, "The era of big government is over." Today, the era of big government is back. The mid-1990s efforts of GOP Speaker Newt Gingrich, R-Ga., and other congressional Republicans to downsize government and devolve power to the states have waned. The administration of Republican president George W. Bush increased the size of the federal government, triggered in part by new domestic security, law enforcement, and military requirements brought about in response to the September 11, 2001, terrorist attacks. Exclaimed journalist David S. Broder,

> Bush is presiding over the biggest, most expensive federal government in history. He has created a mammoth Cabinet department [the Department of Homeland Security], increased federal spending, imposed new federal rules on local and state governments, and injected federal requirements into every public school in America. Meanwhile [in the aftermath of September 11, 2001] the U.S. military is expanding, too, [to track down terrorists and foster the security conditions essential for democratic nation building in Iraq and elsewhere].[1]

Many conservatives inside and outside Congress are dismayed that the Bush administration has sponsored significant increases in federal spending, escalating fiscal deficits, and enactment of a costly prescription drug program under Medicare (the largest expansion of an entitlement program since the days of President Lyndon B. Johnson's Great Society). As conservative representative Mike Pence, R-Ind., stated: "The Republican majority, left to its own devices from 1995 to 2000, was a party committed to limited government and restoring the balance of federalism with the states. Clearly, President Bush has had a different vision, and that vision has resulted in education and welfare policies that have increased the size and scope of government."[2] Or as Pence said in opposing Bush's Medicare drug benefit plan and the president's signature education initiative (the No Child Left Behind Act): "I was concerned that the ship of conservative governance was veering off course into the dangerous uncharted waters of big government Republicanism."[3]

Why is it so difficult for presidents or Congress to shrink the size, role, or reach of the federal government? Setting aside war or other national crises, one basic reason is the ambivalence of the citizenry. Although professing to want to get government off their backs, Americans of virtually all ideological persuasions often turn to government to fulfill their goals and to provide assistance during times of need. As William S. Cohen, former GOP senator from Maine (1979–1997) and defense secretary during the Clinton administration, put it: "The government is the enemy until one needs a friend."[4] The paradox, then, is that citizens understandably oppose the general idea of big government (after all, few people like to pay taxes), but they support the government's specific roles—and may even welcome their selective expansion—in ensuring clean air and water, a strong national defense, quality health care, the safety of prescription drugs, crime prevention, and safety from terrorist attacks. Understandably, lawmakers typically defend governmental programs supported by their constituents.

Even when the GOP vowed to devolve power to the states and localities, many officials in state capitals noted "how limited the transfer of power to the states has been so far, at least compared with the scale of the promises once held out for the idea."[5] As a GOP senator said, "It's much easier to devolve when someone else is in power. When you've got the ball, the temptation is to replace those bad, old regulations with your good, new regulations, instead of sending it back to the states."[6]

The national government is not reluctant to preempt state authority to regulate electricity, define what constitutes drunk driving, or combat child abductions. Moreover, nationwide corporations often lobby for federal regulation so they do not have to contend with the different rules of the fifty states. Businesses, too, may prefer federal regulations because they may be "considerably weaker than those being imposed these days by many of the tougher states."[7] In short, in today's complex and interdependent world, individuals and entities often look to the national government for such things as security, services, justice, or protection. As former senator Ernest F. Hollings, D-S.C. (1966–2005), said: "We have armies who protect us from enemies from without and the [Federal Bureau of Investigation] protects us from enemies within. We have Social Security to protect us from the ravages of old age. We have Medicare to protect us from ill health. We have clean air and clean water [laws] to protect our environment. We have [laws that mandate] safe working places and safe machinery. Our fundamental duties here are to protect."[8]

CONGRESS ORGANIZES THE EXECUTIVE BRANCH

Both the president and Congress are responsible for the fourth branch of government—the bureaucracy. The Constitution requires the president to implement the laws, and by implication it empowers him to give managerial direction to the executive branch. But just as the president is a key player in the lawmaking process, so Congress "has at least as much to do with executive administration as does an incumbent of the White House."[9] Congress is constitutionally authorized to organize and fund the executive branch. But the framers could not have foreseen that their sparse references to "executive departments" would nurture the huge modern bureaucracy. George Washington supervised only three departments (State, War, and Treasury); George W. Bush heads fifteen. Congress establishes the departments and creates the independent agencies, government corporations, and intergovernmental commissions (see Figure 11-1).

The complex federal structure periodically undergoes four basic forms of reorganization. First, the president can recommend administrative changes, such as new strategies for management improvements. Second, Congress can authorize departments and agencies to reorganize themselves. Sometimes Congress establishes an outside commission to recommend how departments or agencies might be merged or abolished. Third, Congress can authorize the president to reorganize on his own initiative or to propose reorganization plans subject to some form of congressional review. Fourth, executive agencies and departments are created or abolished by law. For example, the Department of Homeland Security (DHS) is the newest cabinet creation (see Table 11-1).

Besides establishing federal entities such as DHS, Congress has an array of other ways to affect bureaucratic behavior. The Senate confirms (or not, as the case might be) high-level administrative officials. Congress authorizes the basic personnel systems of federal entities. It also grants rule making authority to administrative agencies. And some scholars suggest that the two Congresses contribute to an expanding bureaucracy.

Department of Homeland Security

Nine days after September 11, 2001, President Bush announced to a joint session of Congress that by executive order he was establishing an Office of Homeland Security within the White House. He named former Pennsylvania governor Tom Ridge to head the new office and also to be the assistant to the president for homeland security. Under Bush's executive order (E.O. 13228), "[t]he mission of the Office shall be to develop and coordinate the implementation of a comprehensive national strategy to secure the United States from terrorist threats or attacks" and "to coordinate the executive branch's" homeland security efforts.

In establishing the Office of Homeland Security as an entity within the Executive Office of the President, Bush was following the administrative presidency strategy. Under this governing model, Bush not only could act quickly and unilaterally, but he also avoided the legislative hurdles and hassles of dealing with a House and Senate controlled by different parties. The president, however, soon encountered congressional criticism and resistance to his

FIGURE 11-1 **The Government of the United States**

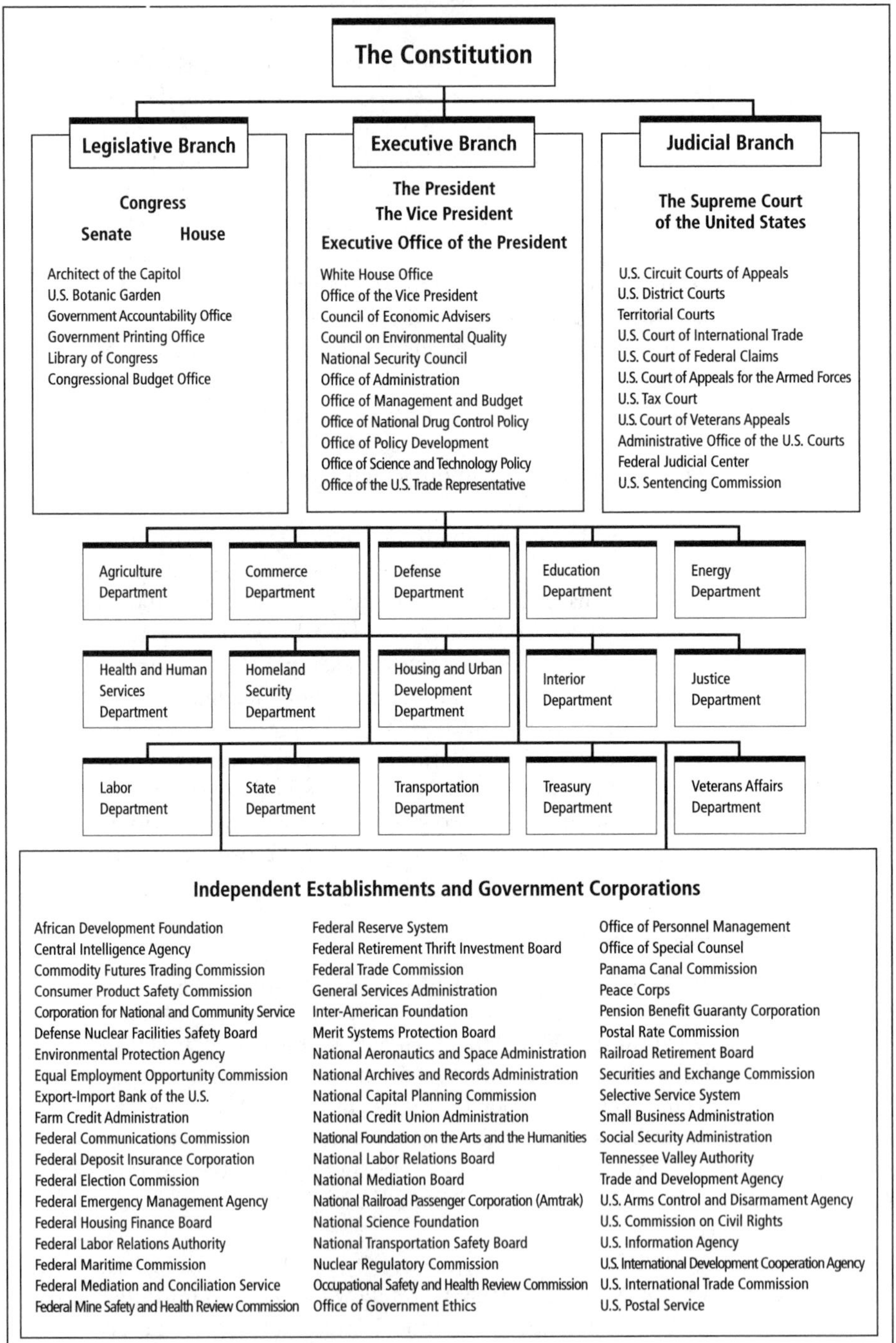

Source: The United States Government Manual, 2004–2005 (Washington, D.C.: U.S. Government Printing Office, 2002), 21.

administrative approach, as both Democrats and Republicans contended that Ridge lacked adequate authority and resources under the executive order to coordinate the government's many agencies involved in antiterrorist activities. Ridge responded that his close access and ties to Bush provided him with all the authority he needed to carry out his mission.

Lawmakers were not convinced. Members such as Sen. Joseph I. Lieberman, D-Conn., and Rep. William M. "Mac" Thornberry, R-Texas, introduced legislation to establish a new homeland security department. They argued that Ridge could not accomplish his coordinative role out of an office in the White House. He needed the budgetary, legal, and human resources provided by a cabinet department. A related legislative-executive dispute soon enveloped the administration. As a personal aide to the president and under orders from Bush, Ridge refused to testify before House and Senate committees.[10] Members of both parties responded to the challenge from the president.

TABLE 11-1 **Growth of the Cabinet**

Department	Year created
State	1789
Treasury	1789
War (reorganized and renamed Defense in 1947)	1789
Interior	1849
Justice (position of attorney general created in 1789)	1870
Agriculture	1889
Commerce (created as Commerce and Labor)	1903
Labor (split from Commerce and Labor)	1913
Health, Education, and Welfare (reorganized and renamed Health and Human Services in 1979)	1953
Housing and Urban Development	1965
Transportation	1966
Energy	1977
Education	1980
Veterans Affairs	1989
Homeland Security	2002

Source: CQ Daily Monitor, January 10, 2003, 3.

For instance, when Ridge refused to testify before GOP Oklahoma representative Ernest Istook's Appropriations subcommittee, Istook threatened to reduce funding for the Executive Office of the President. The result was that Ridge began to meet informally with House and Senate committees and members, a practice that did not satisfy everyone on Capitol Hill.[11]

The controversy over testifying, revelations about failures in executive agencies to analyze or share information that might have prevented terrorist attacks; and Ridge's inability to persuade cabinet members to cede some of their turf finally persuaded the president to support creation of the new department. In April 2002, four administration members—Ridge, Office of Management and Budget (OMB) director Mitchell E. Daniels Jr., White House chief of staff Andrew H. Card Jr., and White House counsel Alberto Gonzales—quickly met in secret to draft legislation to establish the new department.[12] On June 6, 2002, the president went on nationwide television to recommend creation of a new cabinet department on homeland security, something that he had opposed for months. The president sent a draft of his reorganization plan to Congress on June 18, 2002, and it was formally introduced (H.R. 5005) on June 24.[13]

Bush's proposal had no trouble passing the GOP-controlled House, which acted on July 22, 2002, by a 295 to 132 vote. The Senate, controlled by Democrats, was another matter. Initially, many senators hoped that the new department would be created by the September 11 anniversary, but, when that date came and went with no action, many lawmakers became "increasingly doubtful that [it would] . . . get done before the November elections."[14] The stumbling block involved civil service and collective bargaining rights for the tens of thousands of federal employees from twenty-two federal agencies who would be transferred to the new department. President Bush wanted to exempt these employees from civil service protections so he would have the flexibility to hire, fire, or transfer these workers as circumstances dictated. Senate Democrats, backed by their union supporters, vigorously opposed the president on this issue. When it became clear that the Democrats had the fifty-one votes to pass legislation containing civil service protections, Republicans launched a filibuster. Democrats tried five times unsuccessfully to invoke cloture (or closure of debate), which requires sixty votes. In the end, the Senate recessed on October 17, 2002, for the November 5 midterm elections without passing its bill but agreeing to return with the House for a postelection, or lame duck, session in mid-November.

Both parties understood the politics of not having acted on homeland security. President Bush was already on the campaign trail lambasting Democrats, saying they were more concerned about special interests than the nation's security. He repeated this message over and over as he criss-crossed the country on behalf of GOP candidates. Congressional Democrats were unable to neutralize the blame-game politics of the White House by castigating Republicans for their unwillingness to compromise and for preventing Senate

FIGURE 11-2 **The Appointments Process**

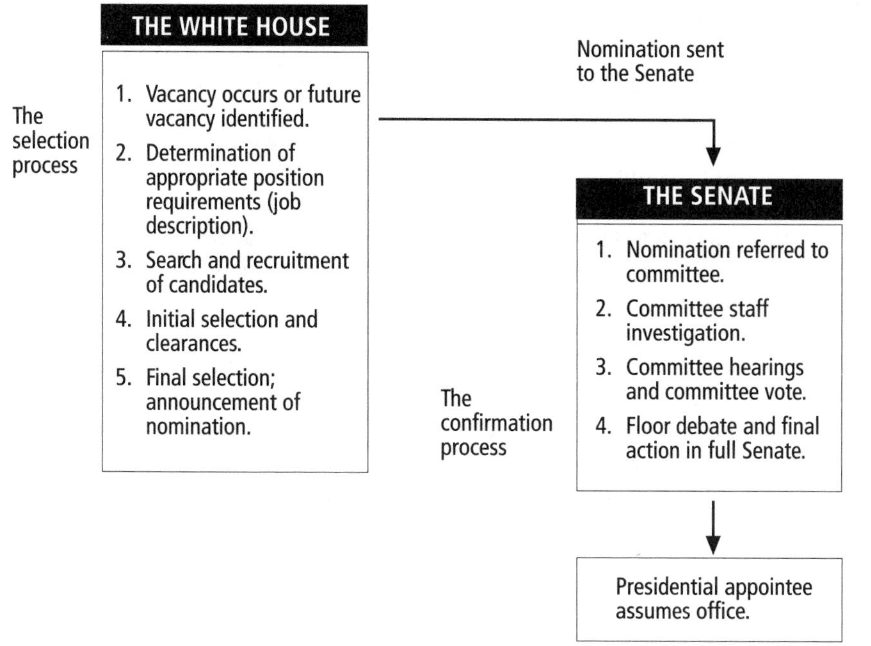

Source: G. Calvin Mackenzie, *The Politics of Presidential Appointments.* Copyright ©1981 by The Free Press. Reprinted with permission of The Free Press, a Division of Simon & Schuster, Inc.

action by filibustering the bill creating the new department. The midterm elections produced a victory for Republicans, who won back control of the Senate and increased the size of their majority in the House. Capitalizing on the electoral victory, Bush used that momentum to push his version of the DHS bill through the lame duck Senate. It passed on November 19 by a 90 to 9 vote. The House agreed to the amended version of the DHS bill, which the president signed into law (P.L. 107-296) on November 25, 2002.

Senate Confirmation of Presidential Appointees

High-level federal appointments—executive, diplomatic, and judicial—are subject to the Senate's "advice and consent" under Article II, Section 2, of the Constitution. After the president has decided whom to nominate, the Senate decides whether to confirm (see Figure 11-2). Senate committees usually elicit the following promise from departmental and agency nominees they have confirmed: "The above nomination [of Michael Chertoff to be secretary of homeland security, for example] was approved subject to the nominee's commitment to respond to requests to appear and testify before any duly constituted committee of the Senate."[15] The confirmation process also reflects the two Congresses principle. As a top Senate official once remarked, "It looks very, very good in California or some place to put out a press release that says, 'Today, I questioned the new Secretary of Transportation about the problems of our area.' "[16]

Presidents sometimes circumvent the Senate's role by making recess appointments during breaks in the Senate's session. (Recess appointees serve until the end of the next Senate session; for example, a person named in 2005 might serve until late 2006.) The Senate resents presidential use of this constitutional option (see Article II, Section 2), and its opposition to some recess appointees has caused some of these appointees to give up their posts. Another way for the administration to circumvent the confirmation process is to appoint officials on an acting basis. Anger at this practice precipitated enactment of the Vacancies Act of 1998. This law identifies individuals subject to the advice and consent of the Senate who can be named on an acting basis and sets limits on the length of their tenure.

Nominations to high-level executive posts today are subject to standards of judgment and evaluation that go beyond questions of competence or conflict of interest. Nominees' personal lives and morality are scrutinized as well. As one commentator explained:

> These days, if you want to run for office or accept a position of public trust, everything is relevant. Your moral, medical, legal and financial background, even your college records, become the subject of public scrutiny. In the old days, the scrutiny was done in private, and certain transgressions could be considered irrelevant.[17]

This shift in standards stems in part from a shift in attitudes by the press and public. The press now reports more aggressively than in years past the private activities of public officials.[18]

Today, there is substantial frustration with the confirmation process. "The nomination system is a national disgrace," wrote a scholar of the presidential appointment process.[19] The problems are many, according to analysts and afflict both Democratic and Republican administrations—even when the same party controls the White House and the Senate. Although most nominees are eventually confirmed by the Senate, three concerns with the process merit mention.

First, it takes longer and longer to fill the full-time cabinet and agency positions requiring Senate confirmation. While President John F. Kennedy had his administrative appointees in place by April 1961, only 2.4 months after his inauguration, "the first Bush administration was not fully confirmed until early October [1991], and the Clinton administration not until mid-October [1993], more than eight months after the start of their respective presidencies."[20] Four months into the first-term administration of George W. Bush, "only 11 percent of its most senior government positions" had been filled.[21] On average, it took George H. W. Bush's administration almost nine months to fill appointed positions that require Senate confirmation compared with the five-month average of the Reagan administration. During George W. Bush's second term, all of his new cabinet secretaries were in place by mid-February 2005, with most confirmed during January. However, many vacancies existed in the national security, diplomatic, and economic departments as senior officials departed at the end of Bush's first term. Some of the delay is attributed to ever-longer background checks required by the White House in the aftermath of the withdrawal of Bernard Kerik (the New York City police chief) as the nominee to head the Department of Homeland Security because of various controversies that surfaced after his nomination. In addition, despite the recommendations of the September 11, 2001, commission, "little has been done to streamline the convoluted process by which the Senate confirms presidential appointments."[22]

Second, bureaucratic developments contribute to the slowness of the confirmation process. Congress and the president have created more executive positions requiring Senate confirmation. For example, President Kennedy nominated fifteen undersecretaries in 1961; President George W. Bush will appoint almost fifty. "Kennedy nominated 87 assistant secretaries; Mr. Bush will appoint more than 220."[23] Further, nominees are required to complete complex and burdensome disclosure forms and undergo lengthy background checks by the Federal Bureau of Investigation (FBI). One result of the onerous review process, according to a study done by the Brookings Institution (a Washington, D.C.-based think tank), is a drop-off in "the number of talented Americans willing to accept the call to presidential service. Presidential recruiters report that it takes more calls to find candidates willing to subject themselves to the process and more work to keep the candidates from bolting once the process begins."[24]

Third, the Senate's confirmation process can be mean and nasty, especially in this period of polarized politics. "With law so hard to make and so hard to change, influencing the choice of the implementers and adjudicators of the law becomes an essential strategic option."[25] Many nominees are subject to rough treatment. Ideological groups, for instance, may organize attack campaigns to defeat nominees who appear unsupportive of their agenda. Sometimes the purpose of Senate confirmation hearings "seems less to ensure that nominees are fit than to cripple the chief executive's political leadership. A defeated nomination can embarrass a president, demoralize his supporters, and reduce public confidence in his judgment."[26] Others argue that the confirmation process may be tough, but so are the positions for which nominees seek assignment. "If you can't fight your way through the process," stated former Central Intelligence Agency (CIA) director Robert Gates, "you might not just do a hot job as director."[27]

Individual senators, too, are not reluctant to threaten filibusters or to place holds on nominations. For example, several Republican senators placed holds

BOX 11-1 A Deal Releases a Senate Hold

Republican leaders in 2005 struck a deal with a Democratic senator to clear a path for the confirmation of Michael O. Leavitt to head the Department of Health and Human Services.

Byron L. Dorgan, D-N.D., had threatened to use a variety of options, including placing a hold on the Leavitt nomination, to spur Senate action on legislation that would allow consumers to import drugs from countries where they often sell for less than in the United States.

Dorgan said Republican leaders promised him that the Health, Education, Labor, and Pensions Committee (HELP) would hold a hearing within ninety days on drug importation legislation that he is cosponsoring with Sen. Olympia J. Snowe, R-Maine.

Dorgan said the promise came from Majority Leader Bill Frist, R-Tenn., and HELP chairman Michael B. Enzi, R-Wyo. Frist confirmed that the committee would hold a hearing within the next ninety days on the Dorgan-Snowe bill.

Source: Adapted from Stephanie C. Weintraub and Mary Agnes Carey, "Leavitt Set for Confirmation as Dorgan Gets a Hearing on Prescription Drug Issues," *CQ Today,* January 26, 2005, 8.

on two Defense Department nominees "to protest what the senators consider Secretary of Defense Donald H. Rumsfeld's lack of communication with Congressional leaders."[28] (See Box 11-1 on holds placed on nominations.) The Senate may also refuse to consider a nominee if members invoke senatorial courtesy. This tradition, dating from President Washington's administration, generally means that the Senate will delay or not act upon nominations for offices in a state if a senator of the president's party from that state opposes them.

The Personnel System

Congress wields wide authority—constitutionally, legally, informally—over the federal personnel system, as the case of DHS shows. Congress authorized both it and the Defense Department to revamp their personnel systems with an eye toward loosening civil service restrictions, such as rewarding employees for the quality of their work instead of their longevity of service. The assassination of President James A. Garfield in 1881 by a disgruntled job seeker prompted Congress to curb the abuses of the spoils system, the practice of handing out federal jobs to supporters of the party that had won the presidency. In 1883 Congress passed the first civil service law that substituted merit for patronage. But the early patronage practices have a modern equivalent: the political-appointee system. Currently, there are a little more than thirty-six hundred key political appointees (see Table 11-2).[29]

Political Appointees. In the 1970s, writes Paul C. Light, "Congress discovered executive structure . . . and began to mine it."[30] Since then Congress and the president have made numerous changes in the top four layers of officials in cabinet departments (secretary, deputy secretary, undersecretary, and assistant secretary). More new job titles in the top echelons of government have been created than ever before. Additional bureaucratic layers result—in some federal agencies there are as many as fifty layers between the president and front-line executive employees—which produce "a bureaucratic fog in which Congress and the president are hopelessly isolated from the people they most need to guide."[31] Among the numerous new titles are deputy associate deputy secretary, principal assistant deputy undersecretary, principal senior deputy assistant secretary, deputy associate assistant secretary, and deputy executive associate administrator.[32] As a result of "title creep," it is becoming "impossible for the bottom to hear the top when messages go through dozens of interpretations on their journey down."[33] Several reasons account for title creep, including the "use of promotions rather than pay raises to reward senior employees, the creation of new positions by Congress and attempts by

TABLE 11-2 **Political Appointee Positions in the Executive Branch**

Type of appointee	Full time	Part time	Total
Presidential appointee requiring Senate confirmation	922[a]	215	1,137
Presidential appointee not requiring Senate confirmation	127	193	320
Non-career Senior Executive Service	691	0	691
Schedule C[b]	1,518	8	1,526
Total	3,258	416	3,674

Source: Figures provided by Henry Hogue, Library of Congress, Congressional Research Service, who is an expert on the presidential appointee process. For presidential appointees, see U.S. House Committee on Government Reform, *United States Government Policy and Supporting Positions,* 108th Cong, 2d sess., November 22, 2004, Committee Print. For non-career Senior Executive Service and Schedule C, see U.S. Office of Personnel Management, Central Personnel Data File. Data as of September 2004, accessed through FedScope, available at www.opm.gov/feddata/. Part-time positions are generally filled by those, subject to term limits, who serve on various federal councils, foundations, commissions, and boards, such as the Harry S. Truman Scholarship Foundation and the National Commission on Libraries and Information Science.

[a] Does not include Foreign Service and diplomatic positions in the Department of State; officer corps positions in the civilian uniformed services of the National Oceanic and Atmospheric Administration in the Department of Commerce; posts in the Public Health Service of the Department of Health and Human Services; the officer corps in the military services; and five positions in the legislative branch (Architect of the Capitol, Comptroller General, Deputy Comptroller General, Librarian of Congress, and the Public Printer).

[b] Employees in policy-determining positions or those who are required to have a close, confidential working relationship with the head of an agency or other key appointed officials.

presidents to tighten their hold on the bureaucracy with a greater number of political appointees."[34]

The number of political appointees is small compared with the total number of federal employees (about 2.7 million civilian employees and 1.4 million uniformed personnel).[35] Yet concern has arisen about the politicization of high-level jobs in the civil service. "We entrust the administration of the largest 'company' in the country . . . to a cast of well-meaning political loyalists with little or no management experience," wrote a career civil servant with thirty-four years of federal service. "We accept the rather mindless notion that any bright and public-spirited dilettante can run a government agency, bureau, or office."[36]

Sens. Russell D. Feingold, D-Wis., and John McCain, R-Ariz., proposed that the number of political appointees be capped at two thousand.[37] In their judgment there are too many for the president to manage effectively. Far from enhancing responsiveness, said GOP senator Trent Lott of Mississippi, the large number of political appointees undermines "presidential control of the executive branch."[38] Not everyone agrees. Some contend that more political appointees are needed "to monitor the permanent government" and "to develop aggressively new policies."[39]

Pay and Other Legal Standards. By law, Congress has wide control over federal employees. It can establish special requirements for holding office; employee performance standards; wages, benefits, and cost-of-living adjustments (COLAs); personnel ceilings; and protections from reprisals for whistleblowers (employees who expose waste and corruption). The 1939 Hatch Act, named for Sen. Carl Hatch, D-N.M. (1933–1949), restricts federal employees' partisan activity. The act was passed during the New Deal after reports that civil servants were being coerced to back President Franklin D. Roosevelt in his reelection efforts. Today, civil servants participate in political activity in accordance with regulations prescribed by the Office of Personnel Management.

Under the Constitution (Article I, Section 6), Congress determines its own pay. Throughout most of its history, Congress enacted stand-alone legislation to hike lawmakers' pay. A second method to raise members' salaries is through a quadrennial salary commission pursuant to a recommendation of the president. Finally, lawmakers may also receive automatic annual cost-of-living adjustments based on presidential recommendation and subject to legislative approval, disapproval, or modification. These automatic adjustments, which are based on the COLAs provided federal employees, were intended to remove politics from the pay hike issue. However, periodic battles are still waged in Congress—often in election years—over the COLAs, and lawmakers have several times been successful in passing legislation to deny the increase. Public criticism of pay hikes is a real concern, as is the threat that potential opponents will seize upon the issue in the next election.[40] (Lawmakers are prohibited from accepting speaking fees, or honorariums, from special interests and other groups.)

In 1992 the Twenty-seventh Amendment to the Constitution (first proposed by James Madison in 1789) was finally ratified: "No law varying the compensation for the services of the Senators and Representatives shall take effect, until an election of Representatives shall have intervened." This amendment permits voters an opportunity to render their verdict on the pay hike before lawmakers receive it.[41]

After leaving public office, members, legislative staffers, and executive officers often pass through the revolving door to jobs with private firms that deal with the government. Responding to procurement abuses at the Pentagon, Congress restricted federal officials who leave public service from immediately joining a private company to work on projects or contracts they managed while in government service. Former federal employees who were "personally and substantially" involved in trade or treaty negotiations with a foreign government cannot lobby on behalf of foreign governments for a year after they leave office. When Congress passed the Lobby Disclosure Act of 1995, it prohibited the U.S. trade representative and his deputies from ever lobbying on behalf of foreign interests. The 1995 act also repealed the Ramspeck Act (named after Rep. Robert C. Ramspeck, D-Ga., 1929–1945), which allowed congressional employees who lost their jobs on Capitol Hill to enter the civil service without meeting the competitive requirements for government positions.

Size of Government. Americans have debated the size and scope of the federal government since the nation's founding. At issue is what functions (law enforcement, welfare, education, and so on) each level of government (local, state, or national) should be responsible for. In addition, people disagree about whether the federal government is bigger or smaller today than it was a few decades ago. Much of the disagreement centers on how governmental size is measured, such as federal expenditures as a share of the gross domestic product, the magnitude of the federal budget, or the number of federal employees. As to the first standard, federal spending relative to the size of the American economy exhibits a mixed picture, from 21.8 percent of gross domestic product in 1990 to 18.4 percent in 2000, 19.8 percent in 2004, and 20.3 percent in 2005. The federal budget keeps growing ($2.6 trillion in 2006), but so, too, have the nation's population and its economy.

Contrary to what many people believe, the federal workforce has remained relatively constant in size. How can the government continue to perform services while keeping its size down? One answer is that much of what the federal government does is to transfer money to eligible recipients, such as the elderly who receive Social Security. This function does not require large numbers of federal workers. Another answer is that federal work is being outsourced, or privatized, to contract firms. The Pentagon, for instance, reached a milestone of sorts at the start of the twenty-first century when the number of its private sector employees (734,000) exceeded its civilian workforce (700,000). These contract employees "perform service jobs from mowing lawns to testing weapons systems."[42] Or consider the Department of Energy, which relies on contractors for "almost everything it does. More than 90 percent of its budget is paid to 100,000 outside workers."[43] A goal of President George W. Bush is to make as many as 850,000 federal jobs subject to private competition.[44] As one analyst explained: "Everybody wants the federal government to look smaller than it really is. By contracting out jobs rather than having civilian workers in those jobs, you can say, 'Look, the government's smaller.' "[45]

When everyone who works directly or indirectly for the federal government is counted, it is much bigger than twenty years or thirty years ago. A scholar puts its "true size" at about 17 million employees: the 4.1 million civilian, military, and postal workers plus the 12.7 million "shadow" workers who are "off the books" because they "work under federal contracts and grants or mandates imposed on state and local governments."[46] An academic dean at Harvard University, however, disagrees. He argues that whom and how many people the federal government employs are "poor surrogates" for the size and scope of government. The conclusion he reaches is that the "federal government—measured by direct and indirect employment, by the dollars it spends and how it spends them—is doing less today than a generation ago."[47]

However this debate about governmental size is reconciled, privatizing (or outsourcing) the work of the federal government has advantages and disadvantages. Because companies under contract to the government are not directly responsible to Congress, the so-called third-party or shadow government presents serious problems of accountability.[48] Some believe certain functions are inherently governmental and ought not to be turned over to outside organizations. Yet third parties are sometimes faster, more flexible, and cheaper than the governmental machine.

Under an e-government initiative, the national government is working to deliver more of its services online. President Bush signed the E-Government Act into law on December 17, 2002. The law establishes an Office of E-Government and Information Technology within the Office of Management and Budget to be responsible for promoting easier online access to the public, for instance, by improving the federal government's Internet site (Firstgov.gov). E-government has implications for the size and work of government because federal employees "are accustomed to working regular business hours, [but] e-government services would operate around the clock."[49] OMB also manages the Regulations.gov Web site, which enables the general public "to comment on the thousands of proposed rules that federal agencies issue each year."[50] In 2006 OMB plans to launch an improved regulatory Web site that will enable citizens "not only to comment on proposed regulations using the Internet—as they do now on the site—but [they] also will have access to supporting agency documents, every public comment and rules that are already in place."[51]

The Rulemaking Process

Although Congress creates executive agencies and lays down their mandates by law, rarely can it specify the details needed to implement policies. The landmark Telecommunications Act of 1996, for example, made it illegal to make "indecent" material available to minors. What material is indecent? That question rests with government regulators (the Federal Communications Commission already bars "seven dirty words" from broadcasts) and ultimately the federal courts. In such cases, specifications must be written, details filled in, and procedures set forth. Thus agencies are empowered to make rules for carrying out the mandates contained in laws.[52] For example, in 2003 a new eleven-hundred-page prescription drug benefit for the elderly became law as part of Medicare. The following year the Department of Health and Human Services issued 1,956 pages of draft regulations (open to public comment for sixty days) to explain how the new prescription drug benefit "will work when it takes effect on January 1, 2006."[53]

In the Administrative Procedures Act of 1946 and later changes to it, Congress established standards for rulemaking by government agencies. Interested parties can take part in the process by testifying in public about the merits or demerits of proposed regulations. Regulations have all the force and effect of law. All regulations, explained Sen. Charles E. Grassley, R-Iowa,

> are based ultimately on authority granted by this Congress. When an agency promulgates a rule, it is engaging in a legislative task—in effect, filling in the gaps on the implementation of policies that we in Congress have established through statute. Accordingly, all regulations must be accountable to this Congress.[54]

In other words, the executive officials who write the rules are lawmakers operating in a bureaucratic context. Federal regulations may be overturned or even declared unconstitutional, as occurred with air quality standards promulgated by the Environmental Protection Agency (EPA). A federal appeals court in May 1999 ruled that Congress had delegated "too much legislative-like authority" to the EPA.[55] However, on February 27, 2001, the U.S. Supreme Court unanimously rejected that claim and upheld EPA's clean air rules as an appropriate exercise of the regulatory authority delegated to it by Congress.[56]

Federal courts also ensure that executive officials cannot by fiat repeal unwanted rules. A federal appeals court, for instance, ruled that the Bush administration acted illegally when it rescinded an efficiency rule for air-conditioners promulgated by the Clinton administration. The court stated that "once a rule is published in the Federal Register, it cannot be reversed without a lengthy administrative process, even if [the rule] has not yet taken effect."[57] Presidents can overturn executive orders of their predecessors with the stroke of a pen, but that is not the case with regulations. "It is not easy for a president to stop a final rule that has been published in the Federal Register short

TABLE 11-3 ***Code of Federal Regulations,* Page Count by Selected Presidencies**

President	Average annual number of pages *Code of Federal Regulations*
Jimmy Carter (1977–1981)	64,483
Ronald Reagan (1981–1989)	50,683
George Bush (1989–1993)	53,843
Bill Clinton (1993–2001)	66,480
George W. Bush (2001–2002)	72,598

Source: Clyde Wayne Crews Jr., *Ten Thousand Commandments: An Annual Snapshot of the Federal Regulatory State, 2003 Edition* (Washington, D.C.: Cato Institute, 2003), 27.

of putting the whole process [as prescribed in the Administrative Procedures Act of 1946] in reverse and beginning the process of rule making anew—with public notices, comment periods and agency reviews that could take years."[58]

Congress and the White House frequently skirmish over rulemaking. During the Clinton administration, Republicans put the rollback of federal regulations high on their agenda. "Regulatory agencies have run amok and need to be reformed," House GOP leader Tom DeLay, R-Texas, declared.[59] This sentiment was triggered in large measure by business's animus toward regulatory growth (see Table 11-3). With a GOP administration, there is an understandable pro-business regulatory tilt, including giving key regulatory jobs to corporate and industry officials who are keen on easing or reducing regulation. The Bush appointees "are achieving what they view as an important goal of eliminating burdensome regulation and freeing companies to grow."[60] Detractors contend that some of the changes weaken worker safety, consumer, and environmental protections.

About six hundred major rules and regulations are issued each year by executive agencies that require review by the White House regulatory czar. The regulatory czar heads the Office of Information and Regulatory Affairs within OMB, which analyzes the costs and benefits of significant regulations (those that "would cost industry more than $100 million to implement") and either rejects them, requires their revision, or approves them as comporting with the president's priorities.[61]

The Bush administration has made it clear that proposed rules and regulations are to be subject to stricter cost-benefit review. Critics of this approach say that it is often easier to quantify costs than benefits because the latter are often intangible and long term, such as future improvements in public health.

The benefits of most public programs, wrote two economists, "are nothing like sales revenues. Rather, the benefits include priceless values such as protection of life, health and nature." However, two risk analysis experts ask what could be fairer than to use neutral decision tools "to sort through a complex world of threats to human and environmental health so we can identify the choices that will do the most people the most good at the least cost?"[62] Needless to say, it is a complex methodological exercise to measure regulatory costs and benefits.

President Bush has another way to undo regulations he opposes: encourage Congress to use laws on the books to overturn unwanted regulations. For example, the Congressional Review Act of 1996 requires regulators to submit all proposed major rules and regulations to the House and Senate. Lawmakers then have sixty legislative days from the time a regulation is published to reject it under expedited procedures by enacting a joint resolution of disapproval. The law was never employed during the Clinton administration. Congress recognized that any disapproval measure would be vetoed by the president, and neither chamber had the two-thirds vote to override. The GOP-controlled House and Senate used the review act shortly after the 107th Congress (2001–2003) convened to repeal a controversial workplace safety rule designed to reduce repetitive stress injuries.[63] Bush signed the repeal measure into law, but that is the only time the review act has been used successfully. (Although seldom employed, the threat of the act's use is not lost on an agency when it crafts rules and regulations.)

This act can also be used with the two Congresses in mind. In March 2005 Sen. Kent Conrad, D-N.D., took the lead in using the review act to block a regulation issued by the Agriculture Department that would lift restrictions on the importation of Canadian beef because of "mad cow" concerns. Up for reelection in November 2006 and representing a "red" state carried by George W. Bush, Senator Conrad responded to North Dakota ranchers who were "worried that the imports will undermine the safety of the state's cattle industry."[64] The joint resolution of disapproval passed the Senate but not the House. Election years are also a time when administrations delay issuing regulations that could be politically controversial or costly—dubbed "slow rolling" by lobbyists and policy makers. "Slow rolling takes place before a presidential election because it is an axiom of political life that agencies take no action that could give an issue to the opponents of the incumbent administration."[65]

How valuable are regulations? Lawmakers, like their constituents, are of two minds. Some, such as Sen. Barbara Boxer, D-Calif., emphasize their positive achievements.

> The purpose of the Federal regulatory process is to improve and protect the high quality of life that we enjoy in our country. Every day, the people of our Nation enjoy the benefits of almost a century of progress in Federal laws and regulations that reduce the threat of ill-

BOX 11-2 **Overturning Federal Rules**

At the urging of business lobbyists, Republican leaders in 2001 dusted off an untested five-year-old statute to use to strike down some of the new regulations issued in the waning days of the Clinton administration.

Lobbyists saw the 1996 Congressional Review Act (P.L. 104-121) as a tool to nullify some of the new rules hustled into the *Federal Register* in President Bill Clinton's final months in office. The law allows Congress to erase regulations by passing a resolution of disapproval by a simple majority vote of both houses. The law was never used during the Clinton presidency because Clinton would have vetoed any disapproval resolution.

Topping the business community's hit list was the hotly debated set of ergonomics rules issued in December 2002 by the Occupational Safety and Health Administration. The rule, many years in the making, was designed to reduce repetitive-motion injuries on the job. The National Association of Manufacturers (NAM) and other trade groups argued that it was too costly and unnecessary.

The review act offers a unique advantage: A resolution of disapproval is not subject to filibuster in the Senate, so its sponsors need only fifty-one votes there.

If Congress wants to disapprove a major regulation—one that costs the economy $100 million or more per year—it has to do so within sixty legislative days after it is entered in the *Federal Register.*

This was the only time so far that the review act was successfully used to overturn a federal regulation.

Source: Adapted from Peter Kaplan, "GOP Eyes 1996 Law in Effort to Overturn Federal Rules," *CQ Daily Monitor,* January 26, 2001, 7.

> ness, injury, and death from consumer products, workplace hazards, and environmental toxins.[66]

Others call for "more rational regulations," with "better analysis of costs, benefits, and risks, so that regulators will issue smarter, more cost-effective regulations."[67] A difficult challenge is to distinguish between inflexible, pointless, or overly burdensome and costly regulations and beneficial regulations that are necessary to promote and protect the public's health and safety. Events, too, shape public attitudes toward regulation. Businesses, for example, often complain about excessive government regulation hampering their initiative and creativity. In the wake of corporate scandals, such as Enron and WorldCom, many individuals and entities recognize the need for federal rules and regulations to protect investors and employee pensions and promote corporate responsibility. (See Box 11-2 on overturning federal rules.)

The Electoral Connection

Some observers suggest that Congress enlarged the executive establishment by passing vague laws that bureaucrats had to embellish with rules and regulations. Regulatory laws, for example, may call for a "reasonable rate," without defining "reasonable." Frustrated by government rules, people turn to their senators and representatives for help. Lawmakers thus "take credit coming and going"—they claim credit for getting programs enacted and then for untangling the bureaucratic snarls they create.[68]

This electoral explanation of overall bureaucratic growth is unproved. There is little support for the argument that members' "incessant quest for local benefits has somehow contributed to growth in government spending." In fact, the most costly federal programs, such as Medicare and Social Security, "deliver benefits as a matter of right, not privilege, and congressmen have fewer opportunities to claim responsibility for them."[69]

Many considerations affect how federal benefits are distributed. An agency may process the requests of the president's congressional backers quickly, while other members' proposals are encased in red tape. Or influential members of the committees with jurisdiction over certain agencies may receive the lion's share of federal benefits. Lawmakers eagerly earmark money in appropriations bills for projects in their states or districts. There has been an explosion of earmarks—designating funds for specific organizations or projects—in appropriations bills. One budget watchdog group estimated that the 2005 federal budget included "an estimated $27 billion to fund 13,965 projects, compared to $17.7 billion for 4,326 projects in 2000, and $10 billion for 1,439 projects a decade ago."[70] Presidential pork is also commonplace as chief executives promise jobs and projects in states crucial to reelection.

Not all federal projects are worth attracting. Members compute the political risks of backing a missile base, hazardous waste dump, nuclear power plant, or other controversial projects strongly resisted by their constituents. Some lawmakers oppose spending for projects even if they are in their own district. Senator McCain is especially vigilant in targeting what he considers to be wasteful spending. McCain's Internet Web site contains his floor statements against legislation containing what he considers pork. Still other members want to challenge unnecessary tax and spending subsidies for businesses and industries (corporate welfare).[71]

Whatever their view of federal projects, legislators must act as intermediaries between constituents and federal agencies. Constituents' problems are handled by personal staff aides called caseworkers. In addition to courting the electoral payoff of effective casework—evidence of the two Congresses once again—some members appreciate its value in oversight. "The very knowledge by executive officials that some Congressman is sure to look into a matter affecting his constituents acts as a healthy check against bureaucratic indifference or arrogance," wrote a former senator.[72]

CONGRESSIONAL CONTROL OF THE BUREAUCRACY

"Congressional power, like chastity," explained a scholar, "is never lost, rarely taken by force, and almost always given away."[73] Congress allows executive officials considerable discretion in interpreting and implementing the laws it passes. This delegation of authority occurs because legislators lack the knowledge and expertise to address the complexities of contemporary society (licensing interstate communications, for example), and no law can be sufficiently detailed to cover every conceivable circumstance.

Congress is often criticized for drafting vague or sloppy legislation that gives executive officials and judges too much leeway in interpretation and administration. "Administration of a statute is, properly speaking, an extension of the legislative process," and therefore Congress must watch over its programs lest they undergo unintended change.[74] Given the size and reach of the executive establishment, Congress's oversight role is more important today than when Woodrow Wilson wrote that "[q]uite as important as lawmaking is vigilant oversight of administration."[75]

The Constitution does not refer explicitly to the oversight role; it is implicit in Congress's right to, among other things, make laws, raise and appropriate money, give advice and consent to executive nominations, and impeach federal officials. Congress, however, has formalized its oversight duties. The Legislative Reorganization Act of 1946 directed all House and Senate committees to exercise "continuous watchfulness" over the programs and agencies under their jurisdiction. Subsequent statutes and House and Senate rules extended Congress's authority and resources for oversight. The Government Accountability Office, the chief investigative arm of Congress, provides the House and Senate with "high risk" reports on the management and accounting practices of federal agencies and departments.

Members understand their review responsibilities. "Congress's duty didn't end in passing this law," remarked a senator. "We have to make sure the law works." Or as Senator Lott said: "I have always felt that one-third of the role of Congress should be in oversight."[76] House Speaker J. Dennis Hastert, R-Ill., has made it clear that he wants committees to focus more of their attention on oversight. The Speaker is "not so much interested in scandal as he is in how departments are being run, what programs work and which don't," said the Speaker's spokesperson.[77]

To ensure that laws are working, Congress utilizes an impressive array of formal and informal processes and techniques. Many of its oversight activities are indirect, ad hoc, and not subject to easy measurement or even recognition. "Oversight isn't necessarily a hearing," said John D. Dingell, D-Mich., a noted House overseer. "Sometimes it's a letter. We find our letters have a special effect on a lot of people."[78]

Hearings and Investigations

Many of Congress's most dramatic moments have occurred in legislative probes into administrative or business misconduct or man-made or natural disasters. Examples include the Teapot Dome inquiry (1923), the Senate Watergate hearings (1973–1974), the Iran-contra investigation (1987), the probes undertaken in 1997–1998 into alleged illegal and improper campaign fund-raising practices during the 1996 election cycle, the 2000 Firestone and Ford hearings into whether vehicle crashes were caused by defective tires, and the 2003 joint hearings into the disintegration of the space shuttle *Columbia* as it was returning to Earth. But Congress's investigative authority is not without limits. Earl Warren, when he was chief justice, wrote in *Watkins v. United States* (1957):

> There is no general authority to expose private affairs of individuals without justification in terms of the functions of Congress. . . . Nor is the Congress a law enforcement or trial agency. These are functions of the executive and judicial departments of government. No inquiry is an end in itself; it must be related to, and in furtherance of, a legitimate task of the Congress.[79]

By collecting and analyzing information, House and Senate inquiries can clarify whether specific legislation is needed to address public problems. They also sharpen Congress's ability to scrutinize executive branch activities, such as the expenditure of funds, the implementation of laws, and the discharge of duties by administrative officials. (The executive branch has a number of ways of not cooperating with congressional investigations, such as inundating Capitol Hill with irrelevant materials or stalling in providing needed information.) And they inform the public by disseminating and revealing information. "Congress provides a forum for disclosing the hidden aspects of governmental conduct," wrote two Senate members of the Iran-contra investigating committee. It allows a "free people to drag realities out into the sunlight and demand a full accounting from those who are permitted to hold and exercise power."[80] Hearings and investigations, in short, are valuable devices for making government accountable to the people. They can spawn new laws or their functional equivalent: unwritten laws that change bureaucratic operations.

Congressional Vetoes

With unelected executive officials necessarily involved in the complexities of modern decision making, Congress has little choice but to delegate sweeping authority to administrative agencies. There are strings attached, however. One of the most popular strings is the legislative veto (or congressional veto), a statutory enactment that permits presidents or agencies to take certain actions subject to later approval or disapproval by one or both houses of Congress (or in some cases by committees of one or both houses). Legislative vetoes are arrangements of convenience for both branches. Executives gain decision-making authority they might not have otherwise, and Congress retains a second chance to examine the decisions.

In 1983, in *Immigration and Naturalization Service v. Chadha,* the Supreme Court declared many forms of the legislative veto unconstitutional. The Court majority held that the device violated the separation of powers, the principle of bicameralism, and the Presentation Clause of the Constitution (legislation passed by both chambers must be presented to the president for his signature or veto). The decision, wrote Justice Byron R. White in a vigorous dissent, "strikes down in one fell swoop provisions in more laws enacted by Congress than the court has cumulatively invalidated in its entire history."[81]

Congress repealed some legislative vetoes, amended others, and employed its wide range of oversight techniques to monitor executive actions. Yet, despite the *Chadha* decision, legislative vetoes continue to be enacted into law. Public law scholar Louis Fisher sums up the status of legislative vetoes:

> Are they constitutional? Not by the Court's definition. Will that fact change the behavior between committees and agencies? Probably not. An agency might advise the committee: "As you know, the requirement in this statute for committee prior-approval is unconstitutional under the Court's test." Perhaps agency and committee staff will nod their heads in agreement. After which the agency will seek prior approval of the committee.[82]

Self-interest requires that agencies pay close attention to the wishes of members of Congress, especially those who sit on their authorizing or appropriating panels.

Mandatory Reports

Congress requires the president, federal agencies, and departments to assess programs and report their findings.[83] Reports can act "as a mechanism to check that laws are having the intended effect." They can "drive a reluctant bureaucracy to comply with laws it would otherwise ignore."[84] The House Permanent Select Intelligence Committee, for instance, threatened to reduce the funds to run the Central Intelligence Agency director's office if the intelligence agency did not "file dozens of overdue reports required by law" within a reasonable period of time.[85] Periodically, Congress passes legislation to eliminate obsolete or unnecessary reports. But, as Senator McCain noted, "Congress assigns about 300 new reports to the agencies each year."[86] By one estimate, executive agencies prepare more than five thousand reports for submission to Congress annually. Occasions also do arise, though, when lawmakers object to the discontinuation of reports that they believe provide useful information to policy makers and the public.

Nonstatutory Controls

Congressional committees also use informal means to review and influence administrative decisions. These range from telephone calls, letters, personal contacts, and informal understandings to statements in committee and conference reports, hearings, and floor debates.[87] Committee reports frequently contain phrases such as "the committee clearly intends that the matter be reconsidered" or "the committee clearly intends for the Secretary to promote" or "the committee clearly expects."

On occasion, OMB directors tell federal agencies to ignore appropriations report language because it is not legally binding. Lawmakers of both parties and chambers (and even executive officials) mobilize to thwart such directives, however. Sometimes they threaten to make all report language legally binding on agencies, thus limiting the agencies' flexibility and discretion in resolving issues.[88] Although there is no measure of their usage, nonstatutory controls may be the most common form of congressional oversight.

Inspectors General

In 1978 Congress created a dozen independent offices for inspectors general (IGs). Since then Congress has established inspector general offices in nearly every federal department and agency. Inspectors general submit directly to Congress reports on their efforts to root out waste, fraud, and abuse. For instance, the IG at the Education Department informed both the secretary and Congress that she had uncovered at least $100 million of fraud in the department's grant and loan programs.[89] "It is the IG's job," said a high-level executive official, "to offer independent analysis to Congress and the public on how the agency and the agency head are doing." Some IGs meet regularly with legislative officials. The State Department's IG, for instance, "meets with congressional staffers at least every other week to discuss his work and, as a result, is often asked by congressional committees to conduct specific audits and investigations."[90]

The Appropriations Process

Congress probably exercises its most effective oversight of agencies and programs through the appropriations process. By cutting off or reducing funds (or threatening to do so), Congress can abolish agencies, curtail programs, or obtain requested information. For example, an agricultural appropriations bill stripped an Agriculture Department undersecretary of his supervisory authority over the U.S. Forest Service and the Natural Resources Conservation Service because of sharp and continuing clashes between GOP appropriators and the appointee.[91] In another case, a House Appropriations subcommittee chairman, angry because the Department of Homeland Security had not provided the panel with reports on its spending priorities, said: "They've just been ignoring us. They'll pay for that."[92] By the same token, Congress can build up program areas by increasing their appropriations—sometimes beyond what the administration has requested.

The appropriations power is exercised mainly through the Appropriations Committees in the House and Senate (and especially through each panel's standing subcommittees). These panels annually recommend funding levels for federal agencies and departments, so they have the money to carry out their program responsibilities. The budgetary recommendations of the Appropriations subcommittees are generally accepted by their parent committee and by the House or Senate.

The Appropriations Committees and their subcommittees, or members from the House or Senate floor, may offer amendments that limit the purposes for which money may be spent or that impose other expenditure restrictions on federal agencies. The spending bills also may contain various policy directives to federal agencies—for example, imposing airline smoking bans or prohibiting agencies from using funds to promulgate or issue certain regulations. Such policy directives are often in the form of floor amendments called riders. "These amendments," wrote two GOP senators, "are an important way for Congress to save taxpayers from wasteful agency spending, and they enjoy a long-standing precedent because of their use by Republican and Democratic Congresses alike to rein in the excesses of Republican and Democratic administrations."[93]

Impeachment

Article II, Section 4, of the Constitution states:

> The President, Vice President, and all Civil Officers of the United States, shall be removed from office on Impeachment for, and Conviction of, Treason, Bribery, or other high Crimes and misdemeanors.

The ultimate governmental check is this removal power, and it is vested exclusively in Congress.[94] The House has the authority to impeach an official by majority vote. It then tries the case before the Senate, where a two-thirds vote is required for conviction.

Only impeached federal judges have been convicted by the Senate. As for presidents, the House impeached President Andrew Johnson in 1868, after Radical Republicans in the House charged that he had violated the Tenure of Office Act by dismissing the secretary of war. The Senate acquitted Johnson by a single vote. President Richard M. Nixon resigned in 1974, after the House Judiciary Committee voted articles of impeachment; he faced probable impeachment and conviction. In December 1998 President Clinton became the first elected president to be impeached by the House. (Johnson was not elected; he became president when Abraham Lincoln was assassinated.) The charges against Clinton were perjury and obstruction of justice. Two months later the Senate voted acquittal on both these articles of impeachment.[95]

Oversight: An Evaluation

Congress's greater willingness in recent years to conduct oversight stems from several factors: the public's dissatisfaction with government; revelations of executive agency abuses; the influx of new legislators skeptical of government's ability to perform effectively; concern that some regulatory agencies are tied too closely to the industries they regulate; the availability of congressional staff; and recognition by Congress that it must make every dollar count.[96]

Electoral, political, and policy incentives also encourage members to oversee the bureaucracy. One of these is the opportunity to claim credit for assisting constituents and to receive favorable publicity back home (the two Congresses connection). Another is prodding by interest groups and the media. Committee and subcommittee chairmen "seek a high pay off—in attention from both the press and other agencies—when selecting federal programs to be their oversight targets."[97] Members on the relevant committees of jurisdiction are also motivated to induce favorable agency and departmental action on pet policies or programs.

Divided government—the president of one party, the Congress of another—fosters vigorous congressional oversight. Opposition lawmakers, for example, may monitor and supervise agency activities and at the same time be on the lookout for ways to bash the administration's policies. They can then highlight these differences ("contrast politics") on the campaign trail per the two Congresses. President Clinton's press secretary complained that House Republicans requested information "not so they can evaluate the effectiveness of the government's performance but so that they can . . . [gum] up the works in order to intimidate and thwart those who might be carrying out the laws as they've been properly passed by Congress." In response, the press secretary to the House majority leader said, "They've gotten nothing from Democratic oversight chairmen [when that party was in charge] but postcards from Hawaii saying, 'Wish you were here.' Now they have to deal with the same type of oversight the Democrats had during the Reagan-Bush years."[98] When Dan Burton, R-Ind., chaired the House Government Reform Committee (1995–2003), he issued nearly one thousand subpoenas investigating the Clinton administration.[99]

With George W. Bush in the White House, the GOP-controlled Congress was less likely to conduct oversight as a way to embarrass the administration. "Our party controls the levers of government. We're not about to go out and look beneath a bunch of rocks to cause heartburn," said Rep. Ray LaHood, R-Ill. "Unless they screw up, we're not going to go after them."[100] However, House Judiciary chairman F. James Sensenbrenner Jr., R-Wis., informed the attorney general and the FBI director that "just because I'm the chairman and the administration is of my party, they don't get a free pass on oversight."[101]

Congressional Republicans highlighted the oversight potential inherent in a little-known law passed by the Democratic-controlled 103d Congress: the

Government Performance and Results Act (GPRA) of 1993. Under the law, federal agencies are required to submit strategic plans to Congress specifying how they intend to measure the achievement of their goals. (The administration also bases funding decisions on how well agencies perform in accomplishing program goals.) Republicans recognize that GPRA gives them "a powerful framework for establishing agency priorities and analyzing how [the agencies] perform."[102] They have urged their committee chairmen to eliminate wasteful and duplicative programs. To make this point a House GOP leader held up a pizza box: "If this were a cheese pizza, it would be inspected by the [Food and Drug Administration]. If it were a pepperoni pizza, it would be inspected by the [U.S. Department of Agriculture].... We definitely have a great deal of duplication here."[103]

On occasion, congressional oversight may not be as tough as some members would wish. Sweetheart alliances can develop among the committees that authorize programs, the agencies that administer them, and the interest groups that benefit from the services. Many committees are biased toward the programs or agencies they oversee. They want to protect and nurture their progeny and make program administration look good. Without concrete allegations of fraud or mismanagement, committees may lack the incentive to scrutinize and reevaluate their programs. This kind of cooperative oversight can dissuade committees from conducting hard-hitting inquiries.

A standard rationale for oversight is that it ensures that laws are carried out according to congressional intent. Because many laws are vague and imprecise, however, they are difficult to assess. Moreover, evidence that programs are working as intended can take years to emerge. Congressional patience may wane as critics conclude that there are no demonstrable payoffs for the taxpayer. Alternatively, oversight may identify program flaws but may not reveal what will work or even whether there is any ready solution.

Each oversight technique has limitations. Hearings, for example, tend to be episodic with minimal follow-up. The appropriations process is usually hemmed in by programmatic needs for financial stability. And statutes are often blunt instruments of control. Other obstacles to effective oversight include inadequate coordination among committees that share jurisdiction over a program; unsystematic review by committees of departmental activities; and frequent turnover among committee staff aides, a situation that limits their understanding of programs passed by Congress.

Critics who fault Congress's oversight may be erecting unattainable standards. Many analysts are looking for what scholars have come to call "police patrol" oversight—active, direct, systematic, regular, and planned surveillance of executive activities. Instead, Congress often waits until "fire alarms" go off from interest groups, the press, staff aides, and others about administrative violations before it begins to review in detail agencies' activities.[104]

Micromanagement

Because oversight tends to be specific instead of general, committees are open to complaints about micromanagement—legislative intrusion into administrative details. Perhaps to the dismay of executive officials, Congress's focus on administrative details is as old as the institution itself. The structural fragmentation of the House and Senate encourages examination of manageable chunks of executive actions. Members understand that power inheres in details, such as prescribing personnel ceilings for agencies. Presidents who oppose certain programs can starve them to death by shifting employees to favored activities. Thus Congress may specify personnel ceilings for some agencies. "It is one of the anomalies of constitutional law and separated powers," writes Louis Fisher, "that executive involvement in legislative affairs is considered acceptable (indeed highly desirable) while legislative involvement in executive affairs screams of encroachment and usurpation."[105]

CONCLUSION

Because of continual shifts in the balance of legislative and executive prerogatives, the age-old issue of executive independence versus congressional scrutiny cannot be settled conclusively. Yet the recent interest in oversight has had little discernible effect on the size and scale of the executive branch or on the main roles and responsibilities of the legislative branch. After all, committees are not disinterested overseers, but rather guardians of the agencies and programs under their jurisdictions. Together with their satellite interest groups, committees and agencies form subgovernments or issue networks that dominate many policy-making areas.

SUGGESTED READINGS

Aberbach, Joel D. *Keeping a Watchful Eye: The Politics of Congressional Oversight.* Washington, D.C.: Brookings Institution, 1990.

Arnold, R. Douglas. *Congress and the Bureaucracy: A Theory of Influence.* New Haven: Yale University Press, 1979.

Foreman, Christopher J., Jr. *Signals from the Hill: Congressional Oversight and the Challenge of Social Regulation.* New Haven: Yale University Press, 1988.

Light, Paul C. *The New Public Service.* Washington, D.C.: Brookings Institution, 1999.

_____. *The True Size of Government.* Washington, D.C.: Brookings Institution, 1999.

Rosenbloom, David. *Building a Legislative-Centered Public Administration: Congress and the Administrative State, 1946–1999.* Tuscaloosa: University of Alabama Press, 2000.

The Senate and House address issues concerning the judiciary (clockwise from the top): Top right, Alberto Gonzales, U.S. attorney general nominee, shakes hands with Vermont's Patrick J. Leahy, ranking Democrat on the Senate Judiciary Committee, before hearings on his nomination. Looking on are Orrin G. Hatch, R-Utah, and chairman Arlen Specter, R-Pa. Center right, Supreme Court justices Clarence Thomas and Anthony Kennedy testify before a House Appropriations subcommittee on funding for the judicial branch. Bottom right, thousands of anti-abortion-rights supporters participate in the annual March for Life on the anniversary of *Roe v. Wade,* the 1973 Supreme Court decision that legalized abortion. Bottom left, Sen. Barbara Boxer, D-Calif., addresses a press conference of the Coalition for a Fair and Independent Judiciary, opposing Janice Rogers Brown's nomination to the D.C. Circuit Court.

chapter 12

Congress and the Courts

"Scarcely any political question arises in the United States that is not resolved, sooner or later, into a judicial one," wrote the famous French chronicler Alexis de Tocqueville in *Democracy in America,* his classic 1835 study of early American life.[1] From the beginnings of the republic, when federal courts handed down decisions that strengthened the national government, to many of today's most hotly debated issues—affirmative action, the war powers, racial redistricting, and abortion—federal judges have been at the storm center of numerous controversies. Bolstered by its prerogative of judicial review that the U.S. Supreme Court asserted in the landmark case of *Marbury v. Madison* (1803)—and the public's perception that the highest court is the primary, but not exclusive, interpreter of the Constitution—federal jurists regularly pass judgment on the compelling issues that confront the nation.[2] Meanwhile, Congress and the White House also interpret the Constitution. As the Supreme Court stated in *United States v. Nixon* (1974): "In the performance of assigned constitutional duties each branch of the Government must initially interpret the Constitution, and the interpretation of its powers by any branch is due great respect from the others."

The American constitutional system of separate institutions sharing power inevitably produces tension between Congress and the courts. While the framers outlined the structure and authority of Congress in some detail in Article I, little by comparison is in Article III dealing with the courts. Thus, the beginnings of the court owe less to constitutional mandates and more to legislation establishing its structure and to the rulings of the early justices, such as Chief Justice John Marshall (1801–1835). As a noted legal scholar explained:

> Congress was created nearly full blown by the Constitution itself. The vast possibilities of the presidency were relatively easy to perceive and soon, inevitably materialized. But the institution of the judiciary needed to be summoned up out of the constitutional vapors, shaped and maintained. And the Great Chief Justice, John Marshall—not single-handed, but first and foremost—was there to do it and did.[3]

These early jurists rebuffed challenges to judicial power and conclusively established the court's right to determine the constitutionality of acts of Congress.

Conflicts between Congress and federal courts are common when the elective branches are called to account by decisions of the nonelective judicial branch, composed of judges with lifetime tenure. A famous instance occurred during the New Deal when the Supreme Court, acting as a super-legislature—making policy through judicial rulings—invalidated thirteen acts of Congress in one term (1935–1936). So frustrated was President Franklin D. Roosevelt that he tried to have Congress pass legislation expanding the size of the Court so he could nominate judges more sympathetic to his program. Widespread legislative opposition to the court-packing plan led to a huge defeat for Roosevelt. Nonetheless, sensitive to the changes under way in the country, the Court soon began to shift its attitude in constitutional interpretation. For example, the Court handed down a decision in 1937 upholding a minimum wage law that only a few months earlier it had ruled unconstitutional.[4] This turnabout by the Court, ending its penchant for limiting congressional power, was, as a wit of the period put it, "the switch in time that saved nine."

CONSTITUTIONAL REVIEW

Whether it is enacting minimum wage, health, or other laws, Congress derives its policy-making authority from two key parts of the Constitution: Article I and the Fourteenth Amendment. Article I, Section 8, grants Congress the right to legislate in a number of specific areas, such as laying and collecting taxes, coining money, and raising and supporting armies. In addition, an elastic clause gives Congress the authority to "make all laws which shall be necessary and proper" to carry out its enumerated powers.

Under the post–Civil War Fourteenth Amendment, no state shall deny any person of life, liberty, or property without due process of law or the equal protection of the laws. The amendment provides that Congress "shall have the power to enforce [these provisions], by appropriate legislation." Congress, as the courts have noted, also has "implied" or "inherent" powers not specifically mentioned in the Constitution, such as its right to conduct investigations as an adjunct to its lawmaking function. Federal courts, however, can impose constraints on the exercise of these constitutional pillars of legislative authority.

As for the courts, Article III of the Constitution states: "[T]he judicial power of the United States shall be vested in one Supreme Court, and in such inferior courts as the Congress may from time to time ordain and establish." Left to Congress was the establishment of the elaborate judicial structure of district and circuit courts of appeals that exist today, not to mention the legislature's authority to create a number of specialized courts, such as bankruptcy courts, where judges serve fixed terms. The Constitution also specifies the "cases and controversies" over which the court has original jurisdiction, such as issues involving the Constitution, federal law, and treaties. In addition, the Supreme Court has appellate jurisdiction (the authority to review cases on appeal) under the Constitution but with such exceptions as Congress may determine. The composition of federal courts is subject to the "advice and consent" of the Senate. Basically, these provisions constitute the core of the federal judiciary.

The judiciary's policy-making role is carried out in three main ways. First, its interpretive decisions can uphold or broaden the legislative powers of Congress. "Congress acted within its authority," said Supreme Court justice Ruth Bader Ginsburg, when the Court upheld a 1998 law further extending copyright privileges for authors, artists, and inventors, such as commercial artist Walt Disney, who created the world-famous animated cartoon character Mickey Mouse.[5] Second, it can check overreaching by Congress through its implied power of judicial review. Third, and equally significant, the Supreme Court can act as a policy-making catalyst, especially when the House or Senate is stymied in making decisions. The landmark civil rights case of *Brown v. Board of Education* (1954) is a classic example. The decision struck down the separate but equal doctrine upholding state laws that permitted racially segregated public schools. Until this decision, majorities in the Senate could not enact civil rights bills because of filibusters conducted by southern senators. The *Brown* case galvanized Congress to enact the Civil Rights Act of 1957, the first civil rights law since 1875. "The genius of a system of divided powers," wrote a law professor, "is that when one branch is closed to the desires of the populace or the demands of justice, another may open up."[6] The *Brown* decision had little impact until Congress began to pass landmark legislation, such as the Civil Rights Act of 1964 prohibiting racial discrimination in public accommodations.

Each national branch of government has the constitutional wherewithal to influence the others. The Supreme Court affects Congress "whenever justices interpret the meaning of the Constitution, treaties, federal statutes, administrative [rules and regulations], and the decisions of [lower] federal and state courts."[7] In turn, Congress has the authority to affect the size, funding, and jurisdiction of federal courts with the Senate directed under the Constitution to approve or reject court nominees chosen by the chief executive. Federal courts issue rulings but they depend on the political branches to enforce those decisions. Alexander Hamilton, in distinguishing judicial power from legislative or executive power, wrote in *The Federalist Papers* No. 78: The judiciary "has no influence over either the sword [the president] or the purse [Congress] . . . and can take no active resolution whatever. It may truly be said to have neither Force nor Will, but merely judgment." Nevertheless, federal courts have issued many rulings that require large financial expenditures in areas such as improvements in prison conditions and mental health institutions. In the area of war, contemporary presidents have taken military action either with or without authority from Congress. Important functions of federal courts in the military arena are to check presidential power and to adjudicate the proper allocation of war-making authority between Congress and the White House.

THE COURT AS REFEREE AND UMPIRE

The Supreme Court serves as both referee between the two nationally elective branches and as the umpire of federal-state relations. Ever since the Court claimed the power of judicial review in 1803 and voided part of an act of Congress, it has considered a large number of separation of power issues, most notably during the New Deal and in the past few decades. Super-legislature, or legislating from the court (the charge of judicial activism), is an oft-repeated epithet used for the Court when it makes decisions that others believe should be settled by the elective branches of government. Someone's view of activism, however, often depends on whether he supports the direction of the court. Decisions that expand Congress's authority to legislate may be opposed by those who prefer matters to be handled by the states. Conversely, decisions that restrict the reach of the legislative branch are likely to be opposed by those who favor a national approach to problems. Criticism has been lodged against conservative judicial activism by the Rehnquist Court, which has struck down "nearly thirty federal enactments since 1995—a record of activism against the national legislative branch."[8]

For example, in *United States v. Lopez* (1995), the Supreme Court overturned a federal law banning guns near school grounds. For the "first time since the New Deal . . . the Court found Congress to have exceeded the bounds of its constitutional authority to regulate interstate commerce"—in this case the movement of guns across state lines that could end up on school playgrounds.[9] Quickly, Congress moved to pass legislation that made clear its authority under the Commerce Clause to restrict guns from school zones. In 1996 it enacted a measure, which the president signed, that said, "It shall be unlawful for any individual knowingly to possess a firearm that has moved in or that otherwise affects interstate or foreign commerce at a place that the individual knows, or has reasonable cause to believe, is a school zone."[10]

Lawmakers are mindful of the court's referee role and seek to employ it for their own goals. Increasingly, members turn to the court to accomplish ends they were unable to achieve in Congress. Often, they ask the court to defend congressional prerogatives against usurpation by the president. War making is the principal example. Not since World War II has Congress declared war, although it may enact legislation that is its functional equivalent. Recent presidents of both parties have committed American troops to combat on their own initiative. As scholar Louis Fisher pointed out with respect to war power suits brought by members:

> From the Vietnam War to the present day, members of Congress have gone to court to contest presidential wars and defend legislative pre-

> rogatives. In most of these cases, the courts held that the lawmakers lacked standing to bring the case. Even when legislators were granted standing, the courts refused relief on numerous grounds. Judges pointed out that the legislators represented only a fraction of the congressional membership and that often another group of legislators had filed a brief defending the president's action. Courts regularly note that Congress as a whole has failed to invoke its institutional powers to confront the president.[11]

Usually, courts dismiss these suits and offer two rationales: (1) the lawsuits raise political questions best left to the elective branches to resolve, and (2) they represent conflicts between groups of lawmakers pitted against each other, not constitutional clashes between Congress and the president.

As the federalism umpire, the Supreme Court has lately taken a more limited view of federal authority in relation to state prerogatives. "The revival of a doctrine of federalism that constrains the power of Congress has been a signature feature of the Rehnquist court, although it is not clear if this will be a long-lasting legacy."[12] The Court revived federalism through use of the Tenth Amendment (powers not delegated to the national government or prohibited to the states are reserved to the states or to the people) and the Eleventh Amendment (states are protected from being sued in federal court by citizens of other states or foreign countries). For example, in *Alabama v. Garrett* (2001) the Supreme Court held that states are immune from suits brought by handicapped state employees under the 1990 Americans with Disabilities Act (ADA). Chief Justice William H. Rehnquist held that states are not required "to make special accommodations for the disabled, so long as their actions toward such individuals had a rational basis." The reason lay in an expanded notion of states' "sovereign immunity" from suits by private citizens—an interpretation disputed by some legal scholars.[13]

Another dispute between the Court's majority and minority in *Alabama v. Garrett* involved opposing views of legislative and judicial powers. Rehnquist asserted "that it is the responsibility of the Supreme Court, not Congress, to define the substance of constitutional guarantees." This claim was far broader than Chief Justice John Marshall's famous 1803 pronouncement in *Marbury v. Madison* that the duty of the courts is "to say what the law is."[14] Evidence of discrimination against disabled state employees had been amassed by congressional panels, but Rehnquist dismissed this evidence as anecdotal.

Justice Stephen G. Breyer, writing for the minority, countered: "In fact, Congress compiled a vast legislative record documenting 'massive, society-wide discrimination' against persons with disabilities." He appended a thirty-nine-page list of findings from the ADA's legislative history. Breyer (a one-time Capitol Hill staff member) went on to remind his colleagues of the constitutional primacy of legislative judgments.

> Unlike courts, Congress can readily gather facts from across the Nation, assess the magnitude of a problem, and more easily find an appropriate remedy. Unlike courts, Congress directly reflects public attitudes and beliefs, enabling Congress to better understand where, and to what extent, refusals to accommodate disability amount to behavior that is callous or unreasonable to the point of lacking constitutional justification. Unlike judges, Members of Congress can directly obtain information from constituents who have first-hand experience with discrimination and related issues.

Federalism cases are filled with complexities. Unsurprisingly, the Court does not exhibit a fixed view as to whether it will read Congress's power broadly or narrowly. Three years later, in *Tennessee v. Lane,* the Court took a different view from *Garrett* with respect to state sovereignty under the ADA. Briefly, George Lane was a paraplegic who had to crawl up two floors to reach a county courtroom in Tennessee because there was no elevator. (Lane had been charged with a crime.) At a subsequent hearing, he refused to crawl up the stairs and was arrested for failure to appear at the hearing on his case. He sued Tennessee under the ADA and won a financial settlement. Why the different outcome in *Lane* compared with *Garrett*? Part of the explanation is that the Court considered a wider range of evidence. In *Garrett,* the Court considered only state employers such as the University of Alabama; in *Lane,* it also examined Tennessee's treatment of the disabled by county and city employers. Significantly, *Lane* involved access to the courts, one of the country's key political institutions. The Court is concerned about access to employment by disabled persons, but it has traditionally demonstrated greater concern for access to political institutions by disadvantaged groups.

Yet another dimension of federal-state tension is the bifurcated career patterns of modern-day judges and elective officials. From Marshall's day through Earl Warren's, the Court typically included members steeped in legislative or executive experience. Today's sitting justices, in contrast, are drawn almost exclusively from lower federal or state courts. (Only one sitting Supreme Court justice had ever held elective office: Sandra Day O'Connor, a onetime Arizona state senator.) The challenge of comprehending the legislative approach to policy questions has plagued the Court's treatment of other politically charged issues, such as racial gerrymandering and campaign finance. As one law professor wrote:

> From reapportionment to campaign finance, gay marriage to abortion, litigants encourage the [Supreme Court] to immerse itself in the political debates of the day, if only to review the decisions of lower courts. Given this reality, shouldn't at least a few of those nine men and women have some experience practicing the subject about which they often have to preach?[15]

Today, as the nation confronts an ongoing terrorist threat against the homeland, it is uncertain whether the Supreme Court's recent tendency to defer to state sovereignty will continue in that direction. "Whenever you see a national emergency, federalism disappears," stated a law professor. "In a national emergency, you give the national government the power to get done what needs to get done."[16] It is the president who gains power during wartime, when the balance between liberty and security tilts toward the latter and not the former.

A condition of perpetual war against terrorists raises a number of important issues: whether and to what extent federal courts will sanction infringements of individual privacy, allow terrorist suspects to be imprisoned without legal protections, permit greater governmental secrecy, and authorize more searches of personal records. After September 11, 2001, federal district judge Gladys Kessler said, "[T]he court fully understands and appreciates that the first priority of the executive branch in time of crisis is to ensure the physical security of its citizens." By the same token, she added, "the first priority of the judicial branch must be to ensure that our government always operates within the statutory and constitutional constraints which distinguish a democracy from a dictatorship."[17] The Supreme Court demonstrated that it can rein in executive power even during wartime when in June 2004 it handed down a series of rulings that denied the president's right to hold citizens or captured terrorists as prisoners without allowing them their day in court.[18]

Congress also must address how to protect the homeland against terrorism without trampling on constituents' civil liberties. The challenge it faces is that partisan polarization in Congress makes it difficult to reach consensus on many issues involving the clash between liberty and security. Polarization on the Supreme Court is also not unusual, as highlighted by its recent spate of 5–4 decisions on the balance of power between national and state governments. (Both *Garrett* and *Lane* were 5–4 judgments.) These and other rulings have raised again the issue of how assertive courts should be in overturning decisions of the popularly elected Congress. Lawmakers are accountable to their constituents every time they face reelection. Although judges are not immune to the tides of public opinion, they do not face accountability through elections. The tension between policy making by lawmakers versus judge-made decisions is perennial. However, it is useful to explore two traditional features of the Congress-court connection: statutory interpretation and legislative checks on the judiciary.

Statutory Interpretation

Communications between Congress and the federal courts are less than perfect. Neither branch understands the workings of the other very well.[19] Judges are generally aware that ambiguity, imprecision, or inconsistency may be the price for winning enactment of legislative measures. The more members try to define the language of a bill, the more they may divide or dissipate congressional support for it. Abner J. Mikva, a four-term House Democrat from Chicago who went on to become a federal judge and later counsel to President Bill Clinton, recounted an example from his Capitol Hill days. The issue involved a controversial strip-mining bill being managed by Arizona Democrat Morris K. Udall, then chairman of the House Interior (now called Resources) Committee:

> They'd put together a very delicate coalition of support. One problem was whether the states or the feds would run the program. One member got up and asked, "Isn't it a fact that under this bill the states would continue to exercise sovereignty over strip mining?" And Mo replied, "You're absolutely right." A little later someone else got up and asked, "Now is it clear that the Federal Government will have the final say on strip mining?" And Mo replied, "You're absolutely right." Later, in the cloakroom, I said, "Mo, they can't both be right." And Mo said, "You're absolutely right."[20]

Called upon to interpret statutes, judges may not appreciate the efforts required to get legislation passed on Capitol Hill or understand how to divine legislative history, as manifested in hearings, reports, and floor debate. For example, prior to House passage in the 109th Congress (2005–2007) of a bill dealing with class action lawsuits, Judiciary chairman F. James Sensenbrenner Jr., R-Wis., and fellow proponents "read into the House record a lengthy colloquy meant to guide federal judges."[21] The courts are debating what is the proper way to approach statutory interpretation. Should judges focus only on the plain meaning of the statutory language or should legislative history be consulted to help judges ascertain what Congress intended when it employed certain statutory phrases?

A group of federal judges, led by Supreme Court justice Antonin Scalia, argues that legislative history is open to manipulation by individual members of Congress, executive officials, congressional staffers, and lobbyists and therefore is unreliable as an indicator of statutory intent. (Decisions by executive and judicial officials are also influenced by the ideas, legal briefs, or written reports submitted to them by lobbyists, law clerks, and others.) Scalia contends that justices should follow a textualist approach and look at the words of laws or constitutional clauses and interpret them according to what they meant at the time of enactment.[22] Other federal judges, including Supreme Court justice Stephen G. Breyer, defend the value of legislative history, finding it useful in statutory interpretation. "It is dangerous," Breyer asserted, "to rely exclusively upon the literal meaning of a statute's words."[23]

The dispute over legislative history is well illustrated by Congress's passage of the Civil Rights Act of 1991. The law overturned, in whole or in part, seven civil rights cases decided by a conservative-leaning Supreme Court.[24] Yet the 1991 legislation was filled with ambiguities, and so lawmakers created their own legislative history during floor debate. A memorandum was even put in the *Congressional Record* stating that the written statement was the exclusive legislative history for certain contested provisions. During debate on the legislation, a Republican senator pointed out the pitfalls of relying on legislative history. His position essentially endorsed Justice Scalia's view that Congress should state clearly what it means or wants in the law instead of in floor debate or other explanatory statements.[25]

Supreme Court justice John Paul Stevens expressed a contrary opinion, saying that a "stubborn insistence on 'clear statements' [in the law] burdens the Congress with unnecessary reenactment of provisions that were already plain enough." Rep. Barney Frank, D-Mass.—who once stopped committee members from putting explanatory language in a committee report by saying "Justice Scalia"—added that, if Scalia's view on legislative history became dominant, Congress would be required to develop a new category of legislation: "the 'No, we really meant it' statute."[26] The disagreement between Congress and federal judges over the utility of legislative history was summed up by the chief counsel of the Senate Judiciary Committee: "The textual interpretation encourages us to write clearer legislation. But unclear bills are still written. If they were not, we would not have this fight over [the confirmation of] judges."[27] Judges who favor the plain meaning principle of statutory construction may still search legislative history to confirm their understanding of the legal language.

Legislative Checks on the Judiciary

Decisions of the Supreme Court can have profound effects on Congress and its members. Cases involving the redistricting of House seats, the line-item veto, and term limits for lawmakers are recent examples. If the court arouses the ire of Congress when it rules on statutory questions, the legislative branch can enact new legislation. Scores of interest groups also monitor court decisions, and, if they disagree with them, these groups are not reluctant to lobby Congress to seek their statutory reversal. Generally, if the court bases its decisions on constitutional grounds, then Congress can change them only by constitutional amendment.[28] Congress has other ways by which it can influence the Supreme Court and lower federal courts. In addition to the Senate's constitutional advice and consent role with respect to judicial nominations, there are four legislative prerogatives that merit some mention.

Withdrawal of Jurisdiction. Under its constitutional authority to determine the court's appellate jurisdiction, Congress may threaten to withdraw the Supreme Court's authority to review certain categories of cases. The cases that promote court jurisdictional-stripping actions by Congress share certain features: they are controversial (abortion and school prayer); they are triggered by state or federal court decisions (the Massachusetts' Supreme Court decision that it is discriminatory to prohibit gay marriages, for example); and they arouse partisan and ideological passions among lawmakers and the electoral groups affiliated with each party. Despite numerous legislative threats to constrict or withdraw jurisdiction, on only one occasion in U.S. history did

Congress prevent the Supreme Court from deciding a case by removing its appellate jurisdiction.

> This extraordinary action was taken by a Congress dominated by Radical Republicans who wanted to prohibit the Supreme Court from reviewing the constitutionality of the Reconstruction Acts of 1867. The acts substituted military rule for civilian government in the ten southern states that initially refused to rejoin the Union and established procedures for those states to follow to gain readmittance and representation in the federal government.[29]

Congress simply passed legislation repealing the Supreme Court's right to hear appeals involving these matters and prevented "a possibly hostile Court from using the power of judicial review to invalidate a piece of legislation that was of vital concern to those who controlled the legislative body."[30]

Recently, a number of lawmakers were offended by certain federal court decisions, and they have strived to remove these issues from judicial review. During the 108th Congress, both chambers expressed strong opposition to a Ninth Circuit Court of Appeals decision that a 1954 federal law adding the phrase "one Nation under God" to the Pledge of Allegiance was unconstitutional on First Amendment grounds. As explained by the House Judiciary Committee in its response to the Ninth Circuit's ruling:

> The purpose of H. Res. 132 . . . is to express the sense of the House of Representatives that the phrase "one Nation under God," should remain in the Pledge of Allegiance; that the Ninth Circuit Court of Appeals ruling in *Newdow v. U.S. Congress* is inconsistent with the Supreme Court's interpretation of the First Amendment; that the Attorney General of the United States should appeal the Ninth Circuit's ruling; and the President should nominate, and the Senate confirm, Federal circuit court judges who will interpret the Constitution consistent with the Constitution's text.[31]

On March 20, 2003, the House adopted H. Res. 132 by a vote of 400 to 17. House majority leader Tom DeLay, R-Texas, reminded the court that Congress could do more than just adopt a sense of the House resolution. "I think that [legislation to limit the court's jurisdiction] would be a very good idea to send a message to the judiciary [that] they ought to keep their hands off the Pledge of Allegiance."[32]

During September 2004, the House passed a bill (H.R. 2028) that barred federal courts, including the Supreme Court, from reviewing cases that challenged the phrase "under God" in the pledge. This bill tracked a similar measure (H.R. 3313), the Marriage Protection Act, that passed the House in July 2004. H.R. 3313 prevented any federal court from hearing cases that grant states the right not to recognize gay marriages. Rep. John Conyers of

Michigan, the ranking Democrat on the Judiciary Committee, pointed out if H.R. 3313 became law—it did not—this would be "the only instance in the history of the Congress that we have totally precluded the federal courts from considering the constitutionality of federal legislation."[33] Members of the House and Senate also proposed constitutional amendments declaring that marriage shall consist only of the union of a man and a woman.

Lawmakers, especially conservative critics of judicial activism, have acted in other ways to curb and challenge federal courts. For example, many members signed on to a House measure chastising the Supreme Court for citing international law in several of its decisions. A bill was introduced allowing Congress to overturn Supreme Court decisions by a two-thirds vote of each chamber. Another measure was proposed to forbid the courts from reviewing the constitutionality of public displays of the Ten Commandments. Congress expanded the work of federal courts by passing a law in the 109th Congress that moved class action lawsuits from state courts to the federal level. And Congress and the courts have clashed over judicial discretion in sentencing convicted criminals.[34]

Members of Congress also employ strong and even threatening rhetoric against federal courts. When federal courts refused to order the reinsertion of feeding tubes for the brain-damaged Terri Schiavo—especially after the GOP-led Congress moved quickly to enact a law shifting jurisdiction for the case from Florida courts to federal courts—conservative lawmakers and outside groups were outraged. Schiavo's death thirteen days after the feeding tubes were removed prompted Majority Leader Tom DeLay to say that "the time will come for the men responsible for this to answer for their behavior." He added: "We will look at an arrogant, out-of-control, unaccountable judiciary that thumbed their nose at Congress and the White House."[35] DeLay asked the House Judiciary Committee to "undertake a broad review of the courts' handling of the Terri Schiavo case."[36] A few weeks later, DeLay said the federal judiciary has "run amok" by overstepping its "authority on countless occasions, overturning and in some cases just ignoring the legitimate will of the people."[37] He blamed Congress in part for not asserting its authority over the courts. (DeLay later apologized for the "inartful" remarks about federal judges.)[38]

Rep. Steve King, R-Iowa, declared that he planned to design a legislative and budget strategy to "put the courts back in their appropriate constitutional place,"[39] noting that Congress has "the constitutional authority to eliminate any and all inferior [district and circuit] courts."[40] The mounting criticism from Congress prompted Chief Justice Rehnquist, in his 2004 annual report on the federal judiciary, to stress the importance of judicial independence and the need to protect judges from political threats because of the decisions they make. Judges "do not always decide cases the way their appointers might have anticipated," he said. "But for over 200 years it has served our democracy well and ensured a commitment to the rule of law."[41]

Impeachment of Judges. Federal judges, like other national civil officers, are subject to impeachment under Article II of the Constitution. They are appointed for life "during good behavior." Only one Supreme Court justice, Samuel Chase, was impeached by the House. This occurred in 1804, during bitter partisan battles between Federalists and Jeffersonian Republicans. The judiciary was the last bastion of Federalist influence after Thomas Jefferson won the presidency in the 1800 election. Intemperate and arrogant behavior on Chase's part, including his having campaigned for John Adams's reelection in 1800, aroused the ire of the president and his Republican allies in Congress. On March 12, 1804, the House voted 73–32 along party lines to impeach Chase. The Senate, however, failed to convict him. The importance of Chase's acquittal by the Senate was underscored by today's chief justice, William Rehnquist.

> The acquittal of Samuel Chase by the Senate had a profound effect on the American judiciary. First, it assured the independence of federal judges from congressional oversight of the decisions they made in the cases that come before them. Second, by assuring that impeachment would not be used in the future as a method to remove members of the Supreme Court for their judicial opinions, it helped to safeguard the independence of that body.[42]

Other Supreme Court justices have either been threatened with impeachment or been the subject of impeachment investigations (for example, William O. Douglas in 1953 and in 1970). Majority Leader DeLay has not been reluctant to suggest the impeachment of federal judges. Nor has Rep. Tom Feeney, R-Fla., who said that judges who base their decisions on international precedents risk being impeached. Rehnquist responded to these impeachment threats by stating that "a judge's *judicial* acts may not serve as the basis for impeachment. Any other rule would destroy judicial independence," given that "judges would be concerned about inflaming any group that might be able to muster the votes in Congress to impeach and convict them."[43]

Fewer than a dozen federal judges have been impeached and even a smaller number have been convicted and removed from office. "The three most recent impeachment efforts led to the removal of Judges Harry E. Claiborne (1986), Walter Nixon (1989), and Alcee L. Hastings (1989)."[44] Claiborne was removed for tax evasion, Nixon for perjury, and Hastings for bribery. None of the three, however, was barred from holding further federal office by a separate Senate vote following their conviction. In 1992 Hastings was elected to the House of Representatives as a Democrat from Florida, where he has served continuously since his first election.

Size, Procedure, and Pay. Historically, on a half-dozen occasions the size of the Supreme Court has varied anywhere from six to ten members. "Generally, laws decreasing the number of justices have been motivated by a desire to punish the president; increases have been aimed at influencing the philosophical balance of the Court itself" (such as Roosevelt's court-packing plan.)[45] Not since 1869 has Congress changed the Supreme Court's size from its current nine justices.

Procedurally, lawmakers have sometimes proposed that court decisions overturning federal laws must be accomplished by a supermajority vote of the justices. Some of the "more extreme proposals have urged that such decisions be unanimous."[46] None of these initiatives has been agreed to by Congress. They are a form of message-sending to highlight lawmakers' dissatisfaction with certain court decisions. Lawmakers are interested, too, in the need for stronger ethical guidelines for judges to ensure their impartiality; security in and away from courthouses in the wake of several murders of judges; the continuity of court operations in the event of a calamity, such as terrorist attacks; and opening courtrooms to television.[47] Justices on the Supreme Court oppose the televising of their proceedings, in part because the cameras might alter decision making and intrude on the privacy of the justices, making them public celebrities.

Recently, concern has arisen about fewer aspirants seeking federal judgeships. Part of the reason for this is pay. "Salaries are far lower [for federal judges] than what fresh-faced law-school grads can make at big corporate firms."[48] Chief Justice Rehnquist said judicial pay is a "most pressing issue facing the federal judiciary today," in part because many qualified candidates cannot afford to serve on the bench.[49] Lawmakers recognize this problem but have been reluctant to boost judicial salaries above their own (currently $162,100).

Constitutional Amendments. On four occasions, Congress successfully used the arduous process of amending the Constitution to overturn decisions of the Supreme Court. In *Chisholm v. Georgia* (1793), the Court held that citizens of one state could sue another state in federal court. To prevent a rash of citizen suits against the states, the Eleventh Amendment reversed this decision. It guarantees the states immunity from suits by citizens outside its borders. The *Dred Scott v. Sandford* (1857) decision that denied African Americans citizenship under the Constitution was nullified by the Thirteenth (abolishing slavery) and Fourteenth (granting African Americans citizenship) Amendments. The Sixteenth Amendment overturned *Pollock v. Farmer's Loan and Trust Co.* (1895), which struck down a federal income tax. The Twenty-sixth Amendment invalidated *Oregon v. Mitchell* (1970), which said that Congress had exceeded its authority by lowering the minimum voting age to eighteen for state elections.[50]

Generally, lawmakers are reluctant to amend the Constitution. Rep. Melvin Watt, D-N.C., reflects the view of many members: "I just think the Constitution has served us very well over a long, long period of time and one needs to make a compelling case before we start amending the Constitution to do anything."[51] However, certain constitutional amendments appear regularly on the legislative agenda, such as a constitutional amendment banning desecration of the American flag. The proposed amendment—which is an especial favorite of many Republicans both inside and outside Congress who view flag burning as highly objectionable behavior—is a response to a 1989 Supreme

Court ruling (*Texas v. Johnson*) that state laws banning flag burning violate the First Amendment right of free speech. Justice William Brennan, who wrote the majority opinion, stated: "We do not consecrate the flag by punishing its desecration, for in doing so we dilute the freedom that this cherished emblem represents." House votes on this proposed constitutional amendment are often scheduled near Flag Day (mid-June) or July 4. The House has passed the legislation several times, but the Senate has never approved the measure.

The issue of life tenure for federal judges is another constitutional change that sometimes surfaces on Capitol Hill. Bitter judicial nomination battles have prompted some to suggest term limits (fifteen years, for example) for federal judges. "If the Senate can't figure out how to reach a [partisan] truce in its battles over these all-important jobs," wrote one analyst, "maybe the best solution is to make the jobs not quite so important."[52] A group of lawyers contends that Supreme Court justices serve too long (18.7 years is the average length of service on the Rehnquist Court), which gives rise to aging justices who may become overly arrogant, out of touch, or too impaired to know it. To avoid the difficulties of winning approval of a constitutional amendment, they propose a complex legislative approach that would "force justices into senior status after roughly 18 years on the high court."[53]

ADVICE AND CONSENT FOR JUDICIAL NOMINEES

Article II, Section 2, of the Constitution states that the president "shall nominate, and by and with the Advice and Consent of the Senate, shall appoint . . . Judges of the Supreme Court." The founders opposed lodging the power to appoint solely in the executive. They also opposed giving it exclusively to Congress as a whole or to the Senate in particular. The framers compromised and provided that judicial selections required joint action by the president and the Senate. The president has the sole prerogative to nominate, but the power to confirm (or not) is the Senate's. Alexander Hamilton, in *The Federalist Papers* No. 66, viewed this division of responsibility in stark terms. "There will, of course, be no exertion of CHOICE on the part of the Senate. They may defeat one choice of the Executive and oblige him to make another; but they cannot themselves CHOOSE—they can only ratify or reject the choice he may have made."

Hamilton's perspective requires modification, however. Giving two elective institutions a voice in the appointments process necessarily meant that nominees would be subject to a political process. Individual senators, House members, interest groups, the American Bar Association (which, since 1952, has rated judicial candidates), the press and media, and even sitting judges all may play a role in influencing both the choice of judicial nominees and Senate action, if any, on those nominees.[54] The fact that federal district and appellate court jurisdictions are geographically based means that senators from those states (especially if they are of the president's party) commonly have a large say in recommending judicial candidates to the White House.

Norms and Practices

Extraconstitutional norms and practices shape the confirmation process. President George Washington quickly learned the importance of the newly emerging norm of senatorial courtesy—an informal practice in which presidents consult home-state senators before submitting nominees for federal positions in their state. When Washington "failed to seek the advice from the Georgia senate delegation regarding a nomination for a federal position in Savannah, Washington was forced to withdraw the nomination in favor of the person recommended by the senators."[55]

Related to senatorial courtesy is the blue-slip policy of the Judiciary Committee, which applies only to district and circuit court nominees. It refers to "blue approval papers that senators are asked to submit on nominees for federal judgeships in their states. For the past few years, both home-state senators had to submit a positive blue slip for a nominee to be considered by the Judiciary Committee."[56] Although exceptions have been made to this policy, it does encourage the president to seek the advice of senators before he submits judicial nominees to the Senate. An array of other Senate practices influence whether any action occurs on judicial nominations, such as holds, the committee chair's prerogative of determining whether hearings will be held, and the majority leader's willingness to schedule floor consideration of the nominations.

An unresolved issue is the balance between advice and consent. Presidents usually favor consent over advice. The Senate tilts in the other direction. "The [George W. Bush] administration seems to think that 'advice and consent' means 'advise and rubber stamp,' " declared Sen. Patrick J. Leahy of Vermont, ranking Democrat on the Judiciary Committee.[57] Adding to the controversy is the lack of agreement on what qualifications are appropriate for service as a federal jurist. The Constitution makes no reference to what presidents or senators should consider when exercising their respective roles. Setting aside the standard qualifications that everyone expects in prospective judges—legal experience, ethical behavior, recognized competence, and so on—an age-old question is whether people should be subject to litmus tests to be either nominated or confirmed for a judicial position. What place should a person's legal philosophy or ideology have in the appointments process? Here, for example, is the approach of the George W. Bush administration.

> The people counseling Bush on judicial appointments are convinced that his father erred in appointing some judges, notably David Souter, who has become a reliable vote for the Supreme Court's moderate wing and cast a pivotal vote for reaffirming *Roe v. Wade* [upholding a woman's right of abortion during the first trimester]. Consequently, Bush's counselors conduct extensive interviews with prospective nominees about their judicial philosophies. Many of the nominees have been active members of the Federalist Society, established in the early 1980s to organize, cultivate and sharpen conserva-

> tive thinking about the Constitution. Activity within the Federalist Society constitutes an important—and sometimes the only—evidence of a young conservative's ideological commitment.[58]

Each party, sensitive to electoral demands from supporters who want judges appointed who share their values and views, confronts a quandary somewhat akin to the one faced by Goldilocks as she sampled the bowls of porridge: Are the judicial nominees too liberal, too conservative, or just right?

Nomination Battles

Over the past two centuries, the Senate has "rejected about 20 percent of all Supreme Court nominees."[59] Most of the rejections occurred in the nineteenth century, with President John Tyler holding the record: Five of his six nominees were rejected by the Senate (see Table 12-1). After the Senate turned down John Parker in 1930, no Supreme Court nominee was rejected until the presidency of Lyndon B. Johnson. In June 1968 Chief Justice Earl Warren informed Johnson of his intention to retire. "Concern that Richard Nixon might win the presidency later that year and get to choose his successor dictated Warren's timing."[60] Johnson nominated his close friend on the court, Associate Justice Abe Fortas, to be the next chief justice. However, when Fortas's ethical violations (accepting private money) came to light, it triggered the first filibuster in the Senate's history on a Supreme Court nomination, which doomed Fortas.[61] Cloture could not be invoked to end the filibuster and Johnson withdrew his nomination for the chief judgeship. The next year, enmeshed in further ethical controversies, Fortas resigned from the Court under threat of impeachment by the House.

Also in 1969 the Senate rejected President Nixon's nominee to fill the Fortas vacancy, Clement Haynsworth, on the grounds of insensitivity to civil rights issues. A year later another Nixon nominee, Harold Carswell, was rejected because of his mediocre record as a lower court judge. President Ronald Reagan's nomination of conservative Robert Bork to the Supreme Court in 1987 sparked the bitter confirmation battles that still continue today. During nationally televised hearings, members of the Democratically controlled Judiciary Committee probed Bork's extensive written record to evaluate his constitutional and philosophical beliefs. Because Bork's nomination came at a time of large public concern about the Supreme Court's ideological balance, and because Bork's views were perceived as too conservative and controversial by many senators and interest groups, the Senate rejected the nominee by a 58 to 42 margin. (Bork's nomination fight gave rise to a made-up verb—"to bork"—which means to attack nominees by launching a politically based campaign against them.)

Even more controversial was President George Bush's 1991 nomination of Clarence Thomas, who was narrowly approved by the Senate on a 52 to 48 vote. Law professor Anita Hill, who previously worked for Thomas, charged that he had sexually harassed her on the job. The charges and countercharges played out on national television during the Judiciary Committee's hearings. Many in the public were glued to their television sets to witness the dramatic testimony of Hill and Thomas. Conservative groups were outraged at the way Bork and Thomas were treated by the Democratically controlled Senate. They bided their time until it was their turn to wreck havoc on Democratic nominees for the federal bench.

In 1995 Republicans took control of the Senate and Democrat Bill Clinton was in the White House. Many of Clinton's nominees never received hearings or waited years before any action took place on their nomination. For example, Richard Paez waited four years from his original nomination before he was confirmed to sit on the Ninth Circuit Court of Appeals. The principal GOP methods for frustrating Clinton's nominees were denying them hearings or floor votes.

During the brief period from June 2001 to November 2002 when Democrats held the Senate because of Vermont senator James M. Jeffords's party switch, they blocked many of President Bush's judicial nominees through holds, blue slips, and other dilatory actions. In the 108th and 109th Congresses, with Democrats again in the minority, unable to control committees or the floor schedule, "they have been compelled to use the more incendiary weapon of the filibuster to stop the Bush nominees they oppose. But the result has been the same: frustration in the White House and rising bitterness in Congress."[62] As one commentator noted, what distinguishes the judicial battles of the Clinton and Bush presidencies from those of earlier eras is that they have come "to resemble political blood feuds, in which each side seeks to avenge the earlier assaults by the other side."[63]

Consent and Dissent

The struggle over who should be a federal judge has intensified in recent years, especially during the Clinton and George W. Bush administrations. Traditionally, little controversy was associated with scrutinizing judges named to serve on the thirteen regional courts of appeals and the ninety district (or trial) courts. Nominees to the Supreme Court often were the focus of sometimes bitter and lengthy confirmation battles between the White House and Senate.

Today, fierce political, strategic, and tactical conflicts between the parties and branches overlay the confirmation process for many judicial nominees, especially for the circuit courts. "The politicization of the judiciary has recently been the most focused, and most virulent, at the appellate, or circuit level," stated federal judge James Robertson.[64] Four main factors explain this development. First, both parties understand that although the Supreme Court is viewed as the "court of last resort," it decides only about 80 cases each year (a decade ago the number was 107). Today, the thirteen "regional appeals courts decide more than 63,000 cases each year."[65] Circuit courts are "playing a more important role in setting law for vast areas of the country. A decision by the 9th Circuit, for example, is binding on nine states, where 19 percent of the nation's

TABLE 12-1 **Supreme Court Nominations Not Confirmed by the Senate**

Nominee	President	Date of nomination	Senate action	Date of Senate action
William Paterson	George Washington	February 27, 1793	Withdrawn[a]	
John Rutledge[b]	Washington	July 1, 1795	Rejected (10–14)	December 15, 1795
Alexander Wolcott	James Madison	February 4, 1811	Rejected (9–24)	February 13, 1811
John J. Crittenden	John Quincy Adams	December 17, 1828	Postponed	February 12, 1829
Roger Brooke Taney	Andrew Jackson	January 15, 1835	Postponed (24–21)[c]	March 3, 1835
John C. Spencer	John Tyler	January 9, 1844	Rejected (21–26)	January 31, 1844
Reuben H. Walworth	Tyler	March 13, 1844	Withdrawn	
Edward King	Tyler	June 5, 1844	Postponed	June 15, 1844
Edward King	Tyler	December 4, 1844	Withdrawn	
John M. Read	Tyler	February 7, 1845	Not acted upon	
George W. Woodward	James K. Polk	December 23, 1845	Rejected (20–29)	January 22, 1846
Edward A. Bradford	Millard Fillmore	August 16,1852	Not acted upon	
George E. Badger	Fillmore	January 10, 1853	Postponed	February 11, 1853
William C. Micou	Fillmore	February 24, 1853	Not acted upon	
Jeremiah S. Black	James Buchanan	February 5, 1861	Rejected (25–26)	February 21, 1861
Henry Stanbery	Andrew Johnson	April 16, 1866	Not acted upon	
Ebenezer R. Hoar	Ulysses S. Grant	December 15, 1869	Rejected (24–33)	February 3,1870
George H. Williams[b]	Grant	December 1, 1873	Withdrawn	

Caleb Cushing[b]	Grant	January 9, 1874	Withdrawn	
Stanley Matthews	Rutherford B. Hayes	January 26, 1881	Not acted upon[a]	
William B. Hornblower	Grover Cleveland	September 19, 1893	Rejected (24–30)	January 15, 1894
Wheeler H. Peckham	Cleveland	January 22, 1894	Rejected (32–41)	February 16, 1894
John J. Parker	Herbert Hoover	March 21, 1930	Rejected (39–41)	May 7, 1930
Abe Fortas[b]	Lyndon B. Johnson	June 26, 1968	Withdrawn	
Homer Thornberry	Johnson	June 26, 1968	Not acted upon	
Clement F. Haynsworth Jr.	Richard M. Nixon	August 18, 1969	Rejected (45–55)	November 21, 1969
G. Harrold Carswell	Nixon	January 19, 1970	Rejected (45–51)	April 8, 1970
Robert H. Bork	Ronald Reagan	July 1, 1987	Rejected (42–58)	October 23, 1987

Source: Joan Biskupic and Elder Witt, *Guide to the U.S. Supreme Court,* 3d ed., vol. 2 (Washington, D.C.: Congressional Quarterly, 1997), 707.

[a] Later nominated and confirmed.
[b] Nominated for chief justice.
[c] Later nominated for chief justice and confirmed.

population lives."[66] The circuit courts, remarked a law professor, are "the Supreme Courts for their region."[67]

Second, circuit courts, especially the District of Columbia Circuit Court of Appeals, are often recruiting grounds for Supreme Court nominees. For example, three of the nine members of today's Supreme Court—Antonin Scalia, Ruth Bader Ginsburg, and Clarence Thomas—served previously on the D.C. circuit court. (Democrats are mindful that President George W. Bush has said that his favorite models as Supreme Court justices are the conservative Scalia and Thomas.)

Third, the contests over circuit court nominees are perceived by many as a warm-up for the impending battles involving Supreme Court vacancies. As Sheldon Goldman, an expert on judicial nominations, observed: "It's very transparent that we're in a high-stakes game, and this is all preparing for fights over the Supreme Court."[68] Conservative and liberal groups already have launched fund-raising, research, and advertising campaigns to be prepared for the expected nomination battles and to influence public opinion. For instance, the Naral Pro-Choice America Foundation was "making a pre-emptive strike with a television campaign . . . that highlights the importance of the court to abortion. The commercial shows a woman gasping as she reads the newspaper headline—'Abortion Outlawed—Court Overturns Right to Choose.'"[69]

Finally, the confirmation battles represent a clash between President Bush and Senate Democrats over who will control the ideological balance of power on the courts. President Bush "has been more consistent and insistent than, say, [Gerald R.] Ford or Reagan" in nominating conservatives to the bench, said a law professor.[70] "If Democrats just rolled over on Bush's nominations," said an analyst, "they would be guilty of oppositional malpractice."[71] There is no doubt that President Bush has been successful in recasting federal courts in a more conservative direction. GOP court appointees "now constitute a majority of judges on 10 of the nation's 13 federal appeals courts" with as few as three more judicial confirmations on key courts giving Bush a majority on all but one federal appeals court: the liberal Ninth Circuit in San Francisco, which many congressional Republicans want to split into several new appeals court circuits on the ground that its workload is too large and cumbersome.[72]

The party label of judicial nominees does not mean, for example, that GOP appointees will decide cases in a way that satisfies Republicans. After all, seven of the nine Supreme Court justices and most appeals court judges are GOP appointees yet conservative lawmakers rail against an "out of control" judiciary. As a journalist pointed out:

> The [judicial confirmation] fight may have more to do with the *kind* of Republican who joins the courts, in particular the Supreme Court. While Democrats are determined to block judicial nominees they see as conservative ideologues, the Republican leadership pushes for right-leaning judges.[73]

The bitter partisan battles and recriminations over judges play out in both the Senate Judiciary Committee and on the Senate floor. The Judiciary Committee is "polarized to a degree that I've never seen," exclaimed Sen. Jeff Sessions, R-Ala., who sits on the panel.[74] Sen. John Cornyn, R-Texas, expressed a comparable view. "I'm very concerned not only about the broken judicial confirmation process, but also how badly it seems to have poisoned relations in the Senate . . . and hurt our ability to do other things as well."[75] Democratic senator Edward M. Kennedy of Massachusetts, who serves on the Judiciary panel, counters that, "What's broken is not the Senate confirmation process, it's the White House nominations process. The process isn't working now because President Bush is trying to stack the courts with right-wing extremists."[76]

Republicans heatedly deny that they are trying to pack the court with conservative activists. They contend that their nominees are highly qualified professionals who represent the mainstream of judicial thinking. These diverse perspectives are difficult to resolve because, unlike the lawmaking process, opportunities for compromise on controversial nominations are limited. It is typically a zero-sum game: President Bush either wins the confirmation battle and Senate Democrats lose, or the reverse scenario plays out.

Several other significant points are important to note about the contemporary confirmation process. Most judicial nominations are approved by the Senate. The approval rate was roughly 85 percent for the period extending from the late 1970s to the late 1990s.[77] Both senatorial parties, however, present dueling and divergent statistics on how each processed a large number of nominations when it was in charge compared with the poor record of the other party when it held the majority.[78]

Recent judicial nominations confront longer confirmation delays. Sheldon Goldman devised an index of obstruction (no action on a nominee) and delay (it takes more than 180 days from the date of nomination to a Senate floor vote) for district and appeals court nominees from 1977 through 2002, accounting for periods of divided or unified government. He found an increasing pattern of delay and obstruction, especially for circuit court nominees. For example, the "average number of days from the date the nomination was reported [by the Judiciary Committee] to the date of confirmation [by the Senate] ranged from a low of 1.8 days for the 97th Congress [1981–1983] for district court appointees and 1.9 days for appeals court nominees to 38.3 days for district court nominees for the 105th Congress [1997–1999] and 68.5 days for appeals court nominees for the 106th [1999–2001]."[79]

A number of reasons account for the delays, especially for the relatively small number of nominees who wait many months or several years for confirmation. Scholars confirm, for instance, that an approaching presidential election, not to mention divided government, usually produces two outcomes: longer delays and more rejections of presidential election-year nominees.[80] A large number of other factors influence whether a nominee is confirmed quickly or subject to lengthy delays or outright rejection—for example, the candidate's race or gender; the position to which a candidate is nominated, especially if it tips the balance of power on the court; the extent of bipartisan support for a nominee; the use of dilatory tactics by senators; the philosophic outlook of candidates; the extent of presidential consultation with senators; the likelihood that a candidate might be nominated to the Supreme Court; and more. President Bush has even offered his own plan to speed Senate action on judicial confirmations.[81]

A New Judicial Front Opens: The "Nuclear Option"

The frustration and anger level over judicial nominees has risen exceptionally high in the Senate, largely over filibusters against a relatively small number (10 judges blocked, 204 confirmed in the president's first term) of George W. Bush nominations. Senate Republicans contend that Democrats are mixing apples and oranges when they say 204 of 214 Bush nominees were confirmed by the Senate in Bush's first term. "When our colleagues on the other side of the aisle talk about the large number of judges that they have approved, they are folding in all of the federal District Court nominees that everybody has always voted for," exclaimed Senate GOP Policy Committee chair Jon Kyl of Arizona.[82] The correct measure, say Republicans, is the number of circuit court nominees blocked by Senate Democrats—seventeen of fifty-two: the lowest confirmation rate (67 percent) in modern times. Over his eight years in office, President Clinton's appellate court confirmation rate was 74 percent.[83]

The best example of a circuit court nominee who sparked unusual partisan acrimony was Miguel Estrada, who came to the United States from Honduras. He was subjected to a "piñata confirmation process," say Republicans, in which the nominee was chastised by critics hoping to "unearth some damning information" about his record.[84] Senate Democrats said that controversy over the Estrada nomination would have been resolved quickly if the Bush administration had supplied "the memos from the Solicitor's Office [of the Department of Justice] while he worked there and that he wrote and [allowed] more questioning of Estrada" at another round of Judiciary Committee hearings.[85] The administration refused to release the memoranda. Meanwhile, Senate GOP leaders forced seven cloture votes on the Estrada nomination to demonstrate to the Hispanic community and others that Democrats were holding back his elevation to the bench. In the end, Estrada withdrew his name from consideration and returned to private law practice.

Furious at the Democratic-led filibusters against several of Bush's judicial nominees, Senate Republicans held hearings on the constitutionality of the filibuster for judicial nominations. They set aside thirty hours (November 12–13, 2003) for the Senate to conduct around-the-clock debate on the state of the nominations process, with Vice President Dick Cheney presiding to underscore the administration's concern. And the majority leader, Bill Frist of Tennessee, sponsored a resolution setting forth a procedure—sixty votes required on the first cloture vote, fifty-seven on the next, fifty-four on the third attempt, and, finally, fifty-one, or majority cloture—to end judicial filibusters.

At the start of his second term, President Bush even resubmitted the names of judicial nominees whom the Democrats filibustered during the 108th Congress (2003–2005), further escalating the tension between Senate Democrats and the White House. One of those blocked by Senate Democrats but resubmitted by the president was William Pryor Jr., a former attorney general of Alabama. Much to the dislike of Democrats, the president bypassed the Senate in February 2004 and granted Pryor a recess appointment to the U.S. Court of Appeals for the Eleventh Circuit; the Senate was in recess for President's Day. (Under the Constitution, the president can make recess appointments to the federal judiciary, including the Supreme Court and to other federal posts requiring the advice and consent of the Senate. See Box 12-1 on Bush's use of recess appointments, which includes Figures 12-1 and 12-2.) The Supreme Court declined to hear challenges to Pryor's appointment.[86] (In June 2005, the Senate confirmed Pryor for the appellate court position.) Bush's recess appointment added to the dismay felt by Senate Democrats about the president's determination to win Senate approval of his judicial nominations without seeking pre-nominating advice from minority members and regardless of the partisan acrimony and ideological strife that his choices may generate.

Upset with Democratic filibusters (and the threat of them) against Bush's judicial selections, Senate majority leader Bill Frist began contemplating a retaliatory procedural action: the so-called nuclear option, later deemed the "constitutional" or "majority rule" option by Republicans. (It was called the "nuclear option" first by Sen. Trent Lott, R-Miss. Because the term implied that something dangerous or harmful was to happen in the Senate, Republicans began to call their procedural maneuver the "constitutional option.") They argue that filibusters impose an unconstitutional supermajority requirement—invoking cloture to end a talkathon—for the confirmation of judges. Judgeships, they say, should be subject to an up-or-down majority vote. Democrats reply that the Constitution authorizes each chamber to "determine the rules of its proceedings," which today means a sixty-vote requirement to end a filibuster under Senate Rule XXII. If cloture is invoked to end debate, then senators have the right to confirm judges by majority vote.

Senate GOP leader Frist and Democratic leader Harry Reid of Nevada devoted weeks trying to reconcile their fundamental differences over how judicial nominees are to be considered by the Senate. Frist, for example, proposed that after one hundred hours of debate every judicial nominee receive an up-or-down vote by the Senate. Reid opposed any curb on the minority's right to filibuster unacceptable judicial nominees. Frist emphasized that filibusters on legislative measures would continue unchanged. A judicial filibuster "is a zero-sum game: you cannot change the shape of a person [as you can bills through

BOX 12-1 Bush Boosting Use of Recess Appointments

President George W. Bush's rate of recess appointments is running somewhat ahead of the pace set by Bill Clinton and George Bush and slightly behind the pace of Ronald Reagan.

Figure 12-1 George W. Bush's Recess Appointments

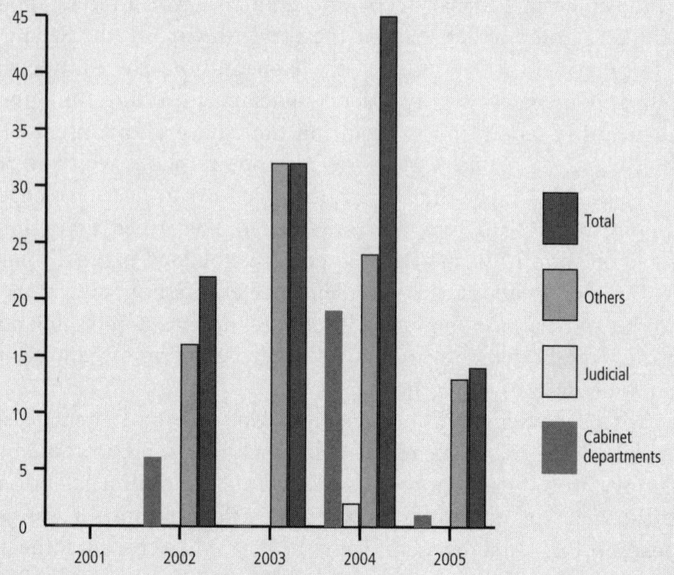

various amendments]. [W]ith the legislative filibuster, the Senate is frustrating its own will; with a judicial one, a minority if interfering with two other branches of government, the executive and the judicial."[87] Opponents of the nuclear option pointed out that it would weaken the Senate's ability to check executive power, undermine the chamber's traditional respect for minority and individual prerogatives, heighten partisan acrimony, and change the ideological makeup of the federal judiciary.

On May 16, 2005, Frist and Reid broke off their talks, with the majority leader declaring that the nuclear trigger would be pulled before the Memorial Day recess. Two days later, Frist called up the controversial nomination of Priscilla Owen to be a federal circuit court judge. Democrats had blocked her ascent to the court for four consecutive years. Timing was an important calculation in Frist's decision to bring up the Owen nomination. The majority leader wanted to have the parliamentary maneuver—called by Democrats

George W. Bush has increased the number each year of his presidency, and the number made as of April 2005 would indicate that this trend has a good chance to continue.

Figure 12-2: Total Recess Appointments

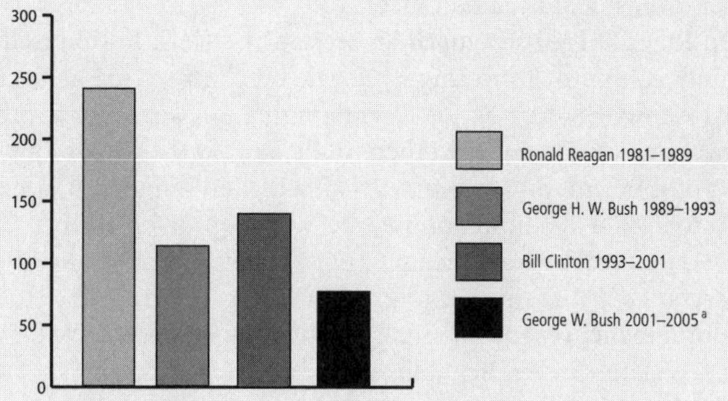

Source: White House and Congressional Research Service.
[a] Through April 20, 2005.

"breaking the rules [a two-thirds vote is required to invoke cloture on proposals to revamp Senate rules] to change the rules"—in place to ensure that the minority could not filibuster the president's future nominations to fill vacancies on the Supreme Court. (Chief Justice William Rehnquist, suffering with thyroid cancer, was expected to announce his retirement by the end of June 2005. Other ailing or elderly high court justices might also retire during Bush's second term in office.)

Majority Leader Frist faced opposition to ending judicial filibusters from within his own party. Sen. John McCain, R-Ariz. (along with Frist a likely 2008 GOP presidential hopeful), did not favor the nuclear option. He argued that Republicans would find themselves in the minority some day and would need the filibuster to protect against the "tyranny of the majority." As Senator McCain noted:

> I say to my conservative friends, someday there will be a liberal Democrat President and a liberal Democrat Congress. Why? Because history shows [that party control of the Senate] goes back and forth. I don't know if it's a hundred years from now, but it will happen. And we do not want a bunch of liberal judges approved by the Senate of the United States with 51 votes if the Democrats are in the majority.[88]

Despite McCain's warning, most Republicans were angry at the "tyranny of the minority" and the Democrats' role in preventing Senate confirmation of a number of Bush's judicial nominees.

On May 23, Frist scheduled an around-the-clock session to demonstrate the GOP's commitment to lengthy debate on controversial judicial nominees. A vote to invoke cloture on the Owen nomination was slated for the next day, but it was expected to fail. Frist then would employ the nuclear option by making "a point of order that no more than a certain number of hours or days is needed to debate a judicial nominee before an up-or-down vote."[89] (The parliamentary scenario would then play out as depicted in the nuclear option box in Chapter 8.) To the surprise of Frist, he never had the chance to execute the procedural maneuver to end judicial filibusters. He was blocked by an ad hoc group of senators: seven Republicans and seven Democrats.

This bipartisan group of moderates, mavericks, and institutionally minded senators had been quietly meeting for days, often in Senator McCain's office, trying to come up with a compromise to break the judicial stalemate and avert use of the nuclear option. Late in the afternoon of May 23, the so-called Gang of 14 signed a memorandum of understanding (see Box 12-2) that ended the looming parliamentary showdown and produced at least a temporary cease-fire over judicial nominations. The agreement, which was to remain in effect through the end of the 109th Congress, had three fundamental features.

First, the fourteen senators would vote to invoke cloture on three of the five most controversial federal appellate court nominees, including Priscilla Owen, virtually assuring the three of Senate approval. The other two would likely face unbreakable filibusters if brought to the floor. On May 24 the Senate voted 84 to 18 to invoke cloture on the Owen nomination. The next day the Senate approved her nomination by a 55 to 43 vote, cast largely along party lines—"a reminder of the deep ideological divisions that persist over President Bush's judicial nominations" despite the deal forged by the Gang of 14.[90]

Second, the seven Republicans promised not to support any initiative to end judicial filibusters, effectively preventing Frist from using the nuclear option and protecting the minority's right to filibuster. In return, the seven Democrats stated they would filibuster future judicial nominees only under "extraordinary circumstances," sidetracking the minority's ability to sustain a

BOX 12-2 Memorandum of Understanding on Judicial Nominations

We respect the diligent, conscientious efforts, to date, rendered to the Senate by Majority Leader Frist and Democratic Leader Reid. This memorandum confirms an understanding among the signatories, based upon mutual trust and confidence, related to pending and future judicial nominations in the 109th Congress.

This memorandum is in two parts. Part I relates to the currently pending judicial nominees; Part II relates to subsequent individual nominations to be made by the President and to be acted upon by the Senate's Judiciary committee.

We have agreed to the following:

Part I: Commitments on Pending Judicial Nominations

A *Votes for Certain Nominees.* We will vote to invoke cloture on the following judicial nominees: Janet Rogers Brown (D.C. Circuit), William Pryor (11th Circuit), and Priscilla Owen (5th Circuit).

B *Status of Other Nominees.* Signatories make no commitment to vote for or against cloture on the following judicial nominees: William Myers (9th Circuit) and Henry Saad (6th Circuit).

Part II: Commitments for Future Nominations

A *Future Nominations.* Signatories will exercise their responsibilities under the Advice and Consent clause of the United States Constitution in good faith. Nominees should only be filibustered under extraordinary circumstances, and each signatory must use his or her own discretion and judgment in determining whether such circumstances exist.

B *Rules Changes.* In light of the spirit and continuing commitments made in this agreement, we commit to oppose the rules changes in the 109th Congress, which we understand to be any amendment to or interpretation of the Rules of the Senate that would force a vote on a judicial nomination by means other than unanimous consent or Rule XXII.

We believe that, under Article II, Section 2, of the United States Constitution, the word "Advice" speaks to consultation between the Senate and the President with regard to the use of the President's power to make nominations. We encourage the Executive branch of government to consult with members of the Senate, both Democratic and Republican, prior to submitting a judicial nomination to the Senate for consideration.

Such a return to the early practices of our government may well serve to reduce the rancor that unfortunately accompanies the advice and consent process in the Senate.

We firmly believe this agreement is consistent with the traditions of the United States Senate that we as Senators seek to uphold.

filibuster. "Extraordinary circumstances" is an ambiguous phrase and soon became a source of some controversy. Republicans suggested that Democratic support of three conservative appellate court justices meant that Democrats would find it difficult to filibuster a conservative Supreme Court nominee. Democratic leader Reid disagreed. "There's nothing in [the agreement] that prevents us from filibustering somebody that's extreme, whether it's on the district court, on a circuit court or the Supreme Court," he said.[91] One of the GOP signers of the accord, Lindsey Graham of South Carolina offered this warning to the seven Democrats: "If one of the seven decides to filibuster, and I believe it's not an extraordinary circumstance for the country, then I have retained my rights under this agreement to change the rules if I think that's best for the country."[92] Adding a two Congresses dimension to the issue, Senator Graham, after receiving numerous critical e-mails and telephone calls from his conservative supporters, exclaimed: "People at home are going to [be] upset with me for a while" for not banning judicial filibusters.[93]

Third, the accord sent a signal to the White House that the president should consult with Senate Democrats and Republicans on prospective judicial candidates. The fourteen senators, led by Robert C. Byrd, D-W.Va., and John W. Warner, R-Va., underscored the importance of the word "advice" in the Advice and Consent Clause of the Constitution. Prior presidential consultation with the Senate could prevent or minimize bitter confirmation fights, especially over Supreme Court nominations. As Sen. Susan Collins, R-Maine, who signed the accord, said: "The White House might have an easier time winning prompt confirmation if it consulted more with members of the Senate. . . . There is a feeling that in the past, the Senate was more involved in giving suggestions and signing off on nominations than it is now."[94]

The agreement aroused consternation inside and outside the Senate, with many wondering whether it would remain in effect for long. "I don't know whether it's something that's here to stay, or just a passing moment," remarked Sen. Edward M. Kennedy, D-Mass.[95] GOP leader Frist, who saw his decision to use the nuclear option circumvented by the Gang of 14, stated flat out that the "constitutional option remains on the table. . . . I will not hesitate to use it" to ensure an up-or-down vote on judicial nominees.[96] Democratic leader Reid contended that the nuclear option was off the table. Whether the promise of the agreement will be met is problematic until it is subject to an inevitable test on a Supreme Court nomination. Ironically, President Bush may hold the fate of the agreement in his hand. "If the president chooses a polarizing figure for the high court, the seven Democrats would face enormous pressure to support a filibuster—and that would pressure the seven Republicans to reverse direction and back the filibuster ban."[97]

Today's battles over judicial appointments, while not a new development in the history of court confirmations, are unique in that they involve a nuclear option with the potential to change the work and character of the Senate. That filibusters are antidemocratic is plain. A majority of the Senate cannot approve judicial nominees unless they can attract supermajority backing to shut down extended debate. However, talkathons do protect political or ideological minorities and encourage or force consensus and compromise.

Many factors help to explain why there is a threat to the fate of judicial filibusters, but three seem especially important. First, the ideological chasm between the two parties is wider than it has been in decades. It is simply far more difficult for the Senate to provide advice and consent for lifetime judicial positions in a polarized environment. Unlike legislation, once the Senate confirms a judicial nominee there is no opportunity for subsequent Senates to reverse that decision except through the arduous impeachment process. A two Congresses component also hampers resolution of the judicial fights. Neither side "sees political gain in compromise. Each energizes its electoral base by standing firm. That translates into money and activism for elections in 2006 and beyond." [98]

Second, a generational shift is under way in the Senate. Many of the newer Republican senators served previously in the House, "where on most questions it doesn't make any difference to the outcome whether Democrats even show up to vote." [99] Senatorial traditions and practices are often less important to these new members than achieving a desired result. "The institution is important," remarked Sen. Jim DeMint, R-S.C., a former House member elected to the Senate in the November 2004 elections, "but the future of the country [as Republicans define it] is what we're here for." [100]

Third, presidents, lawmakers, and others recognize the high stakes involved in appointing judges to federal courts. Politicians and interest group leaders often say they want judges who will not "legislate from the bench." This statement sounds reasonable but in practice it often depends on whether certain lawmakers or groups favor "conservative judicial activism" or "liberal judicial activism." As two scholars state: "Intense ideological disagreement, coupled with the rising importance of a closely balanced federal bench, has brought combatants in the wars of advice and consent to new tactics and new crises, as the two parties struggle to shape the future of the federal courts." [101]

CONCLUSION

Federal courts, like Congress and the president, are important forums for resolving the political, social, and economic conflicts that characterize American society. All three branches of government constantly interact to shape and influence the laws Americans live under. Sometimes, as presidents say, "the buck stops here." In Congress the buck may stop nowhere, and either elective branch may pass the buck to the courts when it is unable to resolve certain issues. "Through this process of interaction among the branches," wrote scholar Louis Fisher, "all three institutions are able to expose weaknesses, hold excesses in check, and gradually forge a consensus on constitutional values." [102]

SUGGESTED READINGS

Berger, Raoul. *Congress v. The Supreme Court.* Cambridge: Harvard University Press, 1969.

Campbell, Colton, and John Stack, eds. *Congress Confronts the Court.* Lanham, Md.: Rowan and Littlefield, 2001.

Fisher, Louis. *Constitutional Dialogues.* Princeton: Princeton University Press, 1988.
Katzmann, Robert A. *Courts and Congress.* Washington, D.C.: Brookings Institution, 1997.
Morgan, Donald. *Congress and the Constitution.* Cambridge: Harvard University Press, 1966.
Noonan, John T., Jr. *Narrowing the Nation's Power: The Supreme Court Sides with the States.* Berkeley: University of California Press, 2002.

The influence of lobbying on the law: Above, in Baton Rouge, Louisiana, a senior citizen talks with former Republican representative Billy Tauzin, president and CEO of PhRMA, the Pharmaceutical Research and Manufacturers Association of America. Under fire for the high cost of medicines, PhRMA launched a nationwide program to assist people who lack prescription drug coverage. Below, thousands gather for the Million Mom March held in 2000 to demand that Congress pass "common sense gun control" laws.

chapter 13

Congress and Organized Interests

"The crush of lobbyists was so large at a hearing of the Senate Finance Committee that the crowd spilled out of the Dirksen Office Building hearing room, filling the corridor and an overflow room four floors below."[1] The lobbyists were on hand to protect the interests of charities, foundations, and other tax-exempt foundations. These groups were facing greater scrutiny by lawmakers who were questioning, among other things, whether tax-free money was being used for expensive vacation trips or huge salaries for group executives and whether charitable contributions were used as tax shelters by wealthy donors. The high-paid lobbyists ($500 or more per hour) who made it into the limited-seating hearing room of the Finance Committee typically hire line-standers who are paid $10 to $20 an hour to wait hours until the lobbyists come to take their places several minutes before the hearing is to start. As one line-stander said, "The lobbyists pay us, and then the interest groups and corporations seeking tax breaks pay the lobbyists."[2]

Capitol Hill lobbyists regularly fill committee hearings and markups, jam into conference committee rooms, and pack House and Senate galleries. These emissaries of organized interests do more than observe congressional events. They wield their vast resources—money, personnel, information, and organization—to win passage of legislation they favor and to reward the politicians who help them. Practically every major corporation, trade association, and professional group has Washington lobbyists. They even have their own associations: the American Society of Association Executives and the American League of Lobbyists. Like many other groups, both are based in Washington, D.C., which is home to more national associations than any other city.

Looking in the Washington telephone directory under "associations" reveals as much about what moves Congress as the Constitution does. More than eighty thousand employees work for various associations. Numerous law firms have moved to the District of Columbia, and growing cadres of consultants and lawyers represent diverse clients, including foreign governments. The lobbying community probably constitutes the third largest industry employer in the nation's capital, behind government and tourism. Several examples of the amount of money spent on lobbying provide a rough measure of special interest efforts to shape public decisions and policies.

A 2005 study by a Washington organization (the Center for Public Integrity) found that, since 1998, lobbyists have spent nearly $13 billion trying to influence Congress, the White House, and more than two hundred federal agencies. "Washington's lobbyists reported billing $2.4 billion in 2003, the most recent year for which complete data exist. That figure will almost certainly go up to more than $3 billion in 2004," more than double the money spent on federal campaigns. "This means two times as much is spent influencing our federal lawmakers as is spent to elect them."[3] The drug industry has "1,274 lobbyists—more than two for every member of Congress."[4] In 2004 the U.S. Chamber of Commerce and an affiliated group (the Institute for Legal Reform) broke a record. The chamber expended $53.4 million on lobbying, more than any other group has ever spent in a single year.[5] The top revenue-generating Washington lobbying firm in 2004 was Patton Boggs. It raked in $30.6 million from clients compared with $13.2 million for the tenth-ranked firm (Hogan and Hartson).[6]

A NATION OF JOINERS

Americans' zest for joining groups was observed long ago by the French observer Alexis de Tocqueville. Americans of all "conditions, minds, and ages daily acquire a general taste for association and grow accustomed to the use of it," he wrote in 1835.[7] During the past decade about 65 percent of the population belonged to at least one organization.[8] All told, the United States is home to more than 138,000 national, regional, and local organizations.[9]

The First Amendment protects the people's right to "petition the Government for a redress of grievances." Throughout American history, groups speaking for different subsets of "the people" have swayed public policies and politics. The nineteenth-century abolitionists fought to end slavery. The Anti-Saloon League crusaded for Prohibition in the 1900s. Movements of the 1960s and 1970s protested the Vietnam War, racial discrimination, and abuse of the environment. Interest groups galvanized support for women's rights and anti-abortion efforts in the 1980s, term limits for lawmakers and balanced-budget amendments in the 1990s, tax cuts in 2001, anti– or pro–Iraqi war in 2003, and Social Security overhaul in 2005.

A free society nurtures politically active groups. "Liberty is to faction what air is to fire," wrote James Madison in *The Federalist Papers* No. 10. In recent years interest groups have grown in number and diversity. In particular, more narrow-based groups focus on single issues such as abortion, gun control, or animal rights. Many factors account for the proliferation of interest groups of all kinds: social and economic complexity; the surge in scientific and technological developments; the government's regulatory role; the competition for federal dollars; and the diffusion of power in Congress and throughout the government, which enhances access for outside interests (see Box 13-1 on theories of interest group formation).

BOX 13-1 Some Theories on Interest Group Formation

Scholars have suggested a number of theories to explain the development of interest groups. Special interests have long been a source of fascination, in part because of their ability to influence policy making even though they may not reflect majority sentiment within the country. The case of intense minorities prevailing over apathetic or disengaged majorities often rivets scholarly attention. Among the various theories of group formation are the following.

- **The proliferation hypothesis** suggests that as society becomes more complex and interdependent, groups naturally form to reflect the country's intricate array of issues and entities. As new conditions, issues, or forces emerge, new groups are formed to reflect or respond to these developments. "The reasoning behind the proliferation hypothesis is straightforward: groups need a clientele from which to draw members."[a]
- **The disturbance hypothesis** posits the notion of an unstable equilibrium among groups. If something disturbs the equilibrium, such as war, technological innovations, the emergence of new concerns (acquired immune deficiency syndrome [AIDS], homeland security, and so on), and the like, then new groups emerge. As two scholars wrote, "Groups organize politically when the existing order is disturbed and certain interests are, in turn, helped or hurt." As an example, they noted: "Mobilization of business interests since the 1960s often has resulted from threats posed by consumer advocates and environmentalists, as well as requirements imposed by the steadily growing role of the federal government."[b]
- **The exchange hypothesis** states that groups form because of the efforts of "entrepreneurs." The argument asserts that "group organizers invest in a set of benefits which they offer to potential members at a price—joining the group. Benefits may be material [private gains], solidarity [camaraderie], or expressive [the reward of belonging to a group with shared values and causes]."[c] The implication is that organized interests are "deemed more powerful than unorganized interests."[d]

---

[a] Scott H. Ainsworth, *Analyzing Interest Groups* (New York: W. W. Norton and Co., 2002), 40.

[b] Alan J. Cigler and Burdett A. Loomis, eds., *Interest Group Politics,* 6th ed. (Washington, D.C.: CQ Press, 2002), 8. See also David S. Truman, *The Governmental Process,* 2d ed. (New York: Knopf, 1971).

[c] Robert Salisbury, "An Exchange Theory of Interest Groups," *Midwest Journal of Political Science* (February 1969): 1. Mancur Olson, in *The Logic of Collective Action* (Cambridge: Harvard University Press, 1965), suggests that many individuals are unlikely to join organizations that may benefit them personally because they will still receive the gains without the costs (fees, attending meetings, and so on) of participating in the group. This is called the free-rider problem. "For Olson, a key to group formation—and especially group survival—was 'selective' benefits. These rewards—for example, travel discounts, informative publications, and cheap insurance—go only to members." See Cigler and Loomis, *Interest Group Politics,* 9.

[d] Ainsworth, *Analyzing Interest Groups,* 39.

For decades the American Medical Association dominated health lobbying. Today hundreds of health advocacy groups woo lawmakers and orchestrate grassroots efforts. In 1975 there were about 90 health groups; today there are nearly 750. "You name a disease, there's probably a Washington lobby for it," said an official of the American Heart Association.[10] Lobbyists for specific diseases sometimes use an innovative technique: placement spots on television shows watched nationwide. For example, they might lobby Hollywood producers to use a story line on television that dramatizes certain afflictions, such as acquired immune deficiency syndrome (AIDS) or Hodgkin's disease. A mention on a hit show encourages viewers to donate money to the relevant health advocacy group.[11]

Some scholars contend, however, that people's civic engagement has declined. Harvard University professor Robert Putnam has argued that citizen participation in associations is on the wane, and he employed a good example to highlight his contention. More people are bowling but they are bowling outside of traditional bowling leagues, resulting in a drop in the number of bowling leagues.[12] "People would rather be alone in front of a television set than out with a group," Putnam wrote.[13] Several years later Putnam presented a more optimistic assess-ment of America's civic life. He spotlighted citizens' engagement in a dozen community-building activities around the country.[14] Other scholars note that, while memberships in older groups such as the Lion's Club, Elks, or Moose are down, membership is rising in newer organizations, such as environmental or youth soccer groups.[15] Many individuals also are using the Internet to form social or political communities. Furthermore, other important indicators of civic engagement—especially volunteering and charitable giving—register increases in participation.[16]

A clear difference, however, is evident in the activity levels of the advantaged and the disadvantaged. A bias in political participation advantages the well-off and the well-educated in U.S. society compared with those who are not so fortunate. Lawmakers hear disproportionately from the former. Each group is interested in different things. The advantaged talk about taxes, government spending, and social issues, while the disadvantaged are primarily concerned about "basic human needs . . .[food], jobs, housing, and health."[17] Elected officials are inundated with messages from groups that represent the politically active (the elderly, veterans, small business owners, for example). Lawmakers receive comparatively little information about the policy preferences of the needy, who often are only marginally engaged in civic life.

PRESSURE GROUP METHODS

Groups have influenced congressional decisions from the beginning. During the nation's early technological and industrial expansion, railroad interests lobbied for federal funds and land grants to build their routes. Some of the lobbyists' methods—offering bribes, for example—helped foster the traditional public suspicion of pressure tactics. In 1874 Sen. Simon Cameron, R-Pa., described an honest politician as one who "when he is bought, stays bought" (or stays "rented" with a long lease).[18] Samuel Ward, the "king of the lobby" for fifteen years after the Civil War, once wrote to his friend Henry Wadsworth Longfellow:

> When I see you again I will tell you how a client, eager to prevent the arrival at a committee of a certain member before it should adjourn, offered me $5,000 to accomplish this purpose, which I did, by having [the member's] boots mislaid while I smoked a cigar and condoled with him until they could be found at 11:45. I had the satisfaction of a good laugh [and] a good fee in my pocket.[19]

Lobbying methods have evolved to become more varied, sophisticated, and subtle. But the move from limited government to big government deepened the mutual dependence of legislators and lobbyists. The legislator-lobbyist connection is a two-way street.

> Groups turn to Congress as an institution where they can be heard, establish their positions, and achieve their policy goals. Members of Congress in turn rely on groups to provide valuable constituency, technical, or political information, to give reelection support, and to assist strategically in passing or blocking legislation that the members support or oppose. Groups need Congress, and Congress needs groups.[20]

Modern-day methods vary according to the nature and visibility of the issue and the groups' resources. Among the most important practices are direct and social lobbying, group alliances, grassroots support, and electronic advocacy.

These diverse techniques typically overlap. For example, business lobbyists regularly meet privately with House GOP leader Tom DeLay of Texas or House majority whip Roy Blunt of Missouri to formulate strategy on the party's issues and goals. The lobbyists then mobilize grassroots support for these initiatives through petition drives, rallies, radio and television advertising blitzes, national door-to-door campaigns, and other techniques.[21] Senate Republicans have their own outreach efforts to the lobbyists on K Street (a street in downtown Washington where many lobbying organizations have their headquarters). Senate GOP Conference chairman Rick Santorum of Pennsylvania is "responsible for coordinating regular meetings with lobbyists who work for firms, while Texas Senator Kay Bailey Hutchison works with trade association lobbyists and Sen. Gordon Smith (R-Ore.) works with in-house lobbyists for corporations and major companies."[22]

Emulating the success of DeLay and Blunt, top Senate Democratic staffers meet bimonthly with "liberal interest groups and lobbyists to seek advice on how to counter the White House bully pulpit."[23] Top leadership aides to House minority leader Nancy Pelosi, D-Calif., also participate in the meetings convened by Senate Democratic aides with various liberal interest groups. Senate Democratic leader Harry Reid of Nevada and House Democratic leader Pelosi in 2005 were "mobilizing Democratic lobbyists to counter Republican lobbyists' efforts to sell the business community on President Bush's Social Security reform plan."[24]

Direct Lobbying

In the traditional method of direct lobbying, lobbyists present their clients' cases directly to members and congressional staff. If a group hired a prominent lawyer or lobbyist, such as Ken Duberstein, Anne Wexler, or Kenneth Kies, the direct approach would involve personal discussions with senators or representatives. An aide to Speaker Thomas P. "Tip" O'Neill Jr., D-Mass. (1977–1987), explained the importance of the personal touch.

> [Lobbyists] know members of Congress are here three nights a week, alone, without their families. So they . . . [s]chmooze with them. Make friends. And they don't lean on it all the time. Every once in a while, they call up—maybe once or twice a year—ask a few questions. . . . Anne Wexler [a former official in the Carter White House, now a lobbyist] will call up and spend half an hour talking about . . . politics, and suddenly she'll pop a question, pick up something. They want that little bit of access. That's what does it. You can hear it. It clicks home. They'll call their chief executive officer, and they've delivered. That's how it works. It's not illegal. They work on a personal basis.[25]

Particularly effective at direct lobbying are Hollywood movie stars, the children and spouses of powerful members, former staff aides and government luminaries, famous sports figures, prominent business executives (such as Microsoft's Bill Gates), and some former members of Congress.[26] "Since I will continue to be active in the Congressional Prayer Breakfast Group, in the House gym, the members' Dining Room and on the House Floor, I will maintain contact with my good friends who affect legislation," a just-retired representative of twenty years wrote to prospective clients. He promised to "unravel red tape, open doors, make appointments, work with the Administration or government agencies, influence legislation, and assist in any other service required."[27]

Member-to-member lobbying can be uniquely effective. No outsider has the same access to lawmakers (or to certain areas of Congress) that former colleagues have. For example, ex–GOP senators who may be lobbyists are invited to attend the regularly scheduled Tuesday Republican Policy Committee lunch "where legislative tactics are plotted on issues ranging from tax cuts to foreign policy," information "that gives them a decided edge over other lobbyists."[28] But some are offended by the entree that former legislators who are lobbyists have to the floor and to other Capitol Hill locations not generally open to the public.[29] Since 1991 former lawmakers have been prohibited for one year from lobbying members of Congress directly, although they may plan strategy and advise others who do so.

Direct lobbying takes many forms. Lobbyists monitor committees and testify (or have their clients function as witnesses) at hearings, interpret Hill decisions to clients and clients' interests to legislators, perform services such as writing speeches for members, and give campaign assistance. The House offers more occasions for contacting members directly than does the Senate, where lobbyists are more likely to target the staff who surround each member. "Essentially, we operate as an extension of congressmen's staff," explained one lobbyist. "Occasionally we come up with the legislation, or speeches—and questions [for lawmakers to ask at hearings] all the time. We look at it as providing staff work for allies."[30] Or, as one of Washington's premier lobbyists, Thomas Hale Boggs Jr. (son of former House majority leader Thomas Hale Boggs Sr., D-La. [1941–1943, 1947–1973], and former representative Lindy Boggs, D-La. [1973–1991]), explained, "Congressional staffs are overworked and underpaid. Lobbyists help fill the information vacuum."[31]

The direct approach is limited, however, by turnover in Congress. Nonetheless, lobbyists are major players in congressional policy making. "Lobbyists contribute a lot to democracy," stated Rep. James P. Moran, D-Va. "They provide continuity and institutional memory. Most of them have been around longer than members."[32] Or as a GOP senator put it: "I would have to say the best information I get in the legislative process comes from people directly involved in the industry that is going to be affected—and from people who represent them: the 'nefarious' lobbyists."[33] Generally, the tendency of lobbyists is to work with lawmakers who share their policy views by providing them with appropriate information, data, and political intelligence.

Social Lobbying

Some lobbyists gain access to members at dinner parties or receptions. "When you want to make an end run, meet someone at a party," explained an experienced power dealer.[34] Because of the public's clamor and members' concern about gifts and free meals and trips from lobbyists, the House and Senate in 1995 imposed tighter restrictions on gift giving. "By themselves, gifts and meals are not sufficient to corrupt the whole system," remarked Sen. Russell D. Feingold, D-Wis. "But they create a psychological feeling that you are obliged. Somebody might not be aware of it, but I think it does have that effect."[35]

Under the amended 1995 House rules, virtually all gifts—free meals, free trips, and presents—were banned. Representatives then complained about the complexities associated with the strict ban on free meals and gifts. (For example, is a gift of a pie or a can of popcorn unacceptable?) This confusion led the House four years later to again amend its gift rules to bring them into alignment with those of the Senate. The Senate's rules include a number of exceptions for meals and gifts. For example, senators may accept a gift, including a meal, if it has a value of less than $50. Senators may not accept a gift, however, from any one source that exceeds $100 annually. Items of little monetary value, such as baseball caps or T-shirts, are exempt from the gift limitation. Neither chamber bans gifts to political organizations or to members' campaigns. Gifts of liquor flow freely to lawmakers' fund-raising events.[36]

In 2003 Republicans amended the House rulebook to relax the ban on gifts from lobbyists. One change permits lobbying firms to provide fancier catered food to House offices (dubbed the "pizza rule" by an aide to Speaker J. Dennis Hastert, R-Ill.). However, criticism of the revision led the Committee on Standards of Official Conduct to issue guidelines on when lawmakers can accept food from interest groups. The committee stated that food "must be refused entirely if the person offering it has a direct interest in the particular legislation or other official business on which the staff is working at the time."[37]

The other change allows charitable groups to pay for lawmakers' travel and lodging expenses for up to two nights if they attend a fund-raising charity function, such as participating in a celebrity golf tournament. Critics have expressed concern that corporations or other entities might underwrite a charity event and then send "its top executives and lobbyists to the event for a weekend of schmoozing with lawmakers." As the chairman of the House ethics committee stated, "I don't want sham charities out there so congressmen can have a nice vacation."[38]

A variation on social lobbying is offering legislators speaking fees (honorariums). Although members now are banned by law from pocketing honorariums, they still may accept speaking fees if they donate them to charities or other tax-exempt groups. Some critics suggest that this arrangement enables members to "obtain political benefits by directing contributions to favored organizations, and some tax-exempt groups are affiliated with politicians."[39]

House and Senate gift rules do permit lawmakers and staff aides to travel on fact-finding missions, attend educational seminars, and make speeches if they are connected with their official duties and the trips are disclosed within thirty days of their completion. Special interests and foundations sponsor many trips to locations throughout the United States and abroad. For example, the American Association of Airport Executives spent about $90,000 to send three House members and six staff aides to a January 2003 conference in Hawaii. "The sessions were substantive and timely, and sure, it was in a warm place," remarked a House member who sent an aide on the trip. "If they held it in Newark, a lot fewer people would go."[40] Business-sponsored trips are on the increase, from more than nineteen hundred trips in 2004 compared with fourteen hundred in 2000.

A fast-growing trend in the business of influencing government is corporate-funded trips carrying lawmakers, their staffs, and often their spouses to attend industry seminars, tour plants, and speak at annual meetings. Because the trips are paid for by corporations and trade associations—and not the hired-guns who lobby for them—such trips are permitted under House and Senate rules. The rules forbid only travel financed by registered lobbyists and foreign agents.[41] (Ethical allegations that arose in 2005 against House majority leader DeLay involved trips he took that allegedly were paid for by lobbyists or foreign agents.)

Members are somewhat wary of overseas travel, however, unless it is on fact-finding missions to places such as Iraq or Afghanistan. "If you travel a lot, your opponent will put a map of the world on the screen and have you, like a ping-pong ball, zigging and zagging all over the world," remarked Rep. Ileana Ros-Lehtinen, R-Fla. No matter who pays for it—special interests or taxpayers—travel can be a political liability, she noted.[42]

Campaign fund-raising events are another important aspect of social lobbying. "With politicians wanting money and lobbyists wanting access, lobbyists are paying big sums to spend time in fancy places with lawmakers." These getaways are legal "because the money comes as a campaign contribution and not as a gift." [43] One lawmaker invited lobbyists to attend a four-day "winter conference" in Vail, Colorado. Here is a chance, the lawmaker said in his invitation, for "members of the PAC [political action committee] community to make a $3,000 . . . contribution to my . . . Leadership PAC." [44] To raise money for their reelection, lawmakers sometimes invite lobbyists to hang out with them informally—on a Super Bowl weekend, a summer trip to Nantucket, or a spring baseball training excursion in Florida, for example.

Coalition Lobbying

"We have no permanent friends or permanent enemies—only permanent interests." This oft-repeated truism helps to explain why "coalitions, like politics, make strange bed fellows." [45] Rival lobbying interests sometimes forge temporary coalitions to promote or defend shared goals. For instance, an unusual coalition of groups—Patriots to Restore Checks and Balances—joined to urge Congress to repeal several provisions of the U.S.A. Patriot Act (passed in the aftermath of the September 11, 2001, terrorist attacks), which in their judgment threaten the civil liberties of individuals. The coalition is made up of diverse groups such as the American Civil Liberties Union and the American Conservative Union. Alliances typically form on either side of an issue to battle against each other. The business-backed Coalition for the Modernization and Protection of America's Social Security (CoMPASS), which included the U.S. Chamber of Commerce, the Business Roundtable, and other advocacy associations, was "operating in 32 states to build public support for President [George W.] Bush's Social Security investment accounts plan." [46] CoMPASS confronted an ad hoc coalition that included the AFL-CIO, the Campaign for America's Future, Rock the Vote, and other groups.[47] It also faced off against the nation's largest lobby—the thirty-five million-member American Association of Retired Persons (AARP)—which opposed the president's overhaul plan.[48]

Coalitions bring advantages—more resources, contacts, and money—to lobbying efforts, but one advantage is especially significant. With the diffusion of power on Capitol Hill, coalitions are better able than a single group to touch all the legislative bases. A drawback is that coalitions are marriages of convenience. It is difficult to keep them working in harness for very long. To coordinate their activities and keep all participants informed, some coalitions post Web sites on the Internet.[49]

Grassroots Lobbying

Instead of contacting members directly, many organizations mobilize citizens in districts and states across the country to pressure their senators and representatives. Grassroots lobbying is perhaps the most effective pressure technique. Masters of grassroots lobbying know how to be specific. Here is what one lobbyist said when he called a sportsman about a proposal to make hunting a nondeductible business expense: "Hello, Johnny Bob? This is J. D. in Washington. Got a pencil handy? Now, this is who your congressman is. This is how you write him."[50]

Interest groups often send mass mailings to targeted congressional districts with enclosed letters or postcards for constituents to sign and mail to their legislators. Legislators understand that lobby groups orchestrate this outpouring of mail, but they do not wholly disregard it.

> Members have to care about this mail, even if it's mail that is almost identically worded. Labor unions do this sort of thing a lot. The congressman has to care that somebody out there in his district has enough power to get hundreds of people to sit down and write a postcard or a letter—because if the guy can get them to do that, he might be able to influence them in other ways. So, a member has no choice but to pay attention. It's suicide if he doesn't.[51]

Lawmakers sometimes have to distinguish between genuine grassroots and astroturf. Many so-called grassroots groups function as front organizations for their financial backers. For example, a group called the Citizens for Sensible Control of Acid Rain was funded by the coal and electric industry to lobby against the Clean Air Act.[52] When the House debated a major telecommunications bill in the mid-1990s, lawmakers were flooded with bogus mail from children, dead people, and constituents who said they had not sent any mailgrams. The uproar from members led to an investigation of the incident by the Capitol police.[53]

Mass mobilizations have become so common that some firms specialize in "grass tops" lobbying. Whereas the goal of grassroots lobbying is to mobilize the masses, the goal of grass tops lobbying "is to figure out to whom a member of Congress cannot say no: his chief donor, his campaign manager, a political mentor. The lobbyist then tries to persuade that person to take his client's side" during talks with the lawmaker.[54] Big corporations may also hire stealth lobbyists—public relations specialists who work quietly to "influence the news media, sponsor grassroots activities and generate favorable scientific reports."[55]

Electronic Lobbying

"Through their computers, [lobbying] groups get to more of my voters, more often, and with more information than any elected official can do," complained one House member. "I'm competing to represent my district against the lobbyists and the special interests."[56] Many lobbyists today orchestrate support at the local level by means of sophisticated electronic technology. As one account noted:

> The mobile telephone allows a lobbyist sitting in a congressional hearing to alert a lobbying group's head office. The fax machine can be used to send out a "broadcast fax" to hundreds of sympathizers with one push of a button. . . . A laptop and printer can be set up at a protest meeting, so that people can type their name, address and a personal message into a standard letter which can then be printed and signed on the spot.[57]

Talk-radio hosts, such as Rush Limbaugh (who is heard weekly on 660 stations by about twenty million listeners), can trigger an outpouring of letters, telegrams, e-mails, and faxes to lawmakers. The potent combination of technology and politics makes "it easier to organize and send a political message across the country at warp speed."[58] Electronic outreach is now incorporated into the advocacy efforts of numerous special interests.

Many groups use computers to identify supporters, target specific constituencies, recruit people, or generate personalized mass mailings. Cyber-lobbying through the Internet is fast becoming an important form of grassroots activism. For example, opponents of a ban on indecent material online rallied Internet users and "orchestrated 20,000 phone, fax or e-mail messages to House and Senate offices in a single day."[59] With the emergence of interactive Web sites, lobbyists can communicate directly with prospective supporters, recruit volunteers, assign tasks, and get immediate feedback on any issue.[60]

With various software programs, computer users—students and homemakers as well as business professionals and interest groups—can send targeted letters to scores of lawmakers or organize a "billion byte march" on Capitol Hill.[61] Worried about cuts in their Medicare fees, doctors organized an e-mail campaign, which included a nationwide network of patients, to lobby lawmakers to "help stop the cuts."[62]

Rep. Jesse L. Jackson Jr., D-Ill., may be the only member to use his Web site (jessejacksonjr.org) to create an electronic network of outside political activists and organizations to lobby Congress on behalf of his policies they support. His e-mail network of external allies can quickly be mobilized to launch lobbying blitzes. Members will be "getting ready to do something against my bill, and I'll go straight to the computer and I'll say, 'All right, folks, we're having a problem over here,' " explained Representative Jackson. "And then, whoomp!"[63] Scores of e-mails, faxes, letters, personal visits, and telephone calls will inundate lawmakers' offices.

A subtle form of electronic lobbying occurs when advocacy groups purchase or establish newspapers and buy radio and television stations to disseminate their views, blurring the "distinction between legitimate media and propaganda to promote their causes."[64] The National Rifle Association (NRA), for example, believes that more advocacy groups will emulate traditional media formats or buy radio stations to present their views to the general public without identifying them as NRA-owned. As NRA's executive director said: "We wouldn't need to any more than NBC needs a disclaimer that it's General Electric-produced or than ABC needs a disclaimer saying it's Disney-produced." He added: "We have as much right to be at the table delivering news and information to the American public as anyone else does."[65]

GROUPS AND THE ELECTORAL CONNECTION

In the fall of 1995 an unusual event occurred. A group of congressional candidates descended on Capitol Hill to learn how to win elections. What made the group unusual was its members. They were not Democratic or Republican recruits but members of the National Federation of Independent Business, an organization that had handpicked them to run for Congress. "It's the final stage of sophistication when [interest groups] train their members to actually run for office," declared a business PAC official.[66] Labor unions, as well as business groups, are making the electoral connection (see Box 13-2 on union workers trained as lobbyists). Today, it is often hard to differentiate the role of interest groups and political parties in electoral politics. "The standard distinction between interest groups and parties used to be that parties were committed to winning elections and that pressure groups let elections happen and then tried to influence the people who got elected," remarked a political scientist. "Now interest groups through their PACs and a variety of other methods are very much involved in the pre-policy arena."[67]

Congressional party leaders and their allied interest groups also connect electorally when they work together to promote the party's message and thereby encourage voters to back preferred candidates in the next election. For instance, the National Association of Manufacturers coordinated with House GOP leaders to generate public support for President George W. Bush's tax-cut proposals. As commonly occurs on Capitol Hill, they assembled a group of average Americans to communicate the point that the tax cuts benefit all taxpayers and not just the well-to-do as the Democrats and their interest group supporters argued in their message offensive.[68]

Interest groups help reelect members to Congress in three other ways. They raise funds and make financial contributions through political action committees, they conduct their own independent campaigns for or against issues and candidates, and they rate the voting record of legislators.

BOX 13-2 Union Workers Trained as Lobbyists

The United Steel Workers brings a group of legislative interns to the capital several times a year. It pays them what they make in their normal jobs plus expense allowances, lodges them in hotels, and gives them desks in the Steel Workers' offices near Dupont Circle. The visitors are technically on sabbaticals authorized by the union's collective bargaining agreements.

The program combines schooling and work. Interns often are sent to Capitol Hill to track down lawmakers or congressional aides to make the union's case on legislative issues. During a typical week, they also study congressional procedures and history, attend hearings, and observe union policy meetings. The purpose is to give rank-and-file workers a deeper knowledge of Congress and to inspire activism at the local level. The union hopes its interns will go home more politically savvy and better prepared to rally coworkers on union issues and at election time.

The steel union's program is unusual in intensity, length, and agenda. The union wants to bolster its grassroots efforts and deepen its pool of potential candidates for elected offices. A spokesman for the Steel Workers said the union hopes the six-year-old program will "get more plumbers and steamfitters and electricians into public office."

Source: Adapted from Matthew Tully, "Union Program Fields Blue-Collar Washington Lobbyists," *CQ Daily Monitor,* March 29, 1999, 7.

Groups and Campaign Fund-Raising

Legislators who dislike raising money—seemingly a majority of them—turn to lobbyists or professional fund-raisers to sponsor parties, luncheons, dinners, or other social events where admission is charged. Lobbyists buy tickets or supply lists of people who should be invited.

Fund-raising events have consumed more and more of legislators' limited time and created new scheduling conflicts—further evidence of the imperatives of the two Congresses, the representative assembly and the lawmaking institution. Members cannot chase money and vote on bills at the same time. To minimize these conflicts between members' electoral and lawmaking responsibilities, "windows" are opened in the Senate schedule.

> A window is a period of time in which it is understood that there will be no roll-call votes. Senators are assured that they won't be embarrassed by being absent for a recorded vote. Windows usually occur between six and eight in the evening, which is the normal time for holding fundraising cocktail parties.[69]

Veteran senator Robert C. Byrd, D-W.Va., complained that members must spend more time raising money than legislating.[70] A former senator said that he "had to become an expert [at fund raising] to survive in California politics."

He described three principles of raising money based on his experiences. First, "people who give once are likely to give again." If you stop asking, they will stop giving or give to someone else. Second, "it's a compliment . . . to ask someone for a large sum." Third, "people who have given to other causes may give to yours." For this reason, "keep track of all who give what to whom."[71] Congressional critics, and even legislators and lobbyists, question the propriety of fund-raising practices. Members are concerned about implied obligations when they accept help or money from groups. For their part, lobbyists resent pressure from members to give repeatedly to congressional campaigns.

Journalists and campaign reform groups often posit a direct linear correlation between a member's vote and the amount he has received from various groups. The Center for Responsive Politics, a nonprofit research group, analyzed fourteen heavily lobbied votes and found that "corporations that poured money into Congress typically got the votes they wanted."[72] The nonpartisan Center for Public Integrity also reported that "lawmakers devote themselves to protecting the industries that do them favors and pay for their campaigns."[73]

Other researchers have had a hard time proving such a cause-and-effect relationship. For one thing, groups tend to give money to members who are already favorably disposed to their objectives. Contributions cement a relationship more often than they create one. Moreover, the influence of money must be weighed against other considerations that influence how members vote. These include constituency pressures, party ties, friendship with fellow legislators or lobbyists, conscience, and personal idiosyncrasies and prejudices. As Rep. Barney Frank, D-Mass., put it:

> Votes will beat money any day. Any politician forced to choose between his campaign contributions and strong public sentiment is going to vote public sentiment. Campaign contributions are fungible, you can get new ones. You can't get new voters.[74]

Access is another matter. "There is no question—if you give a lot of money, you will get a lot of access. All you have to do is send in the check," explained one corporate executive.[75]

Groups and Advocacy Campaigns

To win, congressional candidates must broaden their sights beyond their partisan opponents to well-funded issue advocacy media campaigns. "We don't just run against our opponent anymore," explained the political adviser to a senator. "We run against anybody who wants to come in and run ads."[76] Lobbyists also organize congressional staff focus groups to determine what arguments will most appeal to lawmakers.[77] The president of a telephone trade association underscored the importance of keeping congressional staffers informed. He even organized a retreat for congressional aides, in part to glean political intelligence about how best to frame his association's issues on Capitol Hill.[78]

Something like reverse lobbying also occurs. Lawmakers try to pass legislation designed to appeal to the outside groups aligned with their partisan and policy objectives. To ensure that a minimum wage bill (backed by organized labor) would be made palatable to corporate and small business interests (traditional GOP supporters), Newt Gingrich, R-Ga., then House Speaker, met with officials of the National Federation of Independent Business: "So you guys need to tell us items on your agenda" that will make this bill acceptable. "Just give us the list."[79] In short, lawmakers now lobby the lobbyists. They aggressively solicit from their interest group allies legislative input as well as campaign funds.

GOP congressional leaders also closely monitor the hiring practices of Washington-based special interests. Called the "K Street Project," GOP leaders pressure lobbying firms to hire Republicans over Democrats for plum positions. The pressure on corporations and associations to hire more Republicans for their top lobbying posts began in the mid-1990s as a way to minimize the influence of Democrats in the lobbying community after their party lost the House after four consecutive decades of majority control. The hiring pressure is especially intense now that the GOP controls the House, Senate, and the White House. "My perspective is, we want to have people at . . . associations who will be receptive to our message and be fair to our proposals," exclaimed Senate GOP Conference chairman Rick Santorum.[80] In mid-May 2005, House minority leader Nancy Pelosi unveiled a package of changes titled "Setting a New Ethical Standard for the House." One of her recommendations called for "an end to the 'K Street Project' by prohibiting Members and staff from taking or withholding action 'on the basis of partisan affiliation.' "[81]

Rating Legislators

About a hundred groups keep pressure on legislators by issuing report cards on their voting records. Groups select major issues and then publicize the members' scores (on a scale of zero to one hundred) based on their right or wrong votes on those issues. Members are often warned by colleagues that certain votes will be scored. "You'll hear this as you walk into the chamber: 'This is going to be a scored vote. The environmentalists are going to score this vote, or the AFL-CIO is going to score this vote,' " stated Rep. Joel Hefley, R-Colo.[82] Congressional aides also telephone lobbying groups to determine if certain votes will be scored.

Scorecards not only attract the attention of lawmakers, but they also are used by interest groups to influence members' decisions on selected issues. The liberal Americans for Democratic Action and the conservative American Conservative Union issue score-based ratings that are well known and widely used. One must beware of the ratings game, however. It is always simplistic. The selected issues often are biased, self-serving, and in any case inadequate to judge a member's record. Group strategists, however, defend ratings as "a shorthand way for voters to tell something about their congressman."[83] Many groups that target members for electoral assistance or defeat assign them attention-getting names based on their scorecards: "heroes and zeroes" (from consumer advocates) or the "dirty dozen" (environmental polluters).

Groups use legislative scorecards to determine which candidates will win endorsements and which will receive campaign contributions. Incumbents who hold closely contested seats are usually careful when casting their votes. As a lawmaker who represents a marginal district once said, "If I cast a vote, I might have to answer for it. It may be an issue in the next campaign. Over and over I have to have a response to the question: Why did you do that?"[84] Some of the groups that rate lawmakers maintain Web sites where visitors can register "how they would have voted on the scorecard issues and then compare their own voting record to that of their senators or representatives."[85]

GROUPS AND LEGISLATIVE POLITICS

The lobbyist's job is time-consuming because power in Congress is diffused. "Instead of selling his idea to a few senior members," observed one lobbyist, "he must work all members of a committee, on both sides of the aisle, and repeat that work when legislation reaches the floor."[86] Reflecting on the changing styles of modern lobbying, a lawyer-lobbyist said:

> Because of the increasing sophistication of staff, you have to be armed with facts, precedents and legal points. Sure it's a political environment, but it's much more substantive. The old-style, pat-'em-on-the-back lobbyist is gone, or at least going.[87]

An annual survey conducted by the American League of Lobbyists underscored this observation. Lobbyists rated "good information/analysis" given directly to the member as the most effective way to influence a lawmaker.[88]

An open, decentralized institution, Congress affords lobbyists multiple opportunities to shape the fate of legislation. Groups affect, directly or indirectly, virtually every feature of the congressional environment, such as committee activities, legislative agendas, and floor decision making.

Lobbyists and Committees

Many congressional committees reflect the concerns of specific groups, such as farmers, teachers, or veterans. As long as an outside group wields political clout, Congress is unlikely to eliminate the committee it supports. Members, too, seek assignments to prestigious panels, because they provide a good perch from which to raise money from political action committees. In campaigning for choice committee assignments, legislators sometimes enlist the support of outside organizations. Lobbyists also encourage friendly legislators to bid for committees and subcommittees that handle issues important to their group's interests.

At committee hearings lobbyists employ the usual techniques to win support for their issues. They enlist the assistance of their allies on committees and encourage favorite witnesses to testify. Finding a celebrity witness ensures members' attendance and media attention. An official of a health advocacy group made this observation:

> Let me tell you, at hearings where Elizabeth Taylor has testified about AIDS, there wasn't a seat in the house. There were members there not even on the committee. The minute she left, they left.[89]

Committees often form alliances with the bureaucrats and lobbyists who regularly testify before them and with whom members and staff aides periodically meet. Scholars and journalists use the term *subgovernment* for the three-way, policy-making alliances of committees, executive agencies, and interest groups.

These triangular relationships dominate policy arenas less today than in the past. Other contending forces (citizens groups, aggressive journalists, assertive presidents) have ended their policy monopoly. Fluid issue networks, in which diverse participants and groups influence decision making, better characterize the relationships within and among policy domains. When Democrats ruled Capitol Hill, favored clusters of interest groups embraced such issues as welfare programs, environmental protection, and civil rights. With the GOP in charge, the insiders tend to represent such interests as small business, the family lobby, and the military. But many lobbying clusters—for example, big business and veterans—seem equally at home with both political parties. A few committees even have a formal staff position, such as "director of coalitions," that works with "various coalitions that back legislation" advocated by the committee.[90]

Lobbyists and Legislation

Lobbyists are active throughout all phases of the legislative process. During the committee phase, they draft bills and amendments for members and testify at hearings. They often "help the policy-making process by pointing out how different industries and regions might be affected by various provisions, perhaps in ways unintended by those who drafted them."[91] Sometimes groups blanket Capitol Hill with materials or devices to make a point. The Sierra Club, for instance, sent Hill offices a letter with a condom attached. "I'm sending you this condom," wrote the club's president, "to reinforce our message that international family planning programs, free speech, and environmental protection deserve extra protection."[92] Another group, opposed to a bill titled the Clear Skies Act, sent lawmakers heart-shaped boxes of Valentine's Day candy with the message: "Clearly a sweetheart deal for polluters."[93]

When measures reach the House and Senate floor, groups focus on influencing votes. They prepare arguments for and against expected floor amendments, work to round up their supporters for key votes, draft floor statements and amendments, and plan strategy with friendly lawmakers. "Our approach is a political campaign-approach," stated one lobbyist, including the use of nightly tracking polls to assess how public opinion was influencing lawmakers' views.[94]

Lobbyists and lawmakers also understand that the wording of legislation can be all-important. The deletion of one word—*nonprofit*—from an obscure passage of a four-hundred-page welfare bill produced an immediate scramble for federal dollars. For-profit orphanages competed with nonprofit foster homes "for the billions of dollars that the Government spends each year to support poor children who are taken away from homes judged unfit."[95] Regularly, on behalf of the interests they represent, lobbyists supply lawmakers with the exact legislative language they want enacted into law. For their part, members sponsor bills and amendments that win them group support—again, the two Congresses at work.

On the one hand, groups help to frame Congress's policy and oversight agenda by pushing the House and Senate to address their concerns. Many legislative preoccupations of the past several decades—civil rights, abortion, environmental and consumer protection, deregulation, and child care among them—reflect vigorous lobbying. On the other hand, a lobbyist's job is often to stop things from happening. "Most of the stuff that we do in this business is protection—negative stuff," stated a Washington lobbyist. "For the most part, it's stop this regulation, stop that tax, stop this crazy scheme," including using the courts to challenge or bolster executive or legislative actions.[96] Often, lobbyists exercise more influence on obscure issues compared with topics that receive substantial public and press attention.

INFORMAL GROUPS OF MEMBERS

Congress always has had informal groups, caucuses, coalitions, clubs, alliances, blocs, and cliques. What makes today's informal congressional groups different from earlier ones is their greater number (more than three hundred in the early 2000s), diversity, and capacity to monitor developments that affect their interests.[97]

Some state delegations, often including House and Senate members, meet frequently on either a partisan or bipartisan basis. At a weekly breakfast or lunch they discuss state and national issues and internal congressional politics, plan strategies to capture their share of federal funds and projects, champion colleagues for coveted committee assignments, or back candidates for party leadership positions.

Types of Groups

Many informal congressional groups have ties with outside interests. For example, the Steel Caucus maintains links with the steel industry and the

Textile Caucus with textile manufacturers. Interest groups can be instrumental in forming these informal legislative entities. The idea for the Mushroom Caucus (to protect mushroom producers from foreign imports) originated at a May 1977 luncheon for House members, which was sponsored by the American Mushroom Institute.[98] The black, Hispanic, Asian, and women's caucuses were established to give their national constituencies—and the members themselves—more recognition and clout in Congress.

Other groups have a regional purpose. Members of the Northeast-Midwest Congressional Coalition want to retain their share of energy supplies, encourage federal aid to cities, and promote manufacturing in the Frost Belt states. The Sunbelt Caucus, a southern representative explained, was established in 1979 "in large part to counter lobbying and information-disseminating activities of the Northeast-Midwest Coalition."[99] Each move to protect a region's interests is likely to prompt a countermove from another region.

Caucuses also are formed to focus on issues that overlap several committees' jurisdictions or that fail to receive sufficient committee attention. Sometimes caucuses can buttress their members' strength back home. The House Coal Caucus offered its initiator, Rep. Nick J. Rahall II, D-W.Va., significant political benefits in his coal-producing district, revealing another aspect of the two Congresses.

Legislative Effect of Informal Groups

The effect of informal groups on policy making is not clear. Some legislators believe they undermine party unity and lead to the balkanization of the institution. Nonetheless, informal groups can shape Congress's policy agenda and influence policy making. For example, members of Congress who are on the Internet Caucus—many from rural areas—have been instrumental in shaping telecommunications legislation. The rural members of this caucus want to ensure that their constituencies are not left behind technologically. "There is a common theme with the belief that telecommunications can be a bridge for rural areas into the American economic mainstream," remarked Rep. Rick Boucher, D-Va., cochairman of the Internet Caucus.[100] To be sure, caucus members want to attract high-tech industries to their states or districts.

Informal groups serve as contact points for liaison officers in the executive branch. They provide executive and White House officials with information and can play an essential role in coordinating a legislative strategy and building coalitions. Caucuses permit members to discuss common strategies and join with other groups to pass or defeat legislation. Finally, caucuses enable lawmakers to align themselves publicly with a cause or interest. For many, these memberships are simply another way of taking a position. Paradoxically, informal groups foster both decentralizing and integrative tendencies in Congress.[101]

REGULATION OF LOBBYING

For more than one hundred years Congress intermittently considered ways to regulate lobbying—a right protected by the First Amendment: "the right of the people . . . to petition the Government for a redress of grievances." Not until 1946, however, did Congress enact its first comprehensive lobbying law, the Federal Regulation of Lobbying Act (Title III of the Legislative Reorganization Act of that year). This law's ineffectiveness finally led to passage of the Lobby Disclosure Act of 1995. (A "Guide to the Lobbying Disclosure Act" can be found on the Web site of the clerk of the U.S. House of Representatives: http://clerk.house.gov.)

The 1946 Lobbying Law

The main objective of the 1946 act was to disclose lobbying activities to the public. Persons trying to influence Congress were required to register with the clerk of the House or the secretary of the Senate and to report quarterly on the amount of money received and spent for lobbying. The law's authors, although loath to propose direct control of lobbying, believed that "professionally inspired efforts to put pressure upon Congress cannot be conducive to well-considered legislation." Hence the law stressed registration and reporting.

> The availability of information regarding organized groups and full knowledge of their expenditures for influencing legislation, their membership and the source of contributions to them of large amounts of money, would prove helpful to Congress in evaluating their representations without impairing the rights of any individual or group freely to express its opinion to the Congress.[102]

The lobby law soon proved ineffective. In 1954 the Supreme Court upheld its constitutionality, but the decision *(United States v. Harriss)* significantly weakened the law. First, the Court said that only lobbyists paid to represent someone else must register, exempting lobbyists who spent their own money. Second, the Court held that registration applied only to persons whose "principal purpose" was to influence legislation. As a result, many trade associations, labor unions, professional organizations, consumer groups, and Washington lawyers avoided registering because lobbying was not their principal activity. Some lobbyists claimed immunity from the law on the pretext that their job was to inform, not influence, legislators. Finally, the Court held that the act applied only to lobbyists who contacted members directly. This interpretation excluded indirect lobbying activities that, for example, generated grassroots pressure on Congress.

Lawmakers tried repeatedly to plug the loopholes of the 1946 law. These attempts foundered largely because it was difficult to regulate lobbying without trespassing on citizens' rights to contact their elected representatives. Finally, after repeated efforts to "change the way Washington does business"—

BOX 13-3 **Lobbying Reforms**

The Lobby Disclosure Act of 1995 tightened the rules for lobbyists. The major changes are as follows.

- A lobbyist is defined as anyone who spends 20 percent or more of his time in paid lobbying.
- Lobbying activities include preparation and research intended to influence policy as well as direct contacts with policy makers and their staff.
- Lobbyists are required to register with Congress. They must disclose the names of their clients and the issues on which they are lobbying and state approximately how much clients are paying for their services.[a]
- Lobbyists must file disclosure reports every six months. Those who fail to comply are subject to civil fines up to $50,000.
- Nonprofit groups under Internal Revenue Code Section 501(C)4 that lobby cannot receive direct federal grants.
- Former U.S. trade representatives and deputies are banned for life from lobbying for foreign interests.

Source: Washington Times, November 30, 1995, A14.

[a] There are some exemptions; for example, lobbyists paid $5,000 or less in six months are not required to register.

a campaign theme advocated by many members—the two parties came together to enact the first major overhaul of the 1946 act.

The Lobby Disclosure Act of 1995

Under the Lobby Disclosure Act of 1995, which became effective on January 1, 1996, new rules applied to individuals and firms who lobby Congress and senior executive branch officials (see Box 13-3 on lobbying reforms). The law broadened the definition of people who must register as lobbyists (all those who spend one-fifth of their time trying to influence lawmakers, congressional aides, or high-level executive officials). Registrations of lobbyists quickly soared. A study by the Government Accountability Office determined that when the law took effect "only 6,078 individuals and organizations had registered" under the outdated 1946 act. "After the new law took effect, a total of 14,912 lobbyists registered" with 10,612 being first-time registrants.[103] In 2005, there were 34,785 registered lobbyists.[104] The law is administered by the public records offices of the House and Senate.

Lobbyists are required to "provide semiannual disclosures showing who their clients are, what policies they are trying to influence and roughly how much money they are spending for lobbying."[105] Civil fines of up to $50,000 can be imposed on those who fail to comply. Grassroots lobbying is exempt from the law, as are lobbyists paid $5,000 or less semiannually and organizations that use their own employees to lobby. The 1995 lobby disclosure law was amended three years later to make several technical corrections, such as clarifying the definition of "lobbying contact."

Although the 1995 lobby law is better than the old one, it is minimally enforced. A 2005 report by the Center for Public Integrity noted that the disclosure system is in disarray.[106] As Lee H. Hamilton, former Indiana representative and vice chair of the National Commission on Terrorist Attacks Upon the United States (also known as the 9/11 Commission), noted:

> Roughly one in five of the companies registered to lobby failed to file the required forms, and overall, 14,000 documents that should have been filed are missing, while another fifth of the required lobbying forms were filed late. The Center [on Public Integrity] found that "countless forms are filed with portions that are blank or improperly filled out. An unknown number of lobbyists neglect or refuse to file any disclosure forms whatsoever." In essence, we have a lobby disclosure system in name only.[107]

Some firms and organizations also underreport their lobbying expenditures. "Companies, trade associations, and lobby firms often misreport—intentionally or inadvertently—how much money they shell out or take in."[108]

The problems in enforcing what many lobbyists view as a "voluntary" law, and recent congressional probes into alleged misconduct by several high-profile lobbyists, have triggered proposals for reform, such as expanding the definition of lobbying to include grassroots activities.

> Recruiting citizen-advocates from back home, creating and running commercials, soliciting the writing of speeches and op-ed articles, and paying organizations, such as think tanks, to promote legislative outcomes are also lobbying in every sense of the word. They should finally be considered lobbying in the legal sense and no longer be kept from the public.[109]

The ethical allegations against House majority leader DeLay and his ties to lobbyist Jack Abramoff provided the impetus in spring 2005 for various lawmakers to suggest further lobbying reforms. Among the changes that have been proposed are clarifying the rules with respect to privately funded member travel; requiring lobbyists to more thoroughly disclose their contacts with lawmakers and senior executive branch officials; obligating former lawmakers to wait two years, instead of one, before being able to lobby members of Congress; mandating that the costs of grassroots lobbying be reported on the disclosure forms; hiking the financial penalties for failing to file lobbying reports; and improving the electronic filing of disclosure forms and making them more accessible and searchable by the public.[110] As one journalist noted, Democrats view lobbying overhaul as a political opportunity to lambast DeLay and the GOP in general, while Republicans "are motivated by a sense of political danger."[111]

Foreign Lobbying

The 1995 law also amended the Foreign Agents Registration Act of 1938, which required those who lobby on behalf of foreign governments or political parties to register with the Justice Department. The 1995 law broadened the definition of foreign lobbyists to include individuals who lobby on behalf of foreign-owned commercial enterprises. About five hundred lobbyists have registered with the Justice Department as agents representing foreign governments or parties (see http://www.usdoj.gov/criminal/fara/).

Given the role of the United States in the global economy and in military security, combined with the information technology era, many foreign governments and Americans who work for foreign clients spend considerable time and money lobbying Capitol Hill and promoting their interests nationwide. For example, after September 11, Saudi Arabia spent more than $20 million to improve its image among lawmakers, the press, and the public. (Fifteen of the nineteen airplane hijackers were Saudi-born.) "A major part of the campaign is a direct engagement of Washington lawmakers," noted one account. "Saudi lobbyists are making 500 to 600 visits a year to congressional offices."[112] Many other nations also hire lobbyists to forge closer ties with Congress, the executive branch, and various U.S. industries, such as oil.[113]

The American Israel Public Affairs Committee (AIPAC) is not a registered foreign lobby because it is independent of foreign sponsorship and composed of American citizens who have a keen interest in the mother country. (Ethnic lobbying by citizens of Irish, Greek, or Polish lineage, for instance, is an effective form of advocacy, and it seems sure to grow in this period of increased immigrant flow to the United States.) Yet AIPAC is one of the most influential lobbying groups in the United States. For instance, AIPAC "sponsors tours of Israel for legislators and keeps in touch with all departments of the United States Government with the slightest involvement in Israel. It has student affiliates at more than 200 campuses."[114] Many other nations and international interests also have covered the costs of lawmakers and congressional aides who visit their countries on fact-finding missions.

The globalization of American lobbying efforts is also occurring. Worried that international restrictions and regulations might adversely affect the gun trade and the ability of Americans to acquire firearms, the National Rifle Association formed a transnational organization of gun groups and firearms manufacturers from eleven other countries (the World Forum).[115] The organization's objectives are to fend off international pressure for tighter gun controls in the United States and to defend the right to bear arms worldwide. As another example, multinational cigarette makers "have embarked on a global lobbying campaign to undermine a proposed international treaty that could place tight restrictions on cigarette advertising and smuggling."[116] Many U.S.-based corporations also hire lobbyists who can operate globally to protect their interests in Europe or other parts of the world when disputes arise about trade, agriculture, antitrust laws, the environment, and other issues.[117]

Globalization of the world's economy also influences congressional lobbying. In the late 1990s U.S. antitrust officials approved the Boeing aircraft company's merger with rival McDonnell Douglas in part because the global marketplace seems to require firms to be larger and more efficient to survive. This global imperative enhanced Boeing's political clout on Capitol Hill by broadening its ties beyond lawmakers in its home base in the state of Washington (Boeing's headquarters are now in Chicago) to include "congressional delegations from California, Missouri, Texas, Alabama, and Pennsylvania. . . . Through subcontractors and their employees, they can bring direct influence to bear on virtually every other delegation in Congress."[118] For example, Boeing executives enlisted machine and tool subcontractors in El Monte, California, to lobby their representatives to support the renewal of China's favorable trade status with the United States. Boeing executives said the suppliers readily agreed to lobby Congress because "their firms depend as much as Boeing does on business generated by aircraft sales to China."[119] Boeing was successful in its effort.

CONCLUSION

From the nation's beginning, lobbying and lawmaking have been twin phenomena. Lobbying "has been so deeply woven into the American political fabric that one could, with considerable justice, assert that the history of lobbying comes close to being the history of American legislation."[120]

Recent years have witnessed an explosion in the number and types of groups organized to pursue their ends on Capitol Hill. Compared with a decade ago, more industry associations, public affairs lobbies (such as Common Cause), single-issue groups, political action committees, and foreign agents are engaged in lobbying. Some of these groups employ new grassroots and technological lobbying techniques. Many victories today are won in Washington because of sophisticated lobbying campaigns back in home states or districts.

No one questions that groups and lobbyists have a rightful public role, but some aspects of lobbying warrant concern. Groups push Congress to pass laws that benefit the few and not the many. They exaggerate their members' views and hinder compromise. They frequently misrepresent the voting records of legislators in their rating schemes and pour money into campaigns of their allies (mainly incumbents). Lawmakers who defy single-issue groups find at election time that these organizations pull out all the stops to defeat them.

Built-in checks constrain group pressures, however. Legislators can play one competing group off against another, and knowledgeable staff aides can provide members with reports and studies to counter the lobbyists' arguments. Lawmakers' own expertise is another informal check on lobbyists. Finally, there are self-imposed constraints. Lobbyists who misrepresent issues or mislead members soon find their access permanently closed off.

SUGGESTED READINGS

Birnbaum, Jeffrey H., and Alan S. Murray. *Showdown at Gucci Gulch: Lawmakers, Lobbyists, and the Unlikely Triumph of Tax Reform.* New York: Random House, 1987.

Cigler, Allan J., and Burdett A. Loomis, eds. *Interest Group Politics.* 6th ed. Washington, D.C.: CQ Press, 2002.

Hammond, Susan Webb. *Congressional Caucuses in National Policy Making.* Baltimore: Johns Hopkins University Press, 1998.

Rauch, Jonathan. *Demosclerosis: The Silent Killer of American Government.* New York: Times Books, 1994.

Rozell, Mark, and Clyde Wilcox. *Interest Groups in American Campaigns.* Washington, D.C.: CQ Press, 1999.

Truman, David B. *The Governmental Process, Political Interests, and Public Opinion.* 2d ed. New York: Knopf, 1971.

Policymaking, budgeting, and taxing and spending: Above, a Government Printing Office employee stacks copies of President George W. Bush's 2005 budget. Below, South Carolina representative John M. Spratt Jr., ranking Democrat on the House Budget Committee, points to a chart, as Sen. Jon Corzine, D-N.J., looks on during a press conference challenging the Bush tax policies.

chapter 14

Congress, Budgets, and Domestic Policy Making

In February 2005, President George W. Bush asked Congress to act with dispatch on an emergency supplemental appropriations bill totaling more than $80 million to fund, among other things, military operations and reconstruction efforts in Iraq and Afghanistan. The bill became law in May 2005. The word "emergency" implies the need for immediate action but, as often happens in Congress, lawmakers commonly add extraneous items that slow down enactment of must-pass measures. In this case, the legislation carried changes to immigration law as well as "provisions dealing with oil drilling, forest services, a new baseball stadium for Washington, and economic assistance to Palestinians."[1]

Significantly, if the word "emergency" is affixed to appropriations legislation it allows Congress and the White House to circumvent spending restrictions contained in concurrent budget resolutions. (The House and Senate have rules governing the emergency designation of legislation.) As one budget expert noted: "Classifying something as an emergency allows the White House, House and Senate to avoid cutting other spending or increasing revenues to offset the impact of the additional spending they now want to do. Except in the rarest of circumstances, it is a budget gimmick that allows existing [spending] limits to be ignored."[2]

Lawmakers are mindful that overuse of emergency supplementals for military operations can dilute their power of the purse by providing the Pentagon with a separate revenue stream to fund routine and nonemergency costs.[3] "By sending Congress military spending requests labeled as 'emergencies,' the White House has diminished congressional scrutiny of the details and insulated the funds from any trade-offs that might occur in the regular budget process."[4] The Senate adopted a nonbinding "sense of the Senate" resolution in 2005 urging the president to minimize the use of emergency supplementals and to utilize the regular appropriations process to fund military operations.[5]

Although federal budgeting involves setting priorities, difficult fiscal decisions do not always come easily to either Congress or the president. On the one hand, Congress "does not make hard decisions," exclaimed Sen. George V. Voinovich, R-Ohio. In his judgment, "This place continues to say yes [to tax cuts and spending hikes] without any consideration of the next generation."[6]

On the other hand, presidents confront a comparable circumstance. For instance, President Bush expressed a popular sentiment when he said: "Whatever it costs to defend our country, we will pay it." Yet he refused to ask citizens to pay for it. "On the contrary, in the face of massive new [defense and homeland security] spending, he proposed *additional* tax cuts."[7] A rationale for the proposed tax cuts is that they will stimulate economic growth and produce the revenue to eliminate any deficit. Conflicts about policies and the money to pay for them inhere in the lawmaking process.

DEFINITIONS OF POLICY

Because policies ultimately are what government is about, definitions of policy and policy making—not surprisingly—are diverse and influenced by the beholder's eye. David Easton's celebrated definition of public policy as society's "authoritative allocation" of values or resources is one approach to the question. To put it another way, policies can be regarded as reflecting "who gets what, when, and how" in a society. A more serviceable definition of policy is offered by Randall B. Ripley and Grace A. Franklin: Policy is what the government says and does about perceived problems.[8]

How can one recognize policies? The answer is not as simple as it may seem. Many policies are explicitly labeled and recognized as authoritative statements of what the government is doing, or intends to do, about a particular matter. The measures may be far-reaching (financing the Social Security system, for example); they may be trivial (naming federal buildings after deceased public officials). Nonetheless, they are obvious statements of policy. They are usually written down, often in precise legal language. They boast documented legislative histories in committee hearings, reports, and floor deliberations that indicate what lawmakers had in mind as they hammered out the policy's final provisions.

Not all policies, however, are formal enough to be considered the law of the land. Some are articulated by officials but, for one reason or another, are never set down in laws or rules. The Monroe Doctrine, which declared U.S. resistance to European intervention in the Western Hemisphere, was inserted into the president's 1823 State of the Union report written by Secretary of State John Quincy Adams. It has been adhered to ever since by successive generations of policy makers. Other policies, especially of a symbolic or exhortatory nature, gain currency in the eyes of elites or the public without formal or legal elaboration.

Some policies stress substance—programs designed to build the nation's defense, for example. Others stress procedure, such as those imposing personnel ceilings on federal agencies, mandating program management standards, or requiring contractors' insurance for military weapons. Still others are amalgams of substance and procedure, such as fast-track provisions (renamed "trade promotion authority" by the George W. Bush administration) written into trade laws and other laws that expedite committee and floor action in each house. Ways of putting legislation on a fast track include time limits on committee consideration of a bill and on floor debate of the measure, prohibitions on the offering of floor amendments, and requirements obligating each chamber to pass identical legislation, thus obviating the need for a conference committee to iron out bicameral differences.

Finally, some policies are made by negation. Doing nothing about a problem often has results that are as profound as passing a law about it. The United States had no general immigration law before 1924 and no overall medical care program before 1965, but its policies on those matters—mainly favoring unregulated private activity—were unmistakable.

The process of arriving at these policies is policy making. The process may be simple or complex, highly publicized or nearly invisible, concentrated or diffuse. The policy may happen suddenly, such as military air strikes ordered by the president. Or it may require years or even decades to formulate, as in the case of civil rights or Medicare for the elderly.[9]

STAGES OF POLICY MAKING

Whatever the time frame, policy making normally has four distinct stages: setting the agenda, formulating policy, adopting policy, and implementing policy.

Setting the Agenda

At the initial stage, public problems are spotted and moved onto the national agenda, which can be defined as "the list of subjects to which government officials and those around them are paying serious attention."[10] In a large, pluralistic country such as the United States, the national agenda at any given moment is extensive and vigorously debated.

How do problems get placed on the agenda? Some are heralded by a crisis or some other prominent event—the bombing of a building by terrorists, a schoolyard shooting, a national disaster, or a campaign-funding scandal. Others are occasioned by the gradual accumulation of knowledge; for example, increasing awareness of an environmental hazard such as acid rain or ozone depletion. Still other agenda items represent the accumulation of past problems that no longer can be avoided or ignored.

Agendas, too, may be set in motion by political processes—election results, turnover in Congress, or shifts in public opinion.[11] The 1994 election results gave the GOP control of Congress and a chance to pursue its "revolution" in downsizing government. The next five elections produced a different outcome, reflecting the two Congresses theme, as many Republicans lost their zeal for shrinking the size and reach of government. "Too many people started to believe that the surest path to re-election is to spend money rather than cut government," remarked Rep. Jeff Flake, R-Ariz. "The material that comes from the Republican caucus is not to call for the elimination of this program or that, it's to brag that we have increased the budget for education by 144 percent."[12]

Agenda items are pushed by policy entrepreneurs, people willing to invest time and energy to promote a particular issue. Numerous Washington, D.C., think tanks and interest groups, especially at the beginning of a new president's term, issue reports that seek to influence the economic, social, or foreign policy agenda of the nation. Welfare and Social Security reforms, for instance, have long been advocated by various think tanks. Usually, however, elected officials and their staffs or appointees are more likely to shape agendas than are career bureaucrats or nongovernmental actors.[13] Notable policy entrepreneurs on Capitol Hill are party and committee leaders who push their party's policy initiatives.

Lawmakers frequently are policy entrepreneurs because they are expected to voice the concerns of constituents and organized groups and to seek legislative solutions. Politicians generally gravitate toward issues that are visible, salient, and solvable. Tough, arcane, or conflictual problems may be shunned because they offer few payoffs and little hope of success.

Sometimes only a crisis, such as hikes in gasoline prices in 2005, can compel lawmakers to address difficult questions. Paradoxically, despite the energy-saving innovations introduced in the aftermath of the oil shortages (triggered by an oil boycott led by OPEC—the Organization of Petroleum Exporting Countries) and long gasoline lines of the 1970s, Americans today are as dependent on imported oil as they were over three decades ago and use more energy to power bigger homes and larger trucks and automobiles, such as sports utility vehicles (SUVs). Forecasters predict more short- and long-term energy woes unless steps are taken to develop alternative fuels, change habits of consumption, encourage conservation, and reduce the spiraling demand for oil, especially from the volatile Middle East. This kind of creeping crisis is often difficult for members of Congress to grapple with, in part because of the two Congresses dilemma. As conscientious lawmakers, members might want to forge long-term solutions. But as representatives of their constituents, they must respond to their immediate concerns about rising energy prices.

Formulating Policy

In the second stage of policy making, items on the political agenda are discussed and potential solutions are explored. Members of Congress and their staffs play crucial roles by conducting hearings and writing committee reports. They are aided by policy experts in executive agencies, interest groups, and the private sector.

Another term for this stage is *policy incubation,* which entails "keeping a proposal alive while it picks up support, or waits for a better climate, or while a consensus begins to form that the problem to which it is addressed exists."[14] Sometimes this process takes only a few months; more often it requires years. During Dwight D. Eisenhower's administration, for example, congressional Democrats explored and refined domestic policy options that, while not immediately accepted, were ripe for adoption by the time their party's nominee, John F. Kennedy, was elected president in 1960.[15]

The incubation process not only brings policies to maturity but also refines solutions to the problems. The process may break down if workable solutions are not available. The seeming intractability of many modern issues complicates problem solving. Thomas S. Foley, D-Wash. (Speaker, 1989–1995), held that issues had become far more perplexing since he came to Congress in 1965. At that time "the civil rights issue facing the legislators was whether the right to vote should be federally guaranteed for blacks and Hispanics. Now members are called on to deal with more ambiguous policies like affirmative action and racial quotas."[16] Add to these such complex contemporary topics as stem cell research, genetic discrimination, and global warming.

Solutions to problems normally involve "some fairly simple routines emphasizing the tried and true (or at least not discredited)."[17] A repertoire of proposals—for example, blue-ribbon commissions, trust funds, or pilot projects—can be applied to a variety of unsolved problems. Problem solvers also must guard against recommending solutions that will be viewed as worse than the problem.

Adopting Policy

Laws are ideas whose time has come. The right time for a policy is what scholar John W. Kingdon calls the policy window: the opportunity presented by circumstances and attitudes to enact a policy into law. Policy entrepreneurs must seize the opportunity before the policy window closes and the idea's time has passed.

Once policies are ripe for adoption, they must gain popular acceptance. This is the function of legitimation, the process through which policies come to be viewed by the public as right or proper. Inasmuch as citizens are expected to comply with laws or regulations—pay taxes, observe rules, and make sacrifices of one sort or another—the policies themselves must appear to have been properly considered and enacted. A nation whose policies lack legitimacy is in deep trouble.

Symbolic acts, such as members voting on the House or Senate floor or the president signing a bill, signal to everyone that policies have been duly adopted according to traditional forms. Hearings and debates, moreover, serve to fine-tune policies as well as to cultivate support from affected interests. Responding to critics of Congress's slowness in adopting energy legislation, Sen. Ted Stevens, R-Alaska, asked these questions:

> Would you want an energy bill to flow through the Senate and not have anyone consider the impacts on housing or on the automotive industry or on the energy industries that provide our light and power? Should we ignore the problems of the miner or the producer or the distributor? Our legislative process must reflect all of the problems if the public is to have confidence in the government.[18]

Legitimating, in other words, usually demands a measured pace and attention to procedural details. Another strategy is to move quickly in response to a public outcry—before opposition forces can mobilize—to enact bold changes, knowing that the details will have to be refined and adjusted later.

Implementing Policy

In the final stage, policies shaped by the legislature and at the highest executive levels are put into effect, usually by a federal agency. Policies are not self-executing; they must be promulgated and enforced. A law or executive order rarely spells out exactly how a particular policy should be implemented. Congress and the president usually delegate most decisions about implementation to the responsible agencies under broad but stated guidelines. Implementation determines the ultimate effect of policies. Officials of the executive branch can thwart a policy by foot dragging or sheer inefficiency. By the same token, overzealous administrators can push a policy far beyond its creators' intent.

Congress therefore must exercise its oversight role. It may require executive agencies to report or consult with congressional committees or to follow certain formal procedures. Members of Congress get feedback on the operation of federal programs through a variety of channels: media coverage, interest group protests, and even casework for constituents. With such information Congress can and often does pass judgment by adjusting funding, introducing amendments, or recasting the basic legislation governing a particular policy.

TYPES OF DOMESTIC POLICIES

One way to understand public policies is to analyze the nature of the policies themselves. Scholars have classified policies in many different ways.[19] Our typology identifies three types of domestic policies: distributive, regulatory, and redistributive.

Distributive Policies

Distributive policies or programs are government actions that convey tangible benefits to private individuals, groups, or firms. Invariably, they bestow subsidies, tax breaks, or advantageous regulatory provisions upon favored individuals or groups. The benefits are often called pork (usually special interest spending for projects in members' states or districts), although that appellation is sometimes difficult to define. After all, "one person's pork is another person's steak." The projects come in several varieties.

> Dams, roads and bridges, known as "green pork," are old hat. These days, there is also "academic pork" in the form of research grants to colleges, "defense pork" in the form of geographically specific military expenditures and lately "high-tech pork," for example the intense fight to authorize research into super computers and high-definition television (HDTV).[20]

The presence of distributive politics—which makes many interests better off and few, if any, visibly worse off—is natural in Congress, a nonhierarchical institution that must build coalitions to function. A textbook example was the $1 billion-plus National Parks and Recreation Act of 1978. Dubbed the "Park Barrel Bill," it created so many parks, historical sites, seashores, wilderness areas, wild and scenic rivers, and national trails that it sailed through the Interior (now Resources) Committee and passed the House by a 341–61 vote. "Notice how quiet we are. We all got something in there," said one House member, after the Rules Committee cleared the bill in five minutes flat. Another member quipped, "If it had a blade of grass and a squirrel, it got in the bill."[21] Distributive politics of this kind throws into sharp relief the two Congresses notion: national policy as a mosaic of local interests.

The politics of distribution works best when tax revenues are expanding, fueled by high productivity and economic growth. When productivity declines or tax cuts squeeze revenues, it often becomes difficult to add new benefits or expand old ones. Yet distributive impulses remain strong even in these circumstances as lawmakers in both parties work to ensure that money is spent for particular purposes in their districts or states. For example, amidst concern about rising deficits, the uncertainty of costs associated with reconstructing Iraq, and hikes in the price tag for homeland security, a record number of earmarks—more than twelve thousand totaling $25 billion—were put in the fiscal year 2005 appropriations bills.[22] (Earmarks refer to funds set aside in appropriations measures or committee reports at the request of individual lawmakers for a specific project, activity, institution, or location.) Congressional leaders also use the promise of projects or benefits in bills to secure the votes they need to pass legislation. As House Ways and Means chairman Bill Thomas, R-Calif., stated: "The way you get the votes to pass anything is to ask whoever would possibly vote for something, what do they want. It's an additive process."[23]

Sen. Trent Lott, R-Miss., highlighted the two Congresses theme and the prevailing appeal of distributive policy making to members of Congress when he remarked: "Mississippi is getting tired of dirt roads; we want some asphalt. I also want some more asphalt for my buddies in Florida, Texas, and Alabama."[24] Or, as Lott's colleague Rick Santorum, R-Pa., said: "Republicans feel very strongly about infrastructure. It's an area where we feel real comfortable spending money."[25]

Regulatory Policies

Regulatory policies are designed to protect the public against harm or abuse that might result from unbridled private activity. For example, the Food and Drug Administration monitors standards for foodstuffs and tests drugs for purity, safety, and effectiveness, and the Federal Trade Commission guards against illegal business practices, such as deceptive advertising.

Federal regulation against certain abuses dates from the late nineteenth century, when the Interstate Commerce Act and the Sherman Antitrust Act were enacted to protect against transport and monopoly abuses. As the twentieth century dawned, scandalous practices in slaughterhouses and food-processing plants led to meatpacking, food, and drug regulations. The stock market collapse in 1929 and the Great Depression of the 1930s paved the way for the New Deal legislation that would regulate the banking and securities industries and labor-management relations. Consumer rights and environmental protection came of age in the 1960s and 1970s.

Regulation is not popular with the recent GOP-controlled Congresses. Republicans wanted to cut back the government's role by repealing or modifying many federal regulations that they viewed as overly costly and burdensome, especially to businesses. Much of the clean air debate, for instance, involves the basic issue of costs versus benefits: Do the public health benefits of cleaner air outweigh the financial costs of getting it?[26] Environmentalists and health advocates argue that tougher standards for regulating air pollution would prevent suffering and save the lives of thousands who are afflicted with asthma and other lung diseases. Industries and conservative groups attack these claims and contend that the "regulations are unnecessary, would be too costly and would yield only marginal health benefits."[27]

Redistributive Policies

Redistribution, which visibly shifts resources from one group to another, is the most difficult of all political feats. Because they are controversial, redistributive policies engage a broad spectrum of political actors—not only in the House and Senate chambers but also in the executive branch and among interest groups and the public at large. Redistributive issues tend to be ideological. They often separate liberals and conservatives because they upset relationships between social and economic classes. Theodore R. Marmor described the fight over medical care for the aged as "cast in terms of class conflict."

> The leading adversaries . . . brought into the opposing camps a large number of groups whose interests were not directly affected by the Medicare outcome. . . . Ideological charges and countercharges dominated public discussion, and each side seemed to regard compromise as unacceptable.[28]

Most of the divisive socioeconomic issues of the past generation—civil rights, affirmative action, school busing, welfare, homelessness, tax reform—were redistributive problems. A redistributive issue for the twenty-first century concerns the increasing share of the federal budget that goes to the elderly compared with everyone else in society. Tax dollars spent on entitlement programs, such as Social Security and Medicare, absorb an ever increasing proportion of federal dollars, which then are unavailable for other important social, domestic, or security needs.

Federal budgeting is marked by conflict and by techniques to disguise the redistributions or make them more palatable. Omnibus budget packages permit legislators to approve cuts en bloc instead of one by one, and across-the-board formulas (such as freezes) give the appearance of spreading the misery equally to affected groups. In all such vehicles, distributive elements are added to placate the more vocal opponents of change.

CHARACTERISTICS OF CONGRESSIONAL POLICY MAKING

As a policy-making body, Congress displays the traits and biases of its membership and structure and of the larger political system. Congress is bicameral with divergent electoral and procedural traditions. It is representative, especially where geographic interests are concerned. It is decentralized, having few mechanisms for integrating or coordinating its policy decisions. It sometimes is inclined toward enacting symbolic measures instead of substantive ones. And it is generally reactive, mirroring conventional perceptions of problems.

Bicameralism

Several differences between the House and Senate—their terms of office, the character of their constituencies, and the size of their legislative bodies—powerfully influence the policies they make. Six-year terms, it is argued, allow senators to play the statesman for at least part of each term before they are forced by oncoming elections to concentrate on fence mending. This distinction may be more apparent than real, but empirical studies of senators' voting habits lend some support to it.

The various constituencies unquestionably pull in divergent directions. The more homogeneous House districts often promote clear and unambiguous positions on a narrower range of questions than those reached by an entire state, represented by senators who must weigh the claims of many competing interests on a broad range of matters. The sizes of the two chambers, moreover, dictate procedural characteristics. House rules are designed to allow majorities to have their way. In contrast, Senate rules give individual senators great latitude to influence action. As a GOP senator once said: "The Senate has the strongest minority of any minority on Earth, and the weakest majority of any on Earth."[29]

The two chambers, in short, differ in outlook, constituency, and strategy. Bicameralism is less important in promoting or discouraging particular kinds of policies, writes Benjamin I. Page, than in "the furtherance of deliberation, the production of evidence, and the revealing of error."[30]

Localism

Congressional policies respond to constituents' needs, particularly those that can be mapped geographically. Sometimes these needs are pinpointed with startling directness. For example, an aviation noise control bill required construction of a control tower "at latitude 40 degrees, 43 minutes, 45 seconds north and at longitude 73 degrees, 24 minutes, 50 seconds west"—the location of a Farmingdale, New York, airport in the district of the Democratic representative who requested the provision.[31]

Usually, however, programs are directed toward states, municipalities, counties, or geographic regions. Funds are often transferred directly to local government agencies, which in turn deliver the aid or services to citizens. Lawmakers often require states and localities to fund some national programs. These unfunded mandates strain state budgets and arouse the ire of state and local officials. In 1995 President Bill Clinton signed into law the Unfunded Mandates Reform Act, which governs any proposed mandate that the Congressional Budget Office (CBO) estimates will cost state and local governments $50 million or more. Congress must either "make provision to pay for the mandate . . . or take a separate recorded vote to waive the requirement, thus holding members of Congress accountable for their decision."[32] Lawmakers must now consider the costs of any federal requirements they impose on state and local governments. However, the promise or intent of the law is not always met. The No Child Left Behind education law (P.L. 107-110), for instance, prescribes mandatory testing in all public schools for today's cash-strapped states. School systems in many states are up in arms, charging that the federal government has not provided enough money to cover the expense of meeting the law's requirements. In 2005, the National Education Association (the nation's largest teachers' union), along with school districts in several states, brought suit in federal court to require the Department of Education to fully fund the educational standards imposed on the states.[33]

National and local policies are necessarily intertwined. National policies can be advanced by state and local governments, or states and localities can develop innovations that can spur national action. The threat of terrorist attacks in the United States means that any such calamity will be confronted by first responders—police officers, fire fighters, public health officials, and others on the state and local level. On other issues as well, the states are the testing grounds, or laboratories, for social, economic, and political experiments.

Many policy debates revolve around not only which governmental level can most effectively carry out a responsibility but also which level best promotes particular values. Liberals, for example, seek a significant role for the national government in the enforcement of civil rights and environmental protection. Conservatives support an activist national government on defense and security matters. Although empowerment and decentralization are popular concepts among today's conservatives, in previous decades they were powerful slogans for liberals who supported equal rights for women and local Head Start programs for children. When it suits their purposes, both liberals and conservatives are capable of advocating either national actions or local preferences, depending on which level of government would best serve their objective.

Piecemeal Policy Making

Policies all too often mirror Congress's scattered and decentralized structure. Typically, they are considered piecemeal, reflecting the patchwork of committee and subcommittee jurisdictions. Congress's segmented decision making is typified by authorizing and appropriating processes in which separate committees consider the same programs often without consulting each other.

The structure of a policy frequently depends on which committees have reported it. Working from varying jurisdictions, committees can take different approaches to the same problem. A program from the taxing committees will feature tax provisions, from the Appropriations Committees a fiscal approach, from the commerce panels a regulatory perspective, and so forth. The approach may be well or ill-suited to the policy objective. It all depends on which committee was strategically positioned to promote the bill.

Symbolic Policy Making

At heart, congressional policy making often concerns appearances more than substance. Symbolic actions are important to all politicians. Often bills are passed to give the impression that action is being taken when the impact or efficacy of the measure is wholly unknown. Groups outside Congress continually demand, "Don't just stand there, do something." Doing something is often the only politically feasible choice, even when no one knows what to do or whether inaction might be just as effective.[34]

Reactive Policy Making

Elected officials are seldom far ahead of or far behind the collective views of the citizenry. Hence it would be misguided to expect the national legislature routinely to express radical solutions to problems. Members know that out-of-the-mainstream views are unlikely to attract widespread public support. Congress is essentially a reactive institution. As one House member explained:

> When decision rests on the consent of the governed, it comes slowly, only after consensus has built or crisis has focused public opinion in some unusual way, the representatives in the meantime hanging back until the signs are unmistakable. Government decision, then, is not generally the cutting edge of change but a belated reaction to change.[35]

The reactive character of Congress's policy making is evident in its budget process. Under pressures to reform, Congress reacted in 1974, 1985, and again in the 1990s with changes in the way it makes budget decisions. The current budget process, dating from the mid-1970s, was intended to bring coherence to the way standing committees handle the president's budget. It has decisively shaped both Congress's internal decision making and its relations with the executive.

BOX 14-1 A Budget Glossary

Appropriations. The process by which Congress provides budget authority, usually through the enactment of eleven separate appropriations bills.

Budget authority. The authority for federal agencies to spend or otherwise obligate money, accomplished through enactment into law of appropriations bills.

Budget outlays. Money that is spent in a given fiscal year, as opposed to money that is appropriated for that year. One year's budget authority can result in outlays over several years, and the outlays in any given year result from a mix of budget authority from that year and prior years. Budget authority is similar to putting money into a checking account. Outlays occur when checks are written and cashed.

Discretionary spending. Programs that Congress can finance as it chooses through appropriations. With the exception of paying entitlement benefits to individuals (see mandatory spending below), almost everything the government does is financed by discretionary spending. Examples include all federal agencies, Congress, the White House, the courts, the military, and such programs as space exploration and child nutrition. About a third of all federal spending falls into this category.

Fiscal year. The federal government's budget year. For example, fiscal year 2006 runs from October 1, 2005, through September 30, 2006.

Mandatory spending. Made up mostly of entitlements, which are programs whose eligibility requirements are written into law. Anyone who meets those requirements is entitled to the money until Congress changes the law. Examples are Social Security, Medicare, Medicaid, unemployment benefits, food stamps, and federal pensions. Another major category of mandatory spending is the interest paid to holders of federal government bonds. Social Security and interest payments are permanently appropriated. And although budget authority for some entitlements is provided through the appropriations process, appropriators have little or no control over the money. Mandatory spending accounts for about two-thirds of all federal spending.

Pay-as-you-go (PAYGO) rule. This rule requires that all tax cuts, new entitlement programs, and expansions of existing entitlement programs be budget-neutral—offset either by additional taxes or by cuts in existing entitlement programs.

Reconciliation. The process by which tax laws and spending programs are changed, or reconciled, to reach outlay and revenue targets set in the congressional budget resolution. Established by the 1974 Congressional Budget Act (P.L. 93-344), it was first used in 1980.

Rescission. The cancellation of previously appropriated budget authority. This is a common way to save money that already has been appropriated. A rescissions bill must be passed by Congress and signed by the president (or enacted over his veto), just as an appropriations bill is.

Revenues. Taxes, customs duties, some user fees, and most other receipts paid to the federal government.

Sequester. The cancellation of spending authority as a disciplinary measure to cut off spending above preset limits. Appropriations that exceed annual spending caps can trigger a sequester that will cut all appropriations by the amount of the excess. Similarly, tax cuts and new or expanded entitlement spending programs that are not offset under pay-as-you-go rules will trigger a sequester of nonexempt entitlement programs.

Source: Adapted from Andrew Taylor, "Clinton's Strength Portends a Tough Season for GOP," *CQ Weekly*, February 6, 1999, 293.

CONGRESSIONAL BUDGETING

Congressional budgeting is a complex process that involves virtually all House and Senate members and committees, the president and executive branch officials, and scores of other participants. That congressional budgeting is usually contentious and conflict-laden should come as no surprise considering the high political and policy stakes associated with fiscal decision making. (See Box 14-1 for some of the terminology used in budgeting.)

Authorizations and Appropriations

Congress has a two-step financial procedure: authorizations and appropriations. Generally, Congress first passes authorization laws that establish or continue (reauthorizations) federal agencies and programs, recommend funding them at certain levels, and permit the enactment of appropriations to fund those agencies and programs. Congress then enacts annually appropriation laws that grant agencies legal authority to spend no more than the amount allocated to it. (However, it is not uncommon for appropriations measures to pass before authorization bills. In 2005 the House passed the homeland security appropriations bill before it agreed to the homeland security authorization measure.) An authorization is like an IOU that must be validated by an appropriation.

The authorization-appropriation sequence is an invention of Congress. It is required not by the U.S. Constitution, but by House and Senate rules. The dual procedure dates from the nineteenth century and stems from inordinate delays caused by adding riders—extraneous policy amendments—to appropriation bills. "By 1835," wrote a legislator, "delays caused by injecting legislation [policy] into these [appropriation] bills had become serious and [Democratic Republican representative from Massachusetts] John Quincy Adams suggested that they be stripped of everything save appropriations."[36] Two years later the House required authorizations to precede appropriations. The Senate followed suit.

Authorizations and appropriations can be annual, multiyear, or permanent. Through the end of World War II most federal agencies and programs were permanently authorized. They were reviewed annually by the House and Senate Appropriations Committees but not by the authorizing panels (such as Agriculture or Commerce). Since the 1970s the trend has been toward short-term authorizations, giving the authorizing committees more chances to control agency operations.[37] Agencies and programs are not terminated if their authorization law expires because Congress typically continues to appropriate money for them. In recent years, for example, "the total amount of unauthorized programs has ranged between about $90 billion and $120 billion annually."[38] Authorization (or reauthorization) measures sometimes cannot be passed for various reasons, such as conflicts over policy between the chambers or among the elective branches. Generally, authorizing committees strive to enact their bills, otherwise they cede their power to the appropriating panels. To generate public backing for the reauthorization of the Transportation Equity Act for the 21st Century, House Transportation chairman Don Young, R-Alaska, and ranking Democrat James L. Oberstar, Minn., led a "reauthorization tour" to major media markets "across the country to drum up grass roots support."[39]

The Two Stages. Suppose, for example, that the authorizing committee recommends $20 million for a new Energy Department solar research and development program. Under the authorization-appropriation procedure, before the Energy Department has the authorization to establish the solar program, both houses must pass and the president must sign legislation providing for it.

The House Appropriations Committee (usually one of its ten subcommittees) must propose how much money the solar program should receive. The amount is the budget authority (BA). It is equivalent to depositing money in a checking account. The budget outlay (BO) is the check written by the Treasury to meet a financial commitment. The Appropriations Committee can provide the whole $20 million (but not more), propose cuts, or refuse to fund the program at all. Assume that the House votes to approve $15 million. The Senate Appropriations Committee, acting somewhat like a court of appeals, then hears agency officials asking the Senate to approve the full $20 million. If the Senate accedes, a House-Senate compromise is worked out.

In practice, it is hard to keep the two stages distinct. Authorization bills sometimes carry appropriations, and appropriation bills sometimes contain legislation (or policy provisions). Chamber rules that forbid these maneuvers can be waived. In the House limitation riders make policy under the guise of restricting agency use of funds. Phrased negatively ("None of the funds . . ."), limitations bolster congressional control of bureaucracy. The Senate, too, is not reluctant to add extraneous policy proposals to appropriations bills. Miffed that a major immigration proposal was added to a supplemental appropriations bill, Democratic leader Harry Reid of Nevada exclaimed that "this is the mother of all authorizing legislation on an appropriations bill."[40] Often controversial, policy riders can trigger disputes with the other body and veto threats from the president.

Committee Roles and Continuing Resolutions. Among the authorizing committees, House Ways and Means and Senate Finance have especially powerful roles in the budget process. Both House and Senate tax panels have access to the staff experts of the Joint Taxation Committee. Because the House initiates revenue measures, it usually determines whether Congress will act on legislation to raise, lower, or redistribute taxes. (By custom, the House also initiates appropriations bills.) Occasionally, however, the Senate takes the lead. The Senate technically complies with the Constitution when taking a minor House-passed revenue bill and adding to it a major tax measure. In 1981 the Republican-controlled Senate employed this tactic to act on President Ronald

Reagan's sweeping tax-cut plan. It used the same ploy the next year on the president's tax-increase package. Usually the House jealously guards its constitutional authority to originate tax measures and may return to the Senate any bills that violate the Origination Clause.

Whenever Congress cannot complete action on one or more of the eleven regular appropriations bills (generally one for each subcommittee; under changes agreed to in 2005, the House has ten and the Senate twelve Appropriations subcommittees) by the beginning of the fiscal year (October 1), it provides temporary, stopgap funding for the affected federal agencies through a joint resolution known as a continuing resolution. In the past, continuing resolutions were usually employed to keep a few government agencies in operation for short periods (usually one to three months). Some years Congress has packaged all the regular appropriations bills into one massive continuing resolution. (A record twenty-one continuing resolutions were needed in 2000 before the GOP Congress and President Clinton compromised their differences on several appropriations bills that had not been enacted by the start of the fiscal year.) Each year Congress also passes one or more supplemental appropriations bills to meet unexpected or unforeseen contingencies.

Backdoor Spending Techniques

To sidestep the appropriations ax, authorizing committees evolved backdoor-funding provisions to bypass the front door of the two-step authorization-appropriation sequence. Backdoors are authorization laws that mandate, not simply recommend, the expenditure of federal funds. This type of spending legislation, which is reported solely by the authorizing committees, is called direct (or mandatory) spending as contrasted with the discretionary spending under the jurisdiction of the House and Senate Appropriations Committees. There are three types of backdoor or direct spending legislation. Contract authority permits agencies to enter into contracts that subsequently must be covered by appropriations. Borrowing authority allows agencies to spend money they have borrowed from the public or the Treasury. And entitlement programs grant eligible individuals and governments the right to receive payments from the national government.

The fastest growing of these three techniques is entitlements, which establish legally enforceable rights without reference to dollar amounts. Spending for entitlement programs (Medicare and Social Security, for example) is determined by the number of citizens who qualify and the benefit levels established by law. No fixed dollar amount is established for these programs.

Entitlements are the real force behind the escalation of federal spending (see Figure 14-1). More than half of all federal spending consists of entitlements that avoid the annual appropriations process review. The ratio today of discretionary (determined through yearly appropriations) to mandatory spending represents a dramatic reversal of what it was like four decades ago. Interest on the federal debt is another uncontrollable expenditure. Unlike

FIGURE 14-1 **Federal Spending by Major Category, Fiscal Years 1965 and 2006 (outlays in billions)**

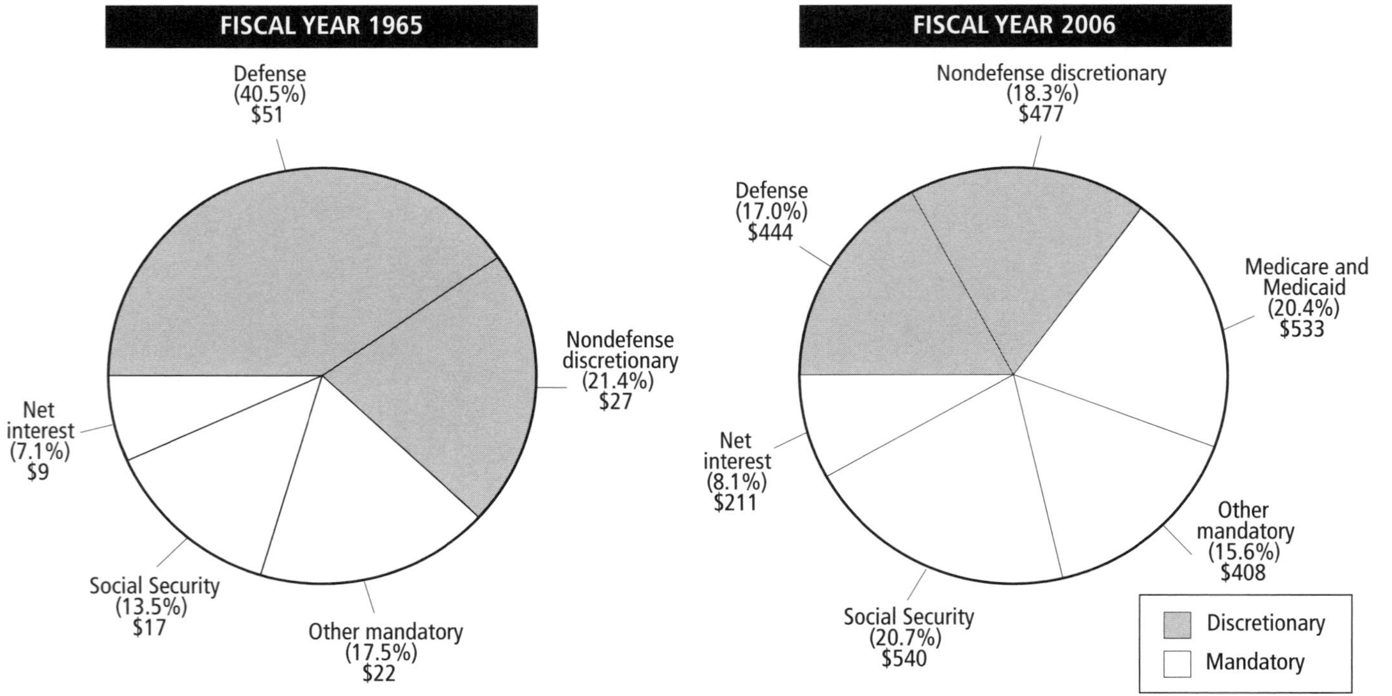

Source: Office of Management and Budget, *Budget of the United States Government: Fiscal Year 2006, Historical Tables* (Washington, D.C.: Government Printing Office, 2005), 125, 134. Charts prepared by Robert Keith, Government Division, Congressional Research Service.

defense or domestic discretionary programs—for which the Appropriations Committees recommend annual amounts and on which all lawmakers may vote—entitlement spending occurs automatically under the terms outlined in the statute. Moreover, around four-fifths of these programs "are not 'means tested,' or linked to the incomes of recipients." [41]

Congress has done a good job of containing discretionary spending. It is trying to rein in expenditures for costly entitlements, a much more difficult task. In 1996 Congress passed legislation ending a decades-old national welfare entitlement program—Aid to Families with Dependent Children.[42] However, benefits to the elderly make up the largest share of entitlement spending, and senior citizens are protective of their entitlement programs and they vote. The top domestic priority of President Bush's second term is to overhaul Social Security to ensure its long-term solvency. (Many Democrats suggest that the president's long-term goal is to transform Social Security from a social insurance program to a largely private investment system in which individuals would be required to take responsibility for managing their retirement income.) Although the president is open, he has said, to a wide range of proposals to revamp Social Security, his signature idea is to allow younger workers to divert part of their payroll taxes into private, or personal, accounts. (President Bush acknowledges that establishing personal investment accounts for workers will not solve Social Security's long-term solvency problem absent other changes.) Despite the president's intense lobbying drive to win public and congressional support for individual investment accounts, he encountered broad opposition to his restructuring plan, especially among Democratic lawmakers. Even some Republicans oppose private accounts. "Social Security became the bedrock of support for seniors," said Sen. Olympia J. Snowe, R-Maine, "precisely because it's defined and guaranteed. What cost and what risk is it worth to erode the guaranteed benefit [through variable stock or bond investments]?" [43]

The long-term demographic challenge confronting Social Security (and Medicare) is that the United States has an aging society with a longer-lived population (thanks to advances in often expensive medical technology). Looming on the horizon is the gradual retirement of the seventy-six million who make up the baby boom generation (those born between 1946 and 1964)—constituting the largest number of retirees in the history of the country—which will lead to huge retirement and medical expenditures for the elderly who are eligible to receive Social Security benefits. Projections are that fewer workers (a birth dearth) will be paying taxes to support retirees' expected benefits. As Senate Budget chairman Judd Gregg, R-N.H., explains:

> [I]n 1950 there were about 16 Americans working for every 1 American retired. That meant programs such as Social Security and Medicare not only generated money to support those who were retired, they actually generated more money than needed to support

> the people who retired. That is happening today even. But the number of people retiring compared to the number of people working has been changing. It has gone from 16 in 1950 down to about 3 and a half today. And further into this century, as the baby boom generation retires, it will drop to 2 people working for every 1 person retired. . . . It becomes pretty obvious, if you have only two people working to pay for one person retired, those two people are going to have to pay a lot more in taxes to support that one person. . . . So this creates a huge . . . unfunded liability [in future years as more money is taken out of Social Security than is paid in]. We do not know how we are going to pay for [Social Security and Medicare] in the outyears.[44]

With fewer workers supporting more retirees (barring some huge influx of immigrants or technological breakthroughs that enhance each worker's productivity), changes are required to address the projected shortage of funds—estimated by the Social Security Administration at nearly $4 trillion over seventy-five years—needed to pay for retirees' full benefits under current law.[45] Enough money is now coming into Social Security to cover the promised benefits to retirees.[46] However, the Social Security Administration projects that by 2017 the retirement system will begin to pay out more in benefits than it receives in payroll taxes. As a result, the Social Security Administration will tap into its reservoir of surplus funds to meet its retirement obligations. The year 2041 is the projected date when the retirement system will be unable to pay full retiree benefits based on current law.[47] Many proposals have been put forth to deal with the long-term funding challenge, but each is controversial. Among several proposed changes are raising the retirement age, reducing benefits for future retirees, increasing the payroll tax rate, requiring affluent retirees to pay taxes on their benefits, and raising the cap on income subject to Social Security payroll taxes. In sum, resolving the long-term solvency problem requires either putting more money into the system, cutting benefits, or doing some combination of the two.

Some analysts contend that the real entitlement budget buster of the future is not Social Security but Medicare. With health care costs rising faster than inflation, the greying of society, and costly new medical technologies, Medicare is already paying out more in benefits than it is receiving in taxes. The gap between promised benefits and Medicare's liabilities in the next seventy-five years is projected to be $27.8 trillion.[48] Compounding the fiscal problem, Congress in 2003 added a prescription drug benefit to Medicare that is projected to cost $1.2 trillion over the next decade.[49] Elective officials decided to focus first on Social Security, because "the steps Congress could take now to restrain Medicare's growth are politically perilous. Deny end-of-life care? Restrict eligibility? Reduce treatments? Raise costs?"[50] Even more frightening from a budget perspective is the prospect of providing long-term nursing home or other care for the elderly. Long-term care, said Rep. Earl Pomeroy, D-N.D., is "the elephant in the living room that no one's talking about."[51] And Medicaid, a federal entitlement program for indigent and low-income persons that is jointly funded by the national and state governments, has "now surged past Medicare to become the nation's largest health care program."[52]

In short, an entitlement revolution is under way as the government today transfers more than half of federal monies to eligible families and individuals. "Call it government by A.T.M.," remarked an analyst, "you walk up, hit the buttons and the cash to which you're entitled pops out."[53] This transformation in the federal budget away from discretionary to direct (or mandatory) spending raises the question of the appropriateness of this funding ratio. Congress and the president face at least a dual fiscal challenge: the battle for scarce resources between entitlements versus discretionary spending and the struggle within the discretionary category between domestic versus defense and homeland security spending. Added to this mix is more than $900 billion in indirect spending called tax expenditures—revenue that is foregone through various tax credits, subsidies, or deductions, such as home mortgage deductions. Tax expenditures receive relatively little public attention compared with direct or discretionary spending, yet in many years, says U.S. Comptroller General David Walker, "the total value of tax preferences exceeds the total value of discretionary spending. These items are off the radar screen, and they should [get the same budgetary attention as discretionary and direct spending]."[54]

THE 1974 BUDGET ACT

Loose control of Congress's purse strings in the 1970s gave rise to charges of financial irresponsibility. President Richard M. Nixon blamed Congress for annual deficits, consumer price hikes, high joblessness, and inflation. He also refused to spend (impounded) monies duly appropriated by Congress. Although his administration lost every court challenge to the impoundments, Nixon won the political high ground. These diverse pressures prompted Congress to restructure its budget procedures.

The Budget and Impoundment Control Act of 1974 created the House Budget Committee, the Senate Budget Committee, and the Congressional Budget Office. The nonpartisan CBO prepares economic forecasts for Congress, scores the costs of proposed legislation, and issues fiscal, monetary, and policy reports. The 1974 act also limited presidential use of impoundments and established a timetable for action on authorization, appropriation, and tax measures. The timetable has been changed periodically, and Congress commonly misses some of the target dates (see Box 14-2 for the timetable).

Among many complex features of the 1974 act, two are central components of Congress's budget process: the concurrent budget resolution and reconciliation. These two features warrant discussion because they orient much of the time-consuming work of each annual legislative session, attract

BOX 14-2 **The Congressional Budget Timetable**

Deadline	Action to be completed
First Monday in February	President submits budget to Congress
February 15	Congressional Budget Office submits economic and budget outlook report to Budget Committees
Six weeks after president submits budget	Committees submit views and estimates to Budget Committees
April 1	Senate Budget Committee reports budget resolution
April 15	Congress completes action on budget resolution
May 15	Annual appropriations bills may be considered in the House, even if action on budget resolution has not been completed
June 10	House Appropriations Committee reports last annual appropriations bill
June 15	House completes action on reconciliation legislation (if required by budget resolution)
June 30	House completes action on annual appropriations bills
July 15	President submits mid-session review of his budget to Congress
October 1	Fiscal year begins

Source: Bill Heniff Jr., *The Congressional Budget Process Timetable,* Congressional Research Service Report No. 98–472 GOV, July 17, 2003.

the attention of many interests and participants clamoring for fiscal resources, and influence policy decisions and outcomes.

Concurrent Budget Resolution

The core of Congress's annual budget process centers on adoption of a concurrent budget resolution. This measure is formulated by the House and Senate Budget Committees, which consider the views and estimates of numerous committees and witnesses. The resolution consists of two basic parts. The first part deals with fiscal aggregates: total federal spending, total federal revenues, and the public debt or surplus for the upcoming fiscal year (October 1 to September 30). The budget resolution also sets multiyear targets for these fiscal aggregates. The second part subdivides the budget aggregates among twenty functional categories, such as national defense, agriculture, and energy, and it establishes spending levels for each. In effect, the budget resolution sets the overall level of discretionary spending for each fiscal year. For fiscal year 2006, the budget resolution set a spending ceiling of $843 billion for appropriations bills in an overall budget of $2.6 trillion.

Under a House rule reinstated at the start of the 108th Congress (January 7, 2003)—it was dropped from the rulebook of the 107th House—"after successful adoption of the budget [resolution] the House would automatically be 'deemed' to have passed a bill to increase the debt ceiling"; that is, the total amount of outstanding public debt (savings bonds, Treasury securities, and other government obligations) permitted by law.[55] Votes to raise the federal debt ceiling are often controversial, in part because campaign challengers can charge lawmakers who support the hike as big spenders. The House's "deeming" procedure avoids this problem.

The Senate has no comparable procedure. However, when the Senate in 2005 adopted the conference report on the fiscal 2006 budget resolution (H. Con. Res. 95), it provided a way to limit debate on the issue. The Senate granted filibuster-proof protection (via the reconciliation procedure) to legislation increasing the national debt from $8.1 trillion to almost $9 trillion. "[M]y friends on the other side of the aisle do not want to have a [lengthy] debate about how exploding budget deficits are piling up our national debt," opined Democratic senator Frank R. Lautenberg of New Jersey.[56] Senate Budget chairman Gregg noted that when Democrats controlled the Senate, they twice raised the debt ceiling using the reconciliation procedure. He went on to say that raising the debt ceiling is "something that as a Government" has to be done "to make sure the Government continues to operate."[57]

The budget resolution is Congress's fiscal blueprint. It establishes the context of congressional budgeting; guides the budgetary actions of the authorizing, appropriating, and taxing committees; and reflects Congress's spending priorities. In a period of polarized politics, partisan considerations dominate debates on these resolutions as Democrats and Republicans battle over spending levels for their competing priorities. "I've always said the budget vote is the toughest vote because we have to carry that budget by ourselves," exclaimed House Speaker J. Dennis Hastert, R-Ill. "We don't get any help from across the aisle."[58] A senator explained the purposes of the budget resolution:

> [The budget] resolution would be analogous to an architect's set of plans for constructing a building. It gives the general direction, framework, and prioritization of Federal fiscal policy each year. Those priorities then drive the individual appropriations and tax measures which will support that architectural plan.[59]

The House and Senate each consider a budget resolution. In the House, budget resolutions are typically considered under special rules from the Rules Committee, which limit debate and impose restrictions on the number and types of amendments. In the Senate, unless members accept a unanimous consent agreement imposing time restrictions, the 1974 budget act sets a fifty-hour limitation for consideration of the budget resolution. However, amendments can be taken up and voted upon after the fifty hours, but without debate. This circumstance often leads to so-called vote-a-ramas, during which senators over several days may "cast back-to-back votes on a dizzying array of dozens of amendments," often with the two Congresses in mind. The votes will "serve as valuable campaign fodder" in the next election.[60]

When each chamber passes budget resolutions that contain different aggregate and functional levels, which is normal practice, House and Senate members usually meet in conference to resolve their disagreements. The conference report is then submitted to both chambers for final action. Congress's budget resolution is not submitted to the president and thus has no legal effect. Instead, it outlines a fiscal framework that enables Congress, through its budget committees, CBO, and other devices, to monitor all budget-related actions taken during the course of a year.

Reconciliation

The 1974 budget act established a special procedure called reconciliation, which is an optional process authorized when Congress adopts the budget resolution. Its basic purpose is to bring revenue and direct spending (entitlement) legislation into conformity (or reconciliation) with the fiscal targets established in the concurrent budget resolution. As Sen. Robert C. Byrd, D-W.Va., declaimed: "[A] budget reconciliation process was established as an optional procedure to enhance Congress's ability to change current law in order to bring revenue and spending levels into conformity with the targets of the budget resolution."[61]

First used in 1980, reconciliation is a controversial and often employed process (nineteen times from 1980 to 2004) that "forces committees that might not want to reduce spending for entitlements under their jurisdiction to act and report legislation."[62] In practice, reconciliation has been used to reduce spending, primarily through entitlement savings, and either to increase revenues or cut taxes.

Reconciliation is a two-step process. In the first step, Congress adopts a budget resolution containing a provision that instructs committees to report legislation that changes existing law. The instructions embody three features. They designate, by name, the committees required to report legislation; they give each committee a dollar figure for mandated savings; and they establish a deadline for reporting legislation to achieve the savings. In the second step, the House and Senate Budget Committees compile into an omnibus reconciliation bill the legislative changes in revenue or direct spending programs recommended by the named committees.

The budget resolution adopted in spring 2005 required three reconciliation bills "later in the year that would provide for $34.7 billion in cuts to mandatory programs, $70 billion in tax cuts and a $781 billion increase in the statutory debt limit."[63] (The debt limit measure applies only to the Senate.)

Politically sensitive to the two Congresses, Republicans wanted separate reconciliation bills for entitlements and tax cuts so as not to encounter electoral fallout. "They would be concerned if tax cuts and cuts in critical services are in the same [reconciliation] bill because people might think spending cuts for programs like Medicaid [approximately $10 billion over the next five years] are being used to fund tax cuts," said the Democratic staff director of the House Budget Committee.[64] Not since 1997 has Congress employed reconciliation to find financial savings in entitlement programs. Unease over rising deficits (a projected record $427 billion in fiscal 2005) galvanized the two chambers to find savings or make reductions in various entitlement programs.

Reconciliation bills are treated in the Senate differently from other bills or amendments. Reconciliation bills cannot be filibustered (a statutory time limit of twenty hours is placed on debate); passage requires a simple majority instead of the supermajority (sixty votes) needed to stop a talkathon; and amendments must be germane (the Senate has no general germaneness rule). Little surprise that measures likely to arouse controversy in the GOP-controlled Senate, such as tax-cut legislation, are attached to filibuster-proof reconciliation measures that could pass with fifty votes, if Vice President Dick Cheney casts the tie-breaking vote. To prevent the Senate from putting issues (abortion, for instance) that are extraneous to deficit reduction into reconciliation bills, senators adopted the so-called Byrd Rule (named after Senator Byrd) in the mid-1980s. Under this complex rule, "measures cannot be included in the Senate reconciliation package [including conference reports] if they do not have revenue or entitlement components or if such components are 'merely incidental' to a broader policy question. It takes 60 votes in the Senate to waive the Byrd Rule."[65] Significantly, changes to Social Security are considered extraneous under the Byrd Rule, which means sixty votes will be necessary in the Senate to overcome a filibuster against legislation revamping the retirement program.

Reconciliation, in sum, is a powerful procedure for fiscal retrenchment. President Reagan and GOP congressional leaders in 1981 used it for the first time on a grand scale. A reconciliation bill dictated deep, multiyear reductions (about $130 billion over three years) in domestic spending. Not long afterward, Congress also agreed to Reagan's tax legislation, the Economic Recovery Tax Act of 1981, which sharply cut tax rates for individuals and businesses. The revenue losses caused by the tax cut, combined with increased defense and entitlement expenditures and insufficient spending reductions in other areas, soon pushed annual budget deficits from double to triple digits. For decades, Congress has grappled statutorily and in other ways with deficits, with only a brief interlude of surpluses.

The Gramm-Rudman-Hollings Plan

The escalating growth of budgetary deficits after 1981 became the prime congressional issue as lawmakers and presidents adapted to a new world: the politics of deficit reduction. As the national debt (the accumulation of annual deficits) mounted, numerous proposals were put forth to deal with the problem. One notable example in the mid-1980s was the Gramm-Rudman-Hollings plan (named after Sens. Phil Gramm, R-Texas; Warren B. Rudman, R-N.H.; and Ernest F. Hollings, D-S.C.).

Its core feature was the establishment in law of annual deficit reduction targets. If Congress did not meet the targets, the president would have to sequester funds; that is, impose automatic across-the-board spending cuts evenly divided between defense and domestic programs. This dire prospect was supposed to create an incentive for Congress and the president to decide how best to achieve deficit reduction. The plan did not work and deficits continued to climb. Congress exempted 70 percent of the budget from the threat of sequestration. Moreover, the yearly targets were met through budgetary gimmicks. Dissatisfaction with this law, despite its value in focusing legislative attention on the deficit, triggered enactment of another major budgetary reform: the Budget Enforcement Act (BEA) of 1990 (the product of a budget summit between President George Bush and congressional leaders). The law was subsequently amended several times but allowed to expire in 2002. Many lawmakers in both parties have tried, so far unsuccessfully, to revive some version of the BEA.

The Budget Enforcement Act

The Budget Enforcement Act once again changed the fiscal procedures of Congress. Three basic features undergird the law. First, it shifted Congress's attention from deficit reduction to spending control. Thus, the law removed the threat of automatic across-the-board reductions if conditions beyond Congress's control (inflation, a worsening economy, or emergency funding for crises or disasters) pushed the deficit upward.

Second, the BEA established caps, or limits, for discretionary spending. The spending caps can be changed, but Congress and the president would have to agree to the modification. If Congress exceeds the spending limits, the law provides for across-the-board reductions to bring spending in line with the caps. However, a loophole in the law enables Congress and the president to escape tight spending caps and avoid a zero-sum dilemma: paying for spending hikes in some discretionary programs by making cuts in other programs. If Congress and the president designate expenditures above the cap as emergency spending, they are exempt from the limits imposed by the BEA.

Third, the BEA subjected tax and entitlement programs to a new pay-as-you-go (PAYGO) procedure, which requires that any tax reductions or any increases in direct spending (that is, entitlement) programs be offset by tax hikes or reductions in other direct spending programs. The enforcement mechanism is the threat of across-the-board cuts in direct spending programs not exempt under BEA. As the chief counsel of the Senate Budget Committee explained: "The 'pay-as-you-go' label implies that Congress and the President may cut taxes or create [new direct spending] programs—that is 'go'—if they also agree to provide offsetting increased revenues or spending reductions—that is 'pay.' "[66]

Throughout much of the 1990s, the GOP-controlled Congress and President Clinton waged fierce battles over deficit reduction. As part of their political game plan, Republicans sent Clinton appropriations and reconciliation bills making deep cuts in federal programs. The president vetoed the measures, forcing two partial shutdowns of the government. The public blamed Republicans for the shutdowns, the longest in congressional history, with the result that GOP congressional leaders changed their combative approach and reopened the government. The bitter fights reflected profound policy differences between the two parties and between Clinton and Congress. Still, the two sides made a fiscal and policy breakthrough when they announced on May 2, 1997, a joint plan to produce a balanced budget by 2002.

SURPLUSES ARRIVE UNEXPECTEDLY

To the surprise of many lawmakers and pundits, who talked regularly about the pain and sacrifice (tax hikes and spending cuts) that balancing the budget would require, a balanced budget became reality sooner than anyone expected. By the end of September 1998, the national budget was $70 billion in the black, something that last occurred in 1969. David A. Stockman, President Reagan's director of the Office of Management and Budget, once predicted deficits as far as the eye could see. Now economic forecasters were predicting surpluses as far as the eye could see.

Why the surge of black ink? Several factors contributed to the fiscal turnaround. First, the end of the cold war led to reductions in defense expenditures. Second, despite some soft spots, the America economy was strong and healthy. This factor, combined with a booming stock market, flooded the federal Treasury with tax and capital gains dollars provided mainly by the richest one percent of the populace. Third, the Federal Reserve kept inflation and interest rates under control through an effective monetary policy that promoted economic expansion. Fourth, presidential and congressional budgetary decisions, such as passage of the BEA of 1990 during the George Bush administration and President Clinton's 1993 economic package, encouraged fiscal restraint and led to budgetary savings. Finally, luck and timing contributed to the fiscal mix. "Just about everything broke right that could have broken right" is how Robert Reischauer, a former CBO director, explained the deficit-free picture.[67]

Not everyone believed that the politics of plenty had arrived or, if so, that it would last indefinitely. Some lawmakers suggested to their colleagues that budget surpluses stood for "b.s." Another economic recession, they said, could be around the corner. Economic forecasts are often unreliable or just plain wrong. A downturn in the domestic economy or an international economic crisis could undermine the optimistic fiscal projections. A military conflict could send defense expenditures skyrocketing and erode any budgetary surplus. Several analysts and lawmakers flatly denied that a surplus existed. "The truth is there is no surplus," exclaimed a senator, citing a national debt at the time of $5.7 trillion.[68]

On January 30, 2001, CBO revised upward its surplus projections over the next decade to $5.6 trillion. This surplus figure was composed of two parts. The first surplus is generated from the payroll taxes of workers and employers, which is earmarked for deposit in the Social Security trust fund. Currently, more payroll taxes are going into the fund than are needed to pay benefits to elderly retirees. Today's excess in Social Security revenues is called the off-budget surplus. This favorable condition is projected to change, when the seventy-six million baby boomers retire in droves and begin to draw down Social Security's extra revenues.

The second surplus is the on-budget surplus. This is the amount of money generated from income taxes and other sources, excluding Social Security. These funds are used to finance federal agencies and programs. Of the estimated $5.6 trillion budget surplus, $2.5 trillion is in Social Security and $3.1 trillion would accumulate from general revenue sources.

Both parties pledged not to touch the off-budget surplus. In 1998 President Clinton promised to "save Social Security first." No longer would Social Security be raided to pay for the general operations of the government. (For decades, both parties had masked the true size of the deficit by using the extra Social Security funds to help pay for general governmental programs.) Not to be outdone, Republicans embraced the lockbox concept. They promised to lock up 100 percent of the Social Security surplus. Their pledges and promises did not last very long.

THE RETURN OF DEFICITS

Given the projected $5.6 trillion surplus, President George W. Bush and congressional Democrats soon began to argue over what to do with the on-budget surplus of $3.1 trillion. Although many lawmakers and pundits recognized that the ten-year projection might be grossly wrong and never materialize because of a slowing economy, international crises, or other reasons, politicians in both parties had their own ideas on how the surplus should be spent. Here was a case of fiscal projections driving policy making, even though the money was not yet in the bank.

President Bush's top priority when he took office was a $1.6 trillion tax cut. And on June 7, 2001, the president signed into law the largest tax cut ($1.35 trillion) since Reagan's. A little more than three months later terrorists attacked the United States and new demands and challenges confronted the country. From a budget perspective, at least three significant developments merit some discussion. First, the rather brief era (1998–2002) of surpluses came to an early end.

What happened to the surplus? It disappeared because the factors that produced it reversed themselves to trigger the return of deficits. Instead of defense cutbacks, the nation was paying for a global war on terrorism, military conflicts in Afghanistan and Iraq and the reconstruction of those countries, and enhanced homeland security. A record ten years of uninterrupted economic growth ended, the economy turned sluggish, and the stock market performed poorly—all of which led to a decline in federal revenues. Another contributor to revenue shortfalls was the large tax cuts pushed by the Bush administration. The Bush White House successfully obtained a new tax cut every year as a way to encourage economic growth, shrink government revenues to pressure lawmakers to reduce spending on unwanted administration programs, and keep the GOP base united.

Finally, Congress's statutory fiscal constraints—spending caps and PAYGO—expired on September 30, 2002. With the return of deficits, Congress now must decide whether to bring back these forms of fiscal discipline, devise new processes, or rely on existing legislative procedures for budgetary control. Lawmakers in both parties have been unsuccessful so far in restoring statutory PAYGO and spending growth budget rules. They have been unsuccessful in part because President Bush wants PAYGO rules to apply only to spending increases but not to tax cuts. This means that if taxes are cut, the lost revenues would not have to be offset, or paid for, by comparable revenue hikes or reductions in entitlement programs. The Senate does have a temporary and narrower (compared with the expired statutory version) PAYGO rule, created as a feature of the concurrent budget resolution. It is slated to expire in 2008. The House has no such provision, but it did add a new point of order provision to its rules.

Some analysts are dismayed by the current state of the congressional budget process. Discretionary spending caps have sometimes been evaded by designating spending, even for the conduct of the decennial census, as emergency. Partisan conflicts frequently delay action on appropriations bills or compel hasty legislative action on omnibus appropriations measures. Budget resolutions may be ignored or cannot be adopted. (In 2002, for the first time ever, the Senate failed to adopt a budget resolution. Four years earlier Congress was unable to agree to a budget resolution.) The lockbox is broken as surpluses in Social Security are once more being used to mask the growing size of the deficit. And the executive branch, in the judgment of various analysts, has seized control of the budget process from start to finish.

> The Constitution gives Congress the power of the purse, and the budget law of 1974, which still governs legislative action, was designed to rein in executive influence. But in recent years, a combination of congressional futility, partisan gridlock, and administration turf-grabbing [the president sets the level of discretionary spending and most congressional Republicans go along, for instance] have

transferred much of the power to the White House. Equally important has been the growth of "mandatory" spending: Programs such as Social Security and Medicare that are outside annual congressional control have come to dominate the budget.[69]

Second, the two parties have switched fiscal positions. Democrats now spotlight the dangers of the deficit and use it on the campaign trail to criticize President Bush's handling of the economy. Many Republicans, contrary to the views of President Reagan, now contend that deficits may be a good thing. "Anything that will help us stop spending money, I'm in favor of," exclaimed conservative representative Sue Myrick, R-N.C. "This place is set up to spend money. . . . And if there's a deficit that may help us."[70] Cutting taxes is an important way for Republicans to reduce the reach of the national government by starving it of funds, even if that means higher deficits. "If we had a little teeny government and a big deficit, I wouldn't care," said conservative GOP strategist Grover Norquist. "It's the size of the government we're focused on. It's also the size of the government the left is focused on."[71]

Conservative Republicans, however, are divided as to whether "the problem is big government or budget deficits. Both philosophies argue for spending cuts. But the deficit hawks see tax increases as an option as well, while those concerned with big government see spending cuts as the only real option."[72] Meanwhile, many Democrats want to reduce the deficit to free up money to spend on scores of favored domestic programs, such as health, education, and environmental protection. Neither party is willing "to sacrifice their priorities for the sake of deficit reduction."[73]

Finally, if deficits continue to escalate in the years ahead, the federal government confronts a serious dilemma in funding competing priorities. President Bush has promised to cut the deficit in half by 2009, but that prediction may not be achievable given the mounting cost of the global war on terrorism, Iraqi reconstruction, and other government programs. How will the government, for instance, address the looming retirement of the baby boomers? "This is a demographic time bomb that we are facing as a society," stated Sen. Kent Conrad, D-N.D.[74] A political consensus currently does not exist on how to deal with the impending explosion in the costs of Social Security, Medicare, and Medicaid, the largest entitlement programs. Some officials argue that a booming economy will generate the bushels of money needed to pay for these and other priorities, that current deficits are relatively small and manageable compared with an over $12 trillion economy, and that various entitlement reforms will reduce the price tag for these programs. The Bush administration's basic plan to deal with the deficit is to cut spending and cut taxes. "Tax cuts and no tax increases are the driving principle of the Republican Party at this point," said GOP representative Michael N. Castle of Delaware.[75] It remains problematic whether reductions in spending and revenue by themselves can stem the flow of red ink and improve the long-term fiscal outlook.

Thus, there is renewed concern about growing deficits. "The deficit is a hard thing to see the effects of. It's not the wolf at the door. . . . [I]t's termites in the woodwork, a constant drag, gnawing away at the capital stock."[76]

CONCLUSION

Today, lawmakers are preoccupied with important policy questions: defense and homeland security in an age of terrorism, economic growth, and the condition of various domestic social programs. Rep. Barney Frank, D-Mass., posed a question that crystallizes the debate over these various concerns: "What is the appropriate level of public activity in our society?"[77] Democrats and Republicans often provide different answers to this question. Governing, however, means making choices. Future decisions about budgeting and national priorities will surely reflect the values, goals, and interests that result from the confrontations and accommodations inherent in America's pluralist policy-making system.

SUGGESTED READINGS

Elving, Ronald D. *Conflict and Compromise: How Congress Makes the Law.* New York: Simon and Schuster, 1995.

Kerwin, Cornelius M. *Rulemaking: How Government Agencies Write Laws and Make Policy.* 3d ed. Washington, D.C.: CQ Press, 2003.

Kingdon, John W. *Agendas, Alternatives, and Public Policies.* Boston: Little, Brown, 1984.

Rubin, Irene S. *Balancing the Federal Budget.* New York: Chatham House, 2003.

Schick, Allen. *The Federal Budget: Politics, Policy, Process.* Rev. ed. Washington, D.C.: Brookings Institution, 2000.

Hard and soft diplomacy (clockwise from top): Above, U.S. secretary of state Condoleezza Rice and Afghan president Hamid Karzai hold a press conference at the Presidential Palace in Kabul, Afghanistan. Top right, food supplies are delivered to needy countries under the Department of State's foreign aid program and the Department of Agriculture's P.L. 480 program, which distributes surplus agricultural products abroad. Bottom right, a U.S. marine runs for cover as another stands watch in Ramadi, Iraq, in late 2004. Bottom left, Dr. Rice testifies during the Senate Foreign Relations Committee hearing on her nomination to be secretary of state.

chapter 15

Congress and National Security Policies

On September 11, 2001, one of the authors of this book was traveling in China. After a day hiking along China's Great Wall and attending the Beijing Opera, he flipped on the TV in his hotel room to witness the scene then unfolding twelve time zones away. The other author was on Capitol Hill, giving a talk to federal executives, when word came to evacuate the building. The members of the group were mystified until they saw the television footage of smoke rising from the Pentagon, across the Potomac River. It was the prelude to a day of terror and uncertainty. The Capitol itself was a possible target, and so he made his way home on the Metro, jammed with people worried that it, too, might be hit.

Not that violence is a stranger to the nation. Its nineteenth-century wars were fought mostly on American soil; and some sixty-odd years ago U.S. military forces stationed at Pearl Harbor, Hawaii, were attacked, pushing the nation into World War II. Violence against innocent or random victims—riots, lynchings, massacres, and other terrorist acts—are part of American history. Furthermore, the United States is not the prime victim of global terrorism: Few nations have escaped its toll in death and destruction.

But Americans cling to the myth that they are a special people set apart from the world's conflicts. Having forsaken old-world wars and rivalries, its citizens—protected by two oceans—historically resolved to remain aloof from other nations' struggles. The most famous passage of President George Washington's 1796 Farewell Address, read dutifully in the chambers of Congress every year on his birthday, counsels that

> [t]he great rule of conduct for us, in regard to foreign nations is in extending our commercial relations to have with them as little political connection as possible. . . . 'Tis our true policy to steer clear of permanent alliances, with any portion of the foreign world. . . . Taking care to keep ourselves, by suitable establishments, on a respectable defensive posture, we may safely trust to temporary alliances for extraordinary emergencies.[1]

This American dream was never fulfilled, and it was grievously shattered by the attacks of September 11.

Such events are a reminder that forming U.S. foreign and national security policies is not an episodic activity but a continual obligation. Congress and the president share in these duties just as they do in domestic and budgetary matters. Congress has broad constitutional authority to take part in foreign and defense decisions. Even the most decisive chief executives can find themselves constrained by active, informed, and determined policy makers on Capitol Hill.

CONSTITUTIONAL POWERS

The U.S. Constitution is "an invitation to struggle for the privilege of directing American foreign policy." [2] In other words, foreign and military powers are divided between the branches. "While the president is usually in a position to *propose,* the Senate and Congress are often in a technical position at least to *dispose.*" [3] The struggle over the proper role of each branch in shaping foreign policy involves conflict over policy as well as over process.

The President Proposes

Chief executives enjoy certain innate advantages in dealing with foreign affairs. As John Jay wrote in *The Federalist Papers* No. 64, the office's unity, its superior information sources, and its capacity for secrecy and dispatch give the president daily charge of foreign intercourse.[4] In Jay's time Congress was not in session the whole year, whereas the president was always on hand to make decisions.

The president's explicit international powers are to negotiate treaties and appoint ambassadors (powers shared with the Senate), to receive ambassadors and other emissaries, and to serve as commander in chief of the armed forces. This last-mentioned power looms large over interbranch politics of the modern period, in which executive agencies possess huge military, security, and intelligence capabilities. Presidents have claimed not only their explicit prerogatives but also others not spelled out in the Constitution. Whether they are called implied, inherent, or emergency powers, they are often invoked by presidents in conducting foreign policy.

The executive branch tends to be favored by foreign policy specialists, who often denigrate legislative involvement in foreign policy. Speaking to his fellow Republicans just after they ascended to power on Capitol Hill in 1995, former secretary of state James Baker cautioned the new majority "not to meddle too much" in the (then Democratic) administration's foreign policy. U.S. leadership in the world, he declared, could be sustained only "if we understand that the president has primary responsibility for the conduct of the nation's foreign policy." [5]

The president's advantages are magnified in times of warfare or crisis. It was Congress's clumsy management of affairs during the Revolutionary War that, among other things, led the founders to champion an independent, energetic executive and to designate the president as commander in chief. Wars and crisis events tend to centralize authority, and at such times presidential powers reach their zenith. This held true during the cold war—hostilities between the United States and the Soviet Union (1947–1989)—and the hot wars that ignited in Korea (1950–1953) and Vietnam (1965–1974). It has been re-ignited by the terrorist attacks of September 2001. Heightened security fears, the assault against terrorism, and wars launched against Afghanistan and Iraq brought new and sometimes unprecedented assertions of executive authority. Congress's voice was muted.

When tensions ease, however, presidential powers usually contract and are subjected to sharper scrutiny from Capitol Hill. Perhaps the most sensible statement of the separation of powers came from Justice Robert Jackson in *Youngstown Sheet and Tube Co. v. Sawyer* (1952), who wrote that "the president might act in external affairs without congressional authority, but not that he might act contrary to an act of Congress."[6]

Congress Reacts

Congress has an impressive arsenal of explicit constitutional duties, such as the power to declare war, to regulate foreign commerce, and to raise and support military forces. Paramount is the power of the purse: "It is within the power of Congress to determine the course of American diplomacy, by virtue of its control over expenditures by the federal government," in the words of Cecil V. Crabb Jr. and his colleagues.[7]

From examining the historical record, Crabb and his colleagues have identified three conditions for congressional activism in foreign and defense affairs: (1) periods of weak presidential leadership in foreign policy, (2) public groundswells of concern over America's international role, and (3) pressing domestic issues that impinge upon foreign affairs. Their assessment of legislative activism in foreign affairs is pessimistic. They contend that legislative activism has been associated with "the least successful and impressive chapters in the annals of American diplomacy."[8]

A sober review of the historical record, however, yields a more balanced assessment of legislative influence on foreign policy. Congress asserted itself following the Revolutionary War and at the outset of the other nineteenth-century wars. At the same time, it moved to rein in excessive presidential assertions of authority both before and after those wars—a revisionist impulse that extends to the more recent wars: Korea, Vietnam, and the Persian Gulf, as well as the later phases of the cold war.

WHO SPEAKS FOR CONGRESS?

The wide-ranging subjects of foreign policy and military affairs fall within the purview of some twenty-three congressional committees. And other House panels and Senate panels consider tangential matters bearing on foreign and military policy.

The foreign affairs and national security panels are among the most visible on Capitol Hill. The Senate Foreign Relations and House International Relations Committees draw more time on the nightly television newscasts than do other committees.[9] The Senate and House Armed Services Committees rank fourth, which still means relatively high TV exposure.

The Senate Foreign Relations Committee considers treaties and nominations of many foreign policy officials. It has normally viewed itself as a working partner and adviser to the president. But, during the height of dispute over the Vietnam War in the late 1960s and early 1970s, the committee became a forum for antiwar debate under the leadership of Chairman J. William Fulbright, D-Ark. (1959–1974). Another chairman, Jesse Helms, R-N.C. (1995–2001), attacked international agencies and thwarted the Clinton administration's diplomatic objectives.

Despite the Senate committee's prestige, however, its subject matter is often regarded—mistakenly, it would seem—as remote from its members' constituencies. Richard G. Lugar, R-Ind., who became chairman in 2003, observed of a recent problem, "There's almost no political sex appeal to issues like Bosnia. For those who get involved it's strictly a pro bono service."[10] The panel's stock fell so low during Helms's regime that the Republican Conference talked about downgrading its status.

For most of its history the House International Relations (formerly Foreign Affairs) Committee worked in the shadow of its Senate counterpart. This situation changed after World War II, when foreign aid programs thrust the House—with its special powers of the purse—into virtual parity with the Senate.[11] Today the House committee addresses nearly as wide a range of issues as does the Senate committee. It tends, however, to attract members who have a more global outlook than the House as a whole. Consequently, its reports sometimes encounter skepticism on the House floor.

The Senate and House Armed Services Committees oversee the nation's military establishment. Annually, they authorize Pentagon spending for research, development, and procurement of weapons systems; construction of military facilities; and civilian and uniformed personnel. This last-mentioned jurisdiction includes the Uniform Code of Military Conduct, which governs the lives of men and women in uniform and which has attracted congressional scrutiny of such diverse matters as sexual harassment, treatment of imprisoned enemy combatants, and the right of Jewish officers to wear yarmulkes with military headgear. Although global strategy may intrigue some of the committees' members, what rivets their attention is structural policy making; that is, force levels, military installations, and defense contracts—issues closer to home. Thus constituency politics often drive military policy.

Because of their funding jurisdictions, House and Senate Appropriations subcommittees exert detailed control over foreign and defense policies. Senate and House oversight committees review intelligence activities. Tariffs and other trade regulations are the province of the taxing committees (House Ways and Means, Senate Finance). Committees involved with banking handle international, financial, and monetary policies; the commerce committees have jurisdiction over foreign commerce generally. With the creation of the Homeland Security Department, nearly every other panel asserts jurisdiction linked in some way to national security.

The House and Senate select intelligence committees were created in the late 1970s, following revelations of widespread abuses, illegalities, and misconduct on the part of intelligence agencies, particularly the Central Intelligence Agency (CIA) and the Federal Bureau of Investigation (FBI). After thirty years, however, the two oversight panels' close ties with the growing intelligence community seemed to hamper vigorous scrutiny. The 2004 report of the 9/11 Commission (National Commission on Terrorist Attacks Upon the United States) called for revitalizing oversight, through either a joint committee or separate House and Senate panels with authorizing and appropriating jurisdiction.[12]

Congress's organization for policy making is far from tidy. The profusion of congressional power centers leads chief executives to complain that they do not know whom to consult when crises arise and that leaks of sensitive information are inevitable with so many players. But chief executives and their emissaries are free to consult with as few or as many lawmakers as they choose—in some cases with only the joint party leaders, in others with chairmen and ranking minority members of the relevant committees.

TYPES OF FOREIGN AND NATIONAL SECURITY POLICIES

Foreign policy is the sum total of decisions and actions governing a nation's relations with other nations. The major foreign policy ingredients are national goals to be achieved and resources for achieving them. Statecraft is the art of selecting preferred outcomes and marshaling appropriate resources to attain them. As former secretary of state Henry A. Kissinger, known as a foreign policy pragmatist, puts it: "Values are essential for defining objections; strategy is what implements them by establishing priorities and defining timing."[13]

Ascertaining a nation's goals is no simple matter. Historically, momentous congressional debates have raged over divergent and even incompatible foreign policy goals—over ties to such old-world powers as England and France during the nation's first decades, over high versus low tariffs, over American expansionism and industrialization abroad, over involvement in foreign wars, and over strategies for combating terrorists. As for resources for meeting such goals, military strength and preparedness (national security policies) probably come first to mind. However, other assets, for example, wealth, productivity, political ideals, and cultural values, are even more potent in the long run.

In balancing national goals and national resources, policy makers confront several different types of foreign and national security policies. Structural policies involve procuring and deploying resources or personnel; strategic policies advance the nation's objectives militarily or diplomatically; and crisis policies protect the nation's safety against specific foreign or domestic threats.

STRUCTURAL POLICIES

National security programs involve millions of workers and expend billions of dollars annually. Decisions about deploying such vast resources are called structural policy decisions. Examples include choices of specific weapons systems, contracts with private suppliers, location of military installations, sales of weapons and surplus goods to foreign countries, and trade policies that affect domestic industries and workers. Structural policy making on foreign and defense issues is virtually the same as distributive policy making in the domestic realm.

The last sixty years have seen a growing imbalance in the weight of military versus nonmilitary elements of foreign policies. The nation's singular military machine (its fiscal year 2006 budget was greater than that of all other nations combined) is, historically speaking, a fairly recent phenomenon. After each of its earlier wars, the United States quickly "sent the boys home" and, under congressional pressure, shrank its armed forces—though each time to somewhat higher plateaus.[14] Following World War II, the nation's global burdens and the cold war threat led to unprecedented levels of peacetime preparedness. By 1960, when retiring president Dwight D. Eisenhower, himself a career officer, warned against the "military-industrial complex," the new militarism was already embedded in the nation's political and economic system.

Department of Defense (DOD) spending—more than $500 billion annually—is the largest controllable portion of the federal budget. As the nation's largest employer, its largest customer, and its largest procurer of equipment and services, DOD controls a huge number of structural outlays, which attract a wide swath of political interests.

The State Department, in contrast, makes relatively few such decisions. Although nearly twenty cents of every federal dollar is spent on the military, slightly more than a penny goes to international affairs, including military assistance, diplomatic representation, foreign development, and humanitarian assistance.[15] The State Department's services and achievements are largely intangible, and in any event it spends much of its energy and money overseas. Little surprise, then, that it has few strong domestic clients and relatively few champions on Capitol Hill.

The Congressional-Military-Industrial Complex

Defense dollars—for projects, contracts, and bases, for example—are pursued by business firms, labor unions, and local communities. The Pentagon's ties to the business community are so cozy that an estimated 40 percent of its contracts are awarded without competitive bidding, according to an independent survey of some 2.2 million contracts.[16] As champions of local interests, members of Congress are naturally drawn into the process. Their impulse is wholly bipartisan.

Weapons Systems. Pentagon procurement officers anticipate congressional needs in planning and designing projects. The perfect weapons system, it is said, is one with a component manufactured in every congressional district in the nation. The Air Force's F/A-22 Raptor jet fighter, each costing nearly $300 million, is assembled at Georgia and Texas factories from parts made by one thousand suppliers in forty-three states. "What it means to the company is the technology and the jobs," explained a factory manager.[17]

Even when military planners decide to phase out a weapon, they may be compelled by lawmakers to keep the item in production. Consider the Marines' V-22 Osprey, a tilt-rotor aircraft that flies like a conventional plane but takes off and lands like a helicopter. Conceived during the cold war, the planes—now some $100 million apiece—were later deemed too costly to be continued. And there were design problems; several planes crashed, claiming the lives of two dozen Marines. But the Osprey lives on. The Tilt-Rotor Caucus, a group of representatives from regions where the plane is manufactured, worked with contractors to keep the project alive.[18] "It is the hardest thing to do, to take a weapon out of the budget," a defense undersecretary noted. "It is just so easy to put one in."[19]

Lawmakers and lobbyists exploit the four services' (Army, Air Force, Navy, Marines) differing priorities, which persist in the face of determined efforts at coordination by civilian managers over several presidencies, Republican and Democratic alike. The Air Force's projects include new jets and space weapons, the Marines want the Osprey, the Navy covets new aircraft carriers, and the Army needs new artillery and combat vehicles.

Military Base Closures. Proliferation and geographic dispersion of military installations are other examples of distributive military policy-making. L. Mendel Rivers, D-S.C., chairman of the House Armed Services Committee (1965–1971), kept defense money flowing to bases in Charleston, South Carolina, campaigning on the slogan "Rivers Delivers!" More recently, Sen. Trent Lott, R-Miss., hailed a Pascagoula, Mississippi, firm that keeps busy building ships for the navy: "It's one of the most important shipyards in the country, and if I were not supportive of my hometown, that shipyard and the workers in that shipyard, I wouldn't deserve to be in Congress, now would I?"[20]

In the post–cold war era, Congress tried to surmount the politically unpalatable problem of closing unneeded military installations. In 1988 Congress passed a law intended to insulate such decisions from congressional pressure by delegating them to a bipartisan Base Realignment and Closing Commission (BRAC). From the defense secretary's recommendations, this agency would draw up a list of installations targeted for closure. To make the decisions hard to overturn, the list had to be accepted or rejected as a whole by the president and Congress.

Four rounds of BRACs (1989–1995) reduced or eliminated hundreds of defense installations. Political pressures were intense. The last commission chair, former senator Alan J. Dixon, D-Ill. (1981–1993), was greeted at base entrances by parents holding children who, they said, would starve if the base closed.[21] Senators and representatives from affected areas fought the closure lists and nearly succeeded in overturning them. Everyone was relieved when the agency closed its doors at the end of 1995, having succeeded in shutting some one hundred major facilities at home and more than six hundred abroad.

The base-closing issue survives. DOD maintains that 20 to 25 percent of the more than four hundred remaining bases are redundant. The Clinton administration called for two more BRAC rounds. "Over my dead body!" exclaimed Joel Hefley, R-Colo., a member of the House Armed Services Committee whose Colorado Springs district bristles with military installations (some of them obsolete).[22]

Secretary Donald H. Rumsfeld renewed the BRAC appeal, finally settling for one in 2005. Leading off the process, he asked the nine-member BRAC commission to shutter thirty-three major domestic sites and shrink twenty-nine more. He predicted savings of nearly $50 billion over twenty years. Some twenty-six thousand jobs were at risk, although most programs and personnel would be transferred to other locations. Lawmakers' cries of anguish were immediate, loud, and bipartisan. "We're going to fight the heck out of this," said Rep. Jack Kingston of Georgia, vice chairman of the House Republican Conference, which sent members a "BRAC Pack" listing direct phone lines for key military officials.[23] And overseeing BRAC's progress was Colorado Springs' Representative Hefley, chair of the Armed Services Subcommittee on Readiness.

Structural decisions, like distributive ones in the domestic realm, are typically brokered in congressional subcommittees. Legislators from areas containing major military installations or contractors lobby with executive agencies for continued support, and subcommittee decisions are reached with local needs in mind. Referring to military bases, Rep. Tom Allen, D-Maine, explained how as a freshman he was attracted to the Armed Services Committee: "There are enough jobs dependent [on defense] that I believed it was important to be present when those issues are discussed."[24] Rarely do these issues spill out on the House or Senate floor. Interested members can usually craft agreements at the subcommittee or committee stage on how to allocate defense resources.

Trade Politics

Another arena for distributive politics is foreign trade. Since the First Congress (1789–1791), the power "to regulate commerce with foreign nations" has been used to protect and enhance the competitive position of domestic goods and industries, whether cotton or wheat or textiles or computer software. Until the 1930s, tariff legislation was fiercely contested on Capitol Hill by political parties and economic regions. Starting with the Reciprocal Trade Agreements Act of 1934, however, Congress began to delegate the details of tariff negotiations to the executive branch.

Protectionist impulses have not waned, however. Myriad trade interests are represented on Capitol Hill. Republicans—reflecting the business community—tend to favor lowering trade barriers at home and combating them abroad, to open world markets for U.S. goods. Democrats from areas of union strength want barriers to slow the loss of jobs to low-wage countries. Specific commodity concerns—steel, textiles, and farm products, for example—are voiced by lawmakers of both parties. Free trade finds more friends in the Senate, which overrepresents export-minded agricultural interests; the House, with its patchwork of local interests, has stronger protectionist leanings.

Most battles over trade bills call forth variations of the above lineups. In the thirteen months preceding completion of the North American Free Trade Agreement (NAFTA) negotiations in 1992, U.S. trade representative Carla A. Hills logged forty consultations with individual lawmakers and no fewer than 199 meetings with congressional groups, from the House Ways and Means and Senate Finance Committees to the Northeast-Midwest Congressional Coalition and the Senate Textile Group.[25]

When the bill implementing NAFTA reached Capitol Hill the next year, a bipartisan effort was needed to approve it. President Clinton launched a high-profile public relations campaign, trumpeted the bill's job-creation benefits, welcomed support from Republican leaders, and cut deals to meet individual legislators' objections. Opposing were many Democrats, including the House majority leader and chief whip. In the end, only 40 percent of House Democrats supported the president, but their 102 votes along with those of 132 Republicans were enough to gain House passage. NAFTA then easily passed the Senate. The final enactment was a huge patchwork of provisions aimed at placating disparate interests.[26] More than a decade later the modest Central American Free Trade Agreement (CAFTA), a centerpiece of President George W. Bush's trade agenda, encountered similar resistance—with many members complaining that the Clinton and Bush administrations had failed to implement promised retraining programs for workers whose jobs went overseas.[27]

Still other foreign policy concerns can fragment these lines even further. In the debate over U.S.-China trade status, for example, representatives splintered across the political spectrum. The lure of China's vast potential market for U.S. goods vied with doubts over China's unpredictable government and its poor human rights, worker safety, and environmental record. Trade policy and negotiations, asserts Rep. Sander M. Levin, D-Mich., "now involve virtually every area of what used to be considered U.S. domestic law—from antitrust and food safety to telecommunications."[28]

Congress, however, confronts a dilemma in dealing with trade. Members realize that trading partners need assurances that agreements can be ratified quickly and as a package. But having delegated most decisions to the executive, lawmakers who want to review specific trade deals must struggle to get back in the game. The Trade Act of 1974 addressed this dilemma. The president, it said, must actively consult, notify, and involve Congress as he negotiates trade agreements. These agreements take effect only after an implementing bill is enacted. Such legislation would be handled under an expedited fast-track procedure, including required steps and deadlines, limits on debate, and prohibition of amendments. Congress's involvement in trade decisions continued with passage of the Omnibus Trade and Competitiveness Act of 1988, which strengthened its oversight of trade agreements.[29]

Most presidents since 1974 have been awarded fast-track (or trade promotion) authority to negotiate trade pacts subject to up-or-down votes in both houses within ninety days. (The authority lapsed during Clinton's presidency and was not renewed by the Republican-led Congress.) After a vigorous lobbying effort, President Bush in August 2002 won a five-year renewal of the fast-track procedure. Even so, the House vote was close—215–212 (the Senate margin was 64–34). To gain the needed House votes, numerous concessions were made, for example, to placate textile workers and citrus growers. "I told the president that we are not going to support anything that leaves us bare on citrus," declared Rep. Mack Foley, R-Fla.[30] The measure also featured a Democratic-sponsored hike in funds for workers who lost jobs to foreign competition.[31]

Distributive politics underlie many other foreign and defense programs. For example, P.L. 480 dispenses agricultural surpluses to needy nations. This law not only serves humanitarian purposes but also provides outlets for subsidized farm products at home. Selling arms to other countries profits the U.S. government and private firms (some $53 billion in the four-year period ending in 1999) and affects civil and military affairs in every corner of the globe.[32]

STRATEGIC POLICIES

To protect the nation's interests, decision makers design strategic policies that address spending levels for international and defense programs; total military force levels; the basic mix of military forces and weapons systems; arms sales to foreign powers; foreign trade inducements or restrictions; allocation of economic, military, and technical aid to developing nations; treaty obligations to other nations; U.S. responses to human rights abuses abroad; and America's basic stance toward international bodies such as the United Nations (UN), the North Atlantic Treaty Organization (NATO), and world financial agencies.

Strategic policies embrace most major foreign policy questions. They engage top-level executive decision makers as well as congressional committees and midlevel executive officers. Such matters can express citizens' ideological, ethnic, racial, or economic interests.[33] Despite their obvious distributive elements, strategic issues typically involve broader themes and invoke policy makers' long-term attitudes and beliefs. The key agencies for strategic decision making include the State Department, the Office of the Secretary of Defense, the intelligence agencies, and the National Security Council—all advisory to the president.

The Power of the Purse

The spending power gives Congress the leverage to establish overall appropriation levels for foreign and defense purposes. Within these ceilings, priorities must be assigned among military services, among weapons systems, between uniformed personnel and military hardware, and on economic, cultural, or military aid, to name just a few of the choices. The president leads by presenting an annual budget, lobbying for the administration's priorities, and threatening to veto options deemed unacceptable. Yet if it chooses, Congress also can write its own budgets down to the smallest detail. And the omnibus character of appropriations measures places pressure on the president to accede to the outcome of legislative bargaining on expenditures. To get the 95 percent of the budget the administration wants, the president may have to swallow the 5 percent he opposes. For example, to support his ambitious post–September 11 military goals, President George W. Bush was obliged to sign military spending bills that included projects he and his defense advisers had resisted.[34]

Post–Cold War Spending: Down and Up. Congress responds both to perceived levels of international tension and to shifting public views about the salience of global engagement. Following the Soviet Union's collapse, a bipartisan consensus in the Pentagon and in Congress agreed that defense funding and force levels could be gradually cut. That consensus arose either from the belief that a sizable "peace dividend" could be realized or from the hope that savings could be gained from smarter planning and trimming waste, fraud, and abuse. However, downsizing the military establishment is politically and economically disruptive.

Congressional worries over defense downsizing flared up in the first year of George W. Bush's presidency. Bush more than once touted military reform that would exceed "marginal improvements" and "skip a generation" of weapons technology. "[G]ood appropriations will really only occur if there is a strategic vision," he explained to Republican House members.[35] Fears mounted when Defense Secretary Rumsfeld launched a thorough and mostly secret strategic review before he would approve specific budget requests. Rumsfeld argued that budgets did not fit weapons, which did not fit strategy. He compared the Pentagon to a factory with "conveyor belts going by and they were loaded four, five, six years ago, and they were not connected with each other."[36] As for creating a high-tech military while supporting conventional forces in combat zones, Rep. John P. Murtha, D-Pa., a senior Appropriations Committee member, said bluntly: "He doesn't have the money to do it."[37]

Footing the bills for combat operations poses dilemmas for Congress. How much money is needed, and how much freedom should the president have in spending it? Lyndon B. Johnson gradually deepened U.S. involvement in

Vietnam, but he hesitated to ask Congress to appropriate the needed funds. Thus the first supplemental funding bill was passed in February 1966, even though Congress had signed onto the war as early as August 1964 (with the Gulf of Tonkin Resolution). Johnson's effort to hide the escalating war costs while maintaining domestic programs elevated both inflation and the federal debt.

After the September 2001 assaults, Congress acted swiftly to pass a $40-billion supplemental appropriations package—one-fourth of which was under the president's near-total control. After the Afghanistan invasion Congress approved another $30 billion, again featuring flexibility. A number of lawmakers, especially on the funding committees, expressed their doubts. "All presidents want unlimited authority. In any time of conflict, there's a tendency to allow a little more leeway," said Rep. David L. Hobson, R-Ohio, an appropriations subcommittee chair. "We have a responsibility to maintain a balance . . . and we're struggling with that."[38] In the four years following the terrorist attacks, however, no less than five supplemental spending packages were approved, totaling more than $300 billion and carrying only marginal congressional adjustments. These were intended to insulate wartime spending from the Pentagon's ongoing procurement and staffing activities.

Spending on Diplomacy. Unlike national defense, international affairs funding represents a relatively small expenditure (see Figure 15-1). Historically, the nation's foreign operations required relatively small outlays. In the immediate post–World War II years, 1947–1951, however, programs to rebuild devastated Europe and Japan consumed as much as 16 percent of U.S. annual spending. Throughout the cold war, the United States was a major provider of economic, military, and technical aid throughout the world.

In recent years, such spending—for Department of State operations, the diplomatic service, and foreign aid—has accounted for around 1 percent of all expenditures. U.S. economic assistance to promote democracy, address poverty, and improve health and education amounts to a fraction of that. And most of this aid goes to a handful of frontline states (Israel, Egypt, Afghanistan, and Iraq most prominently).

U.S. foreign aid, although high in pure dollar terms, ranks low among the world's wealthiest nations as a proportion of gross domestic product.[39] "It's a question of balance," asserted James D. Wolfensohn, the U.S.-appointed World Bank president (1995–2005). "Does it make sense to put all that money . . . into the military when you don't deal with the underlying causes of distress?"[40] (Opinion surveys show that citizens indicate lukewarm support for foreign aid spending but grossly overestimate how much is actually spent.)

In the final analysis, no major foreign or military enterprise can be sustained unless Congress provides money and support. A president can conduct an operation for a time using existing funds and supplies, as Lyndon Johnson did at first in Vietnam, but sooner or later Congress must be asked for funding. The U.S. role in South Vietnam finally ended in 1974, when Congress simply refused to provide emergency aid funds.

FIGURE 15-1 Defense and Foreign Policy Spending as Percentage of Total Budget Outlays, 1940–2005

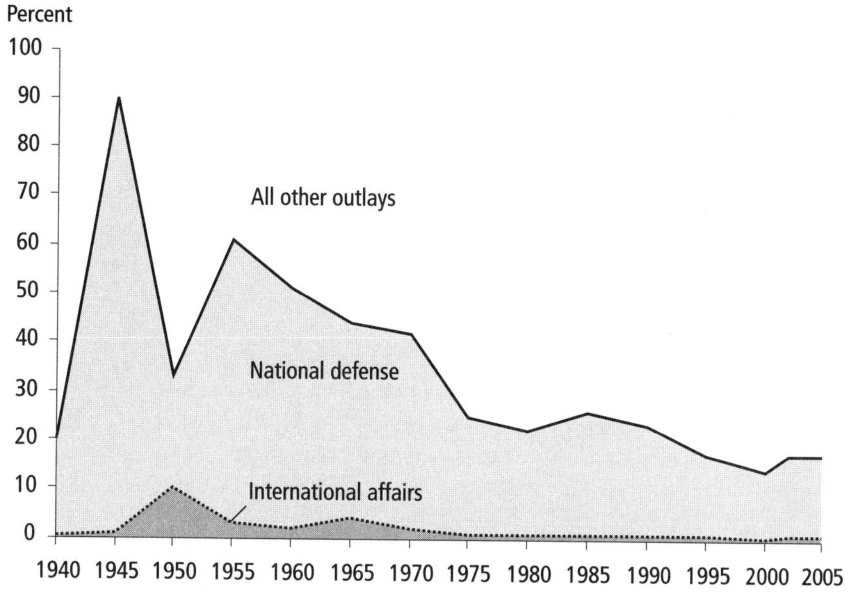

Source: *Budget of the United States Government, Fiscal Year 2006, Historical Tables* (Washington, D.C.: Government Printing Office, 2005), Table 3-2.

Note: Figures are fiscal year outlays, according to current statistical conventions for treating off-budget items. The total budget in billions of dollars was $9.5 in 1940, $42.6 in 1950, $92.2 in 1960, $195.6 in 1970, $590.9 in 1980, $1,253.2 in 1990, $1,825.0 in 2000, and $2,600.0 in 2005.

Treaties and Executive Agreements

The Constitution makes Congress an active partner with the president in a key element of strategic policy: treaties with foreign powers. Although initiated by the president, treaties are made "by and with the advice and consent of the Senate." The Senate's consent is signified by the concurrence of two-thirds of the senators present and voting.

Congress may or may not be taken into the president's confidence when treaties and executive agreements are negotiated. To avoid President Woodrow Wilson's humiliation when the Senate rejected the Treaty of Versailles after World War I, modern chief executives typically inform key senators during the negotiation process. After the pact is sent to the Senate, several courses of action may follow, above and beyond a simple up-or-down vote.

Rarely does the Senate reject a treaty outright. It has turned down only twenty treaties since 1789. One study found that the Senate had approved without change 944 treaties, or 69 percent of those submitted to it.[41] Such was the case in March 2003, when the Senate unanimously approved a U.S.-Russian treaty requiring cuts in the two nations' arsenals of long-range missiles. Despite critics' charges that the deal was "flimsy," senators opted to send a positive signal to Russia during the run-up to the Iraqi war. Despite "many reservations," Sen. Joseph R. Biden Jr., D-Del., ranking minority member on the Foreign Relations Committee, explained that "the reason I'm for this treaty is, failure to ratify [it] would be read as bad faith."[42]

The Senate may attach reservations to a treaty, which, if serious enough, may oblige the president to renegotiate the document. Formal reservations are employed to change policy, according to two scholars who examined the process. "Ratification reservations can dictate how the U.S. will interpret and implement a treaty, how the U.S. will behave on unrelated foreign policy issues, and in some instances can even change the actual text of a treaty."[43]

The Senate may simply decline to act at all. Languishing without Senate approval are some fifty treaties negotiated and signed by various presidents, including pacts dealing with the oceans, women's and children's rights, nuclear weapons testing, global warming, and biological diversity.[44]

The Chemical Weapons Convention, concluded in 1993 just before George Bush left office and signed by 161 nations, illustrates the Senate's active role in ratification. Although the treaty had broad bipartisan support, a group of hawkish lawmakers argued that the agreement was filled with loopholes and would not prevent rogue states such as Iraq or Libya from making and using chemical weapons. Simply to get the measure to the Senate floor required arcane negotiations with the treaty's archenemy, Foreign Relations chairman Helms. Negotiations were spearheaded by Clinton's secretary of state Madeleine K. Albright and mediated by GOP leader Lott. The administration not only agreed to twenty-eight clarifications demanded by the conservatives, but it also made other major concessions—including a State Department reorganization, UN reform, and submission of other arms control treaties to the Senate—aimed at strengthening the Senate's role in future bargaining. During the floor debate, President Clinton and his aides worked the phones, trumpeted support from such Republican luminaries as retired general Colin Powell and former senator Bob Dole, and sent a last-minute letter to Lott promising to withdraw from the treaty if it subverted U.S. interests in any way. The multiple offensive paid off when Lott brought in enough skeptical Republicans to ratify the treaty in April 1997.[45]

A different fate befell another major multilateral pact, the Comprehensive Test Ban Treaty (CTBT) in autumn 1999. From the moment it reached the Senate two years earlier, the pact met widespread resistance from conservatives who held that it would jeopardize the nation's nuclear superiority and weaken deterrence against would-be nuclear powers. Senate Republicans realized from private consultations that they had the votes to kill the treaty. Normally the Senate would have simply taken no action. But when pressed by President Clinton and Democratic leaders to bring the treaty to the floor, Republican leaders suddenly scheduled a flurry of hearings quickly followed by floor debate. No bargaining was evident at either stage.[46] The treaty's foes seemed bent on humiliating the president and signaling a unilateralist approach to future arms control efforts. By the time the treaty's advocates realized they had fallen into a trap (partially of their own making), it was too late to turn back. After debate described as "nasty, brutish, and short," the treaty failed by a 48–51 vote—short of a majority, much less the required two-thirds.[47] "While there was nothing improper or illegal in their parliamentary tactics," one commentator wrote, "it was nonetheless a nasty and contemptuous way of doing business quite out of character with the stately, sometimes ponderous way of doing business."[48]

The hurdle of obtaining a two-thirds Senate vote has led presidents to rely increasingly on executive agreements—international accords that are not submitted to the Senate for its advice and consent. Of the more than fifty-six hundred U.S. international accords signed between 1981 and 1996, 96 percent were executive agreements.[49] Such agreements are enforceable under international law, which regards a treaty as any binding agreement among nations.

Executive agreements should be viewed as congressional-executive instruments. In theory all of them are signed pursuant to some grant of legislative authority, though the laws cited are often outdated and only vaguely linked. Many agreements are subsequently approved by Congress. Kiki Caruson describes the agreements' subject matter:

> The vast majority of executive agreements concern routine procedural matters such as postal agreements, mutual legal assistance, cooperation in the fields of science and technology, conservation, civil aviation agreements, and other relatively non-controversial issues. But the executive agreement has also been used to address important foreign policy issues, such as security and defense matters.[50]

According to the Case-Zablocki Act of 1972, copies of all executive agreements must be transmitted to Congress within sixty days of their going into effect. From time to time a constitutional amendment requiring Senate ratification of executive agreements has been proposed.

Other Policy-Making Powers of Congress

In addition to controlling the purse strings, Congress employs an array of techniques to shape or influence strategic policies. Sometimes the techniques are used to support presidential initiatives. Often, however, Congress ventures on its own and challenges presidents to respond. The most common tools of congressional policy leadership are informal advice, legislative prodding through nonbinding resolutions or policy statements, policy oversight, legislative directives or restrictions, and structural or procedural changes.[51]

Advising, Prodding. Congressional leaders and key members routinely provide the president and other executive officials with informal advice. Sometimes this advice proves decisive. In 1954 President Eisenhower dispatched Secretary of State John Foster Dulles to meet with a small bipartisan group of congressional leaders to determine whether the United States should intervene militarily in Indochina (Vietnam). The leaders unanimously declined to sponsor a resolution favoring involvement until other nations indicated their support of military action. Lacking assurances from either Congress or foreign allies, Eisenhower decided against intervening.[52]

Congress engages in legislative prodding by passing nonbinding resolutions that set forth positions or give advice about foreign policy. Recent Congresses have each approved, on average, more than fifty simple or concurrent resolutions that are not legally binding or enforceable. Such pronouncements may lend support to the executive branch, advance certain policies, or signal assurances or warnings to other nations. Occasionally, nonbinding resolutions put forward fresh policy ideas; at other times they are little more than posturing. Some of both were embedded in the House resolution backing troops for the Kosovo crisis in 1999. The resolution—supported by 174 Democrats, 44 Republicans, and 1 independent—authorized the president to deploy troops with the NATO peacekeeping force, but it also instructed the president to explain to Congress an exit strategy from the area and to ensure that U.S. troops would answer only to American commanders.[53]

Oversight. Congress shapes foreign policy through oversight of the executive branch's performance. Hearings and investigations often focus on foreign policy issues. Recurrent hearings on authorizing and funding State Department and Defense Department programs offer many opportunities for lawmakers to voice their concerns, large and small. Another device is to require that certain decisions or agreements be submitted to Congress before they go into effect. Or Congress and its committees can require reports from the executive that "provide not only information for oversight but also a handle for action."[54] Some six hundred foreign policy reporting requirements are embedded in current statutes.

Oversight in time of war or crisis is especially hazardous. The president resists intrusions, and lawmakers are reluctant to impede the action. "The trick is to rein in the White House but not seem unpatriotic," writes historian Bruce J. Schulman.[55] The boldest legislative foray into wartime oversight occurred during the Civil War. As confederate guns threatened Washington, D.C., the Joint Committee on the Conduct of the War (1861–1865), controlled by Radical Republicans, held hearings on Capitol Hill and published reports that questioned President Abraham Lincoln's war policies, criticized military operations, berated generals who failed to pursue the enemy, and exposed waste and fraud in military procurements.

During World War II, Missouri senator Harry S. Truman's Special Committee to Investigate the National Defense Program (1941–1948) uncovered profiteering, contract abuses, and shoddy workmanship in wartime projects. It saved taxpayers billions of dollars and, not incidentally, boosted the career of its chairman ("Truman Committee," its letterheads proclaimed). Senate Foreign Relations Committee hearings, launched in 1966, raised doubts in the public's mind about the Vietnam War.

In the wake of the 2001 terrorist attacks, a joint House-Senate panel probing intelligence failures met stiff White House resistance. With support from families of the New York attack's victims, Congress pressed a reluctant Bush White House to agree to an independent bipartisan commission to expand on its own inquiries. Sen. John McCain, R-Ariz., who along with Sen. Joseph I. Lieberman, D-Conn., pushed for the panel, called for a "full and frank accounting" and said that administration delays in providing access to materials "creates the appearance of bureaucratic stonewalling."[56]

The result was the bipartisan 9/11 Commission, half of whose ten members were former senators or representatives. The panel's investigations and public hearings drew media and public attention. Its 2004 report faulted intelligence failings and tended to give policy makers a pass, but it was probably the best that could have been hoped for, given the highly charged political atmosphere. Commissioners followed up by lobbying for their proposals, most notably an extensive reorganization of the nation's intelligence agencies, adopted later that year. Congress was not spared in their analysis. "Congressional oversight for intelligence—and counterterrorism—is now dysfunctional," the report warned. "Congress should address this problem."[57]

Legislative Mandates. Congress sometimes makes foreign policy by legislative directives—to launch new programs, to authorize certain actions, or to set guidelines. A landmark enactment of the cold war era was the Jackson-Vanik amendment to the Trade Act of 1974 (named for Sen. Henry M. "Scoop" Jackson, D-Wash., and Rep. Charles Vanik, D-Ohio). Prompted by concern over the Soviet Union's treatment of its Jewish minority, the amendment denied government credits and most-favored-nation (now called normal trade relations) trade status to any communist country that restricted free emigration of its citizens.

Foreign policy statutes may include explicit legislative restrictions, which perhaps are Congress's most effective weapon. Often they are embedded in authorization or appropriation bills that the president is unlikely to veto. Throughout the Ronald Reagan years, for example, Congress passed many limits on military aid to Central American countries. Most notable were the Boland amendments (named for House Intelligence Committee chairman Edward P. Boland, D-Mass.) that were attached to various bills after 1982 to forbid nonhumanitarian aid to the contra rebels in Nicaragua. In the 1987 Iran-contra scandal, President Reagan and his National Security Council staff were accused of violating this prohibition.

Even the threat of passing legislation may bring about the desired result. Dissatisfied with the Reagan administration's weak "constructive engagement" policy toward South African apartheid (a brutal form of racial separation), a pro-civil rights coalition on Capitol Hill threatened to pass legislation imposing economic and other sanctions. Just before a sanctions bill was to be approved in 1985, President Reagan issued an executive order imposing limited sanctions. (The next year, over Reagan's veto, Congress enacted tougher restrictions.)

Legislation also shapes the structures and procedures through which policies are carried out. "Congress changes the structure and procedures of decision making in the executive branch in order to influence the content of policy," writes James M. Lindsay.[58] When lawmakers wanted to reform military procurement, they restructured the Defense Department to clarify and streamline the process; when they wanted more say in trade negotiations, they wrote themselves into the process with the 1974 and 1988 trade laws.

CRISIS POLICIES: THE WAR POWERS

When the nation is directly threatened, national self-preservation pushes aside other foreign policy goals. One definition of an international crisis is a sudden challenge to the nation's safety and security. Examples range from Japan's attack on the U.S. naval fleet in Pearl Harbor in 1941 to the terrorist attacks of September 11, 2001.

Crisis policies engage decision makers at the highest levels: the president, the secretaries of state and defense, the National Security Council, and the Joint Chiefs of Staff. Congressional leaders are sometimes brought into the picture. More rarely, congressional advice is sought out and heeded—as in President Eisenhower's 1954 decision against military intervention in Indochina. Often when executive decision makers fear congressional opposition, they simply neglect to inform Capitol Hill until the planned action is under way. A failed 1980 attempt to rescue American hostages in Iran, for example, was planned in strictest secrecy, and no consultations were undertaken.

As long as a crisis lingers, policy makers keep a tight rein on information flowing upward from line officers. The attention of the media and the public is riveted upon crisis events. Patriotism runs high. Citizens hasten to "rally round the flag" and support whatever course their leaders choose.[59]

Constitutional Powers

War powers are shared by the president and Congress. The president is the commander in chief (Article II, Section 2), but Congress has the power to declare war (Article I, Section 8). Congress has declared war only five times: the War of 1812 (1812–1814), the Mexican War (1846–1848), the Spanish-American War (1898), World War I (1917–1918), and World War II (1941–1945). In four instances, Congress readily assented to the president's call for war, acknowledging in the declaration that a state of war already existed. Only once did Congress delve into the merits of waging war, and that was in 1812, when the vote was close. In two cases—the Mexican and Spanish-American conflicts—lawmakers later had reason to regret their haste.

More problematic than formal declarations of war are the three hundred or so instances in which U.S. military forces have been deployed abroad. (The number is uncertain because of quasi engagements involving military or intelligence advisers.)[60] The examples range from an undeclared naval war with France (1798–1800) to deployment of military forces to Iraq (2003). Since the end of the last declared war—World War II—in 1945, numerous military interventions have taken place abroad. Some of them were massive and even prolonged wars: Korea (1950–1953), Vietnam (1964–1975), Afghanistan (2001), and Iraq (1991, 2003–). Still others were short-lived actions (for example, military coordination of medical and disaster relief after U.S. embassies in Kenya and Tanzania were bombed in 1998) and rescue or peacekeeping missions, some of which involved casualties (Lebanon, 1983; Somalia, 1992–1993).

Most of these interventions were authorized by the president as commander in chief on the pretext of protecting American lives, property, or interests abroad. Some were justified on the grounds of treaty obligations or inherent powers derived from a broad reading of executive prerogatives. Others were peacekeeping efforts under UN or NATO sponsorship. In virtually every armed intervention in U.S. history, constitutional questions have generated "lively disagreement among the president, Congress, and the Supreme Court, and between the central government and the states."[61]

Members of Congress, though wary of armed interventions, are reluctant to halt them: "No one actually wants to cut off funds when American troops are in harm's way," a House leadership aide explained. "The preferred stand is to let the president make the decisions and, if it goes well, praise him, and if it doesn't, criticize him," observed Lee H. Hamilton, D-Ind., former chairman of the House Foreign Affairs Committee (1993–1995) and co-chair of the 9/11 Commission.[62] Interventions go well if they come to a swift, successful conclusion with few American lives lost. Actions that drag on without a satisfactory resolution or that cost many lives will eventually tax lawmakers' patience. As the sense of urgency subsides, competing information appears that may challenge the president's version of the event. Congressional critics thus are emboldened to voice their reservations. This reaction occurred as the undeclared wars in Korea and Vietnam dragged on and after U.S. troops suffered casualties in Lebanon and Somalia.

The War Powers Resolution

Backlash against the Vietnam War made lawmakers skeptical of presidential initiatives abroad. In 1973 Congress passed the War Powers Resolution (WPR, P.L. 93-148) over President Richard M. Nixon's veto. This law requires the president to consult with Congress before introducing U.S. troops into hostilities;

report any commitment of forces to Congress within forty-eight hours; and terminate the use of forces within sixty days if Congress does not declare war, does not extend the period by law, or is unable to meet. (The president may extend the period to ninety days, if necessary.)

Through 2003, presidents had submitted 111 reports to Congress that troops had been deployed abroad.[63] In several other cases the military action was brief, and no report was filed. In still other cases the executive branch claimed that reports were not required because U.S. personnel were not confronting hostilities or imminent hostilities. Thus the Reagan administration declined to comply with congressional reporting requirements when it sent military advisers to El Salvador in 1981 or when it provided protection for oil tankers in the Persian Gulf in 1987 and 1988.

The WPR is an awkward compromise of executive and legislative authority, and presidents still intervene as they see fit. Members of Congress tend to sit on the sidelines, only later questioning presidential initiatives. Sometimes deployments are heatedly debated. President Reagan dispatched two thousand Marines to Lebanon in 1982, but it was not until the troops came under hostile fire in 1983 that Congress seriously debated invoking the War Powers Resolution. Finally, a compromise was reached. The president signed congressional legislation invoking the WPR, and Congress authorized U.S. troops to remain in Lebanon for eighteen months (P.L. 98-119). Shortly afterward, 241 Marines were killed by a suicide truck bombing, raising new complaints from Congress and the public. The president subsequently withdrew the troops.

The law figured prominently in the Persian Gulf War of 1991, a real war involving forces from the United States and the United Nations. A week after Iraqi troops invaded Kuwait in August 1990, President George Bush notified Congress that he had deployed troops to the region. Although the president did not consult with congressional leaders before acting, both chambers later adopted measures supporting the deployment and urging Iraqi withdrawal from Kuwait. Urged by congressional leaders, Bush later asked for a resolution supporting the use of all necessary means to implement the UN decrees. After a lively, high-minded debate, both houses passed a statutory authorization of military action (P.L. 102-1) under the WPR.

Wars against Terrorism

Post–September 11 authorizations under the WPR found Congress in a reactive posture. Three days after the terrorist attacks, with smoke still lingering above the damaged Pentagon building, both chambers passed S. J. Res. 23, authorizing the president "to use all necessary and appropriate force against those nations, organizations, or persons he determines planned, authorized, committed, or aided the terrorist attacks." The single dissenter was Rep. Barbara Lee, D-Calif. The measure included the declaration that "[n]othing in this resolution supercedes any requirement of the War Powers Resolution." Some three weeks later, President Bush notified Congress that he had launched an assault "designed to disrupt the use of Afghanistan as a terrorist base of operations."

After the Afghanistan war ended and its Taliban regime was toppled, the White House resumed its drumbeat of war threats against Saddam Hussein's Iraqi regime, which had survived the 1991 war. The rationale was elusive: Iraq's weapons of mass destruction, its ties to terrorist organizations, and the regime's cruelty to its people were all offered as pretexts. Elite and public opinion agreed that regime change in Iraq would be desirable, but it sharply divided over whether the United States should act unilaterally or work through the UN and a broad coalition of allies, as in 1991. These battles were waged more on media talk shows and editorial pages than in the halls of Congress.

The president's advisers initially asserted that the president could launch a preemptory attack without further approval. But as his father had done before in the Gulf War, George W. Bush bowed to demands that he obtain congressional approval to act. By the standards set in 1991, however, debate in the two chambers was muted and desultory. Sen. Chuck Hagel, R-Neb., voted for the resolution but cautioned against using the military option. "America must understand that it cannot alone win a war against terrorism," he said. "It will require allies, friends and partners."[64] Sen. Bob Graham, D-Fla., Intelligence Committee chair, opposed the resolution because Iraq posed a less urgent threat than terrorist networks: "There are many evils out there, a number of which are substantially more competent, particularly in their ability to attack America here at home, than Iraq is likely to be in the foreseeable future."[65] Sen. Robert C. Byrd, D-W.Va., railed against what he termed the president's demand for "power to launch this nation into war without provocation and without clear evidence of an imminent attack on the United States. And we are going to be foolish enough to give it to him."[66] Lopsided majorities backed the resolution: 296–133 in the House, 77–23 in the Senate (Democrats provided most of the no votes: 126 in the House and 21 in the Senate). In March 2003 the president began the war. Even lawmakers with misgivings signed onto resolutions of "support for the troops."

The final Iraqi authorization (H. J. Res. 114) preserved no more than a fig leaf of congressional prerogatives. The original White House proposal—reminiscent of the infamous Tonkin Gulf Resolution of 1964 and the panicky post–September 11 action—was narrowed somewhat. First, the action made clear that the UN must have time to act before force could be employed. Second, the president had to declare promptly that "diplomatic and other peaceful means" failed and that U.S. action was "consistent with" continuing actions against terrorism by the nation and its allies. Finally, such action would fall under the WPR, requiring reports to Congress at least every sixty days.

Congress's War Powers in Today's World

With each new crisis the War Powers Resolution is attacked or defended, depending on the view held of the proposed intervention. Although presidents are encouraged to pause and consult before acting, experience since 1973 shows that the WPR has not prevented them from boldly exercising military powers, including military responses to sudden threats.

Champions of executive authority—reportedly including Vice President Dick Cheney—think that WPR and other post–Vietnam enactments limit executive flexibility, but recent history belies such a claim. In the case of the war powers, Louis Fisher's careful study of the historical record reveals that a combination of presidential hubris and congressional abdication has caused an "unmistakable . . . drift" away from Capitol Hill. "Congress had made repeated efforts since the 1970s to restore legislative prerogatives, with only moderate success," he concludes. "Presidents continue to wield military power single-handedly, agreeing only to consult with legislators and notify them of completed actions. This is not the framers' model." [67]

For the record, every post–1973 president has denied WPR's legality, but no one is willing to have the courts resolve the question. Lawmakers strive vainly to be consulted. They support the action as long as it is politically feasible. If the crisis persists and the president's actions backfire, however, Congress moves in and sometimes curtails the action by refusing funds.

The resolution has few outright defenders, but lawmakers are not ready to repeal or replace it. Leaders in the last Democratic Congress (1993–1995) vowed to rewrite the statute but fell short. In 1995 Republican leaders in both chambers introduced repeal bills. The House measure, authored by then Judiciary chairman Henry J. Hyde, R-Ill., was brought to the floor. Closing the debate, Speaker Newt Gingrich, R-Ga., argued for passage. But in a rare rebuff to the leadership, the measure was rejected, 217–201. Forty-four Republicans joined 172 Democrats to retain the War Powers Resolution. "The power of the purse is not equivalent to Congress sharing the critical decision, up front, to send troops or not," argued Representative Hamilton, then ranking Democrat on the International Relations Committee. "Congress should hold tenaciously to the power of sharing the decision." Rep. Fred Upton of Michigan, one of three Republicans who spoke against repeal, contended that the resolution, even when not invoked, forces presidents to work with Congress. "The biggest vote that I ever cast was to give President Bush the authority to go into the Gulf War," he said. "I'm not so certain he would have done that [consulted Congress] if there had not been a war powers act." [68]

Although it compromises Congress's constitutional power of declaring war, the WPR has some practical virtues. It accommodates the rapid use of armed force without the traditional but awkward step of formally declaring war on a nation-state and its people—especially when the real target may be, say, a rogue regime or a shadowy terrorist network. "[Y]ou can't just go off and declare war when you don't know who you are declaring war against," Sen. John B. Breaux, D-La., remarked after the September 11 attacks. "It is beneath our dignity to declare war against Osama bin Laden," added Sen. John W. Warner, R-Va.[69]

The WPR bids at least a nodding respect for the framers' belief that Congress, the branch most representative of the people, is the sole source of legal and moral authority for major military enterprises. Presidents may succeed at short-lived actions. But, lacking a legislative mandate, longer and more costly engagements will surely falter—as the Korean and Vietnam wars did. For the time being, then, the enactment stands as a reminder of the ultimate need to gain congressional acquiescence, if not approval, for major military deployments.

CONCLUSION

Some politicians still claim that citizens are preoccupied with domestic concerns and thus uninterested in world affairs. This seems to be a misreading of public sentiment. A strong majority of citizens, for example, endorses an active role for the United States in world affairs. Although people are reluctant to use U.S. troops overseas, they support fights against international terrorism, nuclear proliferation, and drug trafficking.[70]

Congressional actions are disconnected from the views of the public and foreign policy leaders, according to a 2004 survey by the University of Maryland's Program on International Policy Attitudes. "A recurring theme is that the public and leaders show more support for multilateral action than Congress supports."[71] The public and foreign policy elites favored a number of entities rejected by recent congresses, including U.S. participation in the International Criminal Court, the Kyoto treaty on climate change, and a proposed 2002 requirement for UN approval before going to war with Iraq (rejected by a two-to-one House vote, but supported two-to-one by the public). The study found misperceptions in both directions: Capitol Hill respondents assumed that constituents shared their isolationist views, whereas citizens believed their leaders shared a more internationalist outlook.

Unfolding developments, however, ought to enhance Congress's commitment to foreign policy. First, the United States continues to exert influence in every corner of the globe through its actions—and its inactions. Second, post–cold war and post–mideast war conditions could lead the public to expect more legislative dissent in foreign affairs than was previously the case. Legislators are more likely to oppose the president if they believe the voters will not punish them for doing so. Third, global interdependence blurs the line that once demarked domestic policy from foreign policy. Insofar as the resulting issues trespass upon traditional domestic matters, such questions are bound to encourage congressional intervention and influence. Finally, the question of whether the nation is able or willing to underwrite its costly international projects may lead Congress to curtail the nation's global commitments.[72]

Members of Congress dare not abandon their interest in foreign and national security policies. As the world grows ever more interdependent, these policies impinge upon every citizen and every local community. An internationally minded electorate—sensitive to famines and plagues in Africa, deforestation in the Amazon, foreign competition for jobs and trade, and anti–Americanism and terrorism in various regions—may draw fewer distinctions between domestic and global matters than in the past.

Far more than their predecessors, today's legislators do seem to care about world issues. They realize that global developments touch their local constituencies, and they believe (rightly or wrongly) that they will be judged to some degree on their mastery of those subjects. "In Lyndon Johnson's age, you just had to be able to say [Soviet premier Nikita] Khrushchev," remarked Sen. Bob Kerrey, D-Neb. (1989–2001). Now, "you need to know the leaders in sixteen former Soviet Union States." Nebraska's exports, mostly farm-related, go to foreign customers. As Senator Hagel, a Nebraska Republican, told college students in Kearney: "We are living in a global village, undergirded by a global economy." [73]

Paradoxically, however, the militarization of U.S. foreign policy—a contrast between the nation's military superiority and its diplomatic and other resources—works to Congress's detriment. Hot (and cold) wars inevitably tend to elevate the presidency and mute legislative voices. To the extent that U.S. policy is defined in military instead of diplomatic, cultural, or moral terms, the impulse on Capitol Hill is to defer to the commander in chief and, if nothing else, to "support the troops." The following warning by Senate Foreign Relations chair Richard Lugar is aimed at policy makers at both ends of Pennsylvania Avenue:

> Military action will be necessary to deal with serious and immediate threats to our national security, but the war on terrorism will not be won through attrition—particularly because military action will often breed more terrorism. To win this war, the United States must assign to economic and diplomatic capabilities the same strategic priority we assign to military capabilities. What is still missing from the American political discourse is support for the painstaking work of foreign policy and the commitment of resources to vital foreign policy objectives that lack a direct political constituency.[74]

SUGGESTED READINGS

Crabb, Cecil V., Jr., Glenn J. Antizzo, and Leila E. Sarieddine. *Congress and the Foreign Policy Process.* Baton Rouge: Lousiana State University Press, 2000.

Fisher, Louis. *Congressional Abdication on War and Spending.* College Station: Texas A&M University Press, 2000.

Hinckley, Barbara. *Less Than Meets the Eye: Foreign Policy Making and the Myth of the Assertive Congress.* Chicago: University of Chicago Press, 1994.

Lindsay, James. *Congress and the Politics of U.S. Foreign Policy.* Baltimore: Johns Hopkins University Press, 1994.

Mann, Thomas E., ed. *A Question of Balance: The President, the Congress, and Foreign Policy.* Washington, D.C.: Brookings Institution, 1990.

Prelude to the 21st century: Members of Congress take part in a prayer vigil held in the Capitol's Great Rotunda on September 12, 2001, for victims of the previous day's attack by al Qaeda.

chapter 16

The Two Congresses and the American People

On the morning of September 11, 2001, after the terrorist attacks on the World Trade Center in New York City and on the Pentagon had taken place, the president of the United States was hustled aboard *Air Force One.* For most of the day he was flown around to various military installations, while receiving nonstop status reports from all over the world. By nightfall he was back in the White House, where he delivered a brief message to the American people.

Meanwhile, members and staff aides on Capitol Hill were told to evacuate their offices. The Capitol building, like the White House, was a potential terrorist target, and smoke could be seen across the Potomac River, where a hijacked plane had hit the Pentagon. "I remember so vividly racing through this hallway . . . as we departed the building as quickly as we could, having been told that we may be under attack," recalled Senate majority leader Tom Daschle, D-S.D.[1] A month later a staff aide in the Hart Senate Office Building opened a letter addressed to Daschle, and a cloud of fine white dust billowed out. Infected with anthrax, Capitol Hill was virtually shut down for several weeks.

The initial images of the post–September 11 government were starkly symbolic: The president was portrayed as being in charge and in touch; Congress was scattered and for the moment out of the loop.

Granted, the threats were palpable. Capitol Hill was at risk, and a Washington, D.C.-area postal handler died after contact with anthrax-contaminated mail. But the impression remained of a proactive president and a reactive legislature. The deliberative processes of legislatures (and courts) are sorely tested in times of warfare or emergency. Yet the authors of the Constitution—who were under no illusions about the need for a strong commander in chief or the flaws of legislative bodies, especially in fighting wars—nonetheless envisioned the legislative branch as a preeminent maker of public policy in war as well as peace.

The United States is not, as some have claimed, a "presidential nation"; it is a "separated system" marked by the ebb and flow of power among the policy-making branches of government.[2] As Speaker Newt Gingrich, R-Ga. (1995–1999), said about the nation's complex and frustrating governing arrangements:

> We have to get the country to understand that at the heart of the process of freedom is not the presidential press conference. It is the legislative process; it is the give and take of independently elected, free people coming together to try to create a better product by the friction of their passions and the friction of their ideas.[3]

Anxious or fearful citizens, in particular, need to keep in mind the American system's deliberate yet fragile give-and-take among institutions.

Citizens' ambivalent feelings toward the popular branch of government are yet another reminder of the dual character of Congress—the theme that has pervaded our explanations of how Congress and its members work. This notion of the two Congresses manifests itself in public perceptions and assessments. Citizens look at Congress in Washington through lenses different from those they use to view their individual senators and representatives.[4] This same dualism appears in media coverage: The two Congresses are covered by different kinds of reporters working for different kinds of media organizations.

CONGRESS-AS-POLITICIANS

Lawmakers' working conditions and schedules are far from ideal and beg for periodic examination.[5] The hours are killing, the pay comparatively modest, the toll on family life heavy, and the psychic rewards fleeting. "Your schedule is not your own," remarked former senator Fred Thompson, R-Tenn. (1994–2003), on announcing his retirement.[6] For Rep. Joe Scarborough, R-Fla. (1995–2001), "The conflict between being a good congressman and full-time father has grown even greater in recent years."[7]

In addition to the frantic pace and damage to family life, many congressional retirees cite a decline in comity and an erosion of the arts of bargaining and compromise. Incivility became so rife in the House that a bipartisan group of lawmakers sponsored a series of retreats aimed at helping members get along with one another—but without much noticeable result. The Senate, too, has witnessed a rise in incivility. "Civility in this body has eroded over time, and it will take a . . . renewed commitment to regain it," remarked Senate majority leader Bill Frist, R-Tenn.[8]

Members' Bonds with Constituents

Despite their job pressures, elected representatives are by no means an endangered species. Diligence and attentive home styles yield dividends at the polls. If voters regard elected officials as a class as rascals, they tend to be more charitable toward their own elected officials (nearly seven out of ten likely voters in 2004 thought their representative deserved reelection).

Lawmakers forge bonds with voters out of perceived mutual agreement on important issues facing the constituency and the nation. The recruitment process yields lawmakers who reflect local views and prejudices. Contacts with voters during campaigns and while in office reinforce their convergence of views. Citizens tend to regard their own legislators as agents of personal or localized interests. Legislators tend to be judged on their service to the state or district, their communication with constituents, and their home styles. As House Small Business chairman Donald Manzullo, R-Ill., put it: "Members of Congress see the world through people they represent."[9]

Members' unique visibility in their states or districts helps explain their support from potential voters. Large numbers of citizens report having contacts with their lawmakers—by receiving mail from them, reading about them in a newspaper or magazine, or seeing them on television. Incumbents, for their part, miss few opportunities to do favors for constituents, gestures that are remembered or at least appreciated by recipients.

Individual senators and representatives present themselves to constituents largely on their own terms, through advertising, self-promotion, and uncritical coverage by local or regional news media. House Rules chairman David Dreier, R-Calif., explains, for example, that "member web pages serve not only as a basic informational resource [for constituents], but as a tool *advocating,* in the member's own words, their work."[10]

Members and their staffs devote constant attention to generating publicity and local press. "I am never too busy to talk to local TV," said a prominent House member. "Period. Exclamation point."[11] A survey of House press secretaries showed virtually unanimous agreement: "We'd rather get in [the hometown paper] than on the front page of the *New York Times* any day."[12]

Individual lawmakers tend to bask in the flattering light cast by their local media. Hometown reporters, especially for the electronic media, usually work on general assignment and are ill prepared to question the lawmaker in detail about issues or events. Often their primary goal is simply to get the legislator on tape or film. For politicians this is an ideal situation. They can express their views in their own words with a minimum of editing and few challenges from reporters.

Questions of Ethics

As for assessing individual lawmakers, recurrent questions arise about members' personal ethics. Only 20 percent of the respondents in a recent survey ranked the ethics of members of Congress as "high" or "very high"—in the same league with journalists, business executives, and lawyers. (State officeholders and pharmacists are among those seen as most ethical.)[13]

Standards of Conduct. In fact, "Members of Congress behave better than people think," asserts former representative Lee H. Hamilton, D-Ind. (1965–1999).[14] The vast majority of lawmakers are dedicated and ethical in their behavior. There is no reason to think that overall ethical standards are not as high as, or higher than, at any time in history. As Norman J. Ornstein points out, "Most observers would suggest that real corruption on the Hill has in fact *declined* significantly over the past 20 or 30 years, whether the misbehavior is licentiousness or bribery or financial chicanery."[15] Among the reasons he cites are the rising quality of members, broader scrutiny by the public, and reforms in campaign finance, disclosure, and ethics procedures.

Many of the most blatant financial abuses, moreover, have been curtailed or subjected to disclosure requirements. Direct gifts and honoraria are now virtually eliminated, and lobbying by former members or staff is restricted. Money used to flow under the table. "Back in the old days, it was a common occurrence that you walked around with envelopes of cash in your pocket" to hand out to powerful lawmakers, recalled a Washington lobbyist.[16] Today, most contributions—campaign contributions and direct lobbying expenses, for example—are reported and subject to scrutiny by reporters and civic groups. Although loopholes remain, contemporary financial practices unquestionably are tame by the standards common before, say, the 1970s.

Why Ethics Questions Persist. Why, then, do ethical questions continue to loom so large in public and media commentary about members of Congress? First, organized interests and lobbies of all kinds are no less eager than in past eras to manipulate lawmakers and bend public policy to their wishes. The public policy stakes are now higher as government reaches into more sectors of Americans' economic and social lives. Huge sums of money find their way to Capitol Hill in the form of campaign contributions and other perquisites. Fearful of raising their own salaries because of expected backlash from voters, some members fall prey to the blandishments of money and favors.

Second, changing standards of behavior have cast new light upon issues of personal habits and conduct. Sexual misconduct and substance abuse, for example, are less tolerated today than they were a generation ago. Colleagues and journalists are not so inclined to look the other way. Reports of adulterous affairs bedogged the career of House Speaker Newt Gingrich, R-Ga. (1977–1999) and ended the careers of would-be House Speaker Bob Livingston, R-La. (1977–1999) and Rep. Gary A. Condit, D-Calif. (1989–2003). Similar allegations against earlier public figures—for example, Presidents John F. Kennedy and Lyndon B. Johnson—were kept largely out of public view.

Third, ethical lapses and scandals are the glaring exceptions to the rule that the media exert little enterprise or energy in covering individual senators and representatives. The rise of investigative journalism has increased the odds that ethics violations—or even allegations—will be headline news. As a GOP media consultant expressed it, "If I have a choice between announcing a plan to cure cancer or attacking my opponent over some crazy ethical thing, I think the ethical thing will always get coverage. So the need gets fed."[17]

Fourth, intensified regulation of public life has itself opened windows for press coverage and citizens' reaction. Elected officials are scrutinized by the Federal Election Commission, the House and Senate ethics committees, and occasionally by the Justice Department and federal prosecutors (see Box 16-1 on congressional ethics). Reports, investigations, hearings, and even court proceedings are not uncommon. So many rules govern the public activities of law-

BOX 16-1 Congressional Ethics

Members of Congress are bound by the U.S. Constitution, federal laws, party provisions, and House and Senate rules and conduct codes. Although many observers criticize loopholes, the panoply of regulations is extensive.

- **Constitution.** Each chamber has the power to punish its members for "disorderly behavior" and, by a two-thirds vote, to expel a member. Members are immune from arrest during attendance at congressional sessions (except for treason, felony, or breach of peace) and "for any speech or debate in either house, they shall not be questioned in any other place" (Article I, Section 6). This latter provision protects lawmakers from any reprisals for expressing their legislative views.
- **Criminal Laws.** Federal laws make it a crime to solicit or accept a bribe; to solicit or receive "anything of value" for performing any official act or service, or for using influence in any proceeding involving the federal government; to enter into or benefit from any contracts with the government; or to commit any fraud against the United States. Lawmakers involved in the so-called Abscam affair were convicted in 1981 for violating these statutes.
- **Ethics Codes.** Adopted in 1968 and substantially tightened in 1977, 1989, 1995, and 1997, the House and Senate ethics codes apply to members and key staff aides. The codes require extensive financial disclosure; restrict members' outside earned income (to 15 percent of salaries); prohibit unofficial office accounts that many members used to supplement official allowances; impose stricter standards for using the frank for mailings; and ban lawmakers from accepting most meals and gifts from lobbyists. The House Committee on Standards of Official Conduct and the Senate Select Ethics Committee implement the codes, hear charges against members, issue advisory opinions, and recommend disciplinary actions.
- **Party Rules.** Congressional parties can discipline members who run afoul of ethics requirements. House Democratic and Republican rules require a committee leader who is indicted to step aside temporarily; a leader who is censured or convicted is automatically replaced.
- **Federal Election Campaign Act Amendments of 1974.** As amended again in 1976 and 1979, the Federal Election Campaign Act imposes extensive requirements on congressional incumbents as well as challengers. Additional rules and penalties are set in the Bipartisan Campaign Reform Act of 2002.

makers that they can unintentionally run afoul of them. "High-level public officials are particularly good targets for investigation," law professor Cass Sunstein explains, "if only because of the complex network of statutes that regulate their behavior." [18]

Some of these inquiries uncover real wrongdoing that warrants legal punishment or defeat at the polls. Other cases are politically motivated—by electoral foes, by regulators seeking partisan advantage, or by ambitious prosecutors hoping to bag a high-profile trophy. In his study of the impact of what he calls "the ethics culture" on federal appointments, G. Calvin Mackenzie writes:

> Instead of getting out of the way so the winners can govern, the losers begin guerrilla operations that never cease, using every weapon and every opportunity to attack, harass, embarrass, and otherwise weaken those who hold office. If you cannot beat them in an election, current practice now suggests, then do everything in your power to keep the winners from governing and implementing their policy priorities.[19]

In other words, ethics charges and countercharges can become another means of waging political warfare.

Finally, even though a network of laws and rules constrains public behavior, members usually cringe at passing judgment on their peers. At least in the House, the result has been "a moribund ethics process, with occasional spasms of activity when the public embarrassment about an ethical problem became too great."[20] The House made matters worse when it adopted rules for the 109th Congress (2005–2007) that further enfeebled its bipartisan ethics panel (the Committee on Standards of Official Conduct), in part to quash further inquiries concerning Majority Leader Tom DeLay, R-Texas. "These changes were made without consulting the House minority and were passed on a straight party-line vote," the panel's former Republican chairman and ranking Democrat complained. "If the ethics process is dominated by the majority party—whichever party that might be—it will have no credibility."[21] Public protest persuaded the leadership to have the new rules voided.

"A Small Class of People." Do these hazards of public life deter "the best and the brightest" from seeking elective office? It is hard to answer that question. Young people, for example, show lamentably scant interest in government careers; yet their idealism often leads them to pursue other paths of service.[22] Although most congressional seats have no shortage of claimants, many of the ablest individuals—especially in one-party areas—decide to sit on the sidelines. Two political scientists suggest also that if "the public strongly disapproves of Congress, sitting members may decide against seeking reelection and prospective candidates may decide against running for a seat in the first place."[23]

The rising demands and costs of congressional life may lie beyond the reach of average men and women. Reflecting on the multiplicity of presidential duties, Woodrow Wilson once remarked that Americans might be forced to pick their leaders from among "wise and prudent athletes—a small class of people."[24] The same might now be said of senators and representatives. And if the job specifications exceed reasonable dimensions, can even the most qualified citizens be expected to perform these tasks successfully?

CONGRESS-AS-INSTITUTION

People expect an active and productive Congress. Surveys over the years have consistently found that people prefer that Congress play a strong, independent policy-making role. People want Congress to check the president's initiatives and to examine the president's proposals carefully.[25] They have often endorsed the notion of divided government: the White House controlled by one party but checked by another party controlling Capitol Hill.

Noteworthy Achievements. Congress's response to public problems has produced many innovative policies. In an intriguing experiment, Paul C. Light of the Brookings Institution set out to identify the federal government's most influential actions over a fifty-year period.[26] A survey of historians and political scientists served to winnow a preliminary roster of 588 items to a list of fifty "greatest achievements." For the record, the top three successes were judged to be rebuilding Europe after World War II (the Marshall Plan, 1947), expanding the right to vote (Voting Rights Act of 1965), and promoting equal access to public accommodations (Civil Rights Act of 1964).

In every case Light uncovered, Congress played a vital role in the policy's inception, ratification, or implementation. Although Congress was not always the initiator, many programs associated with given presidents—for example, the Marshall Plan (Harry S. Truman) and Medicare (Lyndon Johnson)—began as proposals on Capitol Hill. "No one party, Congress, or president can be credited with any single achievement. . . . Rather, achievement appears to be the direct product of endurance, consensus, and patience."[27]

Congress continues to affect Americans' daily lives. Former representative Hamilton tells the following story.

> [A] group of [young people] visiting my Indiana office told me that Congress was irrelevant. So I asked them a few questions. How had they gotten to my office? On the interstate highway, they said. Had any of them gone to the local university? Yes, they said, admitting they'd got some help from federal student loans. Did any of them have grandparents on Social Security and Medicare? Well sure, they replied, picking up on where I was headed. Their lives had been profoundly affected by Congress. They just hadn't focused on all of the connections before.[28]

Notable Shortcomings. Congress's institutional shortcomings, at the same time, are numerous and obvious. Beyond its structural and procedural complexities, the quality of its deliberations often falls short of democratic ideals. The bottom-line question for citizens probably is: Do the two chambers respond promptly and debate thoroughly the issues upon which the nation needs leadership and resolution?

Most citizens could compile a must-do legislative agenda that would include many items left unattended by recent Congresses. Even routine matters such as annual appropriations bills have been postponed by the passage of continuing resolutions (CRs). Today, government by CRs is a common occurrence. Bills to reauthorize federal agencies and programs often lapse. Agencies and programs thus are funded via the appropriations process without formal scrutiny and review by the appropriate authorizing committees of jurisdiction.

Congressional decision making often leaves much to be desired. Established proceedings have morphed into a wide variety of improvisations—what Barbara Sinclair has termed "unorthodox lawmaking."[29] Committee meetings are frequently poorly attended, with the outcomes laid out by the chairman and his majority-party colleagues. (There are even recent instances in which minority members were barred from the deliberations.) Floor deliberations are usually a series of desultory recitations—public speaking having in this country become a lost art. Again the outcomes are normally predetermined, especially in the House, where majority-party leaders oversee the pre-floor negotiations, craft the rules for debate, and increasingly write modified or closed rules (permitting few if any amendments). The resulting legislation is often so bulky that only a small number of staff aides and members know what provisions have been inserted or left out. House-Senate negotiations have occasionally excluded minority conferees altogether. Some of these dysfunctions are endemic; others are the product of party government.

The decline of comity is a product of several converging factors, most notably the escalating cohesion within, and polarization between, the two parties' officeholders and allied interest groups—a byproduct of partisan realignment. Asked how he worked with Ways and Means chairman Bill Thomas, R-Calif., ranking Democrat Charles B. Rangel, D-N.Y., said: "It's not difficult at all—we just don't talk."[30] Or as Sen. John McCain, R-Ariz., explained: "The environment here is very poisoned. Both parties are playing to their bases and have caused a degree of partisanship and enmity that I haven't seen in the years that I have been here."[31]

Ironically, political scientists of the mid-twentieth century once lamented the absence of "party government," whereby parties would run on coherent platforms and possess the leadership and unity to enact their programs into law. "Oh, those were frustrating years," recalled former Republican leader Robert Michel of Illinois, who served in the minority for all of his thirty-eight years in the House (1957–1989).

> But .. I never really felt I was out of the game or that I had no part to play. Under the rules of the House, the traditions of the House . . . there is a role to play for the minority. . . . We struck a deal, we made a bargain [and worked at] bringing dissident factions together . . . to craft good legislation for the country. That was the joy of it![32]

Michel's successor and former staff aide, Rep. Ray LaHood, R-Ill., says that Michel "taught us by example that the House floor should be a forum for reasoned debate among colleagues equal in dignity. He came to the House every day to do the work of the people, and not to engage in ideological melodramas or political vendettas."[33]

Many elements of the party government model have come to pass. But as Rep. David E. Price, D-N.C., a political scientist, notes, "Unified party control of the organs of government has proved no panacea."[34] To an alarming extent, interparty deliberation and comity have become victims of party government. Commentator David S. Broder remarked that the House, which is "too often these days a cockpit of bitter partisanship," ought to follow the example of such statesmen.[35]

The Perils of Reform. Reforming Congress is often touted as a solution to its organizational or procedural faults. The two chambers themselves periodically engage in self-examination (the last broad-scale inquiry took place in 1993). The historical record, however, shows that major innovations flow from numerous and sometimes conflicting goals—enhancing legislative power and efficiency, to be sure, but also gaining partisan or policy advantage or augmenting individual lawmakers' perquisites.

In his careful survey of forty-two major institutional innovations of the past century, Eric Schickler explains that "preexisting institutions create constituencies for their preservation that typically force reformers with new goals to build upon, rather than dismantle, these structures." [36] An example was the series of new budget procedures piled like so many building blocks on top of the authorization-appropriations process in the 1974–1990 period. Little wonder that such reforms fall short of their sponsors' objectives. Instead of achieving stable, effective arrangements, what results is "a set of institutions that often work at cross-purposes." [37]

Media Coverage

The most open and accessible of the branches of government, Congress is covered by a large press corps containing some of the nation's most skilled journalists. As CBS News reporter Bob Schieffer notes, Capitol Hill is the best news beat in Washington.[38] But neither reporters nor their editors are able to convey in the mass media the internal subtleties or the external pressures that shape lawmaking.

The problem is compounded because the major mass media outlets have curtailed their coverage of Congress and national politics in general. "The market nature of reporting," writes James T. Hamilton, a Duke University political scientist, "leads to simple rules of thumb: Cover the horse race in politics; focus on the human impact of government policies; treat bad news more often than good news; and talk to your targeted audience." [39] Even prestige daily papers and newsmagazines have deemphasized public affairs coverage in favor of stories about celebrities, entertainment, and lifestyle issues. The first cover of *Time* magazine in 1926 portrayed former House Speaker Joseph G. Cannon, R-Ill. (1903–1911). Today, political figures—aside from the president—are rarely seen on the covers of *Time* and its competitors.

The decline has been especially drastic in television (including the so-called all-news channels), where most Americans receive their news about government and politics. "Apart from technology," observes journalist Bill Moyers, "the biggest change in my thirty years in broadcasting has been the shift of content from news about government to consumer-driven information and celebrity features."[40] Radio and TV talk shows are chronic offenders. Although they spend much airtime on issues of one kind or another, their content and style are typically ill informed, combative, and contemptuous of politicians and their work.[41]

Political news has changed in content as well as coverage. Fewer stories appear on policy issues and more on scandal, wrongdoing, or corruption. Following the canons of investigative journalism, reporters play the role of suspicious adversaries on the lookout for good guys and bad guys, winners and losers. Ethical problems, congressional pay and perquisites, campaign war chests, and foreign junkets are frequent targets of their investigations. Their stories reinforce popular negative stereotypes about Congress as an institution.

Former Speaker Thomas S. Foley, D-Wash. (1989–1995), tells a story about how his remarks to a new-member orientation session were covered by the press. Foley counseled that foreign travel, though a cheap political target, was a good way to learn about world conditions and incidentally to get acquainted with colleagues from the opposing party. He also advised the freshmen to avoid the mistake of some former members who had promised perfect attendance for floor votes. He told them to expect to miss a procedural vote someday. Get over it, he said, and do not drive yourself crazy trying to make every vote. The next day's headline proclaimed: "Foley tells freshmen: Take a junket, miss a vote."[42]

Divergent press coverage—local versus national media—widens the gap between the two Congresses' distinct images: more positive for individual members than for the institution. It is still true that "Americans love their congressmen much more than they love their Congress."[43] Individual lawmakers tend to be well known, sympathetically judged, respectfully covered by the local media, and—most important—reelected. Congress the institution, in contrast, is covered by the national press with plenty of skepticism and cynicism. In short, the two Congresses are viewed through different lenses, reported by different channels of communication, and judged by different criteria.

Citizens' Attitudes toward Congress

If individual members get respectable marks, people often seem ready to flunk Congress as a whole (see Table 16-1). The institutional Congress usually ranks well below respondents' own representatives in public esteem. Citizens' ratings of the job Congress is doing fluctuate with economic conditions, wars and crises, scandals, and waves of satisfaction or cynicism (see Figure 16-1). Approval of Congress surged briefly after it handled the Watergate affair in 1974, after the Republican takeover twenty years later, before the Clinton scandal of 1998, and following the terrorist attacks of 2001.

After global terrorism intruded upon U.S. citizens' consciousness, positive appraisals of Congress soared to 62 percent and individual members to 75 percent. Two-thirds of the respondents in a late 2002 survey expressed "high con-

TABLE 16-1 **High Approval for Members, Low Approval for Congress**

Individual members	Congress as an institution
Serve constituents	Resolves national issues only with difficulty or not at all
Run against Congress	Has few defenders
Emphasize personal style and outreach to constituents	Operates as collegial body that is difficult for citizens to understand
Covered by local media in generally positive terms	Covered by national media, often negatively (with focus on scandals and conflicts)
Respond quickly to most constituent needs and inquiries	Moves slowly with cumbersome processes that inhibit rapid responses
Are able to highlight personal goals and accomplishments	Has many voices but none can speak clearly for Congress as a whole

Sources: Timothy E. Cook, "Legislature vs. Legislator: A Note on the Paradox of Congressional Support," *Legislative Studies Quarterly* 4 (February 1979): 43–52; Glenn R. Parker and Roger H. Davidson, "Why Do Americans Love Their Congressmen So Much More Than Their Congress?" *Legislative Studies Quarterly* 4 (February 1979): 53–61; and Richard Born, "The Shared Fortunes of Congress and Congressmen: Members May Run from Congress But They Can't Hide," *Journal of Politics* 52 (November 1990): 1223–1241.

fidence" in the legislative branch. President George W. Bush's popularity soared at the same time.[44] This reflected the well-known "rally around the flag" phenomenon observed by students of public opinion following nearly every national crisis.

The patriotic bubbles eventually burst. A 2005 Gallup Poll found that just 35 percent of Americans approved of the way Congress was handling its job—the worst showing in more than ten years.[45] Other surveys found equally critical attitudes. A Gallup poll found parallel majorities disapproving of Republicans' and Democrats' handling of their jobs in Congress. As for the Senate's disputes over filibustering judicial nominees, majorities thought that both parties were "abusing their powers."[46]

Congress's poor public standing reflected citizen dismay with its focus on divisive social issues instead of pocketbook issues (gasoline prices, jobs, and health care) that were on the voters' minds. (The president's approval ratings also dropped: In mid-2005 only 47 percent of Americans approved of Bush's handling of Iraq, Social Security, and the economy—"tying the lowest marks he ever received.")[47] Unfolding events clearly will determine future levels of citizen support.

Although extensively reported in the media, Congress is not well understood by the average citizen. Partly to blame are the institution's size and complexity, not to mention the arcane twists and turns of the legislative process.

FIGURE 16-1 Public Assessments of the Two Congresses, 1974–2005

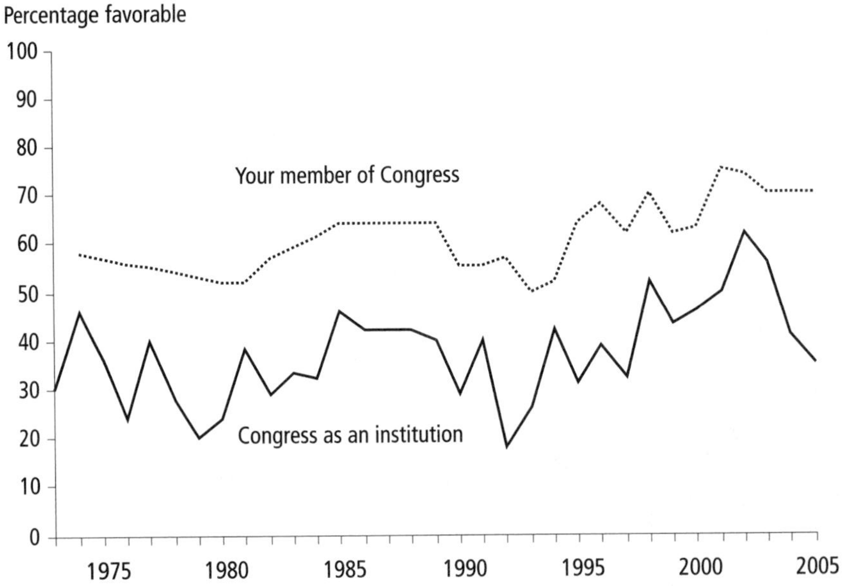

Source: Authors' interpolations of surveys of the Gallup Organization and the Harris Survey. Poll database, Roper Center for Public Opinion, University of Connecticut (www.ropercenter.uconn.edu); the Gallup Organization (www.gallup.com).

Note: The Gallup Organization's questions are "Do you approve of the way the U.S. Congress is handling its job? Do you approve or disapprove of the way the representative from your own congressional district is handling his/her job?" The Harris Survey's questions are "How would you rate the job done this past year by [Congress] [your member of Congress]—excellent, pretty good, only fair, or poor?" Responses are dichotomized as favorable ("excellent," "pretty good") or unfavorable ("only fair," "poor"). The plotted points in the figures indicate respondents having opinions who approve of or are favorable toward congressional performance.

"What Congress does when the subcommittee on acoustics and ventilation meets," remarks Sen. Ron Wyden, D-Ore., "is often achingly dull, which is why most Americans pay scant attention."[48]

Many citizens find more distasteful the core attributes of lawmaking: controversy, messiness, and compromise. In truth, this same messiness is found in the other branches of government. The president speaks with one voice, but fierce competition for the president's ear is unending. President George W. Bush's administration, despite its stress on secrecy and loyalty, witnessed public debates on military reform, the preemptive war doctrine, relations with the

United Nations, and even the Iraqi war. As for the judiciary, opinions are frequently divided or unclear, and they seldom resolve or even clarify great national controversies.

The public's ambivalence toward Congress, however, goes far deeper than unhappiness with specific policies or disgust with scandals, if the sobering conclusions of John R. Hibbing and Elizabeth Theiss-Morse are to be believed.

> People do not wish to see uncertainty, conflicting opinions, long debate, competing interests, confusion, bargaining, and compromised, imperfect solutions. They want government to do its job quietly and efficiently, sans conflict and sans fuss. In short . . . they often seek a patently unrealistic form of democracy.[49]

In other words, people seem to abhor the very attributes that are the hallmarks of robust representative assemblies. As Hibbing and Theiss-Morse observe, Congress "is structured to embody what we dislike about modern democratic government, which is almost everything."[50]

TWENTY-FIRST CENTURY CHALLENGES

The U.S. Congress is now in its third century. Survival for more than two centuries is no mean feat. Perhaps like Dr. Johnson's dog (noted not for its skill at standing on hind legs but for doing so at all), Congress's longevity is proof enough of its worth. Congress has withstood repeated stress and turbulence including a civil war, political assassinations, terrorist attacks, domestic scandals, and contentious foreign involvement. It is sobering to realize that the U.S. constitutional system is far older than most all of the world's existing governments.

Global Threats and Alarms

The physical setting of the U.S. Capitol now mirrors the status of security worldwide. Only a few short years ago, visitors and Hill personnel moved freely in and out of the Capitol and surrounding office buildings. Members of the public may still visit most Capitol Hill facilities, but they will encounter the now-common elements of security: uniformed officers, metal detectors, and concrete barriers. One welcome development, however, will be a long-needed Capitol Visitors' Center—constructed underground on the East Front—that when completed will not only enhance the building's safety but also serve to introduce visitors to Congress and its work.

The possibility of future terrorist attacks forces people to think the unthinkable about the physical continuity of Congress. If the Capitol were attacked, how could deceased House members be quickly replaced? Nearly every state empowers governors to fill Senate seats temporarily, but House seats constitutionally must be elected, which would entail time-consuming special elections. What could be done about incapacitated members?

What would happen if the nation's capital were destroyed or uninhabitable? Could lawmakers, perhaps, conduct business by teleconferencing from remote locations?

Various constitutional amendments have been suggested to allow for the temporary appointment of House members in the event a catastrophe caused mass vacancies. A bipartisan Continuity of Government Commission recommended a constitutional amendment empowering Congress to enact legislation addressing a range of continuity questions.[51] Another constitutional approach suggested by lawmakers would allow "temporary replacements to be chosen on a ballot along with the actual candidate seeking election to Congress in any regular or special election."[52] A House majority has so far opposed the idea of appointing temporary House members to fill vacancies caused by some calamity. Instead the House has passed legislation to require the states to conduct expedited special elections to fill vacancies if, for example, a terrorist attack killed large numbers of lawmakers. It also adopted at the start of the 109th Congress a provisional quorum rule that would allow the House to function if scores of members were incapacitated. The Senate, too, has introduced proposals to allow "each chamber to set terms for replacing members who die or are unable to function."[53]

Mere survival, though, may be the least of Congress's challenges. In a world of uncertain global challenges, Congress continues to face divisive domestic issues, such as energy, health care, economic inequality, and care for aging baby boomers (who reach retirement age beginning in 2008). Such issues are played out in "a narrowly divided House and Senate in which every move by congressional leaders is driven by the desire to win control of both chambers."[54] "Everyone is less secure about what the hell they're doing," remarked former representative Leon Panetta, D-Calif. (1977–1993). "They're basically playing the politics and issues on a day-to-day basis."[55]

On top of these continuing domestic issues are global challenges linked to an ongoing war against terrorists plus war and reconstruction in such states as Afghanistan and Iraq. Among the collateral damages inflicted by wartime conditions is the quality of deliberation—and deliberateness—essential to legislative processes. In its haste to respond to terrorist attacks, Congress gave scant attention to details of the vast grants of power it ceded to the president and the executive branch by approving, for example, open-ended military action, the problematic U.S.A. Patriot Act, and the 180,000-employee Homeland Security Department—actions whose implications were unknown to the lawmakers who voted for them.

Congress shied away from a grand debate in approving the Iraqi war resolution. "We have left the field," confessed Sen. Richard J. Durbin, D-Ill. "This is the largest grant of presidential authority ever given by a Congress."[56] Sen. Robert C. Byrd, D-W.Va., whose Senate career began in 1959, put it this way on the eve of the Iraq war, in an eloquent speech to an almost empty chamber:

> We stand passively mute in the Senate today, paralyzed by our own uncertainty, seemingly stunned by the sheer turmoil of events. Only on the editorial pages of some of our newspapers is there much substantive discussion concerning the prudence or the imprudence of engaging in this particular war. . . . But today we hear nothing, almost nothing, by way of debate. . . .
>
> The rafters should ring. The press galleries should be filled. Senators should be at their seats listening to questions being asked about this war, questions to which the American people out there have a right to expect answers. The American people are longing for information and they are not getting it. This chamber is silent. . . . We are truly sleepwalking through history.[57]

Congress nonetheless showed some signs of regaining its equilibrium once the initial shock waves had subsided from the terrorist attacks and the Afghan and Iraqi wars. Issues of costs, personnel deployments, prisoners' treatment, and foreign policy implications began to be explored.

Following initial military successes in Iraq, for example, congressional committees moved to scrutinize the slow pace and mounting costs of reconstruction and nation-building efforts there. Thwarted by what House International Relations chair Henry J. Hyde, R-Ill., called a "lack of transparency" on the administration's part, the chairmen and ranking minority members of both House and Senate foreign policy committees requested the Government Accountability Office to undertake a thorough study.[58] As a staff aide explained, "The members gave up on getting the administration to share information so they asked for this full investigation."[59] Similar roadblocks were encountered by later probes of intelligence failures, contracting procedures in combat zones, and treatment of detainees held secretly in Iraq, Guantanamo Bay, and elsewhere.

Many lawmakers who had supported the Iraqi endeavor eventually became troubled that the United States was locked in a long-term struggle whose costs were mounting and whose benefits remained unpredictable. As Rep. John Spratt of South Carolina, ranking Democrat on the House Budget Committee, observed, the Iraqi insurgency "is lasting longer, and is more intense, and the cost to keep troops in the theater of operations is proving to be much greater than anyone anticipated."[60]

Checks and Imbalances?

The constitutional system of divided powers and competing branches rarely yields a perfect equilibrium. Powers ebb and flow among the branches. National security crises tend to elevate the presidency, whereas peaceful times are friendlier to congressional power. Activist judges with an agenda can pull the judiciary into the political thickets of policy debate; passivist judges are more inclined to defer to the other branches.

Even before the September 11 attacks, some members of the Bush administration tended to undervalue or dismiss congressional prerogatives. The rationale seemed to spring from Vice President Dick Cheney's historically dubious assertion that chief executives "are weaker today as an institution because of the unwise compromises" on the part of past presidents. Cheney thus vowed "to pass on our offices in better shape than we found them." [61]

The White House's view of executive-legislative relations explained its reluctance, for example, to share documents with Congress, permit certain executive officials to testify before congressional committees, or otherwise cooperate with investigative hearings.[62] By the start of Bush's second term, the vice president could claim that "there has been over time a restoration, if you will, of the power and authority of the president." [63]

In today's world, underlying trends undoubtedly moved in Cheney's direction: toward broader White House prerogatives and narrower legislative involvement. Unified government partially accounts for this development, because the president is his party's leader. Many congressional Republicans, in fact, see their political fate as tied to the president's. This pattern of power flowing toward the White House is clearest in war powers questions.

Through September 10, 2001, White House claims met with considerable resistance on Capitol Hill. The next day, what had up to then been a modestly successful presidency was transformed into a wartime one. The stakes and resources in the ongoing constitutional struggle were profoundly altered—or at least until the terrorist threat fades from the public consciousness.

Executive branch encroachments upon legislative priorities are, in truth, neither new nor confined to crisis periods. President George W. Bush had precedent on his side when he used rulemaking powers to install policies Congress was unlikely to approve. Many of the new rules were written to overturn those instituted by his predecessor, Bill Clinton. Bush also was not the first president to abandon treaties without legislative consultation. Most presidents, moreover, fight for broader leeway in spending appropriated funds and freedom to reorganize agencies and redeploy their personnel. To the extent that lawmakers acquiesce, they have only themselves to blame.

The Bush administration's very success in implementing timeworn practices has tended to impede the work of Congress—especially what Woodrow Wilson called the "informing function." Presidents and their appointees naturally seek to control information about what they are doing. But the Bush administration made secrecy a watchword. A first-ever lawsuit was lodged against the White House—and later abandoned under pressure—by Congress's investigative arm, the Government Accountability Office, in an effort to obtain information on White House consultations leading to the administration's energy plans. (In May 2005 a federal appeals court dismissed a suit brought by two advocacy groups that demanded public disclosure of Cheney's energy task force minutes.)[64] Regarding a range of inquiries, such staunch GOP committee chairmen as Charles E. Grassley of Iowa (Senate

Finance), Henry J. Hyde of Illinois (House International Relations), and F. James Sensenbrenner Jr. of Wisconsin (House Judiciary) protested repeatedly about the executive's failure to provide information. (Sensenbrenner threatened at one point to subpoena information from the Justice Department.)[65]

Congress at the same time faces attacks upon its powers from an activist federal judiciary, which has invalidated federal enactments in some thirty cases since 1995. For the first time since the late 1930s, the courts challenged federal laws in such areas as interstate commerce and civil rights, often in the name of guarding states' rights. By narrow majorities, for example, the U.S. Supreme Court curbed the 1990 Americans with Disabilities Act on grounds it had not dared to apply to earlier civil rights statutes. ("Activism" is often in the eye of the beholder—liberal or conservative. Even with most federal courts filled with GOP appointees, conservative lawmakers and outside groups have attacked the courts over a handful of ideologically tinged issues.)

Few people, however, seem troubled by decisions regarding fundamental state and federal authority. Federal circuit court judge John T. Noonan Jr., a Reagan appointee, argues that the Supreme Court's elevation of states' rights over congressional power has "invented criteria for Congress that invaded the legislative domain."[66] Whatever the constitutional arguments, future activist-controlled courts could constrict legislative powers in much the same way that late-nineteenth-century courts gutted the Civil War constitutional amendments. As Noonan explains, "If five members of the Supreme Court are in agreement on an agenda, they are mightier than five hundred members of Congress with unmobilized or warring constituencies."[67]

We cite such views out of a strong belief in traditional U.S. constitutional values and representative democracy—not from any partisanship that is intentionally liberal or conservative, Democrat or Republican. Historically, it is true, leaders driven by partisan policy agendas have favored one branch over another. Twentieth-century liberals, who generally preferred national power over states' rights, made common cause with activist presidents such as Franklin D. Roosevelt or Lyndon Johnson. On Capitol Hill, leaders of that era's conservative coalition tended to favor state and local power. More recently, the situation is often reversed: Conservative presidents (Ronald Reagan and, especially, George W. Bush) promoted a further rise of big government, but with an ambitious and ideologically polarizing agenda.

Partisans of all stripes have a long-term stake in an active, robust legislative branch. Executive initiatives, however popular, need critical review. Executive programs must be overseen and evaluated. That is why leaders and members of both parties have expressed concern over recent developments. What will the future hold? Much depends on how long the wartime ethos continues and whether Republicans will consolidate their gains to reestablish long-term one-party government in the nation's capital. Answers to such questions must await future developments.

"THE FUNDAMENTAL THINGS APPLY"

Some contend that too much is expected of members of Congress. "Every Congress has its obstacles to tackle," reflects Rep. Walter B. Jones Jr., R-N.C., "but it seems we have more high-stakes matters on our plate today."[68] How can elected generalists render intelligent judgments on the dizzyingly complex problems of governance? "People shouldn't expect those in office to be at the forefront of new developments," observed Rep. Barney Frank, D-Mass. "The best we can do is to be adapters. No one has the intellectual energy to be an elected official and simultaneously break new intellectual ground."[69]

When the First Congress convened, the United States had a tiny population, mostly rural and uneducated. Its social and industrial structure was simple. Changes occurred slowly, and the government's tasks were few. Nothing could be farther from the contemporary situation. "Today," reflected Sen. Nancy Landon Kassebaum, R-Kan. (1978–1997), "there's an almost information overload, a bombardment by news, by faxes. Everything is instantaneous with too little time for thoughtful reflection."[70]

Congress must help the nation compete in a world where all countries increasingly face similar or interrelated problems.[71] National borders and the authority of national governments are becoming less potent than in the past. "The real problem [members of Congress] face," wrote a political observer, "is that local and national politics have now become irretrievably global because their economies are locked into the global system."[72]

In light of all this buzzing confusion, a single national assembly of generalists elected by plurality votes from geographical areas may seem anomalous. Perhaps Congress imperfectly mirrors the real-world "democracy of . . . complex, multiple, and transient minorities."[73] Far from retreating from participation or civic involvement, citizens may simply be moving away from traditional forms—elections, mass political parties, and adversarial courts—and toward more varied, personal, and adaptable modes of participation. Perhaps the movement is away from government itself and toward more fluid, decentralized nongovernmental entities. One thoughtful observer even suggests that "Congress is so unpleasantly noisy these days not because it has too much to do but because it has too little."[74]

We have no confident solutions to these dilemmas, and so we end our discourse with questions for the twenty-first century. Are the two Congresses ultimately compatible? Or are they diverging, each detrimental to the other? Even if the federal government were to be downsized (a doubtful prospect), the burden placed on both Congresses would remain heavy by historical standards. Congress-as-institution is expected to resolve all kinds of problems, not only by processing legislation but also by monitoring programs and serving as an all-purpose watchdog. Legislators struggle to keep abreast of these demands. The question is whether it will be a winning or losing effort.

At the same moment, Congress-as-politicians seems busier than ever. In part because of the sheer scope of modern government, in part because of citizens' empowerment, constituents are insisting that senators and representatives communicate with them more often, serve their states or districts materially, play the role of ombudsmen, and adhere to stricter standards of personal conduct. Legislators have accepted and profited electorally from these functions, but not without misgivings and not without detriment to their legislative tasks.

To maintain its vitality, Congress needs not fewer politicians, but more of them—officeholders who are willing to learn their craft and who will stay around long enough to master it. "To avoid coming apart at the seams," former representative Hamilton declares, "our country needs people who know how to practice the art of politics. That is what good politicians do: they make democratic government possible in a nation alive with competing factions."[75]

If Congress is to fulfill its promise, citizens also must be engaged in politics—learning about issues that concern them and participating by conveying their views. Again former representative Hamilton's assessment is on the mark. Citizens, he says,

> must understand that they need to get involved if they want our system to improve. They need to know that the nature of this relationship between the representative and the represented—and the honesty of the exchange between the two—shapes the strength of our representative democracy.[76]

In the longer view the question is whether an institution embracing so many disparate motives and careers can continue to function as a coherent whole. Can policies patched together from many discrete interests guide the nation on its course? Ever since 1787 people have wondered about this question. History is only mildly reassuring, and the future poses new and delicate challenges for which the margin of error may be narrower than ever before. And yet representative democracy itself is a gamble. The proposition that representation can yield wise policy making remains a daring one. As always, it is an article of faith whose proof lies inevitably in the future.

SUGGESTED READINGS

Bessette, Joseph M. *The Mild Voice of Reason: Deliberative Democracy and American National Government.* Chicago: University of Chicago Press, 1994.

Bok, Derek. *The Trouble with Government.* Cambridge: Harvard University Press, 2001.

Cook, Timothy E. *Making Laws and Making News: Media Strategies in the U.S. House of Representatives.* Washington, D.C.: Brookings Institution, 1989.

Dodd, Lawrence C., and Bruce I. Oppenheimer, eds. *Congress Reconsidered.* 8th ed. Washington, D.C.: CQ Press, 2005.

Mackenzie, G. Calvin, with Michael Hafken. *Scandal Proof: Do Ethics Laws Make Government Ethical?* Washington, D.C.: Brookings Institution Press, 2002.

Mann, Thomas E., and Norman J. Ornstein, eds. *Congress, the Press, and the Public.* Washington, D.C.: Brookings Institution, 1994.

Schickler, Eric. *Disjointed Pluralism: Institutional Innovation and the Development of the U.S. Congress.* Princeton: Princeton University Press, 2001.

Wolfensberger, Donald. *Congress and the People: Deliberative Democracy on Trial.* Washington, D.C.: Woodrow Wilson Center Press, 2000.

Reference Materials

APPENDIX A Party Control: Presidency, Senate, House, 1901–2007

			Senate			House		
Congress	Years	President	D	R	Other	D	R	Other
57th	1901–1903	William McKinley/ Theodore Roosevelt	31	55	4	151	197	9
58th	1903–1905	T. Roosevelt	33	57	—	178	208	—
59th	1905–1907	T. Roosevelt	33	57	—	136	250	—
60th	1907–1909	T. Roosevelt	31	61	—	164	222	—
61st	1909–1911	William Howard Taft	32	61	—	172	219	—
62d	1911–1913	Taft	41	51	—	228	161	1
63d	1913–1915	Woodrow Wilson	51	44	1	291	127	17
64th	1915–1917	Wilson	56	40	—	230	196	9
65th	1917–1919	Wilson	53	42	—	216	210	6
66th	1919–1921	Wilson	47	49	—	190	240	3
67th	1921–1923	Warren G. Harding	37	59	—	131	301	1
68th	1923–1925	Calvin Coolidge	43	51	2	205	225	5
69th	1925–1927	Coolidge	39	56	1	183	247	4
70th	1927–1929	Coolidge	46	49	1	195	237	3
71st	1929–1931	Herbert Hoover	39	56	1	167	267	1
72d	1931–1933	Hoover	47	48	1	220	214	1
73d	1933–1935	Franklin D. Roosevelt	60	35	1	313	117	5
74th	1935–1937	F. D. Roosevelt	69	25	2	319	103	10
75th	1937–1939	F. D. Roosevelt	76	16	4	331	89	13
76th	1939–1941	F. D. Roosevelt	69	23	4	261	164	4
77th	1941–1943	F. D. Roosevelt	66	28	2	268	162	5
78th	1943–1945	F. D. Roosevelt	58	37	1	218	208	4
79th	1945–1947	Harry S. Truman	56	38	1	242	190	2
80th	1947–1949	Truman	45	51	—	188	245	1
81st	1949–1951	Truman	54	42	—	263	171	1
82d	1951–1953	Truman	49	47	—	234	199	1
83d	1953–1955	Dwight D. Eisenhower	47	48	1	211	221	1
84th	1955–1957	Eisenhower	48	47	1	232	203	—
85th	1957–1959	Eisenhower	49	47	—	233	200	—
86th[a]	1959–1961	Eisenhower	65	35	—	284	153	—
87th[a]	1961–1963	John F. Kennedy	65	35	—	263	174	—

Congress	Years	President	Senate D	Senate R	Senate Other	House D	House R	House Other
88th	1963–1965	Kennedy/ Lyndon B. Johnson	67	33	—	258	177	—
89th	1965–1967	Johnson	68	32	—	295	140	—
90th	1967–1969	Johnson	64	36	—	247	187	—
91st	1969–1971	Richard M. Nixon	57	43	—	243	192	—
92d	1971–1973	Nixon	54	44	2	254	180	—
93d	1973–1975	Nixon/ Gerald R. Ford	56	42	2	239	192	1
94th	1975–1977	Ford	60	37	2	291	144	—
95th	1977–1979	Jimmy Carter	61	38	1	292	143	—
96th	1979–1981	Carter	58	41	1	276	157	—
97th	1981–1983	Ronald Reagan	46	53	1	243	192	—
98th	1983–1985	Reagan	45	55	—	267	168	—
99th	1985–1987	Reagan	47	53	—	252	183	—
100th	1987–1989	Reagan	55	45	—	258	177	—
101st	1989–1991	George Bush	55	45	—	260	175	—
102d	1991–1993	Bush	57	43	—	268	166	1
103d	1993–1995	Bill Clinton	56	44	—	258	176	1
104th	1995–1997	Clinton	47	53	—	204	230	1
105th	1997–1999	Clinton	45	55	—	207	227	1
106th	1999–2001	Clinton	45	55	—	211	223	1
107th	2001–2003	George W. Bush	50	49	1	210	222	3
108th	2003–2005	Bush	48	51	1	205	229	1
109th	2005–2007	Bush	44	55	1	202	232	1

Republican control (unshaded) — Democratic control (shaded)

Source: Encyclopedia of the United States Congress, ed. Donald C. Bacon, Roger H. Davidson, and Morton Keller (New York: Simon and Schuster, 1995), 1556–1558.

Note: Figures are for the beginning of the first session of each Congress and do not include vacancies, subsequent shifts, or changes in party affiliation.

Note: Data for the 107th Congress are current as of June 30, 2001. The "other" category for the House includes 2 Independents and 1 vacancy.

[a] The House in the 86th and 87th Congress had 437 members because of an at-large representative given to both Alaska (January 3, 1959) and Hawaii (August 21, 1959) prior to redistricting in 1962.

APPENDIX B **Internships: Getting Experience on Capitol Hill**

Capitol Hill is an excellent place to obtain first-hand experience with the U.S. government. With 540 lawmakers (representatives, senators, delegates, and resident commissioners); hundreds of committees and subcommittees; scores of informal caucuses; and three congressional support agencies (the Congressional Research Service, Government Accountability Office, and Congressional Budget Office), intern opportunities abound for students interested in experiencing Congress and its members up close and personal.

Undergraduates will find useful information about landing an internship on Capitol Hill in several sources. One of the best is published under the auspices of the American Political Science Association and is titled *Studying in Washington: Academic Internships in the Nation's Capital.* Political scientist Stephen E. Frantzich discusses how to get a good internship, make the most of the experience, and find a place to live in Washington, D.C.

From our own years of "soaking and poking" around Capitol Hill, we offer five observations about getting congressional experience. First, no central clearinghouse exists for internships. Every congressional office, committee, caucus, and support agency manages its own internship program. Contact information and intern applications may be found on member and committee websites (www.house.gov and www.senate.gov). Many intern opportunities are available for minority students, such as through the Congressional Hispanic Caucus Institute (www.chci.org) or the minority access internship program (www.minorityaccess.org). You must be persistent, patient, and determined to find a position that will be a rewarding learning experience. Not only should you find out what duties and functions will be assigned to you as a volunteer intern (it is sometimes possible to secure paid internships), but you also need to remember that you have something useful to offer. Most congressional offices and committees are understaffed and subject to high staff turnover. Although the market for interns is competitive, congressional lawmakers, committees, and staffers want and need your talent.

Second, develop some notion as to where you would like to intern. Do research on the committee, lawmaker, support agency, or caucus that interests you. Remember that every office has its own personality. Senate offices, for instance, are often large enterprises with many staff aides, while House offices generally are smaller. Interns thus will have more opportunities for personal, day-to-day contact with House members than with senators. The best way to determine the office environment is by interviewing people who have worked in a particular office, talking with intern coordinators at your college or university, or visiting the office yourself.

Third, target your own representative and senators. Many congressional members prefer interns from their own state or district who are likely to be familiar with the geography and concerns of that area. In addition, potential interns probably will have family and friends who are constituents of the lawmaker. Do not hesitate to use your contacts. You might also volunteer to work in a state or district office of the lawmaker. Before accepting an internship, consider your own views and ideals. If your views are conservative, working for a lawmaker who espouses liberal causes may be difficult. However, if you are tactful and open-minded, working for someone whose views differ from yours may be instructive. Because you are a student, an internship with someone who holds divergent ideological views probably will not be held against you later in landing a position.

Fourth, intern placement opportunities are plentiful. Many colleges and universities sponsor semester programs in Washington. Several schools, including the American University, Boston University, Hamilton College, the State University of New York, the University of Southern California, and the University of California run programs in Washington. Some accept students from other accredited colleges and universities. The Washington Center for Internships and Academic Seminars, in existence since 1975, has placed thousands of students from hundreds of colleges.

Finally, Congress needs and welcomes the influx of new ideas and experiences that interns bring with them. The work at times may be drudgery—answering mail and telephones, entering information into computers, and running errands—but the opportunity to learn about Congress and to pick up political smarts not easily available from textbooks is nearly without equal. You may even want to keep a private journal of your experiences: what you have done and what you have learned. In sum, a volunteer job on Capitol Hill is likely to be rewarding intellectually and in other ways that are impossible to predict.

RESOURCES

The Congressional Intern Handbook. Washington, D.C.: Congressional Management Foundation, 2001.

Fleishman, Sandra. "The Annual Scramble: Washington Interns Line Up for Their First Lesson—in Housing Supply and Demand." *Washington Post,* May 29, 2004, F1.

Frantzich, Stephen E. *Studying in Washington: Academic Internships in the Nation's Capital.* 5th ed. Washington, D.C.: American Political Science Association, 2002.

Gomez, Julissa. *Internships, Fellowships, and Other Work Experience: Opportunities in the Federal Government.* Congressional Research Service Report No. 98–654C, October 28, 2004. Provides useful listings and bibliographies of internships.

Joyce, Amy. "Interns Seek Their Place in the Sun." *Washington Post,* July 11, 2004, F4.

Lee, Jennifer. "Crucial Unpaid Internships Increasingly Separate the Haves from the Have-Nots." *New York Times,* August 10, 2004, 16.

Maxwell, Bruce. *Insider's Guide to Finding a Job in Washington: Contacts and Strategies to Build Your Career in Public Policy.* Washington, D.C.: CQ Press, 1999.

Peterson's Internships. Princeton, N.J.: Peterson's Guides. Annual.

Reeher, Grant, and Mack Mariani, eds. *The Insider's Guide to Political Internships: What to Do Once You're in the Door.* Boulder, Colo.: Westview Press, 2002.

Washington Center for Internships and Academic Seminars. Address: 2301 M Street N.W., Washington, D.C. 20037. Telephone: (202) 336-7600 or (800) 486-8921; Web site: www.twc.edu/internships/index.htm.

Washington Information Directory. Washington, D.C.: Congressional Quarterly. Annual publication that provides information about governmental and nongovernmental groups as well as addresses and phone numbers for congressional offices and committees.

Notes

CHAPTER 1

1. Ben Pershing, "Tragedy Hits Home for New York-Area Members," *Roll Call,* September 13, 2001, 3.
2. Pershing, "Tragedy Hits Home for New York-Area Members."
3. Congressional Quarterly, *CQ's Politics in America 2004* (Washington, D.C.: CQ Press, 2003), 696–697.
4. Paul S. Herrnson, *Congressional Elections: Campaigning at Home and in Washington,* 4th ed. (Washington, D.C.: CQ Press, 2003), 265.
5. Sam Rayburn, *Speak, Mr. Speaker,* ed. H. G. Dulaney and Edward Hake Phillips (Bonham, Texas: Sam Rayburn Foundation, 1978), 263–264. Rayburn was Speaker from 1940 to 1947, 1949 to 1953, and 1955 to 1961.
6. Glenn R. Parker, *Homeward Bound: Explaining Campaign Changes in Congressional Behavior* (Pittsburgh: University of Pittsburgh Press, 1986), 18.
7. U.S. Congress, House Committee on Administrative Review, *Administrative Management and Legislative Management,* 2 vols., H. Doc. 95–232, 95th Cong., 1st sess., September 28, 1977, 2: 18–19.
8. Alan Abramowitz, "A Comparison of Voting for U.S. Senator and Representative in 1978," *American Political Science Review* 74 (September 1980): 633–640; and Richard F. Fenno Jr., *The United States Senate: A Bicameral Perspective* (Washington, D.C.: American Enterprise Institute, 1982), 29ff.
9. U.S. Congress, Joint Committee on the Organization of Congress, *Organization of the Congress, Final Report,* 2 vols., H. Rept. 103–14, 103d Cong., 1st sess., December 1993, 2: 275–287. See Table 5-2 in this book.
10. Glenn R. Parker and Roger H. Davidson, "Why Do Americans Love Their Congressmen So Much More Than Their Congress?" *Legislative Studies Quarterly* 4 (February 1979): 53–61; Kelly D. Patterson and David B. Magleby, "Public Support for Congress," *Public Opinion Quarterly* 56 (winter 1992): 539–540; and Randall B. Ripley, Samuel C. Patterson, Lynn M. Mauer, and Stephen V. Quinlan, "Constituents' Evaluations of U.S. House Members," *American Politics Quarterly* 20 (October 1992): 442–456.
11. Alexander Hamilton, James Madison, and John Jay, *The Federalist Papers,* ed. Clinton Rossiter, No. 51 (New York: Mentor, 1961), 322.
12. *The Federalist Papers,* No. 52, 327.
13. Edmund Burke, "Speech to Electors at Bristol," in *Burke's Politics,* ed. Ross J. S. Hoffman and Paul Levack (New York: Knopf, 1949), 116.
14. Burke, "Speech to Electors at Bristol."
15. Quoted in *Roll Call,* September 9, 1993, 16.
16. Frank E. Smith, *Congressman from Mississippi* (New York: Random House, 1964), 127.
17. David R. Mayhew, *Congress: The Electoral Connection* (New Haven: Yale University Press, 1974), 16.
18. *U.S. Term Limits v. Thornton,* 115 S. Ct. 1842 (1995).
19. Quoted in Mark Carl Rom, "Why Not Assume That Public Officials Seek to Promote the Public Interest?" *Public Affairs Report* 37 (July 1996): 12.
20. Woodrow Wilson, *Congressional Government* (1885; reprint, Baltimore: Johns Hopkins University Press, 1981), 210.
21. Richard F. Fenno Jr., *Home Style: House Members in Their Districts* (New York: Pearson Longman, 2003), 168.

CHAPTER 2

1. Alvin M. Josephy Jr., *On the Hill: A History of the American Congress* (New York: Simon and Schuster, 1980), 41–48.
2. Charles A. Beard and John P. Lewis, "Representative Government in Evolution," *American Political Science Review* (April 1932): 223–240.
3. Jock P. Green, ed., *Great Britain and the American Colonies, 1606–1763* (New York: Harper TorchBooks, 1970), xxxix.
4. Edmund C. Burnett, *Continental Congress* (New York: Norton, 1964).
5. *Congressional Quarterly's Guide to Congress,* 5th ed., vol. I (Washington, D.C.: CQ Press, 2000), 9.
6. Burnett, *Continental Congress,* 171. When quoting the Constitution in this volume, the authors use modern capitalization.
7. Jack N. Rakove, *The Beginnings of National Politics: An Interpretive History of the Continental Congress* (New York: Knopf, 1979), 43.
8. Charles C. Thach Jr., *The Creation of the Presidency, 1775–1789: A Study in Constitutional History* (Baltimore: Johns Hopkins University Press, 1969), 34.
9. James Sterling Young, "America's First Hundred Days," *Miller Center Journal* 1 (winter 1994): 57.
10. John Locke, *Two Tracts on Government,* ed. Philip Abrams (New York: Cambridge University Press, 1967), 374.
11. Alexander Hamilton, James Madison, and John Jay, *The Federalist Papers,* ed. Clinton Rossiter, No. 48 (New York: Mentor, 1961), 308.
12. Joseph Story, *Commentaries on the Constitution of the United States,* 5th ed., vol. 1 (Boston: Little, Brown, 1905), 396. For Justice Robert Jackson's comments, see *Youngstown Sheet and Tube Co. v. Sawyer,* 343 U.S. 579, 635 (1952).
13. *Nixon v. United States,* 506 U.S. 224 (1993).
14. *The Federalist Papers,* No. 65, 396.
15. Van Tassel, Emily Field, and Paul Finkelman, *Impeachable Offenses: A Documentary History from 1787 to the Present* (Washington, D.C.: Congressional Quarterly, 1999).
16. *Marbury v. Madison,* 1 Cranch 137 (1803).
17. *The Constitution of the United States of America: Analysis and Interpretation,* S. Doc. 92–80, 92d Cong., 2d sess., 1973, 1597–1619. Recent figures are courtesy of George Costello, specialist in American law, Congressional Research Service.
18. Quoted in Dana Milbank, "Scalia Showing His Softer Side," *Washingon Post,* March 15, 2005, A2.
19. William N. Eskridge Jr., "Overriding Supreme Court Statutory Interpretation Decisions," *Yale Law Journal* 101 (November 1991): 331–455. See also R. Shep Melnick, *Between the Lines: Interpreting Welfare Rights* (Washington, D.C.: Brookings Institution, 1994).
20. Louis Fisher, *Constitutional Dialogues: Interpretation as Political Process* (Princeton: Princeton University Press, 1988), 275.
21. Quoted in Charles Warren, *The Making of the Constitution* (Boston: Little, Brown, 1928), 162.
22. Quoted in Charles Warren, *The Supreme Court in United States History* (Boston: Little, Brown, 1919), 195.
23. Lindsay Rogers, *The American Senate* (New York: Knopf, 1926).
24. *The Federalist Papers,* No. 55, 343.
25. Charles A. Kromkowski and John A. Kromkowski, "Why 435? A Question of Political Arithmetic," *Polity* 24 (fall 1991): 129–145; and David C. Huckabee, *House of Representatives: Setting the Size at 435,* Congressional Research Service Report No. 95–791GOV, July 11, 1995.
26. *The Federalist Papers,* No. 27, 168.

27. Joe Martin as told to Robert J. Donovan, *My First Fifty Years in Politics* (New York: McGraw-Hill, 1960), 49–50.
28. Norman J. Ornstein, Thomas E. Mann, and Michael J. Malbin, *Vital Statistics on Congress, 2001–2002* (Washington, D.C.: American Enterprise Institute Press, 2002), 149.
29. Ornstein, Mann, and Malbin, *Vital Statistics on Congress,* 146–147.
30. U.S. Congress, House Commission on Administrative Review, *Administrative Reorganization and Legislative Management,* 2 vols., H. Doc. 95–232, 95th Cong., 1st sess., September 28, 1977, 2:17; and U.S. Congress, Senate Commission on the Operation of the Senate, *Senators: Offices, Ethics, and Pressures,* 94th Cong., 2d sess., 1977, Committee Print, xi.
31. See Jefferson's Manual, Section XI; House, *Rules of the House of Representatives,* H. Doc. 105–358, 105th Cong., 2d sess., 1999, 145–148.
32. George B. Galloway, *History of the House of Representatives* (New York: Crowell, 1961), 67.
33. Barbara Sinclair, *Legislators, Leaders, and Lawmaking* (Baltimore: Johns Hopkins University Press, 1995), 75.
34. Neil MacNeil, *Forge of Democracy: The House of Representatives* (New York: McKay, 1963), 306.
35. Elaine K. Swift, *The Making of an American Senate* (Ann Arbor: University of Michigan Press, 1996), 5.
36. David C. King, *Turf Wars: How Congressional Committees Claim Jurisdiction* (Chicago: University of Chicago Press, 1997).
37. Noble Cunningham Jr., ed., *Circular Letters of Congressmen, 1789–1839,* 3 vols. (Chapel Hill: University of North Carolina Press, 1978).
38. Quoted in Galloway, *History of the House,* 122.
39. Quoted in Anthony Champagne, "John Nance Garner," in *Masters of the House: Congressional Leaders over Two Centuries,* ed. Roger H. Davidson, Susan Webb Hammond, and Raymond W. Smock (Boulder, Colo.: Westview Press, 1998), 148.
40. Martin, *My First Fifty Years,* 101.
41. James Sterling Young, *The Washington Community, 1800–1828* (New York: Harcourt Brace Jovanovich, 1966), 89.
42. Cunningham, *Circular Letters of Congressmen,* 57.
43. Roy Swanstrom, *The United States Senate, 1787–1801,* S. Doc. 99–19, 99th Cong., 1st sess., 1985, 80.
44. Nelson W. Polsby, "The Institutionalization of the House of Representatives," *American Political Science Review* 62 (March 1968): 146–147; and Randall B. Ripley, *Power in the Senate* (New York: St. Martin's, 1969), 42–43.
45. Peter Swenson, "The Influence of Recruitment on the Structure of Power in the U.S. House, 1870–1940," *Legislative Studies Quarterly* 7 (February 1982): 7–36.
46. Woodrow Wilson, *Congressional Government* (1885; reprint, Baltimore: Johns Hopkins University Press, 1981).
47. Martin, *My First Fifty Years,* 49.
48. Ripley, *Power in the Senate,* 43–44.
49. David W. Brady, "After the Big Bang House Battles Focused on Committee Issues," *Public Affairs Report* 32 (March 1991): 8. See also Samuel Kernell, "Toward Understanding the Nineteenth Century Congressional Career Patterns: Ambition, Competition, and Rotation," *American Journal of Political Science* 21 (November 1977): 669–693; and Nelson W. Polsby, Miriam Gallagher, and Barry S. Rundquist, "The Growth of the Seniority System in the U.S. House of Representatives," *American Political Science Review* 63 (September 1969): 794.
50. Swanstrom, *The United States Senate,* 283.
51. Young, *The Washington Community,* 126–127.
52. Ornstein, Mann, and Malbin, *Vital Statistics on Congress,* 126–127.
53. Eric Schickler, *Disjointed Pluralism: Institutional Innovation and the Development of the U.S. Congress* (Princeton: Princeton University Press, 2001), 5–12.

54. Schickler, *Disjointed Pluralism,* 267.
55. Schickler, *Disjointed Pluralism,* 267.

CHAPTER 3

1. *U.S. Term Limits v. Thornton,* 514 U.S. 779 (1995).
2. Arend Lijphart, *Democracies: Patterns of Majoritarian and Consensus Government in Twenty-one Countries* (New Haven: Yale University Press, 1984), 174.
3. See Daniel H. Pink, "Givers and Takers," *New York Times,* January 30, 2004, A21.
4. Quoted in Judith Havemann, "Moynihan Poses Questions of Balance," *Washington Post,* August 14, 1995, A15.
5. E. J. Dionne, "Will Republicans Go Nuclear?" *Washington Post,* March 22, 2005, A17.
6. This method is only one of several mathematical formulas that could be employed. Another, the major fractions method, was used from 1911 until 1940. The methods yield slightly different results. For example, in 1992 Montana faced the prospect of losing its second House seat. The state challenged the apportionment formula in the courts but was rejected by the Supreme Court, which found no conclusive answer to the question of "what is the better measure of inequality." *Department of Commerce v. Montana,* 503 U.S. 442 (1992). See Linda Greenhouse, "Supreme Court Upholds Method Used in Apportionment of House," *New York Times,* April 1, 1992, B8.
7. Jonathan Tilove, "Pandora's Box: The Pitfalls of Census 2000," *American Prospect* 11 (April 24, 2000): 39–42.
8. Tilove, "Pandora's Box," 39.
9. Genaro C. Armas, "Census Must Show Adjusted Estimates," *Santa Barbara News-Press,* November 23, 2002, B5.
10. Robin Fields, "State Census Sampling Shows Huge Undercount," *Los Angeles Times,* December 7, 2002, B10.
11. Eric Schmitt, "U.S. Census Bureau Rejects Revision to Nation's Tally," *New York Times,* March 3, 2001, A1. The bureau has continued its strategic retreat from statistical adjustments. Reexamining its numbers three years later, the bureau pronounced its original count a success and claimed it had overcounted the U.S. population by 1.3 million people. However, accuracy varied from state to state, and blacks and Latinos were still undercounted. "Census Bureau Issues Data on Accuracy of 2000 Count," *New York Times,* April 16, 2003, A13.
12. Mark Z. Barabak, "Democrats Rule the Redistricting Roost in California," *Los Angeles Times,* July 25, 2001, A15; and Susan F. Rasky, "Redistricting Defanged by Energy Crisis," *Los Angeles Times,* April 22, 2001, M6.
13. Quoted in Raymond Hernandez, "Lobbying in Albany, New York's Representatives Fight for Their Seats," *New York Times,* February 19, 2001, A16.
14. Mark Z. Barabak, "Redistricting Fuels Partisan Frenzy," *Los Angeles Times,* A1, A14; and Gregory L. Giroux, "GOP in Position to Have Its Say When States Redraw Congressional Districts," *CQ Weekly,* January 6, 2001, 39.
15. *Growe v. Emerson,* 507 U.S. 25 (1993). See Susan B. Glasser, "Supreme Court Voids Minnesota Redistricting," *Roll Call,* February 25, 1993, 1.
16. The classic study is still Gordon E. Baker, *The Reapportionment Revolution: Representation, Political Power, and the Supreme Court* (New York: Random House, 1966).
17. In 2001 Georgia Democrats produced a state legislature redistricting plan testing the notion that a population deviation of plus-or-minus 5 percent would be acceptable at the state level. A circuit court panel invalidated the scheme and eventually drew its own plan, which was ultimately affirmed by the Supreme Court. See *Larios v. Cox,* 300 F. Supp. 2nd 1320 (N.D. Ga. 2004).
18. Alan Ehrenhalt, "Redistricting and the Erosion of Community," *Governing,* June 1992, 10.

19. Chris Cillizza, "Republicans Score Big in Pa.," *Roll Call,* January 7, 2002, 9.
20. Quoted in David G. Savage and Scott Gold, "Justices Order Review of Texas' Political Map," *Los Angeles Times,* October 19, 2004, A10.
21. *Davis v. Bandemer,* 478 U.S. 109 (1986).
22. *Hunt v. Cromartie,* 526 U.S. 541 (1999).
23. *Vieth v. Jubelirer,* 2004 W. L. 894316 (U.S. Pa.). See also Savage and Gold, "Justices Order Review of Texas' Political Map."
24. Rhodes Cook, "Do the Math, and the Result Is: Not Much of a Contest," *Washington Post,* October 6, 2002, B3.
25. Steven Hill, "Schwarzenegger versus Gerrymander," *New York Times,* February 19, 2005, A29. See also Steve Lawrence, "Experts Question Redistricting Plan," *Santa Barbara News-Press,* February 20, 2005, A7.
26. Bruce Oppenheimer's and Alan Abramowitz's recent findings are reported by Bill Bishop, "You Can't Compete With Voters' Feet," *Washington Post,* May 15, 2005, B2.
27. *Thornburg v. Gingles,* 478 U.S. 30 (1986).
28. Charles S. Bullock, "Affirmative Action Districts: In Whose Faces Will They Blow Up?" *Campaigns and Elections* (April 1995): 22.
29. Bullock, "Affirmative Action Districts," 23.
30. David Lublin, *The Paradox of Representation: Racial Gerrymandering and Minority Interests in Congress* (Princeton: Princeton University Press, 1997).
31. Lani Guinier, "What Color Is Your Gerrymander?" *Washington Post,* March 27, 1994, C3.
32. Abigail M. Thernstrom, "A Republican–Civil Rights Conspiracy," *Washington Post,* September 23, 1991, A11. See also Abigail M. Thernstrom, *Whose Votes Count? Affirmative Action and Minority Voting Rights* (Cambridge: Harvard University Press, 1987).
33 . *Shaw v. Reno,* 509 U.S. 630 (1993).
34. Ehrenhalt, "Redistricting and the Erosion of Community," 10.
35. Carol M. Swain, "The Voting Rights Act: Some Unintended Consequences," *Brookings Review* 10 (winter 1992): 51. See also Lublin, *The Paradox of Representation.*
36. Alexander Bolton, "Dems Seek to 'Unpack' Minority Districts," *The Hill,* May 9, 2001, 4.
37. *Gomillion v. Lightfoot,* 364 U.S. 339 (1960).
38. *Shaw v. Reno.*
39. *Miller v. Johnson,* 515 U.S. 900 (1995).
40. Research by Charles S. Bullock and Richard E. Dunn, cited in Adam Clymer, "Shaping the New Math of Racial Redistricting," *New York Times,* July 15, 2001, D16.
41. *Easley v. Cromartie* 121 S. Ct. (2001). The decision was described by Linda Greenhouse in "Court Gives Wiggle Room to Racially Drawn Districts," *New York Times,* May 18, 1999, A12; and in "Justices Reconsider Race and Redistricting," *New York Times,* November 28, 2000, A25.
42. Linda Greenhouse, "Justices Permit Race as a Factor in Redistricting," *New York Times,* April 19, 2001, A1, A16.
43. Mara Caputo and Ragan Narash, "Despite Series of Court Rulings, State Officials Are Left Guessing," *CQ Weekly,* August 11, 2001, 1970.
44. *Georgia v. Ashcroft,* 123 S. Ct. 2498 (2003). See Adam Clymer, "Court Allows a New Approach to Redrawing Districts by Race," *New York Times,* June 27, 2003, A1.
45. *DeWitt v. Wilson,* 515 U.S. 1170 (1995).
46. Louis Sandy Maisel, *From Obscurity to Oblivion: Running in the Congressional Primary* (Knoxville: University of Tennessee Press, 1982), 34.
47. Quoted in Jon Margolis, "The Disappearing Candidates," *American Prospect* 11 (January 31, 2000): 32.
48. Alan Ehrenhalt, *The United States of Ambition* (New York: Random House, 1991), 17.

49. The four Capitol Hill campaign committees are the National Republican Senatorial Committee (NRSC), the Democratic Senatorial Campaign Committee (DSCC), the National Republican Congressional Committee (NRCC), and the Democratic Congressional Campaign Committee (DCCC). See Paul S. Herrnson, *Congressional Elections: Campaigning at Home and in Washington,* 4th ed. (Washington, D.C.: CQ Press, 2004), 90–94.
50. Edward Walsh, "To Every Campaign, There Is a Recruiting Season," *Washington Post,* November 12, 1985, A1.
51. Alice A. Love, "Small Business Group Helps Grow Its Own Grassroots Candidates at Meeting Next Week," *Roll Call,* October 16, 1995, 22.
52. William Claiborne, "In Neb., a Gridiron Hero Scores in Political Arena," *Washington Post,* June 14, 2000, A3.
53. David T. Canon, *Actors, Athletes, and Astronauts: Political Amateurs in the United States Congress* (Chicago: University of Chicago Press, 1990), 2–3, 25–31.
54. Maisel, *From Obscurity to Oblivion,* 23.
55. Michael Janofsky, "Two Congressional Candidates Know They'll Lose, But It's Still Fun," *New York Times,* October 31, 1992, 27.
56. The seminal work on strategic politician theory is Gary C. Jacobson and Samuel Kernell, *Strategy and Choice in Congressional Elections,* 2d ed. (New Haven: Yale University Press, 1983).
57. Jacobson and Kernell, *Strategy and Choice in Congressional Elections,* chapter 3.
58. L. Sandy Maisel, Cherie Maestas, and Walter J. Stone, "The Party Role in Congressional Competition," in *The Parties Respond,* ed. Paul S. Herrnson (Boulder, Colo.: Westview Press, 2002), 129.
59. Lauren W. Whittington, "Scramble Begins for Ohio Special," *Roll Call,* March 21, 2005, 12.
60. Quoted in Jim VandeHei and Tim Curran, "Parties Pushing for Early Money," *Roll Call,* June 14, 1999, 34.
61. Linda L. Fowler and Robert D. McClure, *Political Ambition: Who Decides to Run for Congress* (New Haven: Yale University Press, 1989).
62. Quoted in Burt Solomon, "A Daunting Task: Running for House," *National Journal,* March 21, 1992, 712.
63. Maisel, Maestas, and Stone, "The Party Role in Congressional Competition," 129.
64. Cited in Robin Toner, "Willing Contenders at a Premium in Fierce Fight to Rule Congress," *New York Times,* January 3, 2000, A14.
65. Quoted in Sheryl Gay Stolberg, "Wooed for Congress, Fewer Will Say, 'I Do,' " *New York Times,* October 14, 2003, A22.
66. Maisel, *From Obscurity to Oblivion,* 23.
67. Gary C. Jacobson, *The Politics of Congressional Elections,* 6th ed. (New York: Pearson Longman, 2004), 23.
68. Gary C. Jacobson, "The Marginals Never Vanished: Incumbency and Competition in Elections to the U.S. House of Representatives, 1952–1982," *American Journal of Political Science* 31 (February 1987): 126–141.
69. Norman J. Ornstein, Thomas E. Mann, and Michael J. Malbin, *Vital Statistics on Congress, 1999–2000* (Washington, D.C.: American Enterprise Institute, 2000), 57.
70. Frances E. Lee and Bruce I. Oppenheimer, *Sizing Up the Senate: The Unequal Consequences of Equal Representation* (Chicago: University of Chicago Press, 1999), 95.
71. On the first view mentioned in this paragraph, see Morris P. Fiorina, *Congress: Keystone of the Washington Establishment,* 2d ed. (New Haven: Yale University Press, 1989); and Bruce Cain, John Ferejohn, and Morris Fiorina, *The Personal Vote: Constituency Service and Electoral Independence* (Cambridge: Harvard University Press, 1987), especially chapters 6–7. For more on the second view, see Glenn R. Parker and Roger H. Davidson, "Why Do Americans Love Their Congressmen So Much More Than Their Congress?" *Legislative*

Studies Quarterly 4 (February 1979): 53–61. On the question of whether incumbents' resources are directly tied to votes, see John R. Johannes, *To Serve the People: Congress and Constituency Service* (Lincoln: University of Nebraska Press, 1984), especially chapter 8.

72. Jacobson, *Politics of Congressional Elections,* 38.
73. Quoted in Linda Greenhouse, "Court Rejects One-Ballot Primary as Limit on Party's Right to Shape Its Identity," *New York Times,* June 27, 2000, A19.
74. *California Democratic Party et al. v. Jones,* 99–401 (2000).
75. L. Sandy Maisel, Cary T. Gibson, and Elizabeth J. Ivry, "The Continuing Importance of the Rules of the Game: Subpresidential Nominations in 1994 and 1996," in *The Parties Respond,* 3d ed., ed. L. Sandy Maisel (Boulder, Colo.: Westview Press 1998), 148–151.
76. Harvey L. Schantz, "Contested and Uncontested Primaries for the U.S. House," *Legislative Studies Quarterly* 5 (November 1980): 559. The linkage between interparty and intraparty competition is sometimes referred to as Key's Law. See V. O. Key Jr., *Parties, Politics, and Pressure Groups,* 5th ed. (New York: Crowell, 1964), 438, 447.
77. Maisel, Gibson, and Ivry, "The Continuing Importance of the Rules of the Game," 162–164.
78. Maisel, Maestas, and Stone, "The Party Role in Congressional Competition," 130 ff.
79. Maisel, Maestas, and Stone, "The Party Role in Congressional Competition," 132.
80. John-Thor Dahlburg, "No Harris on the Florida Punch Card," *Los Angeles Times,* January 17, 2004, A9.
81. See, for example, Chris Cillizza, "Club for Growth Favors Schaffer," *Roll Call,* June 17, 2004, 9.
82. Kirk Victor, "Meddling in Minnesota," *National Journal,* May 12, 2001, 1422.
83. Richard A. Oppel Jr., "Despite Big Issues, Primaries Prompted Only 17% to Vote," *New York Times,* September 28, 2002, A12.
84. Austin Ranney, "Parties in State Politics," in *Politics in the American States,* ed. Herbert Jacob and Kenneth Vines (Boston: Little, Brown, 1976), 61–99.
85. John F. Bibby, "State Party Organizations," in *The Parties Respond,* 3d ed., ed. L. Sandy Maisel (Boulder, Colo.: Westview Press, 1998), 20.
86. Herrnson, *Congressional Elections,* 159.
87. Figures for 2003–2004 are derived from Federal Election Commission (FEC) reports, found at fec.gov, and analyses prepared from those data by the Center for Responsive Politics (CRP), available at opensecrets.org. The figures sometimes differ because of CRP's statistical breakdowns of FEC data.
88. See Ornstein, Mann, and Malbin, *Vital Statistics on Congress,* 87–98.
89. Gary C. Jacobson, "Money in the 1980 and 1982 Congressional Elections," in *Money and Politics in the United States,* ed. Michael J. Malbin (Chatham, N.J.: Chatham House, 1984), 58.
90. Christopher Buchanan, "Candidates' Campaign Costs for Congressional Contests Have Gone Up at a Fast Pace," *Congressional Quarterly Weekly Report,* September 29, 1979, 2154–2155.
91. Jacobson, "Money in the 1980 and 1982 Congressional Elections," 57.
92. Committee for Responsive Politics, "Winning versus Spending," www.opensecrets.org. It provides an analysis of FEC data.
93. Quoted in Andy Plattner, "The High Cost of Holding—and Keeping—Public Office," *U.S. News and World Report,* June 22, 1997, 30.
94. See Thomas Romer and James M. Snyder Jr., "An Empirical Investigation of the Dynamics of PAC Contributions," *American Journal of Political Science* 38 (1994): 745–769.
95. Center for Responsive Politics, "Political Parties," www.opensecrets.org. The information is based on Federal Election Commission data released February 18, 2005.
96. Jacobson, "Money in the 1980 and 1982 Congressional Elections," 58–59.
97. Committee for Responsive Politics, based on FEC data as of February 25, 2002.

98. Case studies of political action committees are found in Robert Biersack, Paul Herrnson, and Clyde Wilcox, *Risky Business? PAC Decisionmaking and Congressional Elections* (Armonk, N.Y.: M. E. Sharpe, 1994).
99. Jim VandeHei, "Hastert Starting to Raise Big Bucks," *Roll Call,* June 7, 1999, 1.
100. Quoted in Leslie Wayne, "Business Is Biggest Campaign Spender, Study Says," *New York Times,* October 18, 1996, A1, A26.
101. Center for Responsive Politics, "2004 Election Overview: Top Industries," www .opensecrets.org.
102. Quoted in Jonathan D. Salant, "Business PACs Pick Their Cause," *Congressional Quarterly Weekly Report,* May 6, 1995, 1234.
103. Quoted in Diana F. Dwyer and Victoria A. Farrar-Myers, *Legislative Labyrinth: Congress and Campaign Finance Reform* (Washington, D.C.: CQ Press, 2001), 233.
104. Scott Turow, "The High Court's 20-Year-Old Mistake," *New York Times,* October 12, 1997, E15.
105. E. J. Dionne Jr., "Politics as Public Auction," *Washington Post,* June 19, 1998, A25.
106. Gary C. Jacobson, *Money in Congressional Elections* (New Haven: Yale University Press, 1980).
107. Quoted in Brooks Jackson, "Loopholes Allow Flood of Campaign Giving by Business, Fat Cats," *Wall Street Journal,* July 5, 1984, 1.
108. Dan Balz, "In Long Battle, Small Victories Add Up," *Washington Post,* March 21, 2002, A1.
109. *McConnell v. Federal Election Commission,* No. 02-1674 (2003). See Linda Greenhouse, "Justices, in a 5-to-4 Decision, Back Campaign Finance Law That Curbs Contributions," *New York Times,* December 11, 2003, A1; and David G. Savage, "High Court Upholds Most of Campaign Finance Law," *Los Angeles Times,* December 11, 2003, Al.
110. Glen Justice, "In New Landscape of Campaign Finance, Big Donations Flow to Groups, Not Parties," *New York Times,* December 11, 2003, A25.
111. Quoted in Joe Hadfield, "More Than Survive, Parties Thrive under New Campaign Finance Rules," *Campaigns and Elections* 26 (April 2005): 22–24.
112. Chuck Alston, "A Field Guide to Election Spending Limits," *CQ Weekly,* May 22, 1990, 1621–1626.

CHAPTER 4

1. Sheryl Gay Stolberg, "Chasing a Coveted Democratic Prize across the Plains," *New York Times,* October 24, 2004, A22. Other sources for our account include Charles Babington and Helen Dewar, "8 Senate Races Key to Democrats' Hopes," *Washington Post,* October 18, 2004, A11; and David Kelly, "Daschle Faces Firmly Rooted Rival," *Los Angeles Times,* October 24, 2004, A22.
2. Statistics on money raised and spent in the 2003–2004 electoral cycle were compiled by the Federal Election Commission and released May 12, 2005, as analyzed by the Center for Responsive Politics in "2004 Election Overview: Stats at a Glance" and "Incumbent Advantage," at opensecrets.org.
3. See Richard G. Niemi, Lynda W. Powell, and Patricia L. Bickell, "The Effects of Congruity between Community and District on Salience of U.S. House Candidates," *Legislative Studies Quarterly* 11 (May 1986): 187–201; and Dena Levy and Peverill Squire, "Television Markets and the Competitiveness of U.S. House Elections," *Legislative Studies Quarterly* 25 (May 2000): 313–325.
4. Theodore E. Jackson Jr., "Brand Marketing in Today's Cluttered Political Marketplace," *Campaigns and Elections* 24 (April 2003): 30.
5. Quoted material in this paragraph is from Allison Stevens, "House Candidates in Maryland Striving to Hone Their Messages," *The Hill,* May 8, 2002, 31–32.

6. Quoted in Robin Toner, "In a Cynical Election Season, the Ads Tell an Angry Tale," *New York Times,* October 24, 1994, A1.
7. Chris Cillizza, "Playing It Safe in Carolina," *Roll Call,* October 28, 2004, 1.
8. Kevin McNeill and Cheryl Klock, "Connecticut Upset," *Campaign and Elections* 22 (May 2001): 39, 43.
9. Parke Skelton, quoted in Mary Clare Jalonick, "How to 'Primary' an Incumbent," *Campaigns and Elections* 22 (May 2001): 35.
10. *Notes from EMILY* (December 2004), 5; and *EMILY's List Report to Members 2003–2004* (Washington, D.C., n.d.), 2.
11. Robin Toner, "In Final Rounds, Both Sides Whip Out Bare-Knuckle Ads," *New York Times,* October 21, 1996, B7.
12. Sara Fritz and Dwight Morris, *Gold-Plated Politics: Running for Congress in the 1990s* (Washington, D.C.: Congressional Quarterly, 1992), 28.
13. Raymond Hernandez, "Senator Clinton Piles Up a Fund-Raising Lead for 2006," *New York Times,* April 19, 2005, A21.
14. Statistics on spending in the 2003–2004 electoral cycle are found in "2004 Election Overview: Incumbent Advantage," Center for Responsive Politics, opensecrets.org.
15. Gary C. Jacobson, *The Politics of Congressional Elections,* 6th ed. (New York: Pearson Longman, 2004), 98.
16. Thomas B. Edsall, "In Tight Races, Early Cash Means Staying Competitive," *Washington Post,* July 14, 1998, A6.
17. Gary C. Jacobson, "The Effects of Campaign Spending on Congressional Elections," *American Political Science Review* 72 (June 1978): 469–491.
18. "Total Congressional Campaign Spending," *New York Times,* November 6, 2002, B2.
19. Quoted in Herbert E. Alexander and Brian A. Haggarty, "Misinformation on Media Money," *Public Opinion* 11 (May–June 1988): 7.
20. Edie N. Goldberg and Michael W. Traugott, *Campaigning for Congress* (Washington, D.C.: CQ Press, 1984), 93.
21. Craig Karmin, "Campaign Funds Used for Private Expenses," *The Hill,* September 6, 1995, 1.
22. Philip McCarty, in Democratic Service Club of Santa Barbara, *Newsletter,* December 3, 2004.
23. Larry J. Sabato and Glenn R. Simpson, *Dirty Little Secrets: The Persistence of Corruption in American Politics* (New York: Times Books, 1996), 156.
24. Pew Research Center for the People and the Press, "Voters Liked Campaign 2004, But Too Much 'Mud-Slinging,' " news release, November 11, 2004, 13, www.people-press.org /reports/.
25. University of Southern California, Annenberg School of Communications, Norman Lear Center, "Local TV News Largely Ignores Local Political Races," press release, February 15, 2005.
26. "Media Mix," *Campaigns and Elections* 19 (May 1998): 44.
27. Burdett A. Loomis, "Kansas's Third District: 'Pros from Dover' Set Up Shop," in *The Battle for Congress,* ed. James A. Thurber (Washington, D.C.: Brookings Institution, 1999), 148.
28. Michael Barone and Grant Ujifusa, *The Almanac of American Politics, 1996* (Washington, D.C.: National Journal, 1995), 1445–1446.
29. David T. Canon, "The Wisconsin Second District: History in the Making," in *The Battle for Congress: Consultants, Candidates, and Voters,* ed. James A. Thurber (Washington, D.C.: Brookings Institution Press, 1999), 230.
30. Loomis, "Kansas's Third District," 147–148.
31. Stephen Ansolabehere and Shanto Iyengar, *Going Negative: How Attack Ads Shrink and Polarize the Electorate* (New York: Free Press, 1996), 128.
32. Quoted in David S. Broder, "Death by Negative Ads," *Washington Post,* November 3, °2002, B7.

33. Richard R. Lau and Gerald M. Pomper, "Effects of Negative Campaigning on Turnout in U.S. Senate Elections, 1988–1998," *Journal of Politics* 63 (August 2001) 817.
34. See Howard Kurtz, "Hearing 'Foul,' Stations Pull Political Ads," *Washington Post,* September 20, 2002, A14.
35. Norman J. Ornstein, "Should Liars Be Seated? It's Not Up to Congress," *Roll Call,* May 17, 1993, 12.
36. Quoted in Adam Nagourney, "Politicians Turn to Alternatives to TV Advertising," *New York Times,* October 5, 2002, A1.
37. Quoted in Alexander Bolton, "Grassroots Replacing Soft Cash in Campaigns," *The Hill,* July 29, 2003, 10. Figures are from the Wisconsin Advertising Project, cited in "The Living-Room Campaign," *New York Times,* November 6, 2002, B2. Completed findings will be reported in Ken Goldstein and Joel Rivlin, *Political Advertising in the 2002 Elections* (Cambridge, United Kingdom: Cambridge University Press, forthcoming).
38. Quoted in Nagourney, "Politicians Turn to Alternatives to TV Advertising," A1, A15.
39. Merle Miller, *Lyndon: An Oral Biography* (New York: Putnam, 1980), 120.
40. David S. Broder, "Shoe Leather Politicking," *Washington Post,* June 13, 2001, A29.
41. Donald P. Green and Allen S. Gerber, *Get Out the Vote!* (Washington, D.C.: Brookings Institution Press, 2004), 40.
42. Dan Glickman, as told to Amy Zipkin, "Landing the Job He Wanted," *New York Times,* April 17, 2005, C10.
43. Paul Houston, "TV and High Tech Send Campaign Costs Soaring," *Los Angeles Times,* October 2, 1986, 121.
44. Jamie Stiehm, "Ben and Jerry's State Offers a Choice of Three Flavors," *The Hill,* November 22, 1995, 26.
45. Glenn R. Simpson, "In Rhode Island, Everyone Goes to Bristol Parade," *Roll Call,* July 9, 1990, 1; and Glenn R. Simpson, "Judging from July 4th Bristol Parade in R.I., Chafee Looks Well-Positioned for November," *Roll Call,* July 11, 1994, 21.
46. Ron Faucheux, "Candidate Canvassing," *Campaigns and Elections* (May 1997): 43.
47. Green and Gerber, *Get Out the Vote!* 93–96.
48. Canon, "The Wisconsin Second Congressional District," 229–232.
49. Jonathan E. Kaplan, "Large Voter Turnout Was Key to GOP Victory," *The Hill,* November 7, 2002, 17.
50. David M. Halbfinger, "Improved Ground Game Is Seen as Important Factor in G.O.P. Victories," *New York Times,* November 10, 2002, A24.
51. Ethan Wallison, "GOP Looks to Bush's Grass Roots for Help in '06," *Roll Call,* November 29, 2004, 3.
52. Quoted by E. J. Dionne, "The Democrats' Rove Envy," *Washington Post,* December 14, 2004, A27.
53. Chris Cillizza, "Outside Group Asks Voters to 'Fire' Daschle," *Roll Call,* July 21, 2004, 1.
54. *McConnell v. Federal Election Commission,* No. 02–1674 (2003).
55. Louis Jacobson, "Fighting the Political 'Ground War,'" *National Journal,* October 12, 2002, 2983–2985.
56. Quoted in David S. Broder and Thomas B. Edsall, "Amid Election Apathy, Parties Bet on Core Voters," *Washington Post,* September 7, 1998, A12.
57. Thomas Edsall, "Issues Coalitions Take On Political Party Functions," *Washington Post,* August 9, 1996, A1.
58. Martin P. Wattenberg, "Turnout in the 2004 Presidential Election," *Presidential Studies Quarterly* 36 (March 2005): 138–146.
59. International turnout figures from Institute for Social Research, University of Michigan, reported in Pippa Norris, *Electoral Engineering: Voting Rules and Political Behavior* (Cambridge, United Kingdom: Cambridge University Press, 2004). A sensible review of the

question is found in Martin P. Wattenberg, *Where Have All the Voters Gone?* (Cambridge: Harvard University Press, 2002).

60. Raymond E. Wolfinger and Steven J. Rosenstone, *Who Votes?* (New Haven: Yale University Press, 1980), 18ff.
61. Data on the results of the act are distressingly incomplete. See Raymond E. Wolfinger and Jonathan Hoffman, "Registering and Voting with Motor Voter," *P.S.* 34 (March 2001): 85–92.
62. B. Drummond Ayres Jr., "Easier Voter Registration Doesn't Raise Participation," *New York Times,* December 3, 1995, 22. Registration data are from the Committee for the Study of the American Electorate, news release, November 6, 1998.
63. Richard Morin and Claudia Deane, "As Turnout Falls, Apathy Emerges as Driving Force," *Washington Post,* November 4, 2000, A1.
64. Lyn Ragsdale and Jerrold G. Rusk, "Who Are Nonvoters? Profiles from the 1990 Senate Elections," *American Journal of Political Science* 37 (August 1993): 721–746; and Associated Press, "Many More Non-Voters in '96 Were 'Too Busy,' " *Washington Post,* August 17, 1998, A4.
65. Samuel L. Popkin and Michael P. McDonald, "Turnout's Not as Bad as You Think," *Washington Post,* November 5, 2000, B1.
66. Wolfinger and Rosenstone, *Who Votes?* See also Steven J. Rosenstone and John Mark Hansen, *Mobilization, Participation, and Democracy* (New York: Macmillan, 1993); and Ruy Teixeira, *The Disappearing Voter* (Washington, D.C.: Brookings Institution, 1992).
67. Sidney Verba, Kay Lehman Schlozman, and Henry E. Brady, *Voice and Equality: Civic Voluntarism in American Politics* (Cambridge: Harvard University Press, 1995).
68. M. Margaret Conway, "Political Participation in Midterm Congressional Elections," *American Politics Quarterly* 9 (April 1981): 221–244.
69. Samuel L. Popkin, *The Reasoning Voter* (Chicago: University of Chicago Press, 1994), 7.
70. *Los Angeles Times* exit poll, November 2, 2004. Reported by Ronald Brownstein, "Democrats' Losses Go Far Beyond One Defeat," *Los Angeles Times,* November 4, 2004, A1, 17.
71. Pew Research Center for the People and the Press, "Democrats Gain Edge in Party Identification," July 26, 2004, 2, www.people-press.org/reports/.
72. Quoted in Richard Morin and Claudia Deane, "How Independent Are Independents?" *Washington Post,* August 2, 2002, A1.
73. Gary C. Jacobson, *The Electoral Origins of Divided Government: Competition in U.S. House Elections, 1946–1988* (Boulder, Colo.: Westview Press, 1990), 20.
74. Martin P. Wattenberg, *The Rise of Candidate-Centered Politics* (Cambridge: Harvard University Press, 1991), 36–39.
75. See Bernard Grofman, William Koetzle, Michael P. McDonald, and Thomas L. Brunell, "A New Look at Split-Ticket Outcomes for House and President: The Comparative Midpoints Model," *Journal of Politics* 62 (February 2000): 34–50.
76. Gregory Giroux, "Odds Still Heavily Against Midterm House Takeover," *CQ Weekly,* April 11, 2005, 878–879.
77. Cited in Jeffrey McMurray, "Conservative Southern Dems Disappearing," *Washington Post,* April 25, 2005, A1.
78. Jacobson, *The Politics of Congressional Elections,* 158.
79. Angus Campbell, "Surge and Decline: A Study of Electoral Change," in *Elections and the Political Order,* ed. Angus Campbell, Phillip E. Converse, Warren E. Miller, and Donald E. Stokes (New York: Wiley, 1966), 40–62; and Raymond E. Wolfinger, Steven J. Rosenstone, and Richard A. McIntosh, "Presidential and Congressional Voters Compared," *American Politics Quarterly* 9 (April 1981): 245–255.
80. Eric M. Uslaner and Margaret Conway, "The Responsible Electorate: Watergate, the Economy, and Vote Choice in 1974," *American Political Science Review* 79 (September 1985):

788–803; and Samuel Kernell, "Presidential Popularity and Negative Voting: An Alternative Explanation of the Midterm Congressional Decline of the President's Party," *American Political Science Review* 71 (March 1977): 44–46.

81. Thomas B. Edsall and Claudia Deane, "Poll Shows Democratic Gains with Key Voters," *Washington Post,* November 4, 1998, A27.
82. "The Bush Effect," *New York Times,* November 8, 2002, chart, A20.
83. Committee for the Study of the American Electorate, news release, November 6, 1998, 2.
84. Quoted in Dale Russakoff, "In Tight Arkansas Senate Race, Family Matters," *Washington Post,* August 3, 2002, A1.
85. David Brady, Brian Gaines, and Douglas Rivers, "The Incumbency Advantage in the House and Senate: A Comparative Institutional Analysis," unpublished paper, Stanford University, August 1994; Robert S. Erikson, "The Advantage of Incumbency in Congressional Elections," *Polity* 3 (spring 1971): 395–405; and Robert S. Erikson, "Malapportionment, Gerrymandering, and Party Fortunes in Congressional Elections," *American Political Science Review* 66 (December 1972): 1234–1245.
86. Jacobson, *The Electoral Origins of Divided Government,* 28–29.
87. National Elections Studies, 1980–2002, summarized in Jacobson, *The Politics of Congressional Elections,* 122–125. Thomas E. Mann and Raymond E. Wolfinger, "Candidates and Parties in Congressional Elections," *American Political Science Review* 74 (September 1980): 623.
88. Karlyn Bowman, "POLLitics," *Roll Call,* October 19, 2004, 12.
89. David R. Mayhew, *Congress: The Electoral Connection* 2d ed. (New Haven: Yale University Press, 2004).
90. Michael J. Robinson, "Three Faces of Congressional Media," in *The New Congress,* ed. Thomas E. Mann and Norman J. Ornstein (Washington, D.C.: American Enterprise Institute, 1981), 91.
91. Frances E. Lee and Bruce I. Oppenheimer, *Sizing Up the Senate: The Unequal Consequences of Equal Representation* (Chicago: University of Chicago Press, 1999), chapter 4.
92. Gary C. Jacobson, "Incumbents' Advantages in the 1978 U.S. Congressional Elections," *Legislative Studies Quarterly* 6 (May 1981): 198.
93. Thomas E. Mann, *Unsafe at Any Margin: Interpreting Congressional Elections* (Washington, D.C.: American Enterprise Institute, 1978).
94. John B. Bader, *Taking the Initiative: Leadership Agendas in Congress and the "Contract with America"* (Washington, D.C.: Georgetown University Press, 1996).
95. These quotes are from James G. Gimpel, *Fulfilling the Contract: The First 100 Days* (Boston: Allyn and Bacon, 1996), 28, 29. Gimpel presents a balanced insider's view of the origin, development, and effects of the Contract with America.
96. Quoted by Erin P. Billings and Ben Pershing, "Race for House at Center Stage," *Roll Call,* September 23, 2004, 1.
97. Frank Bruni, "G.O.P. Is Trying to Counter Erosion of Women's Support," *New York Times,* August 1, 2001, A1.
98. Quoted in Judy Newman, "Do Women Vote for Women?" *Public Perspective* 7 (February–March 1996): 10.
99. See Felicia Pratto, Stanford University, and Jim Sidanius, University of California at Los Angeles, e-mail news release, December 2, 1996.
100. Quoted in Barbara Vobejda, "Fragmentation of Society Formidable Challenge to Candidates, Report Says," *Washington Post,* March 7, 1996, A15.
101. Delegates to the parties' national conventions were analyzed in a classic study by Herbert McCloskey, Paul Hoffman, and Rosemary O'Hara, "Issue Conflict and Consensus among Party Leaders and Followers," *American Political Science Review* 54 (1950): 406–427.

102. The "middlingness" of the citizenry is vigorously argued in Morris P. Fiorina, with Samuel J. Abrams and Jeremy C. Pope, *Culture War? The Myth of a Polarized America* (New York: Pearson-Longman, 2005).
103. Pew Research Center for the People and the Press, "The 2004 Political Landscape: Evenly Divided and Increasingly Polarized," survey report, November 5, 2003, 1ff, www.people-press.org/reports/.
104. David W. Brady, "Electoral Realignments in the U.S. House of Representatives," in *Congress and Policy Change,* ed. Gerald C. Wright Jr., Leroy N. Reiselbach, and Lawrence C. Dodd (New York: Agathon Press, 1986), 46–69.
105. Warren E. Miller and Donald E. Stokes, "Constituency Influence in Congress," *American Political Science Review* 57 (March 1963): 45–57.
106. John L. Sullivan and Robert E. O'Connor, "Electoral Choice and Popular Control of Public Policy: The Case of the 1966 House Elections," *American Political Science Review* 66 (December 1972): 1256–1268.
107. Thomas E. Mann and Raymond E. Wolfinger, "Candidates and Parties in Congressional Elections," *American Political Science Review* 74 (September 1980): 629.

CHAPTER 5

1. Michael Barone, with Richard E. Cohen and Grant Ujifusa, *The Almanac of American Politics 2004* (Washington, D.C.: National Journal, 2003), 942. Other sources of material concerning Rep. Roy Blunt, R-Mo., are *CQ's Politics in America 2004* (Washington, DC: CQ Press, 2003), 588–589; and Jonathan Kaplan, "This Is a Tough Business; I Go to the Floor to Win," *The Hill,* September 30, 2003, 12–13.
2. Quoted in Barone, *Almanac of American Politics 2004,* 942.
3. Quoted in Kaplan, "This Is a Tough Business," 13.
4. Quoted in Barone, *Almanac of American Politics 2004,* 942.
5. Richard F. Fenno Jr., *The Making of a Senator: Dan Quayle* (Washington, D.C.: CQ Press, 1989), 119.
6. Commission on Executive, Legislative, and Judicial Salaries, *Fairness for Our Public Servants* (Washington, D.C.: U.S. Government Printing Office, 1988), 23.
7. Data on characteristics of members are found in Mildred L. Amer, *Membership of the 109th Congress: A Profile,* Congressional Research Service Report No. RS22007, February 17, 2005.
8. Joseph Schlesinger, "Lawyers and American Politics: A Clarified View," *Midwest Journal of Political Science* 1 (May 1957): 26–39; and Allen G. Bogue, Jerome M. Clubb, Caroll R. McKibbin, and Santa A. Traugott, "Members of the House of Representatives and the Processes of Modernization, 1789–1960," *Journal of American History* 63 (September 1976): 284.
9. William T. Bianco, "Last Post for 'The Greatest Generation': The Policy Implications of the Decline of Military Experience in the U.S. Congress," *Legislative Studies Quarterly* 30 (February 2005): 85–102.
10. George Gallup Jr., "Religion in America," *Public Perspective,* October–November 1995, 4–5.
11. The pioneering study of this subject is Irwin N. Gertzog, *Congressional Women: Their Recruitment, Treatment, and Behavior* (New York: Praeger, 1984). Two more recent studies are Barbara C. Burrell, *A Women's Place Is in the House* (Ann Arbor: University of Michigan Press, 1994); and Richard Logan Fox, *Gender Dynamics in Congressional Elections* (Thousand Oaks, Calif.: Sage Publications, 1997).
12. Betsy Rothstein, "Congresswomen Press Women's Health Issues," *The Hill,* February 24, 1999, 19; and Maureen Dowd, "Growing Sorority in Congress Edges into the Ol' Boys' Club," *New York Times,* March 5, 1993, A1, A18.
13. Jamie Stiehm, "In Senate, Sisterhood Can Override Party," *The Hill,* November 22, 1995, 16.
14. Kirk Victor, "Still an Old Boys' Club?" *National Journal* 37 (March 12, 2005): 750, 752.

15. Quoted in Erika Niedowski, "Four Walk Out of the Closet and toward the House," *CQ Weekly,* April 25, 1998, 1051.
16. Amer, *Membership of the 109th Congress,* 2.
17. Amer, *Membership of the 109th Congress,* 4–5. For tenure figures, see Table 2-1.
18. Charles S. Bullock and Burdett A. Loomis, "The Changing Congressional Career," in *Congress Reconsidered,* 3d ed., ed. Lawrence C. Dodd and Bruce I. Oppenheimer (Washington, D.C.: CQ Press, 1985), 66–69, 80–82.
19. Allison Stevens, "As More Promises Are Broken, 2004 Election Could Spell Death of the Term Limit Movement," *The Hill,* April 2, 2003, 23.
20. Hannah Finichel Pitkin, *The Concept of Representation* (Berkeley: University of California Press, 1967), 166.
21. Susan Welch and John R. Hibbing, "Hispanic Representation in the U.S. Congress," *Social Science Quarterly* 64 (June 1984): 328–335; and Charles Tien and Dena Levy, "Asian-American and Hispanic Representation in the U.S. House of Representatives," paper presented at the Midwest Political Science Association, Chicago, April 1998.
22. L. Marvin Overby and Kenneth Cosgrove, cited in Carol Swain, "The Future of Black Representation," *American Prospect* 23 (fall 1995): 81.
23. Roger H. Davidson, *The Role of the Congressman* (Indianapolis: Bobbs-Merrill, 1969), 199.
24. Katherine Tate, "The Political Representation of Blacks in Congress: Does Race Matter?" *Legislative Studies Quarterly* 26 (November 2001): 631.
25. Arturo Vega and Juanita Firestone, "The Effects of Gender on Congressional Behavior and the Substantive Representation of Women," *Legislative Studies Quarterly* 20 (May 1995): 213–222.
26. Quoted in Adam Nagourney, "Upbeat Schumer Battles Polls, Turnouts, and His Image," *New York Times,* May 16, 1998, A14.
27. Frank E. Smith, *Congressman from Mississippi* (New York: Pantheon, 1964), 129–130.
28. Donald R. Matthews, *U.S. Senators and Their World* (Chapel Hill: University of North Carolina Press, 1960), chapter 5; and Ross K. Baker, *House and Senate,* 3d ed. (New York: Norton, 2001), chapter 2.
29. Herbert B. Asher, "The Learning of Legislative Norms," *American Political Science Review* 67 (June 1973): 499–513.
30. "Regardless of What Comes Your Way, Just Remain Strong," *The Hill,* November 4, 2004, 20.
31. Quoted from an interview with Jake Tapper, "Retiring, Not Shy," *New York Times Magazine,* September 1, 2002, 25.
32. Thomas E. Cavanagh, "The Two Arenas of Congress," in *The House at Work,* ed. Joseph Cooper and G. Calvin Mackenzie (Austin: University of Texas Press, 1981), 65.
33. Quoted in *New York Times,* August 14, 1980, B9.
34. Damon Chappie, "The New Look of Pork in the 104th," *Roll Call,* January 22, 1996, B19.
35. Quoted in Louis Jacobson, "For Arkansas, No Abundance of Clout," *National Journal,* February 20, 1999, 475.
36. James S. Fleming, "The House Member as Teacher: An Analysis of the Newsletters of Barber B. Conable, Jr.," *Congress and the Presidency* 20 (spring 1993): 53–74.
37. Smith, *Congressman from Mississippi,* 127. See also David Mayhew, *Congress: The Electoral Connection* (New Haven: Yale University Press, 1974).
38. Davidson, *The Role of the Congressman,* 98; Senate Commission on the Operation of the Senate, *Toward a Modern Senate,* S. Doc. 94–278, 94th Cong., 2d sess., committee print, 1997, 27; and House Commission on Administrative Review, *Final Report,* 2 vols., H. Doc. 95–272, 95th Cong., 1st sess., December 31, 1977, 2:874–875.
39. Joint Committee on the Organization of Congress, *Organization of Congress, Final Report,* H. Rept. 103–413, 103d Congress, 1st sess., December 1993, 2:231–232.

40. Ross A. Webber, "U.S. Senators: See How They Run," *Wharton Magazine* (winter 1980–1981): 38.
41. Senate Commission on the Operation of the Senate, *Toward a Modern Senate.*
42. Quoted in Lindsay Sobel, "Former Lawmakers Find Trade Association Gold," *The Hill,* November 26, 1997, 14.
43. Webber, "U.S. Senators," 37.
44. Center for Responsive Politics, *Congressional Operations: Congress Speaks—A Survey of the 100th Congress* (Washington, D.C.: Center for Responsive Politics, 1988), 47–49.
45. Quoted in *Washington Post,* October 18, 1994, B3.
46. Center for Responsive Politics, *Congressional Operations,* 62–64.
47. Joint Committee on the Organization of Congress, *Organization of Congress,* 2:281–287.
48. Quoted in Vernon Louviere, "For Retiring Congressmen, Enough Is Enough," *Nation's Business,* May 1980, 32.
49. John R. Hibbing, *Congressional Careers: Contours of Life in the U.S. House of Representatives* (Chapel Hill: University of North Carolina Press, 1991), 117 (italics in original).
50. Hibbing, *Congressional Careers,* 126, 128.
51. William H. Riker, *The Theory of Political Coalitions* (New Haven: Yale University Press, 1962), 24–38.
52. Pitkin, *The Concept of Representation,* 166.
53. Steven Kull, *Expecting More Say: The American Public on Its Role in Government Decisionmaking* (Washington, D.C.: Center on Policy Attitudes, 1999), 13–14.
54. Davidson, *The Role of the Congressman,* 80.
55. Ross J. S. Hoffman and Paul Levack, eds., *Burke's Politics* (New York: Knopf, 1949), 114–116.
56. Henry J. Hyde, "Advice to Freshmen: 'There Are Things Worth Losing For,' " *Roll Call,* December 3, 1990, 5.
57. Quoted in Jamie Stiehm, "Ex-Rep Mike Synar, Who Fought Lobbyists, Succumbs to Brain Tumor," *The Hill,* January 10, 1996, 5.
58. J. Tobin Grant and Thomas J. Rudolph, "The Job of Representation in Congress: Public Expectations and Representative Approval," *Legislative Studies Quarterly* 29 (August 2004): 442.
59. Thomas E. Cavanagh, "The Calculus of Representation: A Congressional Perspective," *Western Political Quarterly* 35 (March 1982): 120–129.
60. John W. Kingdon, *Congressmen's Voting Decisions,* 3d ed. (Ann Arbor: University of Michigan Press, 1989), 47–54.
61. Lawrence N. Hansen, *Our Turn: Politicians Talk about Themselves, Politics, the Public, the Press, and Reform,* part 2 (Washington, D.C.: Centel Public Accountability Project, 1992), 9.
62. Richard F. Fenno Jr., *Home Style: House Members in Their Districts* (New York: Pearson Longman, 2003), 1.
63. See the discussion of senators' varied constituencies in Frances E. Lee and Bruce I. Oppenheimer, *Sizing Up the Senate* (Chicago: University of Chicago Press, 1999), chapter 3.
64. Congressional Quarterly, *Congressional Districts in the 2000s* (Washington, D.C.: CQ Press. 2003), 1027–1028.
65. Fenno, *Home Style,* 4–8.
66. John F. Bibby and Thomas M. Holbrook, "Parties and Elections," in *Politics in the American States: A Comparative Analysis,* 7th ed., ed. Virginia Gray, Russell L. Hanson, and Herbert Jacob (Washington, D.C.: CQ Press, 1999), 66–112.
67. James L. Payne, "The Personal Electoral Advantage of House Incumbents, 1936–1976," *American Politics Quarterly* 8 (October 1980): 465–482; and Robert S. Erikson, "Is There Such a Thing as a Safe Seat?" *Polity* 8 (summer 1976): 623–632.
68. Thomas E. Mann, *Unsafe at Any Margin: Interpreting Congressional Elections* (Washington, D.C.: American Enterprise Institute, 1978).

69. Fenno, *Home Style,* 8–27.
70. Thomas P. O'Neill Jr., with William Novak, *Man of the House* (New York: St. Martin's, 1987), 25.
71. Nancy Bocskor, "Fundraising Lessons Candidates Can Learn from Tom Sawyer . . . and Other Great American Salesmen," *Campaigns and Elections* 24 (April 2003): 33.
72. Richard F. Fenno Jr., *Senators on the Campaign Trail* (Norman: University of Oklahoma Press, 1996), 131–132.
73. David E. Price, *The Congressional Experience,* 3d ed. (Boulder, Colo.: Westview Press, 2004), 10.
74. Fenno, *Home Style,* 153.
75. Fenno, *Home Style,* 56.
76. Anthony Champagne, *Congressman Sam Rayburn* (New Brunswick: Rutgers University Press, 1984), 28.
77. Kingdon, *Congressmen's Voting Decisions.*
78. Fenno, *Home Style,* 153.
79. Rhodes Cook, "The Safe and the Vulnerable: A Look Behind the Numbers," *Congressional Quarterly Weekly Report,* January 9, 1982, 35–38.
80. E. Michael Myers, "Millions of Miles from Home," *The Hill,* June 14, 1995, 8.
81. Fenno, *Home Style,* 36, 209; and Myers, "Millions of Miles from Home."
82. Hibbing, *Congressional Careers,* 139.
83. Quoted in Jim Wright, *You and Your Congressman* (New York: Coward-McCann, 1965), 35.
84. Betsy Rothstein, "Hey, Congressman! Someone Is Blocking My Driveway!" *The Hill,* June 9, 2004, 18–19.
85. Brian Wingfield, "The Latest Initiative in Congress: Blogging," *New York Times,* February 24, 2005, E4.
86. Amy Keller and Ben Pershing, "Study Faults Hill on E-Mail," *Roll Call,* March 19, 2001, 1.
87. John R. Johannes, *To Serve the People: Congress and Constituency Service* (Lincoln: University of Nebraska Press, 1984), chapter 5.
88. House Commission on Administrative Review, *Final Report,* 1:655; and Janet Breslin, "Constituent Service," in U.S. Senate, Senate Commission on the Operation of the Senate, *Senators: Offices, Ethics, and Pressures,* 94th Cong., 2d sess., committee print, 1977, 21.
89. Lee and Oppenheimer, *Sizing Up the Senate,* 56.
90. Lee and Oppenheimer, *Sizing Up the Senate,* 58.
91. Warren E. Miller, Donald R. Kinder, Steven J. Rosenstone, and the National Election Studies, *American National Election Study, 1990: Post–Election Survey,* 2d ed. (Ann Arbor, Mich.: Inter–University Consortium for Political and Social Research, January 1992), 166–170.
92. Morris P. Fiorina, *Congress: Keystone of the Washington Establishment,* 2d ed. (New Haven: Yale University Press, 1989), 45; and Miller and others, *American National Election Study,* 171.
93. George Serra and David Moon, "Casework, Issue Positions, and Voting in Congressional Elections: A District Analysis," *Journal of Politics* 56 (February 1994): 211.
94. Paul E. Dwyer, *Congressional Salaries and Allowances,* Congressional Research Service Report No. RL30064, October 30, 2002. See also Congressional Management Foundation, *1999 Senate Staff Employment Study* (Washington, D.C.: Congressional Management Foundation, 1999), 82ff; and Congressional Management Foundation, *2000 House Staff Employment Study* (Washington, D.C.: Congressional Management Foundation, 2000), 48–49.
95. Congressional Management Foundation, *1999 Senate Staff Employment Study,* 88–89; and Congressional Management Foundation, *2000 House Staff Employment Study,* 1–2.
96. Amy Keller, "Senate Salaries Lag Behind," *Roll Call,* September 5, 2002, 1, 34; and Congressional Management Foundation, *2000 House Staff Employment Study,* 34–35.

97. Richard Simon, Chuck Neubauer, and Rone Tempest, "Political Payrolls Include Families," *Los Angeles Times,* April 14, 2005, A1.
98. Charles R. Babcock, "Frankly, an Election-Year Avalanche," *Washington Post,* September 19, 1988, A19.
99. John Pontius, *Congressional Official Mail Costs,* Congressional Research Service Report No. RS20671, March 24, 2003, 5.
100. Quoted in David Burnham, "Congress's Computer Subsidy," *New York Times Magazine,* November 2, 1980, 98.
101. U.S. Congress, Committee on Administration, *Campaign Reform and Election Integrity Act of 1999* H. Rept. 106–295, 106th Congress, 1st sess., 22.
102. Editor and Publisher, *International Yearbook 2002* (New York: Editor and Publisher, 2002), vol. I: vi, vol. II: vi; and *Broadcasting and Cable Yearbook 2002* (New York: Reed Elsevier, 2002), xxxii.
103. Charles Bosley, "Senate Communications with the Public," in U.S. Senate, Commission on the Operation of the Senate, *Senate Communications with the Public,* 94th Cong., 2d sess., 1977, 17.
104. For descriptions of the studios, see Michael J. Robinson, "Three Faces of Congressional Media," in *The New Congress,* ed. Thomas E. Mann and Norman J. Ornstein (Washington, D.C.: American Enterprise Institute, 1981), 62–63; and Martin Tolchin, "TV Studio Serves Congress," *New York Times,* March 7, 1984, C22.
105. Marcia Gelbert, "Call-in Show: Hoosiers 'Bark at Mark,' " *The Hill,* February 1, 1995, 41.
106. Tolchin, "TV Studio Serves Congress."
107. Robinson, "Three Faces of Congressional Media," 80–81.
108. Peter Clarke and Susan H. Evans, *Covering Campaigns: Journalism in Congressional Elections* (Stanford: Stanford University Press, 1983). See also Charles M. Tidmarch and Brad S. Karp, "The Missing Beat: Press Coverage of Congressional Elections in Eight Metropolitan Areas," *Congress and the Presidency* 10 (spring 1983): 47–61.
109. Robinson, "Three Faces of Congressional Media," 84.
110. Cokie Roberts, "Leadership and the Media in the 101st Congress," in *Leading Congress: New Styles, New Strategies,* ed. John J. Kornacki (Washington, D.C.: CQ Press, 1990), 94.
111. Quoted in Jeffrey L. Katz, "Studios Beam Members from Hill to Hometown," *CQ Weekly Report,* November 29, 1997, 2946.
112. Fenno, *Home Style,* 99.

CHAPTER 6

1. A. B. Stoddard, "Rejuvenated Gingrich Mounts Media Offensive," *The Hill,* July 10, 1996, 24.
2. See, for example, Bob Gravely and Lori Nitschke, "Shell-Shocked GOP Settles on Hastert as a Source of Calm," *CQ Monitor,* December 21, 1998, 3; Ceci Connolly, "Plain-Talking Hastert Poised to Be Speaker," *Washington Post,* December 21, 1998, A1; and Art Pine, "It's Official: GOP Picks Hastert as New Speaker," *Los Angeles Times,* January 6, 1999, A10.
3. Sheryl Gay Stolberg, "Quietly, But Firmly, Hastert Asserts His Power," *New York Times,* January 3, 2005, A14.
4. Stolberg, "Quietly, But Firmly," A1.
5. *Wall Street Journal,* January 30, 1985, 5.
6. The seminal work on the collective action problem is Mancur Olson, *The Logic of Collective Action, Public Goods, and the Theory of Groups* (Cambridge: Harvard University Press, 1965).
7. Barbara Sinclair, *Legislators, Leaders, and Lawmaking* (Baltimore: Johns Hopkins University Press, 1995), 9.

8. Carl Huse, "Hastert, the Reticent Speaker, Suddenly Has Plenty to Say," *New York Times,* May 24, 2004, A17.
9. Kerry Kantin, "Rep. Rob Portman," *The Hill,* April 10, 2002, 12.
10. Eric Pianin and Helen Dewar, "GOP Leaders on Hill Find Unity Elusive," *Washington Post,* September 30, 2000, A10.
11. Ceci Connolly and Juliet Eilperin, "Hastert Steps Up to Leading Role," *Washington Post,* January 5, 1999, A4.
12. See Graeme Browning, "The Steward," *National Journal,* August 5, 1995, 2004–2007.
13. *U.S. News and World Report,* October 13, 1950, 30.
14. See, for example, Barbara Sinclair, *Majority Leadership in the U.S. House* (Baltimore: Johns Hopkins University Press, 1983).
15. John M. Barry, *The Ambition and the Power: The Fall of Jim Wright* (New York: Viking Penguin, 1989), 4.
16. Tom Kenworthy, "House GOP Signals It's in a Fighting Mood," *Washington Post,* December 26, 1988, A8.
17. Barry, *The Ambition and the Power,* 6.
18. Newt Gingrich, *Lessons Learned the Hard Way* (New York: HarperCollins, 1998), 37.
19. David Rogers, "Gingrich's New Style as Speaker Has a Few Hitches," *Wall Street Journal,* June 2, 1997, A24.
20. Peter King, "Why I Oppose Newt," *Weekly Standard,* March 31, 1997, 23.
21. See, for example, Ceci Connolly, David Broder, and Dan Balz, "GOP's House Divided," *Washington Post,* July 28, 1997, A1; Sandy Hume, "Gingrich Foils Coup by Deputies," *The Hill,* July 16, 1997, 1; and Jackie Koszczuk, "Party Stalwarts Will Determine Gingrich's Long-Term Survival," *Congressional Quarterly Weekly Report,* July 26, 1997, 1751–1755.
22. See Robert Pear, Pam Belluck, and Lizette Alvarez, "Humble Man at the Helm: John Dennis Hastert," *New York Times,* January 7, 1999, A20.
23. Kathy Kiely, " 'Listener' of the House Takes Reins," *USA Today,* June 8, 2001, 11A.
24. Jim VandeHei, "Hastert Takes Gavel, Promises Cooperation," *Roll Call,* January 7, 1999, 22.
25. Ben Pershing, "Smith Spars with Leaders," *Roll Call,* March 26, 2003, 13.
26. Daniel Parks and Andrew Taylor, "House GOP Discord Prompts Fiscal Showdown," *CQ Daily Monitor,* September 13, 2002, 2.
27. Janet Hook, "For Bush, GOP Leaders, Some Policy Paths Diverge," *Los Angeles Times,* January 24, 2005, A10.
28. See, for example, Ronald M. Peters Jr., *The American Speakership: The Office in Historical Perspective,* 2d ed. (Baltimore: Johns Hopkins University Press, 1997); and D. B. Hardeman and Donald C. Bacon, *Rayburn: A Biography* (Austin, Texas: Texas Monthly Press, 1987).
29. Michael Barone, "Slender Is the Newt," *National Review,* November 24, 1997, 28. This quotation leads off David R. Mayhew's *America's Congress: Actions in the Public Sphere, James Madison through Newt Gingrich* (New Haven: Yale University Press, 2000), ix.
30. Quoted in Randall Strahan and Daniel J. Palazzolo, "The Gingrich Effect," *Political Science Quarterly,* 2004, 107.
31. See, for example, Joseph Cooper and David Brady, "Institutional Context and Leadership Style: The House from Cannon to Rayburn," *American Political Science Review* 75 (June 1981): 411–425; David Rohde, *Parties and Leaders in the Postreform House* (Chicago: University of Chicago Press, 1991); and Sinclair, *Legislators, Leaders, and Lawmaking.*
32. John Aldrich and David Rohde, "The Logic of Conditional Party Government: Revisiting the Electoral Connection," in *Congress Reconsidered,* 7th ed., ed. Lawrence Dodd and Bruce Oppenheimer (Washington, D.C.: CQ Press, 2001), 275–276.
33. Jonathan Kaplan, "Hastert, DeLay: Political Pros Get Along to Go Along," *The Hill,* July 22, 2003, 8.

34. Janet Hook, "Conservatives Make Gains in GOP Congress," *Los Angeles Times,* November 11, 2002, A9.
35. Charles Babington, "DeLay Draws Third Rebuke," *Washington Post,* October 7, 2004, A4. See also Richard E. Cohen, "Doubts Over DeLay," *National Journal,* December 18, 2004, 3734–3742.
36. Janet Hook, "Ethics Rebukes Not Sure to Cramp DeLay's Style," *Los Angeles Times,* October 8, 2004, A10. DeLay also confronted the possibility of being indicted by a Texas grand jury. In September 2004, three of DeLay's associates were indicted by the grand jury for campaign fund-raising violations. House Republicans, grateful for all that DeLay had done for the party, voted in November 2004 to change a party rule that required an indicted party leader to step aside until the matter was resolved. However, the adverse political and public fallout of that decision required Republicans to reinstate the party rule just prior to the start of the 109th Congress. Republicans did make several other ethics changes to the House rulebook on the opening day of the 109th Congress, which aroused the ire of Democrats. See U.S. Congress, *Congressional Record,* daily ed., 109th Cong., 1st sess., January 4, 2005, H7–H31; and John Bresnahan and Ben Persing, "GOP Blinks on Ethics Charges," *Roll Call,* January 4, 2005, 1.
37. Carl Hulse, "2 on Ethics Panel Withdraw from Any DeLay Inquiry," *New York Times,* May 5, 2005, A21.
38. Mike Allen, "House GOP Weighs Preapproval of Sponsored Travel," *Washington Post,* May 11, 2005, A5.
39. Gail Russell Chaddock, "DeLay Probe Triggering 'Ethics War,' " *Christian Science Monitor,* May 3, 2005, 1.
40. Jim VandeHei, "DeLay Nears Top of House He Reshaped," *Washington Post,* November 13, 2002, A4.
41. Christopher Madison, "Message Bearer," *National Journal,* December 1, 1990, 2906.
42. Floyd M. Riddick, *Congressional Procedure* (Boston: Chapman and Grimes, 1941), 345–346.
43. *CQ Weekly,* December 30, 2000, 24.
44. See Gebe Martinez, "Solidly Backed by Her Colleagues, Pelosi Faces GOP's Sharpened Barbs," *CQ Weekly,* November 16, 2002, 3008–3013.
45. Susan Ferrechio, "Rep. Nancy Pelosi," *CQ Weekly,* December 28, 2002, 55.
46. Erin Billings, "Pelosi Passes Her First Test, But the Honeymoon Is Over," *Roll Call,* January 24, 2005, 5.
47. Jonathan Kaplan, "New GOP Whip, Roy Blunt Offers Different Style," *The Hill,* November 20, 2002, 4.
48. Juliet Eilperin, "From Freshman to Deputy Whip," *Washington Post,* December 16, 2002, A23.
49. Jonathan Allen, "House GOP's 'Stealth Whip' Know the Power of Listening," *CQ Weekly,* March 29, 2003, 750.
50. Thomas Edsall, "House Majority Whip Exerts Influence by Way of K Street," *Washington Post,* May 17, 2005, A19.
51. Peter Brand, "Hoyer Says He and Pelosi Will Work Well Together," *The Hill,* November 20, 2002, 33.
52. Mark Preston, "Cheney to Help Craft Legislation," *Roll Call,* January 22, 2001, 1. See also Eric Schmitt, "Cheney Assembles Formidable Team," *New York Times,* February 3, 2001, A1.
53. Susan Crabtree, "Cheney Gets Liaison Team," *Roll Call,* February 26, 2001, 1.
54. Woodrow Wilson, *Congressional Government* (Boston: Houghton Mifflin, 1885), 223.
55. David J. Rothman, *Politics and Power: The United States Senate, 1869–1901* (Cambridge: Harvard University Press, 1966), 5–7.
56. Margaret Munk, "Origin and Development of the Party Floor Leadership in the United States Senate," *Capital Studies* 2 (winter 1974): 23–41; and Richard A. Baker and Roger H.

Davidson, eds., *First among Equals: Outstanding Senate Leaders of the Twentieth Century* (Washington, D.C.: Congressional Quarterly, 1991).

57. See Robert Caro, *Master of the Senate* (New York: Random House, 2002).
58. Rowland Evans and Robert Novak, *Lyndon B. Johnson: The Exercise of Power* (New York: New American Library, 1966), 104.
59. See John G. Stewart, "Two Strategies of Leadership: Johnson and Mansfield," in *Congressional Behavior,* ed. Nelson W. Polsby (New York: Random House, 1971), 61–92; William S. White, *Citadel: The Story of the United States Senate* (New York: Harper and Bros., 1956); Joseph S. Clark, *The Senate Establishment* (New York: Hill and Wang, 1963); and Randall B. Ripley, *Power in the Senate* (New York: St. Martin's, 1969).
60. U.S. Congress, *Congressional Record,* daily ed., 96th Cong., 2d sess., April 18, 1980, S3294.
61. David S. Broder, "Don't Bet on Bipartisan Niceties," *Washington Post,* January 1, 2003, A19.
62. Kathy Kiely and Wendy Koch, "Committee Shaped by Party Ties," *USA Today,* October 5, 1998, 2A.
63. Kiely and Koch, "Committee Shaped by Party Ties."
64. Isaiah Poole, "Party Unity Vote Study: Votes Echo Electoral Themes," *CQ Weekly,* December 11, 2004, 2906.
65. Kirk Victor, "Deconstructing Daschle," *National Journal,* June 1, 2002, 610.
66. To review all the provisions of the power-sharing agreement, see U.S. Congress, *Congressional Record,* daily ed., 107th Cong., 1st sess., January 5, 2001, S32–S44; and *U.S. Congress, Congressional Record,* daily ed., 107th Cong., 1st sess., January 8, 2001, S53–S54.
67. U.S. Congress, *Congressional Record,* daily ed., 107th Cong., 1st sess., June 6, 2001, S5844.
68. Dave Boyer, "Lott Rails on Radio against Jeffords' 'Coup of One,' " *Washington Times,* May 31, 2001, A1.
69. Kirk Victor, "Bill Frist, In His Own Words," *National Journal,* January 4, 2003, 37.
70. John Cochran, "Two Years In, Frist Struggles to Tame an Unruly Senate," *CQ Weekly,* October 16, 2004, 2426–2432.
71. Quoted in "Over Breakfast . . . With the Monitor," *Christian Science Monitor,* April 26, 2005, 20.
72. Mark Preston, "Reid to Enlist K Street," *Roll Call,* January 24, 2005, 1.
73. John Cochran and David Nather, "Fast-Moving Events Challenge Frist's Debut at Senate Helm," *CQ Weekly,* January 4, 2003, 17.
74. Geoff Earle, "Reid Grants a Strategy Role to Senior Democrats," *The Hill,* January 19, 2005, 3.
75. *New York Times,* December 6, 1988, B13.
76. Barbara Sinclair, *Majority Leadership in the U.S. House* (Baltimore: Johns Hopkins University Press, 1983).
77. David S. Broder, "Expect to Hear from Hastert," *Washington Post,* January 15, 2003, A19.
78. Ben Pershing, "Hastert Rolls On as Speaker, But for How Long?" *Roll Call* , January 24, 2005, 4.
79. Allison Stevens, "Reid Secures Higher Democratic Funds, Irks Lott," *CQ Today,* January 7, 2005, 1.
80. U.S. Congress, *Congressional Record,* daily ed., 98th Cong., 1st sess., November 15, 1983, H9856.
81. Thomas B. Rosenstiel and Edith Stanley, "For Gingrich, It's 'Mr. Speaker!' " *Los Angeles Times,* November 9, 1994, A2.
82. U.S. Congress, *Congressional Record,* daily ed., 94th Cong., 1st sess., January 26, 1973, S2301.
83. Christopher Madison, "The Heir Presumptive," *National Journal,* April 29, 1989, 1036.
84. Mark Preston and Erin Billings, "Democrats to Cite GOP 'Arrogance,' " *Roll Call,* April 11, 2005, 1.

85. Sidney Waldman, "Majority Leadership in the House of Representatives," *Political Science Quarterly* 95 (fall 1980): 377.
86. Edward Epstein, "Colorful Congressman a Backer of Property Rights," *Washington Times,* January 12, 2003, A3.
87. John Bresnahan, "Ethics Panel in Limbo," *Roll Call,* January 27, 2005, 21.
88. Neil MacNeil, *Dirksen: Portrait of a Public Man* (New York: World, 1970), 168–169.
89. Mark Preston, "Daschle May Write Book Chronicling His Times as Leader," *Roll Call Daily Issue E-newsletter,* May 20, 2002, 3.
90. *New York Times,* June 7, 1984, B16.
91. Noelle Straub and Melanie Fonder, "GOP Shifts Strategy for New Minority Status," *The Hill,* July 18, 2001, 6.
92. Susan Davis, "A Soundbite for Every Faction," *National Journal's CongressDaily/PM,* January 31, 2005, 7.
93. Mark Preston, "Lott Showcases Senators Facing Re-election," *Roll Call,* March 15, 2001, 3.
94. Stephen Gettinger, "Potential Senate Leaders Flex Money Muscles," *Congressional Quarterly Weekly Report,* October 8, 1988, 2776.
95. Susan Crabtree, "Edgy GOP Lawmakers Plot Public Relations Strategy," *CQ Today,* January 31, 2005, 6.
96. Sinclair, *Majority Leadership in the U.S. House,* 96–97.
97. Marc Lacey, "Bush to Attend Democratic Caucuses," *New York Times,* January 27, 2001, A9.
98. Erin Billings, "Pelosi Revamps the Steering Committee," *Roll Call,* March 13, 2003, 3.
99. Stephen Dinan, "Medicare Bill Incites House Conservatives," *Washington Times,* December 23, 2004, A12.
100. Robin Kolodny, *Pursuing Majorities: Congressional Campaign Committees in American Politics* (Norman: University of Oklahoma Press, 1998).
101. See Paul S. Herrnson, "National Party Organizations and the Postreform Congress," in *The Postreform Congress,* ed. Roger H. Davidson (New York: St. Martin's, 1992), 48–70.
102. John J. Pitney Jr., "War on the Floor," *Extension of Remarks,* January 2001, 8.
103. Mark Mellman, "Moderate and Polarized," *The Hill,* January 26, 2005, 18.
104. Cited in "A Polarized Nation?" *Washington Post,* November 14, 2004, B6.
105. Lars-Erik Nelson, "The Republicans' War," *New York Review of Books,* February 4, 1999, 7.
106. David Rogers and Jeannie Cummings, "Democrats Aim to Stir Public as Impeachment Nears," *Wall Street Journal,* December 14, 1998, A20.
107. Alexander Bolton, "House Leaders Tighten Grip, Anger Centrists," *The Hill,* January 15, 2003, 23.
108. David Baumann, "For House Moderates, A Lost Cause?" *National Journal,* January 22, 2005, 189. The views of Speaker Hastert can be found in *The Cannon Centenary Conference: The Changing Nature of the Speakership,* H. Doc. 108–204 (Washington, D.C.: U.S. Government Printing Office, 2004), 62.
109. Jim Hoagland, "The Price of Polarization," *Washington Post,* May 5, 2005, A25.
110. Steve Israel and Timothy Johnson, "Plea From within Congress: Let's Be Civil for a Change," *USA Today,* January 10, 2005, 13A.
111. David S. Broder, "Senate Orientation Aims to Bridge Gap," *Washington Post,* November 7, 2004, A5.
112. Elizabeth Shogren, "Will Welfare Go Way of Health Reform?" *Los Angeles Times,* August 10, 1995, A18.
113. "Sen. Mitch McConnell (R-Ky.)," *The Hill,* January 17, 2001, 24.
114. David Nather and Adriel Bettelheim, "Moderates and Mavericks Hold Key to 107th Congress," *CQ Weekly,* January 6, 2001, 50.
115. Fred Barnes, "Raging Representatives," *New Republic,* June 3, 1985, 9.

116. See David Rohde, *Parties and Leaders in the Postreform Congress* (Chicago: University of Chicago Press, 1991), 27–47.
117. See V. O. Key Jr., *Politics, Parties, and Pressure Groups,* 5th ed. (New York: Crowell, 1964); and Austin Ranney and Willmoore Kendall, *Democracy and the American Party System* (New York: Harcourt Brace, 1956).
118. See Harold Stanley and Richard Niemi, *Vital Statistics on American Politics, 2001–2002* (Washington, D.C.: CQ Press, 2001), 38–39.
119. Susan Crabtree, "House GOP Plans Parliamentary Counterattack," *Roll Call,* June 13, 2002, 3.
120. Mike Allen, "Congressional Republicans Agree to Launch Social Security Campaign," *Washington Post,* January 31, 2005, A4.
121. Ronald Brownstein, "Democrats Are Lost in the Shuffle While GOP Holds All the Cards," *Los Angeles Times,* April 4, 2005, A8.
122. U.S. Congress, *Congressional Record,* daily ed., 104th Cong., 1st sess., October 11, 1995, E1926. Rep. Lee Hamilton, D-Ind., who made the comment, strongly opposed the overuse of omnibus bills.
123. Lee H. Hamilton with Jordan Tama, *A Creative Tension: The Foreign Policy Roles of the President and Congress* (Washington, D.C.: Woodrow Wilson Center Press, 2002), 33.
124. Nick Anderson, "In Shift, GOP Proposes Easing Immigration Rules," *Los Angeles Times,* October 26, 2000, A6.
125. Ralph Hallow, "House Likely to Remain Bush's Base," *Washington Times,* January 6, 2003, A4.
126. Jonathan Kaplan, "Bidding Up the Senate and Bush," *The Hill,* January 15, 2003, 1.
127. Keith Koffler and Martin Vaughan, "McCrery: Everything, Even Bush Plan, Is on the Table for Overhaul Debate," *National Journal's CongressDaily/AM,* January 27, 2005, 15.
128. Richard E. Cohen, "Byrd of West Virginia: A New Job, a New Image," *National Journal,* August 20, 1977, 1294.
129. For an essential guide about members of Congress and their districts, see Jackie Koszczuk and H. Amy Stern, eds. *CQ's Politics in America, 2006: The 109th Congress* (Washington, D.C.: CQ Press, 2005).

CHAPTER 7

1. *Washington Post,* May 14, 1987, A23.
2. U.S. Congress, *Congressional Record,* daily ed., 100th Cong., 1st sess., June 25, 1987, H5564.
3. *Little legislatures* was a term coined by Woodrow Wilson in *Congressional Government* (Boston: Houghton Mifflin, 1885), 79.
4. *New York Times,* July 11, 1988, A14.
5. See, for example, Kenneth A. Shepsle and Barry R. Weingast, "The Institutional Foundations of Committee Power," *American Political Science Review* (March 1987): 85–104.
6. See Keith Krehbiel, *Information and Legislative Organization* (Ann Arbor: University of Michigan Press, 1991); and Bruce Bimber, "Information as a Factor in Congressional Politics," *Legislative Studies Quarterly* (1991): 585–606.
7. John W. Ellwood, "The Great Exception: The Congressional Budget Process in an Age of Decentralization," in *Congress Reconsidered,* 3d ed., ed. Lawrence C. Dodd and Bruce I. Oppenheimer (Washington, D.C.: CQ Press, 1985), 329. For the classic discussion of committee and member roles, see Richard F. Fenno Jr., *Congressmen in Committees* (Boston: Little, Brown, 1973).
8. Roy Swanstrom, *The United States Senate, 1787–1801,* S. Doc. 87–64, 87th Cong., 1st sess., 1962, 224.
9. Lauros G. McConachie, *Congressional Committees* (New York: Crowell, 1898), 124.

10. DeAlva Stanwood Alexander, *History and Procedure of the House of Representatives* (Boston: Houghton Mifflin, 1916), 228; George H. Haynes, *The Senate of the United States: Its History and Practice,* vol. 1 (Boston: Houghton Mifflin, 1938), 272; and Ralph V. Harlow, *The History of Legislative Methods in the Period before 1825* (New Haven: Yale University Press, 1917), 157–158.
11. *Cannon's Procedures in the House of Representatives,* H. Doc. 80–122, 80th Cong., 1st sess., 1959, 83.
12. *Wall Street Journal,* May 3, 1979, 1.
13. Susan Crabtree, "Hastert, in Consultation With Pelosi, Tweaks the Size of 11 House Committees," *CQ Today,* January 6, 2005, 3.
14. Allison Stevens, "Senate Leaders Consider Next Term's Rules, Procedures, and Partisan Edges," *CQ Today,* November 15, 2004, 5.
15. "Chairman Young Announces Homeland Security Reorganization," press release, January 29, 2003, House Committee on Appropriations Web site (house.gov/appropriations).
16. Andrew Taylor, "Sen. Stevens Calls House Appropriators' Reorganization Decision Premature," *CQ Today,* January 30, 2003, 4.
17. U.S. Congress, *Congressional Record,* daily ed., 104th Cong., 1st sess., January 4, 1995, H33.
18. Jackie Koszczuk and Jonathan Allen, "Late-Night Medicare Vote Drama Triggers Some Unexpected Alliances," *CQ Weekly,* November 29, 2003, 2958–2959.
19. Erin Billings, "Pelosi Seeks Rules Change," *Roll Call,* March 22, 2004, 16. See also Erin Billings, "Pelosi to Prevail on Rule," *Roll Call,* March 31, 2004, 1; and Susan Ferrechio, "House Democrats Give Pelosi Authority to Name 'Exclusive' Panel Ranking Members," *CQ Today,* April 1, 2004, 14.
20. Martin Kady, "Select Homeland Security," *CQ Weekly,* January 11, 2003, 95.
21. U.S. Congress, *Congressional Record,* daily ed., 108th Cong., 1st sess., January 7, 2003, H12.
22. Charles L. Clapp, *The Congressman: His Job as He Sees It* (Washington, D.C.: Brookings Institution, 1963), 245.
23. Lawrence D. Longley and Walter J. Oleszek, *Bicameral Politics: Conference Committees in Congress* (New Haven: Yale University Press, 1989), 196.
24. Keith Krehbiel, Kenneth A. Shepsle, and Barry R. Weingast, "Why Are Congressional Committees Powerful?" *American Political Science Review* 81 (September 1987): 935.
25. Roderick Kiewiet and Mathew McCubbins, *The Logic of Delegation: Congressional Parties and the Appropriations Process* (Chicago: University of Chicago Press, 1991).
26. James Bornemeier, "Berman Accepts Seat on House Ethics Panel," *Los Angeles Times,* February 5, 1997, B1; and *CQ Daily Monitor,* December 11, 1999, 1.
27. Mike Allen, "House GOP Leaders Name Loyalist to Replace Ethics Chief," *Washington Post,* February 3, 2005, A1.
28. Mike Allen, "House Rescinds GOP Ethics Changes," *Washington Post,* April 28, 2005, A6.
29. Sonni Efron and Janet Hook, "Lugar Now the Man in the Middle," *Los Angeles Times,* December 23, 2002, A7.
30. Fenno, *Congressmen in Committees* . See also Heinz Eulau, "Legislative Committee Assignments," *Legislative Studies Quarterly* (November 1984): 587–633.
31. Christopher J. Deering and Steven S. Smith, *Committees in Congress,* 3d ed. (Washington, D.C.: CQ Press, 1997), 61–62, 78.
32. Nancy Roman, "Freshman Nets Prized Panel by Seeking Leader's Support," *Washington Times,* December 3, 1996, A4. See also Greg Hitt, "Ways and Means: An Illinois Republican Staged Hard Campaign for Key House Panel," *Wall Street Journal,* January 3, 1997, A1.
33. Office of Rep. Jennifer Dunn, R-Wash., Washington, D.C.
34. Shirley Chisholm, *Unbought and Unbossed* (Boston: Houghton Mifflin, 1970), 84, 86.
35. Susan Ferrechio, "House Democrats Back New Leader as She Spreads Committee Plums Wider," *CQ Today,* January 29, 2003, 15.

36. Susan Davis, "House Dems OK Internal Rules Changes," *National Journal's CongressDaily/AM,* January 4, 2005, 9.
37. Ethan Wallison, "Freshman Democrats Get Panel Waivers," *Roll Call,* June 21, 1999, 20.
38. Martin Vaughn, "A Few Lucky Republicans Secure Ways and Means Spots," *National Journal's CongressDaily/PM,* January 10, 2005, 3.
39. Andrew Beadle, "First Lady's Résumé Won't Impress Seniority System," *CQ Daily Monitor,* November 20, 2000, 9.
40. Peter Kaplan and David Mark, "With Election Day Over, the Campaigns Begin in the House," *CQ Daily Monitor,* November 20, 2000, 3.
41. Jim VandeHei, "Would-Be Chairmen Hit Money Trail," *Roll Call,* July 12, 1999, 1.
42. Hans Nichols, "Leaders Crack Whip on Loyalty," *The Hill,* January 5, 2005, 1; and Susan Crabtree, "Peterson Rehabilitates His Party Credibility in Time to Claim Agriculture Post," *CQ Today,* January 5, 2005, 6. See also Erin Billings, "Democrats on 'Exclusives' Face Review," *Roll Call,* January 24, 2005, 1.
43. Joseph Schatz, "Lewis Wins Coveted Favor of GOP Leaders—And Coveted Appropriations Chair," *CQ Weekly,* January 10, 2005, 71. The campaign fund-raising data are from Susan Crabtree, "If Money Matters, Lewis Has Edge for Appropriations Chair," *CQ Today,* December 20, 2004, 1.
44. Jonathan Allen, "Buyer's Insertion Into Panel Chair Doesn't Sit Well With Veterans," *CQ Weekly,* January 10, 2005, 72.
45. Paul Gigot, "Mack Uses Knife on Old Senate Order," *Wall Street Journal,* July 14, 1995, A12.
46. Matthew Tully and Emily Pierce, "Senate Republicans Adjust Their Committee Term-Limits Rule," *CQ Daily Monitor,* June 26, 2002, 4.
47. Paul Kane, "Republican Conference Clarifies Term-Limit Rules," *The Hill,* June 27, 2002, 23.
48. Keith Perine, "Specter Nears Judiciary Chair as Seniority Wins the Day," *CQ Weekly,* November 20, 2004, 2731–2732.
49. *Washington Post,* November 20, 1983, A9.
50. Amy Fagan, "Thomas Takes Reins on Social Security," *Washington Times,* February 6, 2005, A3.
51. See David King, *Turf Wars* (Chicago: University of Chicago Press, 1997).
52. Allison Stevens, "No Ordinary Power Grab: Chairman Complains of 'Bold' Power Grab," *CQ Today,* June 23, 2004, 1, 9.
53. U.S. Congress, *Congressional Record,* daily ed., 108th Cong., 1st sess., January 7, 2003, H11.
54. Elizabeth Kastor, "The Capital Star System," *Washington Post,* May 9, 1986, D8.
55. Bob Pool, "Survivors Take Stock of Gains against Cancer," *Los Angeles Times,* May 30, 1997, B1.
56. Ralph Vartabedian, "Senate Panel Is Ready to Take IRS to Task," *Los Angeles Times,* September 22, 1997, A1.
57. Sean Piccoli, "Hill Samples 'Third Wave,'" *Washington Times,* June 13, 1995, A8.
58. *Washington Post,* September 23, 1998, A23.
59. Charles Babington, "Democrats Decry Use of Agency in Social Security Battle," *Washington Post,* January 29, 2005, A9.
60. U.S. Congress, *Congressional Record,* daily ed., 107th Cong., 2d sess., July 16, 2002, S6849.
61. *Washington Post,* November 25, 1985, A4. See also Richard L. Hall, *Participation in Congress* (New Haven: Yale University Press, 1997).
62. Quoted in "CQ Midday Update Email," December 14, 2004, 1, www.cq.com.
63. Eric Redman, *The Dance of Legislation* (New York: Simon and Schuster, 1973), 140.
64. Hugh Heclo, "Issue Networks in the Executive Establishment," in *The New American Political System,* ed. Anthony King (Washington, D.C.: American Enterprise Institute, 1978), 87–124. See also David E. Price, "Policy Making in Congressional Committees: The Impact of 'Environmental Factors,'" *American Political Science Review* (fall 1978): 548–574.

65. David Hosansky and Andrew Taylor, "Judiciary's 'Fateful Leap,'" *CQ Weekly,* December 12, 1998, 3290–3294.
66. Erin Billings, "Democrats Seek Expert Advice on Iraq Message," *Roll Call,* February 10, 2005, 20.
67. Norris Cotton, *In the Senate* (New York: Dodd, Mead, 1978), 65.
68. *2004 House Staff Employment Study: Guide for the 109th Congress,* produced for the chief administrative officer, U.S. House of Representatives (Washington, D.C.: Congressional Management Foundation, 2004), 3. The Congressional Management Foundation is a private, nonpartisan group.
69. *Washington Post,* March 20, 1977, E9.
70. David Whiteman, *Communication in Congress: Members, Staff, and the Search for Information* (Lawrence: University Press of Kansas, 1995).
71. Siobhan Gorman and Richard Cohen, "Hurtling toward an Intelligence Overhaul," *National Journal,* September 18, 2004, 2808.
72. *Washington Post,* November 20, 1983, A13.
73. See Eliza Newlin Carney, "Losing Support," *National Journal,* September 23, 1995, 2353–2357.
74. Brett Pulley, "Black Clerics Criticize Torricelli on Minority Hiring for His Staff," *New York Times,* March 21, 1997, A25.
75. See C. Lawrence Evans and Walter J. Oleszek, *Congress under Fire: Reform Politics and the Republican Majority* (Boston: Houghton Mifflin, 1997).
76. Andrew Taylor, "Security Plan Changes Committee Name, Little Else," *CQ Today,* October 8, 2004, 1.
77. Taylor, "Security Plan Changes Committee Name," 4.
78. Walter Pincus, "Plans to Create Senate Intelligence Oversight Panel Run Into Snag," *Washington Post,* February 10, 2005, A21.
79. U.S. Congress, *Congressional Record,* daily ed., 109th Cong., 1st sess., January 4, 2005, H25–H26.
80. Andrew Taylor, "Senate Appropriators Reject Reorganization Plan," *CQ Today,* February 2, 2005, 10.
81. Emily Pierce, "Senate Finalizes Panel Overhaul," *Roll Call,* March 3, 2005, 21. See also Jonathan Allen, "Cochran Cedes Turf to Reshape Landscape of Appropriations Subcommittees," *CQ Today,* March 3, 2005, 4–5.
82. Pierce, "Senate Finalizes Panel Overhaul."
83. Peter Cohn, "House, Senate Agree to More Talks on Approps Changes," *National Journal's CongressDaily/PM,* February 2, 2005, 2.
84. Scott Lilly, "Does Rearranging Appropriations Panels Make Any Sense?" *Roll Call,* January 27, 2005, 11.
85. Emily Pierce and Ben Pershing, "Senators Race to Counter House," *Roll Call,* February 10, 2005, 19.
86. Peter Cohn, "Senate 'Cardinals' Flock in Opposition to House's Reorganization Proposal," *National Journal's CongressDaily/AM,* February 2, 2005, 7. See also Andrew Taylor, "Chambers Spar Over Spending Panels," *CQ Weekly,* February 7, 2005, 306–307.
87. Andrew Taylor, "Another Rejection for Appropriations Revamp Plan," *CQ Today,* February 11, 2005, 8.
88. Quoted in Roger H. Davidson and Walter J. Oleszek, *Congress against Itself* (Bloomington: Indiana University Press, 1977), 263.
89. E. Scott Adler, *Why Congressional Reforms Fail* (Chicago: University of Chicago Press, 2002), 11.
90. Richard Cohen and Marilyn Serfina, "Taxing Times," *National Journal,* December 23, 2000, 3961.

91. Cohen and Serfina, "Taxing Times," 3963.
92. David Firestone, "G.O.P.'s 'Cardinals of Spending' Are Reined In by House Leaders," *New York Times,* December 2, 2002, A16.
93. Alexander Bolton, "House GOP Puts Taylor On Warning," *The Hill,* February 15, 2005, 1.
94. Hans Nichols, "Obey Letter Seeks Deal with Regula," *The Hill,* October 28, 2003, 12. See also Joshua B. Gordon, "The (Dis)Integration of the House Appropriations Committee: Revisiting *The Power of the Purse* in a Partisan Era," in *Congress Reconsidered,* 8th ed., ed. Lawrence C. Dodd and Bruce I. Oppenheimer (Washington, D.C.: CQ Press, 2005), 271–295.
95. David Nather, "Daschle's Soft Touch Lost in Tough Senate Arena," *CQ Weekly,* July 20, 2002, 1922.
96. Noelle Straub, "Senate Finance Panel Faces July 15 Deadline," *The Hill,* July 3, 2002, 6.
97. Susan Crabtree, " 'Moral Values' Session Part of Democrats' Plan to Broaden Their Core Message," *CQ Today,* February 4, 2005, 12.
98. Peter Savodnik, "To Win Social Security Reform, GOP Plans to Reprise Election," *The Hill,* January 19, 2005, 16.
99. U.S. Congress, *Congressional Record,* daily ed., 107th Cong., 1st sess., March 22, 2001, S2718.
100. U.S. Congress, *Congressional Record,* daily ed., 108th Cong., 2nd sess., February 14, 2004, S1496.
101. U.S. Congress, *Congressional Record,* daily ed., 107th Cong., 1st sess., March 22, 2001, H1070.
102. U.S. Congress, *Congressional Record,* daily ed., 109th Cong., 1st sess., February 10, 2005, H567.
103. Nather, "Daschle's Soft Touch Lost in Tough Senate Arena," 1922.
104. *Committee Structure,* hearings before the Joint Committee on the Organization of Congress (Washington, D.C.: U.S. Government Printing Office, 1993), 779.
105. Curt Suplee, "The Science Chairman's Unpredictable Approach," *Washington Post,* October 15, 1991, A21.

CHAPTER 8

1. *Constitution, Jefferson's Manual, and Rules of the House of Representatives,* H. Doc. 107-284, 108th Cong., 2003, 127–128. The rules of the Senate are contained in *Senate Manual,* S. Doc. 107-1, 107th Cong., 2002.
2. Donald R. Matthews, *U.S. Senators and Their World* (Chapel Hill: University of North Carolina Press, 1960), chapter 5.
3. *Wall Street Journal,* October 2, 1987, 1.
4. John Solomon, "Family Crisis Shifts Politics," *USA Today,* August 16, 2001, 15A.
5. Deborah Sontag, "When Politics Is Personal," *New York Times Magazine,* September 15, 2002, 92.
6. *National Journal,* April 10, 1982, 632.
7. Julie Rovner, "Senate Committee Approves Health Warnings on Alcohol," *Congressional Quarterly Weekly Report,* May 24, 1986, 1175.
8. Woodrow Wilson, *Congressional Government* (Boston: Houghton Mifflin, 1885), 320.
9. Theodore Sorensen, *Kennedy* (New York: Harper and Row, 1965), 184.
10. *Wall Street Journal,* June 2, 1988, 56.
11. U.S. Congress, *Congressional Record,* daily ed., 95th Cong., 1st sess., May 17, 1977, E3076.
12. Chuck Todd, "So Many Bills of Rights, So Little Time," *National Journal's CongressDaily/PM,* August 1, 2001, 1.
13. Peter Baker, "White House Finds 'Fast Track' Too Slippery," *Washington Post,* September 14, 1997, A4. See also U.S. Congress, *Congressional Record,* daily ed., 105th Cong., 2d sess.,

September 29, 1998, S11133; U.S. Congress, *Congressional Record,* daily ed., 106th Cong., 1st sess., January 25, 1999, S979; and Ceci Connolly, "Consultant Offers GOP a Language for the Future," *Washington Post,* September 4, 1997, A1.
14. For information on the drafting process, see Lawrence E. Filson, *The Legislative Drafter's Desk Reference* (Washington, D.C.: Congressional Quarterly, 1992).
15. *CQ Monitor,* July 24, 1998, 5.
16. Lawrence J. Haas, "Unauthorized Action," *National Journal,* January 2, 1988, 20.
17. T. R. Reid, *Congressional Odyssey: The Saga of a Senate Bill* (San Francisco: W. H. Freeman, 1980), 17.
18. Carroll J. Doherty, "Lots of Inertia, Little Lawmaking as Election '98 Approaches," *CQ Weekly,* July 18, 1998, 1925.
19. Margaret Kriz, "Still Charging," *National Journal,* December 6, 1997, 2462.
20. Thomas P. Carr, *Suspension of the Rules in the House of Representatives,* Congressional Research Service Report RL32474, February 1, 2005, 11.
21. Donald R. Wolfensberger, "Suspended Partisanship in the House: How Most Laws Are Really Made," paper prepared for the 2002 annual meeting of the American Political Science Association, Boston, Mass., August 29–September 1, 2002, 11.
22. U.S. Congress, *Congressional Record,* daily ed., 109th Cong., 1st sess., January 4, 2005, H34.
23. Jonathan Salant, "Under Open Rules, Discord Rules," *Congressional Quarterly Weekly Report,* January 28, 1995, 277.
24. *National Journal,* January 21, 1995, 183.
25. Lizette Alvarez, "Campaign Finance Measure Soundly Rejected by House," *New York Times,* June 18, 1998, A26.
26. Stanley Bach and Steven Smith, *Managing Uncertainty in the House of Representatives: Adaptation and Innovation in Special Rules* (Washington, D.C.: Brookings Institution, 1988), 87.
27. Alfred Steinberg, *Sam Rayburn* (New York: Hawthorn, 1975), 313.
28. Neil MacNeil, *The Forge of Democracy* (New York: McKay, 1963), 411.
29. Mary Lynn F. Jones, "The Republican Railroad," *American Prospect,* April 2003, 16.
30. Lindsay Sobel, "Democrats Weight Discharge Petition Barrage," *The Hill,* July 1, 1998, 2.
31. Alexander Bolton, "House Leaders Tighten Grip, Anger Centrists," *The Hill,* January 15, 2003, 23.
32. Information courtesy of Richard Beth, specialist in legislative process, Congressional Research Service, Library of Congress.
33. *National Journal's CongressDaily/PM,* January 13, 1995, 4.
34. Robert S. Walker, "Why House Republicans Need a Watchdog," *Roll Call,* January 19, 1987, 10.
35. John F. Bibby, ed., *Congress off the Record* (Washington, D.C.: American Enterprise Institute, 1983), 23.
36. Sen. J. Bennett Johnston, D-La. (1972–1997), quoted in *New York Times,* November 22, 1985, B8.
37. "Democrats to Forgo Control in Brief Edge," *Washington Times,* November 29, 2000, A4.
38. U.S. Congress, *Congressional Record,* daily ed., 101st Cong., 2d sess., July 20, 1990, S10183.
39. Susan F. Rasky, "With Few Bills Passed or Ready for Action, Congress Seems Sluggish," *New York Times,* May 14, 1989, 24.
40. U.S. Congress, *Congressional Record,* daily ed., 98th Cong., 2d sess., January 27, 1984, S328–S329.
41. Walter J. Oleszek, *Congressional Procedures and the Policy Process,* 6th ed. (Washington, D.C.: CQ Press, 2004), 247–251. See also Lewis A. Froman Jr., *The Congressional Process* (Boston: Little, Brown, 1967); and Terry Sullivan, *Procedural Structure: Success and Influence in Congress* (New York: Praeger, 1984).

42. Elizabeth Drew, *Senator* (New York: Simon and Schuster, 1979), 158.
43. U.S. Congress, *Congressional Record,* daily ed., 97th Cong., 2d sess., May 20, 1982, S5648.
44. Mary Dalrymple, "Democrats Say They Are Unified in Opposition Platform," *CQ Today,* January 29, 2002, 5.
45. Gail Russell Chaddock, "Limits on Filibusters Are Already Pervasive," *Christian Science Monitor,* May 24, 2005, 2.
46. U.S. Congress, *Congressional Record,* daily ed., 107th Cong., 2d sess., April 17, 2002, S2850.
47. Helen Dewar, " 'Hold' Likely for IRS Pick, Daschle Says," *Washington Post,* October 30, 1997, A11.
48. See, for example, U.S. Congress, *Congressional Record,* daily ed., 107th Cong., 2d sess., April 17, 2002, S2850.
49. See comments by Alan Cranston of California, then Senate Democratic whip, in *New York Times,* July 17, 1986, A3.
50. Sean Piccoli, "Byrd Still Senate Caesar Despite GOP Takeover," *Washington Times,* February 14, 1995, A11.
51. U.S. Congress, *Operations of the Congress: Testimony of House and Senate Leaders,* hearing before the Joint Committee on the Organization of Congress (Washington, D.C.: U.S. Government Printing Office, 1993), 50.
52. Information for the 108th Congress compiled by the U.S. Senate Library.
53. Jeffrey Toobin, "Blowing Up the Senate," *New Yorker,* March 7, 2005, 46.
54. Maura Reynolds, "Specter Indicates He'll Be His Own Man as Judiciary Chairman," *Los Angeles Times,* February 25, 2005, A9.
55. Testimony of Steven S. Smith, University of Minnesota, before the Joint Committee on the Organization of Congress, 103d Cong., 1st sess., May 20, 1993, 14.
56. U.S. Congress, *Congressional Record,* daily ed., 106th Cong., 2d sess., October 13, 2000, S10520.
57. Philip Shenon, "Democrat Would Appoint McCain to Campaign Finance Panel," *New York Times,* April 2, 2001, A12.
58. Randall B. Ripley, *Power in the Senate* (New York: St. Martin's, 1969), 128.
59. Janet Hook, "In Conference: New Hurdles, Hard Bargaining," *Congressional Quarterly Weekly Report,* September 6, 1986, 2081.
60. U.S. Congress, *Congressional Record,* daily ed., 99th Cong., 2d sess., February 20, 1986, S1463.
61. Barbara Sinclair, *Unorthodox Lawmaking: New Legislative Processes in the U.S. Congress,* 2d ed. (Washington, D.C.: CQ Press, 2000).
62. Barber B. Conable, "Weaving Webs: Lobbying by Charities," *Tax Notes,* November 10, 1975, 27–28.

CHAPTER 9

1. Richard L. Hall, *Participation in Congress* (New Haven: Yale University Press, 1996), 27–30.
2. Quoted in Janet Hook, "Moderates on Outside of GOP Big Tent," *Los Angeles Times,* May 24, 2001, A22.
3. Norman J. Ornstein, "After Shelby Precedent, Bush Had Better Be Careful with Jeffords," *Roll Call,* May 14, 2001, 10.
4. Craig Winneker and Glenn R. Simpson, "Obscure Caucus, Year Five," *Roll Call,* September 12, 1994, A25–26. The listing omits senators: "[S]enators are by definition not obscure, although there are several who seem to strive for it." To be listed in the Obscure Caucus, House members must have served at least three terms.
5. Quoted in *The Hill,* November 15, 2000, 16.

6. David Price, *Who Makes the Laws?* (Cambridge, Mass.: Schenkman Publishing, 1972), 297; and David E. Price *The Congressional Experience,* 3d ed. (Boulder, Colo.: Westview Press, 2004), chapter 6.
7. Quoted in Laura Blumenfeld, "When Politics Becomes Personal," *Washington Post,* June 19, 1996, C1, C2. See also Sarah Pekkanen, "From Drunk Driving to Health Care, Lawmakers' Bills Have Personal Roots," *The Hill,* April 17, 1996, 10.
8. Guy Gugliotta, "On the Hill, Ex-Wrestlers Go to the Mat for the Sport," *Washington Post,* April 30, 1998, A19.
9. Bernard Asbell, *The Senate Nobody Knows* (Garden City, N.Y.: Doubleday, 1978), 210.
10. Richard F. Fenno Jr., "Observation, Context, and Sequence in the Study of Politics," *American Political Science Review* 80 (March 1976): 3–15.
11. Lindsay Sobel, "Early Fast-Track Support Cost Members Leverage," *The Hill,* November 12, 1997, 33.
12. Quoted in Betsy Rothstein, "GOP Leaders Must Cope with Pesky Chafee and Jeffords," *The Hill,* May 16, 2001, 28.
13. Quoted by Joshua Michael Marshall, "Let's (Not) Make a Deal," *American Prospect* 12 (February 26, 2001): 12.
14. Cited in Philippe Shepnick, "Moynihan Is Champion Bill Writer," *The Hill,* March 10, 1999, 6.
15. Rick K. Wilson and Cheryl D. Young, "Cosponsorship in the U.S. Congress," *Legislative Studies Quarterly* 22 (February 1997): 25–43.
16. The study was released by Congressional Connection, an online database. Reported in *Roll Call,* June 16, 1994, 4.
17. Richard F. Fenno Jr., *The Making of a Senator: Dan Quayle* (Washington, D.C.: CQ Press, 1989), 43–45.
18. T. R. Reid, *Congressional Odyssey: The Saga of a Senate Bill* (San Francisco: W. H. Freeman, 1980), 15.
19. Quoted in Hall, *Participation in Congress,* 139; see also 119.
20. Hall, *Participation in Congress,* 126–127.
21. John Cranford, "Heeding the Roll Call Bell," *CQ Weekly,* December 11, 2004, 2910–2911.
22. U.S. Congress, *Congressional Record,* daily ed., 103d Cong., 1st sess., June 23, 1993, H3941–3973.
23. Allan Freedman, "Elimination of NEA Squeaks By as House Passes Interior Rule," *Congressional Quarterly Weekly Report,* July 12, 1997, 1615–1618.
24. John D. Wilkerson, " 'Killer' Amendments in Congress," *American Political Science Review* 93 (September 1999): 535–552.
25. Quoted in Eric Schmitt, "House Votes to Bar Religious Abuse Abroad," *New York Times,* May 15, 1998, A1.
26. Albert R. Hunt, "Balanced-Budget Measure Is Likely to Pass Senate Next Week, Faces Battle in House," *Wall Street Journal,* July 30, 1982, 2.
27. Norman J. Ornstein, Thomas E. Mann, and Michael J. Malbin, *Vital Statistics on Congress, 2001–2002* (Washington, D.C.: American Enterprise Institute, 2002), 172–173.
28. Glenn R. Parker and Suzanne L. Parker, "Factions in Committees: The U.S. House of Representatives," *American Political Science Review* 73 (March 1979): 85–102.
29. For an authoritative analysis of the decline and resurgence of congressional partisanship, see David W. Rohde, *Parties and Leaders in the Postreform House* (Chicago: University of Chicago Press, 1991), especially 3–11.
30. David W. Rohde, "Electoral Forces, Political Agendas, and Partisanship in the House and Senate," in *The Postreform Congress,* ed. Roger H. Davidson (New York: St. Martin's, 1992), especially 34–40.
31. Helmut Norpoth, "Explaining Party Cohesion in Congress: The Case of Shared Policy Attitudes," *American Political Science Review* 70 (December 1976): 1171.

32. John Breaux, "Congress's Lost Art of Compromise," *Roll Call*, April 19, 2005, 17.
33. Morton Kondracke, "Who's Running the House? GOP Freshmen or Newt?" *Roll Call*, December 18, 1995, 5.
34. Rohde, "Electoral Forces," 28.
35. The concept is explained in John H. Aldrich, *Why Parties? The Origin and Transformation of Party Politics in America* (Chicago: University of Chicago Press, 1995).
36. Keith T. Poole and Howard Rosenthal, "Patterns of Congressional Voting," *American Journal of Political Science* 35 (February 1991): 228–278; and Keith T. Poole and Howard Rosenthal, *Congress: A Political-Economic History of Roll-Call Voting* (New York: Oxford University Press, 1997). See Ornstein, Mann, and Malbin, *Vital Statistics on Congress*, 181–182.
37. John F. Manley, "The Conservative Coalition in Congress," *American Behavioral Scientist* 17 (December 1973): 223–247; Barbara Sinclair, *Congressional Realignment: 1925–1978* (Austin: University of Texas Press, 1982); and Mack C. Shelley, *The Permanent Majority: The Conservative Coalition in the United States Congress* (University: University of Alabama Press, 1983).
38. Stephen Gettinger, "R.I.P. to a Conservative Force," *CQ Weekly*, January 9, 1999, 82–83.
39. Sarah A. Binder, "The Disappearing Political Center," *Brookings Review* 15 (fall 1996): 36–39. An extended analysis of the problem and its results is found in Sarah A. Binder, *Stalemate: Causes and Consequences of Legislative Gridlock* (Washington, D.C.: Brookings Institution Press, 2003).
40. Using different measures of more recent data, the same point is made in Morris P. Fiorina, with Samuel J. Adams and Jeremy C. Pope, *Culture War? The Myth of a Polarized America* (New York, Pearson Longman, 2005), 27–32.
41. Sean M. Theriault, "The Case of the Vanishing Moderates: Party Polarization in the Modern Congress," paper presented at the Western Political Science Association, Denver, Colorado, March 27, 2003, Figure 1. Ideology scores from similar years (1969–1970 and 1999–2000) yield virtually the same results. Binder, *Stalemate*, 23–26.
42. Binder, "The Disappearing Political Center," 37.
43. Numbers computed from *CQ Weekly*, December 11, 2004, 2954–2955.
44. Binder, *Stalemate*, 69.
45. James G. Gimpel, *Fulfilling the Contract: The First 100 Days* (Boston: Allyn and Bacon, 1996), 120.
46. Arnold, *The Logic of Congressional Action*, 68.
47. Arnold, *The Logic of Congressional Action*, 84.
48. Joseph J. Schatz, "With a Deft and Light Touch, Bush Finds Ways to Win," *CQ Weekly*, December 11, 2004, 2900–2905.
49. Sen. James M. Jeffords, R-Vt., statement, Burlington, Vermont, May 24, 2001. See Jeffords' Web site at Ussenate.gov/Jeffords.
50. "Presidential Support Background," *CQ Weekly*, December 11, 2004, 2946.
51. See Charles O. Jones, *The Trusteeship Presidency: Jimmy Carter and the United States Congress* (Baton Rouge: Louisiana State University Press, 1988).
52. David Nather, "Clinton's Floor Vote Victories Yielded Few Accomplishments," *CQ Weekly*, January 6, 2001, 52ff.
53. Ornstein, Mann, and Malbin, *Vital Statistics on Congress*, 168–169. Recent figures are reported in *CQ Weekly*, December 11, 2004, 2946–2948.
54. Roger H. Davidson, *The Role of the Congressman* (Indianapolis: Bobbs-Merrill, 1969), 22–23.
55. Robert L. Peabody, "Organization Theory and Legislative Behavior: Bargaining, Hierarchy, and Change in the U.S. House of Representatives," paper presented at the annual meeting of the American Political Science Association, New York, September 4–7, 1963.
56. Carl J. Friedrich, *Constitutional Government and Democracy*, 4th ed. (Waltham, Mass.: Blaisdell Publishing, 1967), 269–270.

57. Ben Pershing, "Boehlert Holding Bush's Feet to Fire," *Roll Call,* April 30, 2001, 28.
58. Mark Preston, "Chafee Remembered as War Hero, Political Giant," *Roll Call,* October 28, 1999, 36.
59. John W. Kingdon, *Congressmen's Voting Decisions,* 3d ed. (Ann Arbor: University of Michigan Press, 1989).
60. Quoted in John F. Bibby, ed., *Congress Off the Record* (Washington, D.C.: American Enterprise Institute, 1983), 22.
61. Quoted in Claudia Dreifus, "Exit Reasonable Right," *New York Times Magazine,* June 2, 1996, 26.
62. Edward J. Derwinski, "The Art of Negotiation within the Congress," in *International Negotiation: Art and Science,* ed. Diane B. Bendahmane and John W. McDonald Jr. (Washington, D.C.: U.S. Department of State, Foreign Service Institute, 1984), 11.
63. Lizette Alvarez, "In Slap at GOP Leadership, House Stops Move to Deny Food Stamps to Immigrants," *New York Times,* May 23, 1998, A9. For background, see John Ferejohn, "Logrolling in an Institutional Context: A Case Study of Food Stamp Legislation," in *Congress and Policy Change,* ed. Gerald C. Wright Jr., Leroy N. Rieselbach, and Lawrence C. Dodd (New York: Agathon Press, 1986), 223–253.
64. Elliott Abrams, "Unforgettable Scoop Jackson," *Reader's Digest,* February 1985. Quotation cited in U.S. Congress, *Congressional Record,* daily ed., 99th Cong., 1st sess., February 20, 1985, E478.
65. David E. Rosenbaum, "The Favors of Rostenkowski: Tax Revision's Quid Pro Quo," *New York Times,* November 27, 1985, B6.
66. Dale Tate, "Use of Omnibus Bills Burgeons Despite Members' Misgivings," *Congressional Quarterly Weekly Report,* September 25, 1982, 2379.
67. The politics of blame avoidance is outlined in R. Kent Weaver, "The Politics of Blame," *Brookings Review* 5 (spring 1987): 43–47. The term *credit claiming* originated with David R. Mayhew, *Congress: The Electoral Connection,* (New Haven: Yale University Press, 2004), 52–61.
68. R. Douglas Arnold, "The Local Roots of Domestic Policy," in *The New Congress,* ed. Thomas E. Mann and Norman J. Ornstein (Washington, D.C.: American Enterprise Institute, 1981), 286.
69. Steve Waldman, *The Bill* (New York: Viking, 1994), 94–95.
70. Quoted in Lindsay Sobel, "NAFTA Supporters Desert Clinton on Fast-Track," *The Hill,* November 12, 1997, 8.
71. Jonathan E. Kaplan, "Horse-Trading on House Floor," *The Hill,* October 5, 2004, 4; and Jackie Koszczuk and Jonathan Allen, "Late-Night Medicare Vote Drama Triggers Some Unexpected Alliances," *CQ Weekly,* November 29, 2003, 2958–2959.
72. Mary Curtius, "House Leader Admonished by Ethics Panel," *Los Angeles Times,* October 1, 2004, A15.
73. Quotes from Jonathan Allen, "Effective House Leadership Makes the Most of Majority," *CQ Weekly,* March 29, 2003, 751.
74. Quoted in Kirk Victor, "Kennedy the Pragmatist," *National Journal,* December 8, 2001, 3791.
75. John B. Gilmour, *Strategic Disagreement: Stalemate in American Politics* (Pittsburgh: University of Pittsburgh Press, 1995), 4.
76. See William H. Riker, *The Theory of Political Coalitions* (New Haven: Yale University Press, 1962), 32. Theorists define legislative bargaining situations formally as *n*- person, zero-sum games in which side payments are permitted. That is, a sizable number of participants are involved; when some participants win, others must lose; and participants can trade items outside the substantive issues under consideration.
77. John G. Stewart, "Two Strategies of Leadership: Johnson and Mansfield," in *Congressional Behavior,* ed. Nelson W. Polsby (New York: Random House, 1971), 67.

78. Russell Hardin, "Hollow Victory: The Minimum Winning Coalition," *American Political Science Review* 79 (December 1976): 1202–1214.
79. Breaux, "Congress's Lost Art of Compromise," 17.
80. Binder, *Stalemate,* 127.
81. Robert J. Dole, remarks to the Senate, March 29, 2000, quoted in *The Hill,* April 5, 2000, 32.

CHAPTER 10

1. The remarks of Rep. Mark Souder, R-Ind., are from Janet Hook, "For Bush, GOP Leaders, Some Policy Paths Diverge," *Los Angeles Times,* January 24, 2005, A10. The comment about the age range of the midterm electorate is from Stuart Rothenberg, "Social Security Has GOP Reaching for Its Worry Beads," *Roll Call,* February 14, 2005, 8.
2. Robin Toner, "Hastert Warns Not to Hurry Overhaul of Social Security," *New York Times,* February 12, 2005, A11.
3. Janet Hook, "GOP Takes to Heartland with Social Security Plan," *Los Angeles Times,* February 19, 2005, A10.
4. Hook, "For Bush, GOP Leaders, Some Policy Paths Diverge," A10.
5. See Stephen Wayne, *The Legislative Presidency* (New York: Harper and Row, 1978).
6. Charles O. Jones, *Separate But Equal Branches: Congress and the Presidency* (Chatham, N.J.: Chatham House, 1995), 138–157.
7. Michael Nelson, "Evaluating the President," in *The Presidency and the Political System,* 7th ed., ed. Michael Nelson (Washington, D.C.: CQ Press, 2003), 21.
8. See Norman J. Ornstein, "Theories of the Presidency," in *Encyclopedia of the American Presidency,* vol. 4, ed. Leonard Levy and Louis Fisher (New York: Simon and Schuster, 1994), 1458–1462.
9. Richard E. Neustadt, *Presidential Power* (New York: John Wiley and Sons, 1960), 23.
10. Neustadt, *Presidential Power,* 16.
11. Leonard D. White, *The Federalist* (New York: Macmillan, 1948), 55.
12. Leonard D. White, *The Jeffersonians* (New York: Macmillan, 1951), 35.
13. John A. Farrell, *Tip O'Neill and the Democratic Century* (Boston: Little, Brown, and Co., 2001), 553.
14. Paul C. Light, *The President's Agenda* (Baltimore: Johns Hopkins University Press, 1982), 230–231.
15. Lyndon B. Johnson, *The Vantage Point* (New York: Popular Library, 1971), 448.
16. Jack Valenti, "Some Advice on the Care and Feeding of Congressional Egos," *Los Angeles Times,* April 23, 1978, 3.
17. Richard Berke, "Courting Congress Nonstop, Clinton Looks for an Alliance," *New York Times,* March 8, 1993, A1.
18. Roy P. Basler, ed., *The Collected Works of Abraham Lincoln,* vol. 3 (New Brunswick: Rutgers University Press, 1953), 27.
19. Samuel Kernell, *Going Public: New Strategies of Presidential Leadership,* 3d ed. (Washington, D.C.: CQ Press, 1997), 2. Also see James Ceaser and others, "The Rise of the Rhetorical Presidency," *Presidential Studies Quarterly* 21 (spring 1981): 158–171.
20. Richard M. Pious, *The American Presidency* (New York: Basic Books, 1979), 194. See also George C. Edwards III, *The Public Presidency* (New York: St. Martin's, 1983).
21. *Wall Street Journal,* December 4, 1987, 8D.
22. Tom Rosenstiel and James Gerstenzang, "Bush Team Rejects Public Relations Techniques of Reagan White House," *Los Angeles Times,* April 30, 1989, 1.
23. George Hager, "For GOP, a New Song—Same Ending," *Congressional Quarterly Weekly Report,* June 14, 1997, 1406.
24. Paul Bedard, "Living, Dying by the Polls," *Washington Times,* April 30, 1993, A1.

25. David S. Broder, "The Reticent President," *Washington Post,* April 22, 2001, B7. See also Mike Allen, "Bush on Stage: Deft or Just Lacking Depth?" *Washington Post,* February 19, 2001, A8–A9.
26. Elisabeth Bumiller, "Keepers of Bush Image Lift Stagecraft to New Heights," *New York Times,* May 16, 2003, A1.
27. Bumiller, "Keepers of Bush Image Lift Stagecraft to New Heights," A20.
28. Jim VandeHei and Peter Baker, "Social Security: On with the Show," *Washington Post,* March 12, 2005, A3.
29. David Barstow and Robin Stein, "Under Bush, a New Age of Prepackaged News," *New York Times,* March 13, 2005, 1.
30. Christopher Lee, "Administration Rejects Ruling on PR Videos," *Washington Post,* March 15, 2005, A21.
31. See, for example, Richard P. Nathan, *The Administrative Presidency* (New York: John Wiley and Sons, 1983); and Robert R. Durant, *The Administrative Presidency Revisited* (Albany: State University of New York Press, 1992).
32. See Kenneth Mayer, *With the Stroke of a Pen: Executive Orders and Presidential Power* (Princeton: Princeton University Press, 2001).
33. Elizabeth Shogren, "President Plans Blitz of Executive Orders Soon," *Los Angeles Times,* July 5, 1998, A11.
34. Susan Page, "When a Law Is Unlikely, Often an Order Will Do," *USA Today,* August 11, 1997, 7A.
35. Dana Milbank and Ellen Nakashima, "Bush Team Has 'Right' Credentials," *Washington Post,* March 25, 2001, A1.
36. Susan Crabtree, "Discordant Voices Need Not Apply as Bush Builds Harmonious Cabinet," *CQ Weekly,* January 10, 2005, 74.
37. Linda Feldmann, "Faith-Based Initiatives Quietly Lunge Forward," *Christian Science Monitor,* February 6, 2003, 2.
38. James Gerstenzang, "Bush Circumventing Congress," *Los Angeles Times,* December 15, 2002, A10.
39. Rebecca Adams, "GOP Adds New Tactics to War on Regulations," *CQ Weekly,* January 31, 2005, 224. See John McKinnon, "White House to Launch Push for Pro-Business Regulation," *Wall Street Journal,* March 9, 2005, A2.
40. For a critique of electoral realignments, see David R. Mayhew, *Electoral Realignments: A Critique of an American Genre* (New Haven: Yale University Press, 2002).
41. James Harding, "A Polarising President Gets His Chance to Become a Republican Roosevelt," *Financial Times,* January 19, 2005, 11.
42. Stephen Skowronek, "Presidential Leadership in Political Time," in *The Presidency and the Political System,* 7th ed., ed. Michael Nelson (Washington, D.C.: CQ Press, 2003), 112.
43. Skowronek, "Presidential Leadership in Political Time," 112.
44. Aaron Wildavsky, "The Two Presidencies," in *The Beleaguered Presidency,* ed. Aaron Wildavsky (Brunswick, N.J.: Transaction Publishers, 1991), 29. Wildavsky's article originally appeared in the December 1966 issue of *Transaction* magazine.
45. Aaron Wildavsky, "The Two Presidencies Thesis Revisited at a Time of Political Dissensus," in *The Beleaguered Presidency,* ed. Aaron Wildavsky (Brunswick, N.J.: Transaction Publishers, 1991), 47–65.
46. Dan Balz, "Bush Lays Out Ambitious Plan for Long Term," *Washington Post,* May 6, 2001, A10.
47. Dana Milbank, "Bush Signs Tax Bill Into Law," *Washington Post,* June 8, 2001, A19.
48. "Bush's Tax-Cut Hardball Seems to Have Paid Off," *USA Today,* May 29, 2001, 9A.
49. Milbank, "Bush Signs Tax Bill Into Law," A19.
50. Norman J. Ornstein,"Bush Faces Strategic Fork in the Road," *Roll Call,* November 14, 2002, 9.

51. Ornstein, "Bush Faces Strategic Fork in the Road," 9.
52. Ronald Brownstein, "Strategies Shift as Bush Drops in Polls," *Los Angeles Times,* July 5, 2001, A9.
53. Ronald Brownstein, "Bush Is a Surprise Hard Liner," *Los Angeles Times,* March 2, 2003, A14.
54. John Harwood and Jeanne Cummings, "Bush's Approval Rating Slips to 50%, a 5-Year Presidential Low," *Wall Street Journal,* June 28, 2001, A18.
55. Ron Faucheux, "Presidential Popularity: A History of Highs and Lows," *CQ Daily Monitor,* February 7, 2002, 14.
56. John M. Donnelly and Helen Fessenden, "Iraq War Poses a Test for Majority Repubicans," *CQ Today,* November 8, 2004, 9.
57. Judy Keen, William Welch, and Andrea Stone, "Tension with Republicans Ties Up Bush's Legislation," *USA Today,* May 13, 2002, 2A.
58. Craig Crawford, "Second Impression," *CQ Weekly,* February 28, 2005, 530.
59. Janet Hook, "Social Security Overhaul Splinters GOP," *Los Angeles Times,* March 6, 2005, 10.
60. E. J. Dionne Jr., "A Wartime Leader Can't Be Partisan as Usual," *Washington Post,* January 26, 2003, B5.
61. Peter Wallsten, "GOP Sees Outreach Potential in Agenda," *Los Angeles Times,* January 20, 2005, A9.
62. Ross K. Baker, "Bush's Plan for the GOP," *USA Today,* February 28, 2005, 15A.
63. Peter Wallsten and Warren Vith, "Dominance on GOP Agenda," *Los Angeles Times,* February 2, 2005, A1.
64. Woodrow Wilson, *Congressional Government* (Boston: Houghton Mifflin, 1885), 52.
65. Frank B. Cross, "The Constitutional Legitimacy and Significance of Presidential 'Signing Statements,'" *Administrative Law Review* 40 (spring 1988): 209–238.
66. *Kennedy v. Sampson,* F2d 430.
67. Robert J. Spitzer, "Veto, Pocket," in *Encyclopedia of the American Presidency,* vol. 4, ed. Leonard Levy and Louis Fisher (New York: Simon and Schuster, 1994), 1552.
68. Ethan Wallison, "Can President Bush Stay Veto-Free for Four More Years?" *Roll Call,* January 24, 2005, 10.
69. Mike Allen, "Bush Signs Corporate Reforms Into Law," *Washington Post,* July 31, 2002, A4. Also see Elizabeth Bumiller, "When Bush Picks Up a Pen, He Drops Names," *New York Times,* December 2, 2002, A16.
70. *Los Angeles Times,* March 18, 1988, part I, 4.
71. Erika Niedowski, "GOP to Skirt Line Item Veto," *The Hill,* February 12, 1997, 24.
72. Andrew Taylor, "Lawmakers File Challenge to Line-Item Veto Law," *Congressional Quarterly Weekly Report,* January 4, 1997, 24.
73. John F. Harris, "Clinton Wields New Authority, Vetoing Three Items," *Washington Post,* August 12, 1997, A1.
74. John Broder, "Clinton Vetoes Eight Projects, Two in States of Leadership," *New York Times,* October 18, 1997, A10.
75. Helen Dewar and Joan Biskupic, "Line-Item Vote Struck Down: Backers Push for Alternative," *Washington Post,* June 26, 1998, A1.
76. U.S. Congress, *Congressional Record,* daily ed., 106th Cong., 1st sess., February 23, 1999, E265.
77. Ethan Wallison, "Can One Word Fix Line-Item Veto?" *Roll Call,* March 14, 2005, 24; and *Analytical Perspectives, Budget of the United States Government, Fiscal Year 2006* (Washington, D.C.: U.S. Government Printing Office, 2005), 241.
78. Richard Neustadt, *Presidential Power,* 187.
79. *National Journal's CongressDaily/AM,* February 27, 2001, 8.
80. *National Journal's CongressDaily/AM,* February 27, 2001.
81. Johnson, *The Vantage Point,* 448.

82. Ethan Wallison, "Adding DeLay Makes It a 'Gang of Five,'" *Roll Call,* March 6, 2003, 3.
83. Wallison, "Can President Bush Stay Veto-Free for Four More Years?" 24.
84. George C. Edwards, III., *At the Margins* (New Haven: Yale University Press, 1989).
85. Ronald Brownstein, "One Slim Win After Another for Bush," *Los Angeles Times,* May 13, 2005, A6.
86. See Joseph P. Harris, *The Advice and Consent of the Senate* (Berkeley: University of California Press, 1953); and G. Calvin Mackenzie, *The Politics of Presidential Appointments* (New York: Free Press, 1981).
87. James MacGregor Burns, *Presidential Government* (Boston: Houghton Mifflin, 1966), 284.
88. See, for example, Stephen J. Wayne, "Great Expectations: What People Want from Presidents," in *Rethinking the Presidency,* ed. Thomas E. Cronin (Boston: Little, Brown, 1982), 185–199.
89. David Broder, "Midterm Jitters in the House," *Washington Post,* May 16, 2001, A23.
90. Arthur M. Schlesinger Jr. and Alfred De Grazia, *Congress and the Presidency: Their Role in Modern Times* (Washington, D.C.: American Enterprise Institute, 1967), 1.
91. Wilson, *Congressional Government;* and Burns, *Presidential Government.*
92. See Joseph S. Clark, *Congress: The Sapless Branch* (New York: Harper and Row, 1964); and Arthur M. Schlesinger Jr., *The Imperial Presidency* (Boston: Houghton Mifflin, 1973).
93. David Mayhew, *Divided We Govern* (New Haven: Yale University Press, 1991), 198.
94. See Wilfred E. Binkley, *President and Congress* (New York: Knopf, 1947); Jones, *Separate But Equal Branches* ; and Richard E. Neustadt, *Presidential Power and the Modern Presidents* (New York: Free Press, 1990).
95. Susan Page, "GAO Chief, Cheney Barreling toward Showdown," *USA Today,* February 18, 2002, 6A.
96. Alexander Bolton, "Members Hit White House Over Secrecy," *The Hill,* August 7, 2002, 1.
97. J. William Fulbright, "The Legislator as Educator," *Foreign Affairs* (spring 1979): 726.

CHAPTER 11

1. David S. Broder, "So, Now Bigger Is Better?" *Washington Post,* January 12, 2003, B1.
2. Jim VandeHei, "Blueprint Calls for Bigger, More Powerful Government," *Washington Post,* February 9, 2005, A7. See Janet Hook, "President Putting 'Big' Back in Government," *Los Angeles Times,* February 8, 2005, A1.
3. Christopher Lee, "Players: Mike Pence," *Washington Post,* March 22, 2005, A15.
4. Quoted in E. J. Dionne Jr., "Back from the Dead: Neoprogressivism in the 90s," *American Prospect* (September–October 1996): 25.
5. Sam Howe Verhovek, "Legislators Meet, Surprised at Limit on Shift of Powers," *New York Times,* January 12, 1997, 1.
6. Eliza Newlin Carney, "Power Grab," *National Journal,* April 11, 1998, 799. See also Timothy Conlan, *From New Federalism to Devolution* (Washington, D.C.: Brookings Institution, 1998).
7. Jonathan Walters, "Preempting Washington," *Governing,* September 2004, 12.
8. U.S. Congress, *Congressional Record,* daily ed., 105th Cong., 1st sess., November 5, 1997, S11737.
9. Richard E. Neustadt, "Politicians and Bureaucrats," in *The Congress and America's Future,* 2d ed., ed. David B. Truman (Englewood Cliffs, N.J.: Prentice-Hall, 1973), 199. See also Louis Fisher, *The Politics of Shared Power: Congress and the Executive,* 3d ed. (Washington, D.C.: CQ Press, 1993).
10. See Dave Boyer, "Ridge Reluctant to Testify in Senate," *Washington Times,* February 27, 2002, A4.
11. George Archibald, "Panel Ties Funding to Ridge Testimony," *Washington Times,* March 22, 2002, A1; and George Archibald, "Ridge Attends Private Meetings on Hill," *Washington Times,* April 11, 2002, A4.

12. See Harold C. Relyea, "Homeland Security: Department Organization and Management—Legislative Phase," Congressional Research Service Report, February 25, 2003.
13. U.S. Congress, *Congressional Record,* daily ed., 107th Cong., 2d sess., June 18, 2002, H3639–H3641. Under forms of reorganization noted in this chapter, the Department of Homeland Security is a statutory creation.
14. Adriel Bettelheim, "Personnel Issues Have Senate Stumbling on Homeland Security," *CQ Weekly,* September 28, 2002, 2515.
15. U.S. Congress, *Congressional Record,* daily ed., 109th Cong., 1st sess., February 15, 2005, S1437.
16. Steven V. Roberts, "In Confirmation Process, Hearings Offer a Stage," *New York Times,* February 8, 1989, B7.
17. William Schneider, "New Rules for the Game of Politics," *National Journal,* April 1, 1989, 830.
18. See Dennis Thompson, *Ethics in Congress* (Washington, D.C.: Brookings Institution, 1995).
19. G. Calvin Mackenzie, "Hung Out to Dry," *Washington Post,* April 1, 2001, B5.
20. Paul Light, "The Glacial Pace of Presidential Appointments," *Wall Street Journal,* April 4, 2001, A20.
21. Al Kamen, "Confirmation Delays Hobble Administration," *Washington Post,* May 20, 2001, A1. See also Laurence McQuillan, "Complex Process Slows Hiring," *USA Today,* May 30, 2001, 10A.
22. "Bush Struggles to Fill Holes in Policymaking Teams," *Financial Times,* March 3, 2005, 2.
23. Light, "The Glacial Pace of Presidential Appointments," A20.
24. Nancy Kassebaum Baker and Franklin Raines, "Uncle Sam Wants a Few Good Appointees," *Los Angeles Times,* April 5, 2001, A17. Baker and Raines are cochairs of the Presidential Appointee Initiative Advisory Board, which is a project of the Brookings Institution. Its basic goal is to propose improvements in the presidential appointments process.
25. G. Calvin Mackenzie, ed., *Innocent until Nominated* (Washington, D.C.: Brookings Institution, 2001), 30.
26. Doyle McManus and Robert Shogun, "Acrid Tone Reflects Long-Term Trend for Nominations," *Los Angeles Times,* March 9, 1997, A6.
27. Peter Grier, "Why Senate Roughs Up Some Cabinet Nominees," *Christian Science Monitor,* March 19, 1997, 3.
28. James Dao, "In Protest, Republican Senators Hold Up Defense Confirmations," *New York Times,* May 10, 2001, A20.
29. Stephen Barr, "Plum Book Counts Political Jobs in Executive, Legislative Branches," *Washington Post,* December 15, 2004, B2.
30. Paul C. Light, *Thickening Government* (Washington, D.C.: Brookings Institution and Governance Institute, 1995), esp. 111–116.
31. Paul Light, "Big Bureaucracy," *Washington Times,* May 10, 2001, A17.
32. Christopher Lee, "Agencies Getting Heavier on Top," *Washington Times,* July 23, 2004, A27.
33. Stephen Barr, "Title Creep Reported at Agencies," *Washington Post,* March 8, 1999, A17.
34. Lee, "Agencies Getting Heavier on Top," A27.
35. Paul Light, "Pressure to Grow," *Government Executive,* October 2000, 24.
36. David M. Cohen, "Amateur Government," *Journal of Public Administration Research and Theory* (October 1998): 451.
37. U.S. Congress, *Congressional Record,* daily ed., 106th Cong., 1st sess., January 19, 1999, S554.
38. U.S. Congress, *Congressional Record,* daily ed., 105th Cong., 1st sess., September 12, 1996, S10367.
39. *Federal Times,* December 12, 1988, 6; and *Washington Post,* August 6, 1987, A2.
40. *Roll Call,* March 11, 1999, 4. See also Amy Keller, "English Targets Members' COLA, Tax Break," *Roll Call,* March 11, 1999, 3.

41. Laura Michaelis, "Judge Upholds Hill Pay Raise; Old, New Congresses Benefit," *Congressional Quarterly Weekly Report,* December 19, 1992, 3880.
42. Ellen Nakashima, "Pentagon Hires Out More Than In," *Washington Post,* April 3, 2001, A19.
43. Joel Brinkley, "Energy Dept. Contractors Due for More Scrutiny," *New York Times,* November 24, 2002, 21.
44. Richard Stevenson, "Government Plan May Make Private Up to 850,000 Jobs," *New York Times,* November 15, 2002, A1.
45. Nakashima, "Pentagon Hires Out More Than In."
46. Paul C. Light, "The True Size of Government," *Government Executive,* January 1999, 20.
47. Peter Zimmerman, "Not So Big," *Government Executive,* February 1999, 39, 42.
48. U.S. Congress, *Congressional Record,* daily ed., 96th Cong., 2d sess., July 1, 1980, E3320.
49. Rebecca Fairley Raney, "Move to Open Government Electronically," *New York Times,* December 23, 2002, nytimes.com/2002.
50. Cindy Skrzycki, "Idea of Electronic Rulemaking Boots Up Slowly," *Washington Post,* October 28, 2003, E1.
51. Shawn Zeller, "E-king Out the Rules," *Government Executive,* January 2005, 24. See Cindy Skrzycki, "Project Aims for One-Stop Online Shopping for Federal Rules," *Washington Post,* March 30, 2004, E1.
52. Cornelius Kerwin, *Rulemaking: How Government Agencies Write Law and Make Policy,* 2d ed. (Washington, D.C.: CQ Press, 1999), 8–9. See also Jeffrey Lubbers, *A Guide to Federal Agency Rulemaking,* 3d ed. (Chicago: ABA Publishing, 1998).
53. Vicki Kemper, "Draft Rules for Medicare Law Unveiled," *Los Angeles Times,* July 27, 2004, A1. For the length of the law, see U.S. Congress, *Congressional Record,* daily ed., 108th Cong., 1st sess., December 8, 2003, H12750.
54. U.S. Congress, *Congressional Record,* daily ed., 100th Cong., 1st sess., July 29, 1987, S10850.
55. Matthew Wald, "Court Overturns Air Quality Rules," *New York Times,* May 15, 1999, A1.
56. Charles Lane, "Clean-Air Authority of EPA Is Upheld," *Washington Post,* February 28, 2001, A1.
57. Matthew Wald, "Court Voids a Bush Move on Energy," *New York Times,* January 14, 2004, A12.
58. Cyril Zaneski, "Escape Artist," *Government Executive,* March 2001, 29.
59. *Roll Call,* December 4, 1995, 15.
60. U.S. Congress, *Congressional Record,* daily ed., 108th Cong., 2d sess., November 20, 2004, E2130.
61. Rebecca Adams, "Regulating the Rule-Makers: John Graham at OIRA," *CQ Weekly,* February 23, 2002, 520.
62. Frank Ackerman, Lisa Heinzerling, James K. Hammitt, and Milton C. Weinstein, "Balancing Lives against Lucre," *Los Angeles Times,* February 25, 2004, A17. Ackerman and Heinzerling are economists, and Hammitt and Weinstein are risk analysis experts.
63. See Helen Dewar and Cindy Skrzycki, "Workplace Health Initiative Rejected," *Washington Post,* March 7, 2001, A1; and Helen Dewar and Cindy Skrzycki, "House Scraps Ergonomics Regulation," *Washington Post,* March 8, 2001, A1.
64. Mary Clare Jalonick, "Bipartisan Senate Effort Forces Vote on Easing Canadian Beef Import Restrictions," *CQ Today,* March 3, 2005, 13.
65. Stephen Labaton, "Agencies Postpone Issuing New Rules as Election Nears," *New York Times,* September 27, 2004, A21.
66. U.S. Congress, *Congressional Record,* daily ed., 104th Cong., 1st sess., July 11, 1995, S9705.
67. U.S. Congress, *Congressional Record,* daily ed., 104th Cong., 1st sess., July 11, 1995, S9697.
68. Morris P. Fiorina, *Congress: Keystone of the Washington Establishment* (New Haven: Yale University Press, 1977), 48.
69. R. Douglas Arnold, "The Local Roots of Domestic Policy," in *The New Congress,* ed. Thomas E. Mann and Norman J. Ornstein (Washington, D.C.: American Enterprise Institute, 1981), 284.

70. Lisa Caruso and Bara Vaida, "Following the Money," *National Journal,* March 5, 2005, 669. See Diana Evans, *Greasing the Wheels: Using Pork Barrel Projects to Build Majority Coalitions in Congress* (Cambridge, U.K.: Cambridge University Press, 2004).
71. *CQ Monitor,* July 15, 1998, 5; and Donald L. Barlett and James B. Steele, "Special Report: Corporate Welfare," *Time,* November 16, 1998, 79–93.
72. Joseph S. Clark, *Congress: The Sapless Branch* (New York: Harper and Row, 1964), 63–64.
73. David B. Frohnmayer, "The Separation of Powers: An Essay on the Vitality of a Constitutional Idea," *Oregon Law Review* (spring 1973): 330.
74. David B. Truman, *The Governmental Process,* rev. ed. (New York: Knopf, 1971), 439.
75. Woodrow Wilson, *Congressional Government* (Boston: Houghton Mifflin, 1885), 297.
76. *Washington Times,* December 29, 1986, A1; and David Rogers, "Sen. Lott Becomes GOP's New Standard-bearer, But His Style Will Be Tested in the Next Congress," *Wall Street Journal,* November 15, 1996, A16.
77. Jackie Koszczuk, "House GOP Is Closing the Door on an Era of Aggressive Inquiry," *CQ Weekly,* February 6, 1999, 328.
78. Rochelle Stanfield, "Plotting Every Move," *National Journal,* March 26, 1988, 796.
79. *Watkins v. United States,* 354 U.S. 178 (1957). See also James Hamilton, *The Power to Probe* (New York: Vantage Books, 1976).
80. William S. Cohen and George J. Mitchell, *Men of Zeal: A Candid Inside Story of the Iran-Contra Hearings* (New York: Viking Penguin, 1988), 305.
81. *Immigration and Naturalization Service v. Chadha,* 462 U.S. 919 (1983).
82. Louis Fisher, in *Extensions,* Carl Albert Congressional Research and Studies Center newsletter (spring 1984): 2.
83. John R. Johannes, "Study and Recommend: Statutory Reporting Requirements as a Technique of Legislative Initiative—A Research Note," *Western Political Quarterly* (December 1976): 589–596.
84. Guy Gugliotta, "Reporting on a Practice That's Ripe for Reform," *Washington Post,* February 11, 1997, A19.
85. Walter Pincus, "Congress Cracks Down on Overdue CIA Reports," *Washington Post,* December 1, 2002, A5.
86. Cindy Skrzycki, "The Regulators," *Washington Post,* January 8, 1999, F7. See also *CQ Monitor,* March 25, 1996, 7.
87. Michael W. Kirst, *Government without Passing Laws* (Chapel Hill: University of North Carolina Press, 1969).
88. Joseph A. Davis, "War Declared Over Report-Language Issue," *Congressional Quarterly Weekly Report,* June 25, 1988, 1752–1753; and David Rapp, "OMB's Miller Backs Away from Report-Language Battle," *Congressional Quarterly Weekly Report,* July 9, 1988, 1928.
89. George Archibald, "Hill Panel Examines Fraud at Education," *Washington Times,* April 4, 2001, A6.
90. "The Inspector General Act: Twenty Years Later," hearing before the Senate Governmental Affairs Committee, September 9, 1998, 32. See also Paul C. Light, *Monitoring Government: Inspectors General and the Search for Accountability* (Washington, D.C.: Brookings Institution, 1993).
91. Steven Holmes, "Amendment Would Strip a Top Official of His Powers," *New York Times,* October 6, 2000, A20.
92. Greta Wodele, "DHS Facing Appropriators' Wrath for Missing Deadlines," *National Journal's CongressDaily/PM,* February 17, 2005, 2.
93. Slade Gorton and Larry Craig, "Congress's Call to Accounting," *Washington Post,* July 27, 1998, A23.
94. U.S. Congress, *Congressional Record,* daily ed., 95th Cong., 1st sess., April 30, 1975, E2080.

95. See Peter Baker, *The Breach: Inside the Impeachment and Trial of William Jefferson Clinton* (New York: Scribner, 2000).
96. See Joel D. Aberbach, *Keeping a Watchful Eye: The Politics of Congressional Oversight* (Washington, D.C.: Brookings Institution, 1990); and James Q. Wilson, *Bureaucracy: What Governmental Agencies Do and Why They Do It* (New York: Basic Books, 1991).
97. Richard Cohen, "King of Oversight," *Government Executive,* September 1988, 17.
98. Paul Bedard, "White House Fumes at Probes," *Washington Times,* April 7, 1995, A1. See also Charles Tiefer, "Congressional Oversight of the Clinton Administration and Congressional Procedure," *Administrative Law Review* (winter 1998): 199–216; Robert Weissman, "Hearings Loss: Oversight in the Republican Congress," *American Prospect* (November–December 1998): 50–55; and William West, "Oversight Subcommittees in the House of Representatives," *Congress and the Presidency* (autumn 1998): 147–160.
99. Ethan Wallison, "Burton Closes In on His 1,000th Subpoena," *Roll Call,* April 2, 2001, 1.
100. David Nather, "Congress as Watchdog: Asleep on the Job?" *CQ Weekly,* May 22, 2004, 1190.
101. Audrey Hudson, "'Tough but Fair' Judiciary Leader Maps Oversight," *Washington Times,* March 19, 2001, A4.
102. Stephen Barr, "GOP Seeking More Control of Programs and Spending," *Washington Post,* February 5, 1997, A25. See also Beryl Radin, "Searching for Performance: The Government Performance and Results Act," *PS,* September 1998, 553–555.
103. Jennifer Kabbany, "Armey Targets Waste in Federal Agencies," *Washington Times,* February 12, 1999, A6.
104. Joel D. Aberbach, "The Congressional Committee Intelligence System: Information, Oversight, and Change," *Congress and the Presidency* 14 (spring 1987): 51–76; and Mathew McCubbins and Thomas Schwartz, "Congressional Oversight Overlooked: Police Patrol versus Fire Alarm," *American Journal of Political Science* (February 1984): 165–177.
105. Louis Fisher, "Micromanagement by Congress: Reality and Mythology," paper presented at a conference sponsored by the American Enterprise Institute, Washington, D.C., April 8–9, 1988, 8. See also David S. Broder and Stephen Barr, "Hill's Micromanagement of Cabinet Blurs Separation of Powers," *Washington Post,* July 25, 1993, A1.

CHAPTER 12

1. Alexis de Tocqueville, *Democracy in America* (New York: American Library, 1956), 72.
2. Richard L. Pacelle Jr., *The Role of the Supreme Court in American Politics: The Least Dangerous Branch?* (Boulder, Colo.: Westview Press, 2001).
3. Alexander Bickel, *The Least Dangerous Branch* (Indianapolis, Ind.: Bobbs-Merrill, 1962), 1.
4. See Dexter Perkins and Glyndon Van Deusen, *The United States of America: A History,* vol. II (New York: Macmillan Co., 1962), 560-566.
5. Joan Biskupic, "Justices Defer to Congress' Power to Extend Copyright," *USA Today,* January 16, 2003, 4A.
6. Jamin Raskin, "Courts v. Citizens," *American Prospect* 14 (March 2003): A25.
7. Colton C. Campbell and John F. Stack Jr., "Diverging Perspectives on Lawmaking: The Delicate Balance between Congress and the Court," in *Congress Confronts the Court,* ed. Colton C. Campbell and John F. Stack Jr. (Lanham, Md.: Rowman and Littlefield, 2001), 2.
8. Cass Sunstein, "The Right-Wing Assault," *American Prospect* 14 (March 2003): A2.
9. Linda Greenhouse, "High Court Faces Moment of Truth in Federalism Cases," *New York Times,* March 28, 1999, 3.
10. Louis Fisher, *American Constitutional Law,* 6th ed. (Durham, N.C.: Carolina Academic Press, 2005), 355.
11. Louis Fisher, "The Law: Litigating the War Power with *Campbell v. Clinton,* " *Presidential Studies Quarterly* (September 2000): 568.

12. Richard Briffault, "A Fickle Federalism," *American Prospect* 14 (March 2003): A26. See John Yoo, "What Became of Federalism?" *Los Angeles Times,* June 21, 2005, 11.
13. The U.S. Supreme Court majority contended, in this and similar rulings, that the Eleventh Amendment granted states "sovereign immunity" from legal suits. But the amendment's plain language protects states only from suits by citizens of other states or foreign nations, not those from its own citizens. Moreover, it is hard to escape the supposition that, whatever the protections afforded by the Eleventh Amendment (ratified in 1798), they were superseded—at least in the realm of civil rights—by the Fourteenth Amendment (ratified in 1868), which not only nationalized basic civil rights but also expressly granted Congress the power of enforcement. For a detailed critique of the Court's activism in such cases, see John T. Noonan Jr., *Narrowing the Nation's Power: The Supreme Court Sides with the States* (Berkeley: University of California Press, 2002).
14. Quotes from the opinions of Chief Justice William H. Rehnquist and Justice Stephen G. Breyer are drawn from "Excerpts from Supreme Court Opinions on Limits of Disabilities Act," *New York Times,* February 22, 2001, A21.
15. Paul A. Sracic, "Politician on Court Isn't a Bad Thing," *USA Today,* March 30, 2005, 13A.
16. Linda Greenhouse, "Will the Court Reassert National Authority?" *New York Times,* September 30, 2001, E14.
17. Linda Greenhouse, "The Imperial Presidency vs. the Imperial Judiciary," *New York Times,* September 8, 2002, E5.
18. Charles Lane, "Justices Back Detainee Access to U.S. Courts," *Washington Post,* June 29, 2004, A1.
19. See Robert A. Katzmann, ed., *Judges and Legislators* (Washington, D.C.: Brookings Institution, 1988); and Robert A. Katzmann, *Courts and Congress* (Washington, D.C.: Brookings Institution, 1997).
20. *New York Times,* May 12, 1983, B8.
21. David Rogers and Monica Langley, "Bush Set to Sign Landmark Bill on Class Actions," *Wall Street Journal,* February 18, 2005, A7.
22. See, for example, Antonin Scalia, *A Matter of Interpretation* (Princeton: Princeton University Press, 1997).
23. Jonathan Kaplan, "High Court to Congress: Say What You Mean," *The Hill,* February 5, 2003, 21.
24. Ruth Marcus, "Lawmakers Override High Court," *Washington Post,* October 31, 1991, A1.
25. U.S. Congress, *Congressional Record,* daily ed., 102d Cong., 1st sess., October 29, 1991, S15324-15325.
26. Joan Biskupic, "Scalia Sees No Justice in Trying to Judge Intent of Congress on a Law," *Washington Post,* May 11, 1993, A4.
27. Kaplan, "High Court to Congress," 21.
28. The First Amendment to the Constitution is shaped by court opinion as well as congressional action. In 1986 the Supreme Court upheld, in *Goldman v. Weinberger,* the constitutionality of a U.S. Air Force regulation that prohibited an Air Force captain from wearing his yarmulke indoors while on duty. The next year, Congress passed legislation telling the Air Force to change its regulation to permit military personnel to wear unobtrusive religious apparel indoors so long as it did not interfere with their military duties. See Fisher, *American Constitutional Law,* 571–572.
29. Joan Biskupic and Elder Witt, *Guide to the U.S. Supreme Court,* 3d ed., vol. II (Washington, D.C.: CQ Press, 1997), 720.
30. William H. Rehnquist, *Grand Inquests: The Historic Impeachment of Justice Samuel Chase and President Andrew Johnson* (New York: William Morrow, 1992), 132.
31. U.S. Congress, House Committee on the Judiciary, *Expressing the Sense of the House of Representatives That the Ninth Circuit Court of Appeals Ruling in NEWDOW V. UNITED*

STATES CONGRESS Is Inconsistent with the Supreme Court's Interpretation of the First Amendment and Should Be Overturned, and for Other Purposes, H. Rept. 108-41, 108th Cong., 1st sess., March 18, 2003, 2.

32. Stephen Dinan, "DeLay Threatens to Curb Courts' Jurisdiction," *Washington Times,* March 6, 2003, A4.
33. U.S. Congress, *Congressional Record,* daily ed., 108th Cong., 2d sess., July 22, 2004, H6581.
34. See, for example, T. R. Goldman, "Full-Court Pressure," *Legal Times,* March 28, 2005, 1; U.S. Congress, *Congressional Record,* daily ed., 108th Cong., 2d sess., March 4, 2004, H845-H846; Jess Bravin, "Congress May Fight Court on Global Front," *Wall Street Journal,* March 21, 2005, A4; Warren Richey, "Court Orders Changes in Sentencing," *Christian Science Monitor,* January 13, 2005, 1; and Laurie Cohen and Gary Fields, "New Sentencing Battle Looms after Court Decision," *Wall Street Journal,* January 14, 2005, A1.
35. Mike Allen, "DeLay Wants Panel to Review Role of Courts," *Washington Post,* April 2, 2005, A9. See David Nather and Seth Stern, "A Classic Creed Supplanted," *CQ Weekly,* March 28, 2005, 778-785.
36. Mike Allen, "DeLay Wants Panel to Review Role of Courts," *Washington Post,* April 2, 2005, A9.
37. Carl Hulse and David Kirkpatrick, "DeLay Says Federal Judiciary Has 'Run Amok,' Adding Congress Is Partly to Blame," *New York Times,* April 8, 2005, A15.
38. Kathy Kiely and Jim Drinkard, "DeLay Apologizes for Judges Remark," *USA Today,* April 14, 2005, 7A.
39. Stephen Dinan and Amy Fagan, "Court Inaction Spurs Vows of Conservative Retaliation," *Washington Times,* March 25, 2005, A9.
40. Charles Babington, "GOP Is Fracturing over Power of Judiciary," *Washington Post,* April 7, 2005, A4.
41. "Rehnquist Backs Life Tenure for Judges," *Washington Times,* January 1, 2005, A5. See David G. Savage, "Rehnquist Sees Threat to Judiciary," *Los Angeles Times,* January 1, 2005, A1; and Linda Greenhouse, "Rehnquist Resumes His Call for Judicial Independence," *New York Times,* January 1, 2005, A10.
42. William Rehnquist, *Grand Inquests: The Historic Impeachments of Justice Samuel Chase and President Andrew Johnson* (New York: William Morrow, 1992), 114.
43. Greenhouse, "Rehnquist Resumes His Call for Judicial Independence," A10.
44. Louis Fisher, "Congressional Checks on the Judiciary," *CRS Report for Congress,* 97-497, April 29, 1997, 4.
45. Biskupic and Witt, *Guide to the U.S. Supreme Court,* 717.
46. Biskupic and Witt, *Guide to the U.S. Supreme Court,* 718.
47. Carol Leonning, "New Rules for Judges Are Weaker, Critics Say," *Washington Post,* December 17, 2004, A31; David Von Drehle, "Scalia Rejects Pleas for Recusal in Cheney Case," *Washington Post,* February 12, 2004, A35; and Eileen Sullivan, "Courts Order Review of Judges' Security," *Federal Times,* March 21, 2005, 12.
48. Seth Stern, "A Career as Federal Judge Isn't What It Used to Be," *Christian Science Monitor,* January 22, 2002, 1.
49. Edward Walsh, "Federal Judicial Pay Called Too Low," *Washington Post,* May 29, 2003, A23.
50. See Fisher, *American Constitutional Law,* 1072.
51. Jennifer Dlouhy, "Congress Reluctant to Change Constitution," *CQ Today,* February 11, 2003, 9.
52. Norman Ornstein, "To Break the Stalemate, Give Judges Less Than Life," *Washington Post,* November 28, 2004, B3.
53. Tony Mauro, "Profs Pitch Plan for Limits on Supreme Court Service," *Legal Times,* January 3, 2005, 1.
54. From 1952 to 2001, the Standing Committee on Federal Judiciary of the American Bar Association (ABA) was consulted by every president with respect to judicial candidates prior

to their formal nomination. President George W. Bush curtailed the ABA's role in providing evaluations of prospective judicial candidates. However, the ABA still provides its evaluations to the Senate and the administration after the candidates' names have been made public. See Amy Goldstein, "Bush Curtails ABA Role in Selecting U.S. Judges," *Washington Post,* March 23, 2001, A1.

55. Brannon Denning, "The 'Blue Slip': Enforcing the Norms of the Judicial Confirmation Process," *William and Mary Bill of Rights Journal* 10 (December 2001): 92.
56. "GOP Move Would Help Nominees," *Washington Post,* January 24, 2003, A25.
57. Janet Hook, "Democrats Spoiling for Estrada Fight," *Los Angeles Times,* February 6, 2003, A10.
58. Michael J. Gerhardt, "Here's What Less Experience Gets You," *Washington Post,* March 2, 2003, B1, B4.
59. Ralph Neas, "United States Needs More Discussion of Judicial Philosophy," *Roll Call,* May 9, 2002, 10.
60. Richard Baker, "Senate Historical Minute," *The Hill,* October 2, 2002, 12.
61. Many Senate Republicans today dispute whether a real filibuster was conducted on Abe Fortas's nomination. "So that was not a real filibuster," stated Sen. Orrin G. Hatch, R-Utah. U.S. Congress, *Congressional Record,* daily ed., 109th Cong., 1st sess., March 1, 2005, S1834. See Charles Babington, "Filibuster Precedent? Democrats Point to '68 and Fortas," *Washington Post,* March 18, 2005, A3.
62. Ronald Brownstein, "To End Battle over Judicial Picks, Each Side Must Lay Down Arms," *Los Angeles Times,* February 21, 2005, A8.
63. Helen Dewar, "Polarized Politics, Confirmation Chaos," *Washington Post,* May 11, 2003, A5.
64. James Robertson, "A Cure for What Ails the Judiciary," *Washington Post,* May 27, 2003, A19.
65. Warren Richey, "Conservatives Near Lock on U.S. Courts," *Christian Science Monitor,* April 14, 2005, 10.
66. Elizabeth Palmer, "Appellate Courts at Center of Fight for Control of Judiciary," *CQ Weekly,* February 23, 2002, 534.
67. Palmer, "Appellate Courts at Center of Fight for Control of Judiciary."
68. Quoted in *Christian Science Monitor,* May 12, 2003, 2.
69. Robin Toner and Neil Lewis, "Lobbying Starts as Groups Foresee Vacancy on Court," *New York Times,* June 8, 2003, 1.
70. R. Jeffrey Smith, "Judge's Fate Could Turn On 1994 Case," *Washington Post,* May 27, 2003, A8.
71. E. J. Dionne Jr., "They Started It," *Washington Post,* February 21, 2003, A27.
72. Richey, "Conservatives Near Lock on U.S. Courts," 1. See Keith Perine, "House Republicans' Plan to Split 9th Circuit Court Is Adopted; No More Action Expected in 108th," *CQ Weekly,* October 9, 2004, 2375.
73. David Savage, "Judges Battle Has a Back Story," *Los Angeles Times,* April 17, 2005, A8.
74. Jennifer Dlouhy and Keith Perine, "Judiciary Committee Agenda Disrupted by Partisan Acrimony," *CQ Weekly,* April 19, 2003, 945.
75. Helen Dewar, "Confirmed Frustration with Judicial Nomination Process," *Washington Post,* March 10, 2003, A19.
76. Amy Goldstein and Helen Dewar, "President Criticizes Filibusters," *Washington Post,* May 10, 2003, A6.
77. Lauren Cohen Bell, "Senatorial Discourtesy: The Senate's Use of Delay to Shape the Federal Judiciary," *Political Research Quarterly* 56 (September 2002): 593.
78. Recent Senate debates on judicial nominations are often filled with each party's analysis of the delays and obstructionism aimed at its president's judicial selections. See, for example, U.S. Congress, *Congressional Record,* 107th Cong., 2d sess., August 1, 2002, S7856-S7857; U.S. Congress, *Congressional Record,* daily ed., 108th Cong., 1st sess., February 26, 2003,

S2724-S2730; and U.S. Congress, *Congressional Record,* daily ed., 108th Cong., 1st sess., March 3, 2003, S2996-S2997.

79. Sheldon Goldman, "Assessing the Senate Judicial Confirmation Process: The Index of Obstruction and Delay," *Judicature* 86 (March-April 2003): 252.
80. See Sarah Binder, "The Senate as a Black Hole: Lessons Learned from the Judicial Appointment Experience," *Brookings Review* 19 (spring 2001): 37-40.
81. Mike Allen and Amy Goldstein, "Bush Has Plan to Speed Judicial Confirmations," *Washington Post,* October 31, 2002, A21.
82. Daphne Retter, "Senators Do the Math . . . Then Someone Else Does the Math," *CQ Today,* April 19, 2005, 9.
83. Donald Lambro, "Misleading Filibuster Myths," *Washington Times,* May 23, 2005, A18.
84. Hook, "Democrats Spoiling for Estrada Fight," A10. Nominees who are the first to serve on the Supreme Court may spark controversy or provoke special attention by senators, such as the 1916 nomination of the first Jewish member (Louis Brandeis) of the high court; the 1967 confirmation of Thurgood Marshall as the first African American to serve on the Supreme Court; and the Senate's unanimous approval in 1981 of Sandra Day O'Connor to be the first female Supreme Court justice.
85. U.S. Congress, *Congressional Record,* 108th Cong., 1st sess., February 25, 2003, S2621.
86. Tony Mauro, "High Court Passes on Pryor Challenges," *Legal Times,* March 28, 2005, 8.
87. "The Filibuster: How It Works," *Economist,* May 21, 2005, 30.
88. Charles Hurt, "McCain Irks Republicans over Anti-Filibuster Option," *Washington Times,* April 16, 2005, A1.
89. Keith Perine, "Daylong Debate to Set Clock Ticking," *CQ Today,* May 23, 2005, 7.
90. Shailag Murray, "Judgeship Deal Called Into Question," *Washington Post,* May 26, 2005, A7.
91. Robin Toner and Richard Stevenson, "Justice Choice Could Rekindle Filibuster Fight," *New York Times,* May 25, 2005, A1.
92. David Hess, "After Deal, Senators Ponder 'Extraordinary Circumstances,'" *National Journal's CongressDaily/PM,*" May 24, 2005, 3.
93. Maura Reynolds and Richard Simon, "Senate Deal Reach on Filibusters," *Los Angeles Times,* May 24, 2005, A8.
94. Ronald Brownstein and Janet Hook, "Senate Truce Faces Test of Bush's Next Nominations," *Los Angeles Times,* May 25, 2005, A8.
95. Jim Drinkard and Kathy Kiely, "Compromise May Spread Beyond Filibuster Agreement," *USA Today,* May 25, 2005, 2A.
96. U.S. Congress, *Congressional Record,* daily ed., 109th Cong., 1st sess., May 24, 2005, S5816.
97. Brownstein and Hook, "Senate Truce Faces Test of Bush's Next Nominations," A8.
98. Brownstein, "To End Battle over Judicial Picks, Each Side Must Lay Down Arms."
99. Karen Tumulty and Massimo Calabresi, "The Freshmen vs. the Varsity," *Time,* May 30, 2005, 45.
100. Tumulty and Calabresi, "The Freshmen vs. the Varsity," 45.
101. Sarah Binder and Forest Maltzman, "Congress and the Politics of Judicial Appointments," in *Congress Reconsidered,* 8th ed., ed. Lawrence Dodd and Bruce Oppenheimer (Washington, D.C.: CQ Press, 2005), 313.
102. Louis Fisher, "Congressional Checks on the Judiciary," in *Congress Confronts the Court,* ed. Colton C. Campbell and John F. Stack Jr. (Lanham, Md.: Rowman and Littlefield, 2001), 35.

CHAPTER 13

1. Jill Barshay, "Fighting to Retain Tax Privileges," *CQ Weekly,* April 18, 2005, 970.

2. Francis Clines, "Among the Not So Well Heeled of Gucci Gulch," *New York Times,* June 22, 1997, A28. See Brian Montopoli, "Do You Know Your Place?" *Los Angeles Times,* April 5, 2004, A13.
3. See Alex Knott, *Special Report: Industry of Influence Nets Almost $13 Billion* (Washington, D.C.: Center for Public Integrity, April 7, 2005); and Paul Singer, "Do the Watchdogs Have It Wrong?" *National Journal,* June 25, 2005, 2068–2070.
4. Jim Drinkard, "Drugmakers Go Further to Sway Congress," *USA Today,* April 26, 2005, 2B.
5. Josephine Hearn, "Chamber's $53.4 Million Breaks Record," *The Hill,* February 15, 2005, 7.
6. Josephine Hearn, "Patton Boggs Tops K St. Money League," *The Hill,* February 17, 2005, 1, 6.
7. Alexis de Tocqueville, *Democracy in America,* ed. Phillips Bradley (New York: Knopf, 1951), 119. See also Richard A. Smith, "Interest Group Influence in the U.S. Congress," *Legislative Studies Quarterly* 20 (February 1995): 89-139.
8. Robert D. Putnam, "The Strange Disappearance of Civic America," *American Prospect* (winter 1996): 35.
9. Roy Rivenburg, "There Is No Such Thing as the Odd Man Out," *Los Angeles Times,* October 1, 1997, B9.
10. Janny Scott, "Medicine's Big Dose of Politics," *Los Angeles Times,* September 25, 1991, A15.
11. Andrea Petersen, "Episodic Illnesses: How Rare Ailments Get on Prime Time," *Wall Street Journal,* April 14, 1998, A1.
12. Putnam, "The Strange Disappearance of Civic America."
13. Suzi Parker, "Civic Clubs: Elks, Lions May Go Way of the Dodo," *Christian Science Monitor,* August 24, 1998, 1.
14. Seth Stern, "No More Bowling Alone," *Christian Science Monitor,* September 4, 2003, 17.
15. Everett Carll Ladd, "The American Way—Civic Engagement—Thrives," *Christian Science Monitor,* March 1, 1999, 9. See Theda Skocpol, *Diminished Democracy: From Membership to Management in American Civic Life* (Norman: University of Oklahoma Press, 2003). Professor Skocpol argues that the decline of broad membership organizations such as the Elks or Moose, which encouraged civic and political participation, occurred in part because many middle-class citizens chose to rely on professionally run advocacy groups to speak on their behalf.
16. Ladd, "The American Way," 9.
17. Sidney Verba, Kay Lehman Schlozman, and Henry Brady, "The Big Tilt: Participatory Inequality in America," *American Prospect* (May-June 1997): 78.
18. Elise D. Garcia, "Money in Politics," *Common Cause,* February 1981, 11.
19. Jeffrey H. Birnbaum, "Lobbyists: Why the Bad Rap?" *American Enterprise,* November-December 1992, 74. See also Jeffrey H. Birnbaum, *The Lobbyists* (New York: Times Books, 1992).
20. Norman J. Ornstein and Shirley Elder, *Interest Groups, Lobbying, and Policymaking* (Washington, D.C.: Congressional Quarterly, 1978), 224.
21. Jeffrey Birnbaum, "The Thursday Group," *Time,* March 27, 1995, 30-31.
22. Kate Ackley and Paul Kane, "Senate, House Jointly Whip K Street," *Roll Call,* April 12, 2005, 28.
23. Mark Preston, "Daschle Starts Monday Meetings," *Roll Call,* February 13, 2003, 1.
24. Alexander Bolton, "Dems Downtown Help against Bush," *The Hill,* February 17, 2005, 1.
25. Hedrick Smith, *The Power Game* (New York: Random House, 1988), 232.
26. See, for example, David Ottaway and Dan Morgan, "Former Top U.S. Aides Seek Caspian Gusher," *Washington Post,* July 6, 1997, A1; and Chuck Neubauer and Ted Rohrlich, "Capitalizing on a Politician's Clout," *Los Angeles Times,* December 19, 2004, A1.
27. Ronald J. Hrebenar and Ruth K. Scott, *Interest Group Politics in America* (Englewood Cliffs, N.J.: Prentice-Hall, 1982), 63.
28. Mark Preston, "Ex-GOP Senators Get Special Access," *Roll Call,* April 3, 2003, 1, 24.

29. Janet Hook, "Ex-Members Have Access, But Not Always Clout," *Congressional Quarterly Weekly Report,* June 18, 1988, 1651-1653. See also Alan Ota, "Top-Tier Lobbyists: Ex-Members' Special Access Becomes an Issue," *CQ Weekly,* February 16, 2002, 455-462; and Melanie Fonder, "Resolution Would Deny Privileges for Lobbyists," *The Hill,* December 12, 2001, 4.
30. *Wall Street Journal,* October 5, 1987, 54.
31. Thomas Hale Boggs Jr., "All Interests Are Special," *New York Times,* February 16, 1993, A17.
32. Sam Walker, "Who's In and Who's Out among Capitol Lobbyists," *Christian Science Monitor,* November 8, 1995, 3.
33. Quoted in *National Journal's CongressDaily/PM,* March 15, 2002, 8.
34. *New York Times,* January 20, 1981, B3.
35. Sam Walker, "Gift Ban Shows New Ethics on Hill," *Christian Science Monitor,* September 19, 1995, 1.
36. Bill McAllister, "Free Liquor Still Flows on Capitol Hill," *Washington Post,* January 17, 1999, A6.
37. Juliet Eilperin, "House Ethics Panel Limits Gifts," *Washington Post,* April 15, 2003, A7.
38. Jim VandeHei and Juliet Eilperin, "House GOP Erodes Its Gift Ban," *Washington Post,* January 21, 2003, A6. In 2005, the House amended its rules to permit a family member other than a spouse or child to travel with the lawmaker at the sponsor's expense.
39. Carol Matlack, "Getting around the Rules," *National Journal,* May 12, 1990, 1139.
40. Juliet Eilperin, "Travel by Lawmakers Scrutinized," *Washington Post,* March 11, 2003, A9.
41. Brody Mullins, "More Lawmakers Take Trips Funded by Corporations," *Wall Street Journal,* April 15, 2005, A1. Jim Drinkard, "Lobbyists Showing Congress the World," *U.S.A. Today,* June 22, 2005, 1A.
42. Nancy E. Roman, "Who Should Pick Up Travel Tab?" *Washington Times,* March 31, 1997, A10. See also Tyler Marshall, "As 'Junket' Becomes Dirty Word, Congress Loses Overseas Interest," *Los Angeles Times,* February 10, 1997, A8.
43. Leslie Wayne, "A Special Deal for Lobbyists: A Getaway with Lawmakers," *New York Times,* January 26, 1997, 1.
44. Al Kamen, "PAC-ed on the Slippery Slopes," *Washington Post,* January 17, 1997, A19.
45. Ernest Wittenberg, "How Lobbying Helps Make Democracy Work," *Vital Speeches of the Day,* November 1, 1982, 47.
46. Donald Lambro, "Coalition to Build Support for Social Security Reform," *Washington Times,* March 25, 2005, A4.
47. Keith Koffler, "Opponents of Bush Plan Get Jump on Lobbying Lawmakers," *National Journal's CongressDaily/AM,* April 5, 2005, 9.
48. Jeffrey Birnbaum, "AARP Leads with Wallet in Fight over Social Security," *Washington Post,* March 30, 2005, A1.
49. Eric Schmitt, "How a Fierce Backlash Saved the 'Made in U.S.A.' Label," *New York Times,* December 6, 1997, A1.
50. *Washington Star,* December 31, 1980, C2.
51. John T. Tierney and Kay Lehman Schlozman, "Congress and Organized Interests," in *Congressional Politics,* ed. Christopher J. Deering (Chicago: Dorsey, 1989), 212.
52. Scott Shepard, " 'Grass-roots' or 'Astroturf'?" *Washington Times,* December 20, 1994, A2.
53. Juliet Eilperin, "Police Track Down Telecom Telegraphs," *Roll Call,* August 7, 1995, 1.
54. Alison Mitchell, "A New Form of Lobbying Puts Public Face on Private Interest," *New York Times,* September 30, 1998, A14. See also Ken Kollman, *Outside Lobbying: Public Opinion and Interest Group Strategies* (Princeton: Princeton University Press, 1998).
55. Sara Fritz and Dan Morain, "Stealth Lobby Drives Fuel-Additive War," *Los Angeles Times,* June 16, 1997, A6.
56. *New York Times,* January 24, 1980, A16.

57. *The Economist,* June 17, 1995, 22.
58. Mitchell, "A New Form of Lobbying Puts Public Face on Private Interest."
59. Craig Karmin, " 'Third Wave' Lobbyists Battle On-line over Smut Ban Proposal," *The Hill,* December 20, 1995, 7.
60. "Trends in Grassroots Lobbying: Consultant Q&A," *Campaigns and Elections,* February 1999, 22.
61. Mary Lynn Jones, "How to Lobby from Home or Office," *The Hill,* January 7, 1998, 7; and " 'Billion Byte March' Trips over E-mail Surge from Trial," *CQ Monitor,* January 20, 1999, 1.
62. Robert Pear, "Doctors Lobbying to Halt Cuts to Medicare Payments," *New York Times,* April 4, 2005, A18.
63. Ethan Wallison, "Jackson Spins Web to Make His Point," *Roll Call,* March 25, 1999, 1.
64. Jeffrey Birnbaum, "Advocacy Groups Blur Media Lines," *Washington Post,* December 6, 2004, A1.
65. Birnbaum, "Advocacy Groups Blur Media Lines," A7.
66. Alice Love, "Small Business Group Helps Grow Its Own Grassroots Candidates at Meeting Next Week," *Roll Call,* October 16, 1995, 22.
67. Jeffrey Birnbaum, "The Forces That Set the Agenda," *Washington Post,* April 24, 2005, B5.
68. Juliet Eilperin and Dan Morgan, "Something Borrowed, Something Blue," *Washington Post,* March 9, 2001, A16.
69. Philip M. Stern, "The Tin Cup Congress," *Washington Monthly,* May 1988, 24.
70. U.S. Congress, *Congressional Record,* daily ed., 100th Cong., 1st sess., August 5, 1987, S11292.
71. "Fundamentals of Fund-raising," *Washington Post,* December 5, 1990, A23.
72. Leslie Wayne, "Lobbyists' Gift to Politicians Reap Benefits, Study Shows," *New York Times,* January 23, 1997, B11.
73. Jim Drinkard, "Report: Interests Are Running Congress," *USA Today,* September 10, 1998, 7A.
74. Claudia Dreifus, "And Then There Was Frank," *New York Times Magazine,* February 4, 1996, 25.
75. Don Van Natta Jr., "$250,000 Buys Donors 'Best Access to Congress,'" *New York Times,* January 27, 1997, A1.
76. Jeanne Cummings, "Candidates Learn to Defuse Outside Groups' Attack Ads," *Wall Street Journal,* July 20, 1998, A20.
77. Sarah Pekkanen, "How Lobbyists Are Changing the Lobbying Game," *The Hill,* February 12, 1997, 21.
78. *National Journal's CongressDaily/PM,* May 30, 1997, 6.
79. Eric Pianin, "How Business Found Benefits in Wage Bill," *Washington Post,* February 11, 1997, A8.
80. John Bresnahan, "GOP Congressional Leaders Continue to Prod Lobbying Firms to Hire More Republicans," *Roll Call,* September 10, 2001, B26. See also Kathleen Day and Jim VandeHei, "Congressman Urges Republican Lobbyist," *Washington Post,* February 15, 2003, A3; and, for a contrary view, Tory Newmyer, "Are Democrats Dinosaurs? Lobby Firms Don't Think So," *Roll Call,* January 24, 2005, 34.
81. Erin P. Billings, "Democratic Leaders to Roll Out Ethics Reform Proposal," *Roll Call,* May 17, 2005, 1.
82. John Brinkley, "Members of Congress Perform under Judging Eyes of Lobbyists," *Washington Times,* March 16, 1994, A16. See John Cochran, "Interest Groups Make Sure Lawmakers Know the 'Score,'" *CQ Weekly,* April 19, 2003, 924-929.
83. Bill Whalen, "Rating Lawmakers' Politics by Looking into Their Eyes," *Insight,* October 20, 1986, 21. See Cochran, "Interest Groups Make Sure Lawmakers Know the 'Score.'"
84. *New York Times,* May 13, 1986, A24.
85. *CQ Monitor,* April 13, 1998, 4.

86. U.S. Congress, *Oversight of the 1946 Federal Regulation of Lobbying Act,* hearings before the Senate Committee on Governmental Affairs, 98th Cong., 1st sess., November 15 and 16, 1983, 228.
87. Kirk Victor, "New Kids on the Block," *National Journal,* October 31, 1987, 2727.
88. Mary Lynn Jones, "Survey Says Lobbyists Find Information Rules the Hill," *The Hill,* November 18, 1998, 8. See also Allan J. Cigler and Burdett Loomis, *Interest Group Politics,* 5th ed. (Washington, D.C.: CQ Press, 1998).
89. Scott, "Medicine's Big Dose of Politics," A12.
90. Alexander Bolton, "House Partisan Conflict Roils Enron Reform," *The Hill,* February 27, 2002, 7.
91. *New York Times,* May 31, 1985, D16.
92. *Roll Call,* March 19, 1998, 1.
93. Michael Janofsky, "Vote Nearing, Clean Air Bill Prompts Rush of Lobbying," *New York Times,* February 15, 2005, A14.
94. Amy Goldstein, "Patients' Rights: A Prescription for Lobbyists," *Washington Post,* June 23, 2001, A7.
95. Nina Bernstein, "Deletion of Word in Welfare Bill Opens Foster Care to Big Business," *New York Times,* May 4, 1997, 1.
96. *CQ Monitor,* January 26, 1998, 3.
97. For a detailed listing of the informal congressional groups active in the 109th Congress, see *Congressional Yellow Book* (New York: Leadership Directories, winter 2005), 931-1012.
98. *Washington Star,* May 22, 1978, A1.
99. U.S. Congress, *Congressional Record,* daily ed., 96th Cong., 1st sess., April 3, 1979, 7065.
100. JoAnn Kelly, "Rural Members Lead Internet Drive," *The Hill,* February 3, 1999, 10.
101. See Susan Webb Hammond, *Congressional Caucuses in National Policy Making* (Baltimore: Johns Hopkins University Press, 1998).
102. U.S. Congress, *Organization of the Congress,* H. Rept. 1675, 79th Cong., 2d sess., 1946, 26.
103. Francesca Contiguaglia, "GAO Finds That Lobbyist Registration Has Soared," *Roll Call,* May 14, 1998, 14.
104. Jeffrey H. Birnbaum, "The Road to Riches Is Called K Street," *Washington Post,* June 22, 2005, A1.
105. Sam Fulwood, "Lobbying Reform Passes House on Unanimous Vote," *Los Angeles Times,* November 30, 1995, A9.
106. Knott, "Special Report: Industry of Influence Nets Almost $13 Billion," 1-4.
107. Lee Hamilton, "Lobbying Murkiness Undermines Our Trust in Congress," Center on Congress at Indiana University, April 11, 2005, 2, http://congress.indiana.edu.
108. Eierdre Shesgreen, "Shining a Dim Light," *Legal Times,* December 21 and 28, 1998, 26, 27.
109. Jeffrey Birnbaum, "Buzz Gets Louder for Tighter Rein on Lobbyists," *Washington Post,* April 18, 2005, E10. See Jonathan Kaplan, "Lobbying Reform Targeted at DeLay, Arbamoff Issues," *The Hill,* April 21, 2005, 4.
110. See, for example, Tory Newmyer, "Lobby Reform Bill Readied," *Roll Call,* May 11, 2005, 1; Joe Crea, "Reforms a Tough Sell among Lobbyists," *Legal Times,* May 16, 2005, 14; and Mike Allen, "House GOP to Consider Tougher Lobbying Rules," *Washington Post,* May 5, 2005, A10. For information on lobbyist Jack Abramoff, see Michael Crowley, "A Lobbyist in Full," *New York Times Magazine,* May 1, 2005, 32-37.
111. Eliza Newlin Carey, "Lobbyists in the Crossfire," *National Journal's CongressDaily/AM,* May 6, 2005, 5.
112. Paul Singer, "The Saudis' $20 Million Image Campaign," *National Journal,* July 17, 2004, 2248.
113. See Ken Silverstein, "Oil Adds Sheen to Kazakh Regime," *Los Angeles Times,* May 12, 2004, A1.

114. Steven Erlanger, "For Forty-seven Years, a Lobby with Muscle Has Tirelessly Tended U.S.-Israeli Ties," *New York Times*, April 26, 1998, 6.
115. Katharine Seelye, "National Rifle Association Is Turning to World Stage to Fight Gun Control," *New York Times*, April 2, 1997, A12.
116. Sam Loewenberg, "Tobacco Lights into WHO," *Legal Times*, September 11, 2000, 1.
117. See Adam Hochschild, "Into the Light from the Heart of Darkness," *Los Angeles Times*, December 6, 1998, M1.
118. Steven Pearlstein and John Mintz, "Too Big to Fly?" *Washington Post*, May 4, 1997, H7.
119. Sara Fritz, "Big Firms Plant Seeds of 'Grass-roots' China Lobby," *Los Angeles Times*, May 12, 1997, A8.
120. Edgar Lane, *Lobbying and the Law* (Berkeley: University of California Press, 1964), 18.

CHAPTER 14

1. David Kirkpatrick, "Military Bill Carries Range of Extra Spending," *New York Times*, April 12, 2005, A14.
2. Stan Collender, "What Emergency?" April 12, 2005, 1, http://nationaljournal.com. See also U.S. Congress, "Conference Report, Concurrent Resolution on the Budget for Fiscal Year 2004," H. Rept. 108-71, April 10, 2003, for an explanation of the emergency designation.
3. William Matthews, "Lawmakers Dispute Items in Emergency Funding Bill," *Federal Times*, February 28, 2005, 10.
4. David Baumann, "King of the Budget," *National Journal*, February 12, 2005, 460.
5. U.S. Congress, *Congressional Record*, daily ed., 109th Cong., 1st sess., April 18, 2005, S3786-S3794.
6. Geoff Earle and Hans Nichols, "Sen. Voinovich," *The Hill*, April 16, 2003, 3.
7. E. J. Dionne Jr., "Now, How Do We Pay for It?" *Washington Post*, February 1, 2002, A25. The italics were in the original, and the quote from Bush is from this article.
8. See David Easton, *The Political System* (New York: Knopf, 1963); Harold D. Lasswell, *Politics: Who Gets What, When, How* (New York: Meridian Books, 1958); and Randall B. Ripley and Grace A. Franklin, *Congress, the Bureaucracy, and Public Policy*, 5th ed. (Pacific Grove, Calif.: Brooks/Cole, 1991).
9. Theodore R. Marmor, *The Politics of Medicare* (Chicago: Aldine Publishing, 1973).
10. John W. Kingdon, *Agendas, Alternatives, and Public Policies* (Boston: Little, Brown, 1984), 3.
11. Kingdon, *Agendas, Alternatives, and Public Policies*, 17-19.
12. Sheryl Gay Stolberg, "The Revolution That Wasn't," *New York Times*, February 13, 2005, E16.
13. Kingdon, *Agendas, Alternatives, and Public Policies*, chapter 2.
14. Nelson W. Polsby, "Strengthening Congress in National Policymaking," *Yale Review* (summer 1970): 481-497.
15. James L. Sundquist, *Politics and Policy: The Eisenhower, Kennedy, and Johnson Years* (Washington, D.C.: Brookings Institution, 1968).
16. Elizabeth Wehr, "Numerous Factors Favoring Good Relationship between Reagan and New Congress," *Congressional Quarterly Weekly Report*, January 24, 1981, 173.
17. Kingdon, *Agendas, Alternatives, and Public Policies*, 148-149.
18. American Enterprise Institute, *The State of the Congress: Tomorrow's Challenges?* (Washington, D.C.: American Enterprise Institute, 1981), 8.
19. Theodore Lowi, "American Business, Public Policy, Case Studies, and Political Theory," *World Politics* (July 1964): 677-715; Theodore Lowi, "Four Systems of Policy, Politics, and Choice," *Public Administration Review* (July-August 1972): 298-310; Samuel P. Huntington, *The Common Defense* (New York: Columbia University Press, 1961); and Ripley and Franklin, *Congress, the Bureaucracy, and Public Policy.*
20. *Wall Street Journal*, May 13, 1988, 17R.

21. Mary Russell, " 'Park-Barrel Bill' Clears House Panel," *Washington Post,* June 22, 1978, A3.
22. Karen Robb, "Pet Projects," *Federal Times,* January 10, 2005, 1.
23. U.S. Congress, *Congressional Record,* daily ed., 108th Cong., 2d sess., April 2, 2004, H2120.
24. Lewis Lord, "Grand Old Pork," *U.S. News and World Report,* March 23, 1998, 7.
25. Edwin Chen, "Senate Fattens Its 'Ice Tea' with Porky Politics," *Los Angeles Times,* March 10, 1998, A6.
26. See, for example, Margaret Kriz, "Heavy Breathing," *National Journal,* January 4, 1997, 8-12.
27. Joby Warrick, "White House Taking a Hands-on Role in Writing New Clean Air Standards," *Washington Post,* May 22, 1997, A10.
28. Marmor, *The Politics of Medicare,* 108-109.
29. Donald Lambro, "Steady GOP Rebound Strategy," *Washington Times,* June 7, 2001, A17.
30. Benjamin I. Page, "Cooling the Legislative Tea," in *American Politics and Public Policy,* ed. Walter Dean Burnham and Martha Wagner Weinberg (Cambridge: MIT Press, 1978), 171-187.
31. Judy Sarasohn, "Money for Lat. 40 N, Long. 73 W," *Congressional Quarterly Weekly Report,* May 12, 1979, 916.
32. Paula Drummond, "Unfunded Mandates Bill Becomes Law," *Kansas Government Journal,* May 1995, 122.
33. William Schneider, "No Lawsuit Left Behind," *National Journal,* April 30, 2005, 1348.
34. "Don't Just Do Something, Sit There," *Economist,* December 23, 1995-January 5, 1996, 11-12.
35. Barber Conable, "Government Is Working," *Roll Call,* April 19, 1984, 3. Congress has initiated change many times. A classic example is the 37th Congress (1861-1863), which drafted "the blueprint for modern America" by enacting measures to finance the Civil War, build the transcontinental railroad, eradicate slavery, promote the land-grant college movement, provide settlers with homesteaded land, and create the Department of Agriculture. See James M. McPherson, *Battle Cry of Freedom: The Civil War Era* (New York: Ballantine, 1988), 452.
36. Robert Luce, *Legislative Problems* (Boston: Houghton Mifflin, 1935), 426. See also Louis Fisher, "The Authorization-Appropriation Process in Congress: Formal Rules and Informal Practices," *Catholic University Law Review* (fall 1979): 51-105; and Richard F. Fenno Jr., *The Power of the Purse* (Boston: Little, Brown, 1966).
37. See Louis Fisher, "Annual Authorizations: Durable Roadblocks to Biennial Budgeting," *Public Budgeting and Finance* (spring 1983): 23-40.
38. David Baumann, "Shirking Duties on the Hill," *National Journal's CongressDaily/AM,* March 27, 2003, 5.
39. *National Journal's CongressDaily/PM,* May 12, 2003, 3.
40. U.S. Congress, *Congressional Record,* daily ed., 109th Cong., 1st sess., May 10, 2005, S4847.
41. Erik Eckholm, "Payments to the Retired Loom Ever Larger," *New York Times,* August 30, 1992, E1, E4.
42. Jason DeParle, "U.S. Welfare System Dies as State Programs Emerge," *New York Times,* June 30, 1997, A1.
43. Jonathan Weisman and Michael Fletcher, "GOP May Be Splintering on Social Security," *Washington Post,* April 27, 2005, A4.
44. U.S. Congress, *Congressional Record,* 109th Cong., 1st sess., February 28, 2005, S1784.
45. Andrew Taylor, "Weighing Nip, Tuck vs. Total Makeover," *CQ Weekly,* April 4, 2005, 843.
46. Dennis Cauchon, "Rethinking Social Security," *USA Today,* March 18, 2005, 4A.
47. Joseph Schatz, "Social Security's Twofold Problem," *CQ Weekly,* April 4, 2005, 833, 835.
48. David Nather and Rebecca Adams, "The Real Crisis Waits Its Turn," *CQ Weekly,* February 21, 2005, 447.
49. Ceci Connolly and Mike Allen, "Medicare Drug Benefit May Cost $1.2 Trillion," *Washington Post,* February 9, 2005, A1.

50. William Welch, "Medicare: The Next Riddle for the Ages," *USA Today,* March 17, 2005, 10A.
51. Julie Rovner, "The Real Budget Buster," *National Journal's CongressDaily/AM,* April 5, 2001, 5.
52. Donald Kettl, "Looking for a Real Crisis: Try Medicaid," *Governing,* April 2005, 20.
53. Matthew Miller, "The Big Federal Freeze," *New York Times Magazine,* October 15, 2000, 94.
54. Gail Russell Chaddock, "Off-Radar Tax Breaks Draw New Scrutiny," *Christian Science Monitor,* March 9, 2005, 11.
55. Andrew Taylor and Alan Ota, "GOP to Seek Budget Deal Now, Tax Cut Decision Later," *CQ Today,* April 10, 2003, 6.
56. U.S. Congress, *Congressional Record,* daily ed., 109th Cong., 1st sess., March 17, 2005, S2917.
57. U.S. Congress, *Congressional Record,* March 17, 2005, S2918.
58. "'You Know What? Democracy Is a Tough Business,'" *The Hill,* April 8, 2003, 3.
59. U.S. Congress, *Congressional Record,* daily ed., 106th Cong., 2d sess., March 2, 2000, S1050.
60. Mark Preston, "'Vote-a-Rama' Keeps Wearing Senate Down," *Roll Call,* March 26, 2003, 1.
61. U.S. Congress, *Congressional Record,* daily ed., 107th Cong., 1st sess., February 15, 2001, S1532.
62. John Ellwood, "Budget Control in a Redistributive Environment," in *Making Economic Policy in Congress,* ed. Allen Schick (Washington, D.C.: American Enterprise Institute, 1983), 93. Data on the number of times reconciliation has been employed were provided by budget expert Robert Keith, Congressional Research Service.
63. Jonathan Allen, "Congress Clears Path to Trim Billions," *CQ Today,* April 29, 2005, 1, 4.
64. Peter Cohn and Martin Vaughan, "GOP Considering Separate Bills for Tax, Entitlement Cuts," *National Journal's CongressDaily/PM,* February 25, 2005, 1.
65. David Rosenbaum, "Democratic Filibuster Hopes Fade," *New York Times,* November 18, 2002, A15; and David Baumann, "The Octopus That Might Eat Congress," *National Journal,* May 14, 2005, 1470-1475.
66. William Dauster, "Budget Process Issues for 1993," *Journal of Law and Politics* 9, no. 9 (1992), 26.
67. Dauster, "Budget Process Issues for 1993," A7.
68. U.S. Congress, *Congressional Record,* daily ed., 107th Cong., 1st sess., January 4, 2001, S19.
69. Baumann, "King of the Budget," 457.
70. David Firestone, "Conservatives Now See Deficits as a Tool to Fight Spending," *New York Times,* February 11, 2003, A22.
71. Robin Toner, "For Republicans, Deficits Are Nothing to Be Ashamed Of," *New York Times,* February 9, 2003, E3.
72. Jonathan Allen, "Divisions Confront Budget Negotiators," *CQ Today,* April 4, 2005, 1.
73. Alan Ota, "Rise of the 'Growth Hawks,'" *CQ Weekly,* November 16, 2002, 2999.
74. U.S. Congress, *Congressional Record,* daily ed., 107th Cong., 2d sess., June 20, 2002, S5810.
75. E. J. Dionne Jr., "Destined for Deficits," *Washington Post,* March 18, 2005, A23.
76. Sue Kirchhoff, "Deficit Warnings Increase in Urgency," *USA Today,* February 27, 2003, 5B.
77. U.S. Congress, *Congressional Record,* daily ed., 107th Cong., 2d sess., July 16, 2002, H4749.

CHAPTER 15

1. Quoted in Samuel Eliot Morison, *The Oxford History of the American People* (New York: Oxford University Press, 1965), 346.
2. Edward S. Corwin, *The President: Office and Powers, 1787-1957,* 4th ed. (New York: New York University Press, 1957), 171. See also Cecil V. Crabb Jr. and Pat M. Holt, *Invitation to Struggle: Congress, the President, and Foreign Policy,* 4th ed. (Washington, D.C.: CQ Press, 1992).
3. Corwin, *The President,* 171; italics are in the original.

4. Alexander Hamilton, James Madison, and John Jay, *The Federalist Papers,* ed. Clinton Rossiter, No. 64 (New York: Mentor Books, 1961), 391-393.
5. Testimony before the House International Relations Committee, January 12, 1995. Reported by Maureen Dowd, *New York Times,* January 13, 1995, A1.
6. *Youngstown Sheet and Tube Co. v. Sawyer,* 343 U.S. 636 (1952).
7. Cecil V. Crabb Jr., Glenn J. Antizzo, and Leila E. Sarieddine, *Congress and the Foreign Policy Process* (Baton Rouge: Louisiana State University Press, 2000), 4.
8. Crabb, Antizzo, and Sarieddine, *Congress and the Foreign Policy Process,* 163.
9. Christopher J. Deering and Steven S. Smith, *Committees in Congress,* 3d ed. (Washington, D.C.: CQ Press, 1997), 92.
10. Quoted in Helen Dewar, "Clinton, Congress at Brink of Foreign Policy Dispute," *Washington Post,* May 16, 1994, A10.
11. Holbert N. Carroll, *The House of Representatives and Foreign Affairs,* rev. ed. (Boston: Little, Brown, 1966), 20.
12. National Commission on Terrorist Attacks Upon the United States, *The 9/11 Report* (New York: St. Martin's Paperbacks, 2004), 596-599.
13. Henry A. Kissinger, "Implementing Bush's Vision," *Washington Post,* May 16, 2005, A17.
14. Christopher J. Deering, "Congress, the President, and Military Policy," in *Congress and the Presidency: Invitation to Struggle,* ed. Roger H. Davidson, *The Annals* 499 (September 1988): 136-147.
15. *Budget of the United States Government, Fiscal Year 2006, Historical Tables* (Washington, D.C.: Government Printing Office, 2005), Table 3.2.
16. Leslie Wayne, "Pentagon Spends without Bids, A Study Finds," *New York Times,* September 30, 2004, C1.
17. Tim Smart, "Getting the F-22 off the Ground," *Washington Post,* April 20, 1998, 12; and Tim Weiner, "Air Superiority at $258 Million a Pop," *New York Times,* October 27, 2004, C1.
18. Tim Weiner, "For Military Plane in Crash, A History of Political Conflict," *New York Times,* April 11, 2000, A1.
19. Quoted in Vernon Loeb, "Weapon Systems Die Hard, Especially on Capitol Hill," *Washington Post,* May 6, 2002, A4.
20. Quoted in Kevin Sack, "For the South, GOP Secures Defense Bounty," *New York Times,* November 18, 1997, A1.
21. Karl Viox, "It's Closing Time for Base Commission," *Washington Post,* December 29, 1995, A21. Scholars regard this as an intriguing example of blame-avoidance politics. See, for example, Christopher J. Deering, "Congress, the President, and Automatic Government: The Case of Military Base Closures," in *Rivals for Power: Presidential-Congressional Relations,* ed. James A. Thurber (Washington, D.C.: CQ Press, 1996).
22. Rep. Joel Hefley, "Base Closings? 'Over My Dead Body,'" *The Hill,* May 2, 1997, 24.
23. John Hedren and Mark Mazzetti, "Military Plans to Shut Down 33 U.S. Bases," *Los Angeles Times,* May 14, 2005, A1; and Mike Allen and Jonathan Weisman, "Legislators Scramble to Reassure Constituents," *Washington Post,* May 14, 2005, A1.
24. Quoted in Robert Schlesinger, "Defense Downsizing Also Impacts Hill Committees," *The Hill,* May 21, 1997, 17.
25. U.S. Congress, *Congressional Record,* daily ed., 102d Cong., 2d sess., August 6, 1992, H7701-7703.
26. Keith Bradsher, "NAFTA: Something to Offend Everyone," *New York Times,* November 14, 1993. See also I. M. Destler, "Protecting Congress or Protecting Trade?" *Foreign Policy* 62 (spring 1986): 96-107.
27. Elizabeth Becker, "Free Trade Pact Faces Trouble in Congress," *New York Times,* May 10, 2005, C1.
28. Sander Levin, "Derailing a Consensus on Trade," *Washington Post,* December 5, 2001, A29.

29. Vladimir Pregelj, *Fast-Track Implementation of Trade Agreements: History, Status, and Other Options,* Congressional Research Service Report No. 97-41E, December 27, 1996.
30. Quoted in Joseph Kahn, "As Vote Nears, Bush Presses for New Trade Powers," *New York Times,* December 5, 2001, A18.
31. Richard Simon and Nancy Cleeland, "Senate OKs Fast-Track Trade Bill," *Los Angeles Times,* August 2, 2002, A1.
32. William A. Orme Jr., "Israeli Armorer in Global Arena," *New York Times,* June 30, 2000, C1.
33. Charles McC. Mathias Jr., "Ethnic Groups and Foreign Policy," *Foreign Affairs* 59 (summer 1981): 975-998.
34. Leslie Wayne, "So Much for the Plan to Scrap Old Weapons," *New York Times,* December 22, 2002, D1.
35. Quoted in James Dao and Steven Lee Myers, "Bush Warning on Spending Cools a Wishful Pentagon," *New York Times,* February 5, 2001, A14.
36. Thom Shanker and Eric Schmitt, "Rumsfeld Seeks Leader Army, And a Full Term," *New York Times,* May 11, 2005, A1
37. Shanker and Schmitt, "Rumsfeld Seeks Leader Army," A15.
38. Joseph J. Schatz, "Has Congress Given Bush Too Free a Spending Hand?" *CQ Weekly,* April 12, 2002, 859.
39. Robin Wright, "Don't Just Fund the War, Shell Out for Peace," *Washington Post,* March 10, 2002, B5; and Stephen Kinzer, "Why They Don't Know Us," *New York Times,* November 11, 2001, D5.
40. Elizabeth Becker, "Chief Urges World Bank to Pick Leader More Carefully," *New York Times,* May 25, 2005, C5.
41. Loch Johnson and James M. McCormick, "Foreign Policy by Executive Fiat," *Foreign Policy* 28 (fall 1977): 118-124.
42. Quoted in Paul Richter, "Senate Approves U.S.-Russian Treaty to Cut Some Nuclear Weapons," *Los Angeles Times,* March 7, 2003, A18.
43. David Auerswald and Forrest Maltzman, "Shaping Foreign Policy through Ratification: The Senate and Treaties," paper delivered at an American Political Science Association meeting, Boston, Massachusetts, August 2002, 6.
44. Peter Grier, "Why 48 Treaties Languish in the Senate," *Christian Science Monitor,* March 20, 1997, 3.
45. Thomas W. Lippman and Peter Baker, "Bipartisanship, But at a Price," *Washington Post,* April 25, 1997, A1.
46. Roger H. Davidson, "Senate Floor Deliberation: A Preliminary Inquiry," in *The Contentious Senate,* ed. Colton C. Campbell and Nicol C. Rae (Lanham, Md.: Rowman and Littlefield, 2001), 22-29.
47. David Silverberg, "Nasty, Brutish and Short: The CTBT Debates," *The Hill,* December 8, 1999, 16.
48. Silverberg, "Nasty, Brutish and Short," 16.
49. Kiki Caruson, "International Agreement-Making and the Executive-Legislative Relationship," *Presidential Research Group Report* 25 (fall 2002): 22.
50. Caruson, "International Agreement-Making and the Executive-Legislative Relationship," 21.
51. This section draws upon the invaluable summary of congressional policy initiation in Ellen C. Collier, *Foreign Policy Roles of the President and Congress,* Congressional Research Service Report No. 93-20F, January 6, 1993, 11-17.
52. The classic account of this incident is Chalmers M. Roberts, "The Day We Didn't Go to War," *The Reporter,* September 14, 1954, 31-35.
53. Alison Mitchell, "In Vote Clinton Sought to Avoid, House Backs a Force for Kosovo," *New York Times,* March 12, 1999, A1.

54. Ellen C. Collier, "Foreign Policy by Reporting Requirement," *Washington Quarterly* 11 (winter 1988): 75.
55. Bruce J. Schulman, "Congress' Wartime Quandary," *Los Angeles Times,* April 27, 2003, M2.
56. Quoted in Dan Eggen, "Lawmakers Urge More Aggressive Sept. 11 Probe," *Washington Post,* May 22, 2002, A1.
57. National Commission on Terrorist Attacks Upon the United States, *The 9/11 Report,* 598.
58. James M. Lindsay, "Congress, Foreign Policy, and the New Institutionalism," *International Studies Quarterly* 38 (June 1994): 281-304.
59. An early, influential analysis of this phenomenon is John E. Mueller, *War, Presidents, and Public Opinion* (New York: Wiley, 1973), 208-213.
60. Richard F. Grimmett, *War Powers Resolution after Thirty Years,* Congressional Research Service Report RL32267, March 11, 2004, 56–75.
61. Harold M. Hyman, *Quiet Past and Stormy Present: War Powers in American History* (Washington, D.C.: American Historical Association Bicentennial Essays on the Constitution, 1986).
62. Quotes from Helen Dewar, "Congress's Reaction to TV Coverage Shows Ambivalence on Foreign Policy," *Washington Post,* October 9, 1993, A14; and Dewar, "Clinton, Congress at Brink of Foreign Policy Dispute," A1.
63. Grimmett, *War Powers Resolution.*
64. U.S. Congress, *Congressional Record,* daily ed., 107th Cong., 2d sess., October 9, 2002, S10175.
65. U.S. Congress, *Congressional Record,* October 9, 2002, S10161.
66. U.S. Congress, *Congressional Record,* daily ed., 107th Cong., 2d sess., October 10, 2002, S10247.
67. Louis Fisher, *Presidential War Power,* 2d ed., revised (Lawrence: University Press of Kansas, 2004), 261.
68. Quotes from Gabriel Kahn, "House Saves Its War Power," *Roll Call,* June 8, 1995, 21.
69. Both these quotes are from "Congress Backs Bush on Emergency Aid," *International Herald-Tribune,* September 15, 2001, 5.
70. John E. Reilly, *Public Opinion and Foreign Policy* (Chicago: Chicago Council on Foreign Relations, April 25, 1999).
71. Program on International Policy Attitudes, *The Hall of Mirrors: Perceptions and Misperceptions in the Congressional Foreign Policy Process* (October 1, 2004), 3. See also Steven Kull and I. M. Destler, *Misreading the Public: The Myth of a New Isolationism* (Washington, D.C.: Brookings Institution Press, 1999), 204.
72. James M. Lindsay, "Congress and Foreign Policy: Why the Hill Matters," *Political Science Quarterly* 107 (winter 1992-1993): 626-627.
73. Quotes from Lindsay Sobel, "Hill Profile: Sen. Bob Kerrey," *The Hill,* October 29, 1997, 24; and Helen Dewar, "Farming Locally, Thinking Globally," *Washington Post,* April 21, 1998, A1.
74. Richard G. Lugar, "Beating Terror," *Washington Post,* January 27, 2003, A19.

CHAPTER 16

1. Quoted in David Nather, "For Congress, A New World—And Business as Usual, *CQ Weekly,* September 7, 2002, 2276.
2. See Charles O. Jones, *The Presidency in a Separated System* (Washington, D.C.: Brookings Institution, 1994).
3. U.S. Congress, *Congressional Record,* daily ed., 105th Cong., 1st sess., May 21, 1997, H3072.
4. Glenn R. Parker and Roger H. Davidson, "Why Do Americans Love Their Congressmen So Much More Than Their Congress?" *Legislative Studies Quarterly* 4 (February 1979): 53–61.

5. See Roger H. Davidson, "The House of Representatives: Managing Legislative Complexity," in *Workways of Governance: Monitoring the Government's Health,* ed. Roger H. Davidson (Washington, D.C.: Governance Institute and Brookings Institution Press, 2003), 24–46; and Sarah A. Binder, "The Senate: Does It Deliberate? Can It Act?" in *Workways of Governance: Monitoring the Government's Health,* ed. Roger H. Davidson, 47–64.
6. Quoted in Mary Lynn F. Jones, "Family Concerns Prompt Early Hill Retirements," *The Hill,* March 20, 2002, 12.
7. Jones, "Family Concerns Prompt Early Hill Retirements."
8. U.S. Congress, *Congressional Record,* daily ed., 108th Cong., 2d sess., November 20, 2004, S11666.
9. Quoted by Jonathan Kaplan, "Not on Speaking Terms," *The Hill,* June 3, 2004, 8.
10. David Dreier, "We've Come a Long Way . . . Maybe," in *Congress and the Internet,* ed. James A. Thurber and Colton C. Campbell (Upper Saddle River, N.J.: Prentice Hall, 2003), 58.
11. Bob Benenson, "Savvy 'Stars' Making Local TV a Potent Tool," *Congressional Quarterly Weekly Report,* July 18, 1987, 1551–1555.
12. Timothy Cook, *Making Laws and Making News: Media Strategies in the U.S. House of Representatives* (Washington, D.C.: Brookings Institution, 1989), 82–83.
13. Joseph Carroll, *Gallup News Service* (Princeton, N.J.: Gallup Organization, December 8, 2004).
14. Lee H. Hamilton, "Ten Things I Wish Political Scientists Would Teach about Congress," Pi Sigma Alpha Lecture, American Political Science Association, August 31, 2000, 7. See also Hamilton's thoughtful book, *How Congress Works and Why You Should Care* (Bloomington: Indiana University Press, 2004).
15. Norman J. Ornstein, "Prosecutors Must End Their Big Game Hunt of Politicians," *Roll Call,* April 26, 1993, 16; italics are in the original.
16. Quoted in T. R. Goldman, "The Influence Industry's Senior Class," *Legal Times,* June 16, 1997, 4.
17. Ronald Brownstein and Alan Miller, "In Politics, Investigation Has Become a Way of Life," *Los Angeles Times,* September 8, 1998, A9.
18. Cass R. Sunstein, "Unchecked and Unbalanced," *American Prospect* 38 (May–June 1998): 23.
19. G. Calvin Mackenzie with Michael Hafken, *Scandal Proof: Do Ethics Laws Make Government Ethical?* (Washington, D.C.: Brookings Institution Press, 2002), 158.
20. Norman Ornstein, "Lax Ethics Enforcement Created Culture of Carelessness in House," *Roll Call,* May 11, 2005, 6.
21. Joel Hefley and Alan B. Mollohan, "Closing a Credibility Gap in Congress," *Washington Post,* April 13, 2005, A17.
22. Paul C. Light, "Measuring the Health of the Public Service," in *Workways of Governance: Monitoring the Government's Health,* ed. Roger H. Davidson, 96–97.
23. John Hibbing and Christopher Larimer, "What the American Public Wants Congress to Be," in *Congress Reconsidered,* 8th ed., eds. Lawrence Dodd and Bruce Oppenheimer (Washington, D.C.: CQ Press, 2005), 55.
24. Woodrow Wilson, *Constitutional Government in the United States* (New York: Columbia University Press, 1908), 79–80.
25. Diane Hollern Harvey, "Who Should Govern? Public Preferences for Congressional and Presidential Power," Ph.D. dissertation, University of Maryland, 1998.
26. Paul C. Light, *Government's Greatest Achievements: From Civil Rights to Homeland Security* (Washington, D.C.: Brookings Institution Press, 2002).
27. Light, *Government's Greatest Achievements,* 63.
28. Hamilton, "Ten Things I Wish Political Scientists Would Teach about Congress," 3.
29. Barbara Sinclair, *Unorthodox Lawmaking: New Legislative Processes in the U.S. Congress,* 2nd ed. (Washington, D.C.: CQ Press, 2000).

30. Terence Samuel, "His Own Ways, His Own Means," *U.S. News and World Report,* March 31, 2005, 26.
31. Richard Cohen, Kirk Victor, and David Baumann, "The State of Congress," *National Journal,* January 10, 2004, 103.
32. Quoted by David S. Broder, "Role Models, Now More than Ever," *Washington Post,* July 13, 2003, B7.
33. Broder, "Role Models."
34. David Price, "Where Political Theory Meets the Sausage Factory," *Roll Call,* May 9, 2005, 1.
35. Broder, "Role Models."
36. Eric Schickler, *Disjointed Pluralism: Institutional Innovation and the Development of the U.S. Congress* (Princeton: Princeton University Press, 2001), 268.
37. Schickler, *Disjointed Pluralism,* 267.
38. Bob Schieffer, *This Just In: What I Couldn't Tell You on TV* (New York: Putnam, 2003).
39. James T. Hamilton, *All the News That's Fit to Sell* (Princeton: Princeton University Press, 2004).
40. Bill Moyers, "Journalism and Democracy," *Nation,* May 7, 2001, 12.
41. Media critic Neal Gabler's commentaries are especially incisive. See his "The Media Bias Myth," *Los Angeles Times,* December 22, 2002, M1.
42. Quoted in Bernard Aronson, "Tired of 'Gotcha' Journalism," *Washington Post,* March 6, 1997, A21.
43. Parker and Davidson, "Why Do Americans Love Their Congressmen So Much More Than Their Congress?"
44. *Washington Post* survey archives, www.washingtonpost.com.politics/polls/vault/stories/data.
45. Isaiah Poole, "Congress Confronts Skeptical Public," *CQ Today,* May 31, 2005, 17; and Gallup Poll, May 10, 2005, www.gallup.com.
46. CNN/*USA Today* /Gallup Poll, May 20, 2005, www.gallup.com.
47. Peter Baker and Jim VandeHei, "Bush's Political Capital Spent, Voices in Both Parties Suggest," *Washington Post,* May 31, 2005, A2.
48. Quoted by Sheryl Gay Stolbert, "The Dangers of Political Theater," *New York Times,* March 27, 2005, D3.
49. John R. Hibbing and Elizabeth Theiss-Morse, *Congress as Public Enemy* (Cambridge, United Kingdom: Cambridge University Press, 1995), 147.
50. Hibbing and Theiss-Morse, *Congress as Public Enemy,* 158.
51. Christopher Lee, "An Amendment to Be Recommended on Continuity of Congress," *Washington Post,* May 25, 2003, A11.
52. Susan Ferrechio, "Despite Some Concerns, House Overwhelmingly Passes Continuity Bill—Again," *CQ Today,* March 4, 2005, 12.
53. Ferrechio, "Despite Some Concerns, House Overwhelmingly Passes Continuity Bill."
54. Nather, "For Congress, a New World," 2274.
55. Nather, "For Congress, a New World," 2274.
56. Quoted in Kirk Victor, "Congress in Eclipse," *National Journal,* April 5, 2003, 1067.
57. U.S. Congress, *Congressional Record,* daily ed., 107th Congress, 2d sess., February 12, 2002, S2268, S2271.
58. James Dao, "Congressman Seeks Review of U.S. Effort to Aid Iraq," *New York Times,* May 16, 2003, A15.
59. Quoted in Elizabeth Becker, "Bipartisan Call to Expand Inquiry Into Occupation," *New York Times,* May 24, 2003, A6.
60. Quoted in Peter Grier, "The Rising Economic Cost of the Iraq War," *Christian Science Monitor,* May 19, 2005, 10.
61. Quoted in Victor, "Congress in Eclipse," 1068.
62. Quoted in Victor, "Congress in Eclipse," 1068.

63. Bob Woodward, "Cheney Upholds Power of the Presidency," *Washington Post,* January 20, 2005, A7.
64. Carol Leonning and Jim VandeHei, "Cheney Wins Court Ruling on Energy Panel Records," *Washington Post,* May 11, 2005, A1.
65. Quoted in Victor, "Congress in Eclipse," 1069.
66. John T. Noonan Jr., *Narrowing the Nation's Power* (Berkeley: University of California, 2002), 11.
67. Noonan, *Narrowing the Nation's Power,* 139.
68. Walter B. Jones Jr., "From Father to Son, And Party to Party," *Roll Call,* May 5, 2005, 13.
69. Interview with Barney Frank, "Lessons on Opposition," *Working Papers Magazine,* May–June 1982, 43.
70. Quoted in Francis X. Clines, "Weary of Political Noise, A Senator Sees a Peaceful Farm in Her Future," *New York Times,* December 3, 1995, 30.
71. The wording of the title of this section, "The Fundamental Things Apply," is from the Herman Hupfeld song "As Time Goes By," which was featured in the 1942 movie *Casablanca.*
72. E. J. Dionne Jr., "All Politics Is Now Global," *Washington Post,* July 13, 1993, A15.
73. Alvin Toffler, "Congress in the Year 2000," *GAO Review* (fall 1980): 44.
74. Alan Ehrenhalt, "Demanding the Right Size Government," *New York Times,* October 4, 1999. A31.
75. Hamilton, "Ten Things I Wish Political Scientists Would Teach about Congress," 7.
76. Hamilton, "Ten Things I Wish Political Scientists Would Teach about Congress," 10.

Index

CONGRESSIONAL TIME LINE: **Eighteenth and Nineteenth Centuries**

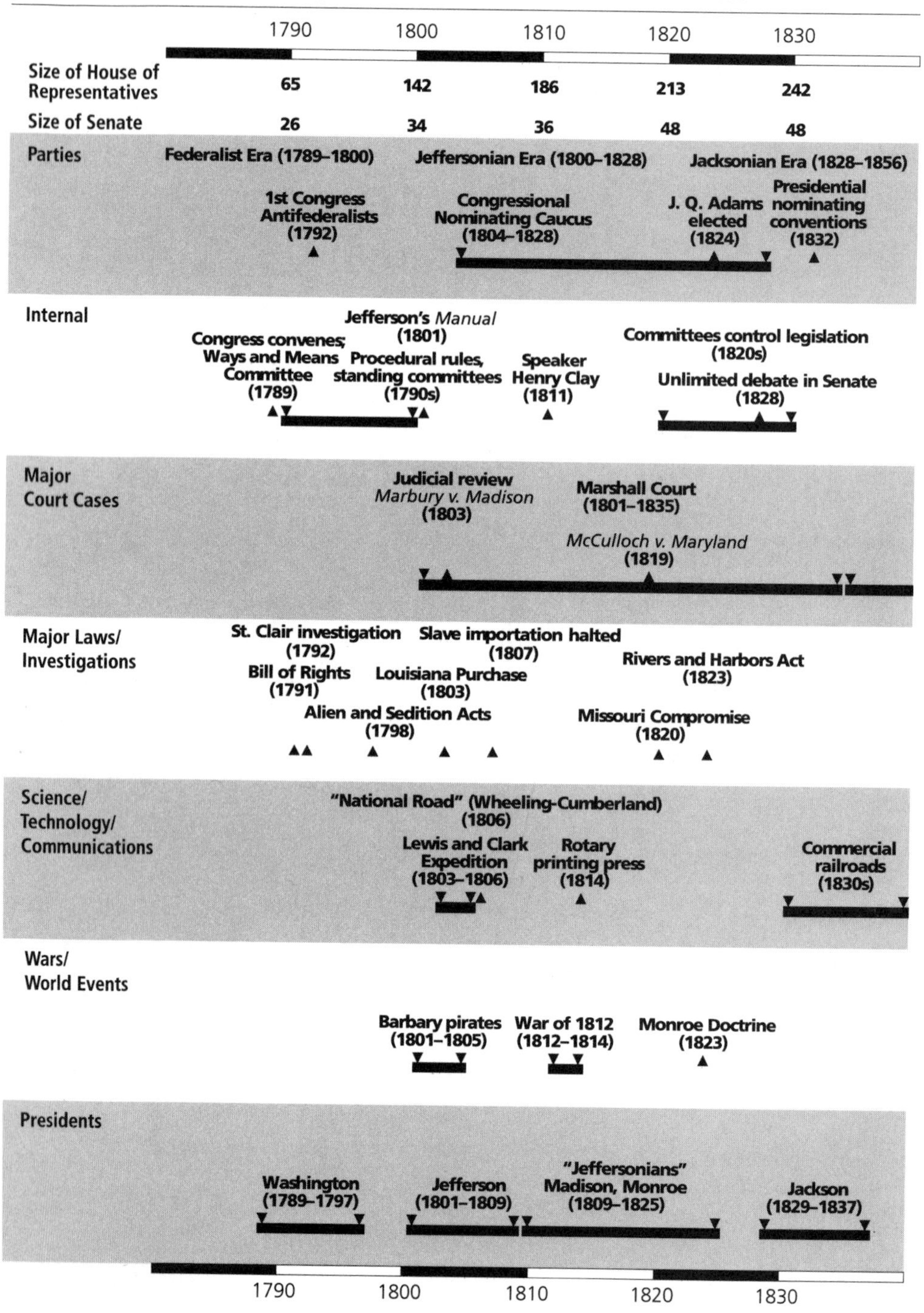